THE

HISTORY OF MASSACHUSETTS.

THE

PROVINCIAL PERIOD.

BY JOHN STETSON BARRY,

MEMBER OF THE MASSACHUSETTS HISTORICAL SOCIETY, AND OF THE NEW ENGLAND
HISTORIC-GENEALOGICAL SOCIETY.

BOSTON:

PHILLIPS, SAMPSON, AND COMPANY.

1857.

STEREOTYPED AT THE
BOSTON STEREOTYPE FOUNDRY.

TO

THE HONORABLE

ROBERT CHARLES WINTHROP, LL. D.

PRESIDENT

OF THE

MASSACHUSETTS HISTORICAL SOCIETY,

THIS SECOND VOLUME OF THE HISTORY OF MASSACHUSETTS, RECORDING

THE DEEDS OF A NOBLE ANCESTRY IN THEIR STRUGGLES

FOR FREEDOM,

IS RESPECTFULLY INSCRIBED,

BY HIS GRATEFUL AND OBLIGED FRIEND,

THE AUTHOR.

INTRODUCTION.

THE flattering reception with which the first volume of this work, covering the period of the Colonial History of Massachusetts, was received, has encouraged the continuance of the author's labors; and the present volume, the second of the series, covering the period of our Provincial History, is now offered to the public. The distinction between the Colonial and the Provincial history of Massachusetts is strikingly marked. During the former period, a large share of independence was enjoyed by the people, who chose their own rulers, and managed their own affairs. Acknowledging their dependence on Great Britain for the charter they held and for the privileges it secured, they yet claimed exemption from the paramount authority of Parliament, and the right to enact their own laws and shape their own policy. Hence the prosperity of the country rapidly increased; commerce was enlarged; industry was fostered; and the simplicity of manners which so generally prevailed threw such attractions around the country, and augured so well for its future advancement, that the jealousy of the statesmen of England was aroused; and to check the spirit of freedom, which was abroad, was urged as the only means by which the people could be kept in subjection. Hence the old charter was overthrown; a new charter was granted, and Massachusetts, from a colony, became a province of England. Under the new charter the governor and a number of other officers were appointed by the king, and were removable at his pleasure; a supervision was exercised over the legislation of the province, and the paramount authority of the crown was asserted. In accepting this charter, however, the people of Massachusetts did not relinquish their natural rights, nor did they yield, without opposition, to innovations upon the customs which had long been established among them. Hence the position of the governors was exceedingly embarrassed ; and the contests between them and the statesmen of the province, so far from resulting in the subjection of the people, tended only to strengthen and develop their love of liberty. The provincial history of Massachusetts is a record of this development ; and these pages are designed to sketch the progress of that struggle, the seeds of which were early sown, and which, when matured, led to a rupture between the colonies and the crown. The prominent characters who figure in our annals were men of unwavering fidelity and courage ; and it was owing to their earnest and persevering efforts, that the tide of oppression was successfully stayed, and the liberties of the people were eventually secured.

All who are acquainted with the difficulties attending the preparation of a work like the present, will readily excuse any trifling inaccuracies, of style or of statement, which may be discovered in its perusal. Such inaccuracies can never be wholly avoided ; and the wide range of subjects brought under discussion, and the perplexities attending the adjustment of rival claims and discrepant authorities, preclude the hope that in all cases the conclusion to which the author has arrived will meet the entire concurrence of his readers. Candid criticism, however, will never be deprecated ; and should mistakes be discovered, no one more cheerfully than the author will acknowledge his indebtedness to those who shall be the means of pointing them out.

The thanks of the author are tendered to those gentlemen who have so kindly encouraged his labors, and to the societies which have afforded him access to their historical treasures. To enumerate these gentlemen, and to specify these societies, would only be to repeat the names given in the first volume. In the hope that the present volume will meet with as favorable a reception as the former, and will prove as acceptable to the people of Massachusetts and to their descendants, it is sent forth on its mission with the diffidence and hesitancy which must ever be felt by one who assumes to write for the benefit of others, and who is conscious of the responsibility attaching to such a position.

CONTENTS.

CHAPTER I.

THE PROVINCE OF THE MASSACHUSETTS BAY.

CHAPTER II.

THE WITCHCRAFT DELUSION.

CHAPTER III.

THE GOVERNMENT OF THE PROVINCE.

CHAPTER IV.

DIFFICULTIES WITH THE FRENCH.

CHAPTER V.

ADMINISTRATIONS OF SHUTE, BURNET, AND BELCHER.

CHAPTER VI.

ADMINISTRATION OF SHIRLEY.   THE GREAT AWAKENING.   CAPTURE
OF LOUISBURG.

CHAPTER VII.

THE FRENCH WAR. 1753–1756.

CHAPTER VIII.

THE FRENCH WAR. 1756–1763.

CHAPTER IX.

CONTESTS WITH THE CROWN.

CHAPTER X.

BEGINNING OF THE STRUGGLE. THE STAMP ACT.

CHAPTER XI.

THE REVENUE ACT. TROOPS IN BOSTON.

CHAPTER XII.

MILITARY RULE. THE BOSTON MASSACRE.

CHAPTER XIII.

PROGRESS OF THE STRUGGLE. COMMITTEES OF CORRESPONDENCE.

CHAPTER XIV.

THE BOSTON TEA PARTY. THE BATTLE OF LEXINGTON.

HISTORY OF MASSACHUSETTS.

CHAPTER I.

THE PROVINCE OF THE MASSACHUSETTS BAY.

THE erection of the Province of the Massachusetts Bay introduced a new era in the history of New England. It was the second act of the great drama, whose third brought freedom to a wide-spread republic. Changes in both hemispheres had been preceded by a revolution in some respects analogous to that which resulted in the independence of America. The revolution of 1688, to England and her dependencies, was a vindication of the rights of the English people against the aggressions of arbitrary power. The revolution of 1776, to America, was a vindication of the rights of the American people against similar oppression. Principles were at stake in both cases — great and momentous principles. But difference of circumstances gave to the latter revolution far higher consequence than to the former.

In reviewing the colonial history of Massachusetts, it will be perceived that the germs of our national greatness inhered in the first settlers ; and the whole of that history is a record of their development. The mission of the Pilgrims, and that of the Puritans, was by no means an aimless mission. They came to these shores for a definite purpose, and shaped their course in accordance with that purpose. And it was the

CHAP.
I.

1692.

noblest purpose which can sway human beings — the enjoyment of religious, in connection with civil, freedom ; as large
a share of both as was attainable, and a share which, if limited at first and tainted with errors, increased with the
enlightenment of the people, and as they became better fitted
to appreciate its blessings.

The development of nations is by the law of progression.
Neither political nor social theories spring into existence
spontaneously ; nor can they be improvised in a moment, like
the songs of Italian minstrels. They are the fruit of perspic-
uous and profound meditation ; the result of the collision of
mind with mind. Not only is the legislation of a community
subject to this law, but it is discernible in more vital affairs,
affecting man's spiritual interests. The world moves on, not
blindly nor by chance, but in accordance with the plans of
Infinite Wisdom. No "spiked gates and impassable barriers"
can be reared to arrest its course. And though its whole
fruitage is mingled and tempered with

"Light and shade, and ill and good,"

alternating in striking but harmonious vicissitude, yet good
grows indestructibly, and propagates itself in spite of, and
even among, the entanglements of evil ; so that none need
despair of the destinies of humanity.

In looking back to the past, and comparing it with the
present, the contrast is so great that the sciolist, in his self-
conceit, is apt to imagine there was nothing good in the olden
times ; and the whole fabric of society, its forms of faith, its
manners and customs, and every thing which gave to it a dis-
tinctive character, are to him of little moment. He forgets
that what is valued to-day may be lightly esteemed to-morrow,
and that the superior enlightenment of the nineteenth century
may be but as a rushlight to the twentieth or the thirtieth
century. It is as absurd to underrate the past as it is foolish
to overrate the present. The past is the parent of the pres-

ent, as the present is of the future ; nor would the present be CHAP.
what it is had it not been for the past. Viewed in this light, I.
trivial incidents become important. Truth has been constantly 1692.
working itself clearer, and depositing the evils resulting from
ignorance.

By the caviller, errors may be pointed out in the history
of every nation ; nor is individual life exempt from their
influence. The question is not, therefore, what were the
errors of the past, but what were its aims. It is by this test
the reflecting mind metes out its judgments. The men who
have preceded us in the race are worthy of credit for all they
accomplished ; and if their achievements appear trifling in
comparison with our own, or if they are mixed up with the
evils incident to humanity, it is to be borne in mind that it
is always a more difficult, as it is a more perilous task, to go
on the forlorn hope of truth ; and it is comparatively easy,
after the breach has been made, to enter the city and seize its
possessions. But he who clears the way is entitled to at least
as much honor as he who follows after. The pioneer must be
a man of unfaltering courage.

That much had been effected for the prosperity of Massachusetts in the less than three fourths of a century which had
elapsed from the settlement of its territory, will be evident
from even a cursory glance at the condition of the colonies.
Plymouth, in the seventy-two years following the landing of
the Pilgrims, had made good progress in wealth and pop- 1620-92.
ulation. The colony was divided into three counties, —
Plymouth, Bristol, and Barnstable, — and contained seventeen
towns[1] and a population of at least seven thousand souls.[2]
Industry, frugality, and an exemplary integrity were the char-

---

[1] These were, Plymouth, Scituate,
Duxbury, Barnstable, Sandwich, Yar-
mouth, Taunton, Marshfield, Rehoboth, Eastham, Bridgewater, Dartmouth, Swansey, Middleborough,
Freetown, Rochester, and Falmouth.

[2] I deduce this from minutes of the
population of different towns, as Plymouth, Scituate, Duxbury, &c. No
general census had been taken at this
date.

CHAP. acteristics of her people ; and, however humble their circum-
  I.   stances or feeble their strength, the noble men who established
1692.   this colony will never cease to be gratefully remembered as
        the fathers of New England and the founders of its glory.

            Massachusetts, in the sixty-six years following the settle-
1626-92. ment of Salem, had advanced with rapid strides in the ca-
        reer of improvement. The colony was divided into four
        counties, — Suffolk, Essex, Middlesex, and Hampshire,[1] — and
        contained fifty-five towns[2] and a population of at least forty
        thousand souls.[3] Boston was the capital ; and this town,
        the largest in New England, contained one thousand build-
        ings and seven thousand persons.[4] Roads radiated in every
        direction from the metropolis to the surrounding villages,
        forming the media of communication with their inhabitants.
        The more distant hamlets were buried in the depths of the pri-
        meval forests, the only paths leading to them being indicated
        by marked trees ; and ragged rocks, piled in heaps, or scattered
        around in commingled confusion, often impeded the progress
        of the wayfarer in reaching those settlements. Yet as many

[1] Part of the towns formerly constituting the county of Old Norfolk
had been joined to New Hampshire ;
the rest were comprised in the county
of Essex.

[2] These were, Salem, Charlestown,
Boston, Medford, Roxbury, Dorches-
ter, Watertown, Cambridge, Ipswich,
Hingham, Weymouth, Dedham, New-
bury, Concord, Springfield, Lynn,
North Chelsea, Sudbury, Salisbury,
Rowley, Braintree, Woburn, Glouces-
ter, Haverhill, Wenham, Hull, Man-
chester, Andover, Malden, Marble-
head, Topsfield, Medfield, Lancaster,
Billerica, Northampton, Marlborough,
Milton, Hadley, Chelmsford, Groton,
Mendon, Amesbury, Beverly, West-
field, Hatfield, Dunstable, Wrentham,
Brookfield, Sherburne, Bradford, Deer-
field, Stow, Worcester, Boxford, and
Newton.

[3] Josselyn, Voy. p. 183, ed. 1675,
extravagantly estimates the population
of New England at "ten hundred

thousand souls." Randolph, in Hutch.
Coll. 484, computes the population
of Massachusetts, Maine, and New
Hampshire at one hundred and fifty
thousand, in 1676. Andros, in N. Y.
Docts. iii. 262, speaks of ten thousand
freemen in Massachusetts in 1678.
From official reports, however, made
to the Board of Trade in 1715, it appears that the population of Massachusetts at that date was but ninety-
four thousand ; and as the population
doubled once in twenty-five or thirty
years, the estimate for 1692 could not
have exceeded forty or fifty thousand.
Compare N. Y. Docts. v. 397 ; Grahame, ii. 92 ; Williamson's Me. ii. 37 ,
Bancroft, ii. 450.

[4] Mather, Magnalia, b. I. Randolph computed the number of houses
in Boston, in 1676, at two thousand.
Hutch. Coll. 487. For further particulars, see Neal's New England,588 ;
Grahame, i. 292, &c.

a scene which, at a distance, looks desert and rockbound, un-
folds itself, when visited, into vales of the rarest beauty, so,
nestled among the hills, were embryo villages, now densely
populated, which, in the Arcadian simplicity of earlier times,
presented points of attraction sufficient to allure thither the
yeomanry of the land, whose diligent toil caused " the wilderness and the solitary place to be glad for them, and the desert
to rejoice and blossom as the rose."

The principal trading towns of the colony were Boston,
Charlestown, and Salem ; and there was " some little trade
for country people at Ipswich and Newberry." [1] The buildings
in the country — irregular in their shape, and of a rude style
of architecture, varying in size and in the quality of their
workmanship — were mostly of timber ; and many of them
were fortified with strong palisades, as a security from the
arrows and small shot of the Indians.   In Boston, though
most of the houses were of timber, there were several of brick,
with " some few of stone, of competent strength and largeness
sutable to the condition of the owners ; " and three churches
or meeting houses, in different localities, sufficed for the religious accommodation of the people. [2]

Manufactures of linen and woollen cloth, shoes, hats, and a
few other articles, were nowhere extensively conducted, but
were principally confined to the family circle, and designed
for home consumption.   The staple commodities were fish and
peltry, with live stock, provisions, and lumber in its various
forms.   Timber for shipping could be had in abundance, with
tar, and pitch, and a variety of naval stores.   Iron was smelt-
ed in a few places, " though in noe great quantity ; " the manufacture of gunpowder had been introduced ; [3] and hemp and
flax grew well, though " labor was so deare that it could not
bee made a commodity to send to other parts, but was only

[1] Comp. Randolph, in Hutch. Coll.
484.
[2] See Hutch. Col. 487, and Josselyn, in 3 M. H. Coll. iii. 319.

[3] Randolph, in Hutch. Coll. 487,
says there were six forges in Massachusetts in 1676. The powder mill was
at Dorchester.

CHAP.
I.

1680.

1678.

improved by the country people for their own occasions."[1] Articles imported from England were "of all sorts generally which that land affords," and amounted in value to forty or fifty thousand pounds per annum.[2] The number of English merchants within the government, bred to the calling, was estimated, in 1680, at only twenty, though there were "near as many others that do trade and merchandise more or less." Of foreign merchants, at the same date, it is affirmed there were none, though a few years later there were certainly several.[3]

There were some slaves in the colony, and had been for many years; but "there hath been no company of blacks or slaves," it is added, "brought into the country since the beginning of this plantation, for the space of fifty yeares; only one small vessell, about two yeares since, after twenty months' voyage to Madagasca, brought hither betwixt forty and fifty negros, most women and children, sold here for ten, fifteen, and twenty pounds apiece, which stood the merchants in neer forty pounds apiece, one with another. Now and then, two or three negros are brought hither from Barbados and other of his majesties plantations, and sold here for about twenty pounds apiece; so that there may be within our government about one hundred, or one hundred and twenty; and it may be as many Scots, brought hither and sold for servants in the time of the warr with Scotland, and most now married and living here; and about halfe so many Irish, brought hither at severall times as servants." Slavery in general, however, was so repugnant to the principles of the Puritans that it was viewed with abhorrence; and, fortunately for New England, it never reached the dignity of a fixed "institution," to be cherished forever.[4]

[1] See Randolph, in Hutch. Coll. 494, 495.
[2] Such is Bradstreet's estimate; that of Randolph is somewhat different.

[3] See Dunton's Journal, in 2 M. H. Coll, ii. 98 et seq.
[4] Randolph, in Hutch. Coll. 485, speaks of two hundred slaves in the colony in 1676. The earliest public

Of the English population the estimates vary. Four or five
hundred whites are said to have been born yearly, taking one
year with another; and the number of marriages was estimated at from two to three hundred per annum. The number
of births exceeded the number of deaths, except during the
prevalence of wars and pestilences.[1] The wealth of the people was quite widely distributed. There were rich merchants
in Boston,[2] but few planters had great estates; and he was
accounted rich among farmers who was worth from ten to
fifteen hundred pounds. The commerce of the country was
remarkably extensive. From one to two hundred [3] ships,
sloops, ketches, and other vessels, belonging to the colony,
either English or home built, were employed in the carrying
trade; and of these, from eight to ten were of a hundred tons
burden and upwards; three or four were of two hundred
tons; the forty or fifty fishing ketches were of from twenty
to forty tons; and six or eight ships, owned in England,
annually visited Boston to trade with the people.

Temporary obstructions to trade frequently arose; and
these originated from an overstocked market, the depredations of pirates, the interruption of the fisheries by the French
at the eastward, and the double custom paid for sugar, indigo,
cotton, wool, and tobacco, first at the places from which these

---

advertisement of slaves for sale I have
met with is in the Boston News Letter for 1704, No. 6; but slaves were
doubtless sold before that time. The
statistics of slavery in Massachusetts
do not, at any period of its history,
show that the people at large viewed
the institution with favor; and the increase of the number of slaves in all
the New England colonies was always
small in comparison with their increase
in the colonies at the south. See
Annals Am. Stat. Ass. vol. i.; Holmes's
Am. Annals; Grahame, vol. ii., &c.

[1] I have seen no published estimates of the deaths in Massachusetts
before 1692; but in the Boston News

Letter, No. 11, the deaths in Boston
were, in 1701, 146 persons; in 1702,
441 persons; and in 1703, 159 persons.

[2] Comp. Randolph, in Hutch. Coll.
484, 485, and Josselyn, Voy. 180.
Also, Bradstreet, in 3 M. H. Coll. viii.
337.

[3] Randolph, in Hutch. Coll. 496,
says there were 730 vessels owned in
Massachusetts in 1676. For the estimate of the General Court in 1665,
see 2 M. H. Coll. vii. 72. See also
3 M. H. Coll. i. 98; Frothingham's
Hist. Charlestown; and Brooks's Hist.
Medford.

CHAP.
I.

1680.

commodities were brought, and again at the places to which they were sent.[1] No rates or duties were imposed in the colony upon goods exported,[2] which were generally the produce of the country, obtained with hard labor, and sold at low prices ; and but one penny per pound value was charged upon goods imported,[3] which, with a like tax on real and personal estate, a capitation tax of twenty pence per head,[4] and a small excise on wines and other spirituous liquors, produced an income of about fifteen hundred pounds per annum[5] — the sole revenue for the support of the government, the salaries of officers, the charges of fortifications, and the maintenance of a garrison at the Castle. During the Indian wars, the expenses and taxes were necessarily increased from ten to fifteen fold, much to the impoverishment of the country, which became burdened with a debt which it required years to cancel.[6]

Besides the college at Cambridge, which was in a comparatively flourishing condition, the interests of education were fostered in every town ; and each town had its ample church and its settled minister, though "some able schollars fit for the ministery rather wanted imploiment." For the religious instruction of the people, the ministers preached generally twice on the Lord's day, besides lecturing in some of the larger towns on the week days, and catechized "the children and youth of the place as they had oppertunity." The maintenance of the ministers in Boston was by voluntary contribution ; in the rest of the towns their salaries were raised by a yearly assessment upon all the inhabitants, " the severall courts

---

[1] Comp. 3 M. H. Coll. i. 98.
[2] Except horses, on which a duty of sixpence each was charged. Hutch. Coll. 497.
[3] For a table of customs, given by Randolph, see Hutch. Coll. 497.
[4] Comp. Hutch. Coll. 496.
[5] Randolph, in Hutch. Coll. 498, sets the revenue at £20,000 per an-

num; but, as Hutchinson well observes, "he has put one cypher more than he should have done. The annual charges never amounted to £2000 until the Indian wars."
[6] Randolph, in Hutch. Coll. 498, estimates this debt at £50,000 ; Bradstreet at "above £40,000."

takeing speciall care that all ministers have comfortable maintenance allowed them, according to the poor ability of the
place and people."[1] "We have no beggars," concludes the
narrative from which most of the foregoing facts have been
gleaned, "and few idle vagabonds, except now and then some
Quakers from Road Island, &c., that much molest us, and
endanger the seducing of the people where they come. And
all townes are enjoined by law to take care of and provide
for all the poor, decayed, and impotent persons within their
respective limits, which accordingly they doe."[2]

This picture of the colony in 1680 is of course imperfect as
applied to its condition in 1692. There had been some growth
in that period, and some important changes. Yet, as a whole,
it is a valuable sketch, emanating from the chief magistrate
of Massachusetts, and one who, for more than sixty years,
participated in its movements and promoted its prosperity.[3]
With the imperfect data furnished by scattered and often conflicting documents, it is obviously difficult to reproduce exactly
the condition of the colonies at the time their territory was
merged into one; but the little that is known of that condition
is sufficient to impress us with a profound conviction of the
eminent worth of the men to whom the destinies of the country
had been confided, and of the value of their services in developing its resources and strengthening the basis upon which
their commonwealth was built. In their connection with the
mother country, every where a strait bond of obedience inflexibly held them down; their yearnings for freedom were
rigidly restrained; and many and desperate had been their
struggles with the Stuarts. Yet it is with colonies as with
trees; the winds which shake serve rather to strengthen their
hold upon the soil than to uproot or prostrate them, and

[1] Randolph, in Hutch. Coll. 501; Josselyn, Voy. 180; 3 M. H. Coll. iii. 331.
[2] 3 M. H. Coll. viii. 332–340.
[3] The venerable Simon Bradstreet, who died at Salem, in 1697, at the advanced age of 94. See Felt's Hist. Salem; Allen's and Eliot's Biog. Dict's; N. E. Hist. Gen. Reg.; Drake's Boston, &c.

CHAP. furnish the exercise which develops their powers, giving to
I.   them an increase of vitality and beauty.

1692.   That is certainly an amiable weakness, if weakness it may
be called, which looks at the past with a slight degree of
enthusiasm ; and such weakness may be excused in the historian, if it does not degenerate into indiscriminate eulogy.
Especially is it excusable in considering the history of Massachusetts ; for much as the Puritans have been decried as illib-
eral fanatics, there were traits in their character of inestima-
ble worth. In tracing their career, it is too often forgotten
that it is necessary to have some toleration for the infirmities
of men whose very excesses sprang from profound reverence
for God and his word. With the Puritan, religion was a
matter of conscience between himself and his God. With a
sincere conviction of the truth of Christianity, and an earnest
desire to conform to its requirements in the minutest particular, he held it to be his duty, and the duty of all, to be
guided by the Scriptures. Life was to be pervaded with the
spirit of piety. There was to be an entire consecration of
its aims to God. Every thing which weakened the sense of
dependence on him was to be scrupulously avoided. Men
were to walk with God. The flesh and its lusts were to be
subdued and crucified : the body was to be a temple meet for
His dwelling. Nothing was innocent which led to forgetful-
ness of Him : nothing was irksome which would purchase His
favor. Religion, with the Puritan, was the Alpha and the
Omega ; the beginning and the end. His faith, it is true, was
cast in the sternest mould. It enthroned God as the Sovereign
of the universe, and made man as clay in the hands of the
potter. To ridicule this creed is to ridicule cherished convictions of millions. Yet, to do justice to the Puritans, no one
is required to indorse all their doctrines. Their integrity,
their piety, their earnestness, will ever be honored, and every
thing else which gave to their characters manliness and vigor.
It would be singular if they exhausted the fountain of truth :

it would be singular if we had sounded its utmost depths. Honesty of conviction and sincerity of purpose are cheerfully conceded to them, and a piety as fervent as ever existed. They lived in an age of general intolerance, an age of intense and violent excitement. They lived, too, at a time when political theories were imperfectly defined, and when monarchs were grudgingly conceding as privileges what the people afterwards understood to be their own, independent of the favor of royalty. And much that has been condemned, and which it is found difficult to excuse, in their conduct, sprang from this source. As we would be judged by our descendants, so should we judge our ancestors.

It is an unfounded charge, however, that the first settlers of New England were universally bigoted ; for many might be named, both in Plymouth and in Massachusetts, who were worthy disciples of the principles of the reformation, and who carried those principles to as high a degree of theoretic perfection as could have then been expected. And it is, perhaps, true, that the right of exercising private judgment in matters of religion was, in terms at least, more generally recognized than many suppose. It is scarcely possible, indeed, to maintain more expressly, as a fundamental principle, the right of every man to think for himself and judge for himself than did some of the most approved leaders of the colonies.[1] True, the gods of Olympus reigned paramount in the Pantheon, and heresy was accounted the greatest of all sins. It was hardly realized that no great harm could result from allowing theological speculation to have free course, and to look fearlessly towards all the thirty-two points of the compass, whithersoever it listed. Hence dissent was denounced as a direful evil ; and if our ancestors were reluctant to concede to others the rights which they claimed for themselves, it was because of their conviction of the truth of their own

[1] Quincy's Hist. H. Coll. i. 49, 50.

opinions, and the conceived impossibility of holding different opinions without overthrowing as well the pillars of their political fabric as the fundamentals of Christian faith, and denying doctrines which had been cherished for centuries as sound and evangelical, and for which the fathers of the church and the early reformers had alike zealously contended.

As society advances, however, it carries men onward in the path of progression; and doctrines once cherished as sacred and venerable give place to new systems, answering to the higher demands of our spiritual nature. The light which at first fitfully gleamed upon a few souls, increases in brilliancy and penetrates other souls, until at last its effulgence, like that of the sun in its meridian splendor, warms and invigorates the whole mass of humanity. The creed of the nineteenth century is not the creed of the seventeenth century, nor is Puritanism in our days what it was in the days of Wilson and Norton.

It is with the political progress of nations, however, that history principally deals. Yet it should never be forgotten that, in all communities, the religious element enters largely into the constitution of civil society, and that the institutions of a country are more or less moulded by the faith of the people upon those subjects which relate to the highest interests of man. Especially is this true of New England, for its foundations were religiously laid.[1] Spiritual forces have predominated here, and above all other forces have they shaped our destiny. The controversies which have arisen have not been mere sectarian wranglings, fields for the display of theological gladiatorship;

---

[1] To some, it may seem the height of folly to assert that the foundations of New England were religiously laid; for, of the hundred passengers of the Mayflower, at least half were women and children; and the other half was composed of adventurers and servants, as well as of members of Mr. Robinson's church. But the character of an enterprise should be judged, not so much by the numbers which espouse it, as by the spirit of its leaders; and few will dispute that Carver, and Bradford, and Winslow, and Brewster were religious men, and came to these shores for religion's sake. These were the fathers of New England. They gave life to its institutions; and its foundations were laid by them in reverence to God.

they are indices of the spiritual activity of the people — an CHAP.
activity which, it is hoped, will never degenerate into mere
latitudinarianism, or cease to exert a healthy and inspiring 1692.
influence.

The connection between the colonial and the provincial history of Massachusetts can be fully understood only by an acquaintance with the political opinions of the people. According to the maxims of English jurisprudence, the civil organization of government resembled a living body ; and every individual existing or arising within that body was part of it as a whole, actually and indissolubly connected with it. No individual or number of individuals, it was contended, from a distinct principle within themselves, or from their own will, could emigrate and quit that community so as to separate and fly off from the body, and effectually dissolve their connection with the same. Besides, the territory upon which the emigrants settled was claimed by the English crown as a part of its dominions ; and although a charter was granted them, which permitted them to form a separate and distinct community, and establish a government having sovereign jurisdiction within its own limits, yet, being settled on the lands and within the dominions of the parent state, it was claimed that they remained " under a certain relation of allegiance to the general and supreme *imperium.*" True, it was by the consent of the king that this emigration was made ; and the emigrants had license from him to transport themselves, their children, their servants, and their goods, but on the implied condition that their lands were to be held of the king, and that they were to remain under the protection of, and in subordination to, his sovereign power.

If these points were conceded, however, as general maxims, it was at the same time contended, on the part of the colonists, that the circumstances of their emigration were peculiar, and such as warranted a construction of these maxims different from that which was ordinarily received. They affirmed — and the correctness of their position was afterwards admitted [1] — that, though they went forth under a charter from the king, yet, as their community consisted of individuals possessing the rights, liberties, and franchises of English subjects, they had a right to political liberty, so far as was consistent with a due subordination to the parent state ; that they were entitled to have, to hold, and to enjoy, within the body of their colony, a free government, of the like privileges, jurisdictions, and preëminences as those of the state from which they emigrated ; that they were entitled to the like power of reasoning and will in a similar legislature, and to a like judicature and executive powers within the bounds of their corporation, as the government of the mother country had within its own realm : in short, that the colony, as a politically free being, had a right to all those internal powers which were essential to its being as a free agent. The power of Parliament to tax them without their consent, since they were unrepresented in that body, was generally denied ; and the right of trial by jury in all cases was inflexibly demanded.[2]

These claims, in their fullest extent, were not, indeed, held valid in England ; for Parliament claimed, if it did not exercise, the right to tax the colonies for the benefit of the mother country ; to regulate their commerce ; and to legislate for them in a general way to secure their dependence. The conviction, however, is forced upon our minds, that the statesmen of England, at this date, had formed no adequate conception of the true nature of the relation of the colonies to the crown. Not only were cabinets at variance in their views, but the advice of eminent jurists was often conflicting.[3] The prevalent opinions, if rigidly applied, would have reduced the colonists to vassals rather than have placed them on the footing of

[1] Pownal, Admin. of the Br. Col's, pt. 2, from which the abstract in the text is principally drawn.

[2] Comp. Franklin's Works, iv. 274; Grahame, Colon. Hist. i. 557.
[3] See the acknowledgment of Chalmers, Revolt, i. 308, 309.

subjects. Hence the policy of the monarchs was selfish and
arrogant ; fatal to the interests of the people, and sure to
awaken a spirit of resistance. It was feared that the colonies,
if unchecked, would become formidable rivals, and cast off their
allegiance. It was not perceived that the ties of consanguinity
were sufficient to bind the children to the parent ; and that
gratitude was a more powerful motive to obedience than fear.
It was supposed that the only way to keep the colonies within
bounds was to cripple them by the arm of physical power.

But the founders of New England were experienced statesmen ; nor as diplomatists were they inferior to the diplomatists
of England. The principal men, of the clergy and of the laity,
possessed disciplined minds, and talents which would have distinguished them in any sphere of action. Trained to take
part in political discussions, and with a sagacity which intui-
tively penetrated the disguises of despotism, they wrought for
posterity ; and the cause in which they engaged was emphatically the cause of freedom and humanity. Not only is America
indebted to them for the blessings of civil liberty, but the world
is indebted to them for initiating the work of popular government and universal improvement : the world is indebted to
them for scattering broadcast the seeds of imperishable political truths, which have been wafted on the wings of every breeze
to the nations of Europe, to ripen in due time to a harvest of
blessings.

The provincial history of Massachusetts is a continuation of
its colonial history under different circumstances. The character of the people was formed before the new government was
instituted ; and the spirit of liberty was too widely diffused to
be easily crushed. The arbitrary reign of the Stuarts was
over ; the struggle for the recognition of Episcopacy had
ceased ; yet Puritanism was still in the ascendant, and the
Puritan principles were as vital as ever. The changes which
had taken place had not materially affected the views of the
people. Freedom was the beacon light guiding them on ; and

CHAP. the desire to enjoy it throbbed high in every heart. Not that
  I.   absolute independence was sought ; nor could it probably have
1692. been secured had it been sought. But the motto of all was, all
freedom consistent with the acknowledged allegiance of subjects. It was impossible to stifle the conviction which had
sprung up that freedom is the inalienable birthright of man,
not to be parted with on any terms whatever. And it was
impossible to check the tendencies towards republicanism which
had grown with their growth and strengthened with their
strength. Time only was needed, with its varied experience,
to lead them to claim freedom in its highest and broadest form.
But it is unjust to our fathers to assert that they were insincere
in their professions of attachment to England ; that the allegiance they acknowledged was not real, but nominal ; and that
they were studiously and systematically laboring to deceive.
If ever men were honest in their views, the people of Massachusetts were honest. Nor was it their fault if, maddened by
oppression, they felt it to be their duty to assert their natural
rights, and to demand what was withheld from them by arbitrary power alone.

The province charter of 1692 differed in many respects from
the charter of Charles I. The government under the latter
instrument, after its transfer, was established by the people ;
and all officers were chosen by the majority of the votes of the
freemen of the colony, attending at Boston, in person or by
proxy, without summons, on the last Wednesday in Easter term
annually. The deputies to the General Court were chosen by
the freemen of each town. No town could send more than two
deputies ; towns having but twenty freemen could send but
one ; and those having less than ten could not send any.
No person being an attorney was eligible as a deputy ; and
all persons aspiring to the immunities of citizenship were required to be church members, in full communion, and approved
by the General Court. The legislative power was seated in
the General Court, from which there was no appeal. This

court was likewise the supreme judicature of the colony, having CHAP. sole power to make laws, raise money, levy taxes, dispose of I. lands, give and confirm property, impeach, sentence, and pardon 1692. criminals, and receive appeals from inferior courts; and it could not be adjourned or dissolved without the consent of the major part of its members.

In ordinary cases the governor and assistants sat apart, and transacted business by themselves, drawing up bills and orders, which, being agreed upon, were sent to the deputies for assent or dissent. The deputies also sat by themselves, consulting upon the common good; and all matters acted upon by them were sent to the magistrates for concurrence or nonconcurrence. No law could be made without the consent of the major part of the magistrates and the greater number of the deputies; and the governor had a casting vote in all courts and assemblies, and could call a General Court, or any other court or council, at his pleasure. The executive power was lodged in the governor and council, of whom seven constituted a quorum, the governor or deputy being one; but in particular emergencies the acts of a less number were valid, so far as related to the impressment of soldiers, seamen, ships, ammunition, provisions, and all other necessaries for the public defence; and warrants could be drawn upon the public treasury for the payment of these expenses. Under this charter, with all its defects, a high degree of political independence had been enjoyed; and its destruction was feared as the precursor of the destruction of all it had secured.[1]

By the terms of the provincial charter, the governor, the lieutenant governor, and the secretary, were appointed by the king; and the powers conferred upon the former were supposed to be sufficient to counterbalance the republican tendencies of the people, and keep them in a state of immediate subjection. But if the powers of the people were circumscribed, they were

[1] See Randolph, in Hutch. Coll. 477, 478; Hutchinson, ii. 15.

ː.ot annihilated. A share in the administration of affairs was conceded to them; nor could it have been withheld without exciting a spirit of rebellion. Yet no act of the legislature was valid without the consent of the governor; and, as the appointment of all military officers was vested in him solely, and it was in his power to reject other officers chosen by the people or their deputies, his influence upon the affairs of the province was great, and might be so wielded as to repress the soarings of the spirit of freedom, and favor the designs entertained by his employers. All laws passed in the province were subjected to revision by the king, and to rejection at his pleasure; and appeals were allowed in personal actions where the matter in dispute exceeded in value the sum of three hundred pounds. Liberty of conscience was assured to all but Papists; and worship in the Episcopal form was placed on the same footing as worship in the Congregational form. Church membership was no longer to be the qualification for citizenship; but all persons of a certain estate were entitled to its immunities, and were eligible to office. In some respects the new charter was preferable to the old; in others it was but its shadow. As a whole, it has been doubted whether its defects were not as great as the defects of the former instrument. Certain it is that, from the powers it reserved to the king, and the extent of his prerogative, many reluctantly consented to its acceptance, and trembled for the consequences of its adoption to the country. Yet it was the supreme law of the land, and continued such, with but slight alterations, until the nation threw off the yoke of bondage, and asserted its title to freedom and self-government.[1]

The circumstances of the country, at the date of the arrival of this charter, have been already partially described. The old institutions, which had grown up under the colonial char-

[1] Mather, Magnalia, b. ii., Life of Phips, § 14; Dummer's Defence, pp. 4, 5, ed. 1721; Minot, i. 57.

ter, yet existed, or were but imperfectly eradicated. The laws of the country had undergone but little alteration. The tenures of lands were substantially such as prevailed when the Body of Liberties was framed. And though a new church and a new ritual had been admitted, which were to be fostered from abroad, the old churches were still in the ascendant, and the old ministers had lost little of their influence. In political affairs, no servile doctrines were eagerly avowed, contrary to the maxims which had long prevailed ; and few were in haste to signalize their loyalty by the basest ingratitude, insolence, and treachery. Differences of opinion, indeed, had arisen ; and there were two parties in the land — the party of freedom, and the party of prerogative : the former exceedingly jealous of all encroachments from the mother country ; the latter inclining to yield to her demands rather than by resistance to arouse her anger, and, without doubt, honestly of opinion that a partial compliance would be for the interest of the country, by commending it to the royal favor, and averting the consequences of discord and confusion. Patriotism, if ever pure, is pure in the hour of trial and discipline. Its senses are quickened by the consciousness of danger. It scents from afar the approach of tyranny, and prepares for the contest with firmness and courage. There was much of such patriotism in the fathers of New England. Unquestionably there were some who were sordid and selfish ; incapable of true friendship ; sensual, frivolous, false, and cold-hearted ; hurried on by the promptings of a lawless ambition. Such possess few qualities which command the esteem of the world ; few which entitle them to be named with respect. Yet the number in Massachusetts who would rank in this category was exceedingly small. The temper of the times was ill suited to their growth.

The people of New England were emphatically a moral people. If the legislation of a community indicates the evils which prevail in its borders, it at the same time indicates the standard of public opinion. Mistakes have been committed in all ages,

CHAP.   perhaps, in legislating for the suppression of vice, and too much
 I.   stress has been laid upon penal enactments.   But over legisla-
1692.   tion is better than none ; for vice, if unchecked, grows like
        weeds.   The precise point beyond which restraint ceases to be
        salutary, it may be difficult to determine ; but it is better to
        suffer the inconvenience of imperfect laws, than to tolerate
        practices subversive of the best interests of all classes of society.
        It is no impeachment, therefore, of the wisdom of our ancestors,
        if, in some things, they went farther than would be approved at
        the present day.   Their motives were good, if their policy was
        defective.   But for their policy they found precedents in the
        writings of the Old Testament ; and their earnestness to pro-
        mote the welfare of the community is an evidence of their
        recognition of the claims of practical religion.   I know not
        where else in the world to look for nobler specimens of unbend-
        ing integrity than among the early settlers of New England.
        All who have written intelligently of those days have concurred
        in awarding them a high share of praise.   Stern they may have
        been, and rigid to a fault ; but better that than the laxity which
        confounds all moral distinctions, and looks with indifference
        upon the decay of substantial virtue, or views unmoved the
        inroads of licentiousness, profligacy, and crime.

        Some may sneer at laws regulating the use of intoxicating
        drinks, punishing incontinency, prohibiting the taking of tobacco
        in the highway, kissing on the Sabbath, and other the like civil
        regulations.   Candid minds see in such things evidence of the
        scrupulousness of the age ; and if such legislation proved inef-
        ficient, it was because human passions are not always suscepti-
        ble of outward control.   The Puritan may have erred in the
        excess of his zeal against what he esteemed the sinful customs
        of the established church ; and he may have condemned too
        severely indulgence in those amusements which the spirit of
        youth naturally craves, and which, within rational bounds, can
        never be deemed criminal.   But it was his desire to build up a
        strong character — strong in the elements of a rigid morality.

To the accomplishment of this object he bent all his energies ; CHAP
and hence he prohibited both dancing and drinking, masses and I.
merriment, hunting and hawking, starched ruffs and stiff petti- 1692.
coats, and every thing else which betrayed, to his eye, a leaning
to the world, or the fashions of the world. And, without doubt,
we owe much to this code of inflexible morals in diffusing
throughout the New England character a reverence for sacred
things, and the subjection of the passions to the control of reason.

In point of intellectual culture, the condition of the colonies
did not admit the classical refinement which distinguished a
later period. Printing was introduced into Massachusetts in
1639 ; [1] yet in 1692 there were but a few presses established,[2]
and not a newspaper was issued until after the opening of the
eighteenth century.[3] Books were comparatively scarce ; and
those which were in circulation were mostly of a religious character, though the libraries of the clergy and of the wealthy
laity were many of them respectable in size and varied in contents. The versification of the age was exceedingly rude. The
poems of Mrs. Anne Bradstreet constitute the principal exception
to this remark.[4] We shall look in vain, among the specimens
which have descended to us from Governor Bradford, Secretary
Morton, Edward Johnson, and John Norton, for pieces equalling in merit those of Milton and Dryden. Anagrams, halting,
limping, and pointless ; epitaphs, ponderous, stiff, and leaden-
winged, were the ordinary evidences of the existence of the
" divine passion." Of few could it be said, —

---

[1] The first press was at Cambridge, and was brought over by Mr. Glover. Pierce's Hist. H. Coll. 6 ; Quincy's Hist. H. Coll. i. 187, 188 ; Drake's Boston, 242, 424.

[2] I find, before 1692, the names of nine printers in Massachusetts, viz. : S. Day, S. Green, S. Sewall, Jno. Foster, Jno. Allen, Benj. Harris, Barth. Green, Jas. Glen, and Marma- duke Johnson. MS. Notes of S. G. Drake, and the Mass. Archives.

[3] The first paper was the Boston News Letter, issued in 1704 ; the sec- ond was the Boston Gazette, printed in 1719 ; and the third was the New England Courant, printed by James Franklin, in 1721. Curious particu- lars concerning these papers may be seen in Thomas's Hist. Printing, the Mass. Hist. Coll's, and Buckingham's Reminiscences.

[4] Her volume was dedicated to her father, Governor Dudley, in a copy of verses dated March 20, 1642. A third edition was published in 1758.

"The poet's eye, in a fine frenzy rolling,
    Doth glance from heaven to earth, from earth to heaven;
    And, as imagination bodies forth
    The forms of things unknown, the poet's pen
    Turns them to shapes, and gives to airy nothing
    A local habitation and a name." [1]

It was an age of too much seriousness to admit of an ardent devotion to the Muses. The company of the Nine was devoutly eschewed. The classics, if not proscribed, were the delight of but few. Men who had before them a wilderness to subdue, cities to build, and a government to frame, had little leisure to devote to the elegances of life ; little time to spend in cultivating the imagination. Their poetry was in action, not in words. Yet there is enough in their character to form an epic of surpassing power ; and when "the hour and the man" come, we shall look for a delineation of their manners as pregnant with interest and as extensive in its influence as the legends of other days, which have immortalized the deeds of men far less earnest, and far less worthy of an undying fame.

The habits of the people were, for the most part, simple. Travelling was principally performed on foot or on horseback, the women mounted on pillions behind the men. Stage coaches were not introduced until near the close of the seventeenth century, and then we hear of but one.[2] Pleasure carriages were rarely seen, save in Boston, until towards the middle of the eighteenth century. The chaise was introduced at about that date.[3] The wagons of the farmers were rude structures, hung on thorough braces or bedded on the axles ; and, from the roughness of the roads, filled with stumps in many cases, riding was far from voluptuously easy, and a trip of a few miles was

[1] Midsummer Night's Dream, Act v. Sc. 1.
[2] In 1687, Lady Andros rode in a coach. Felt's Salem, i. 315 et seq.
[3] In 1753, there were no chaises in the counties of Worcester and Barn-stable ; but one was reported in Bristol ; and there were 47 in Essex, 50 in Middlesex, and about 200 in Suffolk. Felt's Salem, i. 316 ; Ann's Am. Stat. Ass'n, i. 348–358.

a sure cure for the dyspepsia. The roads of New England,
however, were not much worse than those of Old England at
the same date; for, in some of the best counties, at the opening
of the nineteenth century, travellers were subjected to as great,
if not to greater annoyances than existed in Massachusetts.[1]

Among the wealthy, the luxuries of life were indulged as
freely, perhaps, as among persons of like standing in the old
world. Their furniture was of a costly description; their apparel
was sumptuous; their tables groaned with delicacies; and their
hospitality was unbounded.[2] It was contrary, however, to the
sternness of the Puritan character to countenance or encourage
extravagant expenditures in living or dress; and sumptuary
laws prohibited unnecessary profusion, and attempted to pre-
scribe the length of the hair and the fashion of the dress.[3] The
yeomanry, who were the bulk of the people, were hardy, indus-
trious, temperate, and frugal; given to hospitality, and enjoying
the necessaries of life, with a fair share of its luxuries. But
pleasing as those days seem in comparison with our own, we
can hardly claim for them a particular preëminence; and the
more minutely we examine the annals of the past, the more
shall we find to satisfy us that the condition of the people, however simple, was not such as we should voluntarily choose for
our own lot. There is a charm which fancy lends to the past,
and, always, imaginative minds see things painted in colors of
unsurpassed brilliancy and beauty. And it is not, perhaps,
unnatural to desire to invest the lot of those who have preceded
us with some of the rose tints which render it attractive; but
could we go back in reality to any anterior age in the history
of the world, and live in it as it was, we should see enough to
convince us that

"Distance lends enchantment to the view,"

and that the past, so far from excelling the present, is as infe-

---

[1] See Dibdin's Tour, ed. 1801, 4to, vol. i. pp. 46–56.
[2] All travellers concur in commend-ing the hospitality of the people. See Randolph, Josselyn, Dunton, &c.
[3] Mass. Rec's, in different places.

CHAP. rior in comparison as the rough block of marble which the
 I.   sculptor is chiselling into the likeness of man, is inferior to the
1692. statue when finished, in its exquisite symmetry and life-like
expression.

Such were the people whose history is to be traced in these
pages : a peculiar people, zealous of good works : a people
descended from the best English stock ; yearning for freedom ;
far from perfect in their characters ; far from faultless in their
habits ; yet possessing the germs of a higher development, and
earnest to advance in the work of reform : men, who, less than
a century later, made themselves felt as the champions of liberty, and whose deeds of heroic valor challenged the admiration
of statesmen and philosophers.

CHAPTER II.

THE WITCHCRAFT DELUSION.

No event probably in the whole history of New England has furnished grounds for more serious charges affecting the character of the people than the witchcraft delusion, as it has been commonly termed; an episode of thrilling and melancholy interest, impressing the mind with a vivid sense of the evils of superstition, and the unhappy consequences which flow from that morbid excitement of the passion for the marvellous which seems to have had its cycles of recurrence from the earliest period to the present time. The mind of man is a perplexing mystery, which the wisest philosophers have failed to unravel. In its normal state it moves forward generally without much excitement; and the laws which govern its motions are laws of harmony and progressive improvement. But in its abnormal conditions, when its balance is disturbed and its functions are diseased, it soars aloft upon aerial excursions of the wildest description, guided by no chart but that of conjecture, and following, without judgment, the blind promptings of an erratic fancy, which spurns control, and rises higher and higher in its restless flight until, from utter exhaustion, its drooping pinions refuse longer to sustain its course, and it swoops down to earth again, glad to find rest, like the returning dove, from the waves which had swept over its abode in its absence, threatening to wash away the landmarks of ages.

Yet even the follies of our race are not without some compensation; and the discerning will find that

"There is some soul of goodness in things evil,
Would men observingly distil it out."

1692. The lessons which the world is taught by its errors are often of great service; and it would seem as if temporary fits of excitement, like occasional disturbances in the physical world, were necessary to purify the atmosphere, and to scatter the seeds from which new and more vigorous forms of life may spring. All such phenomena are controlled by a Power who has assured us that the wrath of man shall be made to praise him, and that the remainder of wrath he will restrain.

Ps. 76: 10.

From a cursory view of the popular delusions which have prevailed, it will be seen that on no subject has the human mind been more prone to dwell than upon the influence which spiritual agents have been supposed to exert upon beings in the flesh. The belief in such influence is as old as the Bible, and is often alluded to in the sacred writings. How far such belief is founded in truth, every man must judge for himself. Different minds form different conclusions from the same premises; and it would be presumptuous for any one to set up his own opinions as infallible. To many, it seems hardly credible that such belief should have prevailed so extensively without having some foundation;[1] nor can it be doubted that phenomena have occurred and do occur, for which the wisest and best have been and are unable to account. And although it does not necessarily follow that what cannot be accounted for may be legitimately ascribed to causes beyond the present sphere, neither does it follow that nothing can be ascribed to such causes, because such phenomena, when investigated, have been found, in most cases, to fall within the province of recondite laws, imperfectly defined, which have hitherto eluded the grasp of the mind. Profound mystery encircles life on every hand; and

[1] "It seems to me," says Blackstone, Com. b. iv. c. iv., "the most eligible way to conclude, that in general there has been such a thing as witchcraft, though one cannot give credit to any particular modern instance of it."

the world is only in its infancy in knowledge. What the future CHAP.
may unfold, it is impossible to say.   Time may bring wisdom II.
and increasing light ; and the prudent will suspend judgment 1692.
until such light appears. Nor can harm result from that cautious reserve which, while it leaves the mind open to conviction,
reposes calmly upon the power of truth. Wisdom will ever be
justified of her children.

Before sketching the progress of the witchcraft delusion in
Massachusetts, it may be proper to remark that the belief in
witchcraft was by no means confined to America, nor was it
the indigenous growth of the soil of New England.[1] Long
before the settlement of this country, all nations, civilized and
uncivilized, gave more or less credence to marvellous tales of
ghosts and witches ; and in England, within the bosom of the
national church, there had not been wanting a high degree of
credulity relative to the invisible world, and the supposed
power of demons and departed spirits to visit earth, to terrify
the timid and torment the helpless. The theories of ancient
philosophers, developed in the writings of Hesiod, Plato, Aris-
totle, Pythagoras, and Empedocles, incorporated into the poetry
of Homer, Virgil, Ovid, and Horace, and adopted, to some
extent, by the Jewish rabbis, peopled earth and sky with a
race of demons — beings between the gods and men, and the
channels or media through which intelligence was communicated from the one to the other.   Clothed with air, wander-
ing over heaven, hovering over the stars, or abiding in this
sphere at pleasure, they beheld unveiled the secrets of time,
attended man from the cradle to the grave, and, according to
their character, affected his fortunes for good or for ill. The
agatho dæmons were his good spirits, his wise counsellors, conducting his soul to the abodes of the blest. The *caco dæmons*

---

[1] The Indians, indeed, were supposed to be worshippers of the devil,
and their powwows to be wizards ; but
the form in which witchcraft prevailed
among them was somewhat different
from that of more civilized nations,
though similar in character and in its
pernicious effects. See T. Morton's
N. Eng. Can. ; N. Morton's N. Eng.
Mem. ; Hutchinson, ii. 22, &c.

were his evil spirits, the disturbers of his peace ; horrid phan-
toms which had power to annoy by inflicting diseases, convulsing
the body with frightful spasms, and driving their victims to the
verge of despair.[1]

The introduction of Christianity did not at once eradicate
these opinions, for the writings of the fathers abound in allusions to the doctrine of possessions. In the dark ages, superstition held unlimited sway. Nor at the dawn of the reformation were the mists which had brooded over the mind
wholly dispersed. No spell had been found sufficiently potent
to exorcise the delusions which had seized upon all. " He
that will needs perswade himself that there are no witches,"
says one, " would as faine be perswaded that there is no devill ;
and he that can already beleeve that there is no devill, will ere
long beleeve that there is no God."[2] Hence " every old woman
with a wrinkled face, a furr'd brow, a hairy lip, a gobber tooth,
a squint eye, a squeaking voyce, or a scolding tongue, having a
rugged coate on her back, a skull cap on her head, a spindle in
her hand, and a dog or cat by her side," was not only " suspected, but pronounced for a witch."[3] The young and the
beautiful — the bewitchers of modern times — were rarely accused ; but every town or village had its two or three old
women, who were charged with laming men, killing cattle, and
destroying children.[4] Nay, even a hare could not suddenly
spring from a hedge, or an " ugly weasel " run through one's
yard, or a " fowle great catte " appear in the barn, but it was
suspected as a witch.[5] " A big or a boyl, a wart or a wen, a
push or a pile, a scar or a scabbe, an issue or an ulcer," were

---

[1] For an elaborate sketch of the
opinions of the ancients, see Cud-
worth's Intellectual System of the
Universe.

[2] Gaule, Cases of Cons. concerning
Witchcraft, p. 1, ed. 1646.

[3] Gaule, pp. 4, 5. Riding through
the air on sticks was another infallible
token of witchcraft. Hale, 31.

[4] "There was not a village in England," says Addison, Spectator, No.
419, " that had not a ghost in it; the
churchyards were all haunted ; every
large common had a circle of fairies
belonging to it; and there was scarcely a shepherd to be met with who had
not seen a spirit."

[5] Gifford's Dialogue concerning
Witches, Lond. 1593.

"palpable witches markes;" and "every new disease, notable CHAP. accident, mirable of nature, rarity of art, and strange work or II. just judgment of God," was "accounted for no other but an 1692. act or effect of witchcraft." [1]

Hence England, in the seventeenth century, and every other nation of Europe, believed in the agency of evil spirits; and, guided by the statute of Moses, — "Thou shalt not suffer a Ex. 22: witch to live," — the penal code of every state recognized the 18. existence and the criminality of witchcraft; persons suspected as witches or wizards were frequently tried, condemned, and executed; and the most eminent judges, as Sir Matthew Hale, distinguished for his learning as well as for his piety, sided with the multitude, and passed the sentence of death upon the accused. [2]   Commerce with the devil, indeed, was an article of faith firmly embedded in the popular belief; and thousands were ready to testify that they had caught glimpses of Satan and his allies when

> "Down the glen strange shadows sprang,
> Mortal and fiend, a wizard gang,
> Seen dimly side by side.
> They gathered there from every land
> That sleepeth in the sun;
> They came with spell and charm in hand,
> Waiting their master's high command —
> Slaves to the evil one." [3]

The earliest trial for witchcraft in Massachusetts occurred in 1648, when Margaret Jones was charged with this crime, found 1648. Jun. 15. guilty, and executed. [4] Nor was this an isolated case; for, during a period of forty years, there were similar instances in Massachusetts and Connecticut. [5] Under the administration 1688.

---

[1] Gaule, pp. 5, 6.
[2] Hutchinson, ii. 27; Grahame, i. 274; Holmes, Ann. i. 439.
[3] Legends of New England.
[4] Mass. Rec's, ii. 242; Winthrop, ii. 397; Hubbard, 530; Hale, 16;

Hutchinson, i. 141. The year previous, there was an execution at Hartford for witchcraft. Savage, on Winthrop, ii. 374.
[5] Hale's Modest Inquiry, pp. 16–21, ed. 1771; Hutchinson, ii. 22–24.

CHAP. of Andros, however, a case occurred, which seems to have been
  II.   the precursor of the delusion which soon after spread so widely.

1688. A child about thirteen years of age, the daughter of John
Goodwin, "a grave man and a good liver at the north part of
Boston," charged a laundress residing in her father's family
with having stolen some linen. The mother of this laundress,
"Goody Glover," an illiterate Irish woman, and a Catholic
withal, repelled the accusation, and gave Goodwin's daughter
"harsh language," soon after which she fell into fits, which
were said to have "something diabolical in them." A sister
and two brothers of the girl, the youngest but five years old,
"followed her example," and the infection spread until the
excitement was general. Weird faces and giant goblins haunted
the imagination of many a little one, as the life blood curdled
with horror in its veins; and trembling crones began to
deliberate upon the propriety of nailing horseshoes to the
door posts to preserve them from the enchantments of evil
spirits. The evidences of bewitchment were such as were
usually adduced. "Sometimes they would be deaf, then dumb,
then blind; and sometimes all these disorders together would
come upon them. Their tongues would be drawn down their
throats, then pulled out upon their chins. Their jaws, necks,
shoulders, elbows, and all their joints would appear to be dislo-
cated, and they would make most piteous outcries of burnings,
of being cut with knives, beat, &c., and the marks of wounds
were afterwards to be seen." Yet the children "slept comfortably at night," notwithstanding they were "struck dead" in
the daytime "at the sight of the Assembly's Catechism, Cotton's Milk for Babes, and some other good books," though they
could read fluently enough in "Oxford's Jests, Popish and
Quaker books, and the Common Prayer."

The ministers of Boston, Cotton Mather, Willard, Allen, and
Moody, with Symmes of Charlestown, anxious to investigate
the case, "kept a day of fasting and prayer at the troubled
house," and with such success that "the youngest child made

no more complaints." But the others were not relieved ; upon CHAP
which the magistrates interposed ; the woman was apprehended, II.
examined, and executed ; and an account of the whole affair 1688.
was published by Cotton Mather, and reprinted in England,
with a preface by Richard Baxter, who says, " The evidence is
so convincing that he must be a very obdurate Sadducee who
will not believe." [1]

It is highly probable, as Hutchinson suggests, that the outbreak of this delusion in New England was principally caused
by certain books which had been circulated in England, copies
of which had reached this country.[2] Superstition is an epi-
demic easily produced, and its power increases the longer it
prevails, until it reaches its climax, after which it subsides.
And the history of the witchcraft delusion in New England
proves the correctness of this statement.

It was before the arrival of Sir William Phips that the first 1691-92.
symptoms of delusion appeared, at which date a daughter and Feb.
a niece of Mr. Parris, formerly a merchant, but then the minister of Salem Village, (now North Danvers,) with one or two
other girls in the neighborhood, beginning to act " in a strange
and unusual manner," the physicians of the place pronounced
them bewitched. Mr. Parris, the father of one of the sufferers,
who is charged as " the beginner and procurer of the sore
affliction to Salem Village and the whole country,"[3] had, for
some time, been at such variance with a portion of his parish-
ioners, that the strife between them had attracted the attention
of the General Court ; [4] and upon the occurrence of these cases,
he eagerly availed himself of the opportunity to gratify his

[1] Hale, 21; Calef, 299; Remarks on Calef, 38, 62 ; Mather's Magnalia, b. vi. c. vii.; Hutchinson, ii. 25. Cotton Mather published, in 1685, an account of the cases which had occurred in New England, with arguments to prove that they were the effects of familiarity with the devil.

[2] As Glanvil's Witch Stories, and the essays of Perkins, Gaule, and Bernard, with the trials of the witches in Suffolk. Three of these works — those of Perkins, Gaule, and Bernard — are referred to by Cotton Mather in his Enchantments Encountered.

[3] Calef, 136, ed. 1823 ; Hale, 22.

[4] Calef, 187, 188 ; Hutchinson, ii. 18.

CHAP. spite by involving his opponents in disgrace. Tituba, an Indian
II.   servant in his employ, who had been accustomed to practise
1692. "wild incantations," was the first person accused ;[1] and two
Mar. 1. others being complained of, — Sarah Good and Sarah Osborn,
the one "melancholy or distracted," and the other "old and
Mar. 11. bedridden," — the ministers of the neighborhood were called
in, private fasts were held at the house of Mr. Parris, another
Mar. 31. in public at the village, and, finally, a general fast was proclaimed throughout the colony, "to seek the Lord that he
would rebuke Satan, and be a light unto his people in this day
of darkness."[2]

The notoriety thus given to the affair, like flax cast upon a
smouldering fire, caused the latent credulity of the people to
burst forth into a blaze. Bewitched persons alarmingly multi-
plied ; and the ministers increased the evil by inflammatory
discourses delivered from their pulpits, in which they declared
that God had lengthened the chains of the spirits of darkness,
and let loose the devil upon New England, who often appeared
in the shape of a black man, as a punishment for the wicked-
ness and "Sadducism" of the people.[3]

To whom the largest share of responsibility attaches for the
melancholy events which followed, it may be difficult to say.
It would be easy to bring plausible proofs to show that those
who were most forward in the work were intentionally guilty ;
and it would be especially easy to lay upon Cotton Mather, the
"thaumaturgus" of the province, a burden of blame which, it
may be supposed, properly belongs to him as a principal actor
in the terrible tragedy. And there may have been, on his
part, and on the part of Parris, and Noyes, and Stoughton,
inordinate eagerness in fostering the delusion which, without

---

[1] Calef, 189, says Parris abused
her, to make her confess. In her incantations, rye meal was mixed with
human urine and given the children
to eat.

[2] Lawson's Brief Narr. 8; Calef,
188, 189, 193; Hale, 22, 24.
[3] Vide Lawson's Sermon, pub. in
1692. Parris, Noyes, and C. Mather
also delivered sermons, and probably
others.

their coöperation, would probably have soon languished; but CHAP.
it does not thence follow that they were wilfully culpable. It   II.
requires, indeed, no extraordinary stretch of charity to believe 1692.
that, for the most part, they were honest in their views, and
acted from a sincere conviction of duty. That they were deceived, there can be little doubt, and that they were blinded by
credulity; but the errors into which they fell would seem to
have been such as Have been often witnessed among men of an
impulsive temperament and strong conceit.

Besides, the people themselves, or a majority of them at
least, were as fervent believers in the reality of witchcraft as
the ministers and magistrates, and had certainly some agency
in producing and prolonging the excitement which prevailed.
When the spell of superstition is cast over a community, it is
impossible to tell who will be able to resist its enchantment;
for, oftentimes, men of sober judgment are captivated by its
power, and, in such cases, are hurried into greater excesses
than those who might, from the weakness of their faculties,
be supposed more susceptible to the infirmities of a disturbed
and heated imagination. Upon all who participated in these
scenes a portion of responsibility rests; for the delusion was
wide-spread, and the seeds of fanaticism, every where scattered, were so prolific that a harvest of bitterness was the
natural result.

Few dared gainsay the popular belief. There were some,
indeed, whose views were in advance of the rest of their age;[1]
but their appeals had little influence at the time. They did
all they could, consistently with their own safety, to stem
the current of popular prejudice. But the power was not
theirs to say to the boisterous waves of passion, "Peace, be

---

[1] As Brattle and Calef, but especially Willard, the pastor of the South
Church, to whom the pamphlet entitled "Some Miscellany Observations" is attributed by Calef. Brattle
also commends the course of Simon

Bradstreet, Thomas Danforth, Increase
Mather, and Nathaniel Saltonstall,
and affirms that most of the ministers
and several of the justices were dissatisfied with the proceedings instituted. 1 M. H. Coll. v. 75.

CHAP.
II.

1692.

still!" nor could they quell in an instant the furious rage of the storm of imposture which swept over the land. Some things had also occurred for which even the sceptical were unable to account — incidents analogous to those of our own day. And if such incidents, in the nineteenth century, have been attributed to spiritual agents, is it surprising that, in the seventeenth century, they should have been deemed convincing proofs of the reality of witchcraft? The delusion, if it may be called such, was neither wholly unnatural nor wholly inexplicable. It originated, without doubt, in that subtle and mysterious influence which is found, at times, to thrill with awe the stoutest heart, bewildering the senses, confounding the judgment, and baffling the skill of philosophy to explain. It requires deeper thinkers than any that have yet appeared to solve all the problems which psychology presents, and to read the Sphinx riddles it throws in our path.

The interest awakened by the first outburst of "Satan's assaults" was not suffered to subside for the want of support;

Mar. 31.

for, before the end of March, the number of the afflicted had increased to ten;[1] and, as the public mind became more excited, after some preliminary examinations six of the magis-

Apr. 11.

trates were convened at Salem, and more formal proceedings were instituted. The ministers, as usual, were present on the occasion, and Parris was conspicuous for the officiousness of his zeal. It was chiefly through his means that the prosecutions were conducted; and it was observed, as a proof of his partiality, that, while accusations against his friends were carefully "stifled," charges against his enemies were "vigilantly promoted."[2] His own record, still extant, shows plainly his feelings; and from this it is evident that he was neither an impartial advocate nor an unbiased judge. Leading questions were asked, whose drift the dullest could not fail to perceive, until a number of persons, hitherto of

---

[1] Lawson's Narr. 4; Calef, 190.   [2] Calef, 135, 194; Hutchinson, ii. 31.

unblemished reputation — principally females — were attaint- CHAP.
ed and imprisoned. Yet the cautious Hale remarks that he II.
observed in the conduct of the parties in general, "jus- 1692.
tices, judges, and others, a conscientious endeavor to do the
thing that was right;"[1] and the venerable Higginson, when
bending beneath the weight of more than fourscore years,
bears similar testimony to their integrity, though he very
properly adds, "There is a question yet unresolved, whether
some of the laws, customs, and principles used by the judges
and juries in the trials of witches in England, which were
followed as patterns here, were not insufficient and unsafe."[2]

The door once opened, the number of prisoners rapidly
increased. It was not "the poor, and vile, and ragged beggars upon earth" that were alone accused. Even ministers
of the gospel did not escape ; and George Burroughs, who
had formerly preached in Salem Village, and who was hated
by Parris as a rival, was committed and executed.[3] No one,
it was found, was safe so long as convictions could be so
easily procured. "Neither age nor sex, neither ignorance
nor innocence, neither learning nor piety, neither reputation
nor office," could shield the suspected from the grasp of the
law. The only avenue of escape that seemed to be left was
confession, which, it was intimated, might avert from the ac- May 11.
cused the sentence of death.[4] The gallows was set up, not
for professed witches, but for those who rebuked the delusion,
and persisted in asserting their personal innocence.[5]

Upon the organization of the new government, those who
were imprisoned for witchcraft were ironed, and the sad work
of prosecution proceeded with increased violence. Sir William
Phips, the governor, himself a man of but ordinary abilities,
had been indebted for his office more to the favor of the

---

[1] Modest Inquiry, 25.
[2] Preface to Hale's Inquiry, p. 5.
[3] See C. Mather's Wonders of the
Invisible World, 94–104 ; Calef, 212,
213, 231–242 ; Hutchinson, ii. 57–59.
[4] Grahame, i. 277 ; Hutchinson, ii.
34.
[5] Bancroft, iii. 87.

CHAP. Mathers than to his own qualifications; and William Stough-
II. ton, the lieutenant governor, was also indebted to the Mathers
1692. for his elevation, though personally fitted for the station he
filled by his talents, which were at least of average respectability. Both of these gentlemen, though differing from each
other in most respects, had one trait in common — a regard
to their private interests; and both, being thoroughly imbued
with the spirit of the age, fell in with the popular sentiment,
and lent to it the weight of their official support.

It is singular to notice the facility with which fanaticism
dupes its victims. Not only did the number of the accused
increase, but some, of irreproachable life, fancied themselves
possessed with the devil, and confessed that they had entered
into a compact with Satan, signed with their own blood.[1]
The occurrence of phenomena such as, in our own day, have
been attributed to a morbid excitement of the nervous system,
to a disturbed state of the electric forces of the body, to
animal magnetism, and to the agency of spirits, added to the
confusion. Some were lifted from the ground by an invisible
power, and suspended in the air.[2] Others displayed feats of
remarkable, if not of preternatural, strength.[3] Others, by a
look, struck with convulsions those upon whom their glance
fell, or deprived them of speech.[4] Even physical objects were
mysteriously affected. Buildings were shaken; furniture was
destroyed; and things inanimate seemed to have been endued
with the instincts of life.[5] The phenomena of somnambulism
and clairvoyance were likewise exhibited.[6]

It is not enough to assert that all these were delusions;
for if the evidence of the senses is utterly unreliable, the whole
fabric of society is at once overthrown. The most cautious
scepticism did not deny what was confirmed, not only by

[1] See Mather and Calef, and comp.
Glanvil, Gaule, &c.
[2] See Calef, 61, 62.
[3] See C. Mather and Calef.
[4] See Hale, 52, and Brattle, in 1
M. H. Coll. v. 62, 63.
[5] Calef and Mather relate instances
of this kind.
[6] Calef, 29; Upham; Bancroft, &c.

credible witnesses, but by the irresistible convictions of per- CHAP.
sonal inspection. And that must be a hopeless state of incre- II.
dulity which, when any thing out of the usual course occurs, 1692.
refuses to believe in its reality because of its unaccountable-
ness, or because it has never fallen within the range of individual experience.

One of the earliest acts of the new administration was the
institution of a Court of Oyer and Terminer ; and a session
of the same was held at Salem, where the excitement most June 2.
prevailed.[1] Bridget Bishop, a friendless woman, was the first
person brought forward for trial. The charges against her
were preferred by Parris, conviction followed, and eight days Jun. 10.
after she was hanged.[2] It has been remarked as worthy of
special notice, that not one of the magistrates at that time
held office by popular suffrage, and that the tribunal which
had been created had no other sanction but an extraordinary
and an illegal commission, for which the people were not
responsible.[3] Yet the magistrates were not the originators
of this delusion, however readily they may have lent to it their
influence. Nor were the ministers of the country solely culpable, however greatly or justly they may be blamed. For there
were not wanting many, of inferior rank, who approved their
course and sanctioned their proceedings. If the ministers rec- Jun. 15.
ommended "the speedy and vigorous prosecution of such as
had rendered themselves obnoxious," they, at the same time,
urged the "need of a very critical and exquisite caution, lest,
by too much credulity for things received only upon the devil's
authority, there be a door opened for a long train of miserable
consequences, and Satan get an advantage over us."[4] And
if the magistrates, forgetting the caution, adopted the recommendation, the people were present to witness the executions.[5]

---

[1] Calef, 207. The officers of this
Court were William Stoughton, Nathaniel Saltonstall, John Richards,
Bartholomew Gedney, Wait Winthrop, Samuel Sewall, and Peter Sargent. See Quincy, Hist. H. Coll. i.
178.

[2] C. Mather, Wonders, &c., 104–
114; Hutchinson, 51, 52.
[3] Calef, 225; Hutchinson, ii. 51;
Bancroft, iii. 88.
[4] I. Mather, Cases of Conscience;
Calef, 207, 208; Hutchinson, ii. 52.
[5] Comp. Hutchinson, ii. 54.

CHAP.   As the excitement increased, the number of victims multi-
 II.   plied ; and at the next session of the court, five were condemned
1692.   and hanged. In the next month, six more were convicted, all
Jun. 30.
July 19. of whom were executed but one — Elizabeth Proctor, who was
Aug. 5.
Aug.19. soon to become a mother.[1] In the following month, a like
Sept. 9.
Sep. 16. number were sentenced ; and a week later, Giles Cory, a ven-
         erable octogenarian, for refusing to plead was pressed to death
         — the first and the only instance of this horrible punishment
Sep. 17. inflicted in New England.[2] The next day nine others were
Sep. 22. sentenced, and eight of them suffered at the gallows — Noyes,
         the minister of Salem, exclaiming, as their bodies swung in the
         air, "There hang eight firebrands of hell."[3] Never, perhaps,
         was the memorable prediction of our Saviour more strikingly
         verified than at these trials : " From henceforth there shall be
         five in one house divided, three against two, and two against
         three. The father shall be divided against the son, and the
         son against the father ; the mother against the daughter, and
         the daughter against the mother ; the mother-in-law against
Luk.12: her daughter-in-law, and the daughter-in-law against her moth-
52, 53. er-in-law." Children were brought forward as accusers of
         their parents, grandchildren accused their grandparents, and
         wives their husbands. Not that the ties of natural affection
         were sundered, for in most cases the accusations were extorted
         through fear. The only alternative left to the suspected was
         to accuse those of their own household, or suffer themselves ;
         and if, under such circumstances, they were " dragooned " into
         a confession which it was difficult to resist, upon recovering
         their self-possession many retracted and besought forgiveness.[4]

---

[1] Calef, 208, 212 ; Hutchinson, ii.
57.
[2] Calef, 218, 311, 312 ; Hutchinson, ii. 60.
[3] Calef, 221. In justice to Mr.
Noyes, however, it should be stated
that Brattle, in 1 M. H. Coll. v. 64,
speaks of him as "a learned, a chari-
table, and a good man, though all the

devils in hell, and all the possessed in
Salem, should assert the contrary."
[4] Hale, 29, 32 ; Calef, 214 et seq. ;
Hutchinson, ii. 42–46, 59. In cases
where women were accused, a jury of
one doctor and eight women examined
their bodies for witch marks, and a
fleabite would pass for a teat at which
imps sucked.

That there was some imposture mixed with this affair can CHAP
hardly be doubted; for manifestations of art and contrivance, II.
of deliberate cunning and cool malice, are said to have been 1692.
palpably exhibited; and in one or two instances the accusers
were "caught in their own snare, and nothing but the blindness of the bewildered community saved them from disgraceful
exposure and well-deserved punishment."[1] Personal resentments may likewise have been gratified by procuring the conviction of those it hated; and in every respect there may have
been too much precipitancy in listening to the accusations of
irresponsible persons. Yet, as a whole, it may probably be
with justice conceded, that, however frightful the excesses into
which the people were hurried, they acted under honest convictions of duty; though their sincerity by no means exoner-
ates them from the charge of acting injudiciously, nor does it
relieve them from the imputation of yielding too readily to
the power of delusion. Without doubt, they condemned, upon
grounds whose insufficiency was afterwards acknowledged,
many of the worthiest and best of the age.

By this time nineteen persons had been hanged, one had Oct.
been pressed to death, and eight more were under sentence;
while of fifty-five who had confessed, not one had suffered.
One third at least of those who perished were church members; and more than half are said to have been persons "of
a good conversation in general." A few of the accused, by
the connivance of their friends, escaped by flight; yet the
prisons were crowded with victims to the number of at least
one hundred and fifty, and above two hundred more were
accused.[2] It was a season of the deepest gloom and anxiety;
the people were shivering with superstitious awe; and the
thoughtful trembled, and were panic-struck, as they pictured

[1] Upham's Lectures, 52.
[2] Calef, 225; Hale, 33; Brattle, in 1 M. H. Coll. v. 76, 78. The delusion was not confined to Salem, though it originated there; but it had spread to Boston, Charlestown, Andover, and other places.

CHAP.
II.

1692.

to themselves the probable results — for the "generation of the children of God were in danger."[1] But the storm was at its height; and the crisis was produced by charges against persons of whose innocence every one was satisfied. Well might those who had never before doubted, and who had expressed the utmost confidence in the real agency of Satan, pause, and become sceptical, when they found their own friends accused ; and well might Cotton Mather, officious in his zeal for the detection of satanic influence, learn wisdom from the experience of the past, and exclaim, "The whole business is hereupon become so snarled, and the determination of the question, one way or another, so dismal, that our honorable judges have room for Jehoshaphat's exclamation, We know not what to do. They have used, as judges have heretofore done, the spectral evidences, to introduce their further inquiries into the lives of the persons accused ; and they have thereupon, by the wonderful providence of God, been so strengthened with other evidences, that some of the witch gang have been fairly executed. But what shall be done as to those against whom the evidence is found chiefly in the dark world ? Here they do solemnly demand our addresses to the Father of Lights on their behalf. But in the mean time the devil improves the darkness of this affair to push us into a blind man's buffet ; and we are even ready to be sinfully, yea, hotly and madly, mauling one another in the dark. The consequence of these things every considerate man trembles at ; and the more, because the frequent cheats of passion and rumor do precipitate so many, that I wish I could say the most were considerate."[2]

[1] Hale, 33.
[2] Wonders of the Invisible World, 52, 53, ed. 1692. Comp. Hale, 34–37. In the pamphlet in reply to Calef, p. 42, Mather also says, "For my own part, I know not that ever I have advanced any opinion in the matter of witchcraft but what all the ministers of the Lord that I know of in the world, whether English, or Scotch, or French, or Dutch, (and I know many,) are of the same opinion." My friend Rev. Chandler Robbins, of Boston, first called my attention to the above, from the copy in the library of Harvard College.

At this juncture the court adjourned; and before it re- CHAP.
assembled the spell was broken. The wife of Mr. Hale, of II.
Beverly, was among the accused; insinuations had been 1692.
thrown out against Mr. Willard, the excellent pastor of the
South Church in Boston, and Mr. Deane of Andover; and
even the wife of Sir William Phips did not escape suspicion.[1]
Under these circumstances, the revulsion was electrical. If
mere accusations were in themselves plenary proofs of guilt,
then might the best fall; and, in this view, was it not time to
inquire whether the whole subject was not open to doubt?
The antidote for delusion is an enlightened reason, which
calmly weighs in the balance of truth conflicting opinions,
avoids hasty judgments, and pronounces its verdicts only after
mature deliberation, basing them upon safe and reliable data.
Had such reason been exercised at the outset, the wildest
excesses of the delusion would have been prevented, and the
gallows would have been despoiled of its numerous victims.
But the sober second thought of the community was awakening; and outraged justice, casting aside the Mokanna veil
which had distorted its vision, stood forth once more in the
open light of day, and wielded its powers, not to crush, but to
preserve.

Mr. Brattle, in the mean time, was not idle. " The court,"
says he, " is adjourned to the first Tuesday in November, then
to be kept at Salem; between this and then will be the great
assembly, in which this subject will be peculiarly agitated. I
think it is matter of earnest supplication and prayer to
Almighty God, that he would afford his gracious presence to
the said assembly, and direct them aright in so weighty an
affair. Our hopes are here; and if, at this juncture, God does
not graciously appear for us, I think we may conclude that
New England is undone, and undone."[2] Mr. Hale was likewise wavering, and was inclined to suspect that he had been

[1] Calef, Hale, &c.   [2] 1 M. H. Coll. v. 76.

CHAP.
II.
1692.
"walking in a wrong path." And even Cotton Mather, deeply as he was involved in the affair, had stepped forward with a proposal that, "if the possessed people, who were under accusation, might be scattered far asunder, he would singly provide for six of them, and see whether, without more bitter methods, prayer with fasting would not put an end to these heavy trials." [1]

Oct. 18.
A large share of credit, however, is due to the people of Andover, who openly remonstrated against the doings of the tribunals. "We know not," say they, "who can think himself safe, if the accusations of children, and others under a diabolical influence, shall be received against persons of good fame." Nor was this remonstrance ill timed, for a large number of the inhabitants of Andover had been accused. Dudley Bradstreet, a justice of the peace, and a son of the venerable Simon Bradstreet, had "granted warrants against and committed thirty or forty to prison for the supposed witchcrafts;" but becoming dissatisfied, and refusing to proceed farther, he and his wife were both "cried out against," and he "found it his safest course to make his escape." Those who had been committed, knowing themselves innocent, were "all exceedingly astonished and amazed, and affrighted even out of their reason" into confession. "Our understanding, our reason, and our faculties almost gone," say they, "we were not capable of judging our condition, as also the hard measure they used with us rendered us uncapable of making our defence; but said any thing and every thing which they desired, and most of what we said was but in effect a consenting to what they said." [2]

Is it surprising that such excesses were no longer endurable? Yet it is to the credit of the people that no tumultuous modes of redress were adopted, and that they did not retaliate

[1] Comp. Robbins's Hist. Second Church, Boston, p. 107, with Brattle, in 1 M. H. Coll. v. 76, 77, and Calef, 36–38. See also the pamphlet entitled "Some few Remarks," &c., in reply to Calef, p. 39.

[2] Calef, 224–228; Hutchinson, ii. 43–47, 61; Abbot's Andover, 164.

upon their accusers, meeting violence with violence. Restraining their passions, and appealing with calmness to Almighty
God to witness their innocence, they trusted that the blindness
of fanaticism, which had seized upon the community, was not
wholly impenetrable by the light of truth, and that the cry of
justice would make itself heard. And the result vindicated
their wisdom; for when the Superior Court met at Salem, six
women of Andover, at once renouncing their confessions, did
not scruple to treat the whole affair as a frightful delusion;
and of the presentments against those who were still in prison,
the grand jury dismissed more than half without hesitation;
and if they found bills against a few, they were all acquitted
upon trial except three of the worst, and even these were
reprieved by the governor, and recommended to mercy. "Such
a gaol delivery was made this court, as has never been known
at any other time in New England."[1]

Yet one more attempt was made to convict; and Sarah Das-
ton, a woman eighty years old, was brought to trial at Charlestown, in the presence of a crowd greater than had collected on
any previous occasion. But, though the evidence against her
would have been deemed sufficient six months before, the people
had seen enough to awaken mistrust, and a verdict of acquittal
was promptly rendered.[2] Nor could the case of Margaret
Rule, which occurred not long after in Boston itself, and under
the inspection of Cotton Mather, revive the delusion. The
excess of the evil wrought its cure. Its days were numbered,
and the community was happily delivered from its power.[3]

As the excitement subsided, the prominent actors in the terrible tragedy began to reflect, and a few made public acknowledgment of their error. Sewall, in particular, openly confessed
his mistake, and sought the forgiveness of those he had wronged.[4]

CHAP
II.

1692.

1693.
Sept.10.

---

[1] Calef, 226–228; Hutchinson, ii.
61, 62; Abbot's Andover, 163–167.
[2] Bancroft, iii. 96.

[3] Calef, p. 23 et seq.; C. Mather,
More Wonders, &c.
[4] Hutchinson, ii. 62; Holmes's Am.
Ann. i. 440; Drake's Boston, 502.

CHAP.
  II.

1694.
Nov. 26.
And Hale, in his "Modest Inquiry," made a similar confession.[1] But the confession of Parris was deemed less sincere, and was rather extorted through fear of suspension than from an honest conviction that he had been in the wrong.[2] Stoughton alone refused to retract, and to the day of his death never regretted the part he had taken.[3]

The evils resulting from this delusion were felt for a long time, and it is difficult to conceive the excitement which prevailed, and the suffering and sorrow it brought to all. Some have spoken of this whole affair in terms of contempt; others have unsparingly denounced its participants; very few have considered the subject calmly and dispassionately, or given due credit to the honesty of the parties. It was an unhappy affair, at the best; but it can be said with truth, that the delusion was less extensive, and caused less suffering, in New England than in Old; for there the belief in witchcraft prevailed until the middle of the eighteenth century, and persons were hanged, or otherwise put to death, as witches, long after such executions had ceased in America.[4]

[1] Published in 1697. A second edition was issued in 1771, from which I quote.

[2] Calef, 123–128.
[3] Hutchinson, ii. 62.
[4] Hutchinson, ii. 22, 28.

CHAPTER III.

THE GOVERNMENT OF THE PROVINCE.

THE arrival of Sir William Phips was followed by the organization of the government under the new charter. At once the question arose — and a serious question it was — how far that instrument extended in its effects upon the laws which had been enacted under the colonial charter. Obviously, if it invalidated all those laws, a new code must be framed, or the old code must be revived. Accordingly, at the first session of the General Court, an act was passed confirming the former laws until the following November ; and during the recess of the court it was proposed that the members should take this subject in charge, and " consider of such laws as were necessary to be established." [1] It was unfortunate for the people that a select committee was not appointed to attend to this duty ; and the subject itself was of such consequence that the wisest and best should have been placed on that committee. But the necessity for this step was not then foreseen. Hence, when the laws were revised, instead of framing a general code to be forwarded to England, only detached acts were presented, several of which were rejected by the king. This led to confusion ; whereas, had the whole subject been acted upon at once, such alterations would have been proposed as might have issued in a consistent and digested body of laws ; and in case of the rejection of particular acts, temporary provisions might have

---

[1] Mass. Rec's. MS. Continuation of Chalmers's Polit. Annals, Pt. II.; Hutchinson, ii. 18, 21, 63.

CHAP.
III.
been made until the pleasure of his majesty was further known, or until laws were passed which met his approval.

1692. The principal acts rejected by the king were those which asserted the views of the people upon points on which differences of opinion existed between them and the crown. Among these was one which set forth that "no aid, tax, tallage, assessment, custom, loan, benevolence, or imposition, should be laid, assessed, or levied on any of their majesties' subjects, or their estates, on any pretence whatsoever, but by the act and consent of the governor, council, and representatives of the people, assembled in General Court."[1] This act, which was, in effect, a denial of the right of Parliament to tax the colonies for any purpose, was of course obnoxious to all who asserted that right; and it is not surprising that it was rejected. Yet it is worthy of notice that thus early did Massachusetts reiterate her views, and, as under the colonial, so under the provincial charter, join issue with the parent state upon the vital point which, throughout our whole history, was never lost sight of, and which led eventually to the rupture which issued in the independence of the colonies.

The enactment claiming the benefit of the writ of habeas corpus was likewise rejected, on the ground that "the privilege had not yet been granted to the plantations." Yet if the colonists were Englishmen, and entitled to the immunities of Englishmen, it is difficult to conceive with what propriety this right could be withheld. It was enjoyed in the old world: why should it not be in the new?[2] Part of the criminal code of the province was also disallowed, especially the act for pun-

---

[1] Hutchinson, ii. 64. It is singular to notice the unanimity with which the doctrine of the text was avowed in all the colonies about this time; and when it is borne in mind that these colonies were settled at different periods, and by persons of different nations and of different religious persuasions, it is evident that the doc- trine itself must be regarded as according with the principles of natural justice, else would it never have been so generally approved. Comp. Gordon's Am. Revolution, i. 20, 42, 52, 54, 55, 63, 64, 73.

[2] MS. Continuation of Chalmers's Polit. Annals, Pt. II.; Hutchinson, ii. 65; Grahame, vol. i.

ishing capital offenders, which was founded upon the Mosaic, CHAP.
rather than upon the English law.[1] It was not the design of   III.
the mother country to allow her provinces too much latitude 1692.
in their affairs ; and Massachusetts, for her former refractori-
ness, was made to feel at the outset that she had passed from a
state of comparative independence to one of comparative subjection and control. Is it surprising, under these circumstances,
that " the colonial administration of William, contradictory in
principle and inconsiderate in conduct," by the representation
of a pleader against the colonies, " necessarily weakened the
jurisdiction of England over her plantations "?[2]

Of the acts approved by the king, some were of great importance. These provided for the settlement and distribution
of the estates of intestates ; the prevention of frauds and per-
juries ; the observance of the Lord's day ; the solemnization of
marriages by ministers or justices ; the settlement and support
of ministers and schoolmasters ; the settlement of county
bounds, and the regulation of towns ; the administration of the
oaths of allegiance and supremacy ; the regulation of the fees
of civil and judicial officers ; ascertaining the number, and regulating the House of Representatives ; and the prevention of
danger from the French.[3] Two of these acts merit particular
attention. That which related to the observance of the Lord's
day forbade all labor and amusements, works of necessity and
charity only excepted, under a penalty of five shillings for each
offence, and all travelling for business purposes under a penalty of twenty shillings. It also forbade vintners entertaining

---

[1] Hutchinson, ii. 65.
[2] Chalmers, Revolt, i. 315.
[3] Province Laws, ed. 1726, pp. 1–
34 ; Hutchinson, ii. 65. Governor
Phips, in his letter to England at the
date of the transmission of the laws of
the province, gives the first intimation
of the controversy which, for so long a
period, agitated the community, relative to the salary of the chief magistrate. A gratuity of £500 was granted to him, but "no salary was settled
or intended." Hence he petitioned
" the royal recommendation of this
object, which, he conceived, would
prove effectual." But little did he
know the temper or policy of the people if he supposed such a recommendation would succeed ; for no future
governor or king was able to accomplish the object. See under chap. v.

CHAP. others than strangers or lodgers, under a penalty of five shil
 III.   lings. All masters and governors of families were required
1692.   to "take effectual care that their children, servants, and others
under their immediate government, do not transgress in any of
the foregoing particulars;" and justices of the peace, constables, and tithingmen were required to "take effectual care" for
the observance of the act, "as also to restrain all persons from
swimming in the water, unnecessary and unseasonable walking
in the streets or fields in the town of Boston, or other places,
keeping open their shops, or following their secular occasions
or recreations in the evening preceding the Lord's day, or any
part of the said day or evening following."[1] These regulations
evince the scrupulousness of the age, and the reverence for
Sunday which was a prominent trait of the Puritan character.
How striking the contrast between such legislation and that
which sanctioned "dancing, archery, leaping, vaulting, having
May games, Whitson-ales, morrice dances, setting up May poles,
and other sports therewith used, or any other harmless recreations on Sundays after divine service."[2] If the one was too
strict, the other was assuredly sufficiently lax. An enlightened
reverence will always hold sacred things in proper esteem;
and an intelligent regard for Sunday, and for all seasons of
special religious improvement, will point out the path of propriety and decorum.

The act for the settlement and support of ministers and
schoolmasters had also its peculiarities. By its terms, every
town was required to be constantly provided with an "able,
learned, and orthodox minister or ministers, of good conversation, to dispense the word of God to them," who were to
be "suitably encouraged and sufficiently supported and maintained by the inhabitants of such town." All contracts made

---

[1] The power of "restraint" men-   or stocks not exceeding three hours."
tioned in this act was interpreted in   Laws, pp. 14, 15.
1704 to be "understood of imprison-   [2] King James's Book of Sports, 4to,
ment, not exceeding the space of   1618.
twelve hours, or by sitting in the cage

for the support of ministers or schoolmasters were to remain
"good and valid according to the true intent thereof;" and in case of neglect by any town, for the space of six months, to provide for the maintenance of a minister, the Court of Quarter Sessions was empowered to "order a competent allowance unto such minister according to the estate and ability of the town." It was likewise ordered — though the order was subsequently modified — that the churches in the several towns of the province should "use, exercise, and enjoy all their privileges and freedoms respecting divine worship, church order and discipline," and be "encouraged in the peaceable and regular profession and practice thereof;" and "every minister, being a person of good conversation, chosen by the major part of the inhabitants in any town at a town meeting duly warned for that purpose," was to be "the minister of such town," and the whole town was to "pay towards his settlement and maintenance, each man his several proportion thereof." Every town of one hundred families, in addition to its common school, was to support a grammar school; and every town of fifty families, neglecting for one year to provide for the constant support of a schoolmaster, incurred a penalty of ten pounds, to be levied towards the support of such schools within the county as were most in need, at the discretion of the justices in Quarter Sessions.[1]

Such were the provisions for education and religion; and it is to the credit of our fathers that they paid such attention to the vital and permanent interests of society. It is to this foresight we owe our prosperity; and we shall look in vain into the contemporary legislation of any country out of New England for similar provisions for the widest diffusion of intelligence and morality. Massachusetts enjoys the distinguished honor of having led in the work of universal education; and

[1] Laws, ed. 1726, p. 17. See further 4 and 5 W. and M. c. 21; 7 W. c. 9; 1 A. c. 4; 2 G. c. 5; 4 G. c. 6; and 8 G. c. 6.

CHAP.
III.

1692.

the deference of her people to the support of religion is as creditable to their wisdom as it is commendable to their piety. The Bay Province alone is said to have contained at this time eighty churches; and the whole number in New England was computed at one hundred and twenty.[1] Most of the ministers had been educated at Harvard, the "school of the prophets," and until 1691 the only college in America.[2] One hundred and fifty ministers had been graduated from its halls; and though some sought employment abroad, and settled in England, the greater part remained in the country, and were the principal pastors of the churches of New England.[3] There were some dissenters in the province, and dissenting churches had been established.[4] Episcopacy had likewise effected a lodgment, and there was an Episcopal church in Boston.[5] But the majority of the churches were of the Puritan stamp, and Puritanism was the prevalent and popular religion. Some may regret that its sway has since lessened; but in the progress of society changes must be expected; and though different opinions may be entertained of the tendency of these changes, few, perhaps, would be satisfied with the systems of the past if revived in their original form, and few would admit their complete adaptation to the wants of the present age. Yet truly enlightened minds will never cease to reverence all that was excellent in the faith or the practice of the past; and there was much in the faith and practice of the Puritans worthy of the highest praise.

[1] Holmes, Am. Ann. i. 459, gives the number of churches in 1696 as 130; but ibid. 480, he says that in 1701 there were but 120 ministers. Comp. Hildreth, U. S. ii. 168.

[2] William and Mary College, in Virginia, was founded in 1691. See its charter, and comp. Trott's Laws, art. Virginia; Holmes, Am. Ann. i. 443; 1 M. H. Coll. v. 164–166.

[3] See the catalogues for lists of the graduates. There was early complaint that many of the graduates

went to England. Hazard, ii. 74; Quincy's Hist. i. 16.

[4] The first Baptist church in Massachusetts was established in Swansey in 1663; the first in Boston was established in 1665. Benedict, i. 354, 381.

[5] An Episcopal church was built during the administration of Andros. See vol. i. of this work, and the authorities there cited; and comp. 1 M. H. Coll. iii. 259.

The members of the new government had, many of them, CHAP.
held office under the old charter. Bradstreet, Saltonstall, III.
Wait Winthrop, Russell, Sewall, Appleton, Gedney, Hathorne, 1692.
Hutchinson, Pike, Joyliffe, Hinckley, Bradford, Walley, and
Lathrop, had all been assistants in Massachusetts or Plymouth,
and most of them had been distinguished for their zealous
defence of the liberties of the people, and their uncompromising resistance to the aggressions of the Stuarts. Of the new
members, Phillips, Curwin, Adam Winthrop, Middlecot, Foster, Sergeant, Lynde, Hayman, Mason, Alcot, Donnell, and
Davis, were less known, and had been less conspicuous. One
of the number, Mason, was a merchant in London, friendly to
New England, but never a resident of the country ; and his
name was probably inserted in the charter chiefly from respect.
The last three were from Maine and the more distant east.[1]

Sir William Phips, the governor, was a native of New England, and owed his elevation more to a concurrence of favorable circumstances than to the dignity of his character or the
strength of his intellect. Born in an obscure village on the 1650-51.
banks of the Kennebec, and apprenticed to a ship carpenter at Feb. 2.
the age of eighteen, a few years after attaining his majority he 1668.
embarked on the ocean, for the recovery of a Spanish wreck 1683.
laden with treasures. His success in this expedition, which
certainly evinced an enterprising genius, was the foundation
of his fortune, and procured him the honor of knighthood 1687.
from the king. Receiving an appointment as high sheriff
of New England, he returned to his native land, and settled
in Boston towards the close of the administration of Andros. 1689.
Here he joined the North Church, of which Cotton Mather 1690.
was pastor ; and his zeal for Puritanism and the advantages
of his position so far commended him to the favor of the
aspiring minister, then in the zenith of his power and at
the height of popularity, that, conceiving him to be one whose

[1] For sketches of these gentlemen, see Hutchinson, ii. 20, 21, 69, 70 ;
and comp. Williamson's Maine, vol. i.

administration would, in many respects, be serviceable to the church and agreeable to the people, his name was sent in as a candidate for the chief magistracy by Increase Mather, the agent of the colony in England,[1] to whom, as a matter of conciliation, the nomination of the first officers under the new charter had been left.[2]

The qualifications of Phips, which influenced the Mathers to espouse his cause, were, that from the warmth of the neophyte they were assured of his favor to the congregational churches, and that there would be less danger of innovations in religion than under the administration of one less friendly to the Puritan creed ; that in political affairs, as his experience was trifling and his opportunities had been limited, he might be inclined to listen with deference to the advice of his spiritual guides, who were among the most prominent politicians of the day ; and that as a native of the country, who had served in the French wars, and who was well known to the people, he would be more acceptable than a stranger, and more confidence could be placed in his fidelity to their interests.

That the Mathers were honest in their views, has been doubted by some ; and their characters have been subjected to a scrutiny as severe, perhaps, as ever was known. Yet no men stood higher with their contemporaries than they, and none were looked up to with greater respect. The attachment of the people to them was general and sincere ; nor, from a review of their history, do we see cause to doubt the brilliancy of their talents or the purity of their intentions.[3] In some things, it is true, their zeal may have been excessive ; and the credulity of Cotton Mather was certainly unbounded. Yet, when even his political enemies acknowledged his worth, and

[1] Mr. Phips was in England at this time, as well as Mr. Mather.
[2] Mather, Magnalia, b. ii., Life of Phips, § 14.
[3] " We have not lived so but that, through the grace of Christ, we can defy all the malice of our enemies." I. and C. M., Postscript to Remarks on Calef, p. 70. See also ibid. p. 33.

his religious opponents commended his piety, it will, perhaps, CHAP. be conceded, that there must have been qualities in the man III. which commanded respect, else would he never have been held 1692. in such esteem. That both father and son were confirmed politicians, no one can doubt ; and that they were thoroughly convinced of the truth of their creed, will probably be also admitted ; nor would it be strange, considering their tempera- ment and the circumstances in which they were placed, if, in some instances, they overstepped the bounds of that moderation, which is the golden mean between fanaticism on the one hand, and the excessive conservatism which clings tenaciously to old institutions, both of which disturb the harmonious action of the mind, and give to it a tinge of partiality and onesidedness. But if the Mathers had their failings, they were lovers of lib- erty. New England, to them, was a terrestrial paradise. Attached to its creed, and attached to its policy, they devoted themselves zealously to the promotion of its welfare. They were never found wanting in patriotism or loyalty. They were respected at home, and respected abroad. And every where their talents secured to them friends.[1]

Had Sir William Phips been less under the influence of the Mathers, it might, perhaps, have been better for him, and better for the country. The chief magistrate of a commonwealth should, of all men, be free from the bias which dependence cre- ates. He should possess, personally, the decision and energy becoming his station ; the political wisdom which marks the true statesman ; and that dignity of character and moral sensi- bility, which, equally removed from haughtiness on the one hand and vehemence on the other, give him the command at all times of his own temper, and render him self-possessed, affa- ble, and courteous. In most of these qualities Sir William was

---

[1] For a noble tribute to the mem- ory of Cotton Mather, see Robbins's Hist. Second Church, Boston. Abun- dant testimony could be easily pro- duced from the writings of contempo- raries, commending the piety of both father and son. The eulogies at their decease speak highly in their praise.

CHAP.
III.

1692.

wanting. He had energy enough, but not of the right kind ; he was comparatively destitute of political wisdom ; he had enjoyed few advantages for literary culture ; and so violent was his temper that he was hurried into excesses which weakened his influence, and eventually led to his recall from his government. No one impeaches his honesty or his courage. No one doubts that he was benevolent and friendly. Yet good judges have pronounced him " much better fitted to manage the crew of a man-of-war than to sit at the helm of the ship of state." [1]

Justice, however, requires the concession that, whatever may have been his disqualifications for the office of governor, while in that office, " according to the best of his apprehension, he ever sought the good of his country." And if the statement of his biographer may be credited,[2] " he would often speak to the members of the General Assembly in such terms as these : Gentlemen, you may make yourselves as easy as you will forever. Consider what may have any tendency to your welfare, and you may be sure that, whatever bills you offer to me, consistent with the honor and interest of the crown, I will pass them readily. I do but seek opportunities to serve you. Had it not been for this, I had never accepted the government of this province. And whenever you have settled such a body of good laws, that no person coming after me may make you uneasy, I shall desire not one day longer to continue in the government."

These sentiments are certainly liberal ; and had the administration of Sir William corresponded to his professions, some little allowance might have been made for his personal deficiencies. Perhaps some allowance may at all events be claimed

[1] Hutchinson, ii. 74 ; Holmes, Am. Ann. i. 456, 457, note.

[2] Mather, Magnalia, Life of Phips, § 15. Calef, More Wonders, &c., p. 287 et seq., admits that Phips " aimed at the good of the people ; " but, at the same time, he thinks the statements of Mather are a little exaggerated, and that achievements are ascribed to the governor which he never performed.

for him, on the score of inexperience, the peculiarities of his CHAP III. situation, and his embarrassments from the party opposed to his government. For there were men in the province — at the 1692. head of whom stood Cooke and Oakes, both friends to the old charter, and averse to its surrender — who had organized a party vigilant to scrutinize the movements of the new government, and determined to oppose it wherever it swerved from the line of fealty to the liberties of the people.[1] From this time forward, indeed, party spirit will be found more prevalent than ever under the old charter. The struggle for the continued ascendency of Puritanism against the aggressions of a more liberal theology ; the change in political relations, which had given birth to the parties of freedom and prerogative ; and the naturally progressive tendencies, springing from the activity of thought and the yearning for a higher freedom, which characterized the people of Massachusetts, — all these, combined, give to the period of our history now entered upon a singular complexity ; and the involution and evolution of the elements of strife and the germs of advancement render the labor of the historian, onerous enough under any circumstances, one of increasing perplexity, from the difficulty of penetrating the disguises of dogmatists, and detecting truth amidst the conflicting and fluctuating statements of those whose interests inclined them to gloss over the faults which they wished to conceal, or depreciate the virtues which they were unwilling to acknowledge.[2]

The part taken by Sir William in the extraordinary delusion which overspread the country at the date of his arrival has been already noticed ; and there were some who thought he had yielded too readily to popular feeling, and shown too much deference

---

[1] Both Cooke and Oakes were chosen councillors by the people in 1693; but the governor refused his assent to Mr. Cooke, who, when in England, had opposed his appointment to the chief magistracy. Hutchinson, ii. 69, 70.

[2] Even the statements of Hutchinson must be taken *cum grano salis*, especially in those parts of his narrative in which he was personally interested. Without doubt he designed to be impartial, nor was he probably conscious that he was not so.

CHAP. to the opinions of the clergy. But if charity mantles the fail-
III.   ings of his associates, the hem of that mantle should touch the
1692. chief magistrate, who was guilty of no greater excesses than
many, his superiors in ability, who partook of his error.[1] His
vigilance in checking the inroads of the Indians, who were rav-
aging the eastern settlements, was a commendable feature of
his administration. It was at his instance, likewise, and under
his inspection, that a fort was built at Pemaquid, as a barrier
to these encroachments.[2] And the league which he formed
1693. with the Indians, had it been kept, would have restored peace
Aug.11. to many desolated homes, and have delivered the people from
that state of alarm in which they were involved for about
twenty years.[3]

The difficulties which led to the recall of Governor Phips
originated from his collision with Mr. Brenton, of Rhode Island,
who had been appointed collector for the port of Boston.[4] A
vessel had arrived from Bermudas, laden with fustic, which was
purchased on speculation by Colonel Foster, a member of the
council and a friend to the governor. From an alleged infor-
mality in the captain's proceedings both vessel and goods were
seized by the collector ; and upon Foster's complaint to the
governor, he, from his commission as vice admiral claiming the
right to exercise admiralty jurisdiction, which the king had
reserved to himself, charged the collector with having overstepped the bounds of his office, and upon his refusal to release
the ship, went in person to the wharf and forced him to yield.[5]

---

[1] See chap. ii.
[2] On the fort at Pemaquid, see
Niles's Indian Wars, in 3 M. H. Coll.
vi. 231; Dummer's Defence, 25, ed.
1721; Mather, Life of Phips, § 17;
Hutchinson, ii. 68; Neal's N. E. ii.
118; Holmes, Am. Ann. i. 442; Williamson's Me., i. 635, &c. Massachusetts disliked the erection of this fort.
Hutchinson, ii. 68. It was called Fort
William Henry, and was garrisoned
with 60 men.

[3] Mather, Life of Phips, § 17;
Neal's N. E. 543; Charlevoix, vol.
iii.; Hutchinson, ii. 72; Belknap's N.
H. i. 265; N. H. Hist. Coll. ii. 235,
236.
[4] This was before the establishment
of custom houses in the plantations by
act of Parliament. Hutchinson, ii. 74.
[5] Mass. Rec's, and Hutchinson, ii.
74, 75.

There had been a misunderstanding, also, between the governor and Captain Short, of the Nonsuch frigate, which ended in his caning Short, and committing him to prison.[1] In consequence of these difficulties complaints were instituted against the gov- ernor, and he was ordered to England to answer to the same.[2] 1694.
Nov.17.

The prejudice against him in England was great ; and it was not a little aggravated by the conduct of Dudley, himself anxious for the governorship, who, in connection with Brenton, instituted suits in actions of twenty thousand pounds damages ; but by the intervention of Sir Henry Ashhurst, the agent of the province, Sir William was bailed, and his friends were anticipating an accommodation of his affairs, and that he would be permitted to return to resume his government, when, partly in consequence of the humiliation of his arrest, a fever set in which terminated his life.[3] 1694-95.
Feb. 18

One incident, which occurred before the close of his administration, merits particular notice. In the choice of deputies to the General Court, it had been customary to allow the country towns the privilege of choosing for their representatives residents of Boston ; but this year, upon a motion for an address to the king against the removal of Phips, that motion was carried by a bare majority, twenty-six voting for it, and twenty-four against it. Most of the inhabitants of Boston who represented the country towns voted against the address ; whereupon the friends of Phips, to prevent future trouble, inserted a clause in a bill then pending requiring residence as a qualification for 1694.

---

[1] N. Eng. Ent's, iv. 76, quoted by Chalmers, MS. Pt. II.; Hutchinson, ii. 75, 76, and 78, note. Mather, in his Life of Phips, omits to notice either of these cases, perhaps because he felt that the conduct of the governor was open to censure.

[2] Mather, Life of Phips, § 20. Chalmers, MS. Pt. II., says Phips was informed of the charges against him in February, 1694, and quotes N. Eng. Ent's, 4, 92, &c.

[3] Mather, Life of Phips, § 20 ; Neal's N. Eng. 544, 545 ; Hutchinson, ii. 77, 82. Chalmers, MS. Pt. II., on the authority of 7 Jour. 401, and 4 N. Eng. Ent's, 95, says Phips arrived in England in January, 1695, but before his case could be inquired into he died. The cause of his death was attributed by the lords justices to his "want of a fixed salary, which put him upon improper modes of supporting himself"!

CHAP. town representatives. The change thus introduced by the pre-
III. rogative, or court party, for merely personal ends, was highly
1694. important; for, by requiring towns to choose one of their own
citizens as delegates to the General Court, it brought the questions of the day directly to their doors, and compelled them to
take an immediate interest in political discussions. By this
means the people were trained to investigate constitutional
principles; and from the country towns were sent to the
legislature men of the first talents, to participate in its
discussions, and in the exciting events which afterwards
occurred.[1]

Upon the departure of Mr. Phips, the care of the government devolved upon William Stoughton, the lieutenant governor, who, though his sympathies were with the court party,
enjoyed in a high degree the confidence of the people, from his
supposed attachment to their civil and religious interests. A
1650. graduate of Harvard College,[2] employed as an agent for the
1676. colony in England, and interested for many years in political
affairs, he was not only acquainted with the views of the English government, but knew also what suited the temper of his
countrymen.[3] Some, indeed, were opposed to him, because of
his conduct as a councillor under Andros, and because of his
participation in the persecutions for witchcraft; yet, on the
whole, perhaps, it would have been difficult to have found one
more acceptable; and hence his administration was comparatively tranquil. None of his measures awakened jealousy; the

---

[1] Mass. Rec's; Hutchinson, ii. 77,
78; Everett's Orations, 495, ed. 1836.
Douglass insinuates that this step was
taken at the instance of the Mathers.
[2] Mr. Stoughton was educated for
the ministry, in which he continued
above twenty years; but "the people
judged him proper to take his father's
place as a magistrate," and the rest of
his life was devoted to politics. Hutchinson, ii. 118; Quincy's Hist. H. Coll.
i. 172.
[3] Randolph, in 1686, said of him,

"Mr. Stoughton is inclined to the
Nonconformist ministers, yet stands
right to his majesty's interests."
Hutch. Coll. 548. Cotton Mather, in
his letter to his father, written to favor the appointment of Stoughton to
office, says, "Mr. Stoughton is a real
friend to New England, and willing to
make any amendment for the miscarriages of the late government. I wish
that you might be able to do any thing
to restore him to the favor of his country." Hutchinson, i. 365, note.

affairs of the government were conducted with prudence ; and CHAP. a spirit of general contentment prevailed. III.

Mr. Stoughton was a Puritan of the commonwealth mould. 1695. Of a phlegmatic temperament ; rigidly attached to the Puritan creed ; thoroughly versed in the knowledge of men ; knowing how to accommodate himself to a variety of circumstances, yet superior to all ; he was one who, in any situation, was calculated to succeed. Prudently deferring to the counsels of others, that they might share the responsibility of his measures, he rarely acted from impulse, but always from the maxims of a judicious policy. Possessing none of the softness which springs from a warm heart, and uninspired by the influences of domestic life, he looked upon men from his isolated position as beings to be governed by minds of a superior cast ; and if he succeeded in ruling them, it was by humoring their prejudices, and conciliating the favor of the most influential. If he occasionally lost the confidence of the community, he had the address to recover it by the gravity of his deportment, and by studiously avoiding all that might offend. Hence, to the day of his death, notwithstanding there were some whose 1701. friendship he could never secure, the body of the people regarded him with favor ; and he left as few enemies as any one who had taken so active a part in the government, and who had passed through so many eventful vicissitudes.[1]

At the commencement of Mr. Stoughton's administration, it was not expected that it would be of long continuance ; for, if Governor Phips did not return, it was supposed that a new chief magistrate would soon be appointed. Joseph Dudley, a native of Massachusetts, and conspicuous for his zeal in the overthrow of the old charter, aspired to this office ; and, upon the death of Phips, he solicited for it with strong hopes of

[1] For an elaborate notice of Stoughton, see Quincy's Hist. H. C. i. 172–180. Mr. Stoughton was a munificent benefactor of the college ; and before his death a building was reared at his expense, which took the name of Stoughton Hall.

CHAP. success. The character of Mr. Dudley is one of that class
III. which it is difficult to portray, because the anomalies it pre-
1695. sents embarrass the judgment in forming an estimate of its
failings and its virtues. That he was inordinately ambitious,
no one can deny; and that he was not over-burdened with
principle, his whole life proves. Yet, from the gracefulness of
his person and the politeness of his address, he possessed in a
remarkable degree the power of influencing those who were susceptible to flattery, and of imposing upon those least acquainted
with his true disposition; though there were some whom, with
all the "uncommon elegancies and charms of his conversation,"
he was unable to deceive. It is often the case with such men
that religion is used as a cloak to conceal their vices, or rather
to invest them with an air of respectability; and there may
have been, with Mr. Dudley, that commingling of fervor and
respect to the forms of godliness often witnessed in minds of a
worldly stamp, while, at the same time, judged by the standard
which raises spirit above forms, he may have been lacking in
the constituents of genuine piety, however zealous and devoted
as a religionist.[1] Let it not be supposed, however, that he was
destitute of good qualities. He was frugal in his habits, gen-
tlemanly in his manners, accomplished as a scholar, and talented
as a lawyer; and in his private relations he was affectionate to
his children, affable to his servants, and agreeable in his address. Few men are without friends; and Mr. Dudley had
his, who clung to him through life, from sympathy or policy.
But his conduct while president of the colony was generally
condemned; and it is apparent, from his course when Andros
came into power, that, if he had any regard for his country, he
had more regard for himself; that his patriotism was of the
questionable kind which expends itself on one person; and
that it was not so absorbing a passion as to prevent him from

[1] His eulogist, indeed, says of him, "He truly honored and loved the religion, learning, and virtue of New Eng-
land, and was himself a worthy patron
and example of them all." Boston
News Letter, No. 834.

loving the crumbs from the royal table. He was as honest as CHAP.
one can be who loves himself and loves office above all things III.
else, and lays his holocaust on the shrine of ambition.[1]   1695.

Upon the overthrow of Andros, Mr. Dudley was one whom
the patriots of Boston seized and imprisoned. The result of
that imprisonment has been elsewhere noticed. At his release
he was commissioned chief justice of New York, and held that   1690.
office for three years, when he returned to England. A royal-   1693.
ist at heart, his sympathies did not flow in the same channel
as those of the fathers of New England, with whom resistance
to tyrants was obedience to God. Yet his situation in England was far from pleasant. He was distant from his childhood's home ; and, with all his faults, he loved the spot which
had cradled his infancy.[2] Had he loved the institutions of his
country as well as its soil ; had he drank in the free spirit
which breathed from its hills ; had he identified his own interests with the interests of the people, he would have been eminently fitted to have adorned the highest station ; and his
appointment as governor would have been welcomed with joy.
But he sought office for the power it conferred, and for the
consequence it gave him. Hence he was constantly scheming
to secure his return to America, and to secure it in such a way
as to gratify his pride. But his plans were not immediately
successful ; for Ashhurst, and Constantine Phips, the agents of
the province in England, vigilant to defeat his appointment,
drew up a bill, which was passed, for reversing the attainder
of Leisler, the former governor of New York, and Milborne,
his son-in-law, who had been barbarously executed with the   1691

---

[1] Mr. Dudley seems to have inher-
ited a large share of his father's tena-
city of purpose, joined to an innate
pride, and love of power, which led
him to esteem more highly the notice
of the great, than to covet a place in
the affections of the humble. See the
pamphlet entitled "The Deplorable
State of New England," &c., printed
at London in 1708, and reprinted in
1721. A curious correspondence between him and the Mathers may be
seen in 1 M. H. Coll. iii. 126–138,
which furnishes some insight into the
character of both parties.

[2] Hutchinson, ii. 114.

CHAP.
III.

1693.

concurrence of Dudley.[1] By this intervention he failed to obtain the government of Massachusetts ; and having been appointed lieutenant governor of the Isle of Wight by the interest of Lord Cutts, whose friendship he had secured, he continued to hold that office for a period of eight years, and was elected a member of the Parliament of William.[2]

1695.
June.

1697.
Jun. 18.

The Earl of Bellamont was the next most prominent candidate for the governorship ; and during the summer he received the appointment, though his commission was not dated until two years later, nor did he take up his residence in the country until the year following, during which time the administration continued in the hands of Mr. Stoughton.[3] Lord Bellamont was probably indebted for his appointment to the fact that he was supposed to be the most competent person to enforce obedience to the laws of trade, which had been so much neglected that the seas swarmed with buccaneers, who, in times of peace, made their depredations upon the Spanish ships and settlements, and brought their plunder to New York and other ports.[4] The adventures of Captain Kid give an air of romance to the proceedings of these freebooters ; and the treasures which were supposed to have been hidden by him on Long Island, and at other haunts, gave rise to many Quixotic enterprises to search for concealed riches, conducted with the mystery with which the superstition of the age invested such deposits, watched as they were by spirits of darkness, whom it was necessary to circumvent by meeting at midnight, and observing the ceremonies requisite on such occasions.[5]

[1] I. Mather, in 1 M. H. Coll. iii. 127 ; Deplorable State of N. Eng. p. 5 ; Hutchinson, ii. 83, and note ; Bancroft's U. S. iii. 55 ; Hildreth's U. S. ii. 185. On the other side of this subject, see the " Modest and Impartial Narr. of several Grievances and great Oppressions to the Inhab's of N. Y. under Leisler," in Lib. Mass. Hist. Soc., shelf 3, vol. 8, tract 4.

[2] Boston News Letter, No. 834, for April 4–11, 1720 ; Hutchinson, ii. 114.

[3] MS. Continuation of Chalmers's Polit. Annals ; Hutchinson, ii. 84, 96, notes, and 103 ; Lodge's Peerage of Ireland, i. 390, where is a notice of the earl ; Smith's N. Y. 150, ed. 1814 ; N. Y. Colon. Doc'ts, iv. 266–273 ; Dunlap's N. York, i. 229 ; Drake's Hist. Boston, 516, 517.

[4] Chalmers, Revolt, i. 269, 279.

[5] Hutchinson, ii. 83, 84, 109–113 ; Dunlap's N. York, i. 231, 232.

Finally, the new governor embarked to assume the duties of CHAP.
his office ; but as his commission included New York as well III.
as Massachusetts,[1] he touched first at the port of New York,[2] 1697.
where he was waited upon by a committee from Massachusetts, 1698.
Apr. 2.
who tendered him the congratulations of the people upon his
arrival. During his residence in that province, he was frequently consulted by the magistrates of Massachusetts, all
matters of importance were communicated to him, and his
advice and direction were generally followed ; but the administration of the government continued in the name of the lieutenant governor, as commander-in-chief.[3] It is not improbable
that the cordiality with which Lord Bellamont was welcomed
by the Bay Province arose, in part, from the joy of the people
in escaping from the rule of Dudley, who was nearly as obnoxious as the memorable Kirke.   Certain it is that the new governor was so desirous to conciliate esteem, that he maintained
a constant correspondence with Mr. Cooke, whose election as
a councillor had been opposed by Governor Phips, but allowed
by Mr. Stoughton. By this step he secured the coöperation
of that gentleman ; and he is said to have had more confidence
in Cooke than in Stoughton, who was ever, at heart, attached
to the Dudley party.[4]

Before the arrival of Lord Bellamont in America, a step was
taken by the English government pregnant with importance in
its bearings upon the colonies. This was the organization of 1696.
May 15.
a Board of Trade and Plantations, consisting of a president
and seven members, known as the "lords of trade," who succeeded to the authority first exercised by the Council for Trade
and Foreign Plantations, and afterwards by the plantation
committees of the privy council. This board, whose powers
were somewhat extensive, continued till towards the close of

---

[1] New Hampshire was likewise included. Hutchinson, ii. 84.
[2] N. Y. Colon. Doc'ts, iv. 302;
Dunlap, N. York, i. 229; Holmes,
Am. Ann. i. 468.

[3] Mass. Rec's, and Hutchinson, ii.
103.
[4] Hutchinson, ii. 103.

the American revolution to exercise an oversight of the affairs of the colonies; yet as it had neither a voice in the deliberations of the cabinet, nor access to the king, and was often controlled in its movements by interested parties without, its course tended to involve the colonies in ever-increasing confusion.[1]

Concurrently with the establishment of this board, the laws of trade were revived, new and more stringent regulations were adopted, and, to effect their execution in the most thorough manner, the paramount authority of Parliament was asserted. An oath was likewise imposed on the governors of the several provinces obliging them to enforce these acts; all statutes in conflict with the same, past or future, were declared void; officers of the revenue, whose number was increased, were invested with the same powers possessed by the like officers in England; and the persevering Randolph was intrusted with the duties of surveyor general, as a reward for his loyalty.[2]

It is surprising that the statesmen of England had not the wisdom to foresee the consequences which must inevitably result from the adoption of such measures. The experience of the past seems to have been lost on them. How could they expect that a people who had uniformly resisted encroachments from abroad, and who had denied in the most express terms the right of Parliament to legislate adversely to their interests, should now quietly acquiesce, and bow their necks meekly to

[1] Chalmers, MS. Contin. Polit. Ann. Pt. II.; Anderson, Hist. Com. ii. 622, 623; Chalmers, Revolt, i. 269, 270; Grahame, i. 561; Dummer's Defence, 44, 46; New York Colon. Doc'ts, iii. xiii. et seq.; Bancroft's U. S. iii. 104, iv. 17; Hildreth's U. S. ii. 197. Chalmers, of course, applauds the action of the Board of Trade, for he was a pleader against the colonies. Hence he says, "Of this respectable commission it has ever been the praise that they have exerted themselves as the guardians of the national interests, as the patrons of the colonies, as the supporters of the commercial system of Britain, though their success hath not been always equal to their intentions and their efforts, because their power was not proportionate to the extent of their will." Revolt, ii. 43.

[2] Chalmers, MS. Contin. Political Ann. Pt. II., and Revolt, i. 272, 273; Acts 7 and 8 W. and M. chap. 22; Bancroft's U. S. iii. 104, 105; Hildreth's U. S. ii. 197, 198.

the yoke of subjection, without uttering a single remonstrance, or without evincing the least displeasure ? But the experiment was to be tried ; and it had been resolved to enforce submission, cost what it might. Massachusetts, as usual, protested against the acts of the board ; and the merchants of Boston expressed " their indignation at the acts of navigation," and insisted, with the " spirit of pristine times," that " they were as much Englishmen as those in England, and had a right, therefore, to all the privileges which the people of England enjoyed." [1]

Upon the arrival of Lord Bellamont at Boston, he was received with unusual respect.[2] Condescending, affable, and courteous in his manners, he was admirably fitted to ingratiate himself with the people. If he was flattered by the attentions which he received, he had the good sense to conceal it, and in all things conducted with that wise moderation which marks the man of the world, acquainted with its foibles, and willing to humor them for his personal benefit. " We should treat these gentlemen well, for they give us our bread," was his language to his wife ; [3] and he acted accordingly. An Episcopalian in England, he was enough of a Congregationalist in America to attend with becoming reverence the weekly lecture at Boston ; and if he professed great esteem for the clergy of the metropolis, it was because he was sensible they had the ears of the people. The prudent flatters whom he wishes to win.[4]

In consequence of this temporizing complaisance of the governor, he became generally popular. If his inclination led him to side with the opposers of Dudley, his prudence prevented him from neglecting his friends. Hence there was

[1] Chalmers, Revolt, i. 284.
[2] For a sketch of the ceremonies on this occasion, see Grahame, ii. 10 ; Allen's Biog. Dict. art. Bellingham.
[3] Hutchinson, ii. 107.
[4] The address of the ministers of Boston to his excellency, dated May 31, 1699, was printed by Bartholomew Green, on a small folio sheet of four pages, signed by I. Mather, for himself and his brethren ; and the speech of the governor, dated May 29, was printed by the same house.

CHAP.
III.

1699.

harmony in the councils of the province. Every thing moved on quietly and smoothly. His lordship, indeed, had the vanity of caste ; and, presuming from his official position that he was entitled to lead in the government, and, like a second Atlas, bear the chief burden of the state, he concerned himself directly in the debates of the court, proposed all business, and frequently recommended bills which he wished to have passed. But the court took good care to stand upon their reserved rights, and refused, in some cases, to pass objectionable bills, on the ground that " they were too much cramped in their liberties already, and they would be great fools to abridge, by a law of their own, the little that was left them." [1] Yet all was done good naturedly, without giving offence ; and it is a proof of the popularity of his excellency that, though but a small sum had been assigned for the support of former governors, the grants of the General Court, during his stay in the province, amounted to the sum of twenty-five hundred pounds, lawful money — about eight thousand dollars of the currency of the United States. [2]

1700.
May.
1700-1.
March.

The administration of Lord Bellamont was exceedingly brief ; for the year after his arrival he left for New York, where he died in the following March. [3] By this event the charge of the government again devolved upon Mr. Stoughton ; but he took the chair with great reluctance. His advanced age and declining health prompted him to seek for ease and retirement ; and four months after he, too, was numbered with the dead. [4]

1701.
July 7.

Upon the receipt in England of the intelligence of the death of Governor Bellamont, Mr. Dudley renewed his solicitations for the office of chief magistrate, and this time with better success. By fair promises to gentlemen in England and

---

[1] Chalmers, Revolt, i. 283, and MS. Continuation of his Polit. Ann.
[2] Mass. Rec's ; Collection of Proceedings of Gen. Court, ed. 1729, pp. 4, 5 ; Hutchinson, ii. 109 ; Chalmers, Revolt, i. 283.
[3] Hutchinson, ii. 114 ; Dunlap's N. York, i. 243, 244.
[4] Hutchinson, ii. 117.

America, and by his conduct during the probationary period which had elapsed from his former rejection, he had ingratiated himself into favor, especially with the dissenting clergy ; and by his professions of piety he had succeeded in enlisting the sympathies of Cotton Mather, who waived all objections to his appointment, and even wrote a letter to the king favoring his cause.[1] But his majesty professed an unwillingness to confirm his appointment while he was obnoxious to the people. A petition was accordingly procured from several of the merchants in New England, and others then resident in London ; and as this obviated the scruples of the king, his commission passed the seals a few months before the death of the monarch, and was renewed by Queen Anne upon her accession to the throne.[2]

Thus Mr. Dudley reached the summit of his ambition. He would be the first man in Massachusetts rather than the second in England.[3] On his arrival, he was received with ceremonious respect even by his opponents. Winthrop, Cooke, Hutchinson, Foster, Addington, Russell, Phillips, Brown, Sargent, and others of the council which imprisoned him in 1689, were of the council at his return in 1702. They had no desire to remind him of the past ; and it would not, perhaps, have been politic for them to have done so ; but he had not forgotten it, and this they soon felt.

At the first election, when the list of councillors was presented for confirmation, the names of five were stricken from the list. Cooke, Sargent, Oakes, Saffin, and Bradford, were those upon whom the stroke of decapitation fell ; and, however acceptable these gentlemen were to the people, it was enough for his excellency that they were objectionable to

CHAP.
III.

1701.

1701-02.
Mar. 8.

1702.
Jun. 11

1703.
May.

---

[1] Deplorable State of N. Eng., &c., p. 6; Hutchinson, ii. 114, 115, and notes ; 1 M. H. Coll. iii. 128, 129.
[2] Hutchinson, ii. 115, 116. The province would have preferred Wait Winthrop for governor, and voted to send him to England as agent, in hope of his appointment. Hutchinson, ii. 120.
[3] Hutchinson, ii. The queen's instructions to Mr. Dudley may be seen in 3 M. H. Coll. ix. 101.

CHAP.
III.

1702.

July.

1703.
Jun. 20.

1705.

1704.

1705.

him.[1] But if the governor, instead of Sejanus, chose to be Tiberius, he was soon made sensible that he was not omnipotent, and that, if he was capable of governing without a prompter, and had the disposition of offices at his command, he could not delegate the affections of the people. In the summer of 1702, he visited the eastward, to negotiate with the Indians and view Fort Pemaquid; and in the following summer, he made a second visit, and, meeting at Casco delegates from the Indian tribes, confirmed the league which had been previously made with them. The gentlemen who accompanied him on these journeys were not appointed by the court, but were selected by Mr. Dudley from among his friends; and, as he had been instructed by the queen to insist upon the rebuilding of the fort at Pemaquid, and had promised to effect that object, at his return his friends reported in favor of that measure, and the council accepted their report; but the house refused concurrence.[2]

Two years later the question was again brought before the house; but as the governor had seen fit a second time, notwithstanding the remonstrance of the house, to reject Cooke and Sawyer, who had been elected to the council, and had now negatived the choice of Oakes as speaker, that body, indignant at his interference, was in no mood to gratify his wishes, and refused to consent either to rebuild the fort at Pemaquid, or to contribute to the support of the fort at Piscataqua, or to establish the salaries of the principal officers of the government — all which subjects he had commended to their attention.[3]

[1] Mass. Rec's; Hutchinson, ii. 124 –126; Chalmers, Revolt, i. 329; 3 M. H. Coll. vii. 230.

[2] Mass. Rec's; Collection of Proceedings of Gen. Court, ed. 1729, pp. 9, 12, 16; Hutchinson, ii. 124, 125; Chalmers, Revolt, i. 315, 328; 3 M. H. Coll. vi. 247; Williamson's Me., ii. 34; N. H. Hist. Coll. ii. 236.

[3] Mass. Rec's; Collection of Proceedings of Gen. Court, ed. 1729, pp. 15–22; Hutchinson, ii. 137–140; Chalmers, Revolt, i. 329, 332. The house refused, so early as June 25, 1702, to settle a salary upon the governor. Collection of Proceedings of Gen. Court, ed. 1729, p. 6.

The majority of the people had always believed that the CHAP.
sympathies of Mr. Dudley were wholly with the court party; III.
and that his professions of regard for the liberties of America 1705.
were but a specious pretence. Cotton Mather, too, who had
waived his objections to his appointment, had become suspicious of the sincerity of his professions of piety, and believed
him to be at heart as arbitrary as ever, and as readily disposed
to deeds of oppression.[1] And there was much in his own conduct, and in the conduct of his family, which justified such
suspicions. "This country," wrote Paul Dudley, the son of 1703-4.
the governor, and the attorney-general of the province, in a Jan. 12.
letter to a " dear kinsman" in England, — " this country will
never be worth living in for lawyers and gentlemen, till the
charter is taken away. My father and I sometimes talk of
the queen's establishing a court of chancery here. I have
wrote about it to Mr. Blathwayt."[2]

Is it surprising that an attempt was made to supplant one
so obnoxious, and that a man of inferior ability was preferred
in his stead?[3] Complaints of "unheard-of corruptions and 1707.
oppressions, and unjust and partial practices" were instituted;
pamphlets were published in London charging Mr. Dudley 1708.
with "treasonable correspondence;" and a petition was forwarded to the queen, signed by a number of respectable
citizens, professing their belief in the truth of these charges,
and requesting his removal.[4] The council and house, indeed,
apparently non-concurred in this petition, and declared their
belief that the accusations were "scandalous and wicked," and
that they were "sensible of his indefatigable care and protection
of her majesty's good subjects;" but these votes were alleged

[1] Hutchinson, ii. 135, 148, notes;
1 M. H. Coll. iii. 129. Chalmers, Revolt, i. 329, acknowledges that Mr.
D. "looked to England for support."
[2] Deplorable State of N. Eng. pp.
8, 9; P. Dudley's Original Letter to
W. Wharton, printed at London, with
some Necessary Queries; Hutchinson,
ii. 140; 1 M. H. C. 3, 126.

[3] Sir Charles Hobby was the person proposed; Hutchinson, ii. 140.
Grahame, ii. 15, 16, thinks the politicians of the province went a little too
far in this matter; but he may not
have seen all the evidence in the case.
[4] Deplorable State of N. Eng., &c.;
Hutchinson, ii. 145, note; Chalmers,
Revolt, i. 334.

CHAP.
III.

1707.
Nov.25.

to have been obtained by disgraceful and coercive measures; and the uncompromising Sewall, satisfied that there was something wrong, entered his dissent, and assigned as his reasons that the vote was hastily pushed by the governor, who was the interested party; that the charges had not been sufficiently investigated; and that the censure of the petitioners might be of "ill consequence to the province in the time to come, by discouraging persons of worth and probity to venture in appearing for them, though the necessity should be ever so great."[1] Mr. Dudley, however, had the address to allay the storm which would have overwhelmed most men; and though Mr. Povey, the lieutenant governor, who had returned to England, wrote him that he must "prepare to receive the news of his being superseded," the matter was not further prosecuted, and the governor escaped.[2]

For the next few years, the war with the French so engrossed the attention of the people that their political tranquillity was but little disturbed. The party opposed to the

1708.
governor still pursued in England their schemes for his removal; but in the province, by the policy of rejecting his opponents and favoring his friends, the party in his favor was perceptibly strengthening. Not that there was in reality an increase of confidence in his integrity or patriotism; but many were wearied with the protracted struggle, and those who still held out found little encouragement at home, and less countenance abroad.[3]

---

[1] Deplorable State of N. Eng., &c., § ii. iii.; Hutchinson, ii. 146, 147, notes. Comp. 1 M. H. Coll. 3, 131. Brown and Pain, two other members of the council, are said to have deprecated, with Sewall, the haste with which the vote was passed in that body; and in the house, it was twice negatived by a majority of the members, before it was carried through.

[2] Deplorable State of N. Eng., &c.; Hutchinson, ii. 147, 148, and notes.

[3] The methods adopted by Mr. Dudley to win popular favor are hinted at as follows: "Besides the caresses of the table, which are enough to dazzle an honest countryman, who thinks every body means what he speaks, the influence which *preferments* and *commissions* have upon little men is inexpressible. It must needs be a mortal sin to disoblige a governor, that has enabled a man to command a whole country town, and to strut among his neighbors with the illustrious titles of, our major, and the captain, or his worship." Deplorable State, &c., 20.

The change in the ministry, which took place in England at CHAP. III. this time, caused some excitement in Massachusetts, and rendered it necessary to choose a new agent. Sir William 1709. Ashhurst was first appointed, but he refused to accept; upon which Jeremiah Dummer was chosen, and accepted. Contrary to the expectation of his constituents, however, the new agent devoted himself to the persons in power, was employed by Lord Bolingbroke in some secret negotiations, and had assurances of promotion to a place of profit; but the death of the queen blasted his hopes. In the mean time, Mr. Dudley, whose rule it was to gain his enemies, for he was sure of his friends,[1] succeeded in removing the prejudices of Sir William Ashhurst, and in securing his favor; and Mr. Dummer also espoused his cause. Mr. Phips, the old agent, had for some time been friendly to him, and the governor would gladly have continued him in office had he been acceptable to the ministry; but as he was not, he was obliged to consent to his removal. Thus Mr. Dudley had powerful allies in England; and, as he had managed at home with unusual address, he felt quite secure in the position he held.[2]

The latter years of Mr. Dudley's administration were disturbed by a controversy upon the currency of the province. The wars with France, which had continued for a period of nearly twenty years, had not only burdened England with debt, but had impoverished her colonies, and weakened their resources. The bills of credit, issued in 1690, had depreciated in value; and a large part of the specie in circulation had been drained from the country for the payment of its debts. This stringency in money affairs was seriously felt; and merchants and politicians were busily employed in devising schemes to remedy the evil. A few advocated a return to the gold and silver currency, the only sure basis of value in their estimation; others were in favor of the formation of a private bank;

1710 to 1715.

---

[1] Hutchinson, ii. 171.   [2] Hutchinson, ii. 169–171.

CHAP.
III.

1710
to
1715.

and a third party argued for the establishment of a public bank. A majority of the council favored the public bank; but the house was divided in opinion, the influence of the Boston members and others from the country rather inclining them to favor the private bank. The controversy was wide spread, and the whole community was agitated by it. Towns, parishes, and families took part in the discussion; and for a long time it seemed doubtful which way it would be decided. The party for the public bank finally prevailed; and a loan of fifty thousand pounds in bills of credit was agreed to by the General Court, which were placed in the hands of trustees, and loaned for five years, at five per cent. interest, one fifth of the principal to be paid in yearly.[1] This disposition of the question was far from satisfying all. If it diminished the number of the friends of the private bank, it increased their zeal; and the resentment which defeat awakened was not only lasting, but it seriously affected the politics of the country.

1714.
Aug. 1.

The close of Mr. Dudley's administration was more quiet than might have been anticipated. Upon the death of the queen, and the accession of George I., of the house of Hanover,[2] it was expected that he would be displaced, and a new governor appointed; and he seems to have prepared himself to submit with composure. Some change had taken place in public feeling towards him; and many, who had been his greatest opposers, had been won to his interests. His friends, therefore, were in the ascendant, and would have probably acquiesced in the continuance of his government. As if, too, to do all in his power to conciliate, he had consented to con-

---

[1] Province Laws, ed. 1726; Hutchinson, ii. 187–190.

[2] See Boston News Letter, Nos. 544, 545. "On Thursday evening, September 23," says this document, (No. 545,) "Mr. Jonathan Belcher, a gentleman who had been twice at the court of Hanover, on the occasion of his majesty King George's accession, made a very splendid entertainment for his excellency the governor, and council, with a great many other gentlemen, at his house in Hanover St., where were drank his majesty's health, the prince, royal family, &c., the house being all over very finely illuminated." Mr. Belcher, whose advertisements often appear in the News Letter, was a dealer in hardware, and he was afterwards governor of the province.

firm the election of Mr. Cooke, whom he had so often nega- CHAP.
tived. Age was likewise creeping upon him ; he was close   III.
upon the bounds of threescore and ten ; and few are so indif- 1715.
ferent to what may be thought of them after they are dead, as
not to desire to be remembered with kindness.[1] Hence his last
days were his best ; and when he vacated his office, and went Nov.
to his rest, though he left behind many who could neither for- 1720.
get his oppressions nor forgive his misconduct, he left also   April 2,
many who preserved their affection for his family and posterity, and who spoke of him in terms of general respect. His
faults were the faults of an ambitious mind. He can hardly
be ranked among the champions of liberty, and was far more
a lover of royalty than of freedom.[2]

[1] See his letter written in 1716, after the appointment of Shute, in 4 M.
H. Coll. ii. 308.

[2] The eulogist of Governor Dudley
says of him, " He was a man of rare
endowments and shining accomplishments ; a singular honor to his country, and in many respects the glory of
it. He was early its darling, always
its ornament, and in his age its crown.

The scholar, the divine, the philosopher, and the lawyer all met in him.
He was visibly formed for government ; and under his administration,
by the blessing of Almighty God, we
enjoyed great quietness, and were
safely steered through a long and difficult French and Indian war." Boston News Letter, No. 834.

CHAPTER IV.

DIFFICULTIES WITH THE FRENCH.

FRANCE and England were early competitors in the American seas. Their hereditary hatred, which had existed for centuries, had been deepened and intensified by repeated collisions; and upon the discovery of the new world each claimed a portion of its territory, assumed jurisdiction over the country, and attempted its colonization. Differences of religion increased their animosity. Catholic France denounced England as heretic and apostate. Protestant England retorted the ecclesiastical anathemas of its neighbor. The nations were so opposite in their language and habits, their philosophy and government, their opinions and customs, that no very friendly feelings could be expected to subsist between them. They were rivals in the old world, and rivals in the new; rivals in the East Indies, and rivals in the West; rivals in Africa, and rivals in Europe; rivals in politics, in commerce, and the arts; rivals in ambition for conquest and supremacy. Each sought its own aggrandizement at the expense of the other; each claimed to be superior to the other in the elements of national glory and the appliances of national strength. The gayety of the former was in contrast with the gravity and sobriety of the latter. The impetuosity of the one was the counterpart to the coolness and cautiousness of the other. Time, instead of softening, had hardened their prejudices; and for a century and a half from the date of the establishment of the first
French colony at the north, the two nations, with but slight interruptions, were constantly in the attitude of opposition and defiance. (74)

England, without doubt, preceded France in the career of CHAP.
discovery ; and the voyage of the Cabots gave to the former ⁀IV.
her claims to the regions visited by their vessels. But the 1497.
interval which elapsed between the voyage of the Cabots and
the earliest authenticated voyage of the French was exceedingly 1504.
brief ; and the two nations, if not contemporaries, were equals
in the race — neither being able to boast of any great advantage over the other, and neither, at the opening of the seventeenth century, being able to point to any permanent settle- 1602.
ment northward of forty degrees as the fruit of its enterprise.
Matched quite evenly in maritime skill, it was not until near
the close of the reign of Elizabeth that the scale turned in
favor of England. Yet under James I. the balance of power
could hardly be said to incline very strongly towards England ;
and France, undaunted by the prowess of her rival, continued,
with indomitable courage, to prosecute her plans ; succeeded,
even before England, in settling a colony to the north ; and
the foundations of Quebec were laid before the landing of the 1620.
Pilgrims, and before the settlement of Boston.   1630.

In consequence of this rivalry of England and France, the
colonies at the north were early involved in difficulties and
contentions ; and these difficulties increased as the conflict of
interests brought them into collision. Hence before the confederacy of 1643, apprehensions of hostilities were entertained 1632-43.
in Massachusetts ; and from that date to the union of the colonies of Plymouth and Massachusetts, these apprehensions 1692.
continued to disturb the people, and resulted, at length, in vigorous action on the part of the English to uproot their rivals,
and drive them from their possessions.

If New England was the "key of America," [1] New France
might, with equal propriety, claim to be the lock ; for Canada,
with the chain of fresh water lakes bordering upon its territory, opened a communication with the distant west ; and the

[1] 3 M. H. Coll. i. 100.

CHAP.
IV.

1673-98. Jesuit missionaries, Marquette, Joliet, La Salle, and Hennepin, by their explorations on the Mississippi, the "Father of Waters," brought the vast region watered by that stream and its tributaries under the dominion of the Bourbons, and backed all British America with a cordon of military posts, hovering upon the outskirts of the northern settlements with their savage allies, greatly to the alarm of the English, who were exposed to their depredations, and from whose incursions they could defend themselves only by an expenditure of money and strength which impoverished them in their weakness and imperilled their safety.

Behold, then, the two nations, rivals for centuries, upon the eve of a fresh struggle upon the new field of action. Acadia 1629. and Canada were wrested from the French before the settle- 1632.
Mar. 29. ment of Boston, but were restored by the treaty of St. Ger- 1654. main.[1] Acadia was again conquered under the commonwealth, 1669. but by the treaty of Breda was subsequently restored.[2] Under 1666. Charles II. the conquest of Canada was a second time attempted; but the difficulties of the enterprise prevented its 1686. success.[3] Again, under James II., a third attempt for its conquest was made, but with a like want of success.[4] The accession of William of Orange to the English throne was 1689.
May 7. the signal for a new war with France, growing out of a "root of enmity," which Marlborough described as "irreconcilable to the government and the religion" of Great Britain;[5] and on the occurrence of this war, a fourth expedition to Canada was projected, which was attended with important results.

[1] Hazard, i. 285–287; Charlevoix, vol. iii. ; Importance of Cape Breton, &c., 15, 16; 3 M. H. Coll. i. 232, and vi. 215; Haliburton's Nova Scotia, vol. i.; Williamson's Me. vol. i.; Bancroft's U. S. i. 335; Hildreth, vol. i.
[2] Palairet, Concise Description, p. 18, ed. 1755; Mems. Last War, p. 12, 3d ed. ; Importance of Cape Breton, &c., p. 17; 3 M. H. Coll. i. 233; Haliburton's N. S. i.; Beginning, Progress, &c., of Late War, Lond. 1770, 4to., p. 4; Williamson's Me. i.; N. H. Hist. Coll. i. 63.
[3] 2 M. H. Coll. viii. 109.
[4] Bancroft's U. S. ii. 422.
[5] Bancroft's U. S. iii. 175.

The settlers of New England, as Protestants, had, for a long time, viewed with jealousy the insidious advances of their Catholic neighbors at the north and at the west. In point of population, indeed, the English outnumbered the French at least ten to one.[1] It was not, therefore, in this respect that their power was dreaded. They were more formidable from their influence over the Indians within their borders. Their missionaries, with a zeal which has been highly applauded, had planted the cross in every village, and had scores of converts in every tribe ;[2] yet, with the craft and duplicity which distinguished the Jesuits, instead of seeking to allay the brutal ferocity of the savages, they had instilled into them their own hatred of the English and their religion. The natural aversion of the tribes to the progress of the white race facilitated their plans ; and no mass so vast and so combustible ever waited long for a spark to inflame it. As rivals in the fur trade, and rivals in the fisheries, collisions had frequently arisen ; and the fires of discord were smouldering in New England, and in Acadia and Canada.

In one respect, the difference in the condition of the colonies was of striking significance. The colonies of the French were planted by the crown, and were founded and fostered for the extension of its dominions, and the increase of its commerce. Their dependence upon the parent state was direct and immediate ; and their connection with the propagation of the Catholic faith was open and avowed. These colonies were parts

---

[1] Bradstreet, in 3 M. H. Coll. viii. 334, computes the population of New France in 1680 at 5000 men. Haliburton, N. S. i. 68, estimates it, in 1690, at 5815 souls. But Bancroft, U. S. iii. 177, estimates it, in 1688, at 11,249 persons. The tract entitled "The Importance of Cape Breton," &c., published in 1746, p. 102, contains extracts from a letter of M. Vaudreuil, estimating the soldiers of New France, in 1714, at 4480. See also Charlevoix, iv. 150.

[2] Parkman, Conspiracy of Pontiac, 49, says, "The zealous fathers reckoned the number of conversions by the number of baptisms ; and, as Le Clercq observes, with no less truth than candor, an Indian would be baptized ten times a day for a pint of brandy or a pound of tobacco." Bancroft, U. S. iii. c. 20, gives a characteristically glowing description of the progress of the Jesuit missions, equalling in fervor the accounts of the Jesuits themselves.

CHAP. of the dominion of France, controlled by the government, and
IV. subject to its decrees.   The colonies of the English were more
1690. independent.   Established for religion's sake, they were founded
by the people ; and the charters, which were the sanction of
their authority, were the chief bond of union between them
and the parent state.   They looked less abroad for aid, and
relied more upon their own resources.   Living within themselves, and shaping their own destiny in a measure, it was
always with reluctance that they submitted to interference in
their affairs ; and up to this date they had gone on, with very
little help from England, settling their own disputes and fighting their own battles.

The offer of colonial neutrality made by France at the opening of the war being rejected by England, the project of the
invasion of Acadia and Canada was conceived by Massachusetts ; and, in the winter of the same year that Andros was
1689. overthrown, the General Court, inspired with dazzling dreams
of conquest, meditated an attack upon Port Royal and Quebec.
Sir William Phips, afterwards governor of the province, and
a native of Pemaquid, had recently arrived in the country
under his appointment as high sheriff for New England; and,
as he was an experienced seaman, the command of the colonial
forces was intrusted to his care.   Eight small vessels and
seven or eight hundred men constituted the armament sent to
1690. Port Royal ; and sailing from Boston early in the spring, in
Apr. 28.
May 10. about two weeks he reached his destination ; the fort surrendered with but little resistance, yielding plunder sufficient to
pay expenses ; Sir William took possession of the whole sea
coast from Port Royal to New England ; [1] and three weeks
May 30. later he returned to Boston.

The success of this enterprise encouraged the prosecution of
the design upon Canada ; and the expedition was hastened

[1] MS. Continuation of Chalmers's   N. Y. Colon. Doc'ts, iii. 720, and ix.
Polit. Ann. Pt. II. ; Mather, Life of   474, 475 ; Williamson's Me. i. 596.
Phips, § 10 ; Dummer's Defence, 29 ;

by the horrible ravages of the Indians and French upon the frontier settlements, and by the desire of the colonists to commend themselves to the favor of the king, from whom they were expecting a renewal of their charter. So early as April,[1] a small vessel had been sent to England with despatches informing his majesty of the proposed expedition to Port Royal, and of the contemplated invasion of Canada, should it meet his approval, and praying for a supply of arms and ammunition, and a number of the king's frigates to attack the French by sea, while the forces of the colony attacked them by land. Engrossed by the war in Ireland, however,[2] the circumstances of the mother country were such that the request could not be complied with ; and Massachusetts, forming an immediate alliance with Connecticut and New York, at a " congress " held in the latter colony determined to proceed on her own responsibility, and, while a land army of eight hundred men was to march by Lake Champlain to attack Montreal, her forces, consisting of upwards of thirty vessels, and about two thousand men, were to fall upon Quebec.[3]

It was late in the season when this fleet sailed from Nantasket, and contrary winds delayed its progress, so that it did not reach Quebec until the opening of autumn. Intelligence of the proceedings of the troops from Connecticut and New York had, in the mean time, reached Montreal ; and the aged Frontenac, being informed by La Plaque, an Indian runner, that the Iroquois, the enemies of the French, were busy in constructing canoes on Lake George, prepared, without a moment's delay, for the defence of the place ; and placing the hatchet in the hands of La Plaque, and grasping in his own hands the death-

---

[1] MS. Letter of Governor Bradstreet to Lord Shrewsbury.

[2] On the 30th of May, Cooke and Oakes requested of the committee of plantations that a vessel should be sent, &c. 3 N. Eng. Ent's, in the state paper office, bund. 5, quoted in

the MS. Continuation of Chalmers's Polit. Ann. Pt. II.

[3] MS. Continuation of Chalmers's Polit. Ann. Mather, Life of Phips, § 11, and Dummer, Defence, 30, say the land expedition consisted of 1000 English, from New York and Connecticut, and 1500 Indians.

CHAP.
IV.

1690.

Oct. 4.

dealing tomahawk, he chanted the war song and danced the war dance as a pledge of coöperation in repelling the invaders.[1] But the alarm was premature ; for, by dissensions among the English, which ended in mutual recriminations, and other disappointments which paralyzed their strength, the land forces retreated, and fell back to Albany. Had it not been for this discomfiture, or had the fleet under Phips arrived three days earlier, the fate of Quebec would have been sealed. But the failure of the land expedition gave Frontenac time to rally ; and, hastening to the post of honor at the Castle of St. Louis, by his orders M. de Ramsey and M. de Callières mustered the militia of Three Rivers and the adjoining settlements, and marched to reënforce him with all possible despatch.

Major Provost, the commandant at Quebec, had previously prepared for the defence of the town, so that it was only necessary to continue the works, and render them more tenable. A party under M. de Longueuil was accordingly sent down the river to watch the motions of the English, and prevent their landing ; two canoes were despatched by the Isle of Orleans to seek for the supply ships which were daily expected from France ; and the soldiers and militia were employed on the fortifications. The castle itself was, by its natural position, almost impregnable ; but for further security, lines of palisades, armed with small batteries, were formed round the crown of the lofty headland environing the town ; the gates were barricaded with beams of timber, of massive size, and casks filled with earth ; cannon were mounted at every advantageous position ; and a large windmill of solid masonry was filled up as a cavalier. The lower town was protected by two batteries, each of three guns ; and the streets leading up the steep, rocky face of the height were embarrassed with intrenchments and rows of chevaux-de-frise. With these arrangements completed, Frontenac awaited the approach of the fleet.[2]

[1] Charlevoix, iii. 87 ; N. Y. Colon. Doc'ts, ix. 455.

[2] N. Y. Colon. Doc'ts, ix. 455, 484, 485.

At daylight on the fifth of October the white sails of the English ships were descried rounding the headland of Point Levi, and crowding to the northern shore of the river near the vil- lage of Beauport. At ten o'clock they dropped anchor, lowered their canvas, and swung round with the tide. In this position they remained until the following morning, when Sir William Phips, the commander-in-chief, despatched a messenger with a summons to the French general imperiously demanding an unconditional surrender in the name of King William. "Your answer positive in an hour, by your own trumpet, with the return of mine," were the closing words of the summons, " is required upon the peril that will ensue." [1]

The officer who bore this summons was led blindfold through the town, and, on reaching the castle, was ushered into the presence of the aged Frontenac, who was surrounded by the Jesuit bishop, the intendant, and the military officers composing his council. "Read your message," was his direction to the envoy. It was read; and at its conclusion the English officer, taking out his watch,[2] added, "It is now ten; I await your answer for one hour." A burst of indignation greeted the close of this speech; and Frontenac, with difficulty suppressing his own rage, exclaimed, "I know not King William; but I know that the Prince of Orange is a usurper, who has violated the most sacred rights of blood and religion. He has destroyed the laws and privileges of the kingdom, and overthrown the English church; and the Divine Justice will one day punish him for his crimes."[3] Unmoved by this outburst of fury and passion, the officer requested a written answer to return to his chief. "I will answer him at the cannon's mouth," was the haughty reply; and the conference ended.

On the return of the messenger an immediate attack was

[1] Charlevoix, iii. 115, 116; Mather, Life of Phips, § 11; N. Y. Colon. Doc'ts, ix. 455, 486.

[2] Charlevoix, iii., and the N. Y. Colon. Doct's, ix. 456.

[3] Charlevoix, iii. 117, 118, and Mather, Life of Phips, § 11, give an account of this interview. See also N. Y. Colon. Doc'ts, ix. 456, 486.

CHAP.
IV.

1690.
Oct. 8.

determined; and at noon on the eighth, thirteen hundred men [1] were embarked in the boats of the squadron, under the command of Major Walley. These landed without opposition at La Canardière, a little to the east of the St. Charles; and, while the main body formed on the muddy shores, four companies pushed on towards the town in skirmishing order to clear the way. But scarcely had they begun the ascent of the sloping banks when a galling fire was poured in upon them by two or three hundred of the Canadian militia, securely posted among the rocks and bushes on both flanks, and in a small hamlet to the right. The English were, for a moment, thrown into confusion; but the officers rallying, and gallantly leading the way in person, the soldiers followed at a quick pace, and the French troops scattered. Major Walley then advanced with his whole force to the St. Charles, where he bivouacked for the night, while the enemy, for security, retreated to their garrisons.

Oct. 8.

The same evening the four principal vessels of the squadron, having pushed boldly up the river, anchored before the town, and, opening their batteries, commenced firing. Their shot, however, which were chiefly directed against the lofty eminence of the upper town, fell almost harmless; while a vigorous cannonade from the numerous guns of the fortress, under the skilful direction of St. Helène, replied with overwhelming power. By eight o'clock the firing from the English vessels ceased, and on examination it was found that they had suffered severely from the enemy's shot, the rigging being badly

Oct. 9.

torn, and many of their best men slain. At daybreak the attack was renewed, but with no better success. The black muzzles of the cannon thrust from the bastions of the castle poured forth incessant volleys, while the guns of the ships, though constantly plied, made little impression. By noon, fully satisfied that the contest was hopeless, the assailants weighed

---

[4] Walley, in Hutchinson, i. 472, says 1300 men; Mather, Life of Phips, § 11, says 1400; Charlevoix, iii. 120, says 1500; and the N. Y. Colon. Doc'ts, ix. 457, 487, say 2000 men.

anchor, and, with the receding tide, floated their crippled vessels
out of the reach of the enemy's fire ; but not without the loss
of the flag of the rear admiral, which was shot away, and, as
it drifted towards the shore, was seized by a Canadian, who
swam out into the stream and brought it in triumph to the
castle, where, for many years, it was hung up as a trophy in
the church of Quebec.[1]

The troops under Major Walley, through some unaccount-
able delay, remained inactive during this combat with the
squadron of Phips ; but at length, about noon,[2] they advanced
upon the stronghold on the left bank of the St. Charles, preceded by their savage allies, who plunged into the bushes to
prevent an ambuscade. For some time their march was unmolested ; but suddenly they were attacked by two hundred
Canadian volunteers, under De Longueuil and St. Helène ; the
Indians were swept away, the skirmishers were overpowered,
and the English column itself was forced back by the impetuous charge. Walley, however, rallied his reserve, and, by a
quick movement, checked the enemy, and compelled them to
retreat. Frontenac at this time was posted upon the opposite
bank of the river, but evinced no disposition to cross the
stream ; and at night the English troops, wearied from the
fatigues of the day, depressed in spirits, and suffering from
hunger, again bivouacked in the marshes, exposed to the frosts,
which, at that season, are remarkably severe, and which still
farther weakened them, and increased their distress.

Undaunted by former reverses, on the following day Walley
once more advanced upon the French positions, in the hope of
breaching their palisades by the firing of his field pieces ; but
the attempt was unsuccessful. His flanking parties were am-
bushed, and the main body of his troops was repulsed by a
severe fire from a fortified house on a commanding eminence,

---

[1] N. Y. Colon. Doc'ts, ix. 457, 488 ;   Doc'ts, ix. 457, says this was on the
Hawkins, Picture of Quebec.   20th, N. S., corresponding to the
[2] The account in the N. Y. Colon.   10th, O. S.

to which the enemy had retreated, and which he ventured to attack. Utterly discouraged, the assailants withdrew; and reëmbarking in their vessels in the utmost confusion, exposed to the fire of the French, and abandoning their guns and the remnant of their stores, they prepared to return home, humbled and disappointed. Nor was the return voyage without damage; for, unacquainted with the passes of the river, nine vessels were wrecked among the shoals of the St. Lawrence.[1]

The arrival of Sir William at Boston, with the remnant of his fleet, spread an unusual gloom over the community. He had gone forth rejoicing, sanguine of success; he returned broken spirited, and with his men in a mutinous state, demanding their pay. The distress of the government, impoverished by Philip's war, and burdened with debt, was at its height; and finding it impracticable to raise money by ordinary means, bills of credit were issued — the first paper currency of New England.[2] The joy of the French at the withdrawal of the assailants was unbounded; and with a proud heart the gallant Frontenac penned the despatch which informed his master of the victory which had been achieved. To commemorate this victory a medal was struck, bearing the inscription, "*Francia in novo orbe victrix :* Kebeca liberata.— A. D., M. D. C. X. C.;" and in the lower town a church was built, which was dedicated to "Notre Dame de la Victoire."[3]

Thus ended the Canada expedition of 1690 — disastrously to New England, which was humiliated by its defeat. The bor-

[1] On this expedition, see N. Y. Colon. Doc'ts; Hutchinson, i. 352–356, and Walley's Narr. in ibid. 470–478; 2 M. H. Coll. iii. 256–260; Dummer's Defence, 30. The original journal of Phips's expedition was given to Admiral Walker, in 1711, who was then about to sail for Quebec, and was lost, with other papers, on board the Edgar. Walker's Journal, 87.

[2] Dummer, Defence, 30, says the cost of the expedition was £150,000 in money, and the loss of 1000 men.

In 2 M. H. Coll. iii. 260, it is said the expedition brought Massachusetts alone £50,000 in debt. The form of the bills issued at this time may be seen in ibid. 261. See further Mather, Life of Phips, § 12.

[3] The letter of Frontenac is given in full in N. Y. Colon. Doc'ts, ix. 459 –462. Comp. also Warburton's Conquest of Canada, i. c. 14. The sketch of Warburton is exceedingly graphic, and I have been indebted to it for several particulars given in the text.

der towns of the colonies were once more exposed to the forays CHAP.
of the French; and, from the exasperation of feeling which IV.
the invasion had awakened, nothing could be expected but a 1690.
series of retaliatory incursions, marked with the barbarities
inflicted by the Indians, who, involved in disputes relative to
their lands, had wrongs of their own to avenge, as well as to
prove their fidelity to their confederates.[1] The war at the
eastward, however, which followed, and which occupied the
time of the last ten years of the seventeenth century, belongs
more properly to the history of Maine than to that of Massachusetts, although Maine soon became, and for a long period
continued, a part of the Province of the Massachusetts Bay, and
was defended from the incursions of the Indians by the troops
of the province, especially by the gallant Church, who had
already signalized himself by his courage in Philip's war.[2]
That the sufferings of the people were severe, will be doubted
by no one who reads the narratives of their perils and massacre.
In a few cases, as at Groton, Billerica, Newbury, Lancaster, 1694-98.
Andover, Haverhill, and elsewhere, the savages penetrated
nearer Boston; and the escape of Hannah Dustin, the heroine
of Haverhill, is an episode of thrilling interest, showing what
a mother will do, when torn from her family, to restore herself
to the embraces of her husband and children.[3]

The defeat of the expedition of 1690 was probably attributable to the want of concert on the part of the troops from Con-

[1] For an account of the origin of these difficulties, see Belknap's N. H. ii. 43 et seq. This writer represents the inhabitants of the eastern parts of New England as "not of the best character for religion," and "ill adapt-ed to engage the affections of the In-dians by their example." Without doubt, there is some truth in this charge; yet, when it is borne in mind that the people of New England gen-erally purchased of the Indians the lands on which they settled, and the latter had little knowledge of the Eng-lish modes of transacting business, and each generation renewed the claims of its predecessor for a compensation, it will appear quite likely that a share of the blame of these disturbances is to be attributed to the Indians, and to the French, who instilled into them their own hatred of the English.

[2] Life of Church.

[3] Hutchinson, ii. 80, 86, 100–102; Neal's N. E. 553, 554; 3 M. H. Coll. vi. 240; Mirick, Hist. Haverhill, 86–95.

CHAP. necticut and New York and those from Massachusetts, and the
 IV.   failure of the supplies which were sought from England. Had
1690. the forces which were levied to march to Montreal succeeded
       in reaching their destination, or had they remained at Lake
       George, Frontenac would have been sufficiently occupied to
       have prevented his relieving Quebec ; and had seasonable sup-
       plies been forwarded from the mother country, and the fleet
       under Phips arrived sooner before the fortress, while the gar-
       rison was small and the works were incomplete, the place
       would doubtless have speedily fallen into his hands, and Can-
       ada would have been conquered. But there was mismanage-
       ment on all hands in the conduct of the expedition ; and it
       seems to have been predestinated that New England should
       not be delivered from the presence of the French at the north,
       until time had wrought the necessary changes which were to
       render the conquest of that country available for the promo-
       tion of still more important ends. Hence a new expedition,
1692. projected two years later, and resolved to be prosecuted in the
1693. following year, was attended with the like circumstances of
       mortification and defeat.

          England herself participated in this enterprise, and, by
1692-93. advices from Mr. Blathwayt, the government was informed
Feb. 20. that it had " pleased the king, out of his great goodness, and
       disposition for the welfare of all his subjects, to send a consid-
       erable strength of ships and men into the West Indies, and to
       direct Sir Francis Wheeler, the admiral, to sail to New Eng-
       land from the Caribbee Islands, so as to be there by the last
       of May or the middle of June at furthest, with a strength suffi-
       cient to overcome the enemy, if joined and seconded by the
       forces of New England." " There can never," continues the
       letter of the secretary, " be such an occasion for the people of
       New England to show their zeal for their religion and love to
       their king and country. His majesty has taken care, besides
       the ships of war, to send to you a thousand soldiers, if their
       number be not diminished by their service in the West Indies,

under a commander who has looked the same enemy in the face, and will show an example worthy to be followed. Sir William Phips, I suppose, will be at the head of the New England volunteers, and will readily acquiesce, according to the rules of war, in leaving the chief command as his majesty has determined it."[1]

CHAP. IV.

1693.

Unfortunately for the success of these plans, the letter, which should have reached Boston by the first of April, did not arrive until July ; and the mortality which prevailed in the fleet during its stay in the West Indies was so great that, when the commander-in-chief, Sir Francis Wheeler, anchored off Nantasket, — bringing himself the news of the projected invasion, — he had lost thirteen hundred out of twenty-one hundred sailors, and eighteen hundred out of twenty-four hundred soldiers. All thoughts of reducing Canada were therefore abandoned ; but a plan for another year was settled with the governor, the details of which were, that two thousand land forces should be sent from England to Canseau by the first of June, to be joined by two thousand from the colonies, and that the whole force should go up the St. Lawrence, divide, and simultaneously attack Montreal and Quebec. Changes in the government of the province, however, and other causes, prevented the execution of this plan, whose success was problematical even if it had been attempted.[2]

Jı

Juı

16ٵ
June

But if the plans of the English for the reduction of Canada were doomed to disappointment, the plans of the French for the recovery of Acadia were more successful. For the first year after the conquest of that country, indeed, the French were as little concerned to regain, as the English were to retain, the possession of its territory ; nor was Massachusetts

1692.

---

[1] This letter, addressed to Increase Mather, is given in Hutchinson, ii. 70, note. The letter to Admiral Wheeler, directing him to repair to the north, was dated November, 1692. MS. Letter of Governor Phips.

[2] Burchett's Mems. of Transactions at Sea, ed. 1703, p. 173 ; Walker's Journal, 32 ; Hutchinson, ii. 70–72 ; Harris, Voy. ii. 924 ; Holmes, Am. Ann. i. 447.

CHAP.
IV.

1691.

Nov. 26.

1692.

1696.
July 14.

1697.

able to bear the charge of a sufficient military force to keep its inhabitants in subjection, though she issued commissions to judges and other officers, and required the administration of the oath of fidelity. In the course of that year, authority was given to Mr. John Nelson, of Boston, who had taken an active part in the overthrow of Andros, and who was bound thither on a trading voyage, to be commander-in-chief of Acadia ;[1] but, as he neared the mouth of the St. John's, he was taken by Monsieur Villebon, who, under a commission from the French king, had touched at Port Royal, and ordered the English flag to be struck, and the French flag to be raised in its place. The next year an attempt was made to dislodge Villebon, but without success ; and Massachusetts, convinced of her inability to keep the country, though unwilling to relinquish its jurisdiction, petitioned the crown that the province might be freed from further expense in the defence of Port Royal and St. John's, and that garrisons might be placed there at the national charge. In the summer of 1696, Pemaquid was taken by the French, under D'Iberville and Castine, and the frontier of the dominion of France was extended into Maine; and by the treaty of the following year Acadia was re-ceded to France, and the English relinquished their claims to the country.[2]

The last year of "King William's war," as it was long termed in New England, was a year of especial alarm to the province, and rumors were rife that the French were on the eve

---

[1] Nelson, who was a moderate Episcopalian, rendered important service to the province at this time, by communicating intelligence of the designs of the French and their contemplated attacks. When he was taken prisoner, he was sent to France, where he was treated with the utmost rigor, being confined in the Bastile. Circumstances requiring his presence in England, he was at length liberated on parole, and, after transacting the business for which he left prison, he prepared to return. The king interfered, and commanded him, on his allegiance, to remain ; but his noble reply was, "Please God I live, I'll go ; " and go he did. The character of Nelson was a marked one ; and, had he sympathized in his religious opinions with the dominant party, he would doubtless have occupied a more conspicuous place in our annals. MS. notes communicated by E. H. Derby, Esq.

[2] Mass. Rec's, v. 579 ; Hutchinson, ii. 87–95 ; Williamson's Me. ii. 23 ; Bancroft's U. S. iii. 189.

of fitting out a formidable fleet for the invasion of the colonies CHAP.
and the conquest of New York.[1] The year previous, there had IV.
been intimations that an armament from Europe, joined by 1696.
land forces from Canada, was to make a descent upon the
coast; and application had been made to the French mon- 1695.
arch by the governor of Canada for ten or twelve men-of-war
to be sent to encounter an English squadron, which was shortly
expected to arrive ; but, as the intentions of the French court
were principally to secure the possession of Newfoundland, and
recover Acadia, — both which objects were accomplished, — no
design was prosecuted upon Boston, nor was any particular
alarm created by the expedition.

The new expedition was more dreaded ; and for several 1697.
weeks the arrival of the French fleet was daily expected. It
was supposed, on the part of France, that a strong squadron
would be sent from England to recover the ports in Newfoundland, and great preparations were made for its defeat. Frontenac, the governor of Canada, though advanced in years,
received orders to raise fifteen hundred men, in readiness to
march at a moment's warning ; and the command of the French
fleet, consisting of ten men-of-war, a galiot, and two frigates,
was intrusted to the Marquis de Nesmond, an officer of great
reputation, who was to leave Brest by the twenty-fifth of April Apr. 25.
at farthest, with his own vessels, to join those at Rochelle under
Commodore de Magnon, and, with the utmost despatch, proceed
to the Bay of Placentia, in Newfoundland, and from thence sail
for Penobscot, first sending a packet boat to Quebec to inform
Frontenac of his route. Upon his arrival, the troops were to
be immediately embarked for Boston ; and when that town was
taken, they were to range the coast to Piscataqua, destroying
the settlements as far back into the country as possible.

---

[1] " Je prendrai encore la liberté de
vous dire, que la prise de Manhatte
étoit beaucoup plus utile pour la sû-
reté de cette colonie, et pour la déli-
vrer des Iroquois, que celle de Bas-
ton," i. e., Boston. Charlevoix, iii.
318, ed. 1744, 12mo.

CHAP.
IV.

1697.

July 24.

Should there be time for further acquisitions, they were next to go to New York, and upon its reduction the Canadian troops were to march overland to Quebec, laying waste the country as they proceeded.[1]

Tidings of this contemplated invasion reached Boston before the arrival of the fleet on the coast, and the inhabitants were in the greatest consternation. But feeble hopes were entertained of aid from England; yet Mr. Stoughton, the lieutenant governor, making the best preparations in his power, caused the militia of the province to be held in readiness to march for the seaports; and the Castle in the harbor, which was in a comparatively defenceless condition, was strengthened as fully as time would permit. But the schemes of the French were not destined to succeed. De Nesmond, on reaching Placentia, found there a letter awaiting him from M. le Comte de Pontchartrain, informing him that eighteen English ships from Lisbon, laden with salt, under the convoy of a man-of-war, purposed to proceed to Newfoundland to be employed in the cod fishery; and he was instructed to do every thing in his power to prevent their escaping him before leaving for Boston. Detained by contrary winds, however, his passage from France was so long, and his arrival so late, that nothing could be heard of the English fleet; and when a council of war was held to consider the expediency of proceeding to Boston, the proposal was unanimously negatived. The grounds of this decision were, that they were entirely ignorant of the situation and circumstances of the enemy, and that, with whatever despatch messengers were sent to Frontenac, the Canadian forces could not be expected at Penobscot before the tenth of September, and by that time the provisions of the fleet would be so far expended that they would be in no capacity to prosecute such an enterprise.[2]

---

[1] Charlevoix, iii. 318–321; Hutchinson, ii. 96–99.

[2] Charlevoix, iii. 321, 322; Hutchinson, ii. 99; Holmes, Am. Ann. i. 463, 464.

The peace of Ryswick, which soon followed, led to a tem- CHAP.
porary suspension of hostilities.[1]   France, anxious to secure as IV.
large a share of territory in America as possible, retained the 1697.
whole coast and adjacent islands from Maine to Labrador and Sep. 20
Hudson's Bay, with Canada, and the valley of the Mississippi.
The possessions of England were southward from the St. Croix.
But the bounds between the nations were imperfectly defined,
and were, for a long time, a subject of dispute and negotiation.
Each nation had land enough for all practical purposes, and
more than it could colonize or suitably protect.   Yet the ambition for territorial aggrandizement seems to be an inherent
passion ; and, where national honor and private interest are involved, mutual jealousies are sure to arise, nor can they be allayed
until one party or the other is constrained by more powerful
motives to modify or relinquish its extravagant claims.   Without doubt, both parties would gladly have assumed jurisdiction
over the whole North American continent, could they have
done so with the prospect of maintaining their assumptions ;
nor did the French exhibit a greater desire to encroach upon
the English, than the English exhibited to encroach upon the
French.   Each accused the other of trespassing upon its
dominions, and neither was content that the other should gain
the least advantage, or secure to itself a monopoly of the fishery or the fur trade.[2]

The suspension of hostilities in Europe was but temporary ; 1702.
for in 1702 war was again declared.   In the mean time the May 4.
French were secretly employed in encouraging the Indians bordering upon New England to violate the leagues which had
been formed with them, and ravage the country.[3]   It may 1698.

---

[1] Notice of the peace was transmitted to the colonies in October, 1697,
with orders for its proclamation, which
were obeyed in December.   Stoughton, MS. Letter to England, and MS.
Contin. of Chalmers's Polit. Ann. Pt.
II.

[2] Chalmers, Revolt, i. 276 ; Coke's

Detection of the Court and State of
England, iii. 57 ; Hutchinson, ii. 104 ;
Haliburton's N. S. vol. i.

[3] On these leagues, made in 1698,
see Hutchinson, ii. 104 ; Holmes,
Ann. i. 473 ; N. H. Hist. Coll. ii. 265
–267.

CHAP. seem hardly credible that so treacherous a design should have
IV. been deliberately conceived by a nation which boasted of its
1703. superior enlightenment; but the testimony of Charlevoix, the
Jesuit historian of New France, abundantly proves the correctness of the charge, for he glories in the conduct of his countrymen, and speaks of it in terms of extravagant eulogy.[1] Thus
countenanced, it may well be supposed that the fierce Abenakis
manifested no reluctance to avail themselves of this opportunity to satiate their revenge; and in a very short time they
burst like an avalanche upon the country, spreading desolation
wherever they went.

1703-4. Their first principal attack was upon Deerfield, one of the
Feb. pleasantest of the western villages, which had suffered severely
in Philip's war, and which had been recently rebuilt and partially fortified.[2] The assailants, three hundred in number,
French and Indians, under Hertel de Rouville, a merciless mis-
creant, with the aid of snow shoes skimmed over the snow,
which was four feet deep, and, on the evening of the last day
Feb. 28. but one of February,[3] reached the dark pine forest which
loomed up at the outskirt of the village, where they were sheltered for the night.[4] Trembling hearts and tearful eyes were
in the settlement, for the inhabitants had been warned of impending danger by Colonel Schuyler, of New York, and the
Mohawks. A body of twenty soldiers had been sent to defend
the place, and sentinels were posted at different points, who
kept anxious watch until two hours before day, when they
Feb. 29. retired. Immediately the enemy, who had been secretly recon-
noitring, perceiving all to be quiet, crept stealthily up to the

[1] Charlevoix, Nouv. Fr. See also
Dummer's Defence; 3 M. H. Coll. i.
233, and vi. 247; Chalmers, Revolt,
i. 277; Penhallow, in N. H. Hist.
Coll. i. 22, 44.
[2] MS. Letter of John Pynchon to
Governor Dudley, dated August 3,
1702, in the possession of J. W.
Thornton, Esq.

[3] Bancroft, from oversight, says the
last day of February. That year was
leap year.
[4] Holland, Hist. Western Mass. i.
148, says the spot where the Indians
lodged was "at a pine bluff overlooking Deerfield meadow, about two
miles north of the village — a locality
known as Petty's Plain."

palisades, and, aided by the drifts, which were piled up nearly CHAP.
to their top, sprang into the enclosure, and the wild war whoop IV.
pealed upon the air. The garrison house was first surprised; 1704.
and another party breaking into the house of Mr. Williams,
the minister, he was seized, with his wife, and five of his children; his house was plundered, and two children and a negro
woman were cruelly murdered. Falling upon other houses,
upwards of forty persons were slain, and more than a hundred
were made prisoners.[1] When the sun was an hour high the
work was finished, and the enemy took their departure, leaving
the snow reddened with blood, and the deserted village envel-
oped in flames. The sufferings of the prisoners who can portray? Children who grew weary, and women who tottered
from weakness and hunger, were remorselessly slain and scalped
by their captors. A Bible had been saved, which was read to
them at night as they halted for rest; and its inspiring truths
were never more cheering than then. The strength of Mrs.
Williams, who had been recently confined, rapidly failed, and a
blow from a tomahawk ended her sorrows. Mr. Williams, her
husband, was carried to Canada, but eventually returned, with 1706.
four of his children. The youngest, a daughter of but seven
years old, remained, was adopted into a village of Indians
near Montreal, and became a proselyte to the Catholic faith,
and the wife of a Cahnewaga chief. After many years she
revisited her childhood's home, with her husband, clad in an
Indian dress; but neither the entreaties of her friends nor the
prayers of the people could induce her to tarry with them.
She returned to her wigwam, and to the love of her children.[2]

The same summer of the attack on Deerfield, a body of four 1704. July 31.

---

[1] The accurate Prince, in his Appendix to Williams's Redeemed Captive, p. 109, 6th ed. 1795, computes
the number of killed at 49, and the
number of captives at 109, and gives
the names of the persons. See also
Holland's Hist. Western Mass. i. 151,
note.

[2] The narrative of Mr. Williams,
entitled the "Redeemed Captive,"
first published in 1706–7, is the principal authority. See also Hutchinson,
ii. 127–129, 140, 141; Penhallow, in
2 N. H. Hist. Coll. i. 29, 30; Holmes,
Ann. i. 487, 488, and notes; Holland's
Hist. Western Mass. i. 148–156.

CHAP.
IV.

1704.
Aug.
1705-6.

1708.

hundred French and Indians fell upon Lancaster, and burned the meeting house and several dwellings;[1] another party way-laid a scout sent from Northampton to Westfield, and killed one man and took two prisoners;[2] and during this and the two following years, other towns in the Bay province suffered by their depredations.[3] The barbarities perpetrated in this war equalled, if they did not exceed, those of Philip's war. Women, far advanced in pregnancy, were violently delivered, and the tender babes dashed to the ground. Infants were despatched in the same manner; or sometimes, half strangled, they were thrown to their mothers to quiet. Of the captives, some were roasted alive; others were gashed in all parts of their bodies, brands were thrust into the wounds, and then set on fire. The condition of those who fared the best was far from enviable. They were subjected to the hardship of travelling, barefoot and half naked, through pathless deserts, over craggy mountains, through horrible swamps and thickets. They were obliged to endure frost, rain, and snow, and all the inclemencies of the season, both by night and by day. No pity was shown, nor allowance made, for the aged or infirm. Such as, through infirmity, hunger, fatigue, or sorrow, fainted under their burdens, or could not keep pace with the enemy, were despatched with the tomahawk.[4]

The attack upon Haverhill is memorable in the annals of that town. The little village contained about thirty cottages, mostly of logs, clustered upon the slope of the hill whose base is bathed by the beautiful Merrimac. In the centre stood a new meeting house, the pride of the settlers, within whose walls they gathered from Sabbath to Sabbath, to listen to the word of life dispensed from the lips of the amiable Rolfe. Like most of the villages of New England, it was tenanted by the

[1] Boston News Letter, Nos. 16 and 31.
[2] 3 M. H. Coll. vi. 259; N. H. Hist. Coll. i. 39, 40.
[3] N. H. Hist. Coll. i. 42, 49, 50.
[4] Trumbull's U. S. i. 228, 229.

yeomanry of the land, who industriously cultivated their patches CHAP.
of maize, on the few acres which the hand of toil had redeemed IV.
from the wild magnificence of towering forests. The scene 1708.
was one of rural quietude, too peaceful to be invaded by the
ruthless destroyer. Yet at the dawn of a summer's day, whose Aug.29.
eve had closed in with no warning of the danger which threatened, the bloodthirsty Rouville, with his desperate followers,
after impiously calling upon God to sanction his deed, raised the
shrill war cry, and sprang upon the village which his murderous heart had devoted to destruction. The crack of the rifle,
and the crash of the tomahawk as it broke through the skull
of its helpless victim, were mingled with shouts and groans
of despair. The family of Rolfe were among the first sufferers, and the father was beaten to death; the hatchet sank
deep into the brain of the mother; her infant was snatched
from her dying grasp, and its head dashed against a stone.
Two children escaped, who were secreted in the cellar by a
negro slave. Vain was the attempt to drive out the foe.
The surprise was so sudden as to admit of no concert. Each
fought for his own family, and was shot down in their midst,
struggling for their defence. A few only escaped the general
massacre, indebted for their deliverance to the gallantry of
Davis, and others from Salem, posted in the neighborhood and
hastily mustered, who, as the destroyers retired, hung on their
rear to rescue the captives. At the close of the day the
tragedy was over; the bodies of the slain were mournfully
interred; and though nearly a century and a half has elapsed
since they fell, an ancient mound marks their resting-place,
and a moss-grown stone, with its rude inscription, stands by
the grave of Rolfe and his family.[1]

Is it surprising that such cruelties inspired the deepest hate 1697.
towards the French and their missionaries? Scarcely had Dec.

---

[1] Charlevoix; Hutchinson, ii. 157;
Penhallow, in N. H. Hist. Coll. i. 59;
Mirick, Hist. Haverhill, 117–134;
Bancroft, iii. 215, 216. A second at-
tack was made upon Haverhill shortly
after, but without much damage. Bos-
ton News Letter, No. 233, Sept. 27 to
Oct. 4, 1708.

CHAP.
IV.

1698.
Sept. 5.

peace been proclaimed in New England, when the designs of the French against the English were renewed ; and Villebon, the governor at St. John's, forwarded a letter containing his instructions to seize and defend the whole country to the Kennebec. The Board of Trade was informed of these proceedings ; but the only result was a message, insisting on the right of the English as far as the St. Croix, and urging Massachusetts to rebuild the fort at Pemaquid.[1] With this order the General Court was reluctant to comply. It was not a "reprehensible parsimony" which prompted their refusal.[2] The place was so distant that the force of the province was inadequate for its defence, and the funds of the government were needed for other purposes. Besides, it was contended that the work of rebuilding the fort was entirely uncalled for, as it would prove insufficient for the protection of the frontier.[3]

Before long, however, it became evident that a more decided course must be taken. The encroachments of the French were daily increasing ; and their connection with the Indians, whom they had prompted to ravage the country, demanded some action to check their proceedings. Accordingly, intelligence

1707. having been received that an armament from England was to be sent against Acadia or Canada, it was resolved that one thousand men should be raised in Massachusetts to aid in the prosecution of that design. Proposals were made to the other provinces to join in the project ; but Connecticut declined rendering assistance, though New Hampshire and Rhode Island promptly responded to the call. The forces from England did not arrive, the war with Spain preventing their departure. Hence the whole charge of the expedition devolved upon New England. The command of the troops, consisting of two regiments, was intrusted to Colonel March ; and the fleet,

---

[1] Stoughton's Lett. to Board of Trade; Hutchinson, ii. 105, 106; Chalmers, MS. copy of his Polit. Ann. Pt. II., and Revolt, i. 278; 3 M. H. Coll. i. 135; Grahame, ii. 12; Holmes, i. 470; Williamson's Me. ii. 26, 27.

[2] Discov. and Sett. of the English in Amer. quoted in Hutchinson, ii. 68; Williamson's Me. i. 636.

[3] Mass. Rec's; Collection of Proceedings of Gen. Court, ed. 1729, pp. 20, 21; Hutchinson, ii. 138.

which consisted of three transport ships, five brigantines, CHAP.
and fifteen sloops, with "whaleboats answerable," attended IV.
by her majesty's ship the Deptford and the province galley, 1707.
sailed from Boston early in May,[1] and reached Port Royal May 13.
towards the close of the month.[2] Here the soldiers were May 26.
landed, and the fort was attacked; but after several skirmishes, which resulted disastrously, the siege was abandoned, June 7.
and the army reëmbarked — Colonels Rednap and Appleton
returning to Boston for further instructions, and the rest proceeding to Casco Bay. The orders of the governor, returned
by the messengers, were, that the attempt should be renewed.
The army once more sailed, and landing opposite the fort, Aug.10.
prepared for an attack. But the troops were dispirited; the
weather was unfavorable; sickness was spreading; the men
were incapable of sustaining the fatigues of a siege; and ten
days after, the design was relinquished, and the fleet returned Aug.20
to Boston.[3]

Not thus, however, was the attempt to be abandoned; and
England, resolved on increasing her colonial acquisitions, and
punishing the audacity and insolence of the French, prepared 1709.
to send a fleet to America for the reduction of Canada, Acadia, and Newfoundland. The plan was extensive. A squadron of ships was to be at Boston by the middle of May. Five May.
regiments of regular troops, numbering three thousand men,
were to embark in this fleet, and twelve hundred men were to
be raised in the northern colonies to ally with them on their
arrival. Massachusetts and Rhode Island were expected to
raise these men; and the governments were to provide transports, boats, pilots, and provisions. With this force Quebec

---

[1] Penhallow, in N. H. Hist. Coll.
i. 54, says the fleet sailed March 13 —
a misprint, probably, for May 13.

[2] Haliburton, N. S. i. 84, says the
fleet arrived May 17. This must be
a mistake.

[3] On this expedition, see Charlevoix; Hutchinson, ii. 150–155; Pen-

hallow, in N. H. Hist. Coll. i. 54–56;
Chalmers, Revolt, i. 335, 336; Haliburton's N. S. i. 83, 84; Holmes,
Ann. i. 496, 497, and notes. In the
pamphlet entitled "The Deplorable
State of N. Eng.," &c., the blame of
the failure of this expedition is charged
to Governor Dudley.

CHAP. was to be attacked ; and in Connecticut, New York, and New
IV.   Jersey, fifteen hundred men were to be raised, — including the
1709. four independent companies of one hundred men each, the regular garrison of New York, — who were to march by the lakes
and attack Montreal. The expedition from the northern colonies was to be commanded by Colonel Vetch, an officer who
had already been engaged against the French ; and it was left
to Lord Lovelace, the governor of New York, to appoint the
general officer for the troops from the southern department ;
but by his death the power devolved upon Ingoldsby, the lieutenant governor, and Francis Nicholson, successively lieutenant
governor of New York, of Maryland, and of Virginia, was
selected, and marched with his forces to Wood Creek, near
the head of Lake Champlain.

The transports and troops from Massachusetts and Rhode
May   Island waited at Boston from May to September, every day
to   expecting the fleet from England ; but no intelligence arriving,
Sept. Colonel Vetch, satisfied that it was too late to set out at that
season of the year, proposed a conference of the governors at
Oct. 11. Rhode Island. A few days before this meeting, a ship arrived
at Boston from England, with advices from Lord Sunderland
that the forces intended for America had been ordered to Portugal, and with directions to consult upon the expediency of
attacking Port Royal ; but by the refusal of the English ships
then in the harbor to join in the expedition, the General Court,
then in session, desired the governor to discharge the transports and disband the men, who had been kept under pay five
months, greatly to the embarrassment of the finances of the
province. Thus the new scheme of conquest, like others which
had been devised, through the negligence of England proved
an abortion, expensive to the colonists and injurious to their
interests.[1]

[1] On this expedition, see Mass. i. 61 ; Chalmers, Revolt, i. 343 ; Gra-
Rec's, vii. 426 ; Dummer, in 3 M. H. hame, ii. 26 ; Holmes, Ann. i. 500 ;
Coll. i. 234 ; Hutchinson, ii. 160– Williamson's Me. ii. 58 ; Dunlap's N.
163 ; Penhallow, in N. H. Hist. Col. York, i. 266 ; Hildreth's U. S. ii. 261.

The next expedition was more successful. At the instance of Nicholson, Colonel Schuyler, of New York, had visited England with five Iroquois sachems, fantastically attired, who were conducted in state to an audience with the queen, and attracted the attention of the journalists of the day.[1] The government of New York, through these agents, renewed its appeal for aid in the reduction of Canada; and, as the measure was one which demanded attention, the Dragon and Falmouth, two of her majesty's fifty gun frigates, with the bomb ship Star, a tender, and several transports, left England in the spring, and arrived at Boston in the middle of July. Joined here by the Lowestoff and the Feversham, from New York, and the Chester, of fifty guns, with the province galley, and fourteen transports in the pay of Massachusetts, five from Connecticut, two from New Hampshire, and three from Rhode Island, the whole fleet, consisting of thirty-six vessels, sailed from Nantasket for Port Royal, having on board, besides the regiment from England, commanded by Colonel Redding, four regiments raised in New England, two of which were commanded by Sir Charles Hobby and Colonel Tailer of Massachusetts, one by Colonel Whiting of Connecticut, and one by Colonel Walton of New Hampshire, with Nicholson as general of the forces, and Vetch as adjutant general. In six days the fleet anchored before Port Royal, and the troops were landed without opposition. The forces of Subercase, the governor of the French fortress, consisted of but two hundred and sixty men, most of whom were so insubordinate that they could not be trusted. The siege continued three or four days, the French throwing shells and shot from their fort, and the bomb ship replying with signal effect, when, finding the place too warm for them, a flag of truce was sent from Subercase, praying leave for the ladies in the fort to be sheltered in the English camp. This request was granted; but two days after, the

Marginal notes:
CHAP. IV.

1709-10.
March.
1710.
Apr. 19.

May 8.
July 15.
Sept. 9.

Sep. 18.

Sep. 24.

Sep. 29.

---

[1] Coke's Detection, iii. 382, where are the names of the chiefs; Smith's N. Y. i. 121–123; Trumbull, vol. i.; Holmes, i. 502, note.

CHAP. English engineers, Forbes and Rednap, having thrown up
IV. three batteries within one hundred yards of the walls, mount-
1710. ing two mortars and twenty-four cohorn mortars, the attack
Oct. 1. was renewed. At length Colonel Tailer and Captain Abercrombie were sent to the French commandant with a summons
to surrender; a cessation was agreed upon; terms of capitulation
Oct. 2. were settled; on the following day the articles were signed;
Oct. 5. Port Royal was delivered into the hands of the victors; in
honor of her majesty, Queen Anne, the name of the place was
changed to Annapolis; and General Nicholson, having made
himself master of all Acadia, left a garrison at the fortress
under the command of Colonel Vetch, and returned with his
Oct. 26. fleet and army to Boston.[1]

Flushed with success, the ardent Nicholson, panting for
1711. greater triumphs, again visited England, to urge the conquest
of Canada; and being joined there by Jeremiah Dummer, a
young man of superior abilities and accomplishments, afterwards conspicuous in the history of Massachusetts, a memorial
was presented to the queen, begging her, " in compassion to
the plantations, to send an armament against Canada," in
which enterprise he represented that not only Massachusetts,
but the other provinces, " even Virginia," would be ready to
aid.[2] Massachusetts, however, had faint hopes of the success
of this appeal; for, as the change in the ministry, alluded to
in a previous chapter, had just taken place, — the tories under
Harley and St. John having raised themselves to power, —
with what confidence could the colonists look for favor from
a party adverse to their views, when their prayers had been
treated with neglect by their friends? Greatly to their surprise, however, and as greatly to their joy, prompt attention
1711.
June 8. was paid to their request; and, at the return of Nicholson,

---

[1] On this expedition, see Mass.
Rec's; Charlevoix; Lediard's Naval
Hist. Eng. 848, 849; Hutchinson, ii.
164–167; Penhallow, in N. H. Hist.
Coll. i. 63–66; Chalmers, Revolt, i.
348, 349; Haliburton's N. S. i. 85–
88; 1 M. H. Coll. vi. 120; Dummer's
Defence, 32; Williamson's Me. ii. 59.
[2] Chalmers, Revolt, i. 349; Hildreth's U. S. ii. 169.

they were informed that a fleet of from twelve to fifteen ships CHAP. of war and forty transports, under the command of Sir Hoven-IV. den Walker,[1] and seven veteran regiments from Marlborough's 1711. army, under General Hill, with a battalion of marines six hundred in number, was to sail immediately from England, and would probably arrive on the coast in a very few days.

By the same messenger, orders were forwarded from the queen to the governments of New England, New York, the Jerseys, and Pennsylvania, to raise the quotas assigned to them, in readiness to join the fleet without delay, with provisions for the army sufficient for ten weeks' supply.[2] The reason assigned for the last order was, that there might be no suspicions in Europe of the destination of the fleet, which was kept secret; but the government of Massachusetts, aware of the difficulty of procuring such a quantity of provisions at so short a notice, began to suspect that it was not seriously designed in England that Canada should be taken, and that this unusual course had been adopted to shift the blame of the expedition, in case of its failure, from the mother country to the colonies. To anticipate this charge, the governor, and even private persons, put forth vigorous exertions to secure the requisite supplies; and the people, though with some reluctance, acquiesced in their demands.

Upon the arrival of the fleet,[3] with six thousand seamen and Jun. 25. marines, and five thousand five hundred soldiers, as money, the "sinews of war," was necessary for the expedition, the General Court of the province, notwithstanding the embarrassment of the finances, determined to issue forthwith forty thousand

[1] His commission is in his Journal, App. 159, 160, and his instructions are in ibid. 166–174.

[2] A meeting of the governors of the several colonies was held at New London on Thursday, June 20; and in three days' time the necessary orders, &c., were agreed upon. Boston News Letter, No. 376. The New England forces consisted of 1500 men. Walker's Journal, 85.

[3] The Boston News Letter, No. 379, says, on Monday, 25th June, the Castle gave alarm of several ships in the Bay, and General Hill arrived. His excellency was absent at the congress at New London. Walker, Journal, 35, says he arrived at Nantasket June 24.

CHAP. pounds in bills of credit, to be loaned to merchants and others
IV. for the term of two years, for the purchase of bills of exchange
1711. on the treasury of England. As provisions were held at extravagant rates, in consequence of the sudden and enormous
demand, an order was likewise issued regulating the prices at
which different articles should be sold. The dealers, upon
this, closed their stores, or concealed their goods. The government authorized an impressment of provisions, in case of
refusal to sell; and this brought the malcontents to terms.[1]

Nor were these the only difficulties encountered. Soldiers
and seamen began to desert; and Admiral Walker demanded
their return, or a supply equal to the loss. All the evils incident to the quartering of a large force suddenly upon the country began to manifest themselves; and it was soon evident
that, unless the departure of the expedition was hastened, the
whole design must end in discomfiture or disgrace.[2]

July 30. At length, after a month's delay, the fleet, consisting of about
eighty vessels in all, sailed; but scarcely had it begun to ascend
Aug.23. the St. Lawrence, when eight ships were wrecked, and nearly
a thousand men found a watery grave. A council of war voted
unanimously that it was impossible to proceed; and, without
attempting any thing against Placentia, or striking a single

---

[1] The speech of Governor Dudley of July 5 to the General Court, to forward the expedition, is given in the Boston News Letter, No. 377; and Walker's Journal, 72, 73, commends his interest in the enterprise. A fast was proclaimed July 16, to be held July 26, and on the last Thursday in each month afterwards during the continuance of the expedition. Ibid. No. 379. Walker, Journal, 36, 64, 65, complains of "the prices of provisions, and other necessaries for the fleet and army, in New England," and unjustly charges the government with enhancing the expenses of the expedition "to make an advantage of our necessities;" but it would seem from his own account, pp. 76–78, and from other authorities, that the quantity required for his fleet was greater than Boston or the province could supply. Jonathan Belcher was the principal contractor to furnish provisions for the fleet, and Peter Faneuil provided the military stores. Ibid.

[2] The General Court of Massachusetts, in anticipation of the arrival of Admiral Walker, issued an order, May 30, 1711, to prevent the desertion of sailors, marines, and soldiers; and at a later date, July 16, a second order of the same purport was issued. See Mass. Rec's, and comp. Walker's Journal, 198, 199, 229, 230.

blow against the French, the bows of the vessels were turned
homeward, and the enterprise was abandoned.[1]

Upon whom the responsibility of the failure of this expedition rests, it may be difficult to say.   Admiral Walker charged
it to the misconduct of the colonists; the colonists imputed it
to his own mismanagement.   The disappointment and loss were
so grievous to New England, that "it affected the whole country seven years after," and some abandoned all hopes of the
reduction of Canada.   So many failures indicated, as they conceived, that "Providence never designed the whole northern
continent of America to be under the dominion of one nation."
But the "fulness of times" had not then come.   He who sits
at the helm of the universe, guiding events in accordance with
his own plans, had not issued the mandate which was to conduct England to victory, and, by that very triumph, open the
way for the independence of her colonies.   Truly,

> "There's a divinity that shapes our ends,
> Roughhew them as we will."

---

[1] On this expedition, see Mass. Rec's; Walker's Journal, passim; Rapin, iv. 215, 216, and notes; Charlevoix; Boston News Letter, No. 379, 380, 381; Dummer's Letter to a Noble Lord; Lediard, Naval Hist. 851–856; Hutchinson, ii.; Chalmers, Revolt, i. 349–352, 354; Penhallow, in N. H. Hist. Coll. i. 72–77; Dummer's Defence, 32; Holmes, Ann. i. 504, 505; Williamson's Me. ii. 63; Grahame, ii. 30, 33; Bancroft, U. S. iii. 218–224; Hildreth, ii. 265–267.

CHAPTER V.

ADMINISTRATIONS OF SHUTE, BURNET, AND BELCHER.

THE removal of Mr. Dudley took place soon after the accession of George I. ; and the government of Massachusetts, for which there was usually a sufficient number of aspirants, was conferred on Colonel Burgess, who had fought under Stanhope, the new secretary of state, but who, from his "necessitous condition," and the looseness of his manners, but especially from his friendliness to the private bank party, was particularly obnoxious to many of the people. Hence, through the influence of Jonathan Belcher, a prominent opponent of the private bank, and Jeremiah Dummer, the agent of the province in England, and with the assistance of Sir William Ashhurst, a warm friend to America, Mr. Burgess was persuaded, for the sum of one thousand pounds, to resign his commission in favor of Samuel Shute, an officer in the wars of William and Anne, who, from the respectability of his connections, and his professed religious and political principles, was more acceptable than Burgess.[1] By no means a man of "natural imbecility,"[2] the new governor was one who was well esteemed at court. Destitute of the intriguing disposition of Dudley, he had the character of a "friend to liberty;" and if not possessed of extraordinary or even brilliant talents, or if, like Phips, somewhat passionate at times, and a lover of ease, he was of an "open, generous, and humane disposition," and possessed many qualities which not only commended him to popular favor, but

[1] Boston News Letter, Nos. 633, 634.

[2] Such is the charge of Chalmers, Revolt, ii. 11.

(104)

which fitted him for the office to which he was appointed.[1] CHAP.
Unfortunately for him, and for all others, however, who held V.
the office of chief magistrate of the Province of the Massachu- 1716.
setts Bay, there were insuperable obstacles to perfect success
in the administration of affairs. These obstacles arose from
the conflict of opinion between the province and the crown,
and the natural jealousy that those who were placed over them
at the pleasure of the king were, from that very fact, inimical to
their liberties, and disposed to uphold the prerogatives of royalty. Whatever abilities, therefore, the chief magistrate might
bring to the discharge of his duties, something more was needed
than splendid administrative talents to overcome the prejudices
of the politicians of New England. They could say, with
Pericles, —

> "Kings are earth's gods; in vice their law's their will;
> And if Jove stray, who dares say, Jove doth ill?"[2]

Hence, as the governors of the province were appointed by the
king, and were his representatives, bound to conform to his
instructions at the peril of displacement, if his measures were
arbitrary, theirs must be of the same character ; and if he
sought to oppress his subjects, they must assist in fastening the
yoke.

Agreeably to the expectations which had been formed of
him, Governor Shute, upon his arrival, allied himself with the 1716.
opposers of the private bank ; and with the family of Governor Oct. 4.
Dudley, in particular, he was soon on quite friendly terms,
taking his lodgings at the house of Mr. Paul Dudley. The
friends of the private bank were exceedingly chagrined, for
they had counted upon securing his influence. Hence their
opposition to his administration was bitter from the outset, and
increased in violence as years rolled on.[3]

[1] See C. Mather's Letter to Lord
Barrington, in 1 M. H. Coll. i. 105,
106.
[2] Pericles, Prince of Tyre, Act i.
Sc. 1.

[3] Hutchinson, ii. 197. Col. Shute
sailed from the Downs August 2, 1716,
on board the Lusitania, and reached
Boston on Thursday, October 4. Boston News Letter, Nos. 650, 651.

CHAP.
V.

1716.

The population of the province in the early part of Mr. Shute's administration was much greater than at the date of the grant of the charter. The official reports represent Massachusetts as "inhabited by ninety-four thousand white persons, who possessed two thousand slaves, and by twelve hundred civilized Indians, who professed Christianity, and tilled their lands in peace."[1] The commerce of the country had proportionally increased; and from one hundred and forty to one hundred and sixty vessels, of the aggregate burden of six thousand tons, are said to have been annually built, which formed part of their remittance to England. Massachusetts owned at least one hundred and ninety vessels, of the aggregate burden of eight thousand tons, which were navigated by eleven hundred men; and one hundred and fifty "boats," employing six hundred men "in the fisheries" on the coast. The manufactures of cotton and woollen goods, and of linen by Scotch-Irish families settled at the eastward,[2] supplied the ordinary demands of the people; and, "though necessity, not choice," led to the establishment of these manufactures, the vigor with which they were prosecuted awakened the jealousy of the merchants of England, and representations were made to the Board of Trade that, if these things continued, "they will be able in a little time to live without Great Britain, and their ability, joined to their inclination, will be of very ill consequence."[3] The value of the annual imports to all the American plantations at this

1717.

date is estimated at "one million sterling, in British products and manufactures, and foreign goods," the conveyance of which employed at least a fourth part of the shipping cleared from the kingdom. The exports, at the same date, amounted to eight hundred thousand pounds sterling; and the balance of

---

[1] N. Y. Colon. Doc'ts, v. 597; Chalmers, Revolt, ii. 7, 14. The population of all the colonies was estimated at 434,600.

[2] These families — mostly Scotch Presbyterians, settled in the province of Ulster in the reign of James I. — established themselves in New Hampshire and Maine. Belknap's N. H. ii. 35 et seq; Williamson's Me.; Chalmers, Revolt, ii. 14.

[3] N. Y. Colon. Doc'ts, v. 598; Chalmers, Revolt, ii. 12.

two hundred thousand pounds " fell upon the provinces to the CHAP.
northward of Maryland, who were enabled to discharge the   V.
same by the trade they were permitted to carry on in America
and to Europe, in commodities not enumerated in the Acts of
Trade." [1] From Boston alone, in the three years ending June Jun. 24,
24, 1717, there were cleared, for the West Indies, including   1714,
                                                                 to
the British islands, five hundred and eighteen ships, sloops, Jun. 24,
                                                                 1717.
and other vessels ; for the Bay of Campeachy, twenty-five vessels ; for foreign plantations, fifty-eight vessels ; for Newfoundland, forty-five vessels ; for Europe, forty-three vessels ; for
Madeira, the Azores, &c., thirty-four vessels ; for Great Britain,
one hundred and forty-three vessels ; for British plantations on
the continent, three hundred and ninety vessels ; and eleven
vessels for " ports unknown ; " — an aggregate of twelve hundred and forty-seven vessels, amounting to sixty-two thousand
seven hundred and eighty-eight tons of shipping, and employing eight thousand six hundred and ninety-seven men. [2]   Salem,
in the same period, cleared two hundred and thirty-two vessels,
having an aggregate of thirteen thousand four hundred and
thirty-one tons, and employing one thousand seven hundred and
eighty-two men ; while from New York there were cleared,
from 1715 to 1718, but six hundred and forty-five vessels, having an aggregate of twenty-two thousand three hundred and
ninety-two tons, and employing four thousand five hundred and
thirteen men. [3]

These details, though imperfect, furnish some insight into
the commercial activity of the province, and tend to show that

[1] N. Y. Colon. Doc'ts, v. 614, 615.
Dummer, Defence, 10, estimates the
annual value of the exports from
New England, previous to 1721, at
£300,000.
[2] N. Y. Colon. Doc'ts, v. 618.
Chalmers, Revolt, ii. 41, characterizes
these details as " fallacious." Of the
1247 vessels alluded to in the text,
1199 were plantation built. The following scraps are given in further il-

lustration of the text : From May 12
to 19, 1707, fifteen vessels entered at
Boston, and eight cleared. News Letter, No. 161.   From May 26 to June
2, nine entered and fifteen cleared.
Ibid. No. 163.   From June 9 to 16,
thirteen entered and eleven cleared.
Ibid. No. 165.
[3] N. Y. Colon. Doc'ts, v. 618;
Hutchinson, ii. 320, note.

Massachusetts, more than a century ago, was the same busy
and enterprising community as at present, and that the energies
of her people flowed in substantially the same channels. Is it
strange that such a people were regarded with envy, and that
the statesmen of England, unable to solve the startling problems
which this unparalleled progress presented, became fearful lest
the new world should outstrip the old? Under these circumstances, the policy which was adopted was neither unnatural nor
inexplicable. "If the colonies are so prosperous," — thus reasoned the ministers of the king, (for ministers, like other men,
reason and act from the circumstances in which they are
placed,) — "we should reap the benefit of that prosperity ; and
they, as subjects, are bound to contribute to the relief of
our necessities. If England is burdened with debt, America
must aid in paying that debt ; and if the colonies will not voluntarily submit, they must be forced to obey. We can make
our power felt ; and if they refuse to yield, we must punish
their stubbornness by retrenching their privileges." Few had
the sagacity to perceive that the prosperity of America was
the prosperity of England, and that more benefit could be
derived to the mother country by leaving the colonies to their
own way than by hampering their commerce with burdensome
restrictions, and checking their industry by discouraging manufactures.

It was the popular complaint of the age, however, not only
in relation to the charter, but also to the proprietary governments, that they showed "too great an inclination to be
independent of their mother country, and carried on a trade
destructive to that of Great Britain ; " and these evils it was
proposed to remedy by "bringing them all under his majesty's
immediate government, and compelling them, by proper laws,
to follow the commands sent them by the crown." "It hath
ever been the wisdom," — thus they reasoned, — "not only of
Great Britain, but likewise of all other states, to secure, by all
possible means, the entire, absolute, and immediate dependency

of their colonies;" and hence the attempts to reduce the colo- CHAP.
nies of America.[1] V.

A dispute with Mr. Bridger, his majesty's surveyor of the 1717.
woods, who came to New England by the way of New York,
in the same ship with Lord Bellamont, to "inquire into the
state of the country, and its capacity for producing naval
stores, particularly masts, and oak timber for ship building,"
was the precursor of difficulties which disturbed the province
for a series of years. The inhabitants of Maine, conceiving
that Mr. Bridger had infringed upon their rights by forbidding
them to cut trees suitable for masts, — though necessary to
make way for the operations of tillage, — strenuously opposed
his course, and were joined by Mr. Cooke, a zealous politician,
who charged the surveyor with malconduct, in compounding Nov.
with trespassers for his personal emolument — "permitting such
persons as would pay him for it to cut down the trees which
were said to belong to the king."[2] The governor took the
part of the surveyor, and the next year refused to approve the 1718.
choice of Cooke as a member of the Council. Indignant at
this interference, the rejected candidate memorialized the Council, justifying his conduct. That body at first inclined to pass
the matter by; but subsequently a committee was appointed
on their part, to join a committee of the House, to consider this
memorial; and the joint committee reported in favor of Cooke.
An account of these proceedings was transmitted to England;

---

[1] N. Y. Colon. Doc'ts, v. 628; Chalmers, Revolt, ii. 42, 43.
[2] Cooke's Vindication, 2d ed. pp. 5,
6; Hutchinson, ii. 201. By the charter, all trees suitable for masts were
reserved to the crown; and as early as
1668, the government of Massachusetts had reserved for public use all
pine trees twenty-four inches in diameter at three feet from the ground.
Mass. Rec's. In the reign of King
William, a "surveyor of the woods"
was appointed by the crown; and Lord
Bellamont, the governor of Massachusetts, was ordered to cause acts to be
passed for the preservation of the trees
in his jurisdiction. In the next reign,
— that of Queen Anne, — trees fit for
the navy were to be marked with the
broad arrow, and a register of the
same was to be kept. This whole
matter was more fruitful in disputes
than in benefits, however; and, by
mismanagement, it tended to exasperate rather than to conciliate. See
Province Laws, 12, ed. 1726; Belknap's N. H. ii. 26–29, 32; Williamson's Me.

CHAP. and the Board of Trade, in their reply, censured the conduct
V. of the House, and justified the governor ; but the House re-
1719. fused to submit to this censure, alleging that it was occasioned
by " sending home the papers on one side only, whereby their
lordships were informed *ex parte*." At the next election, the
conduct of the governor was publicly disapproved by the choice
of new representatives for Boston, and by a change in other
towns adverse to his interests.[1]

For some time, the English government had resolved upon
the policy of restricting manufactures in the plantations, on the
plea that they " tended to lessen their dependence on Great
Britain." Nearly every branch of industry was subjected to
these restrictions, and every form of competition was discouraged or forbidden. Through the intervention of the hatters
1719. of London, Parliament forbade the transportation of hats from
one plantation to another.[2] At the instance of the proprietors
of iron works, it was decreed that "none in the plantations
should manufacture iron wares of any kind whatsoever ; " and
every " forge going by water, for making bar or rod iron," was
proposed to be prohibited by the Peers.[3] Massachusetts, ever
vigilant to protect her own interests, had anticipated this
1718. action of the mother country, by passing an impost bill,
approved by the governor, levying a duty, not only upon West
India goods, wines, &c., but of one per cent. upon English
manufactures and English ships. This ordinance was promptly
denounced as " a great hardship on British owners," and was
negatived by the king ; but before the receipt of his instructions to " give all encouragement to the manufactures of Great
Britain," and the warning of the Board of Trade that the
" passage of such acts might endanger their charter," the
House passed a second bill of the same tenor, and sent it to

---

[1] On this controversy, see Mass. Rec's ; Cooke's Vindication, 2d ed. p. 5 et seq. ; Hutchinson, vol. ii. ; Chalmers, Revolt, ii. 15–17.

[2] Act 5 G. I. c. 22.

[3] Anderson, Hist. Commerce, iii. 88, 89 ; Bancroft's U. S. iii. 384. This act was defeated by the vigilance of the colonies.

the Council for concurrence. The Council proposed as an CHAP.
amendment to leave out the duty on English vessels and goods ; __V.__
but the House adhered to the original bill. A conference 1719.
ensued ; but the House insisted on their former vote. The
discussion lasted several weeks, both parties refusing to yield ;
until the governor, in a " mild and healing speech," suggested
that the House, by their too great pertinacity, might " rather
destroy than preserve those privileges so justly prized ; " when
the controverted clause was dropped, and, after some further
debate, the matter was so adjusted as to allay the excitement
which had prevailed, and restore harmony to the action of the
government.[1]

The embarrassment of the finances of the province was a 1720.
fruitful source of dissension and debate. Trade, if not in a
languishing condition, was suffering from the derangement in
the currency, which had continued to increase notwithstanding
an additional issue of one hundred thousand pounds in bills of 1716.
credit. Indeed, not only at this juncture, but for a period of
at least thirty years, serious evils resulted from the depreciation
in the value of the bills in circulation ; and all who depended
on their income for support — clergymen, salaried officers, and
widows and orphans of limited means — were reduced to a
state of suffering and want. Public institutions, supported by
funds, and with which the interests of literature and religion
were blended, tended to decay ; the settlement of estates was
delayed by administrators ; trade was, in a great measure,
reduced to a state of barter ; the rich were becoming richer ;
the poor were becoming poorer ; and the province, to many,
seemed on the verge of bankruptcy and ruin.[2]

The conduct of the governor in this emergency was not

[1] On this affair, see Mass. Rec's, and Hutchinson, ii. 204–209.
[2] On the finances, see the tracts published from 1716 to 1720, and comp. Hutchinson, ii. 210 et seq. ; Minot, i. c. v ; Felt's Currency of N.
Eng. ; Bancroft's U. S. iii. 387–390. Similar embarrassments prevailed in the other colonies, originating from the same source — an over issue of bills of credit.

CHAP.   eminently calculated to conciliate the people ; and, by his
V.   attempts to censure the press,[1] and other impolitic steps, a for-
1720.   midable opposition was organized against him.   His rejection
May.   of Cooke as speaker of the House exasperated that body ; and
May 30. on their refusing to proceed to a second election, the court
        was hastily dissolved.[2]   Writs for a new assembly were imme-
July 13. diately issued, which was to meet in July ; but when convened,
        though for the despatch of business a new speaker was chosen,[3]
        a protest was entered against the conduct of the governor in
        dissolving the former body for "asserting and maintaining
        their just and ancient privilege of choosing their speaker," and
        the House refused to acknowledge "his excellency's power to
        negative" such choice.   Nor did their resentment cease here.
        The new House assumed the choice of notaries public ; nega-
        tived the negotiations of the governor with the Penobscot
        tribe ; reduced his semiannual salary from six hundred to five
        hundred pounds ; and, "considering the low circumstances of
        the province," they ordered that "no draft should be made
        upon the treasury for expenses at times of public rejoicing for
        the future."   Dissatisfied with these proceedings, the governor
July 23. again interposed, and in less than two weeks put an end to
        the session.[4]

1720-21.   In the following year the controversy was renewed.   The
Mar. 15. governor, in his speech at the opening of the court, recom-
        mended a series of measures to which, in his estimation, the
        exigencies of the public demanded attention.   These were,
        that steps should be taken to prevent the depreciation of the
        currency ; to suppress unlawful trade with the French at Cape
        Breton ; to punish the authors of factious and seditious pa-
        pers ; to provide a present for the Five Nations in New York ;

[1] On this affair, see the Mass. Rec's, Hutchinson, Grahame, &c.
[2] Boston News Letter, No. 846; Cooke's Vindication, 2d ed. passim ; Hutchinson, vol. ii.
[3] Timothy Lendall, Esq. The elec- tion in Boston was held on Friday, June 10. Boston News Letter, Nos. 848, 853 ; Hutchinson, ii.
[4] Mass. Rec's ; Boston News Let- ter, Nos. 854, 855 ; Hutchinson, ii.

and to enlarge his salary, which they had seen fit to retrench ; CHAP.
but the House refused to consent to either proposal.[1]   V.

Nor was any disposition evinced in other respects to con-   1721.
form to his requirements ; for at the next session of the court   May.
a new speaker was chosen, and, to prevent his being negatived,
a message was sent to the Governor and Council acquainting
them that " John Clarke, Esq., is chosen speaker of the House,
and is now sitting in the chair." At this message his excellency was exceedingly exasperated, and was on the point of
dissolving the court, when he was reminded by his friends that
no choice of councillors had been made, and that, if the court
was adjourned without such choice, the government would be
suspended for a year. This brought him to his senses ; and,
in consequence of the prevalence of the small pox in Boston,
after a little business had been transacted, the court was ad- May 31.
journed to Cambridge.[2]

Here a new system of tactics was adopted. The governor, June 6.
in his despatches to the ministers in England, saw fit to inform
them " that the assembly, composed of men more fit for the
affairs of farming than for the duty of legislators, showed no
regard to the royal prerogative or instructions, but endeavored
to transgress the limits of the charter, though he was, indeed,
supported by the Council, who themselves wanted assistance."[3]
Such representations could but widen the breach between the
parties ; and the House neglected to make provisions for the
support of his excellency and other officers, until they saw
what action he would take upon the votes they had passed.
But the governor had his revenge ; for when the House asked
leave to adjourn, he negatived the request. The House then
adjourned from Wednesday to the following Tuesday ; but this, July 12.
                                                              July 18.

[1] Mass. Rec's; Collection of Pro- through this. Collection of Proceed-
ceedings of General Court, 30, 31; ings of Gen. Court, ed. 1729, p. 26 et
Hutchinson, ii. The controversy upon seq.
the establishment of a fixed salary for   [2] Mass. Rec's; Boston News Let-
the governor, begun under Mr. Dud- ter, No. 903.
ley's administration, was continued   [3] Chalmers's Revolt.

CHAP. so far from mending matters, only made them worse. The
V.   course of the House was censured as "irregular," and was
1721.   afterwards made the ground of a serious charge against that
body.[1] In vain did Mr. Dummer, the agent of the province,
venture to remonstrate. In vaid did he assure the House that
their conduct was displeasing to the ministers of the king, who,
" when they found a governor, fitted to make any people happy,
was made uneasy in New England, concluded that the people
would have no governor at all from England, but wanted to
be independent of the crown."[2] Such remonstrances were
unwelcome ; and the agent was dismissed. His able "Defence
of the Charters of New England" was published about this
time ; but the value of his services to the cause of his country,
which would perhaps have been appreciated under more favorable circumstances, was lessened in the public estimation by
reason of his interference in the difficulties with Mr. Shute.[3]

The prevalence of the small pox, which, after an interval of
April.   about twenty years,[4] broke out again in Massachusetts, was
attended with the usual horrors of that loathsome disease ;
for, out of five thousand eight hundred and eighty-nine persons
who were attacked in Boston, eight hundred and forty-four
died.[5] The practice of inoculation had been recently introduced into Europe ; and Cotton Mather, one of the ministers
of Boston, having read, in the Transactions of the Royal

[1] Mass. Rec's ; Jour. Ho. of Rep. ;
Proceedings of the Mass. Bay, &c.

[2] His Letters to the Province, and
Hutchinson, vol. ii.

[3] The first edition of this able work
was published in 1721. There had
been several attempts before this date
to annul the charter of Massachusetts,
as in 1701, &c. ; but, by the intervention of friends, they were happily frustrated ; and the liberties of the people, in that respect at least, remained
unmolested. Hutchinson, ii. 120, 121.

[4] Douglas, in 4 M. H. Coll. ii. 168.
The small pox had prevailed in Massachusetts four times, at least, before

the year 1700 ; and in 1702–3, it
broke out again. Drake's Boston, 526.

[5] I here follow the Boston News
Letter, No. 943, Douglas, in 4 M. H.
Coll. ii. 168, and Hutchinson, ii. 247.
But in 1 M. H. Coll. v. 207, is an extract from an "old almanac," which
states that 5813 persons were attacked,
and 771 died. The same extract estimates the population of Boston at
this date at 10,567, of whom 6018
lived to the south of the "mill creek,"
and 4549 to the north. Of the former, 3217 had the small pox, and 490
died ; and of the latter, 2596 were attacked, and 281 died.

Society of England, of which he was a member, letters from
Constantinople and Smyrna, giving an account of this practice
and its success, interested himself to introduce it into America ;[1] but his application to the physicians of the town was at
first unsuccessful. At length Dr. Boylston consented to try
the experiment upon his own children and servants. His success was encouraging. But the practice was opposed, not only
by the medical faculty generally, — among whom Douglas, a
Scotchman, and Dolhonde,[2] a Frenchman, were conspicuous for
their zeal, — but also by many "pious people," as well as the
"vulgar," who insinuated that, if his patients died, he "should
be treated as a murderer."[3] The magistrates of Boston
were equally deluded ; and, upon consultation with the physicians, a manifesto was put forth showing the dangers of the
practice.[4] Even the House of Representatives did not display
their usual wisdom, and brought in a bill prohibiting inoculation ; but the Council hesitated, and the bill stopped.[5] It
must not be supposed, however, that there were none in the
province possessed of sufficient intelligence to comprehend so
simple a subject. Several of the ministers, as Increase Mather
and Dr. Colman, espoused the cause of inoculation, and wrote
in its favor.[6] But Cotton Mather, the patron of the movement,

[1] One of these letters was repub-
lished in the Boston News Letter, No.
945, and both were issued in a pamphlet form by Dr. Boylston. Douglas, in 4 M. H. Coll. ii. 169, asserts
that he lent to Dr. Mather the numbers of the Philosophical Transactions
containing this account.

[2] Hutchinson, ii. 248, says Dal-
honde ; but his autograph, in my possession, gives the spelling of the text.
Douglas says he opposed the practice
as "not being sufficiently assured of
its safety and consequences ; " and he
reckoned it "a sin against society to
propagate infection by this means,"
&c.

[3] The pamphlet of Douglas was entitled " Inoculation of the Small Pox
as practised in Boston, considered in

a Letter to A— S—, M. D. and F.
R. S., in London," and was " printed
by J. Franklin, at his Printing House
in Queen St., over against Mr. Sheaf's
School, 1722." A reply to Douglas
was published, entitled " A Friendly
Debate," &c., by Academicus.

[4] Hutchinson, &c.

[5] Mass. Rec's.

[6] The title of I. Mather's pamphlet
I am unable to give ; but that of Dr.
Colman was entitled " Some Observations on the New Method of receiving the Small Pox by Inoculating or
Grafting." I have seen also an anonymous pamphlet, attributed to Walter Grainger, entitled "The Proposition of Inoculation as a Duty religiously considered."

CHAP.   did not escape without experiencing the evil effects of popular
V.   prejudice.   Not only was he personally assailed in vituperative
1721.   pamphlets, but mobs paraded the streets, with halters in their
hands, uttering violent and inflammatory language; and a
hand grenade was thrown in at his window, for the destruction
of his nephew, Mr. Walter, the minister of Roxbury, who had
been privately inoculated in his house.[1]   Yet the practice was
continued, in spite of opposition; and in the end its defenders
effectually triumphed.[2]

It was during the height of this controversy that the court,
Aug.23. which had been dissolved in July, assembled upon a new summons at the George Tavern, at the extreme part of the town.
Mr. Clarke was chosen speaker; and a message was sent to
the governor informing him of this choice, which he saw fit to
approve.[3]   Apprehensive of danger, however, from the proximity of the contagion, the House passed a vote for removing
the court to Cambridge; but the Council non-concurred.   The
governor immediately informed the House that he would willingly consent to their removal, "if he was applied to in such
a manner as should consist with the sole right in him of
adjourning, proroguing, and dissolving the court;" but the
House would not concede this right, and a quorum chose to
risk their lives in Boston rather than acknowledge the power
of the governor to control their motions at pleasure.[4]

Nor did the House hesitate to join issue with the statesmen
of England, who sanctioned the course of the governor; for,
notwithstanding the opinion of the attorney general was forwarded, that "he had good right to negative the speaker,"

[1] In the Boston News Letter, No.
929, are full particulars of this affair.
Douglas, in 4 M. H. Coll. ii. 169,
says, by November 18 one hundred
persons had been inoculated.   One
of the pamphlets issued against the
practice of inoculation was by John
Williams, and was entitled "Several
Arguments proving that Inoculating
the Small Pox is not contained in the

Law of Physick, either Natural or Divine, and therefore unlawful."
[2] Boylston's Account, Lond. ed.
1726; Trans. Royal Soc. vol. xxx.;
Hutchinson, ii.; Pemberton, in 1 M.
H. Coll. 4.
[3] Mass. Rec's; Hutchinson, ii. 241.
[4] Mass. Rec's; Hutchinson, ii. 241.
242.

and the lords of trade approved his proceedings, the House CHAP.
drew up a remonstrance, justifying their own conduct, and V.
declaring, temperately yet firmly, that, "with all deference to 1721.
the opinion of the attorney general, they must still claim the
right of solely electing and constituting their speaker ; and
they humbly presumed that their so doing could not be accounted a slight of, or a disaffection to, his majesty's instructions, or as bearing upon the royal prerogative."[1]

Pending the progress of these disputes, serious difficulties
had arisen with the eastern Indians, who, highly incensed at
the conceived encroachments of the New England colonies,
were instigated by the French to invade the territories of the
English. Sebastian Rasles, a Jesuit missionary, and an accomplished scholar, was the spiritual guide of the tribes ; and, as
he was in close correspondence with the governor of Canada,
it was with his consent, if not with his approval, that these
ravages were committed.[2] The people of Massachusetts resented his conduct ; and Governor Shute was not a little
displeased at the treatment he had personally experienced
during his visit to the eastward, with several of the Council 1717.
of New Hampshire, to negotiate with the Indians at Arrowsick Aug. 9 to 12.
Island.[3] In 1720, the House resolved that one hundred and 1720. Nov. 2.
fifty men should be sent to Norridgewock to "compel the
Indians to make full satisfaction for the damages they had
done ; " and a warrant was issued to Captain Leighton, the
high sheriff of York, for the apprehension of Rasles. The
governor, however, esteemed this resolve as a declaration of
war, and an invasion of the prerogative ; and the Council
rejected it.[4]

In the following year, two hundred Indians, under French 1721 Aug. 17.

[1] Mass. Rec's ; Hutchinson, ii. 242.
[2] Part of this correspondence may
be seen in the M. H. Coll's. Comp.
also Hutchinson, ii. ; Belknap's N. H.
ii. 49 ; Franklin's Works, iv. 7, note.
[3] Shute's Letter to Rallé, in 1 M.
H. Coll. v. 112–119 ; Belknap's N.
H. ii. 47 ; Williamson's Me. ii. ; N.
H. Hist. Col. ii. 242–257.
[4] Mass. Rec's ; Boston Gazette, No.
47 ; News Letter, No. 869 ; Belknap,
ii. 51.

CHAP.
V.

1721.

Nov. 3.

1722.
Jun. 13.

Aug.

colors, came to Georgetown, upon the Arrowsick Island, accompanied by two Jesuits, and left a threatening message for the governor.[1] The House took notice of this affair; and towards the close of the session the governor was prevailed upon to consent that three hundred men should be sent to the head quarters of the Indians with a proclamation, commanding them to "deliver up the Jesuits, and the other heads and fomenters of this rebellion, and to make satisfaction for damages." The prosecution of this enterprise was delayed from time to time, when the House took the matter in hand, and a party was sent to Norridgewock, under Colonel Thomas Westabrooke, who returned with the papers of Rasles, but not his person, "his faithful disciples having taken care to secure his person, and to fly with him into the woods."[2] The seizure of Castine, a natural son of the Baron Castine, who was brought to Boston and put in close confinement, tended further to exasperate the French; and in the ensuing year, sixty Indians, in twenty canoes, went to Merry Meeting Bay, and took nine families prisoners, while other parties made an attempt upon a fishing vessel from Ipswich, lying in one of the eastern harbors, and burned a sloop at St. George's River. These hostile acts were followed by the burning of Brunswick; and in the following August a declaration of war was issued; but the House presuming to determine the service in which the troops were to be employed, the governor informed them that "the king, his master, and the royal charter, had given him the sole command and direction of the militia, and all the forces which might be raised on any emergency; and that he should not suffer himself to be under any direction but his own, and those officers he should think fit to appoint."[3] The controversy which ensued upon this point, as well as upon the attempt of the House to assume the management of the war, and to call

[1] Boston News Letter, No. 917;   [2] Boston News Letter, No. 946
Belknap, ii. 51.   Belknap, ii. 51, 52.
                                [3] Belknap, ii. 52.

to their bar Colonel Walton, to "render his reasons why the CHAP.
orders relating to the expedition to Penobscot had not been V.
executed," was continued for some time, when the governor, 1722-23.
who had secretly obtained leave to return to England, left the Jan. 1.
province, unknown to nearly every one, to lay his grievances
before the king.[1]

At the departure of Colonel Shute, the functions of the chief
magistracy devolved upon William Dummer, the lieutenant governor, who remained at the head of affairs for the next six
years. In his first speech to the court, reluctant to renew the Jan. 2.
controversy which had imbittered the administration of his
predecessor, he expressed his willingness to "concur with them
in any measure for his majesty's service, and the good of the
province." Samuel Sewall, the sole surviving assistant under
the charter of Charles I., and the uncompromising advocate
of the liberties of the people, replied to this speech ; and his
reply was characteristic of the man and of the past. "Although
the unerring providence of God" — such were his words —
"has brought your honor to the chair of government in a
cloudy and tempestuous season, yet you have this for your
encouragement, that the people you have to do with are part
of the Israel of God, and you may expect to have of the prudence and patience of Moses communicated to you for your
conduct. It is evident, that our almighty Saviour counselled
the first planters to remove hither and settle here ; and they
dutifully followed his advice, and therefore he will never leave
nor forsake them nor theirs ; so that your honor must needs
be happy in sincerely seeking their happiness and welfare,
which your birth and education will incline you to do. *Diffi-
cilia quæ pulchra.* I promise myself, that they who sit at this
board will yield their faithful advice to your honor, according
to the duty of their place." [2]

As the object of Governor Shute's return to England was to

---

[1] Boston News Letter, Nos. 987,   [2] Boston News Letter, No. 989;
988, 989; Hutchinson, ii. 260, 261.   Hutchinson, ii. 264.

CHAP.
V.

1723.

May.

Oct. 23.

Oct. 26.

July.

1724.
July 10.

Aug. 12.

complain of the conduct of the legislature, measures for defence were promptly taken. Mr. Anthony Sanderson was recommended by Mr. Popple, of the plantation office, as qualified for agent of the province; and the House sent their papers to him to be used as they should order.[1] At the next annual court, no advices had been received from England. Accordingly, the House chose their speaker, and placed him in the chair without presenting him to the governor for confirmation; and in other matters saw fit to assert their own rights.[2] By the fall, the heads of complaint against the province were received.[3] The House immediately voted that these were groundless, and ordered one hundred pounds sterling to be remitted to Mr. Sanderson, to employ counsel to justify their proceedings; but the Council non-concurred. The House then prepared an answer to the complaint, and an address to the king; but these, too, the Council refused to approve. Upon this the speaker was ordered to sign the papers, and they were forwarded to England. The Council prepared a separate address, which was forwarded to Colonel Shute. At the same time, with the consent of the Council, agents were sent to England on behalf of the province to appear in its defence; and Jeremiah Dummer and Elisha Cooke were chosen for that purpose.[4]

Meanwhile the depredations of the Indians were continued at the eastward; and Canseau was surprised, and sixteen or seventeen vessels belonging to Massachusetts were taken.[5] In the following year further incursions were made, and the war raged fiercely. Father Rasles had hitherto escaped; but at length he was surprised at his head quarters at Norridgewock, and, being fired upon, was slain. The Indians, panic-struck,

---

[1] Hutchinson.
[2] Mass. Rec's, and Hutchinson, vol. ii.
[3] Collection of Proceedings of Gen. Court, 36, 37.
[4] Mass. Rec's; Boston News Letter, No. 1041; Collection of Proceedings of Gen. Court, 36, 37; Hutchinson, ii. 271–273.
[5] Hutchinson, ii. 266, 267; Haliburton's N. S. i. 102, 103.

hastily fled. The English pursued until they took to the CHAP
woods, when ·they returned, plundered the village, and ran-   V.
sacked the church.[1] Subsequently the government of the 1724.
province increased the premium on Indian scalps to one hundred pounds of the ordinary currency. John Lovewell, an
enterprising partisan warrior, encouraged by this bounty raised
a company of volunteers, and made one or two successful expe- 1724-25
ditions; but venturing out a third time, to a place called   Jan.
Pigwacket, he was surprised and slain, with several of his   Feb.
followers.[2] A cessation of arms followed; a treaty of peace 1725.
was agreed upon at Boston; in the following year, the lieuten-   Dec.
ant governor in person, attended by gentlemen of the court,
the lieutenant governor of New Hampshire, and General Mas-
carene, of Nova Scotia, ratified the same at Falmouth; a long 1726.
peace ensued; and provisions were made for the erection of   Aug. 5
trading houses on the St. George, the Kennebec, and the Saco
Rivers, where the Indians were supplied with goods on more
favorable terms than they had been furnished by the French.
Thus ended the Indian difficulties, which had lasted nearly
forty years; and for the twenty years following but little disturbance occurred.[3]

The affairs of the province abroad were still in an unsettled
state. Soon after the arrival of the new agents in England, a
second memorial was presented by Governor Shute, complain-
ing of matters transacted subsequently to his departure from
Massachusetts. Upon this memorial hearings were had; but June 5,
the determination of the lords of trade, and of his majesty in   &c.
council, were, for the most part, unfavorable to the province.

---

[1] Boston News Letter, Nos. 1074,
1085; Hutchinson, ii. 273–284; Charlevoix; Belknap, ii. 60; Haliburton's
N. S. i. 104, 105.
[2] This was long known as the Pigwacket Fight; and a narrative of the
same, by Thomas Symmes, was afterwards published. See also Penhallow,
in N. H. Hist. Coll.; Belknap's N.

H. vol. i.; Holmes, Am. Ann. i. 536,
537.
[3] Colman's Mems. in 1 M. H. Coll.
vi. 108; Hutchinson, ii.; Belknap, vol.
i.; Holmes, i. 538; N. H. Hist. Coll.
ii. 257, 258. Articles of peace with
the Indians were subscribed July 25,
1727. N. H. Hist. Coll. ii. 260–263.

CHAP.
V.
1726.

Aug.12.
1725-26.
Jan. 15.

1725.
May 27.

1727.
June.

The acts and votes relative to the king's woods and the regulation of military affairs were adjudged indefensible, and the
agents were advised to a humble acknowledgment of the
same.   The power of the governor to negative the speaker,
however, and to prevent the adjournment of the House, was
not esteemed so clear ; and an explanatory charter was drawn
up, which the province saw fit to accept.   By this instrument,
the power to negative the speaker was expressly conceded to
the governor, and the time to which the House might adjourn
was limited to two days.[1]   The affair of the synod, which
occurred about this time, was less important in its bearings,
and is chiefly interesting as indicating the change which was
taking place in public sentiment, and the successful resistance
of the mother country to the paramount influence of the provincial clergy.[2]

The decision of the questions brought ·by Colonel Shute
before the lords of trade left him at liberty to return to his
government.[3]   But he was unwilling to embark save in a man-
of-war, and no vessel of that class was then ready to leave.
Hence his departure was delayed until the summer of 1727,
when, just as he was on the eve of sailing, the king suddenly
deceased.   Upon the accession of George II. a change in the
ministry followed ; a pension of six hundred pounds was settled
on Colonel Shute ; and the office of governor of Massachusetts
was conferred on William Burnet, formerly governor of New
York, and a son of Bishop Burnet, the historian of the reformation, conspicuous in the revolution of 1688, and a steadfast
friend of the house of Hanover.[4]

[1] Report, in Lib. Mass. Hist. Soc.,
shelf 3, 32, tract 12 ; Charter and
Laws, ed. 1726, pp. 13, 14 ; Hutchinson, ii. 288–290 ; Chalmers, Revolt, ii.
27–30 ; Minot, i. 60 ; Letter of John
Colman, in 1 M. H. Coll. ii. 31–35.

[2] Hutchinson, ii. 291, 292 ; Chalmers, Revolt, ii. 31.

[3] "I hear the governor saith, he
will try who shall be governor, he or

Mr. Cooke, and that he will see New
England again, let it cost what it will.
Nay, a gentleman here told me he
heard him swear it, which he wondered
at, for he had never heard him swear
an oath before in his life."   Colman's
Letter, in 1 M. H. Coll. ii. 33.

[4] Hutchinson, ii. 293, 294.   Notices of Bishop Burnet may be seen in
the Boston News Letter, Nos. 1081,

Pe ding the arrival of Mr. Burnet, the administration of affairs continued in the hands of Lieutenant Governor Dummer; and, as complaints of the decline of trade continued, a fresh issue of sixty thousand pounds in bills of credit was voted. This bill his excellency at first refused to sanction; but, upon his salary's being withheld, he was prevailed upon to sign it, notwithstanding it was contrary to the king's instructions.[1] Nor was this the only way in which the spirit of the House was manifested, as their contests with the Council evince, upon the election of civil officers, and the decision of private causes heard before both houses.[2] The land fever, which raged at this time with a fury nearly equal to that of the famous Mississippi scheme, gave rise to chimerical projects for the improvement of the waste parts of the province; and for the first, not for the last time, the speculation in eastern lands became a mania, and was pursued with a zeal which ended, in many cases, in the ruin of the projectors, and to the detriment of the province.[3]

Never was governor more pompously received than was Governor Burnet. The press and the pulpit labored with addresses; and men seemed to vie with each other in outward expressions of joy. No poet laureate, indeed, was paid to announce his arrival; but the poet of the province, and the wittiest of his day, put forth his best efforts to celebrate the event.[4] Nor were the people behind him in testifying their

CHAP.
V.

1727-28.

Feb.

1728.
May.

July.

July 13

1082. Chalmers, Revolt, ii. 124, says Burnet was sent to Massachusetts, "not so much as a favor as a punishment, because he had offended the Board of Trade by printing their proceedings, and Horatio Walpole by unsuccessful support."

[1] Mass. Rec's; Charter and Laws of the Province; Hutchinson, ii. 295–298; Douglas, in 4 M. H. Coll. ii. 176.

[2] Mass. Rec's; Hutchinson, ii. 298.

[3] Mass. Rec's; Hutchinson, ii. 299, 300; Williamson's Me. ii.

[4] Mather Byles. The following is a specimen of his effusion on the occasion: —

"Welcome, great man, to our desiring eyes;
  Thou earth! proclaim it; and resound, ye
    skies!
Voice answering voice, in joyful consort
    meet,
The hills all echo, and the rocks repeat.
And thou, O Boston, mistress of the towns,
Whom the pleas'd Bay with am'rous arms
    surrounds,
Let thy warm transports blaze in num'rous
    fires,
And beaming glories glitter on thy spires;
Let rockets streaming up the ether glare,
And flaming serpents hiss along the air."

Drake's Hist. Bost. 581.

CHAP.   respect ; for gay cavalcades paraded the streets, which were
  V.   crowded with people, and the concourse was greater than had
1728.   ever been known.[1] But these flattering attentions, dictated
        by policy, neither blinded the governor to the real state of
        feeling, nor did they deter him from prosecuting his predeter-
        mined plans. The very parade with which he was received
        was used as an argument to prove the ability of the people to
        grant him a liberal support ; and, as this was a matter upon
        which the monarchs had insisted, and which he was instructed
July 24. to enforce, in his first speech he acquainted the court with his
        majesty's directions, and his intention to adhere to them. The
        House was not intimidated. Yet, as it was not their design at
        the outset to push things to an extremity, a grant of seventeen
July 27. hundred pounds was made towards his support, and to defray
July 30. the charge of his journey ; but this he refused to accept. A
Aug. 6. special grant of three hundred pounds was then made for the
        charge of his journey, which he received ; but the court refused
        to establish a fixed salary. In vain did the governor remon-
        strate ; in vain did he threaten. The representatives of the
        people understood their interests too well to sacrifice them at
        the royal pleasure ; and by settling a fixed salary, they saw at
        once that the governor would be independent of the legisla-
        ture, whereas by the system of annual grants he could not at
        pleasure control their proceedings, and a barrier would be
        maintained against the encroachments of the prerogative.[2]

        The refractoriness of the House did not pass unrebuked ;
Aug.28. and when a message was sent to the governor asking permis-
        sion to rise, it was refused until they had " finished the business
        for which the court was then sitting." Messages passed to
        and fro, and the affair became serious ; but the governor was

---

[1] For an account of these civilities, see Drake's Boston, 581.

[2] Mass. Rec's ; Collection of Proceedings of General Court, 39–51 ; Hutchinson, ii. ; Minot, i. 59 ; Chalmers, Revolt, ii. 125. The letter of Douglas to Colden, in 4 M. H. Coll. ii. 175–177, is significant, and shows the system of management which was recommended to Burnet to "bias" the people.

firm, and the House was intractable. In vain did his excel- CHAP
lency insinuate that, if the House persisted in their refusal, V.
"the legislature of Great Britain would take into consider-   1728.
ation the support of the government, and perhaps something   Sept. 2
besides" — meaning the charter. This message added fuel to
the flame; and the House, in their own vindication, drew up a
paper to transmit to the towns for their instruction, giving an Sep 11.
account of the state of the controversy, and the reasons which
influenced them in refusing to submit to his demand.[1] The
towns responded to this call; and Boston, in particular, ever
foremost to support liberty, avowed its aversion to the proposals of the king.[2] A few persons, indeed, counselled compliance; and, friendly to the prerogative principally from
interested motives, they urged that the present controversy
must terminate, like the last, in favor of the crown; and that,
if the province would not peaceably yield, more forcible measures might be adopted, or a change be made in the charter, as
under the administration of Shute. Besides, Governor Burnet
himself was an amiable gentleman; in his manners he was
easy, and his talents were conspicuous. His conversational
powers were the delight of intelligent circles; and, aside from
his official position, he was in most respects as acceptable to
the people as either of his predecessors. Why, then, it was
asked, drive from us so excellent a magistrate? Why not meet
him half way? But the majority of the House was still firm;
and all that could be obtained was a vote granting the gov- Sep. 20
ernor the sum of three thousand pounds of the currency of the
province, equal to one thousand pounds sterling, for half a

---

[1] Mass. Rec's; Collection of Proceedings of General Court, 51–65;
Hutchinson, ii.
[2] A general meeting was held, at
which a vote was passed, and ordered
to be printed, called "the unanimous
declaration of the inhabitants of Boston against fixing a salary upon the
governor." Hutchinson, ii. 315. It
is a somewhat singular coincidence,
that, whilst Massachusetts was contending with Governor Burnet against
granting a fixed salary, a similar controversy was contemporaneously agitating the people of Barbadoes. Hutchinson, ii. 313, 314.

CHAP. year, for the management of public affairs; but this he refused
V.   to accept.

1728.   Soon the affair reached its crisis; and, in consequence of the
Oct. 24. vote of the people of Boston, the governor adjourned the court
to Salem — jocosely remarking, as he did so, that "there might
be a choice in the names of places, and he was at a loss whether
to carry them to Salem or to Concord." [1] But the House viewed
the matter seriously; and, so far from approving the adjournment, denounced it as a further hardship, and an earnest of the
intention of the governor to harass them into compliance.
Oct. 31. Their first vote on assembling at Salem was in accordance with
this feeling; and, after censuring the course of his excellency
Nov.14. as "illegal and a great grievance," they requested to be permitted to meet again in Boston; but this was refused. No
alternative was left, therefore, but to remain in Salem; and
they did remain, supported by their constituents, who voted to
defray their expenses, and who provided for them liberally. [2]

Nov.22.   At length, wearied with the altercation, and persuaded of
the justness of their cause, the House resolved to apply to his
Dec. 20. majesty for redress. Mr. Francis Wilkes, a New England
merchant then resident in London, was selected as their agent,
and Mr. Jonathan Belcher, a member of the Council, and a
young man of pleasing address, was joined with him. Grants
Dec. 20, were made to defray their expenses; but the Council refused
1728,
and   to sanction these grants. Immediately the people of Boston
Apr. 10,
1729. interposed, and, by a subscription among the merchants and
Apr. 16. others, a sufficient sum was raised and placed at the disposal
of the House. For this a vote of thanks was returned, with a
promise of the repayment of the loan at some future date. [3]

May.   The appeal to England was unsuccessful. The Board of
Trade severely censured the course of the House, and approved

---

[1] Hutchinson, ii. 316.   [3] Mass. Rec's; Coll. Proceedings
[2] Mass. Rec's; Coll. Proceedings Gen. Court, 96–109; Hutchinson, ii.
Gen. Court, 90–95; Chalmers, Re- 318.
volt, ii. 127; Hutchinson, ii. 317, 318.

that of the governor; and the agents informed them that, if CHAP.
they persisted in refusing to comply with the king's demands, V.
the affair would be carried before Parliament; but the House 1729.
thought it better, should such a course be taken, that a "salary
should be fixed by the supreme legislature than by the legislature of the province : better the liberties of the people should
be taken away from them, than given up by their own act."
Nor were they without friends to sustain them in this course.
Already the storm was rising which threatened the overthrow
of Walpole ; and if the matter was brought before Parliament,
support was promised by the opponents of the ministry.[1]

The other matters in dispute with Mr. Burnet were of less
importance, and occupied less of the time of the House. His
refusal to sign the warrant for the payment of their expenses
was a retaliation for their refusal to pay his salary ; and his
attempt to establish a new fee from a "let pass" on vessels,
which was resisted by the House, was disallowed by the lords
of trade. His refusal to submit to the choice of an attorney
general, unless nominated by himself, and his attempt to control the treasury, awakened further opposition ; but the settlement of this controversy was left to his successor.[2]

The decision of the lords of trade was adverse to the prov- May 22.

<hr/>

[1] Hutchinson, ii. 320; Chalmers's
Revolt, ii. 128; Hildreth, ii. 347.
Mr. Dummer wrote a letter on this
occasion, dated August 10, 1729, advising compliance with his majesty's
instructions. "I am not afraid," he
says, "to add my hearty wishes that
the assembly would, of choice and by
their own consent, comply with his
majesty's instructions, and fix the governor's salary for the time of his government, or for a term of years. I
am of opinion that they cannot do a
wiser or better thing in their present
circumstances. As they have agreed
on the quantum, and have determined
to give it annually, it's a pity they
won't go a step farther, and make it a
resolve of the House, by which they

will at once restore themselves to his
majesty's favor, and put an end to
the confusions and distractions among
themselves. New England justly
boasts of her loyalty; but methinks it
would not be amiss if to that we added a little complaisance to the crown,
if such an expression may be allowed.
. . . I am afraid if we don't do it
willingly, we shall be compelled to do
it unwillingly. The ministers are determined to lay it before Parliament;
and if they bring in the bill, who will
undertake to get it thrown out?"
Lett. in Lib. Mass. Hist. Soc., shelf 3,
8, tract 2.

[2] Hutchinson, ii. 321, 322; Hildreth, ii. 347.

CHAP.
V.

1729.

Sept. 7.

ince; and a demand was made that "a salary of one thousand pounds sterling per annum should be settled upon the governor during the whole time of his government." The governor attempted to enforce this demand by adjourning the court from time to time; but to no purpose. The House grew warmer in their votes and messages, and complained that they were to be "compelled to measures against their judgment, by being harassed and driven from one part of the province to another." In the midst of the struggle the governor died. Some attributed his death to chagrin; others to a cold caught by the overturning of his carriage as he was crossing the causeway at Cambridge, by which he was thrown into the water, and thoroughly chilled. His funeral was pompously celebrated at the charge of the province, and the administration again passed into the hands of Mr. Dummer.[1]

At the death of Mr. Burnet, Jonathan Belcher, a native of Massachusetts, and a gentleman of aspiring talents and abundant wealth, who had been recently sent to England as the agent of the province, applied for the commission of the government, and, through the influence of Shute, whom he had aided on a similar occasion, he received the appointment. The ministry, it is said, were the more willing to accede to his appointment from the difficulty of finding a person of suitable qualifications, who, in the distracted state of the affairs of the province, would accept the office. Besides, from the fact that Mr. Belcher was a citizen of Boston, and popular among his countrymen, it was supposed that the people might be more easily prevailed upon by him than by a stranger to comply with his majesty's demands, which, the longer they were refused, increased in importance, and which it concerned his prerogative peremptorily to enforce. But if the ministry reck-

[1] Mass. Rec's; N. Eng. Weekly Journal of Sept. 8; Hutchinson, ii. 324–326; Drake's Boston, 582. Chalmers, Revolt, ii. 131, censures the conduct of Governor Burnet in harassing the House as "equally unconstitutional and contrary to principle."

oned upon cajoling the people by flattery, they were destined
to find themselves sadly mistaken. The statesmen of New
England were too wary to be easily insnared, and the liberties
of the people were too precious to be voluntarily relinquished.[1]

The arrival of Governor Belcher was signalized by the
usual professions of loyalty and respect, and ministers welcomed him in public discourses.[2] At the first session of the
General Court, however, it was evident from his speech that,
whatever expectations had been formed of him, he was resolved, equally with Governor Burnet, to insist upon a compliance with his majesty's instructions for the settlement of a
salary, which was fixed at a thousand pounds, to be paid out
of the annual grants. In case of the refusal of the House to
comply, he was not only required to return immediately to
England, but, it was added, "his majesty will find himself
under a necessity of laying the undutiful behavior of the province before the legislature of Great Britain, not only in this
single instance, but in many others of the same nature and tendency, whereby it manifestly appears that this assembly, for
some years last past, has attempted, by unwarrantable practices,
to weaken, if not to cast off, the obedience they owe to the
crown, and the dependence which all colonies ought to have
on their mother country."[3]

The House met these demands as they had those of former
years, making a grant to Mr. Belcher of one thousand pounds,
as a gratuity for his services in England and to defray the
expense of his voyage, and another thousand to enable him " to
manage the public affairs." The Council concurred in these
votes, but desired a specification that the last sum should be
granted annually ; but the House refused to accept this amend-

[1] Hutchinson, ii. 328 ; Chalmers's
Revolt, ii. 132–134.

[2] Mr. Gay, of Hingham, preached
a sermon on the occasion.

[3] Mass. Rec's ; Hutchinson, ii. 333,
334. "Governor Belcher's returning
with the same instructions which he

went to oppose, is a little surprising ;
but some providences, like Hebrew
letters, must be read backwards, as
Mr. Flavel well remarks." MS. Letter of Josiah Smith, of Feb. 8, 1730,
in Mass. Hist. Soc., MS. Letters and
Papers, 1721–1760.

CHAP. ment, and rejected a second, that the sum should be paid an-
V. nually " during his excellency's continuance in the government."
1730. A conference ensued in the presence of the governor, who,
partly by threats and partly by flattery, attempted to shake
their resolution ; but neither his speech, nor the arguments of
the Council, produced any effect. The Boston members were
the most resolute, while many from the country were inclined
to yield ; and, as the governor himself was not unpopular, it
is possible that the settlement of a salary during his administration might have been effected, had it not been for establishing a precedent for the future.[1] But the governor was an
adroit politician, and knew how to accommodate himself to
the prejudices of his countrymen, without, at the same time,
relinquishing the attempt to enforce his majesty's instructions.
Hence, by adopting the policy of appointing to office those
whose favor he was anxious to secure, the number of his adherents rapidly increased, and the Council, in particular, was
remarkably complaisant.

1731.   A year rolled by, and but little had been effected. The governor continued, though prudently, to press the instructions
of the king ; but the House insisted that the settlement of
a salary would " deprive the people of their rights as Englishmen." Besides, the English press had told the Bostonians
" how much their noble stand against the unconstitutional
demands of Burnet had endeared them to all lovers and asser-
ors of liberty in Britain," and this encouragement strengthened
their opposition.[2] At length a bill was prepared, which, after
granting the sum of thirty-four hundred pounds of the currency

[1] Mass. Rec's; Hutchinson, ii. 334, 335. A further grant of £500 was made to the governor for his services as agent in England ; and the sum of £1500, which had been advanced by the merchants of Boston, was ordered to be paid. The House likewise passed a vote appropriating £500 additional to be deposited in the Bank of England for the use of the prov-ince ; but when the governor found that this very money was afterwards employed to promote complaints against himself, he regretted having given his consent to the bill, and saw too late the advantage it conferred upon his opponents in effecting his removal.

[2] Hutchinson, ii. 335, 336 ; Chalmers, Revolt, ii. 134; Hildreth, ii. 350.

of the province, equal to about a thousand pounds sterling, for CHAP.
the salary of the governor, proceeded to enact, that, as his   V.
majesty had been graciously pleased to appoint Jonathan Bel-   1731.
cher, Esq., to be their governor, who was a native of the country, whose fortune was here, and who, when a member of the
Council as well as in a private station, had always consulted
the true interest of his country as well as the honor and dignity of the crown, therefore it is most solemnly promised, that
there shall be granted the like sum for the like purpose at the
beginning of the sessions in May, every year during the governor's continuance in the administration and residence within
the province, "provided this act shall not be pleaded as a precedent, or binding on any future assembly, for fixing a salary
on any succeeding governor." [1]

The governor approved this bill, but it failed to pass ; and
from that time forward, despairing of success, he applied him- April.
self to obtain a relaxation of his instructions. In this he succeeded so far as to have leave from the Duke of Newcastle to Aug.
receive the sum granted for one year, and eventually a general
leave to receive such sums as should be granted was forwarded 1735.
to him. Thus terminated one of the most memorable, and in Aug.
some respects interesting, conflicts, between the crown and the
province, which its political history hitherto affords. The
Gordian knot remained untied. [2]

The war with Spain, which broke out before the close of 1739.
the administration of Mr. Belcher, exerted some influence upon Oct. 23.
the destinies of New England. It was resolved by the British
court to undertake an expedition to Cuba ; and Governor
Belcher received orders to encourage the enlistment of men 1740.
from Massachusetts. Admiral Vernon had already appeared Apr. 29.
before Porto Bello ; in a few days he took possession of the 1739.
town and the castle, and subsequently took and demolished Fort Nov.
Chagre. It was for his relief that the present supplies were

[1] Hutchinson, ii. 337.
[2] Hutchinson, ii. 338; Minot, i. 62; Chalmers, Revolt, ii. 134, 139.

CHAP. destined; and the northern colonies were required to contrib-
V. ute four battalions to the armament. No colony refused its
1740. quota; and Massachusetts, ever prompt to testify her loyalty,
sent forth, both from the old colony and from towns in the
vicinity of Boston, a body of five hundred of her young men,
many of whom fell victims to the unhealthiness of the climate,
or came home with shattered constitutions to die.[1] The result
of this war was still further to impoverish the province, and
embarrass its finances.

The pecuniary controversies which followed filled up the
remainder of the administration of Mr. Belcher. He had been
instructed by the king not to consent to the issue of bills of
credit to remain current beyond the year 1741; but, in spite
of these instructions, and as a protection against the legislation of Rhode Island, which had issued one hundred thousand
1733. pounds in bills of credit, a number of the merchants of Boston
organized a company, and issued one hundred and ten thousand
pounds, redeemable in ten years at a certain fixed rate.[2] At a
1739 later period a new scheme was devised, said to have been
to
1741. approved by Rev. Mr. Colman, and a company of eight hundred members was organized, known as the "Land Bank
Company," with a capital of one hundred and fifty thousand
pounds lawful money.[3] This scheme was opposed by the governor, and a large number of the statesmen of the province
apprehended evil from it; but it was popular with many, perhaps with a majority; and threats of civil disturbance were
made if its operations were suspended.[4] At this stage Parliament interposed, and declared that "the act of King George

[1] Mass. Rec's; Belknap's N. H. ii.
173, 174; Marshall's Washington, i.
333; Chalmers, Revolt, ii. 235; Bancroft, iii. 438–442; Hildreth, ii. 377–
379; Winsor's Duxbury, 116, 117.
Franklin, Works, iv. 188, says the
colonies sent 3000 men to join the
army in the expedition against Car-
thagena.

[2] Laws of the Province, ed. 1726;
Mass. Rec's; Hutchinson, ii.
[3] Mass. Rec's; MS. documents in
the possession of the author; Account
of the Rise, Progress, and Consequences of the Land Bank Scheme,
pub. 1744; Hutchinson, ii.
[4] Hobart's Hist. Abington, 170.

I., chap. 18, did, does, and shall extend to the colonies and plantations in America ; " and the company was dissolved.[1]

The boundary lines between Massachusetts and New Hampshire, and Plymouth and Rhode Island, had been in dispute from the first settlement of the country ; and though frequent attempts had been made for their adjustment, one party or the other remained dissatisfied, and the controversy was opened afresh. These lines were settled during this administration, adversely to Massachusetts, which lost a large tract to the north, assigned to New Hampshire, and another to the south, assigned to Rhode Island.[2]

The opposition of Mr. Belcher to the currency schemes of the province, and his agency in their defeat, rendered him obnoxious to their numerous favorers ; and these, joined to other measures, afforded a sufficient inducement to his enemies to solicit his removal. By forged and anonymous letters, and the help of unscrupulous falsehoods, his friends in England were prejudiced against him ; and, as he had failed to fulfil the expectations which had been formed of him, little difficulty was experienced in obtaining the consent of the lords of trade to his displacement.[3] How far he would have succeeded in the management of affairs under the new state of things, about to be introduced, it may be difficult to say. His qualifications for the chief magistracy were certainly as good as those of his predecessors. He was a native of New England, acquainted with its institutions, and to a certain extent imbued with its prejudices. He had early enjoyed the advantages of a good education, which were improved by travel, and by intercourse with intelligent circles in Europe. Graceful in his person, and generous in his hospitality, he was a favorite with all with whom he associated ; and, ambitious of distinction, he was enabled by his wealth to gratify his taste for public display.

---

[1] Hutchinson, ii. 352–355.
[2] Hutchinson, ii. 342–350, 358–360.
[3] Hutchinson, ii. 355–358 ; Belknap's N. H. ii. 174–180 ; Hildreth, ii. 380.

CHAP. Condescending in his manners, he was popular with the mass
V.   es ; and, though he was a known friend to the prerogative, and
1741. a moderate supporter of the claims of the crown, he was not
suspected of disloyalty to liberty, or of a want of regard to the
welfare of New England. Perhaps, on the whole, it was fortunate for him, and fortunate for the province, that his administration terminated before he had done any thing to deserve
the public censure. To the weak points in his character little
prominence had been given ; but had he been involved in some
sterner conflict, in which the crown and the province were
alike interested, he would have been compelled to elect between
the frowns of the monarch and the aversion of his countrymen
— to " luff for the one or bear away for the other ; "[1] and
whichever way his choice fell, his position would have been
embarrassing. His integrity was vindicated in England ; and,
1747. receiving an appointment as governor of New Jersey, there
he passed the remainder of his life in comparative repose.[2]

[1] Governor Belcher to the Earl of
Leven after his appointment as governor of New Jersey.
[2] Hutchinson, ii. ; Belknap's N. H.

ii. 180 ; Mulford's New Jersey, 349.
His death occurred in August, 1757.
Mulford, 360.

CHAPTER VI.

ADMINISTRATION OF SHIRLEY.   THE GREAT AWAKENING.
CAPTURE OF LOUISBURG.

THE successor of Mr. Belcher, destined for a long time to
act a conspicuous part in American affairs, was William Shirley,
a native of Sussex, in England, and a lawyer of respectable
talents, who had resided in Boston for the last eight years.
The news of his appointment arrived during his absence at
Rhode Island, as counsel before the commissioners to adjust
the boundary line in dispute between the governments; and
immediately upon its reception he hastened home, to assume
the charge confided to his trust.   The affairs of the province
were sadly perplexed.   The derangement in the finances had
been increased by the expenses of the late Spanish war; the
difficulties with the Land Bank party were at their height;
and in this dark hour it devolved upon him, as the chief magistrate, to point out a remedy for the evils which existed, and
evolve from chaos order and harmony.   By his instructions, he
was to consent to no act continuing the bills in circulation
beyond the time fixed for their redemption; but as this would
have burdened the people with an unusual tax, a substitute
was devised, which, while it preserved the spirit of his majesty's commands, violated their letter for the public relief.   The
project reported by the House, in which the governor concurred, provided that all special contracts should be payable
in silver at six shillings and eight pence per ounce, or gold in
proportion; and bills of a new form were issued, which were
to be received in payment of public and private dues, with the
understanding that, if they depreciated in value, a proportion-

CHAP. ate addition should be made to the debts contracted for their
VI.   equitable cancelment.   But this bill was unpopular, nor would
1741. it have effectually prevented the depreciation of the currency.
Besides, the act of Parliament was stringent in its requirements ; and, however strenuous the exertions for relief from its
severity, no measures could be adopted which were sure to be
sanctioned in England.   By prudent management, however,
immediate dangers were obviated, and the governor had the
good fortune to allay the storm which threatened ruin, without
losing the confidence of the people, or exciting a formidable
opposition to his measures.[1]

1740-43.   It was during the administration of Mr. Shirley that the
religious movement known as " the great awakening " agitated
America.   Massachusetts, as has been elsewhere remarked, was
founded by Puritans, whose creed was the rigorous creed of
Calvin.   Their system of theology, whose influence is yet felt,
and whose doctrines, in a modified form, are believed in our
own day, was admirably adapted to the temper of the times,
and was in keeping with the principles and policy of its advocates.   It had its strong points, as has every system based
upon the Scriptures ; and, if it did not contain the essence of
all truth, it had enough to give to it vitality.   Upon it the
churches of the country had been reared.   It had moulded the
customs and laws of the colony.   And no other faith, perhaps,
would have been more serviceable at the time in strengthening
and developing the character of the people.   But, with the
progress of settlement, and with the advancement of society,
new forms of faith began to spring up ; and, before the close
1699. of the seventeenth century, a church was established,[2] which
has continued to this day to advocate views differing essentially from those of the Puritan creed.   Indeed, entire uniformity of belief never existed in New England.   The first

---

[1] Hutchinson, ii. 361–363.
[2] The Brattle Street Church, sketches of whose history have been published by Drs. Palfrey and Lothrop.
See also 1 M. H. Coll. iii. 260, and
Drake's Boston, 519.

president of Harvard College was "heretical" on some points, and his successor was equally obnoxious to censure.[1]   Antinomians, Anabaptists, Gortonists, and Quakers were early introduced into the colony ; the advocates of Episcopacy followed ; and, when Arminian and Socinian doctrines were advanced, it seemed to those who had been brought up in the "straitest sect" of former days as if the floodgates of degeneracy were opened upon the world, and as if New England was to be buried beneath the waves of infidelity and apostasy.

Nor were such fears unnatural.   Not that the new doctrines were in themselves reprehensible, — for there is, doubtless, more or less truth in all sectarian organizations, and each has its mission to perform in the world, — but changes in religion, in politics, and in natural science have been always denounced as rash and uncalled for ; and so deeply rooted is the conservative spirit, that a long time elapses before the world can be convinced that what is new is not necessarily evil, and may be an advance upon what had been formerly received.

The controversy once opened, it raged fiercely for years. The pens of the disputants were dipped in gall.   To acrimonious language succeeded bitterness of feeling.   Neither party was remarkable for the moderation of its censures ; and the excesses of sectarian zeal, which were unhappily exhibited, furnish additional proof of the necessity of charity to temper our judgment of the past, to prevent us from hastily condemning what was rather the fruit of sincere conviction than the offspring of malignity or personal depravity.   It is refreshing to find occasionally one whose catholic spirit overlooked external forms, and discerned and commended the spirit of internal goodness.   But if such cases were rare, they were not wholly wanting.   There were a few who were willing that discussion should be tolerated, and who had no fears of the ultimate triumph of truth.   It augurs well for the advancement of Chris-

[1] Presidents Dunster and Chauncy, both of whom differed in opinion from the Puritan fathers on the subject of baptism.

CHAP. tianity when an eclectic spirit like this is displayed ; and when
VI.   men, reverencing the Scriptures above all creeds, seek to imbue
their lives with the spirit of Jesus. The "millennium" will
come when society is thus regenerated, but hardly before.

The advent of Whitefield brought to a crisis the struggle
1734. which had 'been secretly convulsing the community. Already
Dec. " the Spirit of God" had begun " extraordinarily to set
in, and wonderfully to work ;" and quite an excitement had
been induced by the preaching and writings of Jonathan
Edwards.[1] By the giant intellect of this eminent man form
was given to the faith of the past, and fluctuating opinions were
reduced to a system which, if its premises are admitted, leads
to conclusions of the highest importance. Perhaps, at a later
date, the system of Hopkins, the ablest of his disciples, was
more bold and startling. That of Edwards, if severe, was
exquisitely symmetrical ; and all must respect the mind which
framed it. It embodied the essence of Puritanism in its best
days, and asserted the doctrines of the sovereignty of God and
justification by faith.[2]

But if the system of Edwards was metaphysically exact, it
was lacking in the elements which appeal to the affectional
nature. In this respect Whitefield had greatly the advantage
of him. His ardent enthusiasm wrought powerfully upon all.
Gifted as an orator, and vain of his eloquence, which delighted
the multitude, every where his progress was an ovation and a
triumph. The excitement which his preaching produced was
violent and intense ; and if it led to some extravagances, it
was what might have been expected when the inflammable
nature of our passions is considered, and the nervous diathesis
developed by revivals. The ministers of the province were
divided in opinion ; and, while some welcomed him as an ally,
others denounced him as an "itinerant scourge." His adherents were the "new lights ;" his opponents were the " old

[1] Edwards, Narr. Surprising Con-   [2] See the published works of Ed-
versions ; the Great Awakening, 12.   wards and Hopkins.

lights ; " and between the two lay the party of reform, with CHAP.
Chauncy at its head, who by his abilities was admirably fitted ___VI.___
to be the champion of progress. Edwards and Chauncy dif- 1743.
fered in opinion as to the measures of Whitefield. The former
was the advocate of the most rigid Calvinism. The tendencies
of the latter were towards Universalism.[1] The clergy who
opposed Whitefield were chiefly Arminians. A few Calvinists
joined in his censure ; but the body of the followers of Edwards
were his friends.[2]

The dispute lasted long ; and the press teemed with pamphlets and more ponderous works,[3] which were poured out in
profusion upon the community. Nearly every clergyman in
the country participated in the controversy, and wrote or
preached on the one side or the other. Indeed, it was the
most thorough "awakening" hitherto known in New England ;
and, while it was attended with the evils which usually flow
from such sources, there can be no doubt that its influence was
in many respects salutary. It led to discussion, and hastened
the progress of light and truth.[4]

The difficulties with France, which had broken out at intervals from the peace of Utrecht, were renewed by the declara- 1713.
tion of war in 1744. Previously to the reception of this dec- Mar. 31.
laration in Boston, an armament was fitted out at Louisburg 1744.
under Duvivier, which surprised the English garrison at Can- Mar. 20.
seau, took eighty prisoners, and broke up the fishery.[5] Annap- June 2.
olis, in Nova Scotia, was likewise threatened ; and, as its May 13.
defences were in a ruinous condition, at the solicitation of Mas-
carene, the commander-in-chief, four companies of sixty men
each were ordered to be raised in Massachusetts, and sent

---

[1] See the writings of Chauncy, and
Whittemore's Hist. of Modern Universalism.

[2] Hutchinson, Grahame, &c.

[3] It would be impossible to enumerate these pamphlets, which amounted
to some hundreds. I have seen and
read a very large number on both
sides of the controversy.

[4] The details of this controversy
can be best learned from consulting
the contemporary pamphlets already
alluded to.

[5] Mems. Last War, 19, 20, 3d ed.,
1758 ; Hutchinson, ii. 364 ; Belknap's
N. H. ii. 189 ; Haliburton's N. S. i.
107 ; Minot, i. 74.

CHAP.
VI.

1744.

April 9.

Nov.

1744-45.
Jan.

Jan. 25.

thither for the protection of the place.[1] Louisburg, on Cape
Breton, was at this time the stronghold of the French at the
east; and, as the fortress was unfinished, and its capture was
deemed of the utmost importance to New England, projects for
its surprise were simultaneously started by several persons.
Judge Auchmuty, of Boston, submitted proposals to the English ministry for this object;[2] and William Vaughan, of New
Hampshire, advocated a like course;[3] but Governor Shirley
has been usually considered the planner of the expedition
which was finally sent.[4] Having learned the condition of the
fortress from prisoners liberated on parole, and having sent to
England for vessels of war to protect the east, and communicated with Commodore Warren at the Leeward Islands, soliciting his aid, early in the winter, under an injunction of
secrecy, the details of his plan were submitted to the legislature
of the province for approval; but so visionary did the scheme
appear to many, that it was at first rejected, though, upon a
reconsideration of the vote, at the urgent petition of merchants
of Boston and Salem and the fishermen of Marblehead, it was
carried by a majority of a single vote. Arrangements were
made for the immediate prosecution of the enterprise,[5] and circulars were addressed to the other colonies, as far south as
Pennsylvania, soliciting their aid; but, with the exceptions of
a grant of provisions from Pennsylvania and New Jersey, and
a train of artillery from New York, no general assistance was
furnished, and the charge of the expedition devolved upon New
England.[6]

[1] Mass. Rec's; Mems. Last War,
20–29; Hutchinson, ii. 364; Belknap's N. H. ii. 189; Haliburton's
N. S. i. 108–110; Marshall's Washington, i. 345.

[2] See 1 M. H. Coll. v. 202–205.

[3] Importance of Cape Breton, &c.,
Lond. 1746, p. 128; Journal of Proceedings of N. Eng. Forces, pub. at
Exeter; Hutchinson, ii. 364; Belknap's N. H. ii. 197, 198.

[4] Prince's Sermon, Boston, 1745;

Chauncy's Sermon, p. 9; 1 M. H.
Coll. vii. 69.

[5] Mass. Rec's; Am. Mag. ii. 166;
Mems. Last War, 34–37; Gibson's
Jour. 16–19; Hutchinson, ii. 365–
368; Grahame, ii. 166–168. The
proclamation of the governor for enlistments was issued January 26.

[6] Mass. Rec's; Hutchinson, ii. 369;
Marshall's Washington, i. 348–351;
Parsons's Life of Pepperrell, 57.

The troops from Massachusetts consisted of three thousand CHAP.
two hundred and fifty men, exclusive of commissioned officers; VI.
Connecticut furnished five hundred and sixteen men; New 1745.
Hampshire furnished three hundred and four; and Rhode
Island three hundred, but the contingent of the latter did not
arrive until the enemy had surrendered.[1] The naval force,
besides transports, consisted of three frigates of twenty guns
each, a "snow" of sixteen guns, a brigantine of twelve guns,
and five sloops mounting from eight to twelve carriage guns,
provided at the expense of Massachusetts; the armed sloops
of Connecticut and Rhode Island, each of sixteen guns; and
a small vessel from New Hampshire. The military munitions
consisted of eight cannon carrying twenty-two pound balls,
twelve carrying nine pound balls, two twelve inch mortars, and
two of less diameter, taken from the Castle, and ten eighteen
pound cannon borrowed from New York.[2]

Such was the armament which left Boston, under the convoy
of Captain Rous, for the capture of a fortress so formidable
as to be styled the "Dunkirk of America."[3] Soon after reach- Mar. 24
ing Canseau, however, by order of the Duke of Bedford, first to
lord of the admiralty, and afterwards secretary of state, the   April 4.

[1] Mems. Last War, 42; Gibson's
Jour. 14–19; Prince's Sermon, 24;
Journal of the Siege, 17; Shirley's
Speech of April 3, 1745, in Am. Mag.
ii. 167; Hutchinson, ii. 371. Among
the Pepperrell MSS. is a letter from
Brigadier Waldo, dated July 4, 1745,
in which he says that Massachusetts
sent 3027 men; New Hampshire, 500,
of whom 150 were in the pay of Massachusetts; and Connecticut, 500.

[2] Mems. Last War, 37; Am. Mag.
ii. 169. Rolts's Impartial Representation, iv. 13, is quoted in 1 M. H.
Coll. i. 110, as giving an account of
this expedition and of the number of
troops engaged in it. Also, attached
to a volume of sermons on the expedition to Louisburg, in Lib. Mass.
Hist. Soc., is a list of the naval armament, which says Massachusetts sent

3 ships of 20 guns, 2 vessels of 16
guns, and 2 of 8 guns, with about 100
transports, besides 1 vessel of 20 guns
and 1 of 16 hired from Rhode Island.
1 M. H. Coll. i. 15, speaks of 2 vessels from Rhode Island, both which
were "miserable sailers." Bancroft,
iii. 460, says the N. Eng. forces had
but "18 cannon and 3 mortars;" but
Parsons, Life of Pepperrell, 50, says the
whole number of guns in the fleet was
204, which is probably nearly correct.
Perhaps Mr. Bancroft makes a distinction between the land and sea
forces; but even in this case, his
estimate is below that given in the
text.

[3] Pepperrell MSS.; Prince's Sermon; Belknap's N. H. ii. 195; Grahame, ii. 164.

CHAP.   fleet from New England was joined by several of his majesty's
VI.   ships which had been cruising on the coast, and by the squad-
1745.   ron under Commodore Warren, which sailed to the north to
Apr. 23. act against the French.[1]

The command of this expedition, destined to shed · lustre
upon the valor of the provincialists, after some hesitation on
his part, on account of the circumstances of his family and
business, was intrusted to William Pepperrell, a native of Kit-
tery, who, familiar with the perils of Indian warfare, had
served as a colonel in a regiment of militia, and who, by his
unblemished reputation and engaging manners, was popular in
the Bay province as well as elsewhere in New England.
Whitefield, as Wesley had done to Oglethorpe, gave to New
Hampshire the motto its flag bore — "Nil desperandum, Christo
Duce;" and, as the expedition was viewed partly as a crusade
against heretics, one of the chaplains, "Parson Moody," bore
with him a hatchet to hew down the altars and images in the
French churches.[2] Not a cloud dimmed the prospect of the
adventurers as they embarked. A "guardian angel preserved
the troops from the small pox," which was imported in one of
the sloops taken into the service.[3] The French, so far from
April 4. crediting the rumors of an invasion, treated them as idle and
visionary tales. And, upon reaching Canseau, every thing was
found quiet; and the soldiers had only to wait the arrival of
their allies and the melting of the ice, to proceed to the attack.
It was observed, as a mark of the uncertainty of the enterprise,
that, "if any one circumstance had taken a wrong turn on the
side of the English, and if any one circumstance had not taken

[1] Letters in 1 M. H. Coll. i. 20, 21;
Journal of the Siege, 19; Mems. Last
War, 40–43; Am. Mag. ii. 167, 168;
Hutchinson, ii. 371; Belknap, ii. 196;
Minot's Mass. i. 75; Haliburton's N.
S. i. 115; Parsons's Life of Pepperrell,
59. The forces from New Hampshire
arrived first at Canseau; those from
Massachusetts followed; and those
from Connecticut arrived April 24.

[2] Chauncy's Sermon, 10; Hutchinson, ii. 369; Belknap's N. H. ii. 202
–205; Haliburton's N. S. i. 115;
Gordon's Am. Rev. i. 82; Grahame,
ii. 169, 170; Parsons's Life of Pepperrell, 51, 52, 128.

[3] Douglas; Prince's Thanks. Ser.
24; Prentice's Sermon, 33; Chauncy's Sermon, 15; Belknap, ii. 206.

a wrong turn on the side of the French, the expedition must CHAP.
have miscarried." But it was destined to succeed, notwith- VI.
standing the inexperience of both officers and men. Fortune 1745.
smiles sometimes upon even the novice in war.[1]

The scheme of Governor Shirley does not evince on his part
extraordinary knowledge of military affairs. "Our success,"
says he, in a letter to Wentworth, the lieutenant governor of
New Hampshire, "will depend on the execution of the first
night after the arrival of our forces. The fleet must make
Chapeau-Rouge by nine o'clock in the evening, when they cannot be easily seen, and from thence push into the bay, that all
the men may be landed before midnight. The troops, divided
into four companies, are to scale the walls at different points,
and to attack the grand battery. The formation of these companies will take up at least two hours' time, and the march
another two hours; so that it will be four in the morning
before the attack can be commenced. This will be a late
hour; so that the fleet must arrive punctually, or all may
fail."[2]

It requires no uncommon sagacity to perceive that, if success
depended on such conditions, the prospect was dubious. For
how could the arrival of the vessels be so accurately timed?
How could the troops be landed on a strange coast in the
darkness as readily as by daylight? And how could the
march be made through thickets and bogs, and the attack conducted, by men ignorant of the situation of the fortress, who
had never been in action, and who were incompletely furnished
with the necessary weapons? Fortunately for New England,
success did not depend on the preconcerted plan of the governor. The intended "surprisal" was frustrated by the arrival
of the vessels in the daytime, and their only alternative was a Apr. 30.
regular siege.

[1] Prince's Thanks. Ser. 15; Chaun-   [2] Belknap's N. H. ii. 209, 210.
cy's Sermon, 15, 16; Eliot's Sermon,   Comp. 1 M. H. Coll. i. 5–11.
12; Douglas.

CHAP.
VI.
1745.
The place before which the army was seated merits description. The town itself, about two miles and a quarter in circumference,[1] was built upon a neck of land on the south side of a beautiful basin of water four hundred fathoms broad at its mouth, and was fortified in its accessible parts with a rampart from thirty to thirty-six feet high, and a ditch eighty feet wide. A space of two hundred yards without the rampart, seaward, which was inaccessible to ships, was enclosed by a dike and a line of pickets; and the spot was secured from attack by the side fire from the bastions. These bastions, six in number, with the three batteries, contained embrasures for one hundred and forty-eight cannon, of which sixty-five were mounted, and sixteen mortars. On Goat Island, at the entrance of the harbor, was a battery of thirty cannon, carrying twenty-eight pound shot; and at the bottom of the harbor, opposite the entrance, was the grand or royal battery, of twenty-eight forty-two pounders, and two eighteen pounders. On a high cliff, opposite the island battery, stood a lighthouse, visible in a clear night five leagues off at sea; and within this point, at the north-east part of the harbor, were a careening wharf, completely landlocked and secure from all winds, and a magazine of stores.[2] The town was regularly laid out in squares. The streets were broad; and the houses, partly of wood and partly of stone, corresponded with the general appearance of the place. On the west side, near the rampart, and in the centre of one of the chief bastions, stood the citadel, which was spacious, with a parade near by, and a moat on one side towards the town; and within this building were the apartments of the governor, the arsenal, and bomb-proof barracks for the soldiers. Under the rampart were casemates, to receive the women and children during a siege. The entrance

[1] Some authorities say two miles and a half.
[2] There are curious plans of the forts at Canseau and Louisburg in the possession of Mr. George Follings, of Boston, draughted by his grandfather, who was a gunner in the expedition against Louisburg during the French war.

to the town on the land side was at the west gate, over a drawbridge, near which was a circular battery mounting sixteen twenty-four pounders. Three gates in the north-west walls overlooked the harbor, and had bridges extending to the water, from which goods might at any time be shipped or unshipped. The whole works had been upwards of twenty-five years in building, and, though unfinished, had cost the French government more than thirty millions of livres — upwards of five millions of dollars of the currency of the United States.[1]

The Island of Cape Breton, lying between the forty-fifth and forty-seventh degrees of north latitude, although considered by the English and the French as of the greatest importance, was chiefly so from its central position and the convenience of its ports. The soil, rocky and mountainous, or cold and boggy, was not remarkable for its fertility. The only valuable productions, besides timber, were pit coal and plaster. The atmosphere was laden with fogs in the spring, and the harbors were blocked with ice in the winter. The shores, on the north and west sides, were steep and inaccessible. On the south side were beautiful bays and excellent harbors, capable of receiving and securing ships of any burden. Lying between Canada on the one side and the West Indies on the other, commanding the entrance to the Gulf of St. Lawrence and the highway to New England, a retreat for cruisers, a depot for privateers, and the rendezvous for all ships destined to France from the American seas, its commercial position was favorable to the French, and it was valuable as a fishing station, though less so, perhaps, than several parts of Nova Scotia and Newfoundland.[2] Such was the island whose possession was to be

[1] Theatre of the Present War, 2–5; Beginning, Progress, &c., of Last War, Lond. 1770, 4to, p. 12; Mems. Last War, 13–16; Am. Mag. ii. 216; Hutchinson, ii. ; Belknap's N. H. ii. 193–196; Haliburton's N. S. i. 112, 113; 1 M. H. Coll. v. 202; Marshall's Washington, i. 346.

[2] Mems. Last War, pp. 10, 19, ed. 1758; Importance of Cape Breton, chaps. 3, 4; Theatre of the Present War, 6–10; Belknap's N. H. ii. 191 –193; Minot, i. 76.

CHAP. contested with the French; and such was the fortress which
VI. had been built for its security.

1745.   It was fortunate for the success of the expedition of Governor Shirley that the garrison at Louisburg was discontented
and mutinous; that no succors had arrived from France; and
that the provisions and stores of the fortress were greatly
reduced.[1] The plan of operation, "drawn by a lawyer, to be
executed by a merchant, at the head of a body of husbandmen
and mechanics, destitute of professional skill and experience,"[2]
Apr. 30. as we have seen, was frustrated, and the place was invested for
May 1. a siege. The landing of the troops was effected without much
opposition, and they flew "to shore like eagles to the quarry."
The same day, Colonel Vaughan, of New Hampshire, headed
a detachment of four hundred men, chiefly from that province,
and, passing the town, which he saluted with three cheers,
marched to the north-east part of the harbor, burned the warehouses containing the naval stores, and destroyed a quantity
of spirituous liquors. The smoke of this fire, driven by the
wind into the grand battery, so terrified the French, that they
precipitately abandoned the place, after spiking the guns and
throwing their powder into a well.[3]

May 2.   The next morning Colonel Vaughan took possession of this
battery, and sent for a reënforcement and a flag; but before
either arrived, an adventurous soldier climbed the staff, with a
red coat in his teeth, and fastened it by a nail to the top. A
detachment under Colonel Bradstreet was sent to the assistance of Colonel Vaughan; but the French, in great alarm,
hastily despatched a hundred men in boats to impede his
march; whereupon Colonel Waldo's regiment was ordered to

---

[1] Pepperrell's Letters, in 1 M. H.
Coll. i. 11–17; Belknap's N. H. ii.
207. Duvivier went to France for
supplies in the fall of 1744, but at
this time had not returned.
[2] Belknap's N. H. ii. 214.

[3] Pepperrell MSS.; Shirley's Lett.
p. 7; Pepperrell's Lett. i. 1 M. H.
Coll. i. 27; Journal of the Siege of
Louisburg, 20–22; Mems. Last War,
44, 45; Importance of Cape Breton,
130; Hutchinson, ii. 373.

assist him, and they were repulsed.[1] In vain did the French CHAP.
open a heavy fire on the battery to prevent its being occupied by VI.
the English. By night six companies were lodged there; and 1745.
that of which Seth Pomeroy, of Northampton, a gunsmith by
trade, was major, was immediately employed to drill the cannon
which the enemy had spiked. Before the twelfth of the month May 12.
about twenty were cleared, a portion of which were turned
upon the town with such success that nearly every shot told
with effect, and several pierced the roof of the citadel. The
behavior of the New Hampshire troops, and indeed of all the
provincials, was admirable; and for fourteen nights in succession they were employed in drawing cannon from the landing
to the camp on sleds — the men, with straps on their shoulders,
and sinking to their knees in mud, working like oxen.[2] The
landing and transporting the artillery and stores was a difficult
task, owing to the badness of the ground and the strength of
the surf. But what will not perseverance accomplish? Mortars
and cohorns were dragged through bogs and morasses up the
steep hills, and planted in commanding positions, and fascine May 11
batteries were erected near the west gate.[3]   to 17.

In the mean time councils of war were convened, at which May 7.
Commodore Warren was present; and a summons to surrender
was sent to Duchambon. This was refused; upon which it was
determined to proceed in the most vigorous manner to attack
the island battery, and Commodore Warren offered to send a
number of his sailors and marines to aid in the assault.[4] While
awaiting a favorable opportunity for this movement, despatches May 11.
were sent to Governor Shirley by Pepperrell for a reënforce-

[1] Am. Mag. ii. 223; Prince, Thanks.
Ser. 28; Belknap's N. H. ii. 216, 217;
Parsons's Life of Pepperrell, 65.
[2] Shirley's Lett. 8; Gibson's Journal, 42–46; Chauncy's Sermon, 16;
Belknap's N. H.
[3] Shirley's Letter, 9; Pepperrell's
Lett. 1 M. H. Coll. i. 27; Journal of
the Siege, 20–22, 25; Importance of

Cape Breton, 124, 125; Am. Mag. ii.
224.

"Of all exploits, since first I followed arms,
Ne'er heard I of a warlike enterprise
More venturous, or desperate, than this."
    Alençon, King Henry VI.
        Pt. I. Act. ii. Sc. 1.

[4] Journal of the Siege, 24; 1 M.
H. Coll. i. 27; Am. Mag. ii. 224.

CHAP.
VI.

1745.
May 19.

ment of a thousand men, and for additional military stores. Before these arrived, the Vigilant, a French ship of sixty-four guns, was captured by the squadron under Commodore Warren and the provincial sloops ; and, her crew being made prisoners, she was manned with English seamen. This success was encouraging, as it prevented additional supplies from reaching the fortress.[1]

May 24.

Yet the condition of the besiegers was far from flattering. Nearly fifteen hundred of the troops lay sick at one time ; the army was imperfectly provided with tents ; their "lodgings were turf and brush houses ; " and their provisions and ammunition were rapidly failing.[2] In this posture of affairs, another consultation was held on board the Superb ; and, for the more speedy reduction of the fortress, it was proposed by Commodore Warren that sixteen hundred men should be embarked, and that all his majesty's ships, and the provincial cruisers except two, with the captured ship Vigilant, and the schooners and transports, should enter the harbor, and attack the town and batteries with "the utmost vigor," while the marines, under Captain James M'Donald, were to be landed, and, sustained by the rest of the troops, were to make an attack on shore ;[3] but this plan was not approved by General Pepperrell. From the tenor of the correspondence between Warren and Pepperrell, it is evident that both gentlemen coveted the honor of leading the expedition ; and Commodore Warren was quite as anxious that its success, if effected, should be attributed to his squadron, as General Pepperrell was anxious that it should be achieved by his troops.[4]

[1] Journal of the Siege, 27 ; 1 M. H. Col. i. 43 ; Proclamations of Governor Shirley issued June 1 and June 4 ; Gibson's Journal, 51, 52 ; Am. Mag. ii. 223 ; Parsons, Life of Pepperrell, 67, 68, 72.

[2] Shirley's Lett. 8 ; Journal of the Siege, 23 ; 1 M. H. Coll. i. 32–35 ; Importance of Cape Breton, 126 ; Belknap's N. H. ii. 219. Sickness

seems to have prevailed most in the month of June ; and it was at that date that the 1500 were invalid. Parsons, Life of Pepperrell, 85.

[3] 1 M. H. Coll. i. 52, 53.

[4] 1 M. H. Coll. i. 32 ; Haliburton's N. S. i. 115, note. That part of the correspondence of Pepperrell, preserved by Parsons, in which he uniformly speaks in high praise of War-

In the mean time Pepperrell had not been "idle," as Warren insinuates; for, during the twenty-nine days the siege had continued, five fascine batteries had been erected, from which and from the grand battery considerable breaches had been made in the walls; the west gate was entirely beaten down; the adjoining wall was very much battered, and a breach was made in it about ten feet from the ground. The circular battery, of sixteen twenty-four pounders, was likewise nearly ruined, and all the cannon but three dismounted. The north-east battery, consisting of two lines of forty-two and thirty-two pounders, in all seventeen cannon, was damaged, and the men beaten off from their guns. The west flank of the King's Bastion, belonging to the citadel, and the battery of six twenty-four pounders, which pointed to the land side, were almost demolished; and two cavaliers, of two twenty-four pounders each, raised during the siege, and two other cannon of the same weight of metal, run out at embrasures cut through the parapet near the west gate, were damaged and silenced. The citadel itself was also damaged; several houses in the city were entirely demolished, and almost every one more or less injured. The Maurepas gate, at the east part of the city, was shattered; and, as cross fires from the cannon and mortars, and even from the musketry, ranged through the houses and streets in every part of the city, and through the enemy's parades, by which many were killed, the inhabitants were driven to the casemates, where they were obliged to take refuge for several weeks. Nor was this all; for, during the same period, five unsuccessful attempts were

---

ren, is certainly in favor of his conduct in the enterprise, and proves him to have been actuated by a patriotism as fervent as it was disinterested and pure. He knew what belonged to his office, and maintained his rights with dignity; and he was jealous of the intentions of Warren more for his country's sake than for his own — fearing that the services of the New England troops might be depreciated, and that less notice might be taken of their valor than they rightfully deserved. Governor Shirley seems to have anticipated these difficulties, as appears from one of his letters written at the time. See 1 M. H. Coll. i. 17. It was through the mismanagement of Shirley that these difficulties arose. See his letter to Warren, 1 M. H. Coll. i. 36.

CHAP.
VI.

1745.
May 26:

made upon the island battery, the "palladium of Louisburg," in the last of which one hundred and eighty-nine out of four hundred men were killed or taken prisoners. Scouts had also been kept out to destroy the settlements of the enemy, and to prevent a surprise of the camp.[1] These were certainly brilliant exploits for men who "laughed at zigzags and epaulements," and who conducted their movements "in a random manner ; " and if Commodore Warren was able to boast of his superior knowledge in the science of war, General Pepperrell had no reason to be ashamed of the conduct of his troops.[2]

June 1.

Jun. 11.

June 3.

At length Pepperrell consented that six hundred men should be sent on board the Vigilant, and five hundred on board the other ships, with the understanding that Colonel M'Donald, with his marines, was to assist on shore ; and shortly after, under the direction of Gridley, of Boston, a battery was completed near the lighthouse, containing three embrasures facing the island battery and six facing the sea.[3] The want of ammunition had been seriously felt, that which was used on shore being borrowed from the squadron ; but before this battery was finished welcome supplies arrived from Massachusetts.[4] Thus reënforced, the operations of the besiegers were prosecuted with increased vigor.

One great obstacle to the success of the English arose from the want of exact information of the condition of the fortress ; and Commodore Warren, deeming it "of the utmost consequence to know the situation of the enemy, as to their numbers

[1] Shirley's Letter to the Duke of Newcastle, ed. 1746, pp. 9–11 ; Journal of the Siege, 25–28 ; Mems. Last War, 45–47 ; Gibson's Journal, 56–60 ; 1 M. H. Coll. i. 35 ; Parsons's Life of Pepperrell, 82. Part of the damage referred to in the text was not done until the 6th of June, especially the silencing of the cannon from the parapets. The number of men lost in the attack on the island battery of May 26 is set down in some accounts

at 60 killed, and 112 prisoners. I follow Pepperrell's statement in his letter to Warren.
[2] 1 M. H. Coll. i. 35, 36.
[3] Shirley's Lett. 11 ; Journal of the Siege, 28, 29 ; Gibson's Journal, 62, 67 ; Hutchinson, ii. 376 ; 1 M. H. Coll. i. 38 ; Parsons, Life of Pepperrell, 83, 84.
[4] 1 M. H. Coll. i. 38, 40 ; Parsons, Life of Pepperrell, 85.

and quantity of ammunition and provisions," offered personally CHAP
a reward of from five hundred to a thousand guineas to who- VI.
ever would furnish such information. As one step towards 1745.
securing it, he suggested sending to the French governor
tidings of the capture of the Vigilant ; and, as Pepperrell
approved the plan, a letter written by the former captain of
the Vigilant was forwarded by a flag. The charge of this
letter was confided to Colonel M'Donald, and, by pretending June 7.
ignorance of the French language, he was enabled to listen,
without being suspected, to the discourse of the officers before
whom he was carried, and to observe the effect of his communication upon them.[1]

During the absence of this messenger, a fresh consultation was June 7.
held by Commodore Warren on board the Superb, to consider
the expediency of attempting to enter the harbor and attack the
town before the reduction of. the island battery ; but, after an
examination of the pilots, an inspection of the draughts of the
harbor, and a careful review of the position in which the
squadron would be placed with the battery in its rear, it was
decided to be impracticable. Nothing remained, therefore, but
to determine whether a new attempt should be made upon the
island battery or not ; and it was resolved to make the attempt
with the aid of the forces furnished by General Pepperrell.[2]
The decision of this council was forwarded to Pepperrell ; but,
as he was convinced that no good could result from sending a
few whale boats to the attack, which even musket balls would
sink, he declined seconding the proposal. A general attack by
land and sea was then concerted ; and Commodore Warren,
being strengthened by the arrival of three or four more ships, June 16
was to enter the harbor with his vessels, while General Pep- Jun. 14.
perrell was to open his batteries upon the town ; but before
making this attack, as other French vessels had been captured,

---

[1] 1 M. H. Coll. i. 41–43; Gibson's   H. Coll. i. 41; Parsons, Life of Pep-
Journal, 65.   perrell, 90, 91.
[2] Prince, Thanks. Ser. 30 ; 1 M.

CHAP. which were expected to relieve the fortress, and as the battery
VI. near the lighthouse commanded the island battery, upon which
1745. great reliance had been placed, Duchambon, satisfied that it
Jun. 15. was useless to contend longer, sent hostages to both Warren
and Pepperrell, with letters, proposing to surrender the fortress
on condition that the troops, some sixteen hundred in number,
should be permitted to retain their arms and colors. This
Jun. 16. proposition was accepted ; the fortress was surrendered ; and

> " Bright Hesperus, the harbinger of day,
>   Smiled gently down on Shirley's prosperous sway.
> The prince of light rode in his burning car,
> To see the overtures of peace and war,
> Around the world; and bade his charioteer,
> Who marks the periods of each month and year,
> Rein in his steeds, and rest upon high noon,
> To view our victory at Cape Breton." [1]

Jun. 17.   On the following day the victors entered the city ; and great
was their surprise at beholding the strength of the fortress,
and its capacity for resistance had it been suitably garrisoned.
As chief of the expedition, a large share of the credit of its
success rightfully belonged to Pepperrell ; but he was more
ready to yield the honors of the occasion to Commodore Warren than was Warren to acknowledge the value of his services.
Indeed, such seems to have been the jealousy of Warren, and
such were his fears lest too much credit should be given to
Pepperrell, that, in his personal despatches to England, and by
his representations after his arrival, he challenged to himself
the chief honor of the expedition, and succeeded for a time in

[1] Journal of the Siege, 29–31;
Mems. Last War, 49, 50 ; Gibson's
Journal, 71–74 ; 1 M. H. Coll. i. 43–
46; Hutchinson, ii. 376, 377 ; Haliburton's N. S. i. 119. The rude lines
in the text are taken from a piece inserted in Ames's Almanac for 1746,
commemorating the reduction of Louisburg. There are several volumes of
MSS. in the Lib. of the Mass. Hist.
Soc. comprising the papers of Sir William Pepperrell, his journals of this expedition, muster rolls, &c., from which
an elaborate narrative might be framed.
These papers are in a good state of
preservation, and are quite interesting.

throwing into the shade one who, if his rival, had more mag- CHAP.
nanimity than to descend to such misrepresentations, and who VI.
generously acknowledged the merits of his associate.[1]

1745.

The capture of Louisburg "filled Europe with astonishment
and America with joy." In London, the cannon of the Tower
and Park were fired by order of the lords of the regency; at
night there were great rejoicings, with bonfires and illumina-
tions in the city and its suburbs; and a general gladness was
diffused throughout the kingdom. Indeed, this was the capital
achievement of the war. The prowess of the provincials could
no longer be doubted, and veterans applauded the courage they
had despised.[2] Volumes of congratulatory letters poured in
upon Pepperrell from towns, corporations, and distinguished
citizens, applauding his success. And when the news reached
Boston, two weeks after the surrender, and in New York and July 2.
Philadelphia, unbounded enthusiasm prevailed. Bells rang out
their noisiest peals; cannon boomed; bonfires blazed; and at
night every dwelling was brilliantly illuminated.[3] Two weeks
later, a thanksgiving was celebrated in most of the New Eng- July 18.
land colonies, and patriotic sermons were preached by the
ministers.[4] No event had for a long time created such an
excitement. Many fortunate circumstances preceded and followed the enterprise. A bountiful harvest in the fall had filled
the granaries of the English to overflowing; while a drought,
which prevailed in Canada, cut off the supplies of the French.

[1] Bollan's Lett. in 1 M. H. Coll. i.
53, 54; Lett. to the Earl of Sandwich,
in 1 M. H. Coll. i. 108–111; Chalmers, Revolt, ii. 241; Parsons, Life
of Pepperrell, 101, 102. The jealousy between Warren and Pepperrell
does not seem to have been permanent, nor did it affect the friendliness
of their intercourse. Indeed, the
two officers continued to regard each
other with esteem through life; and
their correspondence indicates that
the rivalry which was called forth during the excitement of the siege was
only such as often springs up on such
occasions; and both gentlemen had
too much good sense to carry the matter so far as to make it the ground of
perpetual contention.

[2] Gibson's Journal, 78–80; Am.
Mag. ii.; 1 M. H. Coll. vii. 69; Parsons, Life of Pepperrell, 144, 145.

[3] Am. Mag. ii. 323; Parsons, Life
of Pepperrell, 108, 109.

[4] A number of these were published, among which that of Prince is
valuable for the information it contains.

CHAP.
VI.
1745.

Favorable weather facilitated the outfit of the troops; and a concurrence of incidents brought together from all parts the vessels of war cruising on the coast. During the siege the weather was unusually pleasant; but the day after the fortress surrendered a storm set in, and the rain fell in torrents for the next ten days.[1] Is it surprising that the French thought "the Virgin Mary was peculiarly kind to the English"?[2] or that the English themselves exclaimed, "The Lord hath done great things for us, whereof we are glad"?[3] Religious enthusiasm had stimulated many to enlist in the war; and, in the fervor of their piety, their success, if not miraculous, was esteemed providential. For a fortress so strong as, in the estimation of good judges, to require thirty thousand men for its capture, to have been taken by about four thousand undisciplined troops, most of whom had never before served in a similar enterprise, was certainly something to awaken astonishment; and one who was present, and who served with the French, observed that, "in all the histories he had read, he never met with an instance of so bold and presumptuous an attempt."[4]

The government of the island, upon the surrender of the fortress, after some controversy was jointly assumed by Warren and Pepperrell; and for his services in the expedition Warren was created vice admiral of the white, and the honors of knighthood were conferred upon Pepperrell.[5] Governor Shir-

Aug.

Dec. 8.

ley, during the summer, visited Louisburg to inquire into the condition of the army and fortress; and at his return he was welcomed with the heartiest rejoicings.[6] The expense of the

---

[1] Prince, Chauncy, Eliot, &c.

[2] Gibson's Journal, 78; Hutchinson, ii. 377.

[3] Prince's Ser. 33. "I scarce know of a conquest," says Chauncy, Ser. 12, "since the days of Joshua and the Judges, wherein the finger of God is more visible."

[4] Gibson's Journal, 78, 79. Comp. Chauncy's Sermon, 18, 19.

[5] MS. Lett. of the Duke of New-

castle to Pepperrell, Aug. 10, 1745; Marshall's Washington, i. 358; Parsons, Life of Pepperrell, 109, 125. The latter, pp. 112–116, gives an account of the difficulties which occurred on this occasion, with extracts from the correspondence on the subject. Warren was created baronet in 1747. Ibid. 165.

[6] Mems. Last War, 52–60. Pepperrell and Warren visited Boston in

expedition amounted to two hundred and sixty-one thousand CHAP.
VI.
seven hundred pounds of the currency of the province, or one
hundred and eighty-three thousand six hundred and forty-nine 1745.
pounds sterling; and this sum, after a vexatious delay, was
reimbursed through the intervention of Mr. Bollan, the son-
in-law of Shirley and the agent of the province. The money
thus received enabled Massachusetts to redeem a large portion 1749.
of her outstanding bills; the condition of the currency was Sep. 18.
temporarily improved; and the commercial activity of the
people was increased.[1]

The reduction of Louisburg was the signal for extensive
plans for the conquest of Canada. Both Shirley and Warren
were at the bottom of this movement;[2] the Duke of Bedford
was deeply interested in its success; and at their solicitation 1745.
a circular letter was addressed by the Duke of Newcastle, then Oct.
secretary of state, to all the governors of the American colo- 1746.
nies as far south as Virginia, requiring them to raise men, and Apr. 19
form them into companies, to be ready to unite and act according to future orders. Eight battalions were to be raised in
England, under Lieutenant General St. Clair, with a squadron
commanded by Rear Admiral Warren; and these, with the New
England troops, were to rendezvous at Louisburg, and from
thence proceed to Quebec. The troops from the southern colonies were to rendezvous at Albany, and from thence proceed
to Montreal.[3]

June, 1746; and on this memorable occasion they were received at Long Wharf by his majesty's Council and the House of Representatives, and escorted by his excellency's company of cadets to the council chamber, being saluted, as they passed through the streets, by the hurrahs of the people, who crowded the doors, windows, and balconies. Every one testified joy at their arrival; and the congratulations of the legislature of the province were cordially tendered them. Mass. Rec's; Parsons, Life of Pepperrell, 140–143.

[1] Trumbull MSS. vol. i. fols. 2, 17; Observations on Present Circumstances of Prov. of Mass. Bay, ed. 1750, p. 6; Hutchinson, ii.; Bancroft, iv. 50, 51.

[2] Mems. Last War, 60, 61; 1 M. H. Coll. vii. 70; Hutchinson, ii. 380, 381; Belknap's N. H. ii. 225–227; Marshall's Washington, ii. 360; Parsons, Life of Pepperrell, 129.

[3] Chalmers, Revolt, ii. 242–244; Marshall's Washington, i. 360; Parsons, Life of Pepperrell, 148. The Duke of Bedford, the first lord of the

CHAP.
VI.

1745.
July 3.

May.

Sep. 12.

Aug.

Sep. 20.

In accordance with these plans, as the design was pleasing to the people, the measures of the ministry were cordially approved, and the colonies furnished with alacrity their quotas.[1] But the French, in the mean time, were not inactive ; and an armament was fitted out from Brest and the West Indies, which, in conjunction with a body of land forces to be raised in Canada, was destined for the conquest of Nova Scotia, and the destruction of the settlements from thence to Georgia. This fleet, the most powerful hitherto sent to these shores, was under the command of the Duke D'Anville, an officer of experience and approved ability, and consisted of seventy sail, of which eleven were ships of the line, twenty frigates, five ships and bombs, and the rest transports and tenders, having on board upwards of three thousand disciplined troops.[2] The energy of the French in making these preparations did not prevent the levy of more than eight thousand men from the colonies for the conquest of Canada ; but, as the fleet from England had not arrived, and the season was so far advanced that, if it should arrive, it would be too late to attempt the navigation of the St. Lawrence, it was judged prudent to defer the attack on Quebec, and to turn the attention of the army to the reduction of Crown Point.[3]

At this juncture intelligence was received of the danger which threatened the eastern provinces, from the inroads of the French and Indians at Minas, and the expected revolt of the Acadians ; and shortly after, by additional letters, the whole country was alarmed by reports of the arrival of the fleet from France. In this emergency, the preparations of Massachusetts were promptly made. Several hundred men had been sent to Annapolis to act there ; and, as Castle Wil-

admiralty, and afterwards secretary of state, is said to have favored this project ; and, according to Pitt, the " great and practicable views for America " sprang from him alone. Bancroft, iv. 21.

[1] Mass. Rec's ; Parsons, Life of Pepperrell, 149.
[2] Marshall's Washington, i. 362 ; Parsons, Life of Pepperrell, 146, 147.
[3] Mems. Last War, 62–64 ; Belknap's N. H. ii. 229.

liam had been recently refitted, a large body of troops was CHAP
ordered thither, and nearly ten thousand persons offered their VI.
services to aid in defending Boston. But the operations of 1746.
the French were signally thwarted; for, crippled by tempest
and shipwreck, the gallant fleet, which had set forth sanguine May.
of success, was so shattered after its arrival on the coast as to Sept.
be unable to proceed; and the death of the Duke D'Anville,
and the suicide of his successor, led to the return of the surviving vessels, and the abandonment of the design upon which Nov.
they had been sent.[1]

Thus ended the "expedition of the most formidable armament ever fitted out against the coast of North America" —
an armament "computed to consist of near half the naval force
of France." To complete the series of catastrophes and disasters, some of the vessels were lost, and others were taken, on
the voyage home; and, by an infection among the seamen, a
disease was communicated to the Cape Sable Indians, in the
interest of the French, by which nearly two thirds of them
miserably perished.[2]

In the mean time the arrangements for the contemplated
attack upon Crown Point had been continued, and preparations had proceeded so far that bateaux were provided for the
transportation of the troops and stores across Lake Champlain;
ordnance stores and provisions were sent from Boston, and a
train of artillery from New York to the fort at Saratoga; and
fifteen hundred of the Massachusetts troops set out for Albany Oct.
to join the troops from the southern governments; but the
general alarm occasioned by the appearance of the French
armament suspended the prosecution of the attempt until the
season was so far advanced that a portion of the colonies
judged it too late to proceed, and refused to join with Massachusetts in the execution of the project. Yet Governor Shir-

[1] Mems. Last War, 64–67. Par- Jonquiere, as the successor of the
sons, Life of Pepperrell, 147, gives the Duke D'Anville.
name of D'Estournelle, instead of La [2] Mems. Last War, 68.

CHAP. ley, unwilling to abandon the enterprise, renewed the attempt
VI. to carry it into effect, and induced the legislature to favor his
1746. plans. The governor of New York, equally eager for war,
was likewise inclined to aid in the expedition. But, by the
prudence of the members of the Connecticut assembly, who
deemed the winter an improper season for so great an undertaking, the rash scheme was defeated, and further thoughts of
exterminating the French were reluctantly abandoned. The
troops from New England remained under pay until the follow-
1747. ing fall, when, by order of the ministry, they were disbanded ;
Oct. 31.
the governors drew bills on the British treasury for their support ; and Parliament granted the money to reimburse the
charges of their equipment and subsistence.[1]

1748.   The peace of Aix la Chapelle, concluded in 1748, caused
Oct. 8.
a temporary suspension of hostilities between England and
France. By the terms of this peace, New England had the
mortification to find the fruits of her toil, in the conquest of
Louisburg, wrested from her grasp ; for, under the compromise
for restoring the French conquests in the Low Countries to
the Queen of Hungary and the States General, and for a general restitution of places captured from the other belligerent
powers, the Island of Cape Breton was delivered back to its
1749. former possessors ; and Massachusetts was left to calculate at
July 12.
leisure the expenses of her warfare, and the benefits which had
accrued to her from the loss of her citizens who had fallen a
prey to the ravages of disease, and the damage to her com-

---

[1] Mems. Last War, 68–75; Hutchinson, ii. 386; Belknap's N. H. ii.
234, 235; Minot, i. 80. The total
expenses of the Canada expedition to
the colonies were £224,741 12s. 8¾d.
Of this sum Massachusetts received
£87,434 18s. 7d. ; Connecticut received £17,191 15s. 8½d. ; N. Hampshire received £21,446 10s. 10½d. ;
New York received £84,098 18s. 6d. ;
New Jersey received £2,231 18s.
4½d. ; and Pennsylvania, Virginia, and
Rhode Island received £12,338 0s·
7¾d. Trumbull MSS. in Mass. Hist.
Soc. vol. i. fol. 30. Letters relating
to the share of Connecticut may also
be seen in ibid. fols. 1, 3, 5, 18, 32.
The Connecticut troops were permitted to go home on furlough October
31, 1746; but half pay was demanded
from that date to October 31, 1747,
when the troops of the colonies were
ordered to be dismissed. Ibid. fols.
18, 30.

merce from the interruption to her trade. English policy, CHAP. however, at this time, was little concerned with colonial pros- VI. perity ; and the people of New England, on this as on other 1749. occasions, were made sensible that they were merely dependencies of the crown, and that their interests were to be sacrificed at the caprice of the dominant powers, however prejudicial that sacrifice might be.[1]

The conduct of the English government throughout the war with France did not, to the inhabitants of America, seem to justify the belief that it acted in good faith towards the colonies, or designed to render efficient aid in the conquest of Canada. Nor was the course pursued by the commanders of English vessels of war such as to inspire confidence in their integrity or good will. For, before the conclusion of the peace of Aix la Chapelle, a tumult occurred in Boston, equal to, if 1747. not more threatening than, any which had preceded it. A Nov. 17. number of sailors having deserted from the squadron at Nantasket, Commodore Knowles, who had charge of the same, and who had been active at Louisburg, demanded a supply equal to those he had lost ; and, sending his boats to the town early in the morning, he seized the seamen of the vessels in port, and swept the wharves, impressing some ship carpenters' apprentices and laboring landsmen.[2] This high-handed outrage aroused the indignation of the people, and all united in condemning it. The laboring class, especially, who were the greatest sufferers, were enraged beyond measure ; and, hastily arming with sticks and clubs, they gathered in crowds, clamoring for redress. A lieutenant was the first person seized ; but he was released on the assurance of Mr. Hutchinson, the speaker of the House, that he was guiltless, and was conducted

---

[1] Minot, i. 81 ; 1 M. H. Coll. vii. 69. "Of such consequence to the French was the possession of that important key to their American settlements," says the last authority, "that 'ts restitution was, in reality, the pur-chase of the last general peace in Europe."

[2] Impressment had long been practised in England, though not enforced by law. Address to Inhabitants of Mass. Bay, p. 5.

to a place of safety.   Receiving intelligence that several of the commanders were at the house of the governor, the mob immediately repaired thither.   The house was surrounded, and the adjacent court filled; but no act of violence was committed, until a deputy sheriff presumed to interfere, when he was seized and set in the stocks.   Soldiers had been posted at the head of the stairway, with loaded carbines, to repel an assault; and it was probably owing to this circumstance, and to the persuasions of the prudent, that no more decided measures were taken.

By dusk several thousand people were assembled in King Street, below the town house, where the General Court was sitting, and stones and bricks were thrown into the council chamber; but the governor ventured into the balcony with several of his friends, and, in a well-timed speech, expressed his disapproval of the conduct of the commodore, and promised his utmost endeavors for the discharge of those who had been taken.   Other gentlemen likewise addressed the crowd; but their speeches had no effect.   Even Pepperrell, "with all his personal popularity, was equally unsuccessful in stilling the tumult." [1]   The multitude clamored for the arrest of those who had committed the outrage, and insisted upon this as the only security for the release of the prisoners.

As conciliatory measures were fruitless, it was deemed expedient for the governor to withdraw to his own residence.   But this did not allay the excitement; and, shortly after, a report being raised that a barge from the ships had touched at one of the wharves, the mob flew to the spot, but took, by mistake, a boat belonging to a Scotch ship, which they drew in triumph through the streets to the governor's house, and prepared to burn it.   A consideration of the danger of this proceeding, however, prevented the execution of the design, and the boat was taken to a safer place and burned.

[1] Parsons, Life of Pepperrell, 172.

The next day, the military companies of the neighborhood CHAP. were ordered to be mustered under arms, and a watch was VI. appointed to be kept the succeeding night. The governor, by 1747. this time, was alarmed for his own safety; and, leaving the Nov.18. town privately, he withdrew to the Castle, notwithstanding the assurance of a number of gentlemen that they would stand by him in the maintenance of his authority and the restoration of order. On reaching the Castle, a despatch was sent to Commodore Knowles, representing the confusion occasioned by the misconduct of his officers; but he refused all terms of accommodation until the officers on shore were released, and threatened to bombard the town in case they were not liberated.

For three days the General Court continued in session with- Nov. 17 out directly interfering in the affair; but towards noon of the to 19. latter day, some of the members of the House reflecting upon Nov.19. the serious consequences which might result from leaving the governor unsupported, a series of resolutions was presented and adopted, expressing a determination to "stand by and support, with their lives and estates, his excellency the governor and the executive part of the government, and to exert themselves, by all ways and means possible, in redressing such grievances as his majesty's subjects have been and are under."

With the passage of these resolves the excitement abated; and, at a town meeting held in the afternoon, the "tumultuous and riotous acts of such as had insulted the governor and the other branches of the legislature" were condemned, though deep regret was expressed at the "great injury and insult caused by the misconduct of the naval officers." The governor, not knowing what course the affair might take, had in the mean time issued his orders to the colonels of the regiments of Cambridge, Roxbury, and Milton, and the regiment of horse, to be ready to march at an hour's warning to such rendezvous as he should direct; but the next day he was agreeably sur- Nov.20. prised at the appearance of the militia of Boston, accompanied by many who had never before borne a musket, who assured

CHAP.
VI.

1747.

1749.

him of protection, and conducted him to his residence with great parade. The commodore, upon this, liberated most of those who had been impressed; and the squadron took its departure, to the infinite joy and relief of the people.[1]

Another measure, adopted in England soon after the peace of Aix la Chapelle, was not particularly acceptable to the people of New England. This was the revival of the project of Archbishop Secker for sending episcopal bishops to America, which was favored by Sherlock, the new Bishop of London, by Bedford, the secretary of state, and by Halifax, the president of the Board of Trade. The political reason assigned for this step was, that several nonjuring clergymen, in the interest of the Pretender, had emigrated to the colonies, whose influence it was necessary to counteract and destroy; but the project was opposed by leading persons in the ministry, and was finally laid aside. The Society for Propagating the Gospel then took the matter up; and, conceiving the chief obstruction to arise from the jealousy of ecclesiastical jurisdiction in the colonies, they labored to remove this difficulty by declaring that no coercive power was intended to be exercised over the laity in any case; that it was not designed the bishops should interfere with the dignity or authority of any of the civil officers; that their maintenance was not to be charged to the people; and that no bishops were to be settled in the colonies where the government was in the hands of dissenters. Happily for Massachusetts, this project, though generally unpalatable, did not cause special alarm to her citizens; and the circumstances of the province were such that, if the attempt had been made to foster episcopacy contrary to the wishes of a majority of the laity, it would have been instantly resisted, and must have failed to succeed. Yet the fact that such a measure was devised, and enforced in the colonies less refractory than those of New England, proves that the arbitrariness of the

[1] Mass. Rec's; Address to the Inhab. of Mass. Bay, &c., by Amicus Patriæ; Hutchinson, ii. 386, 390; Chalmers, Revolt, ii. 244–246.

mother country was daily increasing, and that the measures of her statesmen aimed not to enfranchise her Cis-Atlantic subjects, but to reduce them to a state of more complete vassalage.[1]

Yet, notwithstanding the mismanagement of England, the Province of Massachusetts continued to prosper, and the energies of her people it was impossible to repress. Where the spirit of freedom inspires the soul, obstacles are easily surmounted, and success is insured. The advancement of the interests of Massachusetts, during the fifty-six years which had elapsed from its erection into a province, if not equal in every respect to its advancement in the fifty years which followed the confederacy of 1643, was certainly as great as could have been reasonably expected. The population, at this time, was estimated at two hundred thousand souls; and Boston, the metropolis of the province, contained not far from twenty thousand inhabitants.[2] Sixty-eight towns had been incorporated in the different counties, swelling the number, in all, including those of the "old colony," to one hundred and forty — nearly double what it was at the grant of the charter of William and Mary.[3] The value of the imports from Great Britain to North America, for the ten years ending in 1748, amounted, in the aggregate, to about seven and a half millions sterling, or seven hundred and fifty thousand pounds

1692
to
1748.

1643
to
1692.

1748

1738
to
1748.

---

[1] Gordon's Am. Rev. i. 85, 86; Minot, i. 136–138.

[2] Douglas says, by the valuation of 1742, there were reported 16,382 souls in Boston. Governor Shute, in 1723, estimated the population of Boston at 18,000. Chalmers, Revolt, ii. 26. Governor Shirley, in one of his letters to the Board of Trade, speaks of Boston as a "town inhabited by 20,000 persons." Bancroft, iv. 39. Burnaby, Travels, 133, says Boston contained from 18,000 to 20,000 inhabitants in 1759, and 3000 houses.

[3] The names of these towns, in the order of their incorporation, were, Harwich, Attleborough, Framingham, Dracut, Brookline, Plympton, Truro, Needham, Chatham, Norton, Abington, Pembroke, Dighton, Lexington, Weston, Medway, Oxford, Chilmark, Leicester, Northfield, Sunderland, Hopkinton, Littleton, Sutton, Westborough, Bellingham, Rutland, Holliston, Walpole, Methuen, Stoneham, Easton, Kingston, Stoughton, Hanover, Provincetown, Uxbridge, Shrewsbury, Southborough, Middleton, Lunenburg, Westford, Bedford, Wilmington, Brimfield, Raynham, Townsend, Harvard, Dudley, Sheffield, Halifax, Tewksbury, Acton, Berkeley, Grafton, Upton, Sturbridge, Waltham, Bolton, Hardwick, Wareham, Stockbridge, Leominster, Blandford, Holden, Warren, Pelham, Douglass.

CHAP. per annum — upwards of three millions of dollars of the cur-
VI.   rency of the United States.[1] This sum, indeed, is not much
1748. larger than the value of the imports from 1715 to 1718; but
it must not be hence inferred that the commerce of the country
was decreasing. The statement simply indicates that the people were depending more upon their own resources, and that
inter-colonial exchange was taking the place, in a measure, of
the trade with foreign ports. This is evident, not only from
the acts of Parliament restricting manufactures, but also from
the statistics of that period, which show that the shipping of
the colony had largely increased;[2] that the trade with the
West Indies was much more extensive; and that more attention was paid to those interests upon which, after all, every
people must principally depend for support, and without which
no nation can rapidly progress.

The discipline through which the people had passed had
been painful, and such as they would probably have gladly
avoided, had it been in their power. But it was exactly the
discipline adapted to their circumstances, and exactly the discipline which prepared them for the future. They had learned
something of the feelings of Great Britain towards her colonies, and were able to comprehend better the policy of her
statesmen. Wise men, even at this date, foresaw the impending struggle, and predicted that a generation would not pass
before it would commence.[3] The military training, which was
to fit the citizens of New England for the battles of the revolution, had already been begun, and in the next few years it
was surprisingly advanced. Even the taking of Louisburg,

[1] Minot, i. 162; Hildreth, ii. Franklin, Works, iv. 37, makes the value of
the exports from England to the northern colonies, from 1744 to 1748, in-
clusive, £3,486,261, or about $15,-
479,000 — an average of $3,000,000
per annum.

[2] In 1741, there were upon the
stocks in Boston, "at one and the
same time," 40 topsail vessels, amounting to about 7000 tons. Douglas, ii.
18. Oldmixon states that, at the same
date, "near 600 sail of ships" were laden in Boston "for Europe and the
British plantations."

[3] Franklin's Works, and the Writings of John Adams, &c.

notwithstanding its re-cession, had some influence on the desti- CHAP.
nies of America; and "the same old drums" that beat at the VI.
capture of the fortress "rallied the troops in their march to 1748.
Bunker's Hill; and the same Colonel Gridley who planned
Pepperrell's batteries marked and laid out the one where General Warren fell; and when Gage was erecting breastworks
across Boston Neck, the provincial troops sneeringly remarked
that his mud walls were nothing compared with the stone walls
of old Louisburg."[1] "By a way that ye know not I will lead
ye," is ever God's course in his dealings with men. And it is
well that our destinies are always in his hands; for such is our
ignorance, and such is our folly, that we often complain most
of what eventually proves best for us, and have seldom the
sagacity to perceive that temporary evils generally result in
permanent good, and that the chastenings which we experience
at his hands, while they are rebukes for our misconduct, are at
the same time parts of the great scheme which accomplishes the
advancement of the race — setting up one nation, and humbling
another.

[1] Parsons's Life of Pepperrell, 144; Everett's Orations, 366, 368.

CHAPTER VII.

THE FRENCH WAR. 1753–1756.

CHAP. VII.

THE rivalry between England and France was destined to revolutionize the history of America. Both nations, for more than a century, had been struggling for the prize of supremacy on these shores ; but the superior energy of the English, and the habits of industry peculiar to the settlers of New England and the colonies to the south, had augmented their strength and increased their numbers far beyond those of the feeble settlements to the north. Hence, while the plantations on the seaboard contained upwards of a million of souls, the banks of the St. Lawrence and the valley of the Mississippi were peopled by less than a hundred thousand persons, who owned France as their native land, and who were jealous of the prosperity and the advancement of their neighbors.[1]

1748.
Oct. 7.

The peace of Aix la Chapelle was a truce rather than a league ; and the very vagueness of its terms was fruitful in scattering the seeds of discord. France, on the one hand, was reluctant to relinquish a foot of the territory which had been trod by her missionaries and subjected to her flag ; England, on the other, dreading the presence of France and the influence of the Jesuits upon the warlike Indians, was anxious to restrict the bounds of her jurisdiction, and looked forward to the time when she should be able to expel the French from all North

[1] Chalmers, Revolt, ii. 273, 274; Marshall's Washington, i. 373 ; Bancroft, iv. 127, 128; Hildreth, ii. 447. Even Charlevoix could say, in 1721, "Il règne dans la Nouvelle Angle-terre une opulence dont il semble qu'on ne sait point profiter, et dans la Nouvelle France une pauvreté cachée par un air d'aisance."

(166)

America, supply the farthest wigwam from her workshops, and CHAP
assume absolute sway from the Atlantic to the Pacific. France, VII.
without doubt, would have as readily driven the English from 1748.
the continent, had it been in her power ; but such was her fee-
bleness, and such was the paucity of her population in the new
world, notwithstanding she had for as many years been mistress of parts of its territory, and claimed other parts by the
right of discovery, it was hopeless to look for this result, and
she could only exert herself to fortify the stations she already
held, and prevent their being wrested from her by the prowess
of her rival. Hence a chain of posts was proposed to be
erected, connecting the St. Lawrence with the broad Mississippi. This policy she had long cherished ; this policy she now
began seriously to enforce.[1]

Foreseeing the difficulties which must spring from this
source, and the embarrassed position in which her own colonies would be placed, England, on her part, was equally zealous to frustrate the plans of France ; and a company was
formed, consisting chiefly of Virginians, and settlements were
projected on the banks of the Ohio, for the security of the 1749.
territory watered by that stream, and to resist the continued
aggressions of her rival.[2] Each nation was alive to the importance of accomplishing its purpose ; each was determined
to exert itself to the utmost to fortify its possession of the
country and secure its jurisdiction.

By the terms of the treaty of Aix la Chapelle, the bounds Art.IX
of the two nations were to be as before the war. But for
more than a quarter of a century these bounds had been in
dispute. Hence their adjustment was a matter which required
immediate attention ; and as Governor Shirley had returned 1749.
to England to urge the necessity of erecting a fort near Crown Sept.

---

[1] Letters to Two Great Men, 13 ; Franklin's Works, iv. 336 ; Marshall's
Burr's Discourse of Jan. 1, 1755, p. Washington, i. 375 ; Bancroft, iv. 41,
17 ; Marshall's Washington, i. 375. 42.
[2] Archæol. Americana, ii. 535–541 ;

CHAP. Point, which commanded Lake Champlain, and of settling and
VII. fortifying a town in Nova Scotia, — leaving the government
1750. during his absence in the hands of Spencer Phips, — about a
Sept. year after his arrival, in connection with William Mildmay, he
was appointed commissioner by the court of St. James to meet
at Paris with La Gallisonière and Silhouette for the adjustment
of these bounds.[1] The English commissioners, however, soon
found that there was very little hope of arriving at a friendly
arrangement, for the more they advanced in their offers the
more the French claimed ; futile and frivolous objections were
started ; and, as collisions had taken place within the disputed
territory, after nearly two years had been spent in disputation,
and papers had accumulated sufficient to fill two thick quarto
volumes of protocols, the conference ended ; Mr. Shirley re-
1753. turned to England, and soon after to America, bringing with
Aug. 6. him, at the age of sixty, a new wife, the daughter of his land-
lord in Paris, with whose charms he had been smitten, and
whom he had privately married.[2]

In the mean time, the British government, to guard the commerce and fisheries of New England, and to offset the disadvantages of the restoration of Louisburg, conceived a plan,
1749. approved by Cumberland, Pelham, and Fox, for the settlement
Mar. of a town near the harbor of Chibucto, which was called Halifax, in honor of the Earl of Halifax, the new president of the
May. Board of Trade. Early in the spring, a fleet was sent under
Edward Cornwallis, a brother of Lord Cornwallis, to com-
June. mence this settlement; and at the opening of summer he
arrived on the coast.[3] The whole country was at that time
an unbroken wilderness, and the soil was covered with a dense

---

[1] Summary View of Facts, &c., p. 3 ; Pouchot's Introd. xxxvii ; Letter to Two Great Men, 16 ; Bancroft, iv. 73.

[2] Bollan's Letter of April 25, 1750, in MSS. Letters and Papers, 1721–1760, fols. 191, 192, in Mass. Hist.

Soc. Coll. ; Mems. of the English and French Commissioners concerning the Limits of Nova Scotia, &c., ed. 1755 ; Hutchinson, iii. 15 ; Chalmers, Revolt, ii. 260 ; History of the War, 7.

[3] History of the War, 6 ; Halibur-ton's N. S. i. 137 ; Bancroft, iv. 45.

growth of evergreens, — the spruce, the fir, and the murmuring CHAP.
pine, — whose spiry tops pierced the clouds, and whose spread- VII.
ing limbs, bearded with moss which hung in thick festoons from 1750.
the pendulous branches, shaded the ground in every direction,
giving to the scenery an aspect of gloom to which the emigrants, removed from a cultivated district, where verdant
lawns stretched far away, bordered with the graceful beech or
the drooping elm, were wholly unaccustomed. Nature appeared to them in her wildest form ; and the sullen roar of the
waves, as they dashed upon the rock-bound coast, was less
sweet music to their ears than the chimes of the bells of their
native village, or the cawing of the rooks that lodged in the
groves.

Undaunted by the prospect before them, clearings were
speedily made ; buildings were erected with materials brought
from New England ; and before winter set in the people were
comfortably settled ; a government was established ; and provisions were made for the employment of all, until the warmth
of the spring permitted the renewal of their labors. Thus
sprang into being the first town of English origin east of the
Penobscot.[1]

The French were not idle while these movements were pro-
gressing. Indeed, before the arrival of Cornwallis, they had
taken possession of Chiegnecto, now Fort Lawrence, near Chibucto, and erected a fort ; and they claimed the River St.
John, and all Acadia as far as Penobscot. Immediately the
Acadians, who were of French descent, and who for forty years
had acknowledged themselves subjects of England, declared 1710-50.
their revolt, and their adherence to France ; upon which Cornwallis wrote in pressing terms to Spencer Phips, to invoke aid 1749.
from Massachusetts ; but, though his honor recommended to Dec. 18.
the General Court the necessary measures to enable him to
comply with this request, the court declined seconding his

---

[1] Haliburton's N. S. i. 136–142 ; Bancroft, iv. 44–46 ; Hildreth, ii. 435.

CHAP.
VII.

proposals, and the English commander was left to depend on his own resources.[1]

1750.
June 9.

The renown acquired by Governor Shirley in the capture of Louisburg awakened in his mind an earnest desire to gather fresh laurels on the same field of action ; and, as the failure of the commission for the adjustment of boundaries seemed ominous of a renewal of hostilities, he was by no means reluctant to hasten on a war which presented a prospect of forwarding his own interests. A gentleman of great political sagacity, and of indefatigable industry ; the eulogist of Cumberland, of Bedford, and of Halifax ; ardent, intriguing, and of a boundless ambition ; possessing a singular capacity for framing, if not for executing, stupendous designs ; cautious in his movements ; regular in his habits ; and fond of the discipline of military life, — these qualities, joined to his power of imposing upon the credulity of others by an affectation of superior wisdom, gave him great influence both at home and abroad. Standing, also, foremost on the list of colonels in the army ; regarded with confidence by the English government as well as by his own ; and having paid great attention to the condition of all the colonies, he expected, in case of war, to be promoted at once to the charge of a regiment, if not to be made a general officer. Hence, in his despatches to England,

1749.
April.

he not only urged the necessity of opposing the designs of the French, and destroying their settlements at the eastward, but, in his speeches at home, he recommended to Massachusetts to extend her settlements into such parts of that territory as were obviously included in the provincial charter, to be beforehand with her rivals, and to frustrate their schemes.[2]

The possessions of the French at the eastward were much more extensive than those of the English. In Acadia, they

[1] Mass. Archives; History of the War, p. 7; Hutchinson, iii. 12, 13; Haliburton's N. S. i. ; Minot, i. 132, 133; Bancroft, iv. 67–72.

[2] Hutchinson, iii. 18; 1 M. H. Coll. vii. 69; Chalmers, Revolt, ii. 259.

had seized upon the isthmus near Bay Verte, and had built a fort, which secured the passage to Quebec without going upon the ocean. Some thirteen miles distant, towards Chiegnecto, they had a block house ; and three miles farther on they had a large and strong fort, mounting upwards of thirty guns, within half a mile of the basin of Chiegnecto, at the bottom of the Bay of Fundy. Upon the St. John's they had also built two forts before the peace of Utrecht, which were now repaired and strengthened ; and there was a rumor, which obtained credit, though unfounded, that they had begun a settlement upon the Kennebec, which secured to them the carrying place from that river to the Chaudière. The garrisons at these stations were not, indeed, large ; nor were any of the forts of sufficient strength to withstand a long siege. But the indomitable activity of the French, and their influence with the Indian tribes, whose passions they could easily inflame, and whose war chiefs they could readily induce to grasp again the tomahawk, made them a formidable foe ; and the facilities of communication from one point to another enabled them to concentrate their forces wherever an attack was threatened with great expedition. For these reasons, the difficulties to be encountered in dislodging them from the country were much greater than they would have been had the English been well fortified in the parts which they occupied, and had they paid equal attention to the formation of a chain of posts, not distantly separated from each other, and easily accessible.[1]

Nor was it at the east alone that clouds were gathering. It was well known that, for years past, the French had been active at the west and at the south. Before the war of 1744, they had thrown up fortifications upon the back of Virginia, Pennsylvania, and New York, as well as near the crest of the

[1] MS. Report, s. d., in MS. Letters and Papers, 1721–1760, in Mass. Hist. Soc. Coll. ; Letters and Mems. relating to Cape Breton, &c., by an impartial Frenchman, Lond. 1760, p. 294 ; Hutchinson, iii. 19.

CHAP.
VII.
1749.

Green Mountains, in Vermont; and, stretching from these points across the country by the way of Detroit to the banks of the Illinois, and down the Mississippi to the Gulf of Mexico, they had sent out exploring parties, and established military posts and magazines of stores, so that the frontiers of the English were surrounded with their intrenchments, designed as a bulwark against British ambition.[1]

1754.

Such was the state of affairs at the opening of the year 1754. The progress of the English colonies had been so rapid, and their growth so unparalleled in the annals of history, that America was beginning to attract a degree of attention which had not been heretofore bestowed upon her territory; and, as the importance of the settlements, in both a military and a commercial point of view, could not but be evident to every one who considered their position, the difficulties with France, which were upon the eve of convulsing the country to its centre, to the eye of the philosopher opened, in the future, a prospect of surpassing interest, and promised results whose importance was not circumscribed by the narrow limits of one generation, but which have reached onwards to our own day, and which will continue to be felt so long as free institutions shall be supported in this land.

The difference in the condition of the colonies of France and of England is worthy of notice. All the possessions of France in America were united under one governor, whose power was nearly as absolute as the power of the king. The genius of the people and of the government was military; and the blighting influence of feudal organization extended ove the whole country. The priest, the soldier, and the nobl ruled in Canada; the *habitans* were in a state of abject servitude. The hardy *coureurs des bois*, who roamed over the delightful regions extending from the great lakes to the banks

[1] Letters and Mems. relating to   17; Hutchinson, iii. 19; Minot, i. Cape Breton, 295; Burr's Discourse,   181; N. Am. Rev. for July, 1839.

of the Father of Waters, enjoyed, indeed, a degree of inde- CHAP
pendence during their wanderings; but at home, in the winter VII.
season, when confined to their wigwams, they were scarcely the 1754.
same beings, but submitted with listlessness to the sway of the
priesthood. The Indians were the natural allies of the French.
Living with them on terms of familiar intercourse, speaking
their language, adopted into their tribes, and cohabiting with
their squaws, the lower order of the white population of Canada
became deeply enamoured of the charms of a forest life; and
by this means a connecting link was formed between the races,
of which the Jesuits availed themselves to strengthen the bonds
of union, and to secure the coöperation of those whose modes
of warfare, secret and cunning, rendered them dangerous as
foes, but valuable as allies, and serviceable in forwarding their
schemes of aggrandizement.[1]

The British colonies, on the other hand, were scattered over
a wide extent of territory, and were divided into distinct and
independent governments. Unaccustomed to act in concert,
save where a mutual confederacy or a particular exigency
joined together a few neighbors, each had its own ends to
serve and its own interests to advance. They were more
nearly agreed in their jealousy of English encroachment,
though all acknowledged allegiance to the crown, and unitedly
repudiated the charge of disloyalty. In different parts of the
country dissimilar languages were spoken, indicative of the
various origin of the emigrants. From Germany, from Swe-
den, and from Holland, as well as from England, had come
those who settled the regions bordering upon the Atlantic;
and they brought with them to these shores the manners and
customs of the land of their birth, and the opinions and prejudices to which they had been accustomed. They harmonized
chiefly in one purpose — of possessing and subduing the fair
fields before them, and of wresting from the soil by diligent

[1] Minot, i. 177, 178.

CHAP.
VII.
1754.

labor, and from the ocean by an extended commerce, the means of subsistence for themselves and their families. Their intercourse with the Indians was less cordial than that of the French. There were few points of affinity between them, and they had few interests in common. In rare cases they lived in proximity without collision ; but nearly every where their paths were different, and the red man had little sympathy with the pale face, who was driving him back from his accustomed haunts to a new home in the pathless forests of the distant west.[1]

1752.

1753.
Oct. 30.

Dec. 15.

1754.
Feb.

A war between England and France seemed inevitable. Hostilities, indeed, had already commenced at the south ; and the English traders among the Twigtwees, near the Miami, whom Gist had recently visited, being accused of invading the territory of the French, they were seized as prisoners and taken to Presqu'Isle, where a strong fort was building.[2] In the following year, a letter was sent by Governor Dinwiddie, of Virginia, to St. Pierre, the commander of the French forces on the Ohio, requiring him to withdraw from the dominions of England ; and upon his refusal to comply, instant complaint was made to the court of Great Britain, and a body of troops, three hundred in number,[3] was ordered to be raised for the protection of the frontiers. In this expedition George Washington, then just twenty-two, commenced his military career ; and the youthful Virginian, whose days had been spent in the peaceful pursuit of a surveyor of lands, promptly responded to the call of his country, and was appointed lieutenant colonel of the troops raised for the public defence. Little did he

[1] Minot, i. 178, 179.

[2] Olden Times, ii. 9, 10 ; Plain Facts, 42 ; Ramsay's Am. Rev. 36 ; Sparks's Franklin, iv. 71, 330 ; Sparks's Washington ; N. Am. Rev. for July, 1839 ; Parkman's Conspiracy of Pontiac, 87.

[3] Two companies of 100 men each were first ordered to be raised, the one by Captain Trent and the other by

Major Washington, who was to command the whole. Afterwards, 100 more were raised, and the command of the whole was given to Colonel Joshua Fry ; and Washington was appointed lieutenant colonel, and made second in command. Sparks's Washington, ii. 1–4, notes ; Sargent's Braddock's Expedition, 40.

foresee the consequences which were to result from this move- CHAP.
ment; little did his associates dream of the honors which   VII.
awaited him in the future.   Then was the seed sown; the har- 1754.
vest was not far distant.[1]

It was late in the spring, when the wild flowers covered the May 1.
sides of the Alleghanies and the birds were chanting their
merriest songs, that the little army, led by the gallant officer
who had already won golden opinions by his bravery and
merit, took up its line of march towards the head quarters of
the enemy.   At the end of four weeks a skirmish occurred, in May 28.
which ten of the French, under Jumonville, were killed, and
twenty-one made prisoners.[2]   While waiting for reënforce-
ments, the victors intrenched themselves at the Great Meadows,
and gave to their stronghold the name of Fort Necessity.
Soon an alarm was spread that several hundred French and July 1.
Indians were advancing from the Ohio,[3] and two days after an July 3.
engagement ensued.   The English were but a handful compared to their assailants; but when was ever true courage
known to shrink from even a superior force?   The action
lasted nine hours, during which nearly two hundred of the
French and their allies were slain.   The situation of Washington was perilous; and, hemmed in on every side, he found
himself compelled to yield, and to submit to the terms which
were harshly imposed and shamefully broken.   Thus the banks
of the Ohio remained in the possession of the French; forts
were built to secure their advantage; the Indians were confirmed in their defection from the English; and the frontiers
were again exposed to their ravages.[4]

[1] Plain Facts, 45, 46; Ramsay's
Am. Rev. 37; Chalmers, Revolt, ii.
264–267; 1 M. H. Coll. vii. 70–75;
Gordon's Am. Rev. i. 88; Sparks's
Washington, ii. 1, 431, 446; Sparks's
Franklin, iii. 251–263; N. Am. Rev.
for July, 1839; Lord Mahon's Hist.
Eng. i. 307, note.

[2] On this affair, see Sparks's Washington, ii. 26, &c.

[3] Sargent, Hist. Braddock's Exped.
49, 50, says this intelligence was received June 29, while Washington
was at Gist's plantation; and July 1,
his troops returned to the Great
Meadows.

[4] Pouchot's Mems. i. 14–17; Hist.
of the War, 18, 19; 1 M. H. Coll. vi.
138–144, and vii. 73, 74; Chalmers,
Revolt, ii. 268, 269; Minot, i. 184;

CHAP.
VII.

Representations had by this time been made to the English government of the necessity of union in the colonies to resist the aggressions of the French ;[1] and, approving the plan, a "grand congress of commissaries," or delegates from the several provinces, was appointed to be held at Albany, as well to treat with the Six Nations, whose alliance it was important to secure,[2] as to concert a scheme for a general union of the British colonies.   Already, by the statesmen of America,[3] had similar proposals been made ; and Benjamin Franklin, the "Prometheus of modern times,"[4] a native of Boston, but a resident of Philadelphia ; like Washington, distinguished for his personal merit, and, like Washington, imbued with a glowing devotion to liberty ; ingenious, persevering, and profoundly sagacious ; whose attainments in natural science had attracted the attention of the philosophers of the old world, and whose brilliant speculations in political science were destined to be equally conspicuous ; inspired by the genius of advancing civilization, had wrought out in his own mind problems of sublime interest for his country and the world, and was busied in sketching the outlines of a confederacy which should unite the whole American people upon the broad basis of common interests and a mutual dependence.   "A voluntary union," said he, "entered into by the colonies themselves, would be preferable to one imposed by Parliament ; for it would be, perhaps, not much more difficult to procure, and more easy to alter and

1753.
Aug. 28
and
Sep. 19.
1754.
Jun. 14.

1753.
March.

Sparks's Washington, ii. 474 et seq.; Bancroft, iv. 116–121; Conspiracy of Pontiac, 88, 89; Warburton's Conquest of Canada, ii. 7–10; Sargent's Braddock's Expedition, 49–55. "This skirmish," says Lord Mahon, "of small importance, perhaps, in itself, was yet among the principal causes of the war.   It is no less memorable as the first appearance in the pages of history of one of their brightest ornaments — of that great and good man, General Washington."   Hist. England, i. 294, Appleton's ed.

[1] This project was started in 1750. Bancroft, iv. 75.

[2] Johnson, in Doc. Hist. N. Y. ii. 672; Letter of Lieutenant Governor De Lancey, in Trumbull MSS. i. 79; Shirley's Speech of April 2, in Boston Weekly News Letter for April 25.

[3] Penn had concerted a plan for the union of the colonies as early as 1698. N. Y. Colon. Doc'ts, iv. 296, 297.

[4] Kant's Works, quoted in Bancroft, iv. 255.

improve, as circumstances should require and experience di- CHAP.
VII.
rect."[1]

Happily for America, these views, which, had they been 1754.
uttered a half century before, would have been received with
distrust, as leaning towards independence, were forced upon
the notice of the statesmen of England by the condition of the
colonies and the encroachments of France. Hence the proposition for a congress at Albany, acceptable as it was on this
side of the Atlantic, if it originated here, was favored by the
mother country and sanctioned by her authority.[2]

After some delay this congress met. Delegates from seven June 18
or 19.
provinces were present;[3] and messengers had been sent to the
Indian castles to request their attendance, but few of them
arrived until the last of the month. The members of this
assembly, both for abilities and fortune, were among the most
considerable men in America ; and never had there been convened in New York a more eminent body.[4] The first day was
spent in organizing the convention and settling the preliminaries, after which business was promptly despatched. The
negotiations with the Indians were made at intervals, and the
"chain of friendship" was thoroughly brightened. But the
question of a union of the colonies was the all-important theme ;
and on Monday a committee was appointed, of one from each Jun. 24.
province, to "prepare and receive plans or schemes for the
union of the colonies, and to digest them into one general plan

<hr>

[1] Anon. Lett. from Philadelphia,
attributed to Franklin; and Clark's
Lett. in 1 M. H. Coll. iv. 74. Comp.
also Bancroft, iv. 75, 91.

[2] Hutchinson, iii. 20 ; Doc. Hist.
N. Y. ii. 545.

[3] The delegates from NEW YORK
were De Lancey, Murray, Johnson,
Chambers, and Smith ; from MASSA-
CHUSETTS, Welles, Chandler, Hutch-
inson, Partridge, and Worthington ;
from NEW HAMPSHIRE, Atkinson,
Wibird, Weare, and Sherburne ; from
CONNECTICUT, Pitkins, Wolcott, and
Williams ; from RHODE ISLAND, Hop-

kins and Howard ; from MARYLAND,
Tasker and Barnes ; and from PENN-
SYLVANIA, Penn, Peters, Norris, and
Franklin. See Johnson, in Doc. Hist.
N. Y. i. 553, 554 ; and 1 M. H. Coll.
vii. 76, 203. The colonies to the
south of the Potomac were not repre-
sented.

[4] It was compared, at the time, by
a spirited writer, to "one of the ancient Greek conventions for supporting their expiring liberty against the
power of the Persian empire," &c.
1 M. H. Coll. vii. 77. Comp. also
Hutchinson, iii. 20.

CHAP. for the inspection of this board." [1]   The members of this com-
VII. mittee present to us names distinguished in the annals of our
1754. country.   They were Thomas Hutchinson, of Massachusetts,
afterwards governor of the province, a man of splendid abilities, but loving money and office ; Theodore Atkinson, of New
Hampshire, chief justice of that province, conspicuous for his
virtues, and of unassuming modesty ; William Pitkin, of Connecticut, afterwards governor of the colony, active, persevering,
and of excellent abilities ; Stephen Hopkins, of Rhode Island,
governor of that province for nine years, and a signer of the
memorable Declaration of Independence ; Benjamin Franklin,
of Pennsylvania, also a signer of the Declaration of Independence ; Benjamin Tasker, of Maryland ; and William Smith, of
New York, a lawyer of eminence, afterwards a member of his
majesty's Council and a judge of the Court of King's Bench.
Franklin was, without doubt, the master spirit of the committee ; and, as the movement was one in which he was deeply
interested, he had brought with him the "heads" of a plan
which he had personally "projected." [2]

Jun. 28.   On the 28th, "hints of a scheme" of union were presented,
of which copies were taken by the commissioners of the respective provinces.   These "hints" were debated with singular
eloquence for several days, in speeches which were at once
"both nervous and pathetic ;" but, after nearly a fortnight had
July 10. passed, no decision was reached.   At that date "Mr. Franklin
reported the draught in a new form," which was "read paragraph by paragraph and debated, and the further consideration
of it deferred to the afternoon," when it was adopted. [3]   By its
terms, the general government was to be administered by a
president, appointed and supported by the crown, and a council,
chosen by the representatives of the several colonies.   This
council was to consist of forty-eight members ; of which Mas-

---

[1] Johnson, in Doc. Hist. N. Y. ii.   [3] Johnson, in Doc. Hist. N. Y. ii.
564.   570, 571, 589, 591, 605, 611–615;
   [2] Hutchinson, iii. 21.   1 M. H. Coll. vii. 77.

sachusetts and Virginia were each to choose seven, New Hampshire and Rhode Island two each, Connecticut five, New York, Maryland, North Carolina, and South Carolina four each, New Jersey three, and Pennsylvania six. A new election of members was to be made triennially ; and on the death or resignation of any member, his place was to be supplied at the next sitting of the colony he represented. After the first three years, the quota of each province was to be determined by the proportion it paid into the general treasury ; though no province was to be entitled to more than seven, or less than two, councillors. This council was empowered to choose its own speaker, but could neither be dissolved nor prorogued, nor could it continue in session longer than six weeks at one time without the consent of its members or the special command of the crown. The assent of the president was required to all acts of the council to give to them validity ; and it was his duty to cause such acts to be executed. With the advice of the council he could likewise hold treaties with the Indians, regulate trade, make peace or declare war, purchase their lands for the crown if not within the limits of particular provinces, settle such purchases, and make laws for their government until the crown should form them into distinct governments. The council was further authorized to raise and pay soldiers, build forts for public defence, equip vessels to guard the coast and protect the trade on the ocean and lakes, and levy such duties as were necessary to defray the expenses accruing ; but no men were to be impressed in any colony without the consent of its legislature. A quorum of the council was to consist of twenty-five members, among whom there was to be one or more from a majority of the colonies ; and the laws made by that body were not to be repugnant, but " as near as may be agreeable," to the laws of England, and were to be transmitted to the king for approval as soon as practicable. If not disapproved within three years, they were to remain in force. All military officers were to be nominated by the president, and approved by

CHAP.
VII.
1754.
the council before receiving their commissions; and all civil officers were to be nominated by the council, and approved by the president. The first meeting of the government was to be held at Philadelphia, and was to be called by the president as soon as convenient after his appointment.[1]

Such was the confederacy of 1754, framed in July, just twenty-two years before the Declaration of American Independence, and assented to by two persons, at least, whose names are affixed to that memorable instrument. The constitution, as will be seen, was a compromise between the prerogative and popular power. It was by no means easy, in its arrangement, to avoid giving offence to both the crown and the colonies. The jealousy of the latter was as great as that of the former; and concessions leaning either way would have been instantly rejected. It is, therefore, a high tribute to the wisdom of Franklin that the plan, which he had "the principal hand in framing," was seriously opposed by no one on the royalist side but De Lancey, of New York, and that it was approved at the time by every member of the congress but him.[2]

As the commissioners from the several governments were desired to lay the foregoing plan before their constituents, and as copies of the same were ordered to be transmitted to the chief magistrates of the unrepresented colonies, there was nothing binding in the action of the congress until confirmed by the assemblies. Before these the matter was brought; but, when the reports were made by the several delegates, not one was inclined to part with so great a share of power as was to be given to the general government. In England the plan met with a similar fate. It was transmitted, with the other proceedings of the convention, to be laid before the king; but the

[1] Trumbull MSS. i. 93, 94; Johnson, in Doc. Hist. N. Y. ii. 612–615; Minot, i. 188–198; Trumbull's Connecticut, ii. 541–544; Chalmers, Revolt, ii. 271, 272; 1 M. H. Coll. vii. 203–207.

[2] For the alleged cause of De Lancey's opposition, see 1 M. H. Coll. vii. 77.

Board of Trade, on receiving the minutes, were astonished at the CHAP.
character of the draught; and reflecting men in the old world VII.
"dreaded American union as the keystone of independence."[1]   1754.

A few months later, a private correspondence was carried Dec.
on between Governor Shirley, of Massachusetts, and Benjamin
Franklin, who had recently arrived in Boston on a visit to the Oct.
home of his childhood, relative to the plan of a union of the
colonies.[2]   Governor Shirley was in favor of an assembly to
consist of all the governors and a certain number of the Council of the colonies, with power to agree upon measures of
defence, and to draw upon England for money necessary to
execute these measures, to be reimbursed by a tax levied by
Parliament.   To this scheme Franklin objected in several
ingenious letters, which were afterwards published;[3] and,
without opposing a more intimate union with Great Britain by
representatives in Parliament, provided a reasonable number
was allowed, he, at the same time, urged a repeal of the acts
restraining the trade and manufactures of the colonies, as unjust
and impolitic.   It was of no more importance, in his estimation, to the general state, "whether a merchant, a smith, or a
hatter grew rich in Old or in New England," than "whether
an iron manufacturer lived at Birmingham or Sheffield."   If
in both cases they were subjects of the king, whatever liberties the latter enjoyed should be enjoyed also by the former.[4]

Early in this year the attention of the General Court was 1754.
called by Governor Shirley to the encroachments of the French Mar. 28.
within the limits of Massachusetts; and a small army was proposed to be raised, to march to the eastward to break up the

---

[1] Clarke's Lett. in 1 M. H. Coll. iv.
85; Report of Committee of Connecticut, in 1 M. H. Coll. vii. 207–214;
Hutchinson, iii. 23; Trumbull's Connecticut, ii. 355–357; Smith's N. Y.
ii. 180 et seq.
[2] Letter of Oliver Partridge, of
October 21, in MS. Letters of Israel
Williams, vol. i.

[3] In the London Magazine for
February, 1766. Comp. Franklin's
Works, iii. 578, iv. 172; and see Gordon's Am. Rev. i. 91–94.
[4] Hutchinson, iii. 23–25; Franklin's Works, iv. 251; Bancroft, iv.
172–175.

CHAP.
VII.

1754.
April 9.
June 2.

Jun. 26.

Aug.

settlements, or, at all events, to secure by forts the passes from Quebec for New England by the way of Kennebec. The governor was requested to assume the direction of this affair; and embarking for Falmouth, with a quorum of the Council and several of the House, a conference was held, and a treaty was made with the Norridgewock and Penobscot Indians, to prevent their being alarmed. The forces which had been raised, consisting of eight hundred men, under John Winslow, of Marshfield, who had served in the Spanish war, were then ordered to the Kennebec; and a fort, called Fort Halifax, was built about three quarters of a mile below Taconnet Falls, and thirty-seven miles above Fort Richmond. A second fort was likewise built eighteen miles below the first, at a place called Cushnoc, now the site of the city of Augusta, to which the name of Fort Western was given, in honor of an acquaintance of the governor, resident in Sussex, England. The expedition, however, which originated with Governor Shirley, was of little benefit to the province; and both French and Indians, relinquishing the scheme of seizing the British possessions, which had long been agitated, turned their attention to the defence of their own homes.[1]

Four projects were now devised, in three of which Governor Shirley was more or less concerned.[2] Making his own interest his idol, and every thing else subservient, his thirst for renown, which swallowed up all other feelings, led him to scruple at no measures for the attainment of the object which was nearest

[1] Mass. Rec's; Winslow's MS. Journal; Stirling's Vindication of Shirley, 2–5; Hist. of the War, 119; Mortimer's England, iii. 510, ed. 1766; Hutchinson, iii. 25–27; 1 M. H. Coll. vii. 88; Minot, i. 184–187; Warburton's Conquest of Canada, ii. 11. Governor Shirley, at the conclusion of this expedition, sent despatches to England, informing the ministry of the alarming aspect of affairs in the colonies, and soliciting aid to resist

the encroachments of the French. Mortimer's England, iii. 510.

[2] Hist. of the War, 25. It appears that, long before the arrival of Braddock, Governor Shirley had made preparation for the prosecution of these enterprises, and had issued commissions to various officers. See Williams's MSS. i. 107, 108, 113, 114, 115, 117, under dates January 4, February 1, February 10, February 11, March 7, and March 10, 1755.

his heart; and, though the blandishments of power never occasioned in him the exile of common sense, the fervor with which
he entered into the prosecution of his schemes, and the uncommon application which he brought to bear upon every point,
spread an infectious enthusiasm among his associates, and
blinded them to the difficulties which must inevitably be encountered. Mr. Shirley, indeed, seemed never to flag. To
fatigue he was a stranger. He was fertile in expedients to
meet every emergency. He could perform more labor, and
travel more miles, in a given time, than almost any other man
in New England. He was here, there, and every where.
Profuse in embraces, in compliments, and tears, smiles and
caresses were lavished where necessary; flattery was poured
out with prodigal hypocrisy; and with well-feigned wisdom he
could bear his part in the most grave deliberations, duping the
unwary by his brilliant harangues, and seducing the discerning
to an approval of his measures.[1]

The first project for the conduct of the war was that in
which Braddock, a personal favorite of the Duke of Cumberland, was the prominent actor. This officer, whose unfortunate end is to be attributed chiefly to his own folly, embarked
for America in the winter, holding a commission as commander-
in-chief of the colonial forces, and of the English troops which
accompanied him. Negotiations were then pending between
England and France, professedly for an amicable adjustment
of all matters in dispute; but the proposals of England —
which demanded that France should destroy all her forts as
far as the Wabash, raze Niagara and Crown Point, surrender
the peninsula of Nova Scotia, with a strip of land twenty
leagues wide along the Bay of Fundy and the Atlantic, and
leave the intermediate country to the St. Lawrence a neu-

---

[1] Washington, like most others, on his first introduction to Shirley, was "perfectly charmed" by his "charac- ter and appearances." "I think," he says, "his every word and action dis- cover in him the gentleman and poli- tician." Letter to Fairfax, April 20, 1755, in Works, ii. 74.

CHAP. tral desert — seemed so preposterous that they were unhes-
VII. itatingly rejected. The French king was willing to sacrifice
1754. for peace all but honor and the protection due to his subjects;
but he was unwilling to relinquish all for which he had been
so long contending. He would consent that New England
should reach on the east to the Penobscot, and be divided from
Canada on the north by the summit of the intervening high-
lands, and that the valley of the Ohio should be left as neutral
territory; but to ask him to yield more was, in effect, only to
prepare the way for the complete subjugation of his dominions
in the new world.[1]

1755.   Towards the last of February the squadron of Commodore
Feb. 20.
Keppel anchored in Hampton Road; about the middle of
Mar. 14 March the transports arrived; and a month later, by the
–18.
Apr. 13. orders of Braddock, Shirley and the other governors met him
at Alexandria, to consult upon measures for his majesty's service.[2] The general had received positive instructions to conduct in person an expedition to Fort Du Quesne; for the preservation of Oswego and the reduction of Niagara, he proposed
that the regiments of Shirley and Pepperrell should proceed to
Lake Ontario; a portion of the provincial troops, commanded
by General Johnson, was to march to Crown Point; and the
New England troops, assembled by his majesty's directions,
were to sail to the eastward to reduce the French settlements
in Nova Scotia.[3]

The expedition under Braddock, consisting of twenty-two
June 7 hundred men, left Fort Cumberland early in June; and a
to 10.
march of over a hundred miles lay before the army to reach
its destination. The country through which he was to pass

[1] Sargent's Braddock's Expedition, 188, 189, 287; Bancroft, iv. 176, 177.
[2] Shirley set out for Alexandria the last of March. Letter to Ephraim Williams, of March 29, 1755, in Williams's MSS. i. 121.
[3] Journal H. of R. for 1755, 493–

496; Precis des Faits, 160, 168; Pouchot's Mems. i. 44–46; Stirling's Vindication of Shirley, 7–11; 1 M. H. Coll. vii. 90; Hutchinson, iii. 31, 32; Johnson, in Doc. Hist. N. Y. ii. 648–651; Conspiracy of Pontiac, 93, 94; Sargent's Braddock's Expedition, 132, 133, 300–307.

was a trackless waste — a portion of it not inaptly named the
Shades of Death ; and innumerable difficulties were to be surmounted in traversing so desolate a region, across the Alleghanies, through unfrequented woods and dangerous defiles. A
scout of six hundred men had been sent in advance, to open
the roads and collect provisions ; [1] but the main body dragged
slowly along, with military exactness, heedless of the caution
which had been given by Franklin, that " the Indians were dex-
terous in laying and executing ambuscades." " The savages,"
was the self-confident reply of the general, " may be formidable
to your raw American militia ; upon the king's regulars and
disciplined troops it is impossible they should make any impression." Washington had joined the army at Will's Creek,
before it left Fort Cumberland ; and, better acquainted with
the craft of the Indians, he could not but observe with the
deepest concern the fatal delusion which had seized upon his
superior, and trembled for the consequences which must result
from his temerity.

It was no easy task to conduct the movements of an army,
encumbered with a load of needless baggage, threading its way
with ceaseless toil through the intricacies of a forest abound-
ing in quagmires, anon ascending steep, rugged hills, and then
descending headlong declivities ; but at length the advanced
body of twelve hundred men, including the four hundred under
St. Clair and eight hundred under Braddock, reached the
junction of the Monongahela and Youghiogeny, twelve miles
distant from Fort Du Quesne. The nature of the ground here
debarred the crossing of the stream, and a smoother path was
sought. The first passage was easily made ; and the troops,
elated at the prospect before them, though enfeebled by toil
and an unwholesome diet, moved proudly down the margin of

CHAP.
VII.

1755.

May 30.

May 30.

July 8.

July 9.

---

[1] The whole blame of the failure
of this expedition cannot be justly
ascribed to Braddock, as it is admitted
by Mr. Sparks that there was unwarrantable delay in making the necessary arrangements for its prosecution
on the part of the contractors who
were to furnish the army with supplies. Writings of Washington, ii.
77, note.

CHAP. the stream to the stirring music of the drum and the fife, which
VII. pealed for the first time upon those vast solitudes, frightening
1755. the jay, which screamed discordantly as it wheeled through the
air, and driving to their lairs the wolf and the catamount.

Warned of the approach of the invaders, with the consent
of Contrecœur, two hundred and fifty French and Canadians,
and six hundred and fifty Indians[1] under Beaujeu, hastened
early in the morning to a spot near a brook previously selected
for an ambuscade. The narrow road which descended to this
stream was tunnelled through deep and gloomy woods, whose
sepulchral arches stretched far away, like those of a vast Gothic
cathedral; and two ravines, bordered by trees and bushes, furnished a concealment, where the Indians ensconced themselves,
and, levelling their guns through the openings in the branches,
poured a deadly fire upon the advancing columns. The fierce
onset was courageously met, and the general himself pressed
forward to share the danger and animate his troops; but all
was in vain. The combat was desperate, and column after
column of the English were slain. Of eighty-six officers
twenty-six were killed and thirty-seven were wounded; of the
men more than half were killed or wounded. Sir Peter Hal-
ket was among the killed; and young Shirley, the son of the
governor and the secretary of Braddock, was shot through the
head. Gage, who led the vanguard, and who, twenty years
later, saw his routed battalions recoil in disorder before the
murderous fire from the breastwork on Bunker's Hill, was
among the wounded; as were Colonel Burton and Sir John
Sinclair. Gates, the future conqueror of Burgoyne, escaped
unharmed, as did also Washington, though two horses were
shot under him, and four balls pierced his coat. Five horses
were disabled under the commander-in-chief; at last a bullet
pierced his side, and he fell. The rout was complete; and
July 13. four days after, as the army retreated, Braddock died. To

[1] Such is the French account. Doc'ts in Mass. Archives, ix. 211.

the traveller, who passes over the national road, his grave is CHAP
still pointed out, about a mile from Fort Necessity.[1]   VII.

The second expedition, under Shirley and Pepperrell, was to 1755.
proceed to Lake Ontario for the preservation of Oswego and
the reduction of Niagara. Mr. Shirley, after the consultation Apr. 18.
at Alexandria, returned by the way of New York and Hartford May 13.
to Boston, to prepare for the discharge of this trust; and having attended an assembly for the election of councillors, and May 28.
transacted other business relative to the campaign, he left the
capital in the province sloop to proceed to the westward. The Jun. 28.
tidings of Braddock's defeat and death reached Boston subse- July 23.
quent to his departure; and as he arrived at Albany in about July 10.
a fortnight, the news was not communicated to him until he
had left for Oswego. By this event the chief command of the July 30
forces of the country devolved upon him; and he was in the
position to which he had long aspired, with no superior on this
side of the Atlantic, and on the high road to honor and distinction in England. As may well be supposed, to one of his temperament, who had been looking forward for years to this
consummation of his wishes, there was a slight degree of intox-

[1] On Braddock's expedition, see
French Doc'ts in Mass. Archives, ix.
211; Winslow's MS. Journal, fols. 136
–141; Letter to the People of England, 33 et seq.; Hist. of the War,
23–25; Pouchot's Mems. i. 37–44;
Smith's Narr.; Entick, i. 143; Chauncy's Lett. on Ohio Defeat, 4; 1 M. H.
Coll. vii. 91–94; 2 M. H. Coll. viii. 153
–157; Hutchinson, iii. 32; Mortimer's
England, 514; Chalmers, Revolt, ii.
275; Sparks's Washington, ii. 86–88,
473; Warburton's Conquest of Canada, ii. 16–26; Conspiracy of Pontiac,
94–101; Bancroft, iv. 184–192; Hildreth, ii. 459–461. After his return
from this expedition, Washington
wrote from Mount Vernon, August 2,
1755, "It is true we have been beat-
en, shamefully beaten by a handful of
men, who only intended to molest and
disturb our march. Victory was their

smallest expectation. But see the
wondrous works of Providence, and
the uncertainty of human things!
We, but a few moments before, believed our numbers almost equal to
the Canadian force; they only expected to annoy us. Yet, contrary to all
expectation and human probability,
and even to the common course of
things, we were totally defeated, and
sustained the loss of every thing."
Sparks's Washington, ii. 90. The
visit to Braddock's field, which resulted in the discovery of the bones
of the slain, has been often compared
to the discovery of the bones of the
soldiers of the legions of Varus, in the
forest of Teutenburg, as described by
Tacitus, Ann. b. i. ch. 61. Smith's
Discourse of April 5, 1757, pub. at
London, 1759.

CHAP. ication in the possession of such extensive power ; and he could
VII. hold up his head more proudly than ever, under the conscious-
1755. ness that whoever stood in the way of his preferment could
boast less merit than himself in claiming a reward for their
services, and could plead less eloquently for the favor of the
crown.[1] Yet he was never so intent on contemplating his own
grandeur as to lose all patience in laboring to earn it. " *Honor
virtutis præmium*," was the motto of his ancestors ; and this
motto he was ready to adopt for himself, allowing him to inter-
pret it to suit his own wishes.[2]

Albany was the grand theatre of the preparations for the
northern expedition against Fort Frederick, as well as for that
to the westward for the reduction of Niagara. The general,
July 10. on his arrival, however, did not find things in the forwardness
which he had reason to expect. The provincials, discontented
with the inactivity of a long encampment, were anxious to be
in motion ; and his own troops were filing off in different
directions from Schenectady towards Oswego.[3] The distance
of the latter place from Albany is towards three hundred miles.
Over the first sixteen miles, to Schenectady, there was a good
wagon road ; and from thence to the Little Falls, in the Mohawk, at Canajoharie, a distance of sixty-five miles, the communication was by bateaux set against a rapid stream, in dry seasons so shallow that the boatmen were frequently obliged to
turn out and draw their craft over the rifts with inconceivable
labor. At the Little Falls was a portage, a mile wide, over
which the bateaux were transported on sleds, the ground being

---

[1] See Johnson, in Doc. Hist. N. Y.
ii. 684–689.

[2] He would probably have interpreted it, " *Office* is the reward of *good
management*."

[3] Governor Shirley's instructions to
Ephraim Williams to march to Albany were dated May 31, 1755; and
Colonel Williams arrived there early
in July. Letter of Shirley of May 31,
in Williams's MSS. i., and letters of
E. Williams of July 8 and July 15,
in ibid. 150, 153. Seth Pomeroy, in
a letter dated July 15, in ibid., speaks
of Shirley's and Pepperrell's regiments
as then on their march to Oswego, and
of General Johnson's regiment as ready
to march for Crown Point, but as being detained for the want of stores.

too marshy to admit the use of wheeled carriages. The same CHAP.
conveyance was used at the Great Carrying Place, at Oneida, VII.
sixty miles beyond the Little Falls — the current thither being 1755.
still adverse and extremely swift. Taking water again, the
troops entered Wood Creek, which leads into the Oneida Lake,
distant forty miles. This stream, whose banks were fringed
with thick woods, was then much obstructed with old logs and
fallen trees. The Oneida Lake stretches from east to west
some thirty miles, and in calm weather is passed with great
facility. At its western extremity opens the Onondaga River,
leading to Oswego, situated at its entrance, on the south side
of Lake Ontario. The passage through this river, whose current flows with surprising rapidity, and which abounds with
rifts and rocks, was extremely difficult and hazardous. The
principal obstruction is a fall, about eleven feet perpendicular,
twelve miles short of Oswego.[1]

Through this long and "amphibious" march the army proceeded with great risk and fatigue. For the management of
the bateaux, of which at least five hundred were prepared,
General Shirley had engaged all the young men in the county
of Albany, who had been formerly employed in the Indian
trade at Oswego. The fort at Oswego, at first garrisoned by
twenty-five men, and afterwards by fifty, had been strengthened
in the spring by a detachment of two hundred soldiers, besides May
workmen, under Captain King, and Colonel John Bradstreet,
who had fought under Pepperrell at Louisburg.[2] It was to
this point the attention of the general was directed ; and here
his forces were to be concentrated, to proceed to Niagara,
which was represented to be in a ruinous condition.

Schuyler's New Jersey regiment, consisting of five hundred
men, raised at the instance of Governor Shirley, embarked in
two divisions from Schenectady the beginning of July; and July.

---

[1] Stirling's Vindication of Shirley,
14–16; 1 M. H. Coll. vii. 95, 96.
[2] Stirling's Vindication of Shirley,

11. Marching orders were given these
troops April 16.

CHAP.
VII.

1755.

Aug.18.

Sept. 18
and 27.

Sep. 18.

the regiments of Shirley and Pepperrell were preparing to follow, when the news of the defeat of Braddock arrived.[1] This struck a damp on the spirits of the troops, and great numbers deserted ; but the general, aware of the necessity of pushing forward, pursued his march in spite of every disappointment.[2] On reaching Oswego, the necessary preparations for proceeding to Niagara were made ; but, at councils of war held soon after, intelligence was received from Niagara and Frontenac which led to the belief that a descent was contemplated on Oswego itself; and, as the works were much decayed, and the post was of the utmost importance for securing the frontiers of the western colonies and maintaining the British dominion over the great lakes and the country beyond the Apalachian range, it was deemed advisable, for its security, to commence immediately the erection of a second fort, called Ontario, on a high point commanding the old fort; and a third, called Oswego, a short distance west of the old fort. In the mean time an attempt was made to embark troops for Niagara ; but a furious storm, which raged for thirteen days, prevented its success. During this boisterous weather numbers fell sick, whose tents were an insufficient shelter ; and the Indians, well acquainted with the climate, went off, declaring the season too far advanced to admit of an expedition on the lake. The provisions for the army were by this time much reduced, though further supplies were daily expected ; but the many discouragements in the way of the expedition, owing to this and other causes, led to the postponement of the design

---

[1] Stirling's Vindication of Shirley, 12, 25. Comp. also Johnson, in Doc. Hist. N. Y. ii. 666, 684, and 1 M. H. Coll. vii. 97. Ephraim Williams, than whom no braver or more honest man could be found in the army, does not speak in flattering terms of the conduct of Shirley on this occasion, and confirms the charges of malfeasance brought against him by others. See his letters of August 14 and August 17, in Williams's MSS. i. 171, 173.

[2] A letter of Ephraim Williams, dated August 2, 1755, in Williams's MSS. i. 164, gives an account of Braddock's defeat, the news of which had reached Albany eleven days before; and Generals Shirley and Johnson endeavored to keep the matter as private as possible, for fear it should intimidate their men.

until another year ; the troops went into winter quarters ; and CHAP.
General Shirley, after seeing them comfortably settled under VII.
Lieutenant Colonel Mercer, left Oswego, and returned to Mas- 1755.
sachusetts to attend to the affairs of his government, which Oct. 24.
1756.
needed his presence. Thus ended the second project, less dis- Jan. 30.
astrously than the first, yet fruitlessly, so far as the annoyance
of the enemy was concerned.[1]

The execution of the third project, originated by Gov- 1755.
ernor Shirley,[2] was intrusted to General Johnson, of New
York, which was to proceed to Crown Point for the reduction
of Fort Frederick. The history of this extraordinary man is
singularly romantic. A native of Ireland, and a nephew of
Sir Peter Warren, the associate of Pepperrell in the reduction
of Louisburg, he embarked for America at the age of nineteen, 1734.
in consequence, it is said, of the hapless issue of a love affair.
Here he took charge of an extensive tract of wild land belonging to his uncle, and, settling in the beautiful valley of the
Mohawk, carried on a prosperous traffic with the Indians, rapidly rising to wealth and influence. His residences in the valley — for he had two — were known by the names of Johnson
Castle and Johnson Hall ; the latter of which, a substantial
building of wood and stone, is still standing in the village of
Johnstown.[3] The castle was his ordinary abode ; and here he
lived in a state of feudal magnificence, keeping open house, and
welcoming to his board the crowds of Indians who flocked to
his dwelling.[4] He had supplied the place of his first love by
a damsel of Dutch descent, who bore him several children ;
and at her decease, he found another favorite in the person of
Molly Brant, sister of the renowned Mohawk warrior, " whose
black eyes and laughing face caught his fancy, as, fluttering

---

[1] Pouchot's Mems. i. 47 ; Stirling's
Vindication, 27–40 ; 1 M. H. Coll. vii.
96, 116–124 ; Smith's N. Y. ii. 221.
[2] Stirling's Vindication, 7 ; Smith's
N. Y. ii. 206, 210.

[3] Parkman's Conspiracy of Pontiac,
80.
[4] Doc. Hist. N. Y. ii. 646 ; Mems.
of an American Lady, ii. 61.

CHAP.
VII.   with ribbons, she galloped past him at a muster of the Tryon
       county militia."[1]

1755.   No man, probably, that ever lived in America, was more
       popular with the Indians than William Johnson. He was "the
       tribune" of the Six Nations, who almost idolized him, and who
       would listen to his advice when they would scarcely heed the
       advice of their own chiefs.[2] Tall and erect in his person,
       brusque in his manners, upright in his dealings,[3] undaunted in
       his courage, and gifted by nature with brilliant oratorical pow-
       ers, he was every way fitted for the station he filled, and every
       way worthy the confidence he inspired. Some, indeed, moved
       by jealousy, have insinuated that he was "never distinguished
       for his sense or penetration;" that he was a magnificent vapor-
       er, boasting of exploits which he was unable to perform; who,
       "by the splendid representations of his secretary, and the sov-
       ereign decree of his patron," was "exalted into an eminent
       hero;" and who was indebted "to the panegyrical pen of Mr.
       Wraxall, and the *sic volo sic jubeo* of Lieutenant Governor
       De Lancey" for "that mighty renown which echoed through
       the colonies, reverberated to Europe, and elevated a raw, inex-
       perienced youth into a kind of second Marlborough."[4] All
       such representations, however, must pass for what they are
       worth; and it should be remembered that

> " Men that make
> Envy and crooked malice nourishment,
> Dare bite the best."

       Johnson was the competitor of Governor Shirley;[5] and to
       this is doubtless to be attributed much of the ill treatment
       which he experienced from the latter, and the disparaging re-

[1] Parkman's Conspiracy of Pontiac,
81.
[2] Mems. of an American Lady, ii.
61; Warburton's Conquest of Canada, ii. 31.

[3] See Johnson to the Board of
Trade, in Doc. Hist. N. Y. ii. 672.
[4] Review of Military Operations,
in 1 M. H. Coll. vii. 114.
[5] See Johnson, in Doc. Hist. N. Y.
ii. 645, 646, 687.

flections which were cast upon his conduct. Between two such CHAP.
men — the one open and frank-hearted, of a lively, generous, VII.
and impulsive spirit; the other cautious, crafty, and dissem- 1755.
bling his true feelings — no disinterested and self-sacrificing
friendship could be expected to subsist. They could tolerate
each other's presence, because both had sense enough to know
that it would be folly for either to give way to public demonstrations of anger; but beneath this outward interchange of
unmeaning compliments there was a deep-seated feeling of
hate, generated, in the one case, by the success of a rival, and
provoked, in the other, by the treachery of an enemy.[1]

Let it not be supposed, however, that Johnson was faultless;
for the defects in his character were glaring and great. His
mind was of that coarse nature which delights in sensual pleasures. He was vain of his influence with his savage allies, and
vain of the importance accruing from this source. And, possessing no remarkable delicacy of feeling, "in pushing his own
way he was never distinguished by an anxious solicitude for
the rights of others."[2]

Mr. Johnson, whose commission for the present expedition
was signed by Governors Shirley and De Lancey, was at that Apr. 16.
time at the head of Indian affairs in New York.[3] The assembly of that province was convened early in August, and, agree- Aug. 9.
ably to the request of the government of Massachusetts,
resolved to reënforce the army for Crown Point with four
hundred men. The bill for this purpose passed the House, and
was approved by the governor; but when it came before the
Council it was defeated, the design of a reënforcement was
dropped, and the assembly adjourned.[4] This, however, did not

---

[1] Johnson to Shirley, in Doc. Hist.
N. Y. ii. 663.

[2] Parkman's Conspiracy of Pontiac,
82, 83; Allen's Biog. Dict. art. JOHN-
SON; Campbell's Annals of Tryon
County, &c.

[3] Doc. Hist. N. Y. ii. 651–654;

Mass. Rec's; 1 M. H. Coll. vii. 88.

[4] Doc. Hist. N. Y. ii. 669, 670, 675
–678; 1 M. H. Coll. vii. 101, 102;
Smith's N. Y. ii. 214–217; Chauncy's
Letter on Ohio Defeat, 6, note. See
also Mass. Rec's; and Minot, i. 251,
252.

CHAP. defeat the expedition, which was, in fact, already in progress
VII.   at the time supplies were refused.   Major General Lyman, next
1755. in command to Johnson, had advanced with a detachment of
       one thousand men to the portage, or carrying place, about sixty
July 16. miles from Albany, near the head springs of the Sorel, and
Aug.   awaited the arrival of his superior at Fort Lyman, afterwards
       Fort Edward.[1]   Johnson left Albany three days after the
Aug. 8. court adjourned, with the train of artillery, and arrived at the
Aug.14. camp a week later, where a council of war was held, at which
Aug.22. all the field officers of the army were present.[2]   Towards the
Aug. 25 last of the month, with the main body of the army, consisting
or 26.   of New England militia, chiefly from Connecticut and Massa-
       chusetts,[3] he moved fourteen miles farther north, and pitched
Before his camp at the end of Lake George, which the French called
Sept. 3. St. Sacrement.[4]   Here, while his troops were reposing in indo-
       lence, admiring the beautiful and romantic scenery, or engaged
       on the Sabbath in the worship of God, he received intelligence
       that a party of French and Indians had been discovered at
       Ticonderoga, — which is situated on the isthmus between the
       north end of Lake George and the southern part of Lake
       Champlain, — but that no works were there thrown up.   The
       importance of securing this pass, which commanded the route
       to Crown Point through the lake, was so evident that Johnson
Sept. 1. proposed to sail thither ; and a letter was despatched to Shir-
       ley for the requisite bateaux.   Pending their arrival an en-
       gagement occurred, which was greeted both in England and
       America as a signal victory.[5]

[1] MS. Letter of E. Williams, of
July 22, in Williams's MSS. i. 157;
1 M. H. Coll. vii. 105; Minot, i. 251;
Parsons, Life of Pepperrell, 279.
[2] E. Williams's letter, of August
16, in which he says he arrived at
Fort Nicolson August 14; and letter
of August 23, from the Great Carrying Place, in which he speaks of the
proceedings of the council. Williams's
MSS. i. 171, 173. Also, letter of

August 30, in ibid. 174. Johnson, in
a letter dated August 15, 1755, from
the Great Carrying Place, speaks of
his arrival there, with his troops, numbering in all 2850 men. Mass. Archives.
[3] Doc. Hist. N. Y. ii. 652, 678;
Journal H. of R. for 1755, p. 75.
[4] Doc. Hist. N. Y. ii. 678, 680, 682,
683, 684, 689.
[5] Doc. Hist. N. Y. ii. 689.

A French fleet, of twenty-two ships of the line, besides frigates and transports, had been sent from Brest early in the spring, in which six thousand marines, and eighty-five companies of land troops, of the regiments of the Queen, of Artois, Burgundy, Languedoc, Guienne, and Béarn, under the veteran Dieskau, a native of Germany and the favorite of Saxe, were embarked for Cape Breton and Canada. On the passage, eight companies of grenadiers were taken, with the Lys and Alcide men-of-war, the one *armé en flute*, and the other *en guerre*, who fell in with the English fleet off Cape Race, under Admiral Boscawen, despatched to the coast to watch the French squadron. Subsequently, a thousand of the troops were landed at Louisburg ; and the remainder arrived at Quebec, with De Vaudreuil, the governor general of Canada, and Dieskau, the commander of the forces.[1] Dieskau, whose motto was " Boldness wins," had intended, soon after his arrival, by the advice of Vaudreuil, to seize the fort at Oswego, whither Shirley had marched, and had proceeded to Montreal to make the necessary preparations ; but, apprised of Johnson's movements, he altered his plans, crossed Lake Champlain, landed at the South Bay, some sixteen miles from the English encamp-

CHAP.
VII.

1755.
May 6.

Jun. 10
Apr. 23.

Jun. 19

[1] French Doc'ts in Mass. Archives, ix. 205–229 ; Trumbull MSS. i. 101, in Lib. Mass. Hist. Soc. ; Hist. of the War, 21–23 ; Letter to the People of England, 19 et seq. ; Pouchot's Mems. i. 18–28 ; James Grenville to his brother, in Grenville Corresp. i. 136 ; Chalmers, Revolt, ii. 277 ; Doc. Hist. N. Y. ii. 694 ; 1 M. H. Coll. viii. 113 ; Letters and Mems. relating to Cape Breton, 304 et seq. Mortimer, Hist. Eng. i. 511 et seq., says that, by the last of March, there were at Brest one man-of-war of 80 guns, four of 74 guns, six of 64 guns, one of 60 guns, one of 50 guns, one of 46 guns, four of 30 guns, and one of 24 guns ; at Toulon, one of 80 guns, five of 74 guns, three of 64 guns, two of 32 guns, and one of 24 guns ; and at Rochefort, one of 80 guns, one of 74 guns, three of 64 guns, one of 50 guns, and one of 32 guns : in all thirty-eight vessels. This fleet sailed May 6, commanded by Macnamara, an officer of Irish extraction ; but soon after nine of the vessels returned, and the rest, under M. Bois de la Mothe and M. de Salvert, continued on. Macnamara sailed again in June. By the middle of April the English had at Spithead a noble fleet, consisting of ten ships of the line and six frigates, having on board 6000 land forces. This fleet sailed, under Admiral Boscawen, on the 23d. The accounts in different authorities vary both as to the number of vessels in the two fleets, the troops on board, and the date of sailing.

CHAP.
VII.
_____
1755.
Sept. 7.

July 22.

Sept. 8.

ment, and, making a circuit by the way of Wood Creek, gained the rear of the English army, with a force of about two thousand French and Indians.

Johnson was early informed of the approach of the French by his scouts, who were ever abroad to anticipate an attack; and, presuming from their movements that their first design was to surprise the troops at the Carrying Place, it was resolved to detach a thousand English and two hundred Indians "to catch the enemy in their retreat."[1] The command of this detachment was intrusted to Ephraim Williams, a Massachusetts colonel, who, in passing through Albany, had made a bequest of his estate by will to found a free school;[2] and Israel Putnam, of Connecticut, had charge of a small company of the young men of his own neighborhood.[3] The army of Johnson had, some time before, been increased by the accession of a fine regiment from New Hampshire, of five hundred men, under John Stark, a lieutenant, afterwards conspicuous in the annals of the revolution; so that the encampment on Lake George, numbering four thousand men, was of ample strength to withstand the invaders.[4]

About an hour after the departure of Williams, a heavy firing was heard — a signal that he had fallen in with the main body of the enemy, who were posted in ambush. The surprise was complete; and the deadly fire so thinned the ranks of the little army that the detachment was compelled to retreat, with the loss of their commander, who fell at the first charge, and the gray-haired Hendrick, the chieftain of the Six Nations, famed for his clear voice and flashing eye. The retreat was conducted by Nathan Whiting, of Connecticut. By the arrival of fresh troops, under Lieutenant Cole, the pursuers were checked; and the fugitives once more reached the camp from which they had so recently and proudly departed.

[1] Doc. Hist. N. Y. ii. 691.
[2] Holland's Hist. Western Mass. i. 182; 1 M. H. Coll. viii. 48.
[3] Life of Putnam, 25.
[4] Doc. Hist. N. Y. ii. 683; 1 M. H. Coll. vii. 113.

Soon the troops under Dieskau[1] came in sight; and those who looked out at the edge of the woods which bordered the opening in front, saw painted Indians approaching, and the bayonets of the French glittering among the foliage "like a row of icicles on a January morning." Within a hundred and fifty yards of the breastwork of fallen trees, which had been hastily thrown up for the protection of the camp, the brave baron halted; and this halt proved his ruin. Immediately Johnson's artillery, under the direction of Captain Eyre, was brought to bear upon his columns; and the regulars, finding themselves deserted by the Canadian militia and their savage allies, who had skulked to the swamps, took to trees, and maintained for some time a scattering fire upon the flanks of the English with intermitting briskness.[2] With but a handful of his followers left, Dieskau retired. A party from the camp, jumping over the breastwork, eagerly followed; and at a short distance the French general, thrice wounded, was seized as a prisoner. But one English officer was killed in this engagement — the gallant Titcomb, who had fought with such bravery at the siege of Louisburg, and whose name should be transmitted to posterity with honor. General Johnson was wounded at the outset, but the wound was not serious; and for his services on this occasion, which were perhaps over-magnified, he received a gratuity of five thousand pounds, and the honors

---

[1] According to the French accounts, Doc'ts in Mass. Archives, ix. 241–253, the army of Dieskau consisted in all of 3573 men, viz.: the garrison at Fort Frederic, 150; a corps d'observation, 400; the battalion of the queen, 1011; Canadians, 1412; and savages, 600. Only one third of these troops are said to have been with the baron when he attacked General Johnson. Montreuil, in ibid. 265–269, gives an account of the march of Dieskau and the engagement, in letters dated August 31 and October 1, 1755. See also Mortimer's Hist. Eng. iii. 515, 516.

[2] MS. letters of Clarke, Sept. 16, Seth Pomeroy to his wife, Sept. 20, and Perez Marsh, Sept. 25, in Williams's MSS. i. 174, 182, 184; Lett. on Defeat of French at Lake George, p. 8; 1 M. H. Coll. vii. 112. Pomeroy says that, when the French first rushed towards the camp, they fired impetuously upon the English, so that "the hailstones from heaven have not been much thicker than their bullets came." But the fierceness of the first onset was soon checked.

CHAP. of knighthood were conferred upon him by the king.[1] Yet
VII. to Lyman was doubtless "chiefly to be ascribed the honor of
1755. the victory," though his name makes but little display in the
account transmitted to England.[2]

But one other project remains to be noticed — the expedition against Nova Scotia, proposed by Massachusetts, but
undertaken and conducted at the expense of the crown.[3] Two
battalions were raised for this service. The command of the
first was conferred on John Winslow, of Marshfield, great
grandson of Edward Winslow,[4] who held a commission of
major general in the militia, and whose personal influence and
popularity were so great as to effect the raising of two thousand men in two months, to serve for a year if necessary. Of
the second battalion Colonel Scott had the command; and
Lieutenant Colonel Monckton, of Nova Scotia, was designated
by the king to take charge of the expedition.[5]

May 20. The troops from Massachusetts were embarked in May; and
May 26. towards the last of the month they arrived at Annapolis,
June 1. whence, the week after, in a fleet of forty-one vessels, they set
out for Chiegnecto, early in the morning, and the same evening
about sunset anchored five miles from Fort Lawrence. The
next day the troops landed; and the day after, at a council of
June 3. war, it was resolved to push on and lay siege to Beau-Sejour.
June 4. Captain Adams, of the first battalion, with sixty men, led the
advance, followed by Colonel Monckton, with about three
hundred men. Colonel Scott, with his battalion, occupied the

---

[1] Pouchot's Mems. i. 48–54; Hist.
of the War, 27–31; Doc. Hist. N. Y.
ii. 689–703; Hutchinson, iii. 35, 36;
1 M. H. Coll. vii. 104–109; Minot, i.
250–254.

[2] 1 M. H. Coll. vii. 110.

[3] Letter of T. Robinson, of June
21, 1754, to Governor Shirley, approving the plans detailed in his communications of April 19 and May 1, for driving the French from the Kennebec,
pursuant to an act passed by the assembly of Massachusetts, in Williams's

MSS. i. 71; also, extracts from a letter of the lords of trade of July 5, in
ibid. 72.

[4] For his commission, dated February 10, 1755, see his MS. Journal,
fol. 3.

[5] Winslow's MS. Journal, 1–3;
Jour. H. of R. of Mass. 1755–56,
317; Smith's N. Y. ii. 219, 220;
Letter on Ohio Defeat, 13; Stirling's
Vindication of Shirley, 17, 18; Hutch-
inson, iii. 27, 28.

next place ; and in the rear General Winslow marched, with CHAP.
the rest of the first battalion. The route lay over a marsh, VII.
where the dikes had been cut down ; so that the progress of 1755.
the troops was slow and guarded. The bridge over the Mes-
sagouche, the intervening river, had been destroyed ; and on
its opposite bank the French had a block house, and had thrown
up a breastwork, where four hundred men were stationed. An
engagement ensued ; and in about a quarter of an hour the
French set the block house and village on fire. Pushing on,
notwithstanding the annoyance from the musketry of the enemy, the provincial troops gained the top of the hill in about
an hour, and halted for refreshment. From thence, continuing their march, they moved to within two miles of the fort,
and, turning to the right from the main road, halted in the
woods. A few days after, General Winslow, with three hun- June 8.
dred men, advanced within six hundred yards of the fort. In
a short time intrenchments were opened upon the rock border- Jun. 12.
ing on St. Omer's ; and in four days the enemy surrendered — Jun. 16.
the garrison being allowed to march out with the honors of
war, and to be transported to Louisburg, with their effects, at
the expense of Great Britain, on condition of remaining neutral for the space of six months. This capitulation and the
preceding skirmishes were attended with the loss of but three
men from New England, none besides being mortally wounded.
The fort at Gaspereaux, on Bay Verte, surrendered on the
same terms ; and Captain Rous, with three frigates and a Jun. 18
sloop, sailed to the St. John's, for the reduction of the new
fort erected by the French. These successes, at so early a
stage of the war, diffused a general joy through the colonies,
and were welcomed as omens of future good fortune.[1]

The French forts being subdued, but one question remained

[1] Winslow's Journal, fols. 72–106 ;
Bollan's letter of May 4, 1758, in MS.
Letters and Papers, 1721–1760, fol.
187, in Mass. Hist. Soc. Colls.; Letters and Mems. relative to Cape Breton, 318–323 ; Hist. of the War, 26,
27 ; Extract from Letter of Governor
Lawrence to Sir Thomas Robinson,
June 28, 1755, in Mortimer's Eng.
iii. 513.

CHAP. to be decided : What shall be done with the Acadians, some
VII. thousands in number ? The situation of this people was pe-
1755. culiarly distressing. They were the earliest European occupants of the country, and had dwelt in it now for over two
hundred years. Frugal in their habits, and of a mild disposition, their attention had been turned from hunting and fishing,
the delight of their ancestors, to the cultivation of the soil;
and by diligent effort they had reclaimed from the forest and
the ocean the farms on which they dwelt. By the treaty of
1713. Utrecht they had been brought under the dominion of England. But they still loved the language and the usages of
their fathers, and the religion of their childhood was graven
1713-53. upon their souls. For forty years they were neglected by the
English ; and in that time they prospered, and their substance
increased. The crops from their fields were exceedingly rich.
Flocks and herds grazed in the meadows, or roamed over the
hills ; domestic fowls abounded ; and the thickly clustered village of neat, thatched-roof cottages sheltered a frugal, happy
people. The spinning-wheel and the loom were busily plied ;
and, from morn to night, matrons and maidens, young men
and their sires, toiled for the bread which they ate in peace.

This gentle people, distinguished for their benevolence, were
known as " the neutral French," because of the obligation to
which they had subscribed. Happy in their seclusion, they
conducted their affairs in the simplest manner. Each family
provided for its own wants. No locks were needed for their
doors, " no tax gatherer counted their folds, no magistrates
dwelt in their hamlets." They were too inoffensive to require
the interference of the arm of the law, and their disputes were
amicably settled by their elders. The priest of the parish was
their scribe and their judge. He framed their laws, and drew
their wills ; and to him they looked for advice and direction.
Poverty was rare ; early marriages were encouraged ; and
fathers delighted in settling their children in a cottage of

their own. Living in love, their lives glided on "like rivers CHAP.
that water the woodlands, reflecting an image of heaven."[1]   VII.

Since the settlement of the English they had been grievously 1755.
oppressed. Was their property demanded for the public service ? It must be yielded immediately, or "the next courier
would bring an order for military execution upon the delin-
quents." Did they delay in bringing firewood at the bidding of
their masters ? "If they do not do it in proper time," was the
harsh mandate of the governor, "the soldiers shall absolutely
take their houses for fuel."[2] From such a spirit, which witnessed without compunction their humiliation, what could be
expected but continued oppression ?

Such being the circumstances of the unfortunate Acadians, it
will excite little surprise to be told that Lawrence, the lieutenant governor of the province, and his council, aided by Admi-
rals Boscawen and Mostyn, and Belcher, the chief justice, a
son of the former governor of Massachusetts, determined, in Aug.11.
accordance with advices from England, procured at the instance
of Governor Shirley, that the people should be driven from
the homes they loved, and scattered as exiles over the whole
breadth of the continent. The liberty of transmigration was
refused. They were to be treated as captives ; and as captives
were they to be sent out to live among the English.[3]

The execution of this sentence, so harsh and vindictive, was
allotted to the New England forces. Gladly would their commander, himself distinguished for his courtesy and humanity,
have escaped the unpleasant and painful duty ; but the rules
of war are imperative, and, whatever his own feelings, Mr.
Winslow was compelled to suppress them and obey. To persuade the Acadians to a voluntary exile was seen to be
impracticable ; artifice must therefore be resorted to, to kidnap

[1] Longfellow's Evangeline.
[2] Winslow's MS. Journal, fols. 151
–154; Haliburton's N. S. i. 163.
[3] Winslow's MS. Journal, fols. 159
–163; Minot, i. 122; Haliburton, i.
168.

CHAP. and entrap them.[1] A general proclamation ordered all the
VII.   males of the settlements, "both old and young men, as well as
1755. all the lads of ten years of age," to assemble at the church at
Aug. 30
and   Grand Pré on Friday, at three o'clock in the afternoon, then
Sept. 2. and there to hear his majesty's orders communicated ; declaring
       that no excuse would be admitted on any pretence whatever,
       "on pain of forfeiting goods and chattels in default of real
       estate." [2]

           Some, on the reception of this summons, fled to the forest,
       and lurked on its outskirts, with ominous forebodings of the
Sept. 5. fate before them. Yet, on the day appointed, four hundred and
       eighteen unarmed men gathered in the temple, which had for
       some time been occupied by General Winslow as his head quar-
       ters, while without, their wives, with care-worn looks, awaited
       the issue of the strange conference. The doors were closed ;
       and from the lips of Winslow their sentence was slowly but
       firmly pronounced. "It is his majesty's orders," — such were
       his words, — "and they are peremptory, that the whole French
       inhabitants of these districts be removed. Your lands and
       tenements, cattle of all kinds, and live stock of all sorts, are
       forfeited to the crown, with all your other effects, saving your
       money and household goods ; and you yourselves are to be
       removed from this province. I shall do every thing in my
       power that your goods be secured to you, and that you are not
       molested in carrying them off ; also, that whole families shall
       go in the same vessel, and that this removal be made as easy
       as his majesty's service will admit. And I hope that, in
       whatever part of the world you may fall, you may be faithful
       subjects, a peaceable and happy people. Meanwhile you are
       the king's prisoners, and will remain in security under the

---

[1] They were to be collected by *stratagem* or *force*, as circumstances might require ; and no attention was to be paid to remonstrances or memorials from any desirous to stay, but every person was to be embarked, if possible, according to instructions. Winslow's MS. Journal, fol. 171. "The sooner we strike the stroke the better," said Murray. Ibid. 172.

[2] Winslow's MS. Journal, 174 ; Haliburton's N. S. i. 175, 176.

inspection and direction of the troops I have the honor to CHAP.
command." [1]   VII.

Like a whirlwind in the autumn, which spreads desolation in 1755.
its path, came this announcement to the imprisoned captives.
At first there was unbroken silence, as in speechless amazement
they gazed upon each other's countenances; then a loud wail
of anguish echoed through the aisles and arches of the building.
It was, indeed, a cruel sentence; justifiable, perhaps, by the
policy of war, but strangely at variance with the benevolent
spirit of the gospel of Christ. Every heart ached in Grand
Pré that night, and throughout the district of Minas as the
intelligence reached them from the lips of the twenty who
were permitted to go forth.[2] No "angelus" sounded softly at
sunset. The "summer of all saints" lost its beauty. Old men
looked sadly upon the scenes which had so often delighted
them; young men gloomily brooded over the future. Mothers
clasped their little ones closer in their arms; maidens shrank
timidly from the embraces of their lovers. Well might they
utter the complaint of Melibœus : —

> "En, unquam patrios longo post tempore fines,
> Pauperis et tuguri congestum cespite culmen,
> Post aliquot, mea regna, videns mirabor aristas?
> Impius hæc tam culta novalia miles habebit?
> Barbarus has segetes?
> Ite meæ, felix quondam pecus, ite capellæ.
> Non ego vos posthac, viridi projectus in antro,
> Dumosa pendere procul de rupe videbo;
> Carmina nulla canam; non, me pascente, capellæ,
> Florentem cytisum, et salices carpetis amaras." [3]

At the appointed day, the inhabitants of Grand Pré met for Sept.10
the last time — in all one thousand nine hundred and twenty-
three souls.[4] The prisoners in the church were drawn up six

---

[1] Winslow's MS. Journal, 178,
179; Minot, i. 224–226; Haliburton's
N. S. i. 175, 176.
[2] Winslow's MS. Journal, 179, 180.

[3] Virgil, Eclogue I.
[4] Winslow's MS. Journal, 197–
211, where is a list of the inhabitants.

CHAP.
VII.
~~~~~~
1755.

deep; and the young men, one hundred and forty-one in number, were ordered to march first on board the vessels. With frenzied despair they refused to be separated from their parents and companions; and at the point of the bayonet obedience was enforced. Women and children knelt by the way through which they passed, some singing the hymn of farewell, others weeping and praying for blessings on their heads. Next the fathers, one hundred and nine in number, were commanded to embark; and eighty-nine obeyed. Then — most dreadful of all — mothers and little ones were told they must wait until fresh transports arrived. December came before they left; but where should they find those from whom they had been separated?[1]

A large number of the miserable Acadians in the different districts escaped. The rest, seven thousand in number, were scattered from New Hampshire to Georgia. In the land of strangers, with broken hearts, they were to drag out a weary and cheerless existence, saddened in spirit and bereft of hope. Never again were they to return to their homes. Never again were they to gaze upon the scenes which had delighted their infancy. Never again were they to see those who had been torn from them, until they met them in that land where tyranny can no more annoy, and where a more tolerant spirit reigns than on earth.[2]

[1] Winslow's MS. Journal, 191–193.

[2] About a thousand of these Acadians arrived at Boston at the opening of winter, among whom were several aged persons, who would have perished had not generous hearts welcomed them to their homes. The provincial legislature did what it could to alleviate their sufferings. They were provided for like other poor, only the elderly were exempted from labor. When they found there was no hope of being restored to their homes, many went to Hispaniola, and died. Dispersed throughout the world, the poor Acadians became extinct. A few of their descendants, indeed, still live at the south; but they live to us now chiefly in history. Mrs. Williams, of Connecticut, has written a touching tale of their sufferings; and Longfellow's Evangeline is a beautiful tribute to the memory of this people, as honorable to his character as it is creditable to the poetical genius of New England. Comp. Winslow's Journal, passim; Hutchinson, iii. 38–42; Journal H. of R. for 1755, 265, 285, 318, 456; ibid. for 1756, pp. 65, 69, 119. In the Mass. Archives are two folio volumes of MSS. relating exclusively to the French neutrals, besides a large number of other MSS. scattered through other volumes.

CHAPTER VIII.

THE FRENCH WAR. 1756-1763.

CHAP
VIII.

1755.
Dec.

1756.
May.

THE capture of the French posts at the east, and the removal of the Acadians, with the defeat of Dieskau by General Johnson, were the decisive accomplishments of the campaign of 1755. The defeat of Braddock, and the inefficient movements of Shirley, were the disastrous results. But the French were still masters of a large share of their old posts, and, by ceaseless activity, were strengthening their garrisons and preparing for future hostilities. War, at this time, had not been formally declared by England or France; but that event was daily expected, nor was it long delayed.[1] The surviving force employed by the colonies in the expedition under General Johnson returned before winter, except six hundred men posted at Lake George, where a wooden fort, called Fort William Henry, was built, and at Fort Edward, near the Hudson. These, with the garrison of seven hundred at Oswego, where large magazines of stores and provisions had been lodged, were the whole strength of the English upon the western frontiers.[2] The French had a strong fort at Crown Point, with works at Ticonderoga; another fort at Cataraqui, near Lake Ontario, called Fort Frontenac; and another at the Falls of Niagara, called

---

[1] War was declared by England in May, and by France in June. Trumbull MSS. i. 102; Hist. of the War, 44–52; Mortimer's England, iii. 531; Belsham, ii. 396; Trumbull's Connecticut, ii. 373.

[2] At a council of war held at Albany, November 20, 1755, it was agreed that the army under General Johnson directed against Crown Point, except 600, or such further number as should be agreed upon, should be discharged; and that the rest of the troops should garrison Fort Edward and Fort William Henry. Mass. Archives, Letters, 1.

CHAP. Fort Niagara.[1] Still farther west their posts extended in an
VIII. unbroken line to the banks of the Mississippi; and from thence
1756. to the Gulf of Mexico they held undisputed sway. The prospect of subduing an enemy whose advantages were so great,
and who knew how to improve them, was certainly not flattering; nor did any officer of experience entertain the idea that
they could be easily conquered, though magnificent plans of
operation were draughted, and a degree of assurance was attempted to be kept up by those who knew that hitherto but
little had been effected, and who could have but little encouragement of success in the future. Johnson himself, though he
professed the utmost confidence that "the ambitious and deep-
laid schemes of the French" would not only be "frustrated, but
receive a mortal wound," at the same time confessed that, "to
obtain this desirable end, a great expense for perhaps some
years will necessarily arise;" but "the alternatives," he adds,
"in my humble opinion, most glaringly deserve it, and the
beneficial consequences will abundantly repay it."[2] Well
1755. might the earthquakes, which this year shook the whole coun-
Nov. 18.
Nov. 1. try, the first shock of which, on the Festival of All Saints,
destroyed one of the most flourishing cities of Europe, be regarded by the superstitious as an "ominous" event. The age
of signs and wonders had not ceased; and many remembered
Mat. 24: that the Saviour had predicted that "famines, and pestilences,
7, 8. and earthquakes in divers places," should be "the beginning
of sorrows."[3]

Oct. 24.   Governor Shirley left Oswego in October to return to Mas-
Nov. 4. sachusetts. Soon after his arrival at Albany he received his
commission as commander-in-chief;[4] and, by his orders, a grand

[1] Stirling's Vindication, 13; Rogers's Journal, 10; Willard's Lett. in
1 M. H. Coll. vi. 40; Hutchinson, iii.
42; Minot, i. 258.
[2] Doc. Hist. N. Y. ii. 673.
[3] MS. Sermons, in the possession
of the author; Prince's, Mayhew's,
and Winthrop's Lectures; Boston Ga-

zette for Nov. 24; Minot's Mass. i.
261, 262; Mortimer's England, iii.
520; Lord Mahon's England, i. 305-
307.
[4] Official notice of the appointment
of Governor Shirley as commander-
in-chief was made August 28, 1755.
Letter of T. Robinson, in Trumbull

congress of governors and field officers was convened at New York, which continued in session two days. At this congress were present "his Excellency General Shirley, commander-in-chief of all his majesty's forces in North America; his Excellency Sir Charles Hardy, knight, governor and commander-in-chief of the Province of New York; the Hon. Horatio Sharpe, lieutenant governor and commander-in-chief of the Province of Maryland; the Hon. Robert Hunter Morris, lieutenant governor and commander-in-chief of the Province of Pennsylvania; the Hon. Thomas Fitch, governor and commander-in-chief of the Colony of Connecticut; and of the field officers, Colonels Thomas Dunbar and Peter Schuyler, Majors Charles Craven and John Rutherford, and Sir John St. Clair, deputy quarter-master general."[1]

The conference was opened by Governor Shirley, who laid before the council the king's instructions to General Braddock. Shirley's plan of operations was characteristic of the man, and was framed on the gigantic scale which distinguished all his schemes. After remarking, as a preliminary, upon the position and character of the prominent posts, he added, "that the French settlements at the mouth of the Mississippi furnished these northern garrisons neither with provisions nor stores, being not only at two thousand miles' distance from any of them, but embarrassed with insuperable difficulties, by a laborious navigation against a rapid stream;" and hence that, "could the French be dislodged from Frontenac, and the little fort at Toronto, and their entrance into Lake Ontario obstructed, all their other forts and settlements on the Ohio and the western lakes were deprived of their support from Canada, and must ere long be evacuated."[2]

MSS. i. 107. At the instance of Hutchinson, an address was sent to the governor from the legislature of Massachusetts, November 6, congratulating him upon his promotion. Journal H. of R. for 1755, 221, 222.

[1] Trumbull MSS. i. 112; MS. Lett. of Governor Shirley, of Oct. 15, 1755, in Mass. Archives; Stirling's Vindication, 54; 1 M. H. Coll. vii. 127, 131; Journal H. of R. of Mass. for 1755, 213, 214; Smith's N. Y. ii. 224.

[2] Stirling's Vindication, 55; 1 M. H. Coll. vii. 132.

Impressed with the correctness of these views, and fired with the hope of retrieving past failures, he proposed that five thousand men should be assembled early at Oswego, and that four thousand of them should be sent to attack Fort Frontenac, and La Gallette, upon the Iroquois. Upon the reduction of these places, an attempt was to be made upon the forts at Niagara, Presqu'Isle, Rivière aux Bœufs, Detroit, and Michilimackinac; and in the mean time three thousand provincials were to march from Will's Creek for the reduction of Fort Du Quesne. A body of six thousand troops was likewise to proceed to Crown Point, build a fort, and launch vessels in Lake Champlain; and, that the forces of Canada might be still further divided, two thousand men were to ravage the Kennebec, fall upon the settlements adjoining the Chaudière, and proceed to its mouth, within three miles of Quebec. Thence, dividing into small parties along the banks of the St. Lawrence, they were to destroy the scattered settlements in their path, and spread desolation wherever they went.

If the attempts upon Crown Point and the forts upon the lakes and the Ohio River were not simultaneously prosecuted, he observed, perilous, if not fatal, consequences might ensue; and if, in particular, no attempt was made against Crown Point, which was the stronghold of the enemy, the whole force of Canada would march to oppose the English, which would defeat their design, and require so large a body of troops for the war as to render the transportation of supplies to Oswego impracticable. So numerous an army might also march against Albany as effectually to cut off the retreat of the provincials, or, at least, totally obstruct their supplies. On the other hand, should the whole strength of the army be destined for Crown Point, and the western operations be neglected, Oswego, the grand object of the French, would be in the utmost danger of falling into their hands. This irreparable loss would be attended with the loss of the whole country to Albany, with that of the Six Nations, and the French would acquire an

absolute dominion on the lakes and the whole southern CHAP.
country.[1]

These plans, urged with his usual subtlety and eloquence, 1755.
were, in the main, approved by the congress. The council
advised that orders should be given for building immediately
three or four vessels at Oswego ; they were of opinion that ten
thousand men were necessary for the Crown Point expedition,
and six thousand for that on Lake Ontario ; the attempt
against Fort Du Quesne by the western governments, it was
thought, would answer a good purpose, especially in securing
the fidelity of the Indians ; and the feint against Quebec was
approved, if it did not interfere with the other expeditions.
The operations upon Lake Ontario, it was conceived, should
begin with the attack on Frontenac ; and to accomplish all
these purposes, an additional number of regular troops was
adjudged to be necessary, "for effectually recovering and securing his majesty's rights and dominions on the continent."[2]

It was the intention of Governor Shirley, and part of his
plan formally stated at the time, to prosecute a winter's expedition against Ticonderoga ; but frost and snow, necessary for
the transportation of the stores, failing to appear, the enterprise
was abandoned ; and, leaving New York, he returned to Bos- 1756.
ton, where he was received with public demonstrations of Jan. 21.
Jan. 30.
respect from the military and both branches of the legislature ;
and a splendid banquet was provided for his entertainment, at
the instance of his friends, which was made the more ostenta-
tious from a desire to eclipse New York in its honors conferred
upon General Johnson, between whom and Shirley a coolness
had already sprung up.[3]

[1] Journal of H. of R. for 1755–6,
345, 462, 497, 498 ; Stirling's Vindication, 55, 56 ; 1 M. H. Coll. vii. 131–
133 ; Parsons, Life of Pepperrell, 288.
[2] Trumbull MSS. i. 113 ; Stirling's
Vindication, 56 ; 1 M. H. Coll. vii.
133, 134.

[3] Journal of H. of R. of Mass. for
1756, 295, 298 ; Smith's N. Y. ii. 224
–226 ; Stirling's Vindication, 53 ; Rogers's Journal, 13 ; 1 M. H. Coll. vi.
40, and vii. 134 ; Parsons, Life of
Pepperrell, 288, 289.

CHAP.   Shortly after his arrival, the legislature of the province
VIII.   being in session, application was made by Governor Shirley for
1756.   men and munitions to carry out the plans projected at Albany.
Feb. 4.   The province pleaded poverty; but the governor, in reply,
urged that their furnishing a quota of men for the service would
probably free them from the burden of future taxes, as it would
remove the enemy, which rendered them necessary, and would
be an inducement to the crown to remunerate them for what
had been already expended. To obviate the objection of poverty, he offered to loan the government thirty thousand pounds
sterling out of the moneys committed to him for the payment
of the troops, but with the proviso that an act should be passed
for levying a tax, in the two succeeding years, of an equal
amount, as collateral security.

The plea of poverty urged by the province was doubtless a
political pretence; for the credit of the government was good,
and funds could have been easily procured to meet any exigency, had the disposition existed. The offer of Mr. Shirley
was equally politic, and it answered his purpose; for many of
the assembly, glad to shift the responsibility from their shoulders to his, favored his proposal, especially as they were led to
believe that the action of Parliament would indemnify them
against actual loss. Hence resolutions were passed " for raising three thousand men, in order to remove the encroachments
of the French from his majesty's territories at or near Crown
Point, in humble confidence that his majesty will hereafter be
graciously pleased to give orders for defraying the expense of
this expedition, and for establishing such garrisons as may be
needed in order to maintain the possession of the country." [1]
At the same time it was intimated to his excellency, that it
would encourage men to enlist in the service if the chief com-

---

[1] Letter of March 11, 1756, in   Stirling's Vindication, 62–69; Wil-
Mass. Archives, Letters, fol. 141;   lard's Letter, in 1 M. H. Coll. vi. 40,
Mass. Rec's; Journal of H. of R. for   and Bollan's Mem. in ibid. 47; Hutch-
1755–56, 309, 311, 332, 335, 338;   inson, iii. 45, 46; Minot, i. 267–273.

mand was conferred upon a resident of the province; and this CHAP. intimation was the more pleasing to him, inasmuch as he could, VIII. without being accused of intentional disrespect, decline making 1756. the offer to General Johnson, whose views he was resolved to thwart, if possible. Accordingly, in February, he offered the Feb. command to Sir William Pepperrell, knowing his popularity with the people; but, having by this means secured that gentleman's vote for the passage of his favorite measures, on the pretence that his advices from England compelled him to the change, he altered his mind, and conferred the appointment on General Winslow, an officer of high standing and distinguished Feb. 18 abilities.[1]

Parliament, in the mean time, was not inattentive to the con- Feb. 2. dition of the colonies; and, as a measure of temporary expediency, not of permanent policy, one hundred and fifteen thousand pounds were granted, and forwarded to America, as Aug. 28. a reward for the services of the troops for the past year. Of this sum there were paid to Massachusetts fifty-four thousand pounds; to Connecticut, twenty-six thousand; and to New York, fifteen thousand; the remaining twenty-four thousand being apportioned to the other colonies.[2] The next measure of the government wore a less favorable aspect. The plan of military dictatorship, which for nearly sixty years had been 1697 insisted upon as indispensable to systematize the management to of colonial affairs, and repress the insubordinate spirit which, 1756. it was alleged, existed in every province, was now revived and carried into effect.[3] Mr. Shirley, in his eagerness to forward his own interests, had so far disregarded the feelings of others as to have raised many enemies in different parts of the country; and the manner in which he had treated both civil and

---

[1] Winslow's MS. Journal for 1756, fol. 1; Mass. Rec's; Stirling's Vindication, 65, 70; Journal H. of R. for 1755–56, 387, 423; Winslow's Lett. in 1 M. H. Coll. vi. 34; Minot, i. 265, 273; Parsons, Life of Pepperrell, 289.

[2] Journal H. of R. for 1756, p. 74; Trumbull MSS. i. 114; Mass. Arch. Letters, fol. 182; Minot, i. 288; Bancroft, iv. 227.

[3] Doc. Hist. N. Y.; Chalmers, Revolt, i. 269; Bancroft, iv. 227, 228.

CHAP. military officers had led to complaints which reached the ears
VIII. of his employers in England.[1] His services in behalf of the
1756. crown, it was intimated, had been greatly over-estimated, and
that he was lacking in efficiency in the prosecution of his
schemes, and in the urbanity necessary to constitute a successful commander. No one, perhaps, on this side the Atlantic,
expected to succeed him in the command, nor does any one
appear to have been recommended for that purpose. Hence
these complaints carried the more weight; and, at the instance
March. of Cumberland and Fox, Mr. Shirley was displaced, and the
Earl of Loudoun, the friend of Halifax, and an earnest advocate of the subordination of the colonies, was appointed
governor of Virginia, and commander-in-chief of the army
throughout the British continental provinces in America, with
powers superior to and independent of the other provincial
governors.[2]

Nor did the government stop here; for, during the session
of 1756, the authority of Parliament over American affairs was
signally extended. By different acts, approved by the king,
foreign Protestants might be employed as engineers and offi-

[1] In the Williams MSS. i. 256, is a very severe letter from William Williams, dated Albany, September 13, 1756, reflecting upon the conduct of Shirley, in which he calls him the "Massachusetts Dagon." "Many are the conjectures," says he, "what will become of him. Some are apprehensive he is in such situation that he will fall upon his face, and only a stump will be left. Others, to prevent him that honor, are for serving him by a halter, so that he shall not have an opportunity of ending his feats and life in so honorable a manner. This piece of paper would not contain the heads of the sentences pronounced against him by all orders and degrees of men. In short, your Dagon is looked upon as meaner and viler than the mean prince of the power of the air. Men of superior genius to my-self have so placed him, that I have no occasion nor inclination to dislodge him. I wish his idolaters had seen their mistaken worship sooner; nor do I wish any of them so bad a hell as Mr. S. must bear in his mind." Without doubt some allowance is to be made here for the warmth of the writer; yet this is but a specimen of numerous letters I have seen, all more or less severe, and proving that the feeling against the commander-in-chief was not confined to a few persons, nor to those only who could be suspected of sinister motives in their opposition.

[2] Trumbull MSS. i. 114–116, Letters of Fox of March 13, 1756, and of Halifax of May 11; Doc. Hist. N. Y. ii. 710; 1 M. H. Coll. vii. 134, 135, 145; Parsons, Life of Pepperrell, 295.

cers to enlist a regiment of aliens; indented servants might be
accepted as soldiers, and their masters compensated by the several assemblies; volunteers were freed from the process of law
for petty debts; the naval code of England was extended to
all persons employed in the king's service "upon the lakes or
rivers in North America;" and each northern province was
forbidden to negotiate with the Indians — the management
of Indian affairs being intrusted exclusively to Sir William
Johnson, with no subordination but to Loudoun. It was
useless for Massachusetts to object to either of these measures. Whether acceptable or not, they were to be carried
into effect; and an army was raised without their approval;
taxes were levied without their consent; and martial law was
extended to all the settlements. Yet such was the posture of
public affairs, and such was the necessity for overlooking minor
evils whose burden was not pressingly felt, that the provincial
government peacefully submitted to these innovations, and contented itself simply with expressing its dissatisfaction in terms
of the utmost courtesy and propriety.[1]

Before the arrival of the intelligence of the removal of Mr.
Shirley, that gentleman had left Boston for Albany, and soon
after a council of war was held to consider the measures which
were necessary to be taken. The preparations for the western
expedition were somewhat extensive. The naval force upon
the lake consisted of two sloops of ten carriage guns each, and
two row galleys of ten swivels each; and three other vessels,
a "snow" of eighteen carriage guns and twenty swivels, a brigantine of fourteen carriage guns and twelve swivels, and a

---

[1] Acts, &c., 29 Geo. II. chaps. v.
xxxv. xxxvii.; Trumbull MSS. i. 98;
Journal H. of R. for 1756, 82; Bollan's Letters; Chalmers, Revolt, ii.
281; Minot, i. 275–280; Bancroft,
iv. 231, 232. The proposals for the
conduct of the war, when Lord Loudoun took the command, are said to
have been the same as when Braddock
was sent over, viz.: that the provinces
should not only bear the expenses of
the troops they raised for their own
defence, but should likewise supply at
their expense the regular troops sent
for their protection with provisions.
Loudoun's Communication of Feb. 1,
1757, in Williams's MSS. ii. 6.

CHAP.
VIII.

1756.

sloop of six carriage guns, were building. Besides these, there were to be two hundred and fifty whale boats upon the lake, each capable of containing sixteen men. The land forces, then at Oswego and the way stations, or on their march thither, were his own and Pepperrell's regiments, with the regiment raised and supported by New Jersey, the four independent companies of New York, and the four provincial companies of North Carolina — in all about two thousand men. Of these, one hundred and fifty were to be stationed at the magazine of stores and provisions at the Canajoharie Falls, about thirty-five miles from Schenectady; and a like number at the German Flats, to secure another magazine, guard the portage, and convey the provisions through Wood Creek; at the Oneida carrying place two hundred men were to be left; and at the falls near Oswego a fort was to be built and a garrison of forty men established; while four companies, of sixty privates each, were to be raised to scout along the route, and harass the French settlements between Frontenac and Montreal. For the northern expedition, the New England colonies had voted to raise nearly eighty-eight hundred men, including the officers and garrisons at Forts Edward and William Henry; and to these such Indians as could be mustered were to be joined, to harass the enemy upon Lake Champlain, and procure intelligence of their motions in Canada.[1]

Jun. 26.

Jun. 29.

Dated
Mar. 13
and 31.

Jun. 15.

Such were the movements on foot, and such were the plans of General Shirley at the time he was displaced. While at New York he received despatches from Mr. Fox, the secretary of state, signifying his majesty's pleasure that he should return to England, as "his presence might be necessary to consult upon measures for the conduct of the war." Lord Loudoun was expected to leave soon, to take the command of his majesty's forces; and in the mean time that charge was devolved on General Abercrombie, who arrived with Otway's and the

[1] Stirling's Vindication, 13, 41, 57, H. Coll. vi. 34, and vii. 146–149; 75, 76, 79, 90, 94; Winslow, in 1 M. Letter on the Ohio Defeat, 14.

Highland regiments of nine hundred men.[1] But the season CHAP
was fast wearing away, and nothing had been done. Lord VIII.
Loudoun did not leave England until the middle of May, nor 1756.
did the cannon for Lake Ontario arrive until a later date. May 17.
Well might Sharpe, the lieutenant governor of Maryland, ex- Aug.
claim, "We shall have good reason to sing *Te Deum*, at the
conclusion of this campaign, if matters are not then in a worse
situation than they are at present." [2]

Matters were in a worse situation; for the disasters and
reverses of the campaign of 1756 were greater, if possible, than
those of the previous year. At the outset, an incident occurred which came near threatening serious consequences.
General Abercrombie, soon after taking his command, asked
General Winslow, who was just leaving Albany with about July 15
seven thousand men, "What effect the junction of his majesty's
forces would have with the provincials, if ordered to join them
in their intended expedition?" To which, after consultation July 22.
with his officers, he replied, that "he should be extremely
pleased if such a junction could be made, and that he was
under the immediate command of the commander-in-chief; but
apprehended that if, by this junction, the provincial officers
were to lose their command, as the men were raised immediately
under them by the several governments, it would cause almost
an universal discontent, if not desertion." After the arrival
of Lord Loudoun,[3] a similar question was asked, and the same Aug. 4.
answer was returned. The provincial officers unanimously
signified their willingness to "submit to him in all dutiful
obedience, and their readiness and willingness to act in conjunction with his majesty's troops, and put themselves under

[1] Journal H. of R. for 1756, 106;
Stirling's Vindication, 58; Rogers's
Journal, 22, 23; 1 M. H. Coll. vii.
150; Smith's N. Y. ii. 234; Hutchinson, iii. 47; Minot, i. 275. Abercrombie was despatched from England in the beginning of March, with
two regiments, with orders to supersede Shirley. Mortimer's England,
iii. 529.

[2] Quoted in Bancroft, iv. 235.

[3] The Earl of Loudoun arrived at
Albany July 23. Mortimer's Hist.
England, iii. 529; Smith's N. Y. ii.
235.

CHAP. his command as his majesty's commander-in-chief of all his
VIII. forces in North America; but as the troops, raised by the sev-
1756. eral colonies and provinces in New England, had been raised
this year on particular terms, and had proceeded to act thus
far under that form, they humbly begged it as a favor of his
lordship to let those troops act separate, as far as was consistent with his majesty's service." With this reply his excellency
seemed satisfied, the point was not pressed further, and the
separate operation of the troops was permitted.[1]

July 12.   Meanwhile intelligence reached Albany of the threatening
aspect of affairs at Oswego. Colonel John Bradstreet had
thrown into the fort provisions for five or six months, and a
great quantity of stores; and, hastening eastward for addi-
July 3. tional troops, skirmishing by the way, he brought word that
the French army, numbering twelve hundred men, was in
motion to attack the place. Colonel Webb, with the forty-
fourth regiment, was ordered to its relief; but nothing was
Jun. 26. done. Shirley himself had urged the necessity of this measure
some days before, but the mind of Abercrombie was otherwise
occupied. The movements of Loudoun were equally dilatory;
and Oswego fell.[2]

All through the season the French had been active; and
neither the inclemency of the weather nor the apprehension of
danger availed to deter them from prosecuting their designs.
Mar. 17. At spring dawn, while the sides of the mountains were yet clad
with ice, De Lery, at the head of three hundred men, set out
for Montreal, penetrated to Fort Bull at the Oneida portage,
took it after a short struggle, and returned with thirty prison-

[1] Winslow's MS. Journal, ii. 349
et seq., and iii. 13–36; 1 M. H.
Coll. vi. 35–37; Letters of J. Dwight,
of July 26, 1756, and Aug. 16, in
Williams's MSS. i. 237, 241; 1 M.
H. Coll. vii. 157; Letter on Ohio Defeat, 7–9; Stirling's Vindication, 96,
97; Chalmers, Revolt, ii. 305; Minot, i. 283, 284. The difficulty alluded to in the text was not the only
one which prevailed, for there was a
dispute among the provincial officers
themselves relative to their rank.
Letter of Thos. Williams, of July 27,
in Williams's MSS. i. 238.

[2] Stirling's Vindication, 99; Hist.
of the War, 107–109; 1 M. H. Coll.
vii. 156, 157.

ers.[1] The Marquis de Montcalm had by this time reached CHAP.
Quebec, with De Levis, Bourlamaque, and other officers of his VIII.
staff. Hurrying thence to Fort Carillon, at Ticonderoga, his 1756.
practised eye ran over the defences, orders for strengthening
them were issued, and he was ready for Oswego. Collecting
at Montreal three regiments from Quebec, he set out for Fort
Frontenac ; and, posting five hundred men, under De Villiers,
beneath the shelter of a dense thicket, near the mouth of Sandy
Creek, whence he could intercept supplies for Oswego, he embarked for Niagara, and the same evening anchored in Sack- Aug. 5.
ett's Harbor. A week later Oswego was invested ; and the Aug. 12.
next day the gallant Mercer was killed by a cannon ball, and Aug. 13
a breach was made in the walls. In two days the place was Aug. 15.
taken ; the regiments of Shirley and Pepperrell capitulated ;
the forts were razed, and Oswego was a solitude. The joy of
the Canadians vented itself in extravagant ecstasies ; the missionaries planted a cross, on which was inscribed, " This is the
banner of victory ; " and by its side rose a pillar, with the arms
of France, and the inscription, " Bring lilies with full hands."[2]

"Oswego is lost — lost, perhaps, forever ! " was the despairing exclamation of the English. " Would to God this was all,
and we had nothing more to apprehend ! The French can
now, with the utmost facility, secure the inland country, and
confine us to the very brinks of the ocean ; a free communication is opened between Canada and Louisiana, and all our
intercourse with the Indians totally rescinded."[3] This heavy
disaster filled the army with consternation, and every plan of
offensive operations was immediately relinquished. The orders
to General Winslow to march to Ticonderoga were counter- Aug. 20.

---

[1] Pouchot's Mems. i. 67; Stirling's
Vindication, 76 ; Warburton's Conquest of Canada, ii. 43.
[2] Journal H. of R. for 1756, 157,
164, 172; Winslow's MS. Journal,
iii. 142–148; Pouchot's Mems. i. 70,
81; Stirling's Vindication, 110–116;
1 M. H. Coll. vii. 158; Hutchinson,

iii. ; Minot, i. 285; Smith's N. Y. ii.
239, 240; Bancroft, iv. 237–239.
[3] Winslow's MS. Journal, iii. 41,
42, 55, 56, 85, 86 ; Rogers's Journal,
33, 34, 37; Winslow, in 1 M. H. Coll.
vii. 37; Johnson MSS. in Doc. Hist.
N. Y. ii. 732 ; Minot, i. 287 ; Parsons, Life of Pepperrell, 290, 291.

CHAP.
VIII.
‾‾‾
1756.

manded, and he was directed to fortify his own camp at Fort
William Henry ; General Lyman was to remain at Fort Edward ; General Webb, with fourteen hundred men, was posted
at the Great Carrying Place ; and Sir William Johnson, with
five hundred men, was posted at the German Flats. The
expedition to the Kennebec resulted in a scouting party, which
did as much harm as good ; the attempt against Fort Du
Quesne was abandoned ; the troops went into winter quarters, and not a blow was struck which was seriously felt.
When the Massachusetts forces returned to their homes, no
provisions had been made by the government for their pay.
Hence three commissioners were appointed to apply to Lord
Loudoun for relief ; but, though that officer is said to have
"generously supported and enforced our solicitations with his
interest," he declined making any disbursement on his own
account, as the soldiers were enlisted "antecedent to his command ; " and the burden, as usual, fell upon the province.[1]

Dec. 4.

Before the close of this year a change took place in the
English ministry, and a change of momentous importance to
the colonies. The party which, for over forty years, had mis-
managed affairs, and brought disgrace upon the banner of St.
George, went out of power ; and William Pitt, known as "the
great commoner," and afterwards as Earl of Chatham, — the
early, devoted, and consistent friend of America, "distinguished
by his regard for religion, honor, and his country," — assumed
the reins which had fallen from the hands of the Duke of Newcastle. From this time forward the affairs of the war assumed
a new aspect ; a "cheerful bloom of spirit and joy revived in
the countenance of every individual ; " and the cry was echoed,

[1] Mass. Rec's ; Journal H. of R.
for 1756–57, 232 ; Rogers's Journal,
38, 51 ; Hutchinson, iii. 50. The
Journal H. of R. p. 232, says Lord
L. treated the commissioners with
great condescension, and they were
assured he was zealously disposed to
promote the interests of the colonies ;
yet he gave no encouragement to expect the advance of moneys, on the
plea that all he had received was necessary for the support of the regular
troops ; and should he draw upon this,
it must greatly prejudice his majesty's
service.

" Canada — Canada must be destroyed! *Delenda est Cartha-* CHAP
go, or we are undone! We have wasted our strength in lop- VIII.
ping the branches; the axe must be laid to the root of the 1756.
tree."[1]

A military council was held in Alexandria in 1755, another
in New York in 1756; and this year it was proposed that one
should be held in the town of Boston. For this purpose Lord
Loudoun visited the Bay Province, where he was received by 1757.
Governors Lawrence, of Nova Scotia, Fitch, of Connecticut, Jan. 29.
and Hopkins, of Rhode Island.[2] In the absence of Governor
Shirley, who had embarked for England in the preceding fall, 1756.
the chief command in Massachusetts devolved upon Spencer Sep. 12.
Phips, the lieutenant governor; but he declining to act in the
present emergency, a commission was appointed to represent
the province, consisting of Thomas Hutchinson, William Brattle, Thomas Hubbard, John Otis, and Samuel Welles. The
levies called for from New England amounted to four thousand
men; and of these Massachusetts was to raise eighteen hundred,
Connecticut fourteen hundred, Rhode Island four hundred and
fifty, and New Hampshire three hundred and fifty — all of
whom were to be mustered before the last of March, ready for 1757.
service.[3] Mar.25.

The death of Lieutenant Governor Phips occurred while April 4.
this plan for raising and forwarding the forces was in execution; and the Council, upon whom the government devolved,
with Sir William Pepperrell as their president, proceeded in
the necessary public affairs, and, having enlisted, forwarded the
quota of the province, under Colonel Joseph Frye, to the appointed rendezvous.[4] Before the next session of the court, May.

[1] Review of Pitt's Administration, 10, 14, 16; 1 M. H. Coll. vii.; Trumbull MSS. i. 121; Hist. of the War, 110; Bancroft, iv. 247.
[2] Loudoun's Speech of January 29 is given in the Williams MSS. ii. 5.
[3] Journal H. of R. for 1756–7, 271–273, 280; Lord Loudoun's Speech of January 29, 1757, in Winslow's MS.

Journal, iii. 425; Hutchinson, iii. 50, 51; Minot, ii. 11–15. See also the Proclamation of Phips, Feb. 21, 1757, the Letter of Andrew Oliver, March 18, 1757, and the Letter of Phips, March 23, in Williams's MSS. ii. 9, 11, 13.
[4] Proclamation of Council, April 5, 1757; Hutchinson, iii. 52, 53; Minot, ii. 15, 16.

CHAP. letters were received from Mr. Bollan, the son-in-law of Shir
VIII. ley and the agent of the province in England, informing the
Council that his majesty had been pleased to appoint Thomas
1757. Pownall, Esq., governor, in the room of Mr. Shirley, and that
Mar.12.
he was to embark for New England, by the way of Halifax,
the day after the date of his letters.[1]

Mr. Pownall's first visit to America was made in 1754, as
private secretary to Sir Danvers Osborne, the governor of New
York, where he remained until after the adjournment of the
1754. congress at Albany, when he visited Boston, was admitted to
July.
the confidence of Governor Shirley, and sent to New York to
solicit the concurrence of that colony in the plan against Crown
Point, which the legislature of Massachusetts had resolved to
prosecute.[2] Penetrating the designs of Shirley, whom he ex-
celled in political sagacity, Mr. Pownall joined his opposers, and
having acquainted himself with the geography of the country
1755. and its resources, he returned to England to press his own plans
Feb.
upon the notice of the ministry.   When Lord Loudoun came
1756. to America, Mr. Pownall accompanied him, but remained less
July 23.
than two months, when he hastened to England to solicit a
reënforcement of troops for the prosecution of the war.   Here
1757. he received his appointment as governor of Massachusetts,
March.
embarked in the fleet which brought the forces with Lord
Howe to Halifax, and thence proceeded to Boston, where he
Aug. 3. was formally received, and his commission was publicly read.[3]

Nearly every governor in the thirteen British colonies at
this date was a devout supporter of the prerogative ; nor could
any one have been appointed to office who was not a royalist.

---

[1] Letter of Andrew Oliver, of May
11, 1757, in Williams's MSS. ii. 23 ;
Letter of Bollan, in MS. Letters and
Papers, 1721–1760, fol. 186 ; Hutchinson, iii. 53 ; Minot, ii. 19.

[2] Smith's N. Y. ii. 206.

[3] Bollan, in his letter of March 12,
says, " I this day took leave of him,"
i. e., Pownall, "after having had the

pleasure to hear him make the plain-
est and strongest declarations of his
coming to his government with a determined purpose to promote to the
utmost of his power the prosperity of
the province, together with the highest regard for its liberties and charter
privileges."

Hence not the best men were selected to govern the people, but generally the most subservient. It would be ungenerous to insinuate that any one of these gentlemen was destitute of principle ; for men of far purer virtue and of far higher attainments have been often seduced by the flatteries of royalty, and the blandishments of place and power. This should be remembered in forming an estimate of the character of the provincial governors ; and, judged by this standard, Mr. Pownall will not suffer in comparison with his predecessors. Gifted with talents of a superior order, few were better acquainted with the American people than himself ; and his striking predictions of the effects of ministerial measures were, in more than one instance, remarkably verified. It should also be spoken to his credit, that, in his published writings, especially in his " Speech in the House of Commons," [1] his " Rights of the Colonies stated and defended," and his " Administration of the British Colonies," he sought to avert the evils of the revolution when pending ; though he was not the advocate of the independence of the colonies, but of their constitutional subordination to the Parliament of Great Britain.[2]

Long before the arrival of the new governor, important events had occurred at the westward. The French, during the winter of 1756–57, sent out scouting parties for the annoyance of the English ; and the English rangers at Fort William Henry performed gallant exploits. The brave Rogers, accompanied by Stark and others, seventy-four in all, officers included, marched from Carillon. On the way, they met with sledges sent by the French to Crown Point. The rangers attacked them, but were intercepted by a party of two hundred and fifty French and Indians, and in the night retreated, with the loss of fourteen who had fallen, and six who were missing. The survivors were applauded, and Stark was promoted.[3]

At length Montcalm decided upon a more formidable at-

CHAP.
VIII.

1757.

Jan. 15
to 17.

Jan. 21

---

[1] Published in 1769.
[2] Comp. Hutchinson, iii. 56; Minot, ii. 18, 19 ; Grahame, ii. 306, 307.
[3] Rogers's Journal, 38–49.

CHAP. tempt; and a detachment of fifteen hundred French and Indians
VIII. was sent, under Vaudreuil and De Longueuil, to attack Fort
1757. William Henry. At midnight they noiselessly approached the
Mar.19. fortress; but the vigilant sentries discovered them in time, an
alarm was sounded, and, by a brisk fire of cannon and musket-
Mar.20. ry, they were repulsed. The next day they invested the place,
Mar.21. and the day after summoned the commandant, Major Eyres,
1756. who had relieved General Winslow, to surrender. He refused.
Nov.11. The works were then assailed a fourth, and even a fifth time;
but, repulsed in every attack, the enemy could only burn the
vessels of the English, and their storehouses and huts. Strengthening Ticonderoga and Crown Point with two battalions, and
sending Captain Pouchot to Niagara, where he had been
posted most of the time for the year past,[1] Montcalm returned
to Montreal; and shortly after, Colonel Parker, who had been
ordered, at the head of four hundred English, to attack the
advanced guard near Ticonderoga, was led into an ambuscade,
and nearly half his men were captured or slain.[2]

The plan of campaign proposed by Lord Loudoun, and approved by the English ministry and the colonial governors, was
limited to the defence of the frontiers and the capture of Louisburg. Preparations for the latter expedition had been rapidly
1757. pushed in England; and seven regiments of infantry, and a
Jan. detachment of artillery commanded by Major General Hopson,
were assembled at Cork to await the arrival of a powerful
fleet of fourteen line-of-battle ships, which were to bear them to
America. This armament, under Admiral Holborne, was to
May 8. proceed on its voyage, and, on reaching Halifax, was to be
joined by Lord Loudoun with all the forces he could collect.
Jun. 19. In June, Lord Loudoun left New York, with six thousand men,
in the fleet of Sir Charles Hardy, consisting of four ships of
Jun. 29. war and seventy transports; ten days after he reached Hali-
July 9. fax; early in July, the whole armament was assembled; and

[1] Pouchot's Mems. i. 88–90.   38; Warburton's Conquest of Cana-
[2] Review of Pitt's Administration,   da, ii. 58, 59; Bancroft, iv. 252.

nineteen ships of the line and frigates, with innumerable smaller
vessels, and an army of thirteen battalions comprising ten thousand men, were mustered at the disposal of the British leaders.
But the pusillanimous Loudoun, "whom a child might outwit,
or terrify with a popgun," instead of pushing forward immediately to the attack, wasted his time in "making sham fights
and planting cabbages," until the French fleet had been reënforced by a number of ships of the line, when, deeming it useless to proceed, he abandoned the expedition, and returned to
New York.[1]

The relinquishment of the enterprise against Crown Point
was a severe disappointment to the people of the New England
States, who had set their hearts upon its successful prosecution;
and the result of the campaign of the previous year vindicated
the wisdom of their policy, and rebuked the imbecility of the
British commander. It was quite common with the British officers to decry the colonial forces as "inexperienced wood rangers,
who had never seen regular service, and who were wholly unacquainted with the discipline of military life." Hence, vaunting
their own superiority, they could brook no advice from the
provincial officers, but followed their own judgment, and relied
for success on the experience acquired upon the battle fields
of Europe.

Pending the progress of the expedition to Louisburg, Colonel
Webb, with his army of five or six thousand men, had been
left to cope with the vigilant Montcalm. The latter seized the

---

[1] Letter of James Gray, dated Halifax, July 16, 1757, and of Andrew
Oliver of July 14, in Williams's MSS.
ii. 28, 29; Conduct of Lord Loudoun
impartially reviewed, 2d ed. Lond.
1760, pp. 6–10, 20, 25–27; Hist.
of the War, 132–134; Grenville Corresp. i. 200–202; Hopkins's Defence
of the Halifax Libel, Boston, 1765, p.
4; Review of Pitt's Administration,
18, 22, 36, 37; Letts. and Mems. relative to Cape Breton, 331–336; Walpole to Sir H. Mann, Feb. 13, 1757;
Walpole's George II. ii. 231; Lord
Mahon's Hist. England, iv. 168; Mortimer's England, iii. 567; Hutchinson,
iii. 61, 62; Minot, ii. 23, 24; Warburton's Conquest of Canada, ii. 59–
62; Parsons, Life of Pepperrell, 298.
Indecision was the ruling fault of
Loudoun's character. "He is like
St. George upon the signposts," said
a Philadelphian to Dr. Franklin, "always on horseback, but never advances."

CHAP. favorable moment presented by the withdrawal of Lord Lou-
VIII. doun, and concentrated a force of from six to eight thousand
1757. French and Indians at Montreal, who were to ascend Lake
Aug. 2. George, land at its southern extremity, and besiege Fort William Henry. Webb might have saved the place had he
marched promptly to its relief; but, instead of this, he contented himself with sending a letter to Colonel Monro, the
commandant, exaggerating the numbers of the French, and
advising him to capitulate.[1] The latter refused to surrender,
and declared he would defend his post " to the last extremity."

Aug. 9. Nor did he yield until the eve of the Festival of St. Lawrence,
when half his guns were burst, and his ammunition was expended. The Indians, with their usual ferocity, fell upon his
troops after they were disarmed; and in the slaughter which
ensued six hundred dispersed among the woods and fled to
Fort Edward, whither they were followed by their surviving
comrades, one after another. Governor Pownall was informed

July 31. by express of these movements of the French; and appointing
Sir William Pepperrell lieutenant general over all the militia

Aug. 8. in the province, he was hastened to Springfield to forward supplies and collect a magazine of provisions and stores. Soon
after his arrival he learned the fate of the fortress; and though
the regiments of Worthington, Williams, Ruggles, and Chandler, from the counties of Hampshire and Worcester, had
marched to the relief of Monro, and others followed, they were
stopped by General Webb, whose timidity was strikingly manifested throughout the affair, and who was subsequently censured severely for his cowardice.[2]

---

[1] Mortimer, Hist. England, iii. 567,
says, General Webb beheld the preparation of Montcalm " with an indif-
ference and security bordering on infatuation. It is creditably reported
that he had private intelligence of all
the doings and motions of the French
general; yet, either despising his
strength or discrediting the informa-

tion, he neglected collecting the militia in time, and the fortress fell."

[2] Mass. Rec's; Order of Aug. 5,
1757, " for all and every one of his
majestie's well affected subjects, able
to bear arms, to repair to Fort Edward, on the Hudson, to serve with
General Webb for the relief of Fort
William Henry, which still stands out

Thus the English had been driven from the basin of the Ohio, and Montcalm had routed them from the basin of the St. Lawrence. The frontiers were in a defenceless condition, exposed to the ravages of a triumphant foe ; and New York and Massachusetts trembled for their own safety. The provincial troops alone had achieved signal successes ; not a laurel had been won by the British commanders. The opinion began to prevail that, so long as the war was thus conducted, the French would continue to be victorious ; and more than one was ready to echo the impassioned wish of John Adams : " O that we had nothing to do with Great Britain forever ! "[1]

Yet no disloyal wish was openly expressed ; nor was it until the people had been goaded to the point of desperation, that they gave bold utterance to the thoughts which inspired them. Hence when, in the fall of this year, recruiting parties reached Boston from Nova Scotia, and Lord Loudoun, as he had formerly done at New York and Philadelphia,[2] demanded that they should be quartered upon the people, threatening, in case of refusal, to march his regiments from New York and Connecticut to enforce obedience, the assembly passed a special act, similar to the act of Parliament for quartering troops in public houses ; and a message, expressing the sense of the people of the constitutional authority of Parliament, was draughted, which contains these words : " The authority of all acts of Parliament which concern the colonies, and extend to them, is

CHAP.
VIII.

1757.

Nov. 15.

1758.
Jan. 6.

---

fighting against a large and numerous body of the enemy ; " Letter of Worthington, of Aug. 6 ; Order of Pownall to Israel Williams, of Aug. 6 ; Second Letter of Pownall, of Aug. 7, &c., in Williams's MSS. ii. 31–33 ; Letter of N. Whiting, of Aug. 23, giving an account of the taking of the fort, in ibid. ii. 42 ; Review of Pitt's Administration, 38 ; Pouchot's Mems. i. 101–107 ; Walpole to Sir H. Mann, Oct. 12, 1757 ; Hutchinson, iii. 58–61 ; Minot, ii. 21–23 ; Grahame, ii.
[1] Smith's N. Y. ii. 245–249.
[2] Smith's N. Y. ii. 241, 242 ; Hazard's Register, v. 328 ; Bancroft, iv. 240, 241. In the summer session of the General Court, the governor recommended the passage of an act " to empower and require the civil magistrate to take up and assign quarters for such of the king's troops as should come into the province, under such regulations that the troops might be well accommodated, and the province be as little burdened as possible ; " but the court declined complying with the recommendation. Mass. Rec's; Hutchinson, iii. 63.

CHAP.
VIII.

1757.

April 5.

Jun. 29.

Jun. 29.

July.

ever acknowledged in all the courts of law, and made the rule of all judicial proceedings in the province. There is not a member of the General Court, and we know of no inhabitant within the bounds of the government, that ever questioned this authority. To prevent any ill consequences which may result from an opinion of our holding such principles, we now utterly disavow them, as we should readily have done at any time past if there had been occasion for it." [1]

Pitt, who was compelled to resign his office in April, was re-appointed in the following June, and, upon his accession, exerted himself diligently to retrieve the fortunes of England and to humble France.[2] But he labored under great difficulties, owing to the absurd management adopted by his predecessors. Officers had been sent to America to take charge of the forces of England, not because of their fitness, but because their rank entitled them to precedence. " We are undone," said Chesterfield, " both at home and abroad — at home, by our increasing expenses ; abroad, by our ill luck and incapacity. The French are masters to do what they please in America."[3] But Pitt did not despair. " I am sure," said he to the Duke of Devonshire, — " I am sure I can save this country, and no one else can."[4] And he did save it. It was midsummer before the new ministry was thoroughly organized ; then it was too late

[1] Mass. Rec's; Jour. House Reps.; Hutchinson, iii. 65, 66 ; Gordon's Am. Rev. i. 96; Minot, ii. 24–30; Chalmers, Revolt, ii. 307, 308. Lord Loudoun was dissatisfied with this act, and would not allow that the General Court was authorized to take such a step, as *in time of war the rules and customs of war must govern* ; but the court, in reply, declared their opinion that the act of Parliament did not extend to the plantations, and that the rules and customs of war were not the rules which the civil magistrate was to govern himself by, but that a law of the province was necessary for his justification.

[2] History of the War, 114–117 : Grenville Corresp. i. 195, 196 ; Chatham Corresp. i. 236; Lord Mahon's Hist. Eng. i. 338, 344. " From this period," says the editor of the Chatham Correspondence, " commenced the brilliant era justly called Mr. Pitt's administration ;" " the greatest and most glorious, perhaps," adds Lord Mahon, " that England had ever yet known."

[3] Taylor's Corresp. of Earl of Chatham, i. 238, note ; Lord Mahon's Hist. Eng. i. 345.

[4] Lord Orford's Memoirs, ii. 271; Lord Mahon's Hist. Eng. i. 299 ; N. Am. Rev. for Oct. 1842.

to accomplish any thing that year. Hence the reverses of CHAP.
1757 must be charged to the old ministry. Lord George VIII.
Sackville attempted to apologize for Loudoun; but Pitt, with 1757.
keenest scalpel, ripped up his rotten arguments, and exposed
to view the festering corruption which his client's mismanagement had bred. "Nothing has been done," said he; "nothing
attempted. We have lost all the waters; we have not a boat
on the lakes. Every door is open to France." [1]

The work of reform was instantly commenced; and Loudoun,
who had been at Hartford, planning schemes which he was 1758.
incompetent to effect, was recalled. [2] Massachusetts had pre- 1757.
viously proposed to the New England assemblies a meeting of Dec. 30.
commissioners to agree upon measures of mutual defence; but
New Hampshire and Rhode Island refused to respond to the
call. Connecticut alone seconded the proposal, and sent agents
to Boston, where a plan was agreed upon, and New Hampshire
and Rhode Island were invited to accede; but the whole affair
dropped by the neglect of the assemblies to act upon the
report. [3] The attempt of Lord Loudoun was equally unsuccessful; and hastening to Boston, at his instance the governor,
in his speech to the General Court, recommended that provisions should be made "for a suitable body of forces to coöperate in aid and assistance to his majesty's troops at the eastward." This request gave rise to debate. The number of
men solicited was twenty-two hundred; but the assembly hesitated to vote the supply. "How long are the men to continue
in service?" it was asked. "What officers are they to be
placed under? Where is the command to be? How are they
to be paid, armed, and victualled? What is their destination?
What will be the whole force when they shall have joined it?"
The general was displeased with these queries, and would

[1] Bancroft, iv. 291.
[2] A letter from Pitt, announcing
his recall and the appointment of Abercrombie in his stead, may be seen

in the Trumbull MSS. i. 127.
[3] Mass. Rec's; Hutchinson, iii. 67;
Minot, ii. 33.

CHAP. doubtless have publicly manifested his displeasure, had not an
VIII. express from New York brought intelligence that he was re-
1757. called. The very next morning he left the town, in high anger,
to return to New York, and shortly after embarked for England, to advise a magisterial exercise of British authority, and
to vote in Parliament for enforcing American taxation by fire
and sword.

Dec.   Six months after assuming the reins, Pitt succeeded in obtaining the orders of the king that every provincial officer, of
no higher rank than colonel, should have equal command with
the British, according to the date of their commissions.[1] He
had thoroughly acquainted himself with the posture of affairs
in America, and knew that this measure was not only just, but
politic. And the result proved the correctness of his views.
The same letters which informed the government that Lord
Loudoun had been superseded recommended, in the strongest
terms, an exertion on the part of the province to enlist fresh
troops, and gave encouragement that a proper compensation
would be made by Parliament. These forces, it was expected,
would be employed in the reduction of Canada; and at once
the House voted to raise seven thousand men, to be formed
into regiments under provincial officers approved by the captain general, and to continue in session until the first of
November, unless dismissed sooner.[2] Similar letters were sent
to the other colonies, and with a like success; for, before the
May. season ended, twenty thousand provincials were called into service. The contributions from different parts were exceedingly
unequal — the New England colonies, as usual, excelling the
rest. Nearly one third of the effective men of Massachusetts
were enrolled.

France, in the mean time, though thus far successful, trembled for the future safety of Canada. Famine stared the
people in the face, who were cut off from receiving supplies

---

[1] Lord Orford's Memoirs, ii. 261;   [2] Mass. Rec's; Hutchinson, iii. 69
Lord Mahon's Hist. Eng. ii. 363.   Minot, ii. 36, 37; Bancroft, iv. 291.

from abroad. "I shudder," said Montcalm, "when I think of CHAP. provisions. The famine is very great." "For all our success," VIII. he afterwards wrote, "New France needs peace, or sooner or 1758. later it must fall; such are the numbers of the English, such Feb. 23. the difficulty of our receiving supplies."[1]

Three expeditions were planned by the British ministry, the execution of which was intrusted to experienced officers, selected for their coolness, intrepidity, and judgment. The first, under Jeffrey Amherst and James Wolfe, was to join the fleet under Boscawen, and besiege Louisburg. The second, under Joseph Forbes, was to scour the Ohio valley. And the third, under Abercrombie and Lord Howe, was to proceed against Ticonderoga and Crown Point.

Towards the last of May, Amherst, after a long passage, May 23. reached Halifax. Twenty-two ships of the line and fifteen frigates, with one hundred and twenty smaller vessels, composed the fleet under Boscawen; and fourteen battalions of infantry and engineers, in all twelve thousand men, formed the army of Amherst. Wolfe, who while a lad had fought at Dettingen and Fontenoy, and who had won laurels at Laffeldt when just of age, panted for fresh honors on the new scene of action; and Cook, afterwards celebrated as the circumnavigator of the globe, served in this expedition. In five days the June 2. armament arrived off Cape Breton. Wind and fog delayed June 8. the landing for six days more. Four days later the French Jun. 12. withdrew from their outposts, and the lighthouse battery was surprised. At the end of six weeks Louisburg was in ruins, July 26. and the fortress surrendered. More than five thousand prisoners were taken; eleven ships of war were seized or destroyed; two hundred and forty pieces of ordnance, fifteen thousand stand of arms, and a vast amount of ammunition, provisions, and military stores fell into the hands of the victors; and eleven stand of colors were laid at the feet of George II.,

---

[1] Pouchot's Mems. i. 130, 131; Bancroft, iv. 294.

CHAP. and afterwards deposited with great solemnity in the Cathedral
VIII. of St. Paul's.   A few hovels mark the site of the Dunkirk of
1758. America.[1]

Jun. 30.   The expedition under Forbes was equally successful. Twelve
hundred and fifty of Montgomery's Highlanders from South
Carolina, three hundred and fifty Royal Americans, twenty-
seven hundred men from Pennsylvania, sixteen hundred from
Virginia, and about three hundred from Maryland, — in all,
between six and seven thousand men, — placed under Colonel
Nov. 5. Washington, comprised his army. It was late in the season
before the troops reached Loyal Hanna, afterwards Fort Ligo-
nia ; and then Forbes, fast sinking into the grave, determined
to advance no farther. But Washington, unwilling to abandon the enterprise, was impatient to proceed ; and, obtaining
consent, with his brigade of provincials he promptly set forward. As he drew near Fort Du Quesne, the disheartened
garrison, about five hundred in number, set the fort on fire,
and by the light of the flames descended the Ohio. Before the
Nov.25. month closed Washington planted his flag on the deserted
ruins ; and, in honor of the great statesman of England, the
place was named Pittsburg.[2]

   The third expedition was a failure. The troops from New
England and the other northern colonies were detailed for its

[1] Narr. in French Doc'ts, Mass.
Archives, ix. 1–25 ; Grenville Corresp. i. 240–243, 254–256, 265 ; Walpole's Mem. of George II. iii. 134 ;
Hist. of the War, 152, 153 ; Letters and
Mems. relative to Cape Breton, 342
et seq. ; Review of Pitt's Administration, 47–49 ; Knox's Histor. Jour. i.
144 ; Boston Gazette for 1758 ; Mortimer, Hist. Eng. iii. 603, 604 ; Minot, ii. 38 ; Grahame, ii. ; Warburton's Conquest of Canada, ii. 74–80.
   [2] Grenville Corresp. i. 273–275,
289 ; Pouchot's Mems. i. 170–177 ;
Review of Pitt's Administration, 51 ;
Olden Time, ii. 284 ; Public Adverti-
ser of Jan. 20, 1759 ; Lord Mahon's

Hist. Eng. ii. 365 and note ; Chalmers, Revolt, ii. 291 ; Sparks's Washington, ii. 271–327 ; Sargent's Braddock's Expedition, 270–274 ; Warburton's Conquest of Canada, ii. 103–
105. Mortimer, Hist. Eng. iii. 606,
says the expedition under Forbes left
Philadelphia June 13, and advanced
to Ray's Town, 90 miles from Fort
Du Quesne, whence he sent forward
Bouquet, with 2000 men, to Loyal
Hanna, 50 miles farther. The latter
detached 800 men, under Major
Grant, to reconnoitre, who were repulsed ; upon which Forbes advanced,
and the enemy retreated, &c.

prosecution, and were ordered to take the field early in May ; CHAP.
but, owing to the slowness with which the muster proceeded, VIII.
it was the middle of June before any movements were made 1758.
towards the scene of action. Massachusetts had agreed to May.
June.
enlist seven thousand men for the war. Connecticut, rivalling
her zeal, voted to raise five thousand. New Hampshire, a
thinly-settled province, could furnish but nine hundred ; but
she sent from her hills a captain who was a host in himself —
the gallant Stark. At length nine thousand provincials, from
New England, New York, and New Jersey, assembled on the
banks of Lake George. Over six thousand regulars were Jun. 28.
already on the spot, making, in all, an army of fifteen thousand
men.[1] Early in July the cannon and stores arrived ; and the July 5.
whole force, in upwards of a thousand boats, embarked for
Ticonderoga. The spectacle was gorgeous to behold ; the
armament stretching far down the lake, and moving on, with
flashing oars and glittering weapons, to strains of music which
rung shrilly from crags and rocks, or died away in mellowed
strains among the distant mountains. As day closed in, a landing was effected at Sabbath Day Point ; and an hour before
midnight, reëmbarking, the troops once more moved down the
lake, until they reached the point which still preserves the
name of Lord Howe, where they disembarked. Seven thousand July 6
men, in four columns, began the march through the adjacent
wood, with Rogers and his men in advance as scouts. Soon
they were bewildered ; and, falling in with De Trépézée, at
the head of three hundred men, who had likewise lost his way,
a skirmish ensued, in which Lord Howe, the soul of the expedition, was the first to fall, expiring immediately. Massachusetts voted a monument to his memory, and the English nation
mourned his loss.[2]

---

[1] Mortimer, Hist. Eng. iii. 605,
says Abercrombie's army consisted
of 7000 regulars and 10,000 provincials.
[2] Grenville Corresp. i. 261, 262 ;
Review of Pitt's Administration, 50 ;

Bute to Pitt, Aug. 20, 1758, in Chatham Corresp. i. 335; Mass. Rec's;
Hutchinson, iii. 71; Minot, ii. 39.
This monument was placed in Westminster Abbey, the resting-place of
the worthies of England.

CHAP.
VIII.

1758.
July 7.

July 8.

The next morning, Abercrombie, a victim to " the extremest fright and consternation," drew back to the landing-place; but the gallant Bradstreet, ever active, pushed forward with a strong detachment, the British general reluctantly followed, and that night the army encamped a mile and a half from the enemy. On the following day, at an early hour, Clark, the chief engineer, was sent to reconnoitre; his report was favorable, and it was resolved to proceed. Stark, of New Hampshire, and Rogers, the ranger, saw finished works where their comrades saw only an incomplete breastwork; but the orders were given, and the attack began. The result was fatal. Montcalm, at first irresolute, saw the mistake of his assailants, and was prepared to meet them. As the English drew near, pushing forward in hot haste to open the action, a murderous fire poured in upon them, which mowed down officers and men by hundreds. Abercrombie, intimidated, withdrew to a place of safety. In vain did the intrepid Highlanders charge for three hours, without confusion or faltering, hewing with their broadswords a passage among the branches, and striving to retrieve the fortunes of the day. Two thousand were killed or wounded in the battle; the survivors were panic-struck, and rushed hastily to the boats; nor did they pause in their retreat until again far out on the bosom of Lake George.[1] The reduction of Fort Frontenac by Bradstreet, which shortly followed, was but a partial atonement for the failure of Abercrombie. His expedition was abortive; the situation of the troops was embarrassing in the extreme; and well might the government gloomily ask, What will the next year bring forth?[2]

Three expeditions were planned for that year, centring upon Quebec, the "palladium of Canada," itself the citadel of the French dominions. The first was to proceed through the River

[1] Letter of Oliver Partridge, of July 12, 1758, in Williams's MSS. ii. 77; Pouchot's Mems. i. 134–159; Rogers's Journal, 111–120; Hutchinson, iii. 70–74; Smith's N. Y. ii. 265, 266; Warburton's Conquest of Canada, ii. 84–97.

[2] Letter of William Williams, of Sept. 8, in Williams's MSS. ii. 85.

St. Lawrence; the second was to cross Lake Champlain; the third was to attempt the reduction of Niagara, cross Lake Ontario, embark on the St. Lawrence, and proceed to Montreal. In the arrangements for this campaign, not esteeming, like many ministers, the "Army List" as an unerring guide, Pitt disregarded seniority of rank, and conferred appointments upon the ablest men.[1] Stanwix, after whom Fort Stanwix was named, a daring, intrepid, and resolute officer, was to occupy the posts from Pittsburg to Lake Erie; Prideaux, whose name is preserved in Prideaux's Landing, was to reduce Fort Niagara, in conjunction with Johnson; Amherst, now commander-in-chief, at the head of twelve thousand men, was to advance to Lake Champlain; and the gallant Saunders, a "pattern of most sturdy bravery, united with the most unaffected modesty," was to support the attack on Quebec; while Wolfe, "the immortal," was to command the army in the River St. Lawrence. All these movements were esteemed of great consequence, and, if judiciously conducted, it was thought could scarcely fail of success.[2] France saw her danger, and despaired of preserving Canada. Montcalm had informed Belle Isle that, without unexpected good fortune, Canada must be taken this year or the next. The country was in an impoverished condition, and its energies were exhausted. With a population of less than fourscore thousand, only seven thousand of whom were fit for service, and the eight French battalions numbering but thirty-two hundred men, — what were these to the fifty thousand of England and her colonies? Besides, famine still raged; the fields were hardly cultivated; and old men and women, and even little children, were compelled to engage in tilling the soil, and reaping the scanty harvest upon which they were to depend; for supplies were cut off by the vigilance

[1] Letter of Pitt, of Dec. 9, 1758, in Trumbull MSS. i. 137; Lord Mahon's Hist. Eng. ii. 378.

[2] Military critics, indeed, have censured the plan of the prime minister as imprudent, (see Smollett's Hist. Eng. b. iii. c. xi. § 13;) "but," says Lord Mahon, (Hist. Eng. ii. 379,) "let it never be forgotten how much easier it is to cavil than to act."

CHAP. of the English. By the fall of Louisburg and the reduction
VIII. of Acadia, the high road of the St. Lawrence lay open to the
1759. British ; and the capture of Fort Du Quesne had given them
the command of the valley of the Ohio. Hence the Canadian
French were isolated from all aid, and confined within the limits of the country they occupied.[1]

The policy of England in making liberal appropriations for
the conduct of the war was an encouragement to the colonies
to continue their enlistments. Nearly seven thousand men were
raised by Massachusetts ; Connecticut sent five thousand into
the field ; and the other northern colonies put forth their best
exertions for strengthening the army. It has been estimated
that, in all, nearly twenty-five thousand men were furnished by
the colonies, and that England furnished twenty-five thousand
more.[2] The expense of the war to Massachusetts alone, for
1758, was over a hundred and fifty thousand pounds ;[3] and the
burden upon the other colonies was proportionally great. The
exertions of the colonies, therefore, under these circumstances,
evince their loyalty. The colonies to the south, though equally
interested, had done less for carrying on the war. The institution of slavery crippled their energies, and rendered it dangerous to enlist many whites.[4]

The brigade of Prideaux was the first to engage actively.
July 1. At the opening of July, he embarked on Lake Ontario, with
two battalions from New York, a battalion of Royal Americans, and two British regiments, with a detachment of artillery,
and the Indians under Sir William Johnson. Pouchot was the
commandant at Fort Niagara, and the place was speedily in-
July 15. vested. In the midst of the siege Prideaux was killed by the
bursting of a cohorn ; the command devolved upon Sir William
July 25. Johnson ; and ten days after the garrison capitulated. This

[1] Pouchot's Mems. i. 178 et seq. ;   [3] Mass. Rec's ; Minot, ii. 49.
Walpole's George II. 394 ; Warbur-   [4] Trumbull's Connecticut, ii. 371 ;
ton's Conquest of Canada, ii. 108.   Bancroft, iv. 224.
[2] Trumbull MSS. i. 142.

victory was so decisive that the officers and troops sent by CHAP.
Stanwix from Pittsburg took possession of the French posts as VIII.
far as Erie without resistance; and the English were masters 1759.
of Niagara River and of Lake Erie. Colonel Gage, who was
sent to succeed Prideaux, was intrusted to take the fort at La
Gallette; but so many difficulties attended the attempt that it
was laid aside, and no assistance was afforded to the army at
Quebec from that quarter.[1]

In the mean time General Amherst left New York for Apr. 28.
Albany, and, upon his arrival, busied himself in preparations May 3.
for transporting his troops to Lake George. Tedious delays
attended this movement; but at length, towards the last of Jun. 21.
June, he reached the lake, and immediately traced out the
ground for a fort. Four weeks later all was in readiness; his July 21
army, numbering eleven thousand men, embarked upon the
waters, and the next day landed near the site of Abercrombie's
former encampment.

Conscious of his inability to sustain a protracted siege, Bour-
lamarque, the commandant at Ticonderoga, silently abandoned
the fort, leaving every gun loaded and pointed, several mines July 23.
charged for the destruction of the defences, and a lighted fire
communicating with the magazine. Two days after, in the July 26.
night, an awful explosion rent the air; and, from under the
cloud of smoke and the shower of embers, the flames of the
breastworks flashed upon the sky, while at intervals, "from the
mass of fire, the yellow flash of the bursting guns and the ex-
ploding mines varied the tints of the light that fell far and
near upon the lake and the forest." [2]

Five days later Crown Point was abandoned; and the Aug. 1.
French retreated to intrench themselves at Isle-aux-Noix, with Aug. 16
three thousand five hundred men and one hundred cannon.

[1] Pouchot's Mems. ii. 15–131;   293; Smith's N. Y. ii. 275.
Hist. of the War, 190–192; Review   [2] Pouchot's Mems. ii. 13, 14; Roof Pitt's Administration, 107; Hutch-   gers's Journal, 138–142.
inson, iii. 77; Chalmers, Revolt, ii.

CHAP. The position they had taken gave them the command of the
VIII. entrance to the Richelieu River — the most vulnerable, and at
1759. the same time the most vital, part of Canada. Amherst, instead of instantly proceeding to attack this post, contented
himself with his present advantages ; and all August, and the
month of September, and ten days of October passed before
he embarked. Then messages from Quebec arrived, which
caused him to turn back, having done nothing but occupy and
repair deserted forts.[1]

The fleet under Sir Charles Saunders, and the army under
Feb. Wolfe, left England in February, and arrived before Quebec
Jun. 26. the latter part of June. The army of Wolfe, landed on the
Isle of Orleans, consisted of eight regiments, two battalions of
Royal Americans, three companies of rangers, artillery, and a
brigade of engineers — in all, about eight thousand men. The
fleet under Saunders comprised twenty-two ships of the line,
and as many frigates and armed vessels. A noble spectacle this
armament presented, as the ships of war, with sails furled and
pennons streaming, lay at anchor with the numerous transports,
and as the white tents, in which the troops were lodged, stretched
across the island. But far more imposing, to the eye of Wolfe,
was the appearance of the fortress he was about to besiege,
with its frowning bastions and its array of batteries bristling
with guns. What though a storm burst over his head as he
gazed upon that scene, and the teeming rain fell like a veil
between him and the shore? What though the lightning
hissed through the air, and transports and boats were dashed
frightfully together? What though the enemy launched fire
ships, to light up with lurid glare the bosom of the waters, for
the destruction of the fleet? The gallant commander was not

---

[1] Pouchot's Mems. ii. 14. The
occurrences of this campaign, slight as
they were, called forth the warmest
eulogiums from Pitt. "If it was in
Vigetius," cried he, "all the world
would admire; it is in America, and
nobody regards it." Lord Orford's
Memoirs, ii. 398 ; Lord Mahon's Eng.
ii. 381.

one of those who "fret at trifles, and quarrel with their CHAP
toothpicks." [1] The storm could not quench his courage ; the VIII.
lightning flash but stimulated his zeal. The fire ships were 1759.
repulsed ; and, after the excitement of the hour abated, the
"All is well" of the British seamen greeted his ears like music
from home.

The arrangements for the siege were rapidly pushed ; but
the obstacles to be encountered were many and various. Point
Levi was soon occupied ; and from this post heavy ordnance Jun. 30
played upon the city with ruinous effect. Strong intrenchments
were likewise thrown up on the westernmost point of the
Island of Orleans ; and the safety of the fleet in the basin was
assured. A few days later Wolfe encamped upon the eastern July 9.
bank of the Montmorenci, whose beautiful fall is second in
interest only to Niagara. From the batteries at these places
an incessant fire of guns and mortars was poured upon the
city and upon the French lines to the westward. The lower
town was much damaged ; and a fire broke out in the upper July 16.
town where a shell had fallen.

July and August passed thus away. At length, early in
September, Wolfe himself discovered the cove which bears his Sept. 9
name, where the bending promontories form a basin, over
which the hill rises precipitously. A path, so narrow that two
men could hardly walk in it abreast, led to its top. Here he
resolved to surprise the city. On the twelfth of the month Sep. 12
he issued his last orders, and by one o'clock on the morning
of the thirteenth every thing was in readiness. Silently and
swiftly the boats dropped down the stream, favored by the
darkness and by a flowing tide. As they moved on, the
young general, whose mind was full, repeated the lines from
Gray's Elegy, prophetic of the fate to which he was hastening : —

[1] Wolfe to his mother, Nov. 6, 1751, quoted in Lord Mahon's Hist. Eng.
ii. 377.

CHAP.
VIII.
———
1759.

"The boast of heraldry, the pomp of power,
    And all that beauty, all that wealth e'er gave,
    Await alike the inexorable hour —
    The path of glory leads but to the grave."

Sept. 13.   In a short time the boats landed, and the ascent commenced. When morning broke, the army of Wolfe stood upon the Plains of Abraham, ready for battle. Montcalm was bewildered when he learned of their presence ; but at once he resolved to give them battle. Before midday the battle commenced ; before nightfall it was over. Wolfe and Montcalm were both mortally wounded ; the former expired the same day, the latter on the day following. Quebec was taken, and the key of Canada was in the hands of the English. When the tidings reached Boston, they were received with unusual demonstrations of joy. Bonfires blazed from every hill ; every pulpit applauded Wolfe's bravery ; every paper scattered the news ; legislatures vied with each other in congratulatory resolves. In England, the nation triumphed at the victory its general had achieved ; the nation mourned his early decease. France was in double mourning — for the loss of her general, and for the loss of her possessions.[1]

1760.
May.   The attempt of De Levi to regain Quebec was unsuccessful. "The smiles of fortune were turned to frowns." France was not destined to be again mistress of that fortress ; and its capture resulted in the downfall of her dominions in the west. Sept. 9. Amherst closed the war by the reduction of Montreal ; and the Marquis de Vaudreuil signed the capitulation which separated Canada from France forever. Thus the French war was principally ended so far as America was concerned. Peace was not declared until 1763 ; but in the north hostilities had ceased nearly three years before.

[1] Pouchot's Mems. ii. 131–150; Grenville Corresp. i. passim ; Chatham Corresp. i. 425 et seq. ; Review of Pitt's Administration, 93–106 ; Hist. of the War, 171–189 ; Mortimer's Eng. iii. 655–663 ; Grahame, ii. ; Lord Mahon's Eng. ii. 381–390 ; Warburton's Conquest of Canada, ii. 171–222.

The cost of the war to England was enormous — amounting, CHAP.
in all, to seventy millions sterling. The cost to the colonies VIII.
was proportionally great; and Massachusetts lavished her 1759.
treasure and strength for the conquest of Canada. The effect
of that conquest upon the destinies of the colonies will appear
hereafter. It was the *preparatio libertatis* — the stepping-stone
to the revolution; and officers were trained in all parts of the
country to take charge of the armies of the thirteen United
Colonies, enrolled under Washington as commander-in-chief.

CHAPTER IX.

CONTESTS WITH THE CROWN.

ENGLAND lost her colonies by the mismanagement of her ministers. It can hardly be supposed that the bulk of the nation was hostile to America, for the ties of relationship between the countries were too strong to admit of such feelings. Natives of England were frequently passing from the old world to the new; and many descendants of the original planters returned to the mother country and to the homes of their ancestors. To visit England was to go home; and when those who had been born on these shores crossed the Atlantic, and landed at London, or Bristol, or Plymouth, they did not feel that they had landed among strangers, but among those of their own nation, who spoke the same language and owned the same kindred. There could not be, on either side of the ocean, any extensive alienation of feeling. True, differences of religious opinion have been fruitful of discord in the world; and divisions have been produced by such differences in families and among nations. But the Americans were Protestants as well as the English; and if a majority of the former were dissenters from the ritual of the Anglican church, the doctrines professed by that church were generally received. It can never be believed that the English, as a people, were unfriendly to America; and if alienation of feeling led to a rupture between the colonies and the crown, there must have been a cause for that alienation, for which rulers were chiefly responsible. And the history of the times abundantly proves that the counsellors of the king, like the counsellors of Achitophel, were unworthy of his confidence and traitors to his interests.

From the settlement of Massachusetts, there were not wanting men, neither friends to the colony nor to the English
constitution, who busied themselves in secretly traducing and
maliciously representing the loyalty of the people. These
men could always find others to listen to their tales; and,
under the Stuarts, the mischiefs which sprang from this source
threatened serious evils. Those who have been disappointed
in the prosecution of their own schemes can seldom witness without envy the successes of others; and especially if
crossed in their purposes, the wound rankles deeper in their
breasts, and becomes immedicable. Such was the experience
of America at that period; and, by the machinations of her
enemies, Massachusetts lost the charter which, for more than
fifty years, had guarded her liberties and protected her from
harm. When a new charter was granted, her enemies revived,
and, ever vigilant to check her prosperity, their schemes for
her humiliation were prosecuted afresh. The parties responsible for the measures which followed it is not difficult to desig-
nate. Merchants and manufacturers, whose grasping avarice
could brook no rivalry, complained of the commercial and
industrial prosperity of New England; aspirants for office,
eager for preferment and lacking in principle, echoed these
complaints, and deplored the levelling spirit which prevailed;
and purblind statesmen, destitute of political sagacity, though
vaunting their superior wisdom, recommended a course of legislation based upon false premises, supported by misrepresentations, and enforced with a rigor which begat a retaliatory
spirit, and alienated those whom the truly wise would have
sought to conciliate, rather than to repel.

Hooker, the great light of English literature, and the defender of the "ecclesiastical polity" of the church, declares,
that "the lawful power of making laws to command whole
political societies of men belongeth so properly unto the same
entire societies, that for any prince or potentate, of what kind
soever upon earth, to exercise the same of himself, and not

either by express commission immediately and personally received from God, or else authority received at first from their
consent upon whose persons they impose laws, — it is no better
than mere tyranny."[1]   To the correctness of this doctrine the
American people readily subscribed ; and the acts of the king
and of the Parliament of which they complained were, in their
estimation, an infringement of their liberties as Englishmen
and as men.   The history of that legislation, and of its causes
and results, will prepare us to understand the action of the
colonies, and will amply defend them from the charge of
disloyalty.

The instincts of a whole people may sometimes be wrong ;
yet the maxim, *Vox populi vox Dei*, holds true in general. A
few persons may delude themselves with the idea that their
rights are invaded, when, in fact, all that has awakened their
resentment is that wholesome restraint indispensable to the
welfare of every community.   But when the public itself rises
in its might ; when the gifted and the true, as well as the
masses, are burning with a sense of overwhelming injustice,
and no alternative is left but to resist or be enslaved ; then
resistance is lawful — nay, it is imperatively demanded ; and
he who would condemn it must do so by a perverse reasoning,
against which there is no remedy, and which can only be left
to be cured by its own folly.   For nearly a century the American people were the victims of an oppression as systematic as
it was unjust.   They were entitled to the rights of Englishmen
— to the rights of man.   The former were trampled upon ; the
latter were denied.   English jurisprudence bounded its views
of American duty by the narrowest construction of legal fic-
tions.   It seems never to have entered the minds of the majority of British statesmen that there was any thing superior to
human constitutions ; nor was the sacredness of compacts
strictly regarded.   Not only was there a defect in the founda-

---

[1] Eccles. Polity, book viii.

tion of their reasoning, but the superstructure built upon that CHAP. reasoning was equally defective. A gigantic system of fraud IX. and of wrong was reared, which reached such a height that 1748 the whole political fabric tottered under its weight, and the to dismemberment of the colonies was the natural result. 1763.

The restriction of commercial and of manufacturing interests was one of the earliest causes of complaint. There has never existed, perhaps, a more energetic people than the original settlers of British America. Coming to a new country, which was to be subdued by their toil, and compelled to depend, not upon extraneous aid, but upon their own resources, for success, the efforts they put forth were necessarily vigorous; nor would their labors have been crowned with such abundant rewards, had it not been for the diligence with which they were prosecuted. Hence, within fifteen years from the settlement of 1643. Boston, the inhabitants of Massachusetts were noted for their enterprise; they had built up a commerce, both local and foreign, and had laid the foundation for domestic manufactures.[1] And from that time forward these branches of industry were pursued with a zeal which knew no abatement, but which was constantly stimulated by the hope of increased gains; so that, before the charter fell, merchants and manufacturers began to 1676. complain that such "widely-extended traffic, if not checked in season, would not only ruin the trade of this kingdom, but would leave no sort of dependence from that country to this."[2] In consequence of this enterprise, and of the complaints of the disaffected, the commerce of the country was subjected to laws whose authority was resisted and whose constitutionality was denied, though submission was generally, if reluctantly, paid to them.

Before the close of the seventeenth century, at the instance 1696. of Davenant and the principal merchants of Bristol and Liverpool, the "Board of Trade" was established, to regulate the

---

[1] See vol. i. of this work, p. 309.   [2] See vol. i. p. 453.

CHAP. national and colonial commerce. The position of this body,
IX.   even if the expediency of its establishment is conceded, was
1696. peculiarly unfortunate; nor were its members, in all cases,
distinguished for their wisdom. Framed to promote the
commerce of England, which attracted a large share of the
attention of the nation, it had yet no executive power, nor
could it enforce the regulations it saw fit to adopt. It could
only investigate, deliberate, and advise. It could hear complaints from whatever source they came, especially from the
governors of the colonies; but it had little responsibility for
the measures it proposed. The ministers were the responsible
parties, though it was doubtless designed that they should be
advised by the lords of trade, and kept properly informed;
but, from the fact that the power of these lords was purposely
circumscribed, and their importance could be increased only
by alarming the fears or humoring the prejudices of the counsellors of the king, they were tempted to give false information, and to suggest harsh measures, well knowing that either
would result in little harm unless the counsellors were deceived
by their information, and approved their measures. It must
not be supposed, however, that the Board of Trade was utterly
powerless to accomplish the purposes for which it was instituted. On the contrary, as the depositary for all complaints
from home and from abroad, and as bound to be informed of
the state of the colonies in general, and of each province in
particular, its archives were loaded with documents of every
description, and to this day are valuable for the materials they
furnish illustrating the progress of the colonies and the spirit
and purposes of their rulers and officers.[1]

1701   The war against the new charter was commenced at an early
to
1715. date; but, fortunately for the people, by the labors of their

[1] The records of this board are
comprised in upwards of two thousand
folio volumes, relating chiefly to America. The State of New York, with
commendable liberality, has published
several volumes relating to the history
of that state; and the materials from
the same source illustrating the history of Massachusetts are copious and
valuable.

agents and the help of their friends these attempts were frustrated, and the province was left to act under the instrument which had been sanctioned by solemn pledges, and which could not have been violated without the grossest injustice.[1] The character of these attempts evinces the infatuation which had seized upon the statesmen of England, and their ignorance of the principles of natural and civil liberty.

It was a defect in the charter of William and Mary that the governors of the provinces were to be appointed by the king, instead of being chosen by the people. These governors, it was early foreseen, would receive their appointments, not because of their acquaintance with the countries they were to rule, or their fidelity to the interests of the people, but because of their zeal in supporting the prerogative. For the most part strangers to America, having neither estate, nor connections, nor interests there, little dependence could be placed upon their friendliness; and of many it was openly said, "They come only to make money as fast as they can; are sometimes men of vicious characters and broken fortunes, sent by a minister merely to get them out of the way; and, as they intend staying in the country no longer than their government continues, and purpose to leave no family behind them, they are apt to be regardless of the good will of the people, and care not what is said or thought of them after they are gone."[2]

It was on this ground that the legislatures of Massachusetts and New York, as well as of other provinces, refused to settle fixed salaries on their governors. It was only by so doing that their rapacity could be curbed and their fidelity secured. The misrepresentations of these gentlemen had, doubtless, a powerful influence upon the suggestions and actions of the lords of trade, and the secretary for the southern department who stood between them and the crown. They were supposed

---

[1] For an account of these attempts for the subversion of the charter, see Dummer's Defence, Hutchinson, Grahame, &c.; and comp. Franklin's Works, iv. 296.

[2] Franklin's Works; Prior Doc'ts.

CHAP. to be well acquainted with the condition of the colonies and
  IX. the views of the people; and when, in their state papers, they
complained of the "insubordinate spirit" which prevailed, and
accused the people of disloyalty, it is not surprising that their
allegations were received as true, and that an impression went
abroad unfavorable to America. The governors of Massachusetts were not behind those of other provinces in spreading
these misrepresentations; and the official papers of the Board
of Trade prove conclusively that few of them hesitated to
accuse the people of "aiming at independence," and of "resisting the wholesome instructions of the king."

The controversies with the crown under the administrations
of Dudley, of Shute, of Burnet, and of Belcher, have been
already noticed, with the action of Parliament during that
period. Under the administration of Governor Shirley, these
contests were continued; and that gentleman, whose ambition
it was to commend himself to the favor of the king and the
ministry, and who was a zealous supporter of the supremacy of
Parliament, was conspicuous for his zeal in the cause of oppres-
1749. sion — urging a tax to be laid upon the colonies by Parliament
for the support of frontier garrisons, and a revenue to the
crown independent of the people. A large share of responsibility for the measures which followed must attach to Mr.
Shirley and his confederates in the other provinces. It was
at their suggestion that many steps were taken which would
hardly have been thought of, or at least not attempted, had it
not been for their advice. They were busy in inflaming the
prejudices of the enemies of America, and succeeded too well
in poisoning the minds of the counsellors of the king. Hence
a system of oppression was begun and continued, until the
people of America, exasperated beyond endurance, appealed to
the last resort for redress, and submitted their cause to the
arbitration of the sword.

The war with France which terminated with the peace of
1748.
Oct. 8. Aix la Chapelle burdened England with debt. Massachusetts,

in the mean time, though involved in that war, and conducting CHAP
enterprises for the conquest of Canada, had not materially ㅤIX.
increased her burdens ; but, by her commercial activity and
diligence, and by developing her industrial resources, she had
gone on prospering in her circumstances, and had largely extended the area of her operations. The expense of the capture
of Louisburg was indeed great, and at the close of the war the
province was in debt over two hundred thousand pounds sterling ; but as England reimbursed more than one hundred and
eighty thousand pounds, this sum, judiciously applied, placed
the currency upon a sound basis again, and remedied evils
which had long been felt. It is not to be inferred, however,
because the finances of the province were temporarily embarrassed, that the energies of the people were palsied, or that the
channels of trade and commerce were choked. On the contrary, a sense of the necessity for vigorous exertion to prevent
such a calamity had stimulated the activity and industry of all
classes ; societies and schemes for the promotion of domestic
manufactures were organized and established ; and enterprising
merchants sent forth their vessels to all ports where commerce
could be profitably conducted.[1]

Two transactions in Parliament, at this date, indicate the
policy upon which the statesmen of England were preparing to
enter. In 1748–9, a bill was brought in for strengthening the ㅤ1748-9.
ㅤㅤㅤㅤㅤㅤㅤㅤㅤㅤㅤㅤㅤㅤㅤㅤㅤㅤㅤㅤㅤㅤㅤㅤㅤㅤMar. 3.
prerogative, by which all the king's instructions were to be
enforced in the colonies. This bill, had it passed, would have
swept away at once the charters of the provinces without trial
or judgment, and would have established a precedent which
might have been dangerous to England itself. Wise men foresaw these evils, and the bill was defeated. At the instance of
Walpole, an attempt was next made to regulate and restrain
the bills of credit which had been put in circulation. Mr.
Bollan, the agent of Massachusetts, exerted himself, with others,

[1] Minot, i. 135.

CHAP.
IX.

1751.
March.

to defeat this attempt, but without success; for an act was passed which forbade the issue of bills of credit except for the current expenses of the year and in case of an invasion, but in no case were such bills to be a legal tender for the payment of debts, on pain of dismission from office on the part of any provincial governor, and a perpetual incapacity for serving in any public employment.[1]

1750.

The complaint of the West India sugar planters was attended with more serious consequences. The wealthy proprietors who owned those plantations, jealous of the success of their rivals at the north, and of the extent and importance of their commercial adventures, charged them with being the agents of France and other foreign nations — carrying on commerce with Europe and America for their own particular benefit, and against the interests of the mother country.[2] Complaints from so respectable a source could not pass unheeded, especially as the proprietors themselves were persons of influence at court, and many of the merchants of England were interested in their plantations. Rum was, at that date, the "chief manufacture" of Massachusetts; and the arguments adduced in support of its utility were certainly novel, if they were not convincing. It was contended that this "staple commodity" was the "grand support of their trades and fishery, without which they could no longer subsist." As a "standing article in the Indian trade," and the "common drink" of "laborers, timbermen, mastmen, loggers, and fishermen," how deplorable their condition, if deprived of this beverage! They "could not endure the hardships of their employments nor the rigors of the season without it." How cruel, therefore, to restrain such a traffic!

[1] Commons Journals, xxv. 246, and xxvi. 65, 119, 120, 187, 206, 265; Ashley's Mems. on Trade, &c.; Chalmers, Revolt, ii. 257; Minot, i. 146–148; Gordon's Am. Rev. i. 87.

[2] A like petition was presented in 1731, which led to the act of 1733; and in 1739 another petition was presented, in consequence of which a bill was brought into the House for granting liberty to carry sugar directly to foreign markets. Ashley's Mems. on the Trade of the Colonies, chaps. i. and ii.

Besides, rum was the "merchandise" principally made use of CHAP.
to procure "corn and pork;" nay, more, it was exported to IX.
Guinea, and "exchanged for gold and slaves." This gold 1750.
flowed freely into the coffers of England, and these slaves
were carried to the English sugar colonies, and "exchanged for
their commodities, or sold for bills on Great Britain." Rum
was, therefore, an article of vital importance. It aided in
selling "refuse fish" and "low-priced horses," and was indispensable to whalemen, being the "common drink of their profession." [1]

Hence the preëminent importance of rum; and could the
statesmen of England fail to be impressed with such logic?
The reasoning was conclusive; and for the time being the
West India merchants failed of their purpose. Is it surprising
when, a few years later, the legislators of Massachusetts, con- 1754.
sidering the extent and importance of the rum traffic, proposed
an excise upon wines and other spirituous liquors, that this
proposal produced an excitement and provoked a controversy
which disturbed for a long time the peace of the province?
Taxes were becoming burdensome from the increased expenses
of the government; and the House, to relieve the polls and
estates, the subjects of the "dry tax," imposed a duty on the
consumption of spirituous liquors. In the bill for this purpose
— so stringent were its terms — every householder, if required,
was to report, under oath, the quantity consumed in his family
not purchased of some licensed person, in order that the duties
might be accounted for by the consumer. This regulation,
from its invasion of "the liberties of the people," excited great
opposition; in every town the law was more or less denounced; the press teemed with pamphlets, in which the members of the House were attacked with great violence; and

[1] These reasons are urged in Ashley's Mem. on the Trade of the Colonies, published in 1740, and in a
pamphlet, published in 1764, entitled
"Reasons against the Renewal of the
Sugar Act," &c., pp. 12–15. See also
Minot, i. 148–164.

CHAP.
IX.

1754.

prosecutions were instituted against some persons who were most bitter in their opposition. The character of the literature which this controversy called forth reminds one strongly of that of the age of Elizabeth, when Martin Mar-Prelate sent forth his extravagant productions. The titles of some of the present pamphlets were equally significant; and "The Monster of Monsters," "The Cub new licked," and other delectable performances, remain as evidences of the extent of the excitement and the temper of the weapons with which the war was conducted.

In opposition to the law, it was urged that the tax, once submitted to, would be a precedent for other taxes equally obnoxious, and "windows," and "soap," and all other articles would come under the prohibitory ban, until nothing would be free. The virtues of rum were loudly extolled. The nectar of the gods was "trash" in comparison. It was a sovereign specific for the poisonous qualities with which the waters of the country were loaded, flowing as they did "through marshes and fens, spawning with frogs." A tax upon other luxuries would be far less objectionable, as the wealthy would pay a large portion of such tax; but to tax rum, the drink of the poor, the consoler, the vivifier, the "ambrosia from heaven," — this was indeed to touch nearly the people. Boston and the trading towns were the principal opponents of the law; elsewhere in the community it was viewed with more favor; and the House, finding public opinion divided, assumed the responsibility of passing the bill, and the law was enforced.[1]

1750.
Feb.

The complaint of the West India sugar planters was followed by the complaint of the English iron manufacturers, and this was promptly heard. The manufacture of iron in the colonies had become somewhat important; and to check the

---

[1] Speech of Governor Shirley, of June 17, in the Evening Post for June 24, 1754; Freedom the First of Blessings; the Relapse; the Eclipse; Letter to a Merchant in Boston, by a True Friend of Liberty; Minot, i. 201–214.

danger of rivalry, a committee, of which Charles Townshend
was chairman, reported a bill, which permitted the importation
of pig or bar iron duty free, but forbade, under a penalty of
two hundred pounds, and declared to be " nuisances," the erection of mills for slitting or rolling iron, or plating forges to
work with a tilt hammer, or furnaces for making steel. Pennsylvania resisted this act as " an attack on the rights of the
king's subjects in America ; " Massachusetts denounced it as
an infringement of her natural rights. To the English manufacturers it was objectionable in so far as it encouraged the
importation of the raw material ; and, to appease them, such
importation was limited to the port of London. The most
odious clause in the law was, that a return of existing mills
was required, and the number was never to be increased ; and
it was only by a small majority that a proposition for the destruction of every slitting mill was defeated. The indignation
which such a law would excite among the people may be readily conceived ; nor is it surprising that its enactment deepened
their hatred of the tyranny which oppressed them.[1]

False steps, once taken, are not easily retraced ; and the
statesmen of England, having entered upon the task of legislating for the colonies, found that task so congenial to their
ambition that the very opposition their measures awakened
served to confirm them in their course ; and, determined at all
hazard to subdue the refractory people, fresh projects were
devised, in which the lords of trade and the ministry became
deeply interested. An American revenue was imperiously
demanded ; and, to secure it, the sugar act of the early part
of this reign was revived and continued.[2] Nor was this all.
"Persons of consequence," it is said, " had repeatedly, and
without concealment, expressed undigested notions of raising

---

[1] Commons Journals, xxv. 979, 986, 993, 1053, 1091, 1096; Acts 23 Geo. II. c. xxix , and 30 Geo. II. c. xvi.; Plantation Laws for 1750 and 1757; Douglas, ii. 109; Minot, i. 170, 171.

[2] Acts 12 G. II. c. xxx., and 24 G. II. c. lviii.; Chalmers, Revolt, ii. 121.

CHAP.
IX.

1751.

revenues out of the colonies " — some proposing to accomplish this object through the medium of the post office, others by a modification of the acts of trade, and others by a stamp act, to apply to all the colonies. The Board of Trade, equally urgent "for a revenue with which to fix settled salaries on the northern governors, and defray the cost of Indian alliances," heark-

1753.
Mar. 8.

ened not unwillingly to such suggestions, and at length announced to the House of Commons the "want of a colonial revenue," and proposed, as the first step towards securing such revenue, a revision of the acts relating to the West Indies, and to substitute imposts on all West India produce brought into the northern colonies; but, for the "want of information on the subject," the proposal was delayed.[1]

The next step was more decisive. Shirley, indefatigable in his devotion to the crown, continued to urge upon the secretary

1755.
Feb. 4.

of state "the necessity, not only of a parliamentary union, but taxation;" officers in every colony clamored for the same

July.

object; and Halifax, soon after, insisted with the ministry on a "general system to ease the mother country of the great and heavy expenses with which it of late years was burdened." It was accordingly resolved to "raise funds for American affairs by a stamp duty, and a duty on products of the West Indies imported into the continental colonies." A tax upon "stamped paper" was likewise suggested, which was to be "so diffused as to be in a manner insensible."[2] Massachusetts was informed

Nov. 6.

of these proceedings, and immediately instructed her agent to "oppose every thing that shall have the remotest tendency to raise a revenue in the plantations for any public uses or services of government."[3] If, in consequence of such instructions, apprehensions were entertained that the colonies would, "in time, throw off their dependency upon the mother country, and set up one general government among themselves," Shirley was

---

[1] Bancroft, iv. 100, 101.
[2] Shirley to Sir T. Robinson, Feb. 4, 1755; Board of Trade to the Secretary of State, July, 1755; Essay on Course of Great Britain, &c., 89, 92.
[3] Mass. Rec's; Gordon's Am. Rev. i. 95.

at hand to remark that, "whilst his majesty hath seven thou- CHAP.
sand troops kept up within them, with the Indians at command, IX.
it seems easy, provided his governors and principal officers are 1755.
independent of the assemblies for their subsistence, and commonly vigilant, to prevent any step of that kind from being
taken."[1] Such opiates soothed the timid; and the resolute
were more earnest to bring the people into "immediate subjection." The idea of a standing army, already familiar to their
minds, was eagerly seized upon ; and, by an order in council, 1756.
the rule was laid down, without limitation, that troops might July 7.
be kept up in the colonies, and quartered upon the people,
without the consent of the several assemblies. Thus a permanent army was established ; and, before many years, the people
became accustomed to the presence of a hireling soldiery, the
ostensible object of whose enlistment was "to guard the frontiers," but which were actually designed to overawe, should an
independent spirit be manifested.[2]

With an army to enforce its provisions, and "warrants of
distress and imprisonment of persons" in case of resistance, a
law imposing a tax upon the colonies, it was thought, could be
executed without difficulty ; and the British press began to 1757.
defend the scheme which had been "often mentioned in private, Jan.
to introduce a stamp duty on vellum and paper." The project
of a stamp act was pressed upon Pitt; but he "scorned to take
an unjust and ungenerous advantage" of the colonies. Yet,
though the war with France prevented its immediate prosecution, the measure was too important to be laid wholly aside.
Hints in its favor had been repeatedly thrown out by colonial
governors, writers upon political economy, and aspiring office
seekers ; and it was thought the time had arrived when these
hints might be improved upon, and a revenue secured.[3] Hence
a memorable resolve was adopted in the House of Commons,

[1] Shirley to Sir T. Robinson, Aug.
15, 1755 ; Bollan's Lett. to Secretary
Willard, in 1 M. H. Coll. vi. 129.

[2] Bancroft, iv. 229, 230.
[3] Comp. Gordon's Am. Rev. i. 80,
81, 90 ; Bancroft, iv. 58.

CHAP. that "the claim of right in a colonial assembly to raise and
IX. apply public money by its own act alone is derogatory to the
1757. crown, and to the rights of the people of Great Britain." This
was controlling with a high hand the legislation of the colonies; but, as the views of Parliament and the counsellors of
the king did not in all respects harmonize, and the privy council were persuaded that they, with the king, had plenary power
to govern America, the execution of the extreme authority of
Parliament was again postponed.[1]

Upon the accession of Pitt to the ministry, measures of taxation were abandoned, and assurances of protection and encouragement were sent from England. And, without doubt,
the great commoner was sincere in his expressions of good
will; but, unfortunately for him and for America, though much
power was lodged in his hands, he was not supreme; and,
though he threw all his influence upon the side of reform, such
was the weight of existing abuses, and such was the strength
of former prejudices, that, with all his zeal and with all his
eloquence, he was unable to infuse his own spirit into every
branch of the government. Hence the Board of Trade, over
which Halifax still presided, and at which Oswald, Jenyns,
Rigby, and Hamilton sat as members, earnest to enforce the
policy it had long advocated, was preparing a new scheme for
narrowing the power of the colonies, and was courting the
complaints of the royalist governors, who were vehement in
advocating a tax upon the people. Of the secret designs of
this formidable cabal Pitt was for some time ignorant, nor
were the colonies better informed of the impending storm.
Relying implicitly upon the professions of the minister, the citizens of Massachusetts were fully assured that, while he ruled,
nothing would be wilfully done to infringe upon their liberties,
and that his integrity would frown upon, and his vigilance
defeat, every attempt to degrade and enslave them. Nor was

[1] Bancroft, iv. 255.

this confidence misplaced ; for, so great was the love of free- CHAP.
dom with Pitt, he would sooner have sacrificed his own prefer- IX.
ments than have been guilty of abridging the liberties of 1757.
America.

Under these circumstances, Massachusetts acted with characteristic promptness ; and the legislature of the province, to be 1759.
beforehand with the statesmen of England, revived one of its
former acts, and imposed of its own accord a stamp tax upon
vellum and paper, besides assessing a tax on personal estate of
thirteen shillings and fourpence on the pound income, and a
poll tax of nineteen shillings on every male over sixteen.[1]
Governor Pownall, foreseeing the tendency of these measures,
had already predicted, with his usual confidence, the "nearness
of American independence ;" and, aggrieved at the conduct of
the legislature in keeping under its own control the money
which had been raised for the conduct of the war, he laid his
complaints before the Board of Trade. That board, expressing
its deliberate and settled conviction that "the dependence
which the colony of Massachusetts Bay ought to have upon
the sovereignty of the crown stands on a very precarious foot,"
and was "in great danger of being totally lost," unless "some
efficient remedy was timely applied," advised dissimulation ;
and, by heeding this advice, the cloud passed over for a time.[2]

At this juncture Governor Pownall was transferred to South 1760.
Carolina ; and Francis Bernard, the willing friend to the English church and the British authority, was appointed governor
of Massachusetts. The administration of Pownall had been
comparatively short ; but he had proved himself zealous in the
defence of the prerogative. His standing in the community
was remarkably good ; and, by "guiding the people with a

---

[1] Mass. Rec's ; Chauncy's Sermon paper; and on the 18th of June, 1755,
on Repeal of Stamp Act; Gordon's it was renewed for two years. On the
Am. Rev. i. 98. 4th of June, 1756, James Russell was
[2] Bancroft, iv. 299. In January, chosen commissioner of stamps. Jour.
1755, an act was passed for granting H. of R. for 1755–6, 32, 42.
duties upon vellum, parchment, and

CHAP.   silken cord," and conducting prudently in the disbursement of
IX.   the revenues, he had made himself popular.   Easy in his man-
1760. ners, courteous and affable in his intercourse with others, and
       inclining to indulge in the pleasures of fashionable life, he was
       the welcome associate of the wealthy and the gay; and his
       supposed influence in England, and the respectability of his
       connections, gave him great weight in the public councils.
       The extent of his influence with the legislature at large is
       evinced by their respectful and even panegyrical addresses, and
       by the offer of a passage to England in the provincial frigate,
       previous to his entering upon the duties of his new commis-
June 3. sion; and, at his embarkation, both Houses attended him in a
       body to his barge, and took leave of him in terms as compli-
       mentary to his talents as they were creditable to themselves.[1]

           Mr. Bernard, the successor of Pownall, had previously served
       as governor of New Jersey, and was therefore somewhat ac-
       quainted with the spirit of the people.   His advancement to
       Massachusetts was esteemed a reward for his former fidelity;
Aug. 4. and, upon his arrival, he was received with the respect due to
       his office.   In his first address to the General Court, which
       was convened shortly after, he expressed his intention to pre-
       serve the privileges secured by the charter; and, in a subse-
Sept.26. quent speech, he hinted at the "blessings of their subjection to
       Great Britain."   The House, in their replies, joined in extol-
       ling the "happiness of the times;" but, instead of acknowledg-
       ing their "subjection" to Great Britain, they contented them-
       selves simply with expressing their "relation" to that country.
       Yet the English constitution they unanimously applauded — an
       instrument which, in the estimation of the wisest, "approached
       perfection," and of which their own was held to be a "copy,"
       or rather "an improvement, with additional privileges," which
       were not enjoyed by the masses in England.[2]

[1] Minot, ii. 62–65.   uel Adams, quoted in Bancroft, iv. 16,
[2] Blackstone's Commentaries, b. i.   378; Hutchinson, iii. 83; Minot, ii.
c. i. § 5, note 12; Writings of Sam-   76, 77.

The conquest of Canada left England at liberty to listen once more to the artful insinuations of "insubordination" which were spread abroad by the enemies of America. Indeed, from almost every quarter it was urged that "North America could never remain long subject to Great Britain." "It is no gift of prophecy," it was said ; "it is a natural and unavoidable consequence, and must appear so to every one whose head is not too much affected with popular madness or political enthusiasm."[1] "For all what you Americans say of your loyalty," was the declaration of Pratt, afterwards Lord Camden, in conversing with Franklin, "I know you will one day throw off your dependence upon this country, and, notwithstanding your boasted affection to it, will set up for independence." "No such idea," was the prompt reply, "is entertained in the minds of the Americans ; and no such idea will ever enter their heads, unless you grossly abuse them." "Very true," was the rejoinder ; "that is one of the main causes I see will happen, and will produce the event."[2]

The work of "abuse" soon began ; and in Massachusetts its progress was signally marked. For a long time two parties had existed in the province — the party of freedom and the party of prerogative. At the head of the latter were such of the wealthy as hoped, by complaisance, to share the royal favor ; leagued with the former were the sagacious and eloquent champions of the people. ·Two of these characters merit particular notice because of their prominence. Thomas Hutchinson, a native of Massachusetts, and a descendant of Mrs. Anne Hutchinson, was the leader of the royalist party, and held the office of lieutenant governor. Gifted by nature with respectable talents ; plausible, influential, and of a grasping ambition, he had, from his entrance into public life, participated largely in political movements ; by a long course of training

[1] Weare's Lett. in 1 M. H. Coll. i. 72, 76; Almon's Anecdotes, in Bancroft, iv. 365.

[2] Gordon's Am. Rev. i. 97 ; Quincy's Life of Quincy, 269.

CHAP.
IX.

1760.

he had acquainted himself thoroughly with the questions of the day; and, foreseeing the advantages which obsequiousness would secure him, he had devoted himself zealously to the support of the prerogative. A lover of money and a lover of place, he sacrificed the nobility of his nature to acquire and enjoy wealth, and became the flatterer of every one he imagined could forward his interests. Even his professions of piety were a courtly pretence; and, though not wilfully dishonest, his conscience had the peculiar elasticity which distinguishes the demagogue, and which knows how to equivocate, to conceal, and to deceive. He was as sincere in his patriotism as any one can be who sacrifices his country for personal aggrandizement; and, though not devoid of good qualities, though active in business and remarkably polite, his whole nature was corrupted with disingenuousness. Had he written his "History of Massachusetts" alone, — an admirable work and a monument to his genius,[1] — he would have been entitled to great credit, for it is certainly worthy of high commendation; but his unfortunate "Letters," designed only for private circulation, but which were discovered and published, stripped from his face the disguise he had borrowed, and exposed to the public his glaring insincerity.[2]

Born
1725.
1743.
1746.

James Otis, the opponent of Hutchinson and the champion of liberty, was a native of Barnstable, and a graduate of Harvard. At the age of twenty-one he commenced practising law

[1] Relative to the History of Hutchinson, I find the following passage in his Corresp. vol. ii., forming part of a letter dated January 3, 1763. "I design to carry down Mr. Prince's Chronology, and, as Bishop Burnet did, write the history of my own times. I shall paint characters as freely as he did; but it shall not be published while I live; and I expect the same satisfaction which I doubt not the bishop had, of being revenged of some of the r——s [rascals]. After I am dead, I wish you may have the pleasure of reading it." This passage has had the pen passed through it; but it doubtless expresses the views of Governor Hutchinson, and shows that the third volume of his History, at least, which was not published until after his death, was written under the influence of partisan feelings, for which due allowance must be made in its perusal.

[2] On these letters, see Franklin's Works, vol. iv., and the notes of Mr. Sparks.

in Plymouth, in the old colony; but two years after he moved to Boston, where the brilliancy of his talents and his reputation for integrity won for him at once an enviable fame, so that his services were sought in cases of the greatest importance. Sincerely devoted to the cause of his country, keenly alive to the indignities it had endured, and anxious to distinguish himself as the advocate of its rights, he had resented the slight which had been put upon his father, who had been promised a judgeship by Shirley upon the occurrence of a vacancy, and who, upon the death of the venerable Sewall, applied for the office, but was rejected by Bernard in favor of Hutchinson. As yet no opportunity had occurred for the display of his zeal, nor had he evinced the statesmanship for which he afterwards became famous; but he was known as an orator of superior powers, and, from his ardent enthusiasm and the largeness of his heart, great hopes were formed of his future career.[1]

Nor were Hutchinson and Otis the only noted men of the day; for on the side of the royalists were Andrew Oliver, the brother-in-law of Hutchinson, and a man of like principles; the talented Gridley, a lawyer of learning, majestic in his manner, and at the head of his profession; Timothy Ruggles, a man of quick apprehension, and lordly in his manners, yet distinguished for the boldness and strength of his thoughts. And on the side of the people were Samuel Adams, regarded by some as "the father of the revolution," a man of unquestionable devotion to liberty, " of steadfast integrity, exquisite humanity, genteel erudition, engaging manners, real as well as professed piety, and a universal good character;"[2] the elder Otis, speaker of the House and a distinguished politician; Oxenbridge Thacher, a lawyer of merit, and respected for his learning, though somewhat eccentric; James Bowdoin, subsequently governor of Massachusetts, distinguished for his learning, his

CHAP.
IX.

1748.

1760.
Sep. 11.

---

[1] On Otis, see Tudor's Life of Otis; Allen's and Eliot's Biog. Diction's; Hutchinson, iii. 86 et seq.   [2] John Adams, Diary, in Works, ii. 163.

CHAP. courtesy, and his address ; and Thomas Cushing, calm yet con-
IX. stant in his devotion to freedom, and famed for his secrecy and
1760. his talent at procuring the earliest intelligence.

The age called for great men, and great men appeared.
Whenever special instruments are required in a côuntry, God
raises them up ; and, as the battles of freedom were to be
fought on these shores, and a new empire was to grow out of
the violence of the old world, he imparted the courage which
shrinks from no danger, the patriotism which threats cannot
terrify nor blandishments seduce, the chivalrous virtue which
sacrifices ease and personal security for the benefit of others,
the fidelity to principle which falters not in its path, and the
heroic spirit which never quails. It was by men of such temper that the colonies were prepared for their freedom. They
were found, not only in New England, but in New York, and
at the south. In all British America union of feeling began
to spring up ; and, as the meshes of tyranny were drawn closer
and closer, and escape seemed impossible, the resolute clad
themselves in the panoply of war, and the gauntlet of defiance
was thrown at the feet of the king and his ministers.

Oct. 25.   The death of George II., and the accession of George III.,
mark a new era in the history of the colonies. Already were
rumors in circulation of the " fixed design in England to re-
model the provinces ; " [1] and many officers of the army expressed
openly the opinion that " America should be compelled to yield
a revenue at the disposition of the crown." [2] Such proposals
could not but awaken resentment ; and the feeling was expressed, " These Englishmen will overturn every thing. We
must resist them, and that by force." [3] Nor was the character
of the new monarch, then but twenty-two years of age, such as
to inspire the hope that, under his reign, the affairs of the
provinces would be less rigorously conducted. True, Ingersoll,
of Connecticut, who was present at his coronation, carried

[1] John Adams's Works, iv. 6, 7.   [3] John Adams's Works, iv. 6.
[2] Bancroft, iv. 371.

away by the general enthusiasm, described him as "not only, CHAP
as a king, disposed to do all in his power to make his subjects IX.
happy," but as "undoubtedly of a disposition truly religious."[1] 1760.
This was before the arbitrariness of his disposition had had
time to develop itself; for the ruling idea, indelibly branded
in his mind, was the restoration of the prerogative, which, in
America, the provincial assemblies had resisted and defied.
"The young man is very obstinate," was Charles Townshend's
judgment; and facts soon verified the correctness of that
judgment.[2]

The news of the demise of George II. reached Boston in
the winter;[3] and soon after events occurred significant in their Dec. 17
influence upon the liberties of America. The reduction of
Canada, it was hoped by the people, would free them from the
presence of a formidable enemy, and enable them to "sit quiet
under their own vines and fig trees, with none to molest or
make them afraid."[4]   Satisfied, generally, with the government
under their charter, notwithstanding its defects, and sincerely
attached to the English constitution, no people were more loyal
than the inhabitants of the colonies.   Undoubtedly there were
some who had figured to themselves, in the distant future, an
American empire of unlimited extent and unparalleled grandeur; but, while the French held possession of a large portion
of the continent, the people, as a whole, were content with their
present condition, and would probably have continued so had
they been left undisturbed.   When the French were subdued,
a new scene opened.   It was foreseen by English as well as
by colonial statesmen that the pleasantness, fertility, and plenty
of the country, washed by the Atlantic for over two thousand
miles on its coasts, and communicating with a region of exu-

---

[1] Bancroft, iv. 385. Franklin, also, in 1769, speaking of George III., says, "I can scarcely conceive a king of better dispositions, of more exemplary virtues, or more truly desirous of promoting the welfare of his subjects." Works, vii. 440, ed. 1840.
[2] Bancroft, iv. 386, 387.
[3] Boston Gazette for Jan. 1, 1761; Hutchinson, iii. 88.
[4] Walpole's George III. ii. 70; Hutchinson, iii. 84.

CHAP. berant fertility by vast lakes and many navigable rivers,[1] would
IX.   naturally invite, and that there was nothing to obstruct, a
1760. gradual progress of the settlements, already extensive, throughout the continent, from the Atlantic to the Pacific. The population of the colonies was rapidly increasing, and the number
of inhabitants doubled once in about twenty-five years. In less
than a century, therefore, if not within half that time, there
would be "more people in America than in England;"[2] and
would a body so numerous and hardy, "accustomed to more
than British liberty," with whom the "leaven of independency"
was thought to be "irradicable," perpetually submit to foreign
domination, without a thought of bettering their condition by
"setting up for themselves"? These considerations, indeed,
did not of themselves "immediately occasion any plan" to secure "independency;" but they "produced a higher sense of
the grandeur and importance of the colonies," and broader
views of the destiny to which they might attain; and minds
accustomed to reflection could not long resist the impulse
which such thoughts inspired. Hence, every where, "men
were led to inquire, with greater attention than formerly, into
the relation in which the colonies stood to the state from which
they sprang;" and, from various events, they were "prepared
to think more favorably of independency, before any measures
were taken with a professed design of attaining it."

One of these events was the opening of the drama which
soon after followed. By an act of Parliament of the 6th of
1733. George II., a duty of sixpence per gallon was imposed upon
all foreign molasses imported into the colonies; and in case of
forfeiture, one third part went to the king for the use of the
colony where the forfeiture was made, one third to the governor, and one third to the informer. This act had been in
force for nearly thirty years; large sums had been forfeited
under it; and illegal abuses had been committed in the disposal

---

[1] Weare's Lett. in 1 M. H. Coll. i.   [2] Weare, in 1 M. H. Coll. i. 71;
72.   Grahame, ii. 363.

of the fines. The officers of the customs, distinguished for their rapacity, and zealous to meet the approval of the ministry, began to be more vigorous in enforcing the law; and, as it had ever been odious, their conduct was resented, their proceedings were scrutinized, and their authority was questioned. A petition for a hearing was presented by several merchants; the committee reported in their favor, and both branches of the legislature sanctioned their report. The officers of the customs appealed to the governor, and the resolution of the House was negatived. A conference ensued, and the governor acquiesced in the resolution. Immediately an action was brought by the treasurer of the province, and a plea in abatement was made by Mr. Paxton. This plea was overruled in the Inferior Court; but, on the appeal, it was sustained by the Superior Court, and judgment was rendered against the treasurer.[1]

This triumph of the officers prepared them to take stronger grounds; and, as they had been accustomed, under color of the law, forcibly to enter both warehouses and dwelling houses, upon information that contraband goods were concealed in them, one of their number petitioned the Superior Court for writs of assistance to aid in the execution of his duty. Exceptions were taken to this application, and James Otis desired a time might be assigned for a hearing. His request was granted; and, on the day fixed, Thomas Hutchinson, the new chief justice, with his four associates, sat in the crowded council chamber of the old town house, in Boston, for the trial of the cause.[2]

The case for the crown was opened by Gridley, as the king's attorney, and the legality of the writ was learnedly maintained. "The statutes of the 12th and 14th of Charles II., and the 6th

[1] Hutchinson, iii. 89–92; Minot, ii. 80–87. Hutchinson says the cause was "feebly supported" by the plaintiffs.

[2] Hutchinson admits that the authority under which the officers acted in these cases was "assumed," and that the warrants which the governor had been accustomed to issue were "of no value." Hist. iii. 92, 93.

CHAP. of Anne,"— such was his plea, — "allow writs of assistance to
  IX.   be issued by the English Court of Exchequer ; the colonial law
1761. of the 2d William III., chapter 3, devolves the power of that
court on the colonial Superior Court ; and the statutes of the
7th and 8th William III. confer upon colonial revenue officers
the same powers as are exercised by the like officers in England.   To refuse, therefore, the writ of assistance, even if the
common privileges of Englishmen are taken away by it, is to
deny that the Parliament of Great Britain is the sovereign
legislature of the British empire." [1]

Oxenbridge Thacher rose to reply ; and his argument evinces
his wisdom and learning.   " The material question which claims
our attention," said he, " is whether the practice of the Exchequer is good ground for this court.   The court itself has
renounced the chance of jurisdiction which the Exchequer had
in cases where either party was the king's debtor ; and why
depart in the present instance ?   Besides, in England, all infor-
mations of uncustomed or prohibited goods were in the Exchequer ; so that the custom house officers were the officers of
that court, under the eye and discretion of the barons, and
accountable for wanton abuses of power.   The writ now prayed
for is not returnable.   If the seizures were so before their honors, and this court should inquire into them, they would often
find a wanton exercise of power.   In England, the officers
seize at their peril, even with probable cause." [2]

James Otis appeared for the inhabitants of Boston ; and his
speech created an unusual excitement.   " I am determined,"
was his avowal, " to my dying day to oppose, with all the
powers and faculties God has given me, all such instruments
of slavery, on the one hand, and villany, on the other, as this
writ of assistance is.   I argue in favor of British liberties, at
a time when we hear the greatest monarch upon earth declaring
from his throne that he glories in the name of Briton, and that

[1] Hutchinson, iii. 94 ; Minot, ii. 88 ;   [2] Minot, ii. 90, 91.
Bancroft, iv. 414, 415.

the privileges of his people are dearer to him than the most CHAP.
valuable prerogatives of his crown. I oppose the kind of IX.
power the exercise of which, in former periods of English his-1761.
tory, cost one king of England his head and another his throne.
Let the consequences be what they will, I am determined to
proceed, and to the call of my country am ready to sacrifice
estate, ease, health, applause, and even life. The patriot and
the hero will ever do thus ; and if brought to the trial, it will
then be known how far I can reduce to practice principles
which I know to be founded in truth.

"Special writs may be legal ; and the Court of Exchequer
may grant such, upon oath made before the lord treasurer by
those who solicit them. The act of 14 Charles II. conclusively
proves this. On this ground the present writ, being general,
is illegal. Every one, with this writ, may be a tyrant ; and if
this commission be legal, a tyrant, in a legal manner, may also
control, imprison, or murder any one within the realm. Again,
the writ is perpetual. No return is to be made ; and he who
executes it is responsible to no one for his doings. He may
reign secure in his petty tyranny, and spread terror and desolation around him until the trump of the archangel shall excite
different emotions in his soul. Besides, the writ is unlimited.
The officers may enter all houses at will, and command all to
assist him. Nay, even his menials may enforce its provisions.
And what is this but to have the curse of Canaan with a witness upon us ? — to be the servant of servants, the most despicable of God's creation ?

"The freedom of one's house is an essential branch of English liberty. A man's house is his castle ; and while he is
quiet, he is as well guarded as his prince. This writ, if declared legal, annihilates this privilege. Officers and their
menials may enter our houses when they please, and we cannot resist them. Upon bare suspicion they may institute a
search. And that this wanton exercise of power is no chimera
facts fully prove. Reason and the constitution are both

CHAP. against this writ. The only authority that can be found for
IX.   it is a law enacted in the zenith of arbitrary power, when Star
1761. Chamber abuses were pushed to extremity by some ignorant
clerk of the Exchequer. But even if the writ could be elsewhere found, it would be illegal. No act of Parliament can
establish such a writ. Though it should be made in the very
words of the petition, it would be void ; for every act against
the constitution is void." [1]

The audience listened with breathless interest to the stream
of eloquence which, for over four hours, poured from the lips
of the gifted orator. " Otis," says Adams, who was one of his
hearers, " was a flame of fire. With a promptitude of classical
allusions, a depth of research, a rapid summary of historical
events and dates, a profusion of legal authorities, a prophetic
glance of his eyes into futurity, and a rapid torrent of impetuous eloquence, he hurried away all before him. American
independence was then and there born. Every man of an
immense, crowded audience appeared to me to go away, as I
did, ready to take up arms against writs of assistance." [2] The
sketches of his speech which have been preserved give but an
imperfect idea of its volume and meaning. It was an unwrit-
ten performance, and not easily reported, for the sympathy of
his hearers was carried with his theme. Yet the fragments we
possess are certainly powerful ; and we can form some conception of the impression the whole must have made. The very
May. same year the orator was chosen a representative from Boston.
In the estimation of Hutchinson, he was the " great incendia-
ry " of New England ; in the estimation of the people, he was
the guardian of their rights. The inhabitants of Boston were
alive with excitement. Never before had their feelings been
so stirred ; never before had a more vital question been discussed in their presence. John Adams, borne away by the
occasion, felt the spirit of resistance welling up in his breast ;

[1] For this celebrated speech, see   Adams, App. 523, 524.
Minot, ii. 91–99 ; Diary of John   [2] Allen's Biog. Dict. art. Otis.

and from that time forward he could never read the Acts of CHAP
Trade without anger, "nor any section of them without a IX.
curse."[1]

1761.

Yet the eloquence of Otis did not carry the day. The old
members of the Superior Court and the "friends of liberty"
inclined to his side; but the plausible Hutchinson, determined
not to yield to the pressure of public opinion, "prevailed with
his brethren to continue the cause to the next term, and in the
mean time wrote to England" for definite instructions. The
answer was in his favor; and when it came, notwithstanding
the charge of illegality was untouched, writs of assistance were
granted by the court whenever the revenue officers applied for
the same.[2]

Before the controversy was renewed, an ominous change
took place in the ministry. Pitt, the "great commoner," resigned his office, and the Earl of Egremont became his suc- Oct. 2.
cessor.[3] The king, bent on securing "to the court the unlimited and uncontrolled use of its vast influence, under the sole
direction of its private favor,"[4] was seconded in his purpose
by the Earl of Bute, his obsequious friend and willing tool.
Pitt was in the way of the accomplishment of this object. His
unyielding integrity would stoop to no chicanery. Confiding
in his own judgment, and relying too much, perhaps, on its fal-
lible dictates, he was unwilling to listen to the suggestions of
others; and, by taking decided ground in opposition to the
wishes of the court, he provoked the enmity of those who
envied his abilities and hated him for his firmness. His place
was no longer desirable, and he surrendered the seals into the
hands of the king. The friends of Bute wished him "joy of
being delivered of a most impracticable colleague, his majesty

[1] Novanglus, App. 269; Bancroft,
iv. 218.
[2] Hutchinson, iii. 96; Bancroft, iv.
418.
[3] Trumbull MSS. ii. 15; Letter of
Earl of Egremont of Oct. 19, 1761,
announcing the resignation of Pitt;
Review of Pitt's Administration, 143;
Grenville Corresp. i. 391, 409; Walpole's George III. i. 80.
[4] Burke's Works, i. 358; Bancroft.
iv. 387.

CHAP.
IX.
of a most imperious servant, and the country of a most dangerous minister." [1] But there were not wanting those who

1761.
viewed his withdrawal in a different light. The nation was
"thunderstruck, alarmed, and indignant;" the people of
America, who almost idolized him, heard of his resignation with
the deepest regret; and the changes which followed hastened
the period of conflict with the crown.

Not immediately did the storm burst, though the clouds were
gathering and the winds were rising. In this brief interval
Otis again entered the field as the champion of the people;

Sep. 15.
and, resenting a stretch of authority in the governor, who had
presumed to interfere with the rights of the House, by recommending provisions for the continuance of pay to the crews of
the vessels employed for the protection of the province, he
drew up a remonstrance, condemning his conduct as taking
from the House "their most darling privilege, the right of
originating all taxes," and as "annihilating," at a blow, "one
branch of the legislature." [2] In such cases, he urged, it would
be of little consequence to the people "whether they were
subject to George or Louis, the King of Great Britain or the
King of France, if both were arbitrary, as both would be if
they could levy taxes without Parliament."

This remonstrance was sent to the governor, but was returned the same day in a private letter to the speaker, with
the advice that he should recommend to the House not to enter
it upon their records without expunging from it that passage
in which "the king's name was used with a freedom which was
not decent." Otis resisted this proposal, but at length expressed his willingness so far to modify his language as to
insert the saving clause, "with all due reverence to his majesty's sacred person and government;" but the friends of the
governor cried, "Erase them! erase them!" and they were
ordered to be expunged. Otis defended his course in a pam-

---

[1] Doddington's Diary; N. A. Rev.   [2] Hutchinson, iii. 97.
for Oct. 1842; Bancroft, iv. 412.

phlet which he published at the close of the session, and the CHAP.
character of the governor was attacked in the newspapers.[1]

IX.

The controversy upon the currency was of minor impor- 1761.
tance, though it called forth again the energies of Otis. A bill
was reported, and passed in the House, making gold a legal
tender in the payment of debts. The council non-concurred.
A conference ensued; and, after the subject had been fully discussed, the House persisted in adhering to their determination,
and the Council, as firm, refused to sanction the bill. Yet it
passed at a subsequent date; and gold, as well as silver, was
made a lawful tender.[2]

The speech of Mr. Otis at the conclusion of the French war, 1763.
and upon the reception of the news that peace had been proclaimed, may be considered as expressing the views of Massachusetts at that time. " We in America," said he, " have certainly abundant reasons to rejoice. The heathen are not only
driven out, but the Canadians, much more formidable enemies,
are conquered, and become fellow-subjects. The British dominion and power may now be said, literally, to extend from
sea to sea, and from the great river to the ends of the earth.
And we may safely conclude, from his majesty's wise administration hitherto, that liberty and knowledge, civil and religious,
will be coextended, improved, and preserved to the latest posterity. No other constitution of civil government has yet appeared
in the world so admirably adapted to these great purposes as
that of Great Britain. Every British subject in America is,
of common right, by acts of Parliament, and by the laws of
God and nature, entitled to all the essential privileges of
Britons. By particular charters there are peculiar privileges
granted, as in justice they might and ought, in consideration
of the arduous undertaking to begin so glorious an empire as

---

[1] Otis's Vindication, 15. Hutchinson, iii. 97, 98, alters the language,
and with it the sense.

[2] Hutchinson's Corresp. ii.; Boston
Evening Post for Dec. 14, 1761; Con-
siderations on Lowering the Value of
Gold Coins; Hutchinson, iii. 98–100;
Minot, ii. 102–106.

CHAP.
IX.

1763.

British America is rising to. These jealousies, that some weak and wicked minds have endeavored to infuse with regard to the colonies, had their birth in the blackness of darkness; and it is great pity they had not remained there forever. The true interests of Great Britain and her plantations are mutual; and what God in his providence has united let no man dare attempt to pull asunder." [1]

These words, which came from his heart, met with a response as cordial as it was sincere. The loyalty of the colonists at this date stands unimpeached; and, doubtless, their union with the mother country might have continued much longer, had it not been for the misconduct of the counsellors of the king. Upon them must rest the responsibility of the measures which followed, and not upon the people of the thirteen colonies.

[1] Hutchinson, iii. 101, 102.

CHAPTER X.

THE peace of Paris was as joyously welcomed in America as
in England. The seven years' war, which had convulsed the
civilized world, had terminated in favor of the rivals of France,
and the bounds of the Gallican empire in the west had been
largely restricted. Freed from fears of aggressions from the
north, and at peace with the Indians by a judicious policy, the
inhabitants of New England and of the other British colonies
cherished the hope that a brighter day was about to dawn, and
that an unbounded career of happiness was before them. But,
though loyal addresses were forwarded to the king, and public
testimonials of gratitude were offered, the people were destined
quite early to learn that the very successes which had attended
the English arms were ominous of evil to them, and that the
policy which the statesmen of England had long been maturing
was to be more fully developed, and applied with a rigorous-
ness far exceeding any former oppressions. It was unfortunate
for England that the men who at this time managed her political affairs were lacking in the wisdom, and eschewed the mod-
deration, which could alone secure to her the benefit of her
triumphs. Ignorant of the geography of the country and of the
character of its residents, few were familiar with the history of
America, and none fully sympathized with, or even comprehend-
ed, the opinions which prevailed here. Looking at politics from
a different standpoint, the statesmen of the new world, versed
in the principles of natural law, demanded, not as a favor, but
as a matter of justice, equality with their fellow-subjects, and

(271)

CHAP.
X.

1763.

exemption from special and unequal legislation. Had a little more deference been paid to these claims, or had the ministers of the king consented to listen to the statements of grievances sent from these shores, the struggle which issued in the independence of America might, perhaps, have been deferred for a season ; for it was not until they were forced to resistance that the American people renounced their allegiance to England, and declared themselves entitled to the benefits of self-government.[1]

At this period of our history, when a new scene is about opening, it may be proper to pause for a moment, and glance at the condition and prospects of the province. Massachusetts, in 1763, contained a population of two hundred and forty-five thousand white persons, and five thousand blacks.[2] There were thirteen counties and two hundred and forty towns within its limits, including the Province of Maine. The commerce of the country employed at least six hundred vessels, chiefly owned in Boston and Salem and a few other seaboard towns, which were engaged in the fisheries, and in voyages to all parts of the civilized world.[3] Domestic manufactures, in some departments, were vigorously prosecuted ; in others their progress had been comparatively trifling. It was never the policy of the English government to encourage industry in the colonies ; and what was accomplished was accomplished in secret, and by stealth, as it were. But it was difficult to repress the energies

[1] " The colonists," writes Otis in 1764, " know the blood and treasure independence would cost. They will never think of it till driven to it, as the last, fatal resort against ministerial oppression, which will make the wisest mad and the weakest strong. The world is at the eve of the highest scene of earthly power and grandeur that has ever yet been displayed to the view of mankind. Who will win the prize is with God. But human nature must and will be rescued from the general slavery that has so long triumphed over the species."

[2] 1 M. H. Coll. iv. 198 ; 2 M. H. Coll. ii. 95 ; Holmes's Am. Ann. ii. 118 ; Bradford, i. 41 ; Grahame, ii. 38. An order was passed by the legislature of Great Britain requiring a census to be taken of the inhabitants of the colonies ; but the legislature of Massachusetts, suspicious of the object of this order, delayed complying with it ; and when a census was taken, the task was negligently executed. Mass. Rec's ; Journal H. of R.

[3] Bradford, i. 11, 41.

of the people; and, however stringent the legislation which CHAP.
X.
rebuked their activity, they had gone on developing their resources, and rendering available, at least for domestic purposes, 1763.
the produce of their fields and the increase of their flocks.
Wool was a staple of New as of Old England; the spinning
wheel and the loom were found in nearly every dwelling; and
the wives and daughters of the farmers of Massachusetts prided
themselves upon the fabrics which their own industry created,
and were comfortably clad in garments wrought by their own
hands, without being compelled to depend upon foreign supplies.[1]   The extent to which these branches were carried it is
impossible to determine, for the statistics are wanting upon
which to base a reliable judgment.   It can hardly be supposed
that the imports of the province supplied in full all demands;
and, as the inhabitants of New England were noted for their
thrift, it may be safely computed that the products of their
own toil exceeded in value the aggregate of their imports; so
that the balance of trade, though apparently against them, was
actually in their favor.   Owing to these circumstances, the
wealth of the country had rapidly increased; and upon their
ability to sustain additional draughts upon their resources was
based the plea for taxing the colonies for the benefit of the
crown.   But to such taxation they were reluctant to submit,
and the attempt to enforce it was steadily resisted.

The institutions of learning, founded by the wisdom of the
first settlers, had advanced with the general advancement of
society; and the basis upon which they were established was
sufficiently liberal to accommodate the different opinions which

---

[1] The style of living in Boston had somewhat improved, and the dwellings of merchants of the wealthiest class were sumptuously furnished. Thus, John Adams, writing in 1766, says, "Thursday. Dined at Mr. Nich. Boylston's, with the two Mr. Boylstons, two Mr. Smiths, Mr. Hallowell, and their ladies — an elegant dinner indeed!   Went over the house to view the furniture, which alone cost a thousand pounds sterling.   A seat it is for a nobleman, a prince.   The Turkey carpets, the painted hangings, the marble tables, the rich beds with crimson damask curtains and counterpanes, the beautiful chimney clock, the spacious garden, are the most magnificent of any thing I have ever seen." Diary, in Works, ii. 179.

CHAP. prevailed. A controversy had arisen relative to Harvard Col-
X.   lege; but the struggle terminated in favor of the opinions
1763. advocated by such men as Mayhew and Chauncy.[1] The Puritan clergy, indeed, had lost little of their reverence for the
creed of Geneva, and were disposed to exert their utmost
power for the propagation of Christianity as they understood
it. Their piety retained traces of its original asceticism; and,
naturally conservative, it was with forebodings of evil that
they witnessed the prevalence of more liberal views. The
encroachments of episcopal power, viewed always with jealousy, awakened a controversy of remarkable virulence; both
parties, in their eagerness to defend their own side of the question, transgressed the bounds of equitable moderation; and
mutual recriminations and reproaches ensued.[2] Yet the genial
spirit which the diffusion of knowledge usually awakens was
fast wearing away the sharper angles of the Puritan creed, and
smoothing the austerity of the Puritan manners; so that, before
the opening of the war of the revolution, Unitarian views had
become somewhat prevalent, and Murray had advocated the
doctrines of free grace. The religious element, ever prominent
in the New England character, had lost little of its vigor;
and, though forms of faith had been essentially modified, the
progress of society in spiritual affairs had kept pace with its
social and intellectual progress. The press, the great engine
of civilization, which one of the journals of the day proudly
appealed to as "the test of truth, the bulwark of public safety,
and the guardian of freedom,"[3] was permanently established;
and the publishing houses of Boston, though by no means numerous, were extensively engaged in diffusing the productions
of native and foreign authors.[4] But few newspapers were

[1] Quincy's Hist. H. Coll. A portion of the college buildings at Cambridge were destroyed by fire on the
night of the 24th of January, 1764.
Mass. Gaz. for Feb. 2, 1764; Mass.
Rec's; Journal H. of R.; Quincy's
Hist.; Pierce's Hist.

[2] Minot, ii.; Grahame, ii. 350, 351.
[3] Connecticut Commercial Gazette
for Nov. 1, 1765, the day on which
the stamp act was to go into effect.
[4] See Thomas's Hist. of Printing,
Buckingham's Reminiscences, Drake's
Boston, &c.

issued in Massachusetts, and the number in New England was CHAP.
not very large.[1] There are no definite statistics of the number   X.
of volumes annually printed ; but several editions of popular   1763.
works were circulated ; and the people of the province, always
a reading people, were deeply interested in every thing relating
to politics or religion. The speeches of Otis, and the addresses of the General Court, were sent out into every town ;
and the writings of Chauncy, of Mayhew, and of Edwards
were scattered in every village, and read in every house.

Upon the Sabbath, which was consecrated to the worship of
God, the churches of New England, full five hundred and thirty
in number,[2] were thronged with worshippers ; for few staid
at home who were able to attend. The clergy, whose interest
in political affairs had ever been great, discussed from their
pulpits topics of public concern ; on all occasions where a
"word fitly spoken" might give tone to the sentiments of the
people, they were prompt to offer their counsel ; and no men,
probably, did more than they to carry on successfully the work
of the revolution.[3]

The facilities of communication had also been enlarged ; and
intelligence of stirring events was rapidly disseminated through
the medium of "posts," which travelled regularly from Boston
to other towns. The interests of different parts of the country
were not fully identified ; but the interchange of opinion was
wearing away ancient prejudices ; a community of wants and a
community of sufferings were assimilating their feelings ; and
the consciousness that bickerings and dissensions would but
alienate and distract inclined many to hope for a more perfect
union. The spirit of former days — that spirit of freedom, and
of loyalty to liberty, which the tyranny of England had been
unable to crush — was reviving. "Liberty" was the watchword in every one's mouth. And the energy it imparts to a

---

[1] See Thomas's Hist. of Printing ;   [2] Holmes, Grahame, Hildreth.
Buckingham's Reminiscences, the   [3] Holmes, Am. Ann. ii. ; Grahame,
Mass. Hist. Colls.   ii. 341, 342.

CHAP.
X.
—
1763.

nation's genius had inspired the gifted to advocate its claims. If, in some places, there were those who inclined to moderate counsels, and if the supporters of the prerogative encouraged compliance with the demands of the crown,[1] the people at large, though loyal, were jealous of invasions of their charter and its privileges ; discussed with great freedom the projects of the ministry ; and expressed with much fearlessness their dissent from measures conceived to be an encroachment upon their natural rights.

The first step which awakened opposition was the revival of the project for raising a revenue from the colonies, to be disposed of by the ministry at the pleasure of the king. The debt of the English government, at the close of the war, amounted in the aggregate to one hundred and forty millions of pounds sterling, of which seventy millions were borrowed.[2] For relief from the burden of this debt, of which all classes complained, especially the landholders, who were most deeply affected by it, it was authoritatively announced that it was " just and necessary that a revenue be raised in his majesty's dominions in America for defraying the expenses of defending, protecting, and securing the same." [3] How this was to be accomplished will appear hereafter ; but the first charge upon this revenue, partly effected at this time, and favored by Governor Bernard in his later letters,[4] was to be the civil list, by which all officers, both executive and judicial, to be independent of the provincial legislatures, were to be appointed by the king ; and the next charge was to be the support of an army of twenty regiments, or ten thousand men, who were to be kept

[1] The following passage from a letter of Hutchinson to Bollan, dated November 15, 1762, in MS. Corresp. vol. ii., shows his views. "A governor in the plantations," says he, "must support those who are friendly to government, or they cannot long support themselves against their enemies. He [Governor Bernard] is in some measure convinced that this is true, and I hope will be more so."

[2] Walpole's George III. i. 388; Macaulay's England, iii.; Bradford, i. 11.

[3] Grahame, ii. 370; Bancroft, v. 32.

[4] Bancroft, v. 148, 149, notes.

up as a peace establishment, nominally for the defence of the country, but in reality to enforce the king's instructions.[1]

That measures so radical, revolutionizing the government of the colonies, sweeping away their charters, and asserting the unlimited authority of Parliament, should have awakened the most serious apprehensions, will be surprising to no one acquainted with the spirit of the people. New York openly remonstrated; and Massachusetts, unwearied in her opposition to tyranny, bitterly inveighed against the blindness which had seized upon the advisers of the king.[2]

Early in March, Charles Townshend, who, at the instance of Bute and with the concurrence of the king, had taken the place of Lord Sandys at the head of the Board of Trade,[3] and who was distinguished for his impetuous temper, and for his disposition to make "thorough work of it with the colonies," brought forward in the House of Commons the scheme, agreed upon by the committee of which he was a member, for raising a revenue from the plantations by Parliament. By this scheme, the duty of six per cent., formerly levied on molasses imported from the Spanish colonies and the West Indies, was to be reduced to two per cent.; but the bill which was reported failed to pass.[4]

[1] Mauduit's Lett. to the Speaker of the H. of R., March 12, 1763; Commons Journal, xxv. 506; Grahame, ii. 367; Bancroft, v. 83–88, notes. To the establishment of an army in the colonies it was objected, that such an army was unnecessary "even to preserve the obedience of our English subjects to the crown of Great Britain;" and that, if it was designed to secure the new possessions, the "original colonies should not be taxed for the same." The Necessity of Repealing the Stamp Act demonstrated, pp. 12, 13.

[2] Bancroft, v. 84.

[3] Mauduit's Lett. to Sec. Oliver, March 12, 1763.

[4] Mauduit's Lett. to Oliver, March 23, 1763. From the Commons Journal, xxix. 597, 599, 603, 606, 609, 613, 617, 622, 623, 630, 633, 665, it appears that, March 19, 1763, resolves were presented by Alderman Dickinson, extending the acts of 6, 11, 19, 26, 29, and 31 Geo. II., and 1 Geo. III., "for the better securing and encouraging the trade to his majesty's sugar colonies in America," to September 29, 1764, and thence to the end of the next session of Parliament; also extending to May 25, 1770, the acts of 21 and 28 Geo. II., for encouraging the making of indigo in the British plantations in America; and bills were ordered to be brought in in accordance with these resolves. The bill for the latter purpose was presented by the same gentleman March 21, and ordered to a second reading. On the 23d it was read a second time, and referred to a committee of the

CHAP. Grenville, not behind Townshend in his zeal to promote the
X.   maritime greatness of England, contemplated an addition to
1763. this scheme ; and before the end of the month leave was grant-
Mar.24. ed to bring in a bill " for the further improvement of his majesty's revenue of the customs," which provided that all officers
of British ships of war stationed upon the American coast
should act as officers of the customs, and receive a share of the
cargoes confiscated for violation of the revenue laws. This bill
Mar.30. was read the second time in the following week, and referred
Apr.12. to a committee of the whole ; and in the ensuing month it was
to
Apr.18. passed by the House, agreed to by the Lords, and approved by
the king.[1]

Before any thing definite was effected, however, a change
took place in the ministry ; and, after some difficulty, a new
April 8. cabinet was formed.   George Grenville took the place of Bute
at the head of the treasury and the exchequer ; the Earl of
Egremont and Lord Halifax became the two secretaries of
state ; and Charles Jenkinson, the able and indefatigable secretary of Bute, was retained under Grenville as principal secretary of the treasury.[2]

But the new ministry, styled by some " the Athanasian administration," and laughed at by the people as a " sort of
Cerberus," a " three-headed monster, quieted by being gorged
with patronage and office,"[3] found itself powerless to rule the
storm which lowered in the horizon.   The chief minister, in-

whole, to be considered the next day.
On the 30th the bill was ordered to
be engrossed, and in the following
month, April 12 to 19, it was approved
by the Lords and the king. On March
24 the supply bill, covering the matters referred to in the first resolve, was
reported by Alderman Dickinson, and
read the first time. On the 28th, it
was resolved to go into committee of
the whole on Wednesday to consider
this bill; and on the 30th it was postponed.
[1] Commons Journal, xxix. 609,
623, 629, 630, 633, 665 ; Minot, ii.
138 ; Bancroft, v. 88.
[2] Grenville Corresp. ii. 32–41 ;
Walpole's George III. i. 271 ; Aikin's
Anns. of George III. i. 28 ; Lord
Mahon's Hist. Eng. v. 25–29 ; Bancroft, v. 96–102. Jenkinson afterwards rose to be Earl of Liverpool,
and his son to be prime minister of
England. Mahon's Hist. Eng. v. 21.
[3] Wilkes to Earl Temple, in Grenville Corresp. ii. 81. Lord Mahon,
Hist. Eng. v. 34, characterizes Grenville as " an excellent speaker spoiled."

deed, still pushed forward his favorite plans ; yet in justice to CHAP.
him it should be said that it does not appear, from contempo- X.
rary records, that he entered upon them with sinister inten- 1763.
tions, but advocated the taxation of the colonies as a measure
of justice, indispensable to the welfare and prosperity of England.[1] In the person of Richard Jackson, his private secretary
as chancellor of the exchequer, he possessed an able adviser,
distinguished for his frankness, uprightness, and fidelity, and
perfectly acquainted with American affairs. Had Grenville
consented to listen to his remonstrances against the proposed
measures, doubts of their expediency might, perhaps, have been
raised in his mind ; but, relying on his own judgment, and following its promptings, he became the more resolute the more
obstacles he encountered.[2]

In the following month the advice of the lords of trade was May 5.
asked concerning American affairs, the "principal object of
consideration" with the ministry. The questions proposed to
those lords were, I. What new governments shall be established, what forms shall be adopted for them, and where shall
the residence of the governors be fixed ? II. What military
establishments will be requisite, what new forts shall be erected, and what old forts shall be demolished ? And, III. "In
what mode, least burdensome and most palatable to the colonies, can they contribute towards the support of the additional
expense which must attend this civil and military establishment ? "[3] The Earl of Shelburne, who was at the head of the
Board of Trade, and who was an Irish as well as an English
peer, was naturally inclined to limit the authority of Parliament over the outlying dominions of the crown, and in his
answer declined to implicate himself in the plans for taxing
America.[4] But the Earl of Egremont was not to be shaken
in his purpose ; nor was Grenville intimidated. Both of these

[1] Lord Mahon's Hist. Eng. v. 34 ;   [3] Bancroft, v. 107, 108, note.
Bancroft, v. 106.   [4] Bancroft, v. 134–136.
[2] Bancroft, v. 106.

CHAP. gentlemen favored the project of taxation; and to Jenkinson
X. was assigned the duty of preparing the business for Parlia-
1763. ment.[1] The stamp act was not openly included in this project;
and Grenville professed an unwillingness to urge, nay, he even
declared that he should have esteemed himself "unpardonable"
had he "thought of, this measure, without having previously
made every possible inquiry into the condition of America."[2]
Hence information of the state of public feeling was proposed to be sought from the colonial governors, and others in
whom he had confidence;[3] but before any decision was reached
Aug. 20. Egremont died; Lord Shelburne withdrew from his post; and
Sept. 9. the Bedford and Grenville parties formed an alliance with
Halifax as the secretary of the southern department, and the
Earl of Hillsborough, like Shelburne an Irish as well as an
English peer, as the head of the Board of Trade.[4]

Immediately upon the establishment of this ministry, Grenville, as lord treasurer, renewed the attempt for the passage
Sep. 22. of a revenue bill; and, meeting with Lord North and Mr.
Hunter at the board room in Downing Street, a minute was
adopted, directing Jenkinson to "write to the commissioners
of the stamp duties to prepare a draught of a bill to be presented to Parliament for extending the stamp duties to the

[1] Bancroft, v. 136.
[2] Grenville, in Cavendish, i. 494;
Bancroft, v. 136, note.
[3] Possibly Hutchinson was one of
those consulted, as he writes to Richard Jackson, September 2, 1763, "For
my part, I have always wished, whilst
I was in trade myself, for some effectual measures to put a stop to all contraband trade; but I have always
thought it might have been done
without any further provision by the
Parliament. The real cause of the
illicit trade in this province has been
the indulgence of the officers of the
customs; and we are told that the
cause of this indulgence has been that
they have been quartered upon for
more than their legal fee, and that

without bribery and corruption they
must starve. If the fanatics of the
present age will not admit of a reform
in this respect, perhaps the provision
now made may be the next best pro-
cedure. *I wish success to it.*" MS.
Corresp. ii.
[4] Grenville Corresp. ii. 93–99, 104
–112, 115–123, 193–207; Walpole's
George III. i. 288–295; Lord Orford's
Mems. i. 288; Lord Mahon's Hist.
Eng. v. 36 et seq.; Bancroft, v. 138–
148. "Thus," says Walpole, "from
a strange concurrence of jarring circumstances, there sprang out of great
weakness a strong and cemented ministry, who all acquiesced in the predominant power of Grenville."

colonies." The next day Jenkinson attended to this duty, and CHAP.
the stamp act was draughted to be presented to Parliament.[1]   X.

It must be owned that this measure, now for the first time   1763.
distinctly brought forward, was not, at the outset, seriously Sept.23.
opposed by the colonial agents in London. Knox, of Georgia,
publicly defended the act, as "least liable to objection ; "[2] and
Jasper Mauduit, the agent of Massachusetts, through his brother, Israel Mauduit, not only gave to it the weight of his influence, but promised for his constituents a " cheerful submission."[3]
Richard Jackson alone, the secretary of Grenville, had the
courage to oppose the proposition, and refused to take part in
preparing or supporting it.[4] But Jenkinson, the secretary of
the treasury, gave different counsel, and was listened to in
preference because his advice fell in with the preconceived
notions of the minister. For Grenville, the die was cast ; and
whatever odium might attach to the measure, he was prepared
to assume it. Nor is it unjust to impute to him the paternity
of the act. He "brought it into form." It was deliberately
adopted by him. And, from his official position, the burden of
sustaining it must rest on his shoulders.[5] He believed it to
be founded on " the true principles of policy, of commerce, and
of finance ; " and, as it was his highest ambition to frame a
"well-digested, consistent, wise, and salutary plan of colonization and government," the stamp act was fostered as its basis
and ultimatum, as the "one thing needful" to give to it vitality.[6]
The minister knew that the act would be unpalatable ; and no
sooner were his orders issued to the officers of the customs in Oct.
the colonies to assume their posts, with "new and ample instructions enforcing in the strongest manner the strictest atten-

Treasury Minutes, Sept. 22, 1763 ;
Jenkinson's Lett. of Sept. 23, 1763 ;
Bancroft, v. 151, and notes.
  [2] See his pamphlet, published at
London in 1765, entitled "The Claim
of the Colonies to an Exemption from
Internal Tax, &c., considered," p. 2.
  [3] Gordon's Am. Rev. i. 158.

  [4] Letter to Jared Ingersoll, March
22, 1766, in Ingersoll's Letters, 43 ;
Bancroft, v. 155.
  [5] Burke's Speech on Amer. Taxation; Conduct of the late Administration examined, 77 ; Bancroft, v. 156.
  [6] Regulations concerning the Colonies, 5, 114; Bancroft, v. 157.

CHAP.
X.

1763.

Oct. 4.

1764.
Jan. 11.

tion to their duty," than the consequences which were foreseen began to be developed. The " restraint and suppression of practices which had long prevailed " could not but " encounter great difficulties in such distant parts of the king's dominions," so that the whole force of the royal authority was invoked in aid. And when orders were issued to the commander-in-chief in America, that the troops under his command should " give their assistance to the officers of the revenue for the effectual suppression of contraband trade," and when Admiral Colville and his subordinate officers qualified themselves for their new and distinguished duties as excisemen and tidewaiters, and entered upon their discharge, the whole country was aroused ; the proceedings of the officers were bitterly denounced ; the colonists, subjected to vexatious delays and expenses, were stung nearly to madness ; and prudence alone, probably, prevented them from showing their resentment more openly by forcibly resisting such proceedings.[1]

In this posture of affairs, the action of the General Court was prompt and decided ; and a committee of the House, upon a memorial of the merchants of Boston, Plymouth, Marblehead, Salem, and Newbury, presented a report, with instructions to Mr. Mauduit to labor for the repeal of the obnoxious sugar act, and to exert himself to prevent the passage of the stamp act, " or any other impositions or taxes upon this or the other American colonies." [2] It was not upon " mere speculative points in government" that people now took sides; nor is it true that there was " nothing in practice which could give any grounds for forming parties." It was with good cause that the " officers of the crown, and especially all officers of the customs, were considered as engaged in measures more restrictive of the natural rights and liberties of the people than the

---

[1] Grahame, ii. 368 ; Bancroft, v. 362. Proclamations against the clandestine importation of goods were issued December 26, 1763, and published in the newspapers of the following month. Boston Gazette for Jan. 5, 12, and 26, 1764.

[2] Mass. Rec's ; Journal H. of R. for 1764, p. 182 ; Minot, ii. 140, 148.

ends for which government was instituted made necessary." CHAP.
Royalists might content themselves with saying, "We have the X.
law on our side," and they might sneer at the "squibs" which 1764.
were "thrown at their general characters in newspapers, handbills, &c. ; "[1] but the anger of the people which vented itself
in these ways was called forth by the manifest unconstitution-
ality of the measures of which they complained ; and Otis
came forward again as the champion of their rights, which he
vindicated in a pamphlet of signal ability.[2]

As the position of Mr. Mauduit was somewhat equivocal,
and but feeble hopes were entertained of his exerting himself
resolutely to stay the progress of oppressive legislation, it was
proposed, before the adjournment of the General Court, to Jan.
choose a new agent, to be joined with him in remonstrating
with the ministry ; and the choice fell upon Thomas Hutchinson, the lieutenant governor, who by his complaisance had re-
gained the favor of the people, and who was apparently sincere
in his professions of regard to the liberties of his country.
The vote in his favor was nearly unanimous ; but as it was
intimated by Governor Bernard that it would be improper for
him to be absent from the province without permission, — an
opinion in which he seemed to acquiesce, — the House, much
to his chagrin, voted to excuse him from serving as agent ; and Feb. 1.
thenceforth, satisfied that he had little to expect from the province, the current of his feelings turned into a new channel ;
and, like the "waiters upon Providence" of the age of Crom-
well, "he deemed it a high delinquency towards Heaven if he
afforded countenance to any cause longer than it was favored
by fortune." [3]

---

[1] Hutchinson, iii. 103.
[2] His Rights of the Colonies.
Comp. Hutchinson, MS. Corresp. ii.
76, 77 ; Minot, ii. 143 ; Novanglus,
283.
[3] MS. Corresp. of Hutchinson, passim. That Hutchinson, at one time,
stood high in the public favor, is evident from the writings even of those
who differed from him in opinion.
"Has not his merit," says John Adams, (Diary, in Works, ii. 189,) "been
sounded very high by his countrymen
for twenty years ? Have not his countrymen loved, admired, revered, rewarded, nay, almost adored him?

CHAP.   At the opening of the spring the scheme of Grenville for
  X.   the passage of the stamp act was renewed.   But, though there
1764. were many who favored the scheme both in Parliament and
Mar. 9. out, the Americans in London, with very few exceptions, denied both the justice and the right of Parliament to impose
such a tax while the colonies were unrepresented in that body.
Nor were there wanting "members of the House of Commons"
who "declared against the stamp duty while it was a mere
matter of conversation ; " Pitt had steadily and uniformly opposed it ; and even Lord Hillsborough, the first lord of trade,
signified his dissent.[1] It was not, therefore, a measure which
seemed likely to pass without debate ; nor could the minister
deny the force of the objections urged by the colonies.   Yet,
determined not to falter, Grenville persisted in adhering to his
policy.   But one point would he concede ; and this he was
induced to yield at the urgent request of Thomas Penn, one
of the principal proprietors of Pennsylvania, William Allen,
the chief justice of the same province, and Richard Jackson,
his own private secretary.   Declaring that, in their judgment,
the proposed stamp duty was "an internal tax," and that it
would be better to "wait till some sort of consent to it shall
be given by the several assemblies, to prevent a tax of that
nature from being levied without the consent of the colonies,"[2]
Grenville so far listened to these representations as to consent,

Have not ninety-nine in a hundred of them really thought him the greatest man in America? Has not the perpetual language of many members of both Houses, and of a majority of his brother counsellors, been, that Mr. Hutchinson is a great man — a pious, a wise, a learned, a good man, an eminent saint, a philosopher, &c., the greatest man in the province, the greatest on the continent, &c. ? Nay, have not the affection and admiration of his countrymen arisen so high as often to style him the greatest and best man in the world ; that they

never saw, nor heard, nor read of such a man ? a sort of apotheosis, like that of Alexander and that of Cæsar while they lived."

[1] Hutchinson, iii. 116 ; Bancroft, v. 181. "It was the fate of the times," says Walpole, George III. ii. 71, 72, "to stir questions which, for the happiness of the whole, had better have slept in oblivion. From this moment nothing was heard from America but questions of the right of taxation."

[2] Grenville Corresp. ii. 393 ; Mass. Gazette for May 10, 1764 ; Bancroft, v. 183.

" out of tenderness to the colonies," to postpone the tax for one year. His views had not changed; and this consent was but a politic stroke to furnish hereafter additional pretexts for urging his scheme. He was fully aware that the measure, if carried, must be carried by force. The approval of the colonies he neither sought nor expected. It was enough for him if the scheme was favored at home; for, in his estimation, its enforcement was essential to the welfare of the nation, and would be attended with incalculable benefits to its commerce. Hence all his energies were bent to this point. He had committed himself too far to recede; and his only care was to smooth the way for the success of his plans, with which his own triumph was closely identified.

Two steps taken by Grenville at this time were designed to conciliate the northern colonies. The bounties on hemp and flax, first granted in the reign of Anne, were revived;[1] and encouragement was given to the prosecution of the whale fishery, in which the ships of New England were largely engaged.[2] But the bait thus thrown out proved ineffectual to lure the people into the net which had been spread for them. The minister's own course, indeed, was sufficient to convince them that for all favors conferred he expected an equivalent; for, besides giving notice of his intention in the next session to bring in a bill imposing stamp duties in America, a bill was reported by Jenkinson, at his instance, providing that duties be laid on various enumerated foreign commodities, as coffee, indigo, pimento, French and East India goods, and wines from Madeira, Portugal, and Spain, imported into the British colonies

Mar. 9.

Mar.14

---

[1] 3 and 4 Anne, c. x.; 8 Anne, c. xiii. § 30; 12 Anne, c. ix.; Mass. Gazette for July 5, 1764; Commons Jour. xxix. 995, 1011, 1035, 1040, 1041.

[2] 4 Geo. III. c. xxix.; Debates in Parl. iv. 213; Regulations concerning the Colonies, 49–51; Mass. Gazette for May 10, 1764. The petition of the merchants of New England and of London relative to the whale fishery was presented February 24, 1764, reported upon February 29, and referred to a committee of the whole. In the ensuing month a bill was reported, discussed, passed, and approved. Commons Jour. xxix. 877, 885, 912, 946, 953, 956, 977, 986, 994, 995, 1004, 1015, 1018, 1023, 1028, 1031, 1056.

CHAP.
X.

1764.

and plantations in America, and upon other articles, the produce of the colonies, exported to any other place than Great Britain ; that a duty of threepence per gallon be laid on molasses and sirups, and an additional duty of twenty-two shillings per hundred weight upon white sugars, of the growth of any foreign American plantation, imported into the British colonies ; and that the income of this last duty should be paid into his majesty's exchequer, to be disposed of by Parliament towards " defraying the necessary expenses of defending, protecting, and securing the British colonies and plantations in America." The bill thus brought forward was rapidly pushed through its several stages, and, after some slight amendments,

April 4.
April 5.

was agreed to by the Lords, and approved by the king. For the enforcement of its provisions, the jurisdiction of the Vice Admiralty Courts was enlarged ; and penalties for any breaches of the act were made recoverable in these courts, either in the colony in which the offence was committed or in any other, at the election of the informer.[1]

---

[1] Acts 4 Geo. III. c. xv. ; Debates in Parl. iv. 207 et seq. ; Hutchinson, iii. 108 ; Mass. Gazette for May 10, 1764 ; Minot, ii. 155 ; Holmes's Ann. ii. 125, &c. The history of this bill is as follows : February 9, 1764, resolves were presented that the laws relative to encouraging the trade of the sugar colonies, and the liberty to carry sugars to foreign parts, were fit to be continued ; but, though a bill was ordered to be brought in upon the latter subject, the former was postponed. March 1, an account of wines and East India goods exported to America ordered to be brought in ; also, of foreign cambrics, and French lawns, and of the quantity of tea, which was done March 5. On the same day, extracts from papers relative to American trade were presented by Lord Carysfort, pursuant to his majesty's address ; and, on the 9th, further extracts, from messages of the colonial governors, were presented by Lord Charles Spencer, and laid upon the table. These were the preparatory steps ; and, March 9, in committee of the whole, the resolves of February 9, which were postponed, were called up, and, with the preceding documents, and papers for preventing contraband trade, &c., referred to a committee. On the 10th Mr. Whateley presented their report, imposing duties on coffee, indigo, wines, &c., making the sugar act perpetual from and after September 29, 1764, and imposing a duty of 3d. sterling in *money* on molasses, sirups, &c., the income of which was to be paid into the exchequer. Bills were ordered to be brought in in accordance with this report, with a clause to prevent clandestine exportation and importation ; and a bill for charging " certain stamp duties in the said colonies and plantations." On the 13th Mr. Whateley, from the committee on ways and means, reported certain resolves relative to the colonies, upon which bills were ordered. On the 16th the bill on Amer-

Thus the scheme of taxation which Grenville had long cherished, and which Bernard approved, — that scheme which is
said to have been "in conformity to uninterrupted precedent
for near a hundred years,"[1] — was fairly begun. Its very
audacity is a sufficient proof of the perversity of its patrons.
How it would be received by the colonies few stopped to
inquire. From the character of the state papers which had
crossed the Atlantic, it was supposed that the spirit of the people would be easily tamed, and that all that was necessary to
secure submission was a vigorous administration, backed by an
appeal to military force in case of resistance.

The news that the sugar act had passed was not long in
reaching America; and there was "not a man on the continent
who did not consider it a sacrifice made of the northern colonies to the superior interest in Parliament of the West Indies."[2]
Before this date, the town of Boston, at its annual meeting,
passed, at the instance of Samuel Adams, a series of resolves
instructing its representatives what course to pursue, and recommended an appeal to "the other North American colonies"
to add the weight of their protest to "that of this province,

---

ican duties was read a second time, and referred to a committee of the whole. On the 20th persons were sent for to attend this committee; and on the 22d, the supply bill being again under consideration, with Mr. Whateley in the chair, other persons were ordered to attend. Thus the matter continued along until the 30th, when the bill was read the third time, and ordered to be engrossed. It was agreed to by the Lords April 4, and approved by the king April 5. Commons Jour. xxix. 825, 889, 890, 904, 907, 909, 933–935, 940, 945, 958, 968, 979, 981, 983, 987, 1015, 1027, 1029.

[1] Conduct of the late Administration examined, p. 7; Debates in Parl. iv. 251, note. "It had been proposed to Sir Robert Walpole," says Horace Walpole, Mems. George III. ii. 70, "to raise the revenue by imposing taxes on America; but that minister, who could foresee beyond the actual moment, declared it must be a bolder man than himself who should venture on such an expedient. That man was found in Grenville, who, great in daring and little in views, was charmed to have an untrodden field before him of calculation and experiment."

[2] Mass. Gazette for May 10, 1764; Weare's Lett. in 1 M. H. Coll. i. 83. "These colonies," says the Mass. Gazette, "are under very great disadvantages in not being sufficiently interested in Parliament; for the want of which the West Indies have been able to carry every point against them, and their interests are almost totally disregarded."

CHAP. that, by united application, we may happily obtain redress." [1]
X.   The General Court, of which the Council was the conservative
1764. branch, had hitherto maintained a decorous reserve in its appeals to the ministry, and had only suggested that the passage
of such acts would be esteemed a grievance, and that the commerce of the country, already overburdened, would be forced
into unnatural channels.[2] But now that it was compelled to
take stronger grounds, a " Statement of the Rights of the Colonies " was prepared by James Otis, and the " Sentiments of a
British American " were published by Oxenbridge Thacher.[3]

Jun. 13. A new letter of instructions was also draughted to be sent to
Mr. Mauduit, the tone of which indicates the feelings that prevailed. " If all the colonies," say they, " are to be taxed at
pleasure, without any representation in Parliament, what will
there be to distinguish them, in point of liberty, from the subjects of the most absolute prince ? Every charter privilege
may be taken from us by an appendix to a money bill, which, it
seems by the rules on the other side of the water, must not at
any rate be petitioned against. To what purpose will opposition to any resolutions of the ministry be, if they are passed
with such rapidity as to render it impossible for us to be acquainted with them before they have received the sanction of
an act of Parliament ? A people may be free, and tolerably
happy, without a particular branch of trade ; but, without the
privilege of assessing their own taxes, they can be neither." [4]

Jun. 14.   In accordance with the proposal of the representatives of
Boston, a committee was appointed to correspond with the
other colonies. James Otis, Thomas Cushing, Oxenbridge
Thacher, Thomas Gray, and Edward Sheafe were the members
of this committee ; and circulars were sent throughout the
country, in which the dangers that menaced " their most essen-

[1] Mass. Gazette for May 31, 1764;
Hutchinson, iii. 107; Bradford, i. 18–
20; Bancroft, v. 194, 197.
[2] Mass. Rec's; Jour. H. of R.

[3] These were both published in
Boston, in June, 1764.
[4] Minot, ii. 169–175; Bradford, i.
21, 22; Bancroft, v. 198.

tial rights" were set forth, and the "united assistance" of all CHAP.
was desired to obtain a repeal of obnoxious acts, and to X.
"prevent a stamp act, or any other impositions and taxes, upon 1764.
this and the other American provinces." [1]

As may well be supposed, neither Bernard nor Hutchinson
was particularly pleased with these proceedings; and Hutchinson, especially, censured the "madness" of the House in
inserting on their journal the letter to their agent.[2] But the
people viewed the controversy differently, and, excited by the
eloquence of their favorite orators, censured the "madness"
of the ministry, which, in their estimation, exceeded their own.
A recourse to arms was neither thought of nor advised, for
forcible resistance was acknowledged to be treasonable. More
peaceable measures were adopted; and a system of retrench-
ment of unnecessary expenditures was entered upon, and adhered to until the struggle had ended.[3]

The expedient of the governor, to embarrass the action of
the General Court, was to prorogue that body from one month
to another. But the clamor against him became so violent
that he was compelled to accede to the wishes of the people,
and the assembly was convened for the transaction of business. Oct. 18.
It was suspected, — and, as it afterwards appeared, not without

---

[1] Hutchinson, iii. 110; Minot, ii.
175; Bradford, i. 29; Bancroft, v.
200.

[2] "You allow," writes Hutchinson,
July 11, "that it is possible for Parliament to pass acts which may abridge
British subjects of what are generally
called natural rights; and I am willing
to go further, and will suppose that in
some cases it is reasonable and necessary, *even though such rights should
have been strengthened and confirmed
by the most solemn sanctions and engagements.*" MS. Corresp. ii. 90.

[3] Resolves of the People of Boston,
in Mass. Gazette, Supp't, for Sept. 13,
1764. Says the author of Observations on the Present State, &c., of the
British Colonies, pub. in 1769, "As

the inhabitants of New England pride
themselves more than any other people upon earth in that spirit of freedom which first made their ancestors
leave their native country and settle
there, and do really, as individuals,
enjoy more independency, from several peculiar circumstances in their
manners, laws, and situation, it is natural to conceive that, upon the first
apprehension (whether justly founded
or not makes no difference) of any
invasion of that freedom, they should
take fire, and sacrifice to resentment
— may I not say to virtuous principle? — the passions whose gratification consumed their articles of commerce and luxury, and confine themselves to mere necessaries."

CHAP.
X.

1764.

cause, — that, during this interval, the pen of his excellency, as well as that of Mr. Hutchinson,[1] had been busily employed in fomenting the evils which existed, and that, by his misrepresentations and his impeachment of the loyalty of the province, he was responsible in a measure for encouraging the scheme which the ministry was persistently pressing upon Parliament. There were many things in his conduct which were displeasing to the patriots of the province. His sympathies were with the court, not with the people; and the motives to induce him to side with the former were far more powerful than any expectations of advancement from the latter. To minds of his cast, the prospect that the struggle would terminate adversely to England was exceedingly doubtful; and he had no hesitation in abiding the issue. But he was soon made sensible that, with whatever meekness his sway had been thus far submitted to, there were bounds which it would be unwise to transgress. Hence, at the opening of the court, aware of the odium which attached to his proceedings, he had not the courage to persist in his interference, but contented himself with recommending unity in their counsels, and prudence and moderation in the measures they should adopt.[2]

The action of the House was at first undecided. The wishes of the people had been distinctly expressed; but where so much was at stake, caution was advisable. The stillness which portends the earthquake reigned. Yet the deep under current of popular feeling urged the representatives on; and, setting aside private business, the House went into a committee of the whole to consider the letters which had been received from

[1] Hutchinson draughted a long paper on the claims of the colonies; and in a letter, of July 23, to a friend in England, he says, " If I have any where expressed myself with too great freedom, I know you will not suffer it to do me any prejudice. I desire to avoid publicity, and to do nothing out of character. If that were out of the question, yet I could wish it so disguised as to be supposed to come from some other colony rather than from Massachusetts. Whatever you do, I hope you will not let it be known that they come from me." MS. Corresp. ii. 99.

[2] Hutchinson, iii. 112; Bradford, i. 32, 33.

their agents in England; and an address to the king was prepared by a committee, of which Otis was chairman.[1] The tone
of this address was displeasing to the Council, and it was opposed. Mr. Hutchinson was at the bottom of this opposition;[2]
and, after a conference, an address to the House of Commons
was agreed upon, and prepared by a committee of both branches of the court. The tone of this address was much milder
than that to the king. Nothing was said of the right of Parliament to impose a tax, nor of the intention of the people to
evade its operation; but, after setting forth in general terms
the objections which had been urged against the sugar act and
the stamp act, it concluded with a prayer for further delay, and
for a continuance of the privileges which had been hitherto
enjoyed, without which their condition would be deplorably
wretched.

Aware of the feeling against him in America, Mr. Hutchinson was indefatigable to prevent misapprehension of his position in England; and, though he seems to have wavered
between patriotism and loyalty, — between devotion to his own
country and servility to the crown, — he had decided, on the
whole, to side with the oppressors. By taking this course, his
ambition whispered to him there was a reasonable chance of
his elevation to the chief magistracy, should any thing occur to
occasion the removal of Governor Bernard. This was the
elevation to which he aspired; and hence the duplicity of his
conduct was thinly veiled by an outward profession of attachment to liberty.[3]

---

[1] Mass. Rec's; Jour. H. of R. for
1764, p. 102; Mass. Gazette for Mar.
14, 1765.

[2] "I desire, as long as I live," wrote
Hutchinson, March 16, 1765, MS.
Corresp. ii. 132, "to promote entire
concord and harmony, and to prevent
unreasonable and intemperate zeal
against the powers without. This
may be thought, from a short and
imperfect view, to betray diffidence
and want of spirit; but stay till you
see the consequences, and you will
determine it to be well-judged caution and prudence. The misfortune
is, the imprudence of particular governments will probably bring down
destruction upon their neighbors, as
well as themselves."

[3] I am fully aware that there are
difficulties in forming a correct estimate of the character of Hutchinson.

CHAP.
X.

1764.

1765.
Jan.

Jan. 10.

But if the action of Massachusetts was less decided in this trying hour than might have been expected, the zeal of her citizens was soon inflamed to a still higher pitch ; and, upon the receipt of the addresses from New York and Virginia, whose resolute tone strikingly contrasted with their own modest address, the demand for stronger measures became so urgent that the appeal could be no longer resisted.[1] The action of Parliament was likewise calculated to rekindle strife. Grenville, who had postponed his scheme of taxation for a season, now came forward prepared to urge it "upon the most general and acknowledged grounds of whig policy."[2] The king, at the opening of the session, presented the American question as one of "obedience to the laws and respect for the legislative authority of the kingdom ; " and the Lords and Commons, in their reply, declared their intention to pursue every plan calculated for the public advantage, and to proceed

---

It would be easy to quote passages from his correspondence in which liberal sentiments are candidly expressed, and it would be equally easy to quote passages betraying a want of confidence in such sentiments, and a decided leaning towards arbitrary measures. His position was peculiar. On the one hand, his social relations inclined him to espouse the cause of his country ; on the other, his cautiousness whispered to him that perhaps his political interests would be better secured by a little reserve, and that it would be more prudent to appear willing to acquiesce in the measures of the ministry than to express dissent from them. The following passage, from a letter dated April 26, 1765, in MS. Corresp. ii. 136, may give some clew to his motives. "Some men," says he, "it is most evident, of both sides, have not a spark of public spirit, and see the public interest rise or fall with no other pleasure than as their own particular interest is concerned ; and as a bad man of an enterprising genius can always serve himself at the expense of the public, he will never fail doing it unless he finds the temporal advantage will be more than balanced by his particular share of the damage that will accrue to the public." With this conjoin the saying of Lord Bacon : "All rising to great place is by a winding stair ; and if there be factions, it is good to side a man's self whilst he is in the rising, and to balance himself when he is placed."

[1] Hutchinson, iii. 115. "The acts of Parliament have made such impressions on the minds of the northward people, and the men-of-war so steadily enforce them, that there is an entire stagnation of trade. Nothing do they talk of but their own manufactures, the downfall of England, and the rise of America ; as if, in a little time, we should be able to supply ourselves with most of the necessaries we used to take from England." Extract from letter from Virginia, in Mass. Gazette for Jan. 10, 1765.

[2] Bancroft, v. 229.

therein "with that temper and firmness which will best concil- CHAP.
iate and insure due submission to the laws, and reverence to X.
the legislative authority of Great Britain."[1] The prospect 1765.
of carrying his favorite measure was exceedingly gratifying to
the feelings of the chief minister; to the remonstrances of the
agents of the colonies a deaf ear was turned; and, seconded Feb. 2.
by Townshend, Jenyns, and others, a series of resolutions, fifty-
five in number, was proposed to the committee of ways and Feb. 5.
means, embracing the details of the contemplated stamp act.[2]
The opponents of the resolutions were comparatively few;[3] yet
their names are worthy of perpetual remembrance. Beckford,
Conway, Jackson, and Barré were the principal speakers; and
to two of these, Conway and Barré, the thanks of the province
were afterwards tendered.[4] But their eloquence was of no
avail. The resolutions were carried by an overwhelming
majority of five to one, and the triumph of the ministry was
emphatic and complete.[5]

The very next day orders were issued to Grenville and his Feb. 3.

---

[1] Debates in Parl. iv. 244–246; Aikin's Anns. of George III. i. 39.

[2] Walpole's George III. ii. 68; Debates in Parl. iv. 250; Bancroft, v. 236. "The colonies, in truth," says Walpole, "were highly alarmed, and had sent over representations so strong against being taxed here, that it was not thought decent or safe to present their memorial to Parliament."

[3] "We hear that at the debate in the House of Commons, when the resolves passed, not a man spoke who did not declare his opinion that the American people ought to be taxed; nor would any one introduce a petition which should impeach the right of Parliament. Even the most interested, and those who are of the opposition, all refused to present such a petition." Mass. Gazette for April 4, 1765.

[4] Walpole's George III. ii. 67; Providence Gazette of Aug. 14, 1765; Conduct of the late Admin. examined,

30. The speech of Barré was exceedingly spirited. Townshend had said that the American colonies were planted by the care, nourished by the indulgence, and protected by the arms of England; to which Barré replied, *"They planted by your care!* No; your oppressions planted them in America. *They nourished up by your indulgence!* They grew by your neglect of them. *They protected by your arms!* They have nobly taken up arms in your defence. And believe me, the same spirit of freedom which actuated that people at first will accompany them still." Mass. Gazette for May 30, 1765. For further particulars relative to the correspondence between the General Court and Barré see Drake's Boston, 704. An expression used by Barré in his speech furnished to the province the motto of "the Sons of Liberty."

[5] Aikin's George III. i. 40.

CHAP.
X.
1765.
Feb. 27.
Mar. 8.
Mar. 22.

associates to "bring in a stamp bill for America;" and six days after the bill was ready. It was read the first time without debate, and petitions against it were rejected.[1] Two weeks later the bill passed the Commons; early in the following month it was agreed to by the Lords; and a fortnight later it received the royal assent by a commission, his majesty being ill and unable to sign it. Thus, at a time when the light of reason was obscured in the head of the nation, was the measure adopted which laid the foundation of the American revolution.[2]

The tidings of the passage of this act gave great dissatisfaction. Mr. Hutchinson, it is true, still held a seat in the Council, and exerted an influence upon public affairs. But his former popularity was daily declining, and his influence was destined to be counteracted in a way little agreeable to his feelings.[3] The message of the governor, at the opening of the General Court, took no notice of what he knew must be uppermost in the minds of a majority of the representatives;[4] but the House was not daunted, and, at the instance of Otis, voted

June 6.

at once that it was expedient there should be a "meeting, as soon as convenient, of committees from the Houses in the several colonies, to consult together on their present circumstances, and the difficulties to which they were and must be reduced

[1] Conduct of the late Admin. examined, 8; Mass. Gazette for May 23, 1765.

[2] Supp't Mass. Gazette for May 16, 1765; Walpole's George III. ii. 82; Hutchinson, iii. 116, 117; Minot, ii. 200; Bancroft, v. 243–248.

[3] "The ministry," says Hutchinson, in speaking of this act, MS. Corresp. ii. 135, April 9, 1765, "may obtain applause, and the nation be amused a little while by this measure; but I think there is danger that the discouragements, discontents, and dissatisfaction to the mother country, which will be caused in many of the colonies, will eventually more than balance all the profit that will ever be received from taxes," &c. Yet afterwards he wrote,

June 4, 1765, in ibid. 139, "The stamp act is received among us with as much decency as could be expected. Hitherto I have endeavored to state the case of the colonies in the most favorable light, always with submission to the supreme authority. It is now become my duty, as an executive officer, to promote the execution of the act and to prevent any evasion, and I hope there will be as little room for complaint from this as from any colony." Again, June 5, ibid. 140: "The act will execute itself, and there is no room for evasion; and if there was, I am sure the executive court would show no countenance to it."

[4] Jour. H. of R. for 1765, p. 11.

by the operation of the late acts of Parliament." This meeting was proposed to be held on the first Tuesday of October; and circular letters were drawn up to be sent as far south as South Carolina. The opposition of the governor and of Mr. Hutchinson could not check these proceedings, and they were compelled to acquiesce in them with the best grace they could.[1]

It was the intention of Grenville, in the execution of the new act, to " begin with small duties and taxes, and to advance in proportion as it should be found the colonies would bear ; "[2] but his colleagues were urgent for the adoption of additional measures, and, in particular, insisted that the mutiny act should be extended to America, with power to billet troops on private houses. To this Grenville would not consent. Yet the bill passed ; and the colonies were required, at their own expense, to furnish the troops quartered upon them by Parliament with fuel, bedding, utensils for cooking, and various articles of food and drink. To take off the edge from this bill, bounties were granted on the importation of lumber and timber from the plantations ; coffee of domestic growth was exempted from additional duty ; and iron was permitted to be carried to Ireland.[3]

---

[1] Jour. H. of R. for 1765, 108, 109 ; Mass. Gazette for Aug. 29, 1765 ; Hutchinson, iii. 118 ; Minot, ii. 203–207 ; Bradford, i. 54 ; Bancroft, v. 279. The committee to write to the other colonies consisted of Samuel White, James Otis, and —— Lee ; and on the 20th of June, James Otis, Timothy Ruggles, and Oliver Partridge were chosen delegates to the congress. On the 24th, Mr. Cushing, of Boston, Captain Sheafe, and Mr. Gray were chosen to draught a letter to the agent in England, which was done. Jour. H. of R.

[2] Hutchinson's Letter of April 9, 1765, in MS. Corresp. ii. 135 ; Bancroft, v. 248.

[3] Chatham Corresp. iii. 192, 208 ; Acts Geo. III. c. xlv. ; Supp't to Mass. Gazette for June 6, 1765 ; Bancroft, v. 248–251. Hutchinson was one who was confident that the stamp act would execute itself; but he afterwards wrote, Aug. 16, 1765, in MS. Corresp. ii. 145, " I made a poor judgment when I wrote you last, and find I promised myself what I *wished* rather than what I had reason to *expect*. I am now convinced that the people throughout the colonies are impressed with an opinion that they are no longer considered by the people of England as their fellow-subjects, and entitled to English liberties ; and I expect some tragical event in some or other of the colonies, for we are not only in a deplorable situation at present, but have a dismal prospect before us as the commencement of the act approaches. If there be no execution of it, all business must cease ; and yet the general view is, it cannot be carried into execution."

CHAP. But the stamp act itself was the principal grievance ; and it
X. soon became evident to all who had flattered themselves it
1765. would be peacefully executed that they had entirely mistaken
the temper of the colonists, and, from their former submission,
had too hastily concluded that they would continue to submit.
Nor was the policy of Grenville, of selecting the officers who
were to execute the act from among the Americans themselves,
more fortunate. It was well known that enough could be
found who were ready to barter their liberties for office ; and
such were held in deserved execration. True, the agents of
the colonies were invited to make the nominations, and, as a
minor evil, in most cases did so ; nor did any of them, not even
Franklin, express their belief that the act would be resisted.[1]
Otis had said, " It is our duty to submit to all acts of Parliament ; " but he qualified this statement by adding, that all acts
contrary to the constitution were null and void, and consequently not binding even if sanctioned by Parliament.[2] The
1764. General Court, too, in one of its addresses, while they " humbly
Nov. 3. apprehended " they might " propose their objections," acknowledged " their duty to yield obedience to the act while it continued unrepealed." [3] But public opinion cannot always be
hemmed in by conventional restraints ; and the outbreak
which followed was as spontaneous as it was unexpected.

A general determination was early evinced to prevent the
execution of the stamp act at all hazards. Virginia was the
1765. first to " ring the alarm bell ; " but her resolves were so point-
May 29. ed that some pronounced them treasonable.[4] The newspapers
vindicated them ; and, the tide of opinion suddenly changing,
in the end they were applauded as worthy of imitation.[5] The

[1] Conduct of the late Admin. examined, 13–18.

[2] Bancroft, v. 250–252.

[3] Conduct of the late Admin. examined, 17.

[4] Hutchinson's Lett. of Aug. 15 to
the Sec. of State, and to Pownall of
July 19, in MS. Corresp. ii. ; Hutch-

inson's Hist. iii. 119 ; Debates in Parl.
iv. 308 ; Conduct of the late Admin.
examined, 26, 71, 93, 94. A copy of
the Virginia resolutions was transmitted to the ministry so early as the
27th of July. Conduct of late Admin.
examined, 20.

[5] Says Hutchinson to Pownall, July

names of the stamp distributors had been pubilshed in Boston
by Jared Ingersoll, of Connecticut, who had just arrived from
England ; and it was found that Andrew Oliver, the brother-in-
law of Hutchinson, was appointed for Massachusetts. Immediately " the decree seemed to go forth that Boston should
lead the way in the work of compulsion." [1]

A change in the ministry had taken place in England ; and
William Pitt had been again called to office.[2] The birthday
of the Prince of Wales was kept as a holiday ; and the crowd
that assembled on the occasion, as they kindled their bonfire
in King Street, rent the air with tumultuous shouts of " Pitt
and liberty." It was welcome news to all that one in whom
they trusted as the friend of the colonies had been restored to
power ; and, such was the impulse given to the " Sons of Liberty," they would rest satisfied with nothing short of some
signal demonstration of their feelings. It was at once concerted, therefore, to hang in effigy the obnoxious distributor of
stamps ; and on the morning of Wednesday, the fourteenth of
August, the inhabitants of the southerly part of the town, as
they passed to their business, saw suspended from the out-
stretched limb of a majestic elm, long known as the " Liberty
Tree,"[3] an effigy of Oliver,[4] tricked out with the emblems of

---

10, 1765, in MS. Corresp. ii. 143,
" Upon the first arrival of the stamp
act, our political heroes seemed to be
silenced, and acknowledged the address or petition from the province,
which had been much exclaimed
against, was right and well judged ;
but, encouraged by Virginia, they begin to open again, and yesterday we
had published a piece as full of rant
as any which had preceded it." Comp.
Debates in Parl. iv. 311, 312.

[1] Letter of Gage to Conway, Sept.
1765.

[2] The intention of removing the
old ministry was declared in the middle of May, and the new administration came into office in July. Con-

duct, &c., 17 ; Walpole's George III.
ii. 163 ; Mass. Gazette for Aug. 29,
1765.

[3] This tree stood at the corner of Essex and Washington Streets ; and the
Hon. David Sears has erected upon
its site a splendid building, known as
the " Liberty Tree Block," on the
front of which is a representation of
the tree in bass-relief.

[4] The effigy of Oliver was prepared
by the mechanics of Boston, viz., Ben-
jamin Edes, Thomas Crafts, John
Smith, Stephen Cleverly, John Avery,
Jr., Thomas Chase, Henry Bass, and
Henry Welles. Gordon's Am. Rev.
i. 175 ; Diary of John Adams, in
Works, ii. 175 ; Drake's Boston, 695.

CHAP. Bute and Grenville.[1] The news spread like wildfire; and
X.   thousands collected to gaze on the spectacle. Hutchinson, as
1765. the chief justice, ordered the sheriff to remove the images; but
Aug.14. the people interfered, expressing their determination to have
them remain until evening. Governor Bernard summoned his
Council to meet in the afternoon; but what could they do? A
majority was opposed to taking any action; and the minority
was compelled to submit.

Towards evening the excitement increased, and the images
were taken down, placed upon a bier, supported in procession
by six men, and followed by an "amazing multitude" through
the streets to the town house. Here the crowd paused directly
under the council chamber, and shouted at the top of their
voices, "Liberty, property, and no stamps!" Three cheers were
then given; and the crowd moved on to Kilby Street, to Oliver's Dock, where a building was demolished which, it was
supposed, had been erected for a stamp office. The fragments
of this building were carried to Fort Hill, and a bonfire was
made of them in front of Oliver's house, upon which the images
were burned.[2]

The spirit of resistance was fully aroused, and the cry of
the south was echoed at the north. "The stamp act shall
never be executed here," was the determination of the people.
"All the power of Great Britain shall not compel us to submit to it." "We will die on the place first." "We will spend
our last blood in the cause." "The man who offers a stamped
paper to sell will be immediately killed."[3] It was to no purpose that Hutchinson directed an alarm to be sounded, and the

---

[1] Bute, "the favorite," had been frequently burned in effigy in England, under the emblem of a jack-boot — a pun upon his name as John, Earl of Bute. To the jack-boot in these burnings it was not unusual to add a petticoat — a further compliment to the Princess Dowager of Wales. Such bonfires of the jack-boot were renewed during several years, both in England and America, as tokens of hostility to the court. Lord Mahon's Hist. Eng. v. 25.

[2] Mass. Gazette for Aug. 19, 1765, Supp't, and for Aug. 22.

[3] Hutchinson's Narr. in MS. Corresp. ii.; Conduct of the late Admin. examined, 27.

military to be mustered, for " the drummers were in the mob." CHAP.
Nor did his appearance in person, with the sheriff at his heels, X.
cause the crowd to disperse. " Stand by," was the watchword ; 1765.
and the baffled chief justice was compelled to flee. An hour
before midnight the throng repaired to the residence of the
governor, and, after three cheers, quietly dispersed.[1]

The next day a proclamation was issued by the governor, Aug. 15.
offering a reward for the discovery of the offenders ;[2] but no
one was disposed to act as informer, and, if any were seized,
" the prisons," said Mayhew, " would not hold them many
hours." " We have a dismal prospect before us," said Hutchinson ; and he advised that a larger watch should be set at
night ; but the motion was opposed, and the ordinary watch
was not increased. " If Oliver had been found last night,"
said Bernard ruefully, " he would actually have been mur-
thered ; " and Oliver himself inclined to the same opinion. It
was plainly intimated that, if he did not resign his office before
night, his house would be pulled down about his ears ; and,
thoroughly convinced that it would be best to yield, he signed
a paper expressing his willingness to throw up his commission.
This satisfied the crowd, and at night a bonfire celebrated
their victory.[3]

For a short time there was quiet. But at length the distrust of the people fell upon Hutchinson ; and, twelve days
after Oliver had been hanged in effigy, the crowd assembled to Aug. 26
pay him a visit. " He is a prerogative man," was the general
cry. " He grasps all the important offices in the state." " He
himself holds four offices, and his relatives six or seven." " He
had a principal hand in projecting the stamp act."[4] Such

[1] Hutchinson's Lett. of Aug. 15, in
MS. Corresp. ii. ; Hutchinson's Hist.
iii. 120 ; Conduct of the late Admin.
examined, 99–101.
[2] This proclamation is given in
Drake's Bost. 696, note.
[3] Hutchinson's Lett. of Aug. 16, in
MS. Corresp. ii. 145, and Hist. iii.

121 ; Conduct of the late Admin. &c.
101 ; Debates in Parl. iv. 313–316.
[4] That Hutchinson stood ready to
execute the stamp act, if he did not
approve its passage, is evident from
his letter of June 4, 1765, which has
been already quoted.

CHAP. outcries wrought upon their inflammable spirits, and prepared
  X.   them for deeds of greater violence. Their first act was to
1765. enter the office of Mr. Story, the deputy registrar, opposite
the north side of the court house, and burn the records of the
Vice Admiralty Court; next they ravaged the house of Mr.
Hallowell, the comptroller of the customs, situated on Hanover
Street; and then, hastening to the residence of Hutchinson, in
Garden Court Street, and barely giving his family time to
escape, they split open the doors of his palatial mansion, destroyed his furniture, scattered his plate, threw his books and
manuscripts into the streets, ransacked his wine cellar, and at
daybreak left his house a ruin.[1]

Governor Bernard was at the Castle when these events occurred; but, hastening to town the next day, he summoned the
Council to meet immediately to decide what should be done.
Before that body met, the inhabitants of Boston assembled in
Faneuil Hall, and, deprecating the violent proceedings of the
previous night, a series of resolutions was passed, desiring the
selectmen to suppress the like disorders in the future, and
pledging the assistance of the people in the discharge of this
duty. The Council advised a proclamation, offering a reward
of three hundred pounds for the detection of the ringleaders,
and one hundred pounds for other persons, and six or eight
were apprehended; but the attempt to arrest one Mackintosh,
in King Street, was resisted, and those who had been seized
were speedily liberated. The popular excitement was such
that nothing could be effectually done, and the government
was shorn of its usual strength. Few even of the conservative
citizens sympathized with the legislation which had awakened
this resentment, and few were disposed to interrupt the course
of events. Only so much restraint was therefore exercised as
to prevent the passions of the multitude from overleaping all

[1] Hutchinson's Lett. of Aug. 30, in   duct of the late Admin. &c. 102–104;
MS. Corresp. ii. 146, and Hist. iii.;   Debates in Parl. iv. 316–318.
Boston News Letter for Sept. 3; Con-

bounds, and many rejoiced that the abettors of oppression had been signally rebuked.[1]

/ Shortly after the attack upon the house of Mr. Hutchinson, news arrived that another change had taken place in the ministry, the Rockingham whigs having been elevated to power.[2] Great was the joy awakened by these tidings; and the hope was cherished that, as the new cabinet contained some friends to America, a repeal of the stamp act might be effected.[3] "If Astræa were not fled," said Mayhew, "there might be grounds for the hope."[4] But little could be gained by waiting in silence for the repeal. Something must be done to show that the colonies were in earnest in their resistance; that the outbreak which had just passed, if it was an ebullition of passion, was also an indication of the determination of the people not to submit to the obnoxious act; and that, if no open countenance was given to the doings of an excited populace, it was not because the prudent thought or felt differently, but because, conscious of the justice of their cause, they were more disposed to rely upon an appeal to Parliament, by showing that the act, if persisted in and enforced, would be as pernicious to Great Britain as to America.

In accordance with these views, in all the colonies, from Georgia to New Hampshire, the same spirit of opposition was manifested as in Massachusetts. The stamp distributors and

[1] Conduct of the late Admin. &c. 28; Mass. Gazette for Aug. 29, 1765. "The colonists," says Hutchinson, MS. Corresp. ii. 90, "like all the rest of the human race, are of different spirits and dispositions; some more calm and moderate, others more violent and extravagant; and if now and then some rude and indecent things are thrown out in print, in one place and another, I hope such things will not be considered as coming from the colonists in general, but from particular persons, warmed by the intemperate zeal, shall I say? of English-

men, in support of what upon a sudden appear to them to be their rights." This passage was penned more than a year before the attack upon his house, and shows how he could then apologize for the warmth of his countrymen.

[2] Mass. Gazette for Sept. 26, 1765; Hutchinson, iii. 128; Bradford, i. 66; Lord Mahon's Hist. Eng.; Bancroft, v. 296–306, 316.

[3] For an account of the ceremonies on this occasion, see Drake's Boston, 703.

[4] Quoted in Bancroft, v. 316.

CHAP. inspectors, in Connecticut, Rhode Island, New York, and at
X. the south, by the "unconquerable rage of the people," were
1765. compelled to resign.[1] Not one was permitted to hold office
quietly. At all hazards it had been determined to resist the
act. If the question was asked, "What will you do after the
first of November?" the reply was, "We shall do as before."
"Will you, then," it was inquired, "set at defiance the Parliament?" "We are ready," it was answered, "to submit to
constitutional laws; but the stamp act is against Magna
Charta; and Lord Coke says, an act of Parliament against
Magna Charta is for that reason void."[2]

Nor were the statesmen of the province idle. The General
Sep. 25. Court had been prorogued to the last week in September, at
which time the governor, in his message, after alluding to
the late acts of violence, and to the declarations of the people that the stamp act should never be executed, called upon
both houses to support him in the exercise of his authority.
The law, he observed, might be inexpedient; yet it could not
be denied that Parliament had the right both to pass and to
enforce it; and he cautioned them against denying this right,
lest such denial should injure their own interests, and prevent
the repeal of the act. The alarming consequences of a refusal
to submit were also set forth; and, while he insisted that their
submission alone would be insufficient without the concurrence
of the people, he advised them to acquaint themselves well
with the exigencies of the times, and to endeavor to persuade

---

[1] John Adams's Diary, in Works,
ii. 154; Hutchinson, iii. 128; Bancroft, v. 316, 322. "The people,"
wrote J. Adams, in the following December, "even to the lowest ranks,
have been more attentive to their liberties, more inquisitive about them,
and more determined to defend them,
than they were ever before known or
had occasion to be; innumerable have
been the monuments of wit, humor,
sense, learning, spirit, patriotism, and

heroism, erected in the several colonies and provinces in the course of
this year. Our presses have groaned,
our pulpits have thundered, our legislatures have resolved, our towns have
voted; the crown officers have every
where trembled, and all their little
tools and creatures have been afraid
to speak and ashamed to be seen."
[2] Hutchinson, MS. Corresp. ii.;
Bancroft, v. 323.

their constituents to yield. For this purpose he proposed to CHAP.
give them a recess; but the House would ask for no recess, X.
and two days after the governor adjourned the court to the 1765.
last week in October.[1]

Sep. 27.

Already had John Adams, through the medium of the press,
expressed the convictions of his honest heart. "There seems
to be," said he, "a direct and formal design on foot in Great
Britain to enslave all America. Be it remembered, liberty
must at all hazards be defended. Rulers are no more than
attorneys, agents, and trustees for the people; and if the trust
is insidiously betrayed, or wantonly trifled away, the people
have a right to revoke the authority that they themselves have
deputed, and to constitute abler and better agents. We have
an indisputable right to demand our privileges against all the
power and authority on earth."[2] Braintree, his native town,
passed, at his instance, a series of resolves, instructing their Sep. 24.
representatives in relation to the stamps. These resolves were
published; and such was their spirit that they rang through
the whole province, and forty towns, at least, adopted them in
substance as instructions to their representatives.[3] Boston had
previously expressed its abhorrence of the act as "contrary to Sep. 12
the British constitution," and "contrary to the charter of the and 18.
province and the rights of mankind."[4] The voice of a kinsman
of Adams spoke in these words; and Samuel Adams, who "felt

[1] Jour. H. of R. for 1765, pp. 117–123, 129; Mass. Gazette Extra for Sept. 26, 1765; Hutchinson, iii. 129, 130, and App. C.; Bradford, i. 68. "The right of the Parliament of Great Britain to make laws for the American colonies," said the governor, "however it has been controverted in America, remains indisputable at Westminster. If it is yet to be made a question, who shall determine it but the Parliament? If the Parliament declares that the right is inherent in them, are they likely to acquiesce in an open and forcible opposition to the exercise of it? Will they not more probably maintain such right, and support their own authority? Is it in the will, or in the power, or for the interest of this province, to oppose such authority? If such opposition should be made, may it not bring on a contest, which may prove the most detrimental and ruinous event which could happen to this people?"

[2] Bancroft, v. 325.

[3] John Adams's Works, ii. 152, 153. The instructions of other towns are given in Mass. Gazette for Oct. 1⁷ and 24, 1765.

[4] Mass. Gazette for Sept. 19, 1765; Bradford, i. 66, 67; Bancroft, v. 329.

CHAP.
X.

1765.
Oct. 24.
Oct. 28.
Oct. 29.

Oct. 7.

an ambition of doing something extraordinary," acted as the scribe of the people, and gave utterance to their thoughts. Hence, when the court met, after its adjournment, the answer to the message of his excellency was ready ; and, five days after, a series of resolves, fourteen in number, was passed, which were ordered "to be kept in the records of this House, that a just sense of liberty, and the firm sentiments of loyalty, may be transmitted to posterity." [1]

Earlier in the month a congress of delegates from the different provinces had assembled in New York, at which resolutions were passed, based upon the inalienable rights of man, and an address to the king, a memorial to the House of Lords, and a petition to the House of Commons were draughted and signed by the "commissioners, or the major part of them, who were instructed for that purpose." [2] The proceedings of this body were cautious and respectful, yet decisive and firm. The tone of its papers was certainly mild, displaying no spirit of rashness or innovation ; and there was little in either of them to which exception could be taken. The memorialists, indeed, claimed an exemption from all taxes except such as were imposed by the legislatures of the respective colonies ; but, at the same time, they frankly affirmed that "they esteemed their

---

[1] Mass. Gazette for Oct. 31 and Nov. 14, 1765 ; Jour. H. of R. for 1765, 151–153 ; Hutchinson, iii. App. E. ; Bradford's State Papers. Samuel Adams was elected at this time to represent Boston in the place of Oxenbridge Thacher, deceased ; and it was by him, probably, that the address of the House to the governor was penned.

[2] The provinces represented in this congress were, Massachusetts, Rhode Island, Connecticut, Pennsylvania, Maryland, Delaware, New Jersey, New York, and South Carolina. New Hampshire, though unrepresented, agreed to abide by the result ; and Georgia sent for a copy of their proceedings. Virginia and North Carolina were not represented. Pitkin, 130, 136 ; Mulford's New Jersey, 368 ; Story's Comm. i. 175 ; Bancroft, v. 334. Gage, speaking of this congress, says, "Those who compose it are of various characters and opinions ; but in general the spirit of democracy is strong among them, supporting the independence of the provinces as not subject to the legislative power of Great Britain. The question is not of the inexpediency of the stamp act, but that it is unconstitutional, and contrary to their rights." Gage to Conway, Oct. 12, in Bancroft, v. 342. The names of the members are given in Dunlap's N. Y. i. 416, note.

connection with and dependence on Great Britain as one of CHAP.
their greatest blessings, and apprehended the latter would ⎯X.⎯
appear to be sufficiently secure when it was considered that 1765.
the inhabitants in the colonies had the most unbounded affection for his majesty's person, family, and government, as well
as for the mother country, and that their subordination to
Parliament was universally acknowledged." [1]

The ministry, in the mean time, had been informed of the
" riots " in Massachusetts and elsewhere ; and, reluctant to coerce, they shrank from enforcing at the point of the sword
the law which a part of them in their hearts disapproved.
Hence, just one day before the adjournment of the congress at
New York, and one week before the stamp act was to go into Oct. 24.
effect, orders were sent to the American governors, and to
General Gage, recommending " the utmost prudence and lenity," and advising a resort to " persuasive methods." [2]

The first of November dawned upon the province ; and it Nov. 1.
found the people ready and determined to nullify the stamp
act.   In Boston, the bells of the churches tolled its knell ;
minute guns were fired ; the vessels in the harbor displayed
their colors at half-mast ; and children in the streets, catching
from their elders the word as it passed round, swelled the chorus,
and shouted wildly, " Liberty, property, and no stamps ! " [3]   It

[1] Trumbull MSS. ii. 64 ; Lett. of
Gov. Fitch, of Connecticut, dated Nov.
13, 1765 ; Mass. Gazette for March
20, 1766 ; Hutchinson, iii. App. 479–
488 ; Bradford, i. 55–60 ; Lord Mahon's Hist. Eng. v. 126 ; Bancroft, v.
334–345.   Two of the delegates —
Timothy Ruggles, of Massachusetts,
and Joseph Ogden, of New Jersey —
refused to sign the address and memorials ; and the former was censured
by his constituents on his return, and
the latter was hanged in effigy by the
people.   The report of the proceedings of the congress was approved by
the Massachusetts House of Representatives on the 2d of November.
Jour. H. of R. 164.   For Ruggles's
VOL. II.   20

reason for dissenting from the action
of the congress, see Mass. Gazette for
May 1, 1766.

[2] Conway to Gov. Fitch, Oct. 24,
in Trumbull MSS. ii. 65 ; Conway to
Bernard and Gage, and to the other
American governors, in Debates in
Parl. iv. 302–306 ; Mass. Gazette for
Feb. 6, 1766.   The same day that
these letters were dated, viz., October
24, a committee was appointed on the
part of both branches of the Massachusetts legislature to consider some
proper method to prevent difficulties
after the 1st of November.   Journal
H. of R. for 1765, p. 145.

[3] Mass. Gaz. of Oct. 31 gave as its
motto a couplet from Pope's Homer :

CHAP. had been suggested that Mr. Huske, a native of New Hamp-
  X. shire, who had removed to London and obtained a seat in the
1765. House of Commons, had urged upon Grenville the passage of
this act; and his effigy, with that of the late chief minister,
was hung upon Liberty Tree early in the morning. In the
evening both images were cut down, carried to the town house,
and thence to the gallows, where they were suspended a second
time, and then torn in pieces and flung into the air.[1] The
Nov. 5. fifth of the month, the anniversary of the powder plot, which
had been a season of rioting with many in former years, was
this year peaceably observed. A feud, which had long existed
between the residents of the north and of the south part of
Boston, was amicably settled; both parties united in the customary pageants, and the utmost harmony and good feeling
prevailed.[2]

By the operation of the stamp act, the courts of the province
were closed, business was suspended, and an unusual stillness
reigned throughout the country. The provisions of the act
were exceedingly stringent; and, as the people had refused to
use the stamps which had been sent over, nothing remained but
Dec. 18. to abide the consequences.[3] In this crisis a meeting was appointed to be held in Boston; but on the preceding day, as a
precautionary measure, Oliver was compelled to resign his
Dec. 17. office as distributor of stamps, and, in the presence of a multi-

---

"Jove fixed it certain, that whatever day
Makes man a slave takes half his worth away."

On the 1st of November the paper
was not issued; but on the 7th a
sheet was issued, marked No. 0. The
regular publication was resumed May
22, 1766. See the volumes of the
Gazette, in Lib. Mass. Hist. Soc., and
comp. Drake's Boston, 708, note.
   [1] Mass. Gazette for Oct. 31, 1765;
Drake's Boston, 708.
   [2] Mass. Gazette for Nov. 7.
   [3] September 25, the governor sent
a message to the House, informing
them that a vessel had arrived in the
harbor, with stamped papers for Massachusetts, N. Hampshire, and Rhode
Island, and asking what should be
done with them; but the House declined advising him upon the subject.
The stamps were then deposited at the
Castle, and, to prevent their being forcibly seized by the populace, an additional military company was stationed
at the Castle by the governor. The
House protested against this step, and
several messages passed between them
and the Governor and Council. Jour.
H. of R. for 1765, pp. 124–126, 169–
185; Bradford, i. 75.

tude of two thousand persons, an oath was administered to him, CHAP.
under Liberty Tree, to the effect that " he had never taken any X.
measures to act in that office, and that he never would do so, 1765.
directly or indirectly." [1]

Satisfied with this concession, the town meeting convened ;
and a vote was unanimously passed authorizing a committee to
sign and present to his excellency the governor and the honorable Council a memorial requesting that the courts might be
opened.[2] At the same time, the principal merchants of Boston
and other towns, to the number of two hundred, agreed to
import no more goods from England unless the stamp act
should be repealed, and countermanded the orders already sent
abroad.[3]

Thus closed the year 1765. Would the new year bring
forth a repeal of the act ? " This year," wrote John Adams, 1766.
" brings ruin or salvation to the British colonies. The eyes Jan. 1
of all America are fixed on the British Parliament. In short,
Britain and America are staring at each other ; and they will
probably stare more and more for some time." [4] At the opening of the General Court, the House, in their answer to the Jan. 18.
message of the governor, demanded redress for existing grievances. " The custom houses," said they, " are now open, and
the people are permitted to transact their usual business. *The
courts of justice also must be open, — open immediately,* — and
the law, the great rule of right, duly executed in every county
in the province. This stopping of the course of justice is a
grievance which this House must inquire into. Justice must

[1] Mass. Gazette for Dec. 19, 1765 ;
Hutchinson, iii. 139, 140 ; John Adams's Diary, in Works, ii. 156 ; Bancroft, v. 375. The dampness of the
weather on this day did not damp the
ardor of the people.

[2] The members of this committee
were Samuel Adams, Thomas Cushing,
John Hancock, Benjamin Kent, Samuel Sewall, John Rowe, Joshua Henshaw, and Arnold Welles ; and they
were empowered to employ as counsel
Jeremiah Gridley, James Otis, and
John Adams. Diary of John Adams,
in Works, ii. 157 et seq.

[3] Mass. Gazette for Dec. 6, 12, and
19, 1765 ; Bradford, i. 77.

[4] Diary, in Works, ii. 170.

CHAP.
X.
1766.

be fully administered without delay." [1]   This message was followed by a resolve of the House, sent to the Council, declaring that " the shutting up of the courts of justice has a manifest tendency to dissolve the bonds of civil society ; is unjustifiable on the principles of law and reason ; dangerous to his majesty's crown and dignity ; and a very great grievance to the subject that requires immediate redress."   The Council saw fit to lay this address on the table ; but, after some further proceedings, verbal declarations were made that the courts would be opened at the next term, and business be transacted as usual. [2]

Already the question of the repeal of the stamp act had begun to be agitated in England.   Grenville, indeed, towards the close of his life, declared with emphasis that, " had he continued in office, he would have forfeited a thousand lives if the act had been found impracticable." [3]   But Grenville was out of power ; and the new ministry, fortunately for all parties, was neither imbued with his prejudices nor cursed with his stubbornness.   Besides, the people of England, after all, were friendly to liberty ; their attachment to freedom was stronger than their love of arbitrary power ; and their consciences and affections appealed to them loudly to side with those who were struggling to resist the encroachments of absolutism. [4]   Hence,

1765.
Oct. 3.

early in October, finding themselves in an unpleasant dilemma, the ministers had agreed that the American question was too weighty for their decision, though no hope was given that the

[1] Mass. Gazette for Jan. 23, 1766 ; Hutchinson, iii. 143 ; Bradford, i. 77. On the 16th of January, the people of Plymouth, at a town meeting, passed a vote of thanks to their brethren of Boston for their zealous defence of the rights of the province. Mass. Gazette for Jan. 30, 1766.

[2] Jour. H. of R. for 1766 ; Hutchinson, iii. 143–145.

[3] Cavendish Debates, i. 551; Bancroft, v. 363.

[4] That multitudes in England were earnest for the repeal of the stamp act is evident from the petitions presented for that purpose.   Policy, without doubt, had much to do in exciting this feeling, for the commercial interests of the country were suffering.   But combined with this was another feeling, the love of liberty, which the Americans were struggling to secure and enjoy.   Both interest and affection, therefore, prompted the nation to urge the repeal of an act which was as inimical to their own welfare as to the welfare of America.   Comp. Bancroft, v. 366.

act would be repealed, as its cancelment unconditionally would CHAP.
be a "surrender of sovereignty." [1]   X.

Early in the new year, Parliament, after the usual holiday 1766.
recess, reassembled, and was informed by the king that "mat- Jan. 14.
ters of importance had happened in America, and orders been
issued for the support of lawful authority." [2] The Lords, in
reply, expressed their readiness to "assert and support the
king's dignity, and the legislative authority of the kingdom
over its colonies;" but in the House of Commons, which was
full, a debate sprang up, the most striking and memorable in
the annals of England. [3] In the course of this debate William
Pitt unexpectedly entered, having just arrived in town. It was
above a year since he had been seen within those walls; and,
as he walked slowly in, yet lame from gout, the eyes of all
were fastened upon him. The Americans in the gallery, drawn
thither by the importance of the pending debate, viewed him
as their "guardian angel or saviour," [4] and eagerly awaited his
words.

Mr. Nugent (Lord Clare) was the first to address the House;
and he insisted that the honor and dignity of the kingdom
obliged the Parliament to compel the execution of the stamp act,
except the right was acknowledged and the repeal was solicited
as a favor. He then expatiated on the extreme ingratitude of
the colonies, and concluded by charging the ministry with encouraging petitions to Parliament, and instructions to members
from trading and manufacturing towns against the act. [5] Edmund Burke followed, and delivered his maiden speech on
American affairs. [6] Then Pitt rose; and, as the House was

---

[1] Lord Mahon's Hist. England, v.
128; Bancroft, v. 367.
[2] On the 24th of December there
was a warm debate in Parliament "as
to what should be done with the re-
bellious Americans," in which Grenville took part. Mass. Gazette for
Feb. 13, 1766. The speech of the
king is in ibid. for March 27, 1766.
[3] Debates in Parl. iv. 285–287;

Lord Mahon's Hist. England, v. 129.
[4] John Adams's Diary, in Works,
ii.; Henry Seymour, of Connecticut,
in a letter to Gov. Fitch, dated Feb.
26, 1766, in Trumbull MSS. ii. 77
[5] Debates in Parl. iv. 288.
[6] Lord Mahon's Hist. Eng. v. 130.
Bancroft, v. 400, says the maiden
speech of Burke was made at a later
date.

CHAP. greatly agitated, his opening words were scarcely audible.
  X.   But, warming as he proceeded, his voice increased in volume
1766. and power, and he poured forth one of those brilliant harangues
which distinguished him as the most powerful orator of his day.

"I stand up in this place" — such were his words — "single
and unconnected. As to the late ministry," — and here he
turned to Grenville, who sat within one of him, — "every capital measure they have taken has been entirely wrong. As to
the present gentlemen, to those, at least, whom I have in my
eye," — and here he looked at the bench where Conway sat
with the lords of the treasury, — "I have no objection. Their
characters are fair ; but, notwithstanding, I love to be explicit :
I cannot give them my confidence. Pardon me, gentlemen ;
confidence is a plant of slow growth in an aged bosom ; youth
is the season of credulity.

"It is a long time since I have attended in Parliament.
When the resolution was taken in the House to tax America,
I was ill in bed. If I could have endured to have been carried in my bed, so great was the agitation of my mind for the
consequences, I would have solicited some kind hand to have
laid me down on this floor, to have borne my testimony against
it. It is now an act that has passed. I would speak with
decency of every act of this House ; but I must beg the indulgence of the House to speak of it with freedom.

"I hope a day may be soon appointed to consider the state
of the nation with respect to America. I hope gentlemen will
come to this debate with all the temper and impartiality that
his majesty recommends and the importance of the subject
requires — a subject of greater importance than ever engaged
the attention of this House, that subject only excepted, when,
near a century ago, it was the question whether yourselves
were to be bond or free. In the mean time, as I cannot depend upon health for any future day, such is the nature of my
infirmities, I will beg to say a few words at present — leaving
the justice, the equity, the policy, the expediency of the act to

another time. Some gentlemen," alluding to Mr. Nugent, CHAP
" seem to have considered it as a point of honor. If gentle-   X.
men consider it in that light, they leave all measures of right 1766.
and wrong, to follow a delusion that may lead to destruction.
It is my opinion that this kingdom has no right to lay a tax
upon the colonies — to be sovereign and supreme in every circumstance of government and legislation whatsoever. They
are the subjects of this kingdom, equally entitled with yourselves to all the natural rights of mankind and the peculiar
privileges of Englishmen, equally bound by its laws and equally
participating of the constitution of this free country. The
Americans are the sons, not the bastards of England. Taxation is no part of the governing or legislative power. The
taxes are a voluntary gift and grant of the Commons alone.

"There is an idea in some that the colonies are virtually
represented in this House. I would fain know by whom an
American is represented here. Is he represented by any knight
of the shire in any county in this kingdom? Would to God
that respectable representation was augmented to a greater
number. Or will you tell him that he is represented by any
representative of a borough — a borough which, perhaps, no
man ever saw? This is what is called the rotten part of the
constitution. It cannot continue a century. If it does not
drop, it must be amputated. The idea of a virtual representation of America in this House is the most contemptible idea
that ever entered into the head of man. It does not deserve
a serious refutation." [1]

On the close of this speech there was a long pause. Then
General Conway arose, and expressed his concurrence in the
views of Mr. Pitt. Grenville was the next speaker; and he
brought to the task all his energies. In the outset he censured
the ministry severely for not giving earlier notice of the disturbances in America; "for," said he, "they began in July, and

[1] Parl. Hist. Eng. iv. 288–291; Lord Mahon's Hist. Eng. v. 130–132;
Bancroft, v.

CHAP. now we are in the middle of January.   Lately they were only
X.   occurrences ; they are now grown to disturbances, to tumults,
1766. and riots.   I doubt they border on open rebellion ; and, if the
doctrine I have heard this day be confirmed, I fear they will
lose that name, to take that of revolution.   The government
over them being dissolved, a revolution will take place in
America."

"I cannot," he continued, "understand the difference between
external and internal taxes.   They are the same in effect, and
only differ in name.   That this kingdom has the sovereign, the
supreme legislative power over America, is granted ; it cannot
be denied ; and taxation is a part of that sovereign power.
It is one branch of the legislation.   It is, it has been, exercised
over those who are not, who were never represented.   It is
exercised over the India Company, the merchants of London,
the proprietors of the stocks, and over many great manufacturing towns.   It was exercised over the palatinate of Chester
and the bishopric of Durham before they sent any representatives to Parliament.   I appeal for proof to the preambles of
the acts which gave them representatives.

"When I proposed to tax America, I asked the House if
any gentleman would object to the right.   I repeatedly asked
it ; and no man would attempt to deny it.   Protection and
obedience are reciprocal.   Great Britain protects America ;
America is bound to yield obedience.   If not, tell me when
these Americans were emancipated.   When they want the
protection of this kingdom, they are always very ready to ask
it.   That protection has always been afforded them in the most
full and ample manner.   The nation has run itself into an
immense debt to give them their protection ; and now they are
called upon to contribute a small share towards the public
expense, an expense arising from themselves, they renounce
your authority, insult your officers, and break out, I might
almost say, into open rebellion." [1]

[1] Debates in Parl. iv. 292, 293.

No sooner had Grenville closed than Pitt rose to reply, and, CHAP.
by the indulgence of the House, was permitted to proceed. X.
"The gentleman tells us" — such were his words — "America 1766.
is obstinate; America is almost in open rebellion. I rejoice
that America has resisted. Three millions of people, so dead
to all the feelings of liberty as voluntarily to submit to be
slaves, would have been fit instruments to make slaves of the
rest. With the enemy at their back, with our bayonets at their
breasts, in the day of their distress, perhaps the Americans
would have submitted to the imposition; but it would have
been taking an ungenerous, an unjust advantage. I am no
courtier of America; I stand up for this kingdom. I maintain
that the Parliament has a right to bind, to restrain America.
Our legislative power over the colonies is sovereign and supreme. When it ceases to be sovereign and supreme, I would
advise every gentleman to sell his lands, if he can, and embark
for that country. When two countries are connected together,
like England and her colonies, without being incorporated, the
one must necessarily govern; the greater must rule the less;
but so rule it as not to contradict the fundamental principles
that are common to both.

"The gentleman asks, When were the colonies emancipated?
But I desire to know when they were made slaves. He must
not wonder he was not contradicted when, as the minister, he
asserted the right of Parliament to tax the colonies. I know
not how it is, but there is a modesty in this House which does
not choose to contradict a minister. Even your chair, sir,
looks too often towards St. James's. I wish gentlemen would
get the better of this modesty. If they do not, perhaps the
collective body may begin to abate of its respect for the representative.

"A great deal has been said without doors of the power of
America. It is a topic that ought to be cautiously meddled
with. In a good cause, on a sound bottom, the force of this
country can crush America to atoms. I know the valor of

CHAP. your troops ; I know the skill of your officers. There is not
  X.   a company of foot that has served in America, out of which
1766. you may not pick a man of sufficient knowledge and experience
       to make a governor of a colony there. But on this ground,
       on the stamp act, when so many here will think it a crying
       injustice, I am one who will lift up my hands against it. In
       such a cause, your success would be hazardous. America, if
       she fell, would fall like a strong man. She would embrace the
       pillars of the state, and pull down the constitution along with
       her. Let prudence and temper come first from this side ;

                    ' Be to her faults a little blind ;
                      Be to her virtues very kind ; '

       and I will undertake for America that she will follow the
       example.

       " Upon the whole, I will beg leave to tell the House what
       is really my opinion. It is, that the stamp act be repealed —
       absolutely, totally, and immediately ; that the reason for the
       repeal be assigned — because it was founded on an erroneous
       principle. At the same time, let the sovereign authority of
       this country over the colonies be asserted in as strong terms
       as can be devised, and be made to extend to every point of
       legislation whatsoever — that we may bind their trade, con-
       fine their manufactures, and exercise every power whatsoever,
       except that of taking their money out of their pockets without
       their consent." [1]

       Thus he closed ; and his words of fire fixed at once the
Jan. 14. minds of the wavering. The same day, large extracts from
       the recent correspondence with America were laid on the
Jan. 17. table ; [2] and, three days later, petitions for the repeal from the
       merchants of London trading to North America, and similar
       petitions from Birmingham, Coventry, Bristol, Liverpool, Man-

       ---

       [1] Debates in Parl. iv. 294–298 ;   [2] This correspondence is given in
       Mass. Gazette for May 8, 1765.   Parl. Debates, iv. 301 et seq.

chester, and other towns, were presented.[1]   Towards the last
of the month the House resolved itself into a committee of the
whole to consider these petitions ; and the sittings of the committee were continued into the next month.   Before this committee[2] Dr. Franklin was summoned; and his examination
excited the surprise of his auditors.   No previous event,
indeed, had given him such celebrity.   The promptness and
pertinency of his replies, the breadth and soundness of his
political views, and the boldness and candor with which he
expressed them, were regarded with admiration when the results
of the examination were published.[3]   "The American people,"
said he, "will never submit to this act, unless compelled by
force of arms.   Before this act passed the temper of that people
towards Great Britain was the best in the world.   They submitted willingly to the government of the crown, and paid, in
their courts, obedience to the acts of Parliament.   Natives of
Britain were always treated with particular regard.   To be an
Old England man was of itself a character of respect, and
gave a kind of rank among us.   The authority of Parliament
was allowed to be valid in all laws, except such as should lay
internal taxes.   They considered the Parliament as the great
bulwark and security of their liberties and privileges, and
always spoke of it with the utmost respect and veneration.
Arbitrary ministers, they thought, might possibly, at times,
attempt to oppress them ; but they relied on it that the Parliament, on application, would always give redress.   But that
respect is now greatly lessened ; and a concurrence of causes
has contributed to produce this result, among which the stamp
act is most prominent.   This act, even if modified, will never
be submitted to ; and any other act, based upon the same principles, will be received in the same way.   The manufactures

[1] On the 13th December, 1765, the merchants of London waited upon the ministry to solicit a repeal of the stamp act.   Mass. Gaz. for Feb. 13, 1766.

[2] The date is February 3 in Sparks, February 13 in Bancroft.

[3] Sparks's Franklin, iv. 161.

CHAP. of England are not absolutely necessary; for there is not a
X. single article imported into the northern colonies but what
1766. they can either do without or make themselves. With industry
and good management, they may very well supply themselves
with all they want. In manufactures they have made a surprising progress already. And I am of opinion that, before
their old clothes are worn out, they will have new ones of their
own making. In three years wool enough can be raised to
supply their wants. Should a military force be sent to America to enforce this act, it will be of no avail. They will find
no one in arms; what are they then to do? They cannot force
a man to take stamps who chooses to do without them. They
will not *find* a rebellion; they may indeed *make* one. If the
act is not repealed, I foresee a total loss of the respect and
affection the people of America bear to this country, and of all
the commerce that depends on that respect and affection. People will pay as freely to gratify one passion as another — their
resentment as their pride. They will pay no internal tax;
but requisitions may be granted on application in the usual
form. They will never repeal the resolutions which have been
passed in their assemblies, and acknowledge the right of Parliament to lay internal taxes. No power, how great soever,
can force them to change their opinions. And whereas it was
once the pride of the people of America to indulge in the
fashions and manufactures of Great Britain, it is now their
pride to wear their old clothes over again, until they can make
new ones." [1]

For some time the question of repeal remained in suspense.
The friends of Grenville joined with him in denouncing the
measure, and insisted that the stamp act should be rigidly enforced; and once, in both Houses, they succeeded in obtaining
a majority on their side. [2] But the friends of America contin-

---

[1] Sparks's Franklin, iv. 162–198;   or Documents, 64–81, &c.
Debates in Parl. iv. 323–345; Pri-   [2] Bancroft, v. 413, 417.

ued inflexible, and, watching every opportunity to accomplish CHAP
their purpose, when Grenville, to test the temper of the Com-   X.
mons, introduced a resolution tending to enforce the execution 1766.
                                                                 Feb. 7.
of all acts, — meaning specially the stamp act, — Pitt sprang
to his feet, and called on the House not to order the enforcement of the stamp act before they had decided the question of
repeal.   Grenville replied, and denounced bitter curses on the
ministers who should sacrifice the sovereignty of England over
her colonies ; but when the question was taken on his motion
to enforce the act, it was rejected in a full House by more
than two to one.[1] This triumph paved the way for further
measures ; and, two weeks later, the crisis came.   Every seat Feb. 21.
in the House was occupied.   Between four and five hundred
members were present.   Pitt was there, notwithstanding his
illness.   Merchants from all parts thronged the gallery, the
lobby, and the stairs.   Many Americans were likewise in attendance.   Conway led the debate ; and, in the name of the
government, moved for leave to bring in a bill to repeal the
stamp act.   If the act was not repealed, he predicted both
France and Spain would declare war, and protect the malcontents.   Jenkinson, on the other side, moved a modification of
the act, and insisted that its repeal would be the overthrow
of the authority of Great Britain in America.   Burke replied
in his happiest manner ; and a visible impression was made
by his speech.   At length, about eleven, Pitt rose ; and his
speech was at once both fervid and winning.   Avoiding expressions which might give offence, and candidly acknowledging the perplexity of his own mind in choosing between two
ineligible alternatives, he yet pleaded for the repeal of the act
as due to the people of America, and as a measure of leniency
which would tend to conciliate.   The reply of Grenville was
in his customary strain.   " America must learn," said he, in
conclusion, " that prayers are not to be brought to Cæsar
through riot and sedition."[2]

[1] Bancroft, v. 423, 424.   [2] Bancroft, v.

CHAP.   At half past one on the ensuing morning the division took
  X.   place, and Conway's motion was triumphantly carried. The
1766.   votes against it were one hundred and sixty-seven; those in
Feb. 22. its favor were two hundred and seventy-five.[1] As Pitt stepped
forth from the House that night, the huzzas of the crowd
greeted his appearance. Every head was uncovered; and
many, in token of their respect and gratitude, followed his
chair home.[2] But Grenville was saluted with scorn and hisses.
Swelling with rage and mortification, he seized the man nearest to him roughly by the collar. " If I may not hiss," said
he, " at least I may laugh ; " and he laughed aloud in Grenville's face. The jest caught, and the multitude applauded.[3]
The last division on the repeal of the act was still more deci-
Mar. 4. sive ; and at midnight, on the fourth of March, the question,
in the House of Commons, was disposed of by a vote of two
hundred and fifty in favor of the repeal, and one hundred and
twenty-two in opposition.[4] In the House of Lords the bill
Mar. 17. was debated ; but even there it was carried by a majority of
thirty-four.[5]

Mar. 18.   On the eighteenth of March the repeal of the stamp act
was sanctioned by the king. The friends of America were

---

[1] For the names of the members
voting against the repeal, see Debates
in Parl. iv. 346–350.

[2] Bancroft, v.

[3] Lord Orford's Mems. ii. 299;
Lord Mahon's Hist. Eng. v. 141, note.
H. Lyman, of Connecticut, in a letter
to Governor Fitch, dated February
26, gives an account of the repeal of
the act. "This act," says he, " had
taken so strong hold of the people's
minds by the artifice of the late administration and their tools, that but
very few here thought it in the power
of this wise administration to procure
a repeal. Yet, sensible of the justice of the cause, they undertook it,
though they knew it would cost them
their posts if it failed. The merchants
of London, and mechanics throughout
the kingdom, gave all the assistance

in their power, and the Americans who
are here have contributed every thing
they could to the same purpose. The
Grenvillian party did all they could to
defeat the design ; but in spite of their
efforts, a committee of the whole
House of Commons came into the total repeal of the act, by 275 against
167 ; and after reporting to the House,
the dispute was revived by a thinner
House, and was carried, 240 against
133. Every inch of ground was disputed." Trumbull MSS. in Lib. Mass.
Hist. Soc. ii. 78. See also R. Jackson, in ibid. ii. 78, under date Feb.
27 ; and Conway to Fitch, March 1,
in ibid. ii. 79.

[4] Bancroft, v. 445.

[5] Debates in Parl. iv. 367 ; Lord
Mahon's Hist. Eng. v. 142 ; Bancroft,
v. 453.

transported with joy ; Bow Bells merrily clanged the peal of CHAP.
triumph ; the ships on the Thames displayed all their colors ; X.
bonfires blazed as night set in ; and houses were illuminated all 1766.
over the city. It is an honor to the English nation that the
people at large entered so fully into the spirit of the occasion.
Grenville was defeated ; but liberty had triumphed.[1]

[1] For particulars relative to these proceedings, see Mass. Gazette for April 3 and 25, 1766; and comp. Bancroft, v. 454. On the 3d of April a preliminary meeting was held in Boston upon the repeal; but the news of the passage of the bill had not then arrived.

CHAPTER XI.

THE REVENUE ACT. TROOPS IN BOSTON.

CHAP.
XI.

1766.
May 16. THE repeal of the stamp act awakened in America the liveliest joy.[1] The declaratory act with which it was accompanied, which asserted the authority of Parliament to "bind the colonies and people of America in all cases whatsoever," was less acceptable.[2] Intelligent patriots saw in this act enough to excite serious alarm; and the display of lenity on the part of the ministry was viewed as a politic stroke — a sort of specific to close over the wound which was far from being healed. The statesmen of England, at least the advocates of arbitrary measures, could brook no acknowledgment that they had fallen into an error. A majority, indeed, of the House of Commons, and of the House of Lords, chose to temporize rather than resort to open violence. Yet, sincere in their conviction that the power of Parliament was indisputable and absolute, the only questions seriously discussed were the expediency of exercising that power, and how far it should be pushed. To assert without maintaining the supremacy of Parliament, it was acknowledged, would be a dereliction of the honor and dignity of government. Hence the declaratory act was intended to be significant. True, in one sense it was a "salvo to the wounded pride of England," — that "bridge of gold" which,

---

[1] "It hushed into silence almost every popular clamor, and composed every wave of popular disorder into a smooth and peaceful calm." J. Adams's Diary, in Works, ii. 203.

[2] The repeal and the declaratory act were published in the Mass. Gazette for May 22, 1766. See also Conway to the Governor of Connecticut, March 31, 1766, in MS. Letters and Papers, 1761–1776.

according to the French saying, should always be allowed to a CHAP.
retreating assailant,[1] — but, at the same time, it was designed XI.
to preserve the form of authority ; and it was well understood 1766.
that, if it had not been for this, the stamp act would never
have been repealed.[2]

But if the declaratory act was unacceptable to America, it
did not prevent the colonies from acknowledging the relief
afforded by the repeal of the stamp act.   Hence, at the session
of the General Court, an address to the king was prepared Jun. 19.
by a committee, of which Cushing was chairman ;[3] a vote
of thanks to William Pitt was unanimously passed, "for his
noble and generous efforts in behalf of the common rights of
mankind and the liberties of Great Britain and her colonies ;"[4]
and the grateful acknowledgments of the province were tendered to other distinguished gentlemen.[5]   For the rejoicings
of the people a day had been previously appointed and observed.   Liberty Tree was the centre of attraction ; and thither May 19.
the multitude was called at an early hour by the ringing of
bells and the booming of cannon.   Vast crowds paraded the
streets ; pendants waved in every direction ; and the steeples
of churches were hung with banners.   In the evening the whole
town was brilliantly illuminated ; images of the king, of Pitt,
of Camden, and of Barré were exhibited in the houses ; and
Liberty Tree was loaded with lanterns.[6]

[1] Belsham's George III. i. 147;
Grahame, ii. 413 ; Lord Mahon's Hist.
Eng. v. 144.   Comp. Hutchinson, iii.
147, and Bradford, i. 81.

[2] The merchants of London en-
treated their brethren in America to
take no offence at this act, but could
give no assurance that it would not
be enforced. See Hutchinson, iii. 147 ;
Bancroft, v. 456.

[3] For the address, see Bradford's
State Papers, 91.

[4] For this vote, and the reply of
Pitt, see Mass. Gazette for April 16,
1767; and comp. Bradford, i. 84, and
State Papers, 92.

[5] To the Dukes of Newcastle, of
Grafton, and of Richmond, Lord Stanhope, the lord high chancellor, General Conway, the Marquis of Rockingham, Lord Edgcomb, the Earls of
Dartmouth, Powlett, Shelburne, Camden, and Egmont, the Hons. George
Onslow, Arther Onslow, George Howard, Charles Townshend, William
Dowdeswell, and Isaac Barré, Sir
William Meredith, Sir William Baker,
Sir George Saville, and George Cooke,
Esq.   Bradford, i. 84 ; State Papers,
92. For the answers of these gentlemen, see Bradford, i. 395-398.

[6] On the 21st of April, in anticipa-

CHAP.   The annual election took place before the news of the repeal
XI.   of the stamp act arrived ; but, in expectation of that event, the
1766.   people of Boston, vigilant to preserve the liberties of the prov-
May 6 ? ince, selected as their representatives five of the ablest patriots
May 28. of the town.[1] In the House, the list of councillors was revised ;
and the names of five — Hutchinson, the Olivers, Trowbridge,
and Lynde — were dropped.[2] This step, and the course of the
House in choosing for their speaker James Otis, displeased the
governor ; and, as he had given notice of his intention to " play
out his part " as chief magistrate while he had the power, he
negatived the choice of Otis, and rejected six of the new board
of councillors.[3] As the explanatory charter sustained him in
this course, the House acquiesced in the rejection of their
speaker, and chose in his place Thomas Cushing. The rejection of the councillors was also submitted to ; but the governor,
finding no new choice was made, sought to constrain the elec-
May 29. tion of those who had been dropped, and, in his message, not
only predicted the royal displeasure if they persisted in their
course, but accused them of having determined their votes from
" private interests and resentments, and popular discontent."
" It were to be wished," he added, " that a veil could be drawn
over the late disgraceful scenes. But that cannot be done
until a better temper and understanding shall prevail. The
recent election of councillors is an attack on government in
form, depriving it of its best and most able servants, whose

tion of the repeal, the inhabitants of
Boston, at a town meeting duly warned, instructed the selectmen to fix a
time for the general rejoicings ; and
on the 16th of May they appointed
Monday, the 19th. Circular, in Lib.
Mass. Hist. Soc. For an account of
the ceremonies, see J. Adams's Diary,
in Works, ii. 195. " No rejoicings,"
says Hutchinson, iii. 147, " since the
revolution, had been equal to those
on this occasion."

[1] James Otis, Thomas Cushing,
Samuel Adams, John Rowe, and

John Hancock. Drake's Boston,
719.

[2] But four of these were dropped
by the House ; one resigned of his
own accord. The persons chosen in
their stead were S. Dexter, J. Bowers,
J. Otis, J. Gerrish, and T. Saunders.
J. Adams's Diary, in Works, ii. 195 ;
Bradford, i. 87, 88.

[3] Otis, Sparhawk, Dexter, Saunders, Gerrish, and Bowers were the
persons rejected. J. Adams's Diary,
in Works, ii. 196, 204 ; Hutchinson,
iii. 148.

only crime is their fidelity to the crown, and is an ill-judged CHAP.
and ill-timed oppugnation of the king's authority.[1]   XI.

The House, in their reply, repelled the charge of acting 1766.
from private interests and resentments, and declared that it June 3.
had "ever been their pride to cultivate harmony and union,"
and that they had "given their suffrages according to the dictates of their consciences and the best light of their under-
standings."[2] If, by so doing, they had dropped some of the old
board, they had "released the judges from the cares and perplexities of politics, and given them opportunity to make still
further advances in the knowledge of the law;" and this,
surely, "was not to deprive the government of its best and
ablest servants, nor could it be called the oppugnation of any
thing, but of a dangerous union of legislative and executive
powers in the same persons."[3] Thus the controversy continued; but the House was firm, and begged to be "excused from
any unnecessary search for palliatives or expedients." The
vacancies in the board, therefore, remained unfilled; and from
this time forward the Council, which had long been the conservative branch, joined with the House in promoting every measure material to the cause in which they had engaged; and
James Bowdoin, who succeeded Hutchinson as head of the
board, obtained greater influence than his predecessor had enjoyed, and devoted himself warmly to the cause of freedom.[4]

While this discussion was in progress, changes were taking
place in the ministry in England. The Marquis of Rockingham,
the chief minister, however well intentioned, was lacking in the
qualities of a great statesman. The excellence of his measures,
therefore, could not avert from his administration the evils aris-

[1] Mass. Gazette Extra for May 29,
1766; Hutchinson, iii. 148–150;
Bradford, i. 87–89, and State Papers,
74; J. Adams's Diary, in Works, ii.
204.
[2] "They had an undoubted right,"
says Hutchinson, "to vote for whom
they thought fit."

[3] Samuel Adams to De Berdt, 1766;
Hutchinson, iii. 150–156; Bradford's
State Papers, 76–81; Bancroft, vi. 8.
[4] Hutchinson, iii. 156. The House,
at this session, opened a gallery for
the public to attend its debates; Bradford, i. 90; Bancroft, vi. 13.

CHAP. ing from his personal deficiencies. The Duke of Grafton threw
XI.   up the seals as secretary of state; and, after several peers had
1766. refused them in succession, they were conferred upon the self-
May 23. confident Duke of Richmond.[1] At the close of the session, the
June 6. symptoms of dissolution had alarmingly increased; and, in the
July 7. ensuing month, an invitation was extended to Pitt to return
to the cabinet. This invitation was accepted; and, at a later
July 30. date, a new ministry was organized, the chief posts being filled
by the friends of Pitt and the members of the late administration. The Duke of Grafton became the head of the treasury;
Charles Townshend was appointed chancellor of the exchequer;
General Conway was continued secretary of state, with the Earl
of Shelburne as his colleague;[2] Sir Charles Saunders was
placed at the head of the admiralty; Lord Camden became
chancellor, and Lord Northington president of the council;
and, in the lower ranks, places were bestowed on Lord North,
and Mr. James Grenville, brother of Lord Temple, and on
Colonel Barré, the ardent defender of the liberties of America.[3] "If ever a cabinet," wrote one who made politics his
study, "can hope for the rare privilege of unanimity, it is this,
in which Pitt will see none but persons whose imagination he
has subjugated, whose premature advancement is due to his
choice, whose expectations of permanent fortune rest on him
alone."[4]

Behold how shortsighted are the wisest in their speculations
upon the political conduct of men! The seeds of dissolution
were sown in the new ministry at the outset of its career,
and Pitt was the instrument in scattering them abroad. The

[1] MS. Letter of the Duke of Richmond to the Governor of Connecticut,
May 23, 1766, in Trumbull MSS. ii.
87.
[2] Conway was secretary for the
northern department, and Shelburne
for the southern. Lord Mahon's Hist.
Eng. v. 159; Grahame, ii. 420; Bancroft, vi. 5, 21.

[3] Shelburne to the Governor of
Connecticut, Aug. 9, 1766, in Trumbull MSS. ii. 110; Pitt to Shelburne,
July 23, 1766, in Chatham Corresp.
iii. 14; Hist. of the War, 36, 37;
Mass. Gazette for Sept. 25, 1766;
Belsham's George III. i. 154–156.
[4] Durand to Choiseul, July 30
1766, in Bancroft, vi. 22.

"great commoner" had been respected by the people because CHAP.
by his merits he had raised himself from their ranks to a post XI.
of the highest honor and influence. He now signified his 1766.
desire to be raised to the peerage ; and the king, in compliance
with his wishes, created him Earl of Chatham.[1] The colleagues of Pitt, astonished and disheartened, blamed him for
this step ; and, while some lamented it as an error, others denounced it as a crime. Certain it is that it weakened his
influence at court ; and the eclipse of his career dates from this
period. A twilight of popularity lingered around him ; but it
faded away every moment. That he had earned the peerage,
few, perhaps, will dispute, if distinguished merit can ever be
considered as entitling one to that honor ; but he harmed himself by accepting it, for there was a manifest impolicy in his
quitting the House, which needed his presence, and upon whose
floor his laurels had been won. It was esteemed a desertion
of the popular cause ; and many, who had idolized, could never
forgive him. He was no longer the exponent of the enthusiasm of the nation, and had cut himself loose from the sympathy of the masses. None rallied around him as cordially as
before ; and he was left like the storm-beaten oak, scarred by
conflicts waged with the elements, shorn of its primitive vigor
and glory.[2] All his labors in every department of reform
were unsuccessful. His position debarred him from diminish-
ing the ascendency of the aristocracy in England ; the envy of
his associates led them to thwart his favorite plans ; and neither the liberties of America, of which he had been the guar-

---

[1] There had been rumors for some time of Pitt's aspiring to a high-er rank. See Mass. Gazette for 1765, 1766. "A great commoner, it is said, intends speedily to apply for leave to assume the name and arms of a lately deceased baronet, who left him a large fortune." Extract from a letter of March 26, 1765, in Mass. Gazette for May 16, 1765.

[2] On the elevation of Pitt, see Lord Orford's Mems. George III. ii. 338 ; Chatham Corresp. iii. 21 ; Lond. Ga-zette for July 30, 1766 ; Mass. Gazette for Sept. 25, 1766 ; Lord Mahon's Hist. Eng. v. 154–162 ; Belsham's George III. i. 159, 160, 193 ; Ban-croft, vi. 18–25. The Mass. Gazette for Sept. 25 and Oct. 2 contains ex-tracts from London letters, reflecting severely on Pitt for accepting the peerage.

dian, nor the liberties of India, which he was anxious to secure, could be effectually promoted, because there were enough to throw obstacles in his path and to baffle him in the execution of his most promising schemes. The infirmities of age, too, were creeping upon him; his hereditary disease had made sad havoc with the remnants of his strength; and he stood as one tottering on the brink of the grave, grasping the shadow of power for support, while the substance was rapidly vanishing before him.[1]

The repeal of the stamp act had been consented to by the king as a measure of expediency and mercantile convenience; but he ever lamented it as a "fatal compliance" which had "planted thorns" under his pillow, and preferred the hazard of losing the colonies to relinquishing the claim of absolute authority.[2] His natural temperament inclined him to insist upon the maintenance of his prerogative; and if, to some, he realized the idea of a "patriot king,"[3] there were others to whom his course was the embodiment of selfishness. In the colonies, in particular, while a tender regard for his person was expressed, the violence of the measures which had been sanctioned by his seal was severely reproved; and, as the
May 26. means of security against further aggressions, Boston proposed a closer union of the different governments.[4] The necessity of such union had long been foreseen; and if the advances

---

[1] "I wish," wrote Chesterfield to Stanhope, "I could send you all the pamphlets and half-sheets that swarm here upon this occasion; but that is impossible, for every week would make a ship's cargo. It is certain that Mr. Pitt has, by his dignity of earl, lost the greatest part of his popularity, especially in the city; and I believe the opposition will be very strong, and perhaps prevail, next session, in the House of Commons — there being now nobody there who can have the authority and ascendant over them that Pitt had." Chatham Corresp. iii. 21, note. See also an extract from a letter of Sir Andrew Mitchell, in ibid. 42, note.

[2] A Short History, &c., 18, 19; Considerations on the Present State of the Nation, 50; Lloyd's Conduct of the late Admin.

[3] Bernard to the General Court, and the Reply of the House; also, Belsham's George III. i. 3.

[4] Instructions to Representatives, in Mass. Gazette for May 29, 1766; Hutchinson to Jackson, June 11, 1766, in MS. Corresp.; Mayhew to Otis, June 8, 1766, in Bradford's Life of Mayhew, 428, 429.

towards it had hitherto failed, it was not because the scheme CHAP.
was impracticable, but because the time for effecting it had not XI.
arrived. The conduct of the governor hastened this time. 1766.
For years he had insisted upon the more perfect subordination
of the colonies to the crown ; [1] and, as the charters were obstacles in the way, concurrently with Townshend he declared
war against them, and in his letters to the ministry complained
of the elective character of the Council as the " fatal ingredient
in the provincial constitution." " The only anchor of hope,"
he writes, " is the sovereign power, which would secure obe- July 7.
dience to its decrees, if they were properly introduced and
effectually supported." [2]

The effect of these representations was to deepen the displeasure of the people of Massachusetts. The repeal of the
stamp act had led them to hope that their rights and liberties
would be once more restored ; for " every newspaper and pamphlet, every public and private letter, which arrived in America from England, seemed to breathe a spirit of benevolence,
tenderness, and generosity." [3] But the enemies of America
were not silenced ; and, still resolute to enforce the authority
of Parliament, Governor Bernard renewed his complaints of
" illicit trade," and endeavored to compel obedience to the
laws. The anniversary of the outbreak against the stamp act Aug.14
was celebrated in Boston with great parade ; and the reports
sent to England set forth in glowing terms the " treasonable "
conduct of the " Sons of Liberty," who had drunk to the health
of Otis, " the American Hampden, who first proposed the con-

[1] See his letters and speeches.
[2] Bernard to the Lords of Trade,
July 7, 1766 ; Bancroft, vi. 16.
[3] John Adams's Diary, in Works,
ii. 203. " The utmost delicacy," he
adds, " was observed in all the state
papers in the choice of expressions,
that no unkind impression might be
left upon the minds of the people in
America. The letters from the ministry to the governor recommended

the mildest, softest, most lenient and
conciliating measures ; and even the
resolve of the House of Commons and
the recommendation of his majesty,
concerning an indemnification to the
sufferers, was conceived in the most
alluring language. Oblivion of every
disagreeable circumstance which had
happened through the warmth of the
people, in the late unhappy times, was
recommended in the strongest terms."

CHAP.
XI.
1766.

June 3.
Nov.

gress ;" to "the brave sons of liberty throughout America ;" to "the spark of liberty kindling in Spain ;" and "success to Paoli and the struggling Corsicans."[1]

The requisition of the ministry, forwarded in a letter from Secretary Conway,[2] that compensation should be made to the sufferers by the "riots" of the preceding year, was briefly considered by the General Court in the summer, and more fully in the fall; but, though most of the towns left the matter to the discretion of their representatives,[3] a majority of the House determined against a compensation by tax. The discussion on this point was sharp and spirited. Joseph Hawley, a lawyer of Northampton, of unblemished integrity, was the principal speaker ; and he opposed relief except on condition of a general amnesty. "Of those seeking compensation," said he, "the chief," referring to Hutchinson, "is a person of unconstitutional principles, as one day or other he will make appear." The resolves of Parliament were cited in vain. "The Parliament of Great Britain," was the reply, "has no right to legislate for us." At these words Otis sprang to his feet, and, bowing to the speaker, thanked him, saying, "He has gone further than I myself have as yet done in this House."[4] At length, as an act of generosity rather than of justice, a grant was proposed to be passed through the formalities of a law, which should concurrently extend a free pardon to those who

[1] Oliver to ——, May 7, 1767; Mass. Gazette for Aug. 14 and Aug. 21, 1766. Loyal toasts were not forgotten; for the health of the king and his family was drunk, and one of the sentiments expressed the wish that "the union between Great Britain and the colonies" might "never be dissolved."

[2] The letter of Conway, dated March 31, was received May 31, and laid before the House June 3. Mass. Gazette Extra for June 4, and Gazette for June 5 and 12 ; Prior Doc'ts, 103 –108; Bradford State Papers, 81–91,

93–96. The message of Bernard, on presenting this letter, was conceived in the haughtiest terms ; and "it seemed," says Grahame, ii. 414, "as if, in the fervor of his zeal for British dignity, he sought to repudiate every semblance of approach to courtesy or condescension towards the colonists."

[3] The instructions of the town of Boston to its representatives are given in the Mass. Gazette for Oct. 9, 1766.

[4] Hutchinson to Williams, Dec. 7, 1766, in Williams MSS. 161; Bernard to Shelburne, Dec. 24, 1766.

had been engaged in the "riots." The bill for this purpose was ordered to be printed, and sent to the towns; and, after a short recess, when the court again met, it was passed to be enacted by a vote of fifty-three to thirty-five; the Council concurred; and the governor, after some hesitation, gave his assent.[1]

The laws of trade, which the governor sought to enforce, had always been oppressive. It was a narrow policy which led to the passage of these laws; and the distinctions made between citizens of America and citizens of England could not but give offence to the colonies. The duties imposed upon articles imported into the provinces were so high, that, with the added restrictions on commercial enterprise, no profits accrued. To these laws, which had been recently revised in England,[2] attention was now turned; and committees were appointed by the General Court to consider the difficulties which embarrassed the commerce of the country, and to propose measures for remedying these evils.[3]

Nor was this the only step which awakened resentment. Towards the close of the year, two companies of royal artillery were driven into the harbor of Boston by "stress of weather;" and, as the General Court was not then in session, the governor, by advice of Council, directed that provision should be made for them at the barracks, at the expense of the province. For this assumption of authority he was called to an account;

---

[1] Hutchinson, iii. 150–160; Bradford's State Papers, 97–101; Mass. Gazette for Nov. 20, 1766; Prior Doc'ts, 113–118, 123, 134, 135; Shelburne to Pitt, Feb. 1, 1767, in Chatham's Corresp. iii. 186. Some of the towns opposed making a compensation. J. Adams's Diary, in Works, ii. 204. The act was annulled by the king; but the annulment obtained little notice, and produced no effect. Prior Doc'ts, 134–142; Chatham Corresp. iii. 255; Stedman's Am. War, i. 50; Adolphus, i. 260; Lord Mahon's

Hist. Eng. v. 181. According to Hutchinson's statements, Bernard was partly governed by policy in assenting to this bill, as he knew that the clause relating to the compensation of the sufferers would go into immediate effect, and could not be recalled even if the act was subsequently rejected.

[2] Debates in Parl. iv. 354 et seq.; Hutchinson, iii. 164.

[3] Jour. H. of R. for 1766; Mass. Gazette for Nov. 20, 1766; Bradford, i. 93.

and, though he pleaded in his justification the necessity of the case and the act of Parliament, the requirements of which he had followed, the court protested against his proceedings, and declared that with them alone, and not with the chief magistrate, resided the power of raising and appropriating supplies for the public service.[1] The presence of an armed soldiery in their midst the people were little disposed to view with favor; and it was apprehended — and justly — that disturbances would be increased rather than diminished.[2]

Meanwhile, in England, the political elements were in an unsettled state; and the scramble for office and the emoluments of office had reached such a height that patriotism was merged in selfishness and cupidity. The conduct of the ministry was fickle and inconstant. Pitt, who had been driven into retirement by nervous prostration, and who with a trembling hand, but a sincere heart, had attempted to guide the course of affairs, was absent from his post; and events were left to shape themselves. The cabinet was divided; Parliament was unruly; private dissensions and bickerings arose; a deadly jealousy was kindled between Grafton and Shelburne; Townshend assumed to himself airs of importance; and the trustiest men were sadly perplexed.[3] The parties out of office rallied

[1] Bernard to Shelburne, Dec. 6 and 24, 1766; Prior Doc'ts, 126–129, 133, 134; Jour. H. of R. for 1766; Bradford, i. 97, 98, and State Papers, 105 –108; Hutchinson, iii. 168–171; Boston Gazette for Feb. 9, 16, and 23, 1767; Mass. Gazette for Feb. 5, 19, and 26, and March 12, 1767. In May, 1767, a few recruits for the 14th regiment arrived in Boston, and were quartered by the governor at the Castle, and the controversy was renewed. Bradford's State Papers, 109–112.

[2] "Nothing," says Thomas Cushing, (letter of May 9, 1767, in MS. Letters and Papers, 1761–1776, in Lib. Mass. Hist. Soc.,) "would have so direct a tendency to bring us into such a state as sending troops here to enforce an act of Parliament. Nothing would so soon throw the people into a flame. No one measure I could think of would so effectually drive them into resolutions which, in the end, would prove detrimental to Great Britain — I mean, living as much as possible within ourselves, and using as few as possible of your manufactures."

[3] See Chat. Corresp. iii. 136–139, and notes. "Such a state of affairs," wrote Chesterfield, "was never seen before, in this or in any other country. When this ministry shall be settled, it will be the sixth in six years' time." "We have had a busy month," wrote Horace Walpole, "and many grumbles of a state-quake." "Never," wrote Lord Charlemont, Feb. 19,

for a new struggle; and of those in office, some broke loose CHAP
from all restraint. Townshend, in particular, whose indiscre- XI.
tion forbade esteem, but whose good humor dissipated hate, 1767.
as if hurried away by the levity of his temper, delivered in the
House of Commons several speeches, both admired for their
eloquence and censured for their wildness. In one of these
speeches, styled his " Champagne Speech," because delivered
on his return from a convivial dinner, he descanted upon the
times, the parties, and their leaders, and declared that " the
government had become what he himself had been often called
— a *weathercock.*" [1] In another of his vain and capricious
moods, he threw out a pledge that he would find means to Jan. 26
raise a revenue from America which should be free from offence. " I am still," said he, " a firm advocate for the stamp
act — for its principle, and for the duty. I laugh at the distinction between internal and external taxes. I know no such
distinction. It is perfect nonsense." Then, looking to the
galleries, where the agents of the colonies were seated, he added, " I speak this aloud, that all you in the galleries may hear
me." In conclusion, he struck his hand upon the table, and
said, " England is undone, if this taxation in America is given
up." [2] Nor did Townshend stand alone. Even Camden, who

1767, " was known such disunion, such
a want of concert, as visibly appears
on both sides. How it will end Heav-
en only knows. One thing, however,
appears very extraordinary, if not indecent. No member of the opposition
speaks without directly abusing Lord
Chatham, and no friend ever rises to
take his part. *Qui non defendit alio
culpante* is scarcely a degree less black
than *absentem qui rodit amicum.*"
Comp. further the brilliant speech of
Edmund Burke on American taxation, delivered in 1774, especially the
parts referring to Chatham and Townshend.
[1] Lord Orford's Mems. George III.
iii. 24 and 26, note; Lord Mahon's
Hist. Eng. v. 179. " In what little
business has hitherto been done in the

House of Commons, Charles Townshend has given himself more ministerial airs than Lord Chatham will, I
believe, approve of." Chesterfield to
his Son, Feb. 19, 1767, in Chatham
Corresp. iii. 170, note.
[2] Johnson to Pitkin, Feb. 12, 1767;
Cavendish Debates, i. 213; Chatham
Corresp. iii. 178, 184, 185; Belsham's
George III. i. 201, 202; Wirt's Patrick Henry, 96; Lord Mahon's Hist.
Eng. v. 180; Bradford, i. 93. The
Mass. Gazette for July 2, 1767, contains an extract from a letter dated
London, May 11, in which Townshend
is represented as holding entirely different language, declaring that he
would cut off his hand before he
would vote for taxing America.

CHAP.
XI.

1767.
Feb. 25.

Feb. 27.

had once boldly maintained that taxation and representation were clearly inseparable, now retracted, and declared that his "doubt respecting the right of Parliament to tax America was removed by the declaration of Parliament itself, and that its authority must be maintained."[1] Encouraged by this avowal, the friends of Bedford, of Grenville, of Rockingham, and of Newcastle forgot for the moment their personal feuds, uniting "with others, who had county or popular elections," for the overthrow of the ascendency of Chatham; and so well did they succeed in rallying their forces that, in a division on the question of a reduction in the land tax, proposed by Townshend, they were enabled to cast two hundred and six votes against one hundred and eighty-eight for the ministry.[2] This defeat, the first of importance which the government had sustained since the days of Sir Robert Walpole, prepared the way for the withdrawal of Chatham; and, though he continued at the head of the ministry for over a year, from this time forward he remained in seclusion, leaving the factions to shape their own courses and fight their own battles.

Yet the confidence of Massachusetts in the justness of her cause strengthened, instead of wavering, as the schemes of the ministry were more fully developed; and Otis, and Adams, and Hawley, and others scanned more closely and resisted more strenuously every measure which could imply their consent to the right of taxation of the colonies by Parliament.[3] The crown officers, indeed, both here and elsewhere, labored to

---

[1] W. S. Johnson to Roger Sherman, Sept. 28, 1768, in MS. Letters and Papers, 1760–1776, fol. 84; Walpole, ii. 418; Bancroft, vi. 56.

[2] Cooke to Chatham, Feb. 27, 1767, in Chatham Corresp. iii. 222; Grafton to Chatham, Feb. 28, 1767, in ibid. iii. 224; Grenville Corresp. iv. 212–214; Lord Mahon's Hist. Eng. v. 177; Bancroft, vi. 60.

[3] Mass. Gazette for March 9, 1767; Bancroft, vi. 50. Hutchinson says meetings of a select number of the

inhabitants of Boston, with members of the House when the court was in session, were held at least once a week, at regular places; and at these meetings necessary measures were projected and settled, and from hence it was supposed the newspapers were generally furnished with speculations and compositions for the service of the cause in which they were engaged. Hist. iii. 167. Comp. Diary of J. Adams, in Works, ii. passim.

suppress the spirit of freedom ; but with whatever sincerity
Shelburne, as secretary for the southern department, assured
the people they "might be perfectly easy about the enjoyment
of their rights and privileges under the present administration," and sought to relieve the burdens which pressed so
heavily upon them, he could not suspend the declaratory act,
nor insure exemption from further oppressions, but asserted
that " the dignity of the government must be maintained." [1]
He was fully aware that, if the Americans " should be tempted
to resist in the last instance," France and Spain would avail
themselves of the opening to break the "peace, the days of
which they had already begun to count." [2] Prudence, therefore, constrained him to consider the American question, and
to prepare for its solution ; and the ill health of Chatham and
the disorders in the cabinet furnished additional reasons for
diligence.

The course of study upon which he now entered was one
which superior talents alone could pursue with success. The
matters in dispute were such in their nature as to involve the
broadest and most complicated relations. The British constitution, the boasted bulwark of the liberties of the nation, had
not been matured in a single generation, but was the product
of the discussions and struggles of centuries. Based upon
principles which were confirmed by experience and sanctioned
by the happy results which attended them, it was in itself a
tower of strength. But that constitution had reached its maturity before the difficulties with the colonies occurred. The
growth of these colonies had been so rapid that their present
importance could not have been anticipated by the sagest econ-
omist ; and this marvellous expansion of territory and subjects
presented to the philosopher problems which had never before

---

[1] Letter of De Berdt, of Sept. 19, 1766, in Bradford's State Papers, 102 ; Hutchinson, iii. 164, note ; Gra-hame, ii. 421.

[2] Shelburne to Pitt, February 16, 1767, in Chatham Correspondence, iii. 209.

challenged the attention of mankind. No precedents could be found to fall back upon. Official records furnished no guide. Maxims from the files were equally useless. Whatever solution was attempted to be given must spring from the fertile brain of the statesman.

The talents which Shelburne brought to this task were respectable, but not brilliant. His mind could not at a glance sweep the horizon of political science, and take in every thing that crossed the field of vision; nor had he the keen intuition which, from unpromising and apparently incongruous elements, can evolve a consistent, harmonious system. He was honest and well-meaning, but by no means a prophet nor a successful inventor. He proposed, indeed, changes in certain departments which might have allayed the excitement in the colonies, had his colleagues approved them. The billeting act, in his estimation, could be safely modified; and, instead of concentrating the troops in the principal towns, he advised that they should be scattered along the frontiers, where their presence was needed, and where it would provoke neither jealousy nor distrust. The principle upon which this act was based he also condemned, as establishing a " precedent which might hereafter be turned to purposes of oppression." [1] The political dependence of the judges he objected to, and advised that their commissions should conform to the precedents followed in England.[2] He likewise advised the settlement of disputed boundaries.[3] And other matters, of minor importance, which were complained of as grievances, engaged his attention.

The zeal with which the secretary advocated these changes fastened upon him the suspicion of his associates, and led them to view him as " an enemy," who should be watched. The king demanded that submission should precede favor; that the

---

[1] Shelburne to Gage, Dec. 11, 1766, and to Chatham, Feb. 6 and 16, 1767.
[2] Moore to Shelburne, Feb. 1, 1767.

[3] Shelburne to Bernard, Dec. 11, 1766; Bernard to Shelburne, Feb. 28 and March 23, 1767; Hutchinson, iii. 177.

colonies should evince a loyal spirit before attention was paid CHAP.
to their clamors ; "otherwise," said he, "we shall soon be no ~~XI.~~
better than savages."[1] Accordingly, he declared that the bil- 1767.
leting act should be enforced, and that no relaxation of its
provisions should be made.[2] In no other way could the dependence of the colonies be secured. They were already on
the verge of rebellion ; and firmness alone could check the
licentiousness of opinion which was spreading.

De Choiseul, the minister of France at St. James's, was no
inattentive observer of these movements ; and, satisfied that
the crisis was near, at his instance De Kalb, an officer of German extraction, was sent to America, to investigate the condi- Apr. 22.
tion of the colonies and the strength of their purpose to engage
in a revolt. Should he find a plan of operations matured, he
was to report the names of those who were to lead, and the
resources of the government in troops and munitions.[3] But
this commission was premature ; for, such was the forbearance
of the colonies, no open rupture was contemplated or advised.
There were those, indeed, who felt that the struggle must eventually come ; but, had moderate counsels prevailed with the
ministry, its advent would have been delayed, if not prevented.

The conduct of Townshend precipitated this struggle. He
had given a pledge that he would find means to raise a revenue Jan. 27.
from America which should be free from offence ; and Grenville, the "outed proposer of the stamp act,"[4] who had listened
with an almost savage joy to the speech of the chancellor,
demanded the fulfilment of this pledge. In compliance with

---

[1] Grafton's Autobiog. ; George III. to Conway, Sept. 20, 1766.

[2] "The American papers," wrote Beckford to Chatham, April 29, 1767, "are to be taken into consideration on the morrow ; and I hear the quartering act is to be enforced, *in violentiâ, et prava voluntate.* If so, adieu peace and comfort ! A former administration, by their ill-conceived projects, made the Americans stark staring mad ; and at present the devil seems to have taken possession of their understand-ings." Chatham Corresp. iii. 251. See also Shelburne to Chatham, Feb. 1767, in ibid. iii. 187, 207, 209.

[3] Choiseul to De Kalb, April 20 and 22, 1767 ; De Kalb to Choiseul, April 24, 1767, in Bancroft, vi. 67 ; Grahame, ii. 427, 428, and notes.

[4] Franklin's paper of 1768, in Works, iv. 247 ; Prior Doc'ts, 228.

CHAP. XI.

1767.
May 13
to 15.

Jun. 29.

this demand, the chancellor came forward with the scheme he had matured; and, while the doors of the House, by a special order, were shut against the agents of the colonies, and even against every American merchant, he proposed a tax on glass, paper, painters' colors, and tea, to be paid as impost duties, from which an income of from thirty-five to forty thousand pounds a year might be realized. This scheme was agitated for some weeks. Lord Camden objected to it, and Jackson foretold the evils that would follow; but the consent of the ministers was obtained, and the act passed both Houses with but little opposition, and was approved by the king.[1]

It is evident that the passage of this bill, which would hardly have been consented to had Chatham been at his post, was not a little forwarded by the influence of Paxton, a citizen of Boston in the confidence of Townshend, who had been sent from America at the instance of Bernard, and Hutchinson, and Oliver, to appear as the advocate of the officers of the crown, and to mature a scheme for a Board of Customs.[2] Both Bernard and Hutchinson seem, at this time, to have resolved to push matters to the utmost extremity; and the latter, in particular, resenting the conduct of the General Court, which had cen-

[1] 7 Geo. III. c. 46; Walpole's Mems. George III. iii. 28; Belsham's George III. i. 204; Cavendish Debates, i. 38, 39, 213; Mass. Gazette for July 2, 1767; Boston Gazette for Oct. 12, 1767; Hutchinson, iii. 179; Franklin's Works, vii. 333; Grahame, ii. 423, 424; Bradford, i. 93; Lord Mahon's Hist. Eng. v. 180, 181, and Mems. Duke of Grafton, in ibid. App. xvii.; Bancroft, vi. 47, 75–78. "It had ever been uniformly acknowledged," says Belsham, George III. i. 204, "that Great Britain possessed the right of commercial regulation and control; it could not be denied that port duties had been at former periods imposed for the purpose of commercial regulation, particularly by the act passed in the sixth year of the reign of the late king. It could not be pretended with consistency and plausibility that the same power did not now inhere in the British Parliament; but it was at the same time impossible not to discern that this power was, in the present instance, exercised with a very different intention and for the accomplishment of a very different object, and that, by a species of artifice unworthy of a great nation, an attempt was now made to inveigle them into the payment of that revenue which could not be extorted by means more direct and unequivocal."

[2] Bradford, i. 120, 121; Bancroft, vi. 32, 47. There is a portrait of Paxton at the rooms of the Mass. Hist. Soc., deposited by Peter Wainwright, Jr., Esq.

sured his intrusion into the Council, of which he was not a CHAP. member, on the day when the governor read his message, took XI. it as a personal affront, which soured his temper and increased 1767. the violence of his opposition to their proceedings.[1] The gov- Feb. ernor, indeed, from his official position, was expected to side with the ministry ;[2] and, in some cases, his dissent from the action of the court was proper and politic. But, a royalist at heart, and a supporter of the prerogative, his opinions on meas- ures of public concern were too much in unison with those of the enemies of America to admit the supposition that his pro- fessions of regard to the interests of the province were cordial and sincere ; and much of the disturbance of this and the fol- lowing years must be attributed to him. He was in close correspondence with the active advocates of the taxation of the colonies ; and his misrepresentations were eagerly seized and quoted as arguments to prove the necessity of curbing the disloyal spirit by which, it was alleged, the people were animated.

Hutchinson, more cautious and crafty in his movements, dared not so openly avow his opinions ; yet, guarded as was his language in most of his letters, to the eyes of the discerning occasional passages betrayed his real sentiments, and few could mistake his real position. Of the two, Mr. Hutchinson was by far the more dangerous ; for the very duplicity which veiled his conduct, and the air of honesty which he could so well

---

[1] On this affair, see Bradford's State Papers, 102–105, and the letter of the House of March 16, 1767, to Dennys De Berdt ; Bernard to the Secretary of State, Feb. 7 and 21, 1767 ; Oliver to ——, May 7, 1767 ; Hutchinson, iii. 173–177 ; Mass. Gazette for Feb. 12 and 19, 1767 ; Boston Gazette for Feb. 23 and April 6, 1767 ; Bancroft, vi. 50.

[2] "Nothing less," wrote Bernard to Hillsborough, July 18, 1768, "than a general sacrifice of the rights of the sovereign state can make a governor

popular in this place at this time. It has been my misfortune to be gov- ernor of this province during a period when the most favorable representa- tion of the proceedings of the assem- blies and the doings of the people must occasion his majesty's displeas- ure. For these three years past it has been impossible to reconcile the duty of the governor with pleasing the people ; and it would have been so, if a man of greater ability than I pretend to had been in my place."

CHAP.
XI.

1767.

assume, imposed upon many who were ignorant of his true character, and led them to ascribe to him virtues which he never possessed and abilities as a statesman to which he was not entitled. To one unacquainted with the part which he played, his sketch of the transactions which preceded the revolution would appear as an impartial, straightforward narrative. But the inquisitive reader, who compares his account with contemporary annals, will easily detect the gloss which he gives to many of the scenes his pen has portrayed, and the concealments which detract from the truthfulness of his statements. Implicit reliance can never be placed on partisan writers; and students of history need not to be told that he who treats of matters in which he was personally concerned appears as the advocate pleading his own cause, and sitting in judgment on those who were opposed to him.[1]

The new scheme of taxation which Townshend had proposed, conjoined with the establishment of a Board of Customs[2] and the legalization of writs of assistance,[3] was more subversive of the rights of the colonies than the stamp act, which Grenville had pressed upon Parliament.[4] In effect, it was a menace of perpetual servitude. The revenue accruing from the duties imposed was to be disposed of at the king's pleasure, under his sign manual, and, by one of the provisions of the act, was to be principally employed in the support of the officers of the crown, to secure their independence of the colonial legislatures.[5] The power of the king over his cabinet had been sensibly strengthened by recent occurrences; and Grafton, who was left with the position of prime minister, was completely under his con-

---

[1] Comp. Bradford, i. 86.

[2] Acts 7 Geo. III. c. 41. May 26, 1767, it was ordered in the House of Commons that a bill be brought in for establishing a Board of Customs in America. Mass. Gazette for Aug. 27, 1767.

[3] Bancroft, vi. 84.

[4] "It is the opinion of men of dis-

cernment and good judgment that the people through the continent are much more alarmed at the late acts than they were at the stamp act; and it would be vastly more difficult to reconcile the people to them." T. Cushing to De Berdt, July 13, 1768.

[5] Mulford's N. Jersey, 376; Bradford, vi. 96.

trol.[1] Yet the nation at large was a gainer by these factions; CHAP.
and, as the influence of the aristocracy lessened, the people,   XI.
whose intelligence was increasing, demanded fuller knowledge   1767.
of every thing that was passing in Parliament, and the press
was employed to support their claims.[2]

"The die is thrown," cried the patriots of Boston, when the Sept.
news of the passage of the revenue bill arrived. "The Rubi-
con is passed." "We will form an immediate and universal
combination to eat nothing, drink nothing, wear nothing imported from Great Britain."[3] "Our strength consists in union.
Let us, above all, be of one heart and of one mind. Let us
call on our sister colonies to join with us in asserting our
rights. If our opposition to slavery is called rebellion, let us
pursue duty with firmness, and leave the event to Heaven."[4]

The fourteenth of August was celebrated as usual; and the Aug.14.
ceremonies of the day served to intensify the abhorrence with
which the acts of the ministry were viewed.[5] The revenue bill
was to go into effect in November; but in the mean time Nov.20.
Townshend, its author, suddenly died,[6] and Lord North, the Sept. 4.
eldest son of the Earl of Guilford, who had voted for the stamp
act and against its repeal, was appointed to his place.[7] The
new chancellor entered upon his duties at a critical period;
yet for fifteen years he remained in the cabinet, lending his
influence to the measures of the ministry, and standing high in

[1] Lord Mahon's Hist. Eng. v. 184;
Bancroft, vi. 94.

[2] T. Hollis to A. Eliot, Feb. 23,
1767. "Power," wrote Durand to
Choiseul, July 21, 1767, (in Bancroft,
vi. 90,) "has passed into the hands of
the populace and the merchants. The
country is exceedingly jealous of its
liberty."

[3] Hutchinson's Letter of July 18,
1767; Bernard to Shelburne, Sept.
14, 1767.

[4] Mauduit to Hutchinson, Dec. 10,
1767; Boston Gazette for Aug. 31,
1767.

[5] Boston Gazette for Aug. 17, 1767.

[6] W. S. Johnson to Dyer, Sept.
12, 1767; Mass. Gazette Extra for
Feb. 11, 1769; Chatham Corresp. iii.
284 and note; Lord Mahon's Hist.
Eng. v. 184; Walpole's Geo. III. ii.
99; Bancroft, vi. 98.

[7] W. S. Johnson to Gov. Pitkin,
of Conn., 1767; North's Speech in the
House of Commons, March 2, 1769;
Letter to Grafton, Sept. 10, 1767;
Lloyd to Lord Littleton, Sept. 17,
1767; Belsham's George III. i. 215;
Lord Mahon's Hist. Eng. v. 184;
Bancroft, vi. 99, 100.

the favor of the king.[1] How the new act should be enforced
was a question which immediately solicited attention. Should
the merchants of Boston subscribe to an agreement to import
no more goods from England, no revenue, of course, would
be paid into the treasury. But such an agreement Bernard
thought to be "impracticable." Yet he advised that a regiment of soldiers should be sent over, to aid the officers of the
customs in the discharge of their duties. "Ships of war and
a regiment," said Paxton, in England, who echoed his wishes,
" are needed to insure tranquillity." [2]

The board of commissioners was to be established in Boston,
and it was queried throughout the country how Boston would
act. "The commissioners," said the more hasty, "must not be
allowed to land." "Paxton, like Oliver, must be taken to Liberty Tree or the gallows, and obliged to resign." [3] The press
spoke boldly, counselling resistance,[4] and declared that those
who had attempted this barbarous violation of their most
sacred rights deserved "the name of rebels and traitors, not
only against the laws of their country and their king, but
against Heaven itself." Faith in the integrity of Parliament
seemed shaken ; [5] and it was thought that there remained no
alternative but an appeal to Heaven to vindicate their cause.

Oct. 28.   At length the crisis came ; and, towards the last of October,
the inhabitants of Boston, "ever sensitive to the sound of liberty," assembled in town meeting, and voted to dispense with
the importation of a large number of articles of British manufacture, which were particularly specified ; to "adhere to former
agreements respecting funerals ; and to purchase no new clothing for mourning." Committees were appointed to obtain

[1] Bancroft, vi. 100.
[2] Bernard to Shelburne, Aug. 31
and Sept. 7, 1767 ; Bollan to Hutchinson, Aug. 11, 1767 ; Bancroft, vi.
101.
[3] Bernard to Shelburne, Sept. 21,
1767 ; Hutchinson, iii. 181 ; Bancroft,
vi. 102. Yet the commissioners were

suffered to land, and did so on the 5th
of November. Hutchinson, iii. 183.
[4] J. Quincy, under the signature
Hyperion, in the Boston Gazette for
Oct. 5, 1767 ; Rogers to Hutchinson,
Dec. 30, 1767.
[5] Mass. Gazette for Oct. 12, 1767
Boston Gazette for Oct. 19, 1767.

subscribers to this agreement; and the resolves were sent into
all the towns of the province, — many of which returned a
favorable reply,[1] — and abroad to the other colonies.[2] The
twentieth of the ensuing month passed without tumult. Pla-
cards were exhibited and effigies were set up, but the people
in general were unusually quiet. Otis, at the town meeting
held to discountenance riot, delivered a speech in which he
recommended caution, and advised that no opposition should
be made to the new duties. "The king has the right," said
he, "to appoint officers of the customs in what manner he
pleases and by what denominations; and to resist his authority
will but provoke his displeasure."[3] Such counsel was displeasing to the zealous, but it was followed.

The last change in the ministry in this session of Parliament
took place in December. The charge of the colonies, which
had been intrusted to Shelburne, was consigned to a separate
department, and Lord Hillsborough, who had been "laid up in
lavender at the post office"[4] until elsewhere wanted, was made
its secretary; the place which Conway had filled was given to
Lord Weymouth; Earl Gower became lord president; Rigby
was made vice treasurer of Ireland till he could get the pay
office; the post office was promised to Sandwich; and Jenkinson, the former secretary of Grenville, took a seat at the treasury board.[5] Five of the six here named were the personal
friends of the Duke of Bedford; and the principle upon which
they entered the ministry was the maintenance of the authority
of Parliament over the colonies.[6] The resolutions of the peo-

CHAP.
XI.

1767.
Nov.20.

Nov.

Dec. 27

[1] Mass. Gazette for Nov. 2, 1767;
Bradford, i. 122. The plan was also
adopted in Portsmouth, Providence,
New York, Philadelphia, and in some
towns in other colonies.

[2] Hutchinson to Pownall, Nov. 10,
1767; Bernard to Shelburne, Oct. 30,
1767; Boston Gazette for Nov. 2,
1767; Hutchinson, iii. 182; Hist. of
the War, 39.

[3] Boston Evening Post for Nov. 23
and 30, 1767; Bernard to Shelburne,

Nov. 21, 1767; Hutchinson, iii. 180,
181.

[4] Chatham Corresp. iii. 139, note.

[5] Chesterfield's Letter of Dec. 27,
in Chatham Corresp. iii. 302, note;
Mass. Gazette Extra for February 25,
1769; Lord Mahon's Hist. Eng. v.
185; Grahame, ii. 432; Bancroft, vi.
109, 110.

[6] Mauduit to Hutchinson, Dec. 15,
1767; Bancroft, vi. 110.

CHAP.
XI.

1768.
Jan.

ple of Boston, to suspend importations from England and to
encourage domestic manufactures, served to quicken their
anger; and, early in the new year, the intention was avowed
of initiating measures to abrogate the charters, and introduce
uniformity into the government of the colonies.[1] Of the approval of Hillsborough to this scheme his associates were
assured. His professions of regard for the liberties of America
were known to be a pretence; for if any purpose was cherished by him more fondly than all others, it was the purpose
of abridging colonial privileges. Conceited and shallow in
the opinions he held, headstrong and obstinate in defending
and enforcing them, the union of stiffness with affected suavity
gave to his manners an awkwardness and constraint which are
often the accompaniments of craft and duplicity. He had not
the boldness which courage confers; and, if his apologists
esteemed him "honest and well meaning," it was because he
had concealed from them the weak points of his character.[2]

Almost his first act respecting Massachusetts was the grant
of a pension of two hundred pounds to Thomas Hutchinson,
to be paid annually by the commissioners of customs.[3] The
news that such a grant had been made could not be kept secret; and the people of Boston expressed their abhorrence in
no gentle terms. "If such acts are continued," said they, "we
shall be obliged to maintain in luxury sycophants, court para-
sites, and hungry dependants, who will be sent over to watch
and oppress those who oppose them. The governors will be
men rewarded for despicable services, hackneyed in deceit and
avarice, or some noble scoundrel who has spent his fortune in
every kind of debauchery."[4] At this juncture Samuel Adams

---

[1] Bancroft, vi. 111.
[2] Franklin's Works, vii. 507; Bancroft, vi. 116. "His lordship," writes
De Berdt, Aug. 29, 1768, "says laws
must be supported, or we sink into a
state of anarchy, which he thinks must
be avoided at all events."
[3] Hutchinson to Hillsborough, Apr.

18, 1768; Oliver to ——, May 11,
1768; Bancroft, vi. 116.
[4] A. Eliot to T. Hollis, Dec. 10,
1767; A. Eliot to Blackburne, Dec.
15, 1767; Bancroft, vi. 117. Even
Huske, who was hanged in effigy in
1765, in 1758 said, "As to the civil
officers appointed for America, most

drew up a voluminous letter, in the form of a remonstrance CHAP
against the revenue act, to be sent by the province to their   XI.
agent in England. This letter was read in the House of   1768.
Representatives, which had opened its session in the previous   Jan. 6.
month, and was debated for several days. "Seven times it   1767.
was revised; every word was weighed, every sentence consid-   Dec. 30.
ered; each seemingly harsh sentence was tempered and refined;" and, after it had passed this searching ordeal, it was
adopted to be sent to the agent, communicated to the ministry,
and published to the world as expressing the unchangeable
opinion of Massachusetts.[1]

The House having sanctioned this document, letters were
sent to each of the ministers embodying the same sentiments,   1768.
and urging the impracticability of a suitable representation of   Jan. 15
the colonies in Parliament.[2] No memorial was sent to the   to 22.
Lords or the Commons; but an address to the king was pre-   Jan. 20.
pared, and he was appealed to as umpire in the dispute.[3] A
proposition that these proceedings should be laid before the
other colonies, that, "if they thought fit, they might join them,"
was at first negatived; but on maturer consideration it was   Feb. 4.
adopted, and a masterly circular, draughted by Adams, was   Feb. 11
read and accepted.[4]

---

of the places in the gift of the crown
have been filled with broken members
of Parliament, of bad, if any principles, valets de chambre, electioneering
scoundrels, and even livery servants.
In one word, America has been for
many years the hospital of England."
Lord Mahon's Hist. Eng. v. 240.
[1] Prior Doc'ts, 167–175; Bernard
to Shelburne, Jan. 21, 1768, in Letters, &c. 4; T. Cushing to De Berdt,
Jan. 31, 1768; Bradford, i. 124, 134,
and State Papers, 124–133; Boston
Gazette for April 4, 1768; Jour. H.
of R. for 1768, 99, 102, 104, 107,
109; Bancroft, vi. 119, 120.
[2] Boston Gazette for March 21,
1768; Mass. Gazette for March 31
and April 7, 1768; Prior Doc'ts, 177

–191; Bradford's State Papers, 137–
144; Jour. H. of R. for 1768, 128,
144, 164, 204, also the Appendix, in
which all the papers are given in
full.
[3] Prior Doc'ts, 175–177; Bradford's State Papers, 121–123; Jour.
H. of R. for 1768, 121, 122, 124;
Mass. Gazette for March 24, 1768.
[4] Mass. Gazette for Mar. 10, 1768;
T. Cushing to De Berdt, and Bernard to Shelburne, Jan. 30, 1768, in
MS. Letters and Papers, 1761–1776,
in Lib. Mass. Hist. Soc.; Trumbull
MSS. ii. 163; Jour. H. of R. for 1767
–8, 148, 164; Bernard to Shelburne,
Jan. 30 and Feb. 18, 1768; Prior
Doc'ts, 191–199; Bradford, i. 134,
138, 153, and State Papers, 112, 134

CHAP. Nearly at the same time, the revenue board, in secret con-
XI. clave, prepared a memorial to be sent to England. Professing
1768. apprehensions that their own lives were in danger, and com-
Feb. 5. plaining of the licentiousness of the press, of the league to
discountenance the consumption of British manufactures, and
of the New England town meetings, in which "the lowest
mechanics discussed the most important points of government
with the utmost freedom," they declared that they had "every
reason to expect" it would be found "impracticable to enforce
the execution of the revenue laws, until the hand of government should be properly strengthened." "At present," they
added, "there is not one ship of war in the province, nor a
company of soldiers nearer than New York."[1]

This paper, like most of those sent from America by the
minions of power, was artfully framed, and admirably adapted
to inflame the passions of those to whom it was addressed.
The current of feeling in England was beginning to turn.
For more than a year no pains had been spared to irritate the
people, especially the freeholders, and to persuade them that
they were to pay "infinite taxes," and the Americans none;
that they were to be burdened, and the Americans eased; in
a word, that the interests of Britain were to be sacrificed to
those of America.[2] By such misrepresentations, many were
prepared to look with favor upon the arbitrary measures which
were urged upon Parliament, and the friends of those measures
were encouraged to persist in their course. Hence distorted

-136. Bernard wrote to Shelburne, Feb. 18, 1768, that these proceedings expressed the opinions of but a few, and that, after much opposition, they were pushed through by the intrigues and threats of some violent members. Yet he acknowledges that the House "acted in all things, even in their re-monstance," so far as he could learn, "with temper and moderation."

[1] Mem. of the Commissioners of Feb. 12, and Letter of May 3, 1768; Bradford, i. 106; Bancroft, vi. 128. The proclamation of Bernard, requir-ing all civil officers to assist the offi-cers of the customs in the discharge of their duties, is given in the Mass. Gazette for March 14, 1768.

[2] Letter of W. S. Johnson, dated London, March 14, 1767, in Trumbull MSS. ii. 144; Johnson's Diary, March 30, 1767, in Bancroft, vi. 64.

accounts were given of every occurrence in the colonies, and innocent acts were construed as treasonable. Did the legis- lature of Massachusetts, following the lead of the merchants of Boston, with but one dissenting voice pass resolutions discouraging the use of British, and giving the preference to American, manufactures?[1] These resolves, though conceded by Bernard to be "so decently and cautiously worded that at another time they would scarcely have given offence,"[2] were enough to excite the anger of Grenville and his friends; and the House of Commons ordered a full account of the manufac- tures of the colonies since 1734 to be prepared and forwarded to England, with a view to subject such manufactures to addi- tional restrictions.[3]

Considering the position he had taken, disputes with the gov- ernor were of course to be expected; and he was constantly fur- nishing grounds for fresh accusations. An article in the Gazette commented severely upon his "obstinate perseverance in the path of malice," and his "diabolical thirst for mischief."[4] This he pronounced a "virulent libel," and, after it had been pre- sented to the Council and the House, the latter of which passed it over as a matter of little moment, the grand jury were called upon to indict the author; but they refused. Hutchinson, by his own acknowledgment, told them, "almost in plain words, that if they did not find against the paper as containing high treason, they might depend on being damned;" but his menace was laughed at, and the "Sons of Liberty" toasted the jurors.[5]

---

[1] Letter of T. Cushing to De Berdt, April 18, 1768, in MS. Letters and Papers, 1761–1776, in Lib. Mass. Hist. Soc.; Jour. H. of R. for 1767– 8, 198; Mass. Gazette for March 17, 1768; Bradford, i. 145.

[2] Bernard to Shelburne, March 5, 1768.

[3] Trumbull MSS. ii. 175, in Lib. Mass. Hist. Soc.

[4] Otis, in the Boston Gazette for Feb. 29, 1768, Supp't; Prior Doc'ts,

199; Bradford, i. 141, and State Pa- pers, 118, 119. The closing lines of this piece were significant: —

"If such men are by God appointed,
The devil may be the Lord's anointed."
Rochester's Satires.

[5] Hutchinson's Letters of March 23, 26, and 27, and Oct. 4, 1768, and Hist. iii. 186; Bernard to Shelburne, March 5 and 12, 1768; Jour. H. of R. for 1768, 206–210; Mass. Gazette Extra for March 4, and Gazette for

CHAP. On the last day of the session, the legislature came in for a
XI. share of the reproofs of his excellency, and of some of the
1768. members he spoke in terms of the bitterest contempt. "These
Mar. 4. are the men," said he, "to whose importance everlasting contention is necessary. . . . Time and experience will soon
pull the mask off these false patriots, who are sacrificing their
country to the gratification of their own passions." [1]

Nor did he stop here. Satisfied that he had nothing to
expect from either branch of the court, he once more busied
himself in denouncing the charter, and invoked the aid of
troops to assist in the work of oppression. To give point to
his appeal, a scheme was devised which, it was thought, if properly managed, could scarcely fail of success. The anniversary
Mar. 18. of the repeal of the stamp act, it was supposed, would be observed in Boston with some parade; and the governor concerted that reports should be circulated of a designed insurrection on that day, and of danger to his own person and to
the Board of Customs. Aware of his intentions, the "Sons
of Liberty" labored to preserve order; and when, on the
morning of that day, the effigies of Paxton and of Williams
were found suspended from Liberty Tree, they were immediately taken down.[2] The observances of the day were conducted
with decorum. At an early hour, drums were beaten, guns were
fired, and the "whole town was adorned with ships' colors;"
at the public dinner, in Faneuil Hall, toasts were drunk to
the freedom of the press and to the memory of several of

March 7, 1768; Prior Doc'ts, 199–
202. "The time is not yet come,"
wrote Bernard to Shelburne, "when
the House is to be moved against popular printers, however profligate and
flagitious."

[1] Jour. H. of R. for 1768, 214;
Mass. Gazette Extra for March 4,
1768; Hutchinson, iii. 186; Bradford,
Hist. i. 143, and State Papers, 120,
121.

[2] "There was, in the time of it, a

strong suspicion in the minds of many
that these effigies were hung up by
some *particular persons* on that day,
with a design to give a coloring to just
such representations as Governor Bernard now makes. There are persons
here capable of playing such a game;
and there are some circumstances
which make it appear that such a suspicion was not groundless." Vindication of the Town of Boston, 6.

the martyrs of liberty ;[1] but, though public and private dwell- CHAP
ings were generally illuminated, no bonfire was lighted in the XI.
evening ; and the "mob," if there was one, by the acknowledg- 1768.
ment of Hutchinson was only such as had been usual " on the
fifth of November and other holidays."[2] Bernard, however,
was not to be baffled ; and, since, the people would give no
cause of offence, he was determined to make one. Hence, in
his despatches to England, he magnified these occurrences into
a terrible riot. " Many hundreds," he affirms, " paraded the
streets with yells and outcries which were quite terrible ; " and
when the " mob " passed his house, there was " so terrible a yell
that it was apprehended they were breaking in." " I can afford
no protection," he continues, " to the commissioners. I have
not the shadow of authority or power. I am sure to be made
obnoxious to the madness of the people by the testimony I am
obliged to bear against it, and yet left exposed to their resentment without any possible resort of protection."[3] The commissioners of the customs seconded these charges, and, to insure
the arrival of an armed force, earnestly appealed to Commodore Hood, the naval commander at Halifax, for aid, and memorialized the treasury for troops to be sent over.[4]

Before these charges reached England, the Twelfth Parlia- Mar.11.

[1] Boston Gazette for March 21,
1768 ; Mass. Gazette for March 24,
1768 ; Bancroft, vi. 134.

[2] Hutchinson to Jackson, March
23, 1768 ; Hist. iii. 188. Comp. Bernard to Shelburne, March 19, 1768,
and see Mass. Gazette for March 24
— the organ of the government.
Gage to Hillsborough, Oct. 31, 1768,
asserts that, " according to the best information he had been able to procure, the disturbance in March, so far
from being ' terrible,' as the governor
represents it, was in truth trifling."
Vindication of the Town of Boston, 9.
Pownall, also, in his Speech in the
House of Commons, in Feb. 1769, p.
4, says the " disturbance " on the 18th
of March " was nothing more than a

mere procession of a post chariot or
two and some single horse chaises,
with a mob of boys and idle people at
their heels, by way of ovation or triumph over the stamp act. There was
a procession of the very same nature
in London upon the anniversary of the
failure of the excise bill ; and yet the
civil magistrates of the city of London
never had any such severe charge
brought against them for not putting
a stop thereto."

[3] Bernard to Shelburne, March 19
and 21, 1768. Comp. Pownall's Speech
of Feb. 1769, p. 4.

[4] Hood, in Grenville Corresp. iv.
306 ; Mem. of Commissioners, March
28, 1768 ; Bancroft, vi. 136.

CHAP. ment was dissolved. In the election which ensued, the system
XI.   of bribery, which had long been practised, was carried to an
1768 extent never before known. The blood of Africa and the tears
of Hindostan, by a new species of alchemy, were transmuted
into English gold ; and seats in Parliament became an article
of brokerage and merchandise. " There is no such thing as
a borough to be had now," wrote Chesterfield to his son.[1]
" The rich East and West Indians have secured them all at the
rate of three thousand pounds at least, but many at four thousand, and two or three at five thousand." " George Selwyn
sold his borough of Ludgershall to two members for nine thousand pounds." In the borough of Northampton, a contested
election and the petition which followed are said to have cost
the Earl of Spencer no less than seventy thousand pounds.[2]
To a Parliament thus rotten were the liberties of England and
America intrusted. Obviously, it would have been absurd to
have expected from such a body measures of patriotism, of prudence, or of peace.[3] Men who jest at their own corruption
will not, as a general thing, hesitate to sanction the vilest
measures. Is it surprising that the colonies, which had relied
upon the integrity of Parliament, should have henceforth regarded it as their deadliest foe ? " We must be free," was the
word which began to circulate. " Laws are not valid unless
sanctioned by our consent." " We will oppose any minister
who shall innovate an iota in our privileges." Dickinson,

[1] Dec. 19, 1767, and April 12,
1768, in Lord Mahon's Hist. Eng. v.
190, 191.
[2] Lord Orford's Mems. iii. 198,
note ; Franklin's Works, vii. 394 ;
Belsham's George III. i. 232 ; Lord
Mahon's Hist. Eng. v. 191. Comp.
Bancroft, vi. 147. Well might the
poet indignantly exclaim, —

" Corruption ranges with gigantic stride,
   And scarce vouchsafes his shameless front
     to hide ;
The spreading leprosy taints every part,
Infects each limb, and sickens at the heart.

Stern Independence from his glebe retires,
And anxious Freedom eyes her drooping
   fires.
By foreign wealth are British morals
   changed,
And Afric's sons and India's smiles avenged."
                   Epist. to Wilberforce.

[3] " It is at present," wrote De
Berdt, May 11, 1768, " a time of great
confusion ; the heats and animosity of
electing new members of Parliament
are not yet subsided ; universal discontent spreads itself through the
kingdom." Bradford, State Papers,
142.

of Pennsylvania, the author of the "Farmer's Letters," and a CHAP
man of singular calmness and moderation, approved this course. XI.
"Almighty God himself"— such were his words—"will look 1768.
down upon your righteous contest with approbation. You will
be a band of brothers, strengthened with inconceivable supplies
of force and constancy by the sympathetic ardor which animates
good men confederated in a good cause. You are assigned by
Divine Providence, in the appointed order of things, the protectors of unborn ages, whose fate depends upon your virtue."[1]
The people of Boston responded to this appeal; and, in a
meeting convened for the purpose, thanks were voted, and a Mar.24:
committee was appointed, consisting of Samuel Adams, John
Hancock, and Joseph Warren, to greet the author in the name
of the town, as "the friend of Americans and the common benefactor of mankind."[2]

The circular of Massachusetts, sent out in February, reached
England in April; and it was at once denounced as of a "most Apr 15.
dangerous and factious tendency, calculated to inflame the
minds of his majesty's good subjects in the colonies, to promote
an unwarrantable combination, to excite and encourage an
open opposition to and defiance of the authority of Parliament,
and to subvert the true principles of the constitution."[3] Letters were written to all the governors to prevail with the
assemblies to take no notice of this circular;[4] and the General
Court of Massachusetts were required to rescind their resolutions, and to "declare their disapprobation of the rash and
hasty proceeding." Should they refuse to comply, the governor
was "immediately to dissolve them. Upon their next choice,

---

[1] Farmer's Letters, 12; Franklin's Works, i. 282; Bancroft, vi. 139.

[2] Bernard to Hillsborough, March 28, 1768; Boston Gazette for March 28, 1768; Mass. Gazette for March 24, 1768. The Boston Gazette for April 25, Mass. Gazette for April 28, contain the reply of Mr. Dickinson.

[3] Hillsborough to the Governor of Connecticut, April 29, 1768, in Trumbull MSS. ii. 170; Hillsborough to ——, in MS. Letters and Papers, 1761–1776, in Lib. Mass. Hist. Soc.; Letter to the Earl of Hillsborough, pub. in 1769, p. 31; Grahame, ii. 433.

[4] Trumbull MSS. ii. 170; Bancroft, vi. 144.

CHAP.
XI.

1768.

he was again to insist on it; and if then refused, he was to do the like, and as often as the case should happen."[1] As an additional argument to induce obedience, General Gage, the commander-in-chief of his majesty's forces in America, was ordered to maintain the public tranquillity.[2]

For some time Mr. Bernard had corresponded with Hillsborough, the secretary of state, and had acted as informer against the province, under the pledge that no exposure should be made of his letters.[3] "It requires your lordship's distinguished abilities," he wrote, "to accomplish the most arduous task of reducing the colonies into good order;" and he expressed the hope that he would prove successful. This compliment to his talents was sufficient to insure a favorable reception to the proposals of the governor, and the reply of the secretary was as flattering as heart could wish. Hutchinson, anxious to secure his share of applause, chimed in with the statements of Bernard, and rang the refrain in a similar strain. "It only needs," said he, "one steady plan, pursued a little while, and success is sure."[4] Such suggestions were by no means displeasing to the secretary; and, as the letters from the revenue

June 8. officers bore the same burden, Gage was ordered to send a regiment to Boston, to be permanently quartered there for the assistance of the civil officers and the officers of the customs. The admiralty was also directed to send one frigate, two sloops, and two cutters to be stationed in Boston harbor; and, for the accommodation of the troops, the Castle was to be repaired and occupied.[5]

---

[1] Shelburne to Bernard, April 22, 1768; De Berdt to the Speaker of the House of Rep. July 29, 1768, in Bradford's State Papers, 161; Grahame, ii. 435; Bradford, Hist. i. 148; Bancroft, vi. 144.

[2] Hillsborough to Gage, April 23, 1768. "It is become necessary that such measures should be taken as will strengthen the hands of the government in the Province of the Massa-

chusetts Bay, enforce a due obedience to the laws, and protect and support the civil magistrates and the officers of the crown in the execution of their duty."

[3] Bernard to Hillsborough, May 12, 1768.

[4] Hutchinson to Jackson, June 14, 1768.

[5] Hillsborough to Gage, June 8, to the Lords of the Admiralty, June 11,

The annual election occurred before these orders were is- CHAP.
sued ; and the General Court, when convened, though they   XI.
listened to a sermon from Shute, of Hingham, in which the   1768.
absolute authority of Parliament was denied, and resistance to   May 4.
May 25.
inequitable laws was justified, evinced no disposition to stir
afresh the waters of strife, but patiently awaited the result of
their appeal to the king, and continued to confide in his majesty's good will.[1]   Parties, indeed, were so nearly equal, and
the disposition to overlook former miscarriages so far prevailed,
that even Hutchinson, whose friends brought him forward, for
the last time, as a candidate, lacked but three votes of an election to the Council ; but the pension he had accepted caused
his defeat.[2] Stung by this rejection, his arbitrariness increased ;
and the commissioners of the customs — Paxton, in particular,
who was his intimate friend — assumed the haughtiest airs, and
cared not what umbrage was taken at their course.

A ship of war, the Romney, had for a month past lain at
anchor off in the channel ; and her commander, Captain Corner, under the pretence that he was in want of men, had ventured to impress a number of seamen belonging to New England.   One of these was rescued ; but when an attempt was   Jun. 10.
made to obtain the release of another, by offering a substitute,
the captain exclaimed, in a violent rage, " No man shall go out
of this vessel.   The town is a blackguard town — ruled by
mobs.   They have begun with me by rescuing a man whom I
pressed this morning ; and, by the eternal God, I will make
their hearts ache before I leave it." [3]

and to Bernard, June 11; Narr. of
Facts ; Bancroft, vi. 153. " As this
appears to be a service of a delicate
nature," says Hillsborough, " and _pos-
sibly leading to consequences not
easily foreseen_, I am directed by the
king to recommend to you to make
choice of an officer for the command
of these troops upon whose prudence,
resolution, and integrity you can entirely rely."
[1] Hutchinson to ——, July 21,

1768 ; Mass. Gazette for May 26,
1768 ; Bancroft, vi. 151.
[2] Affidavit of N. Waterman. Comp.
Hutchinson to Jackson, June 18, 1768,
and Oliver to ——, May 11, 1767.
Letters from the Earl of Hillsborough
and the Board of Trade were laid before the House, May 31, " concerning
the constitution of an agent for this
province." Jour. H. of R. for 1768, 20.
[3] Affidavit of N. Waterman, annexed to the Mem. presented by De

About sunset of the same day, another step, of a more violent nature, fanned the sparks of excitement into a flame. A sloop, the Liberty, belonging to John Hancock, one of the wealthiest and warmest of the Boston patriots, which had just discharged a cargo of wines and taken in a freight of oil and tar for a new voyage, was seized for an alleged false entry, and, after receiving the broad arrow, preparations were made to remove her from the wharf, to be moored under the shelter of the guns of the Romney. The revenue officers, fearing a rescue, signalled to the Romney ; and a boat, filled with armed men, was sent to their aid. Malcom, a trader at the north part of the town, advised the officers to let the vessel lie at the wharf : but Hallowell, the comptroller, gruffly replied, "I shall not," and orders were given to cut the fasts. "Stop, at least, till the owner comes," was shouted from the crowd ;[1] but the comptroller, with an oath, bade the men "cast her off ;" and the master of the Romney cried, "I'll split the brains of any man that offers to reeve a fast, or stop the vessel." Then, turning to the marines, he commanded them to fire. "What rascal is that," cried one, "who dares to tell the marines to fire ?" Harrison, the collector, witnessed these proceedings, but refused to interfere. "The owner is sent for," it was said ; "you had better let the vessel lie at the wharf till he comes." But Hallowell repeated his orders, and added, "Show me the man who dares oppose." Exasperated at this conduct, Malcom shouted, "We will throw the people from the Romney overboard ;" but Corner, with an oath, swore the vessel should go, and again called to the marines, "Why don't you fire? Fire, I say !" The crowd, on this, fell back, and the sloop was towed away.[2]

Berdt ; Hutchinson to Jackson, June 18, 1768; Jour. H. of R. for 1768, 25, 30 ; Bancroft, vi. 155.

[1] The commissioners represented this as a "numerous mob ;" but the Vindication of the Town of Boston, p. 10, says, "It was not a numerous mob, nor was it of long continuance, neither was there much mischief done."

[2] Affidavits of Joseph Piper, William Ross, Caleb Hopkins, &c., annexed to the memorial of De Berdt of July 21; Deposition of Hallowell,

As the officers of the customs retired, the crowd followed CHAP.
at their heels, pelting them with stones and bricks and dirt; XI.
but, save a few flesh wounds, no serious injury was done.[1] On 1768.
reaching their houses, the mob broke in the windows, and
frightened their families; and, soon after, seizing a pleasure
boat belonging to the custom house, it was dragged in triumph
from the water side to the Common, and burned. Hancock,
Warren, and Samuel Adams had already met to deliberate as
to what should be done; but, an hour before midnight, the
word was given, "Each man to his tent." The crowd dispersed, and all was quiet.[2]

Saturday and Sunday passed without disturbance. The governor convened the Council, to advise with them; and, after
some altercation, a committee was appointed to ascertain the
facts attending the seizure. This, however, did not satisfy the
officers, who trembled for their own safety; and four of the
five went with their families on board the Romney.[3] On
Monday, a placard called upon the "Sons of Liberty" to meet Jun. 13.
the next day at "Liberty Hall," a name given to the space
around Liberty Tree.[4] A vast crowd responded to this call;[5] Jun. 14.
a chairman was chosen; and the selectmen were requested to
call a legal meeting that afternoon at three o'clock. At that
hour the meeting was held; but, finding the concourse so

in Mems. of the Commissioners, June
16, 1768; Hutchinson to ——, June
18, 1768, and Hist. iii. 190; Boston
News Letter for June 16, 1768.
[1] The officers, indeed, alleged more
serious injuries; but their account of
the affair is in most respects exaggerated. See Bernard to Hillsborough,
June 11 and 13, 1768, and Mem. of
the Commissioners, June 16, 1768;
and comp. Mem. of Mass. in Prior
Doc'ts, 222.
[2] Bernard to Hillsborough, June
11, 1768; Hutchinson to ——, June
18 and Aug. 1768, and Hist. iii. 191;
Bancroft, vi. 157.
[3] Mems. of the Commissioners,

June 16, 1768; Hutchinson, Hist.
iii. 191; Grenville Corresp. iv. 322;
Bradford, i. 155. "It has been usual
for the commissioners to affect an apprehension of danger to themselves
and their families, to serve the purposes they had in view." Vindic. of
the Town of Boston, 5; comp. ibid. 14.
[4] Bernard to Hillsborough, June
16, 1768. "This tree," says the governor, "has often put me in mind of
Jack Cade's Oak of Reformation."
[5] See the Commissioners' Report.
Bernard, to Hillsborough, June 16,
1768, says, "at least 4000 men, many
having come out of the country for
that purpose."

VOL. II.   23

CHAP.   great that Faneuil Hall would not hold all, they adjourned
XI.   to the meeting house of the Old South Church, of which Dr.
1768.   Sewall was the pastor.   James Otis was chosen moderator;
and upon his appearance he was "ushered into the hall by an
almost universal clap of hands."   An address to the governor
was unanimously voted; and a committee of twenty-one, of
which Tyler was at the head, was appointed to present it.
Jun. 15. The meeting was then adjourned to the following day, at four
o'clock in the afternoon; and, on reassembling, Otis delivered
a speech, recommending in the strongest terms the preservation of order, and expressing the hope that the grievances they
had suffered would be speedily redressed.   "If not," he added,
"and we are called on to defend our liberties and privileges,
I hope and believe we shall, one and all, resist even unto
blood.   But I pray God Almighty that this may never so
happen." [1]

The committee appointed for that purpose [2] waited upon the
governor at his residence in Roxbury, — proceeding thither in
a procession of eleven chaises, — and presented the address.
The language of this address was pointed and clear.   "To
contend with our parent state" — such were its words — "is,
in our idea, the most shocking and dreadful extremity; but
tamely to relinquish the only security we and our posterity
retain of the enjoyment of our lives and properties, without
one struggle, is so humiliating and base that we cannot support
the reflection.   It is at your option, we apprehend, in your
power, and we would hope in your inclination, to prevent this
distressed and justly-incensed people from effecting too much,
and from the shame and reproach of attempting too little.
. . We flatter ourselves, therefore, that your excellency will,
in tenderness to the people, use the best means in your power

[1] Bernard to Hillsborough, June
11, 16, and 18, 1768; the Commissioners to Commodore Hood, June 15,
1768, in Mems.; also, Letter to the
Commissioners, June 14, 1768, in
ibid.; Boston News Letter for June
16 and 23, 1768.
[2] "Which was in general very respectable," says Bernard.

to remove the other grievances we so justly complain of, and CHAP.
issue your immediate order to the commander of his majesty's XI.
ship Romney to remove from this harbor, till we shall be ascer- 1768.
tained of the success of our application." [1]

The governor received this address with marked obsequiousness; [2] but on the following day, in his reply, he refused to
order the removal of the Romney, which, he said, was not
subject to his direction, and cleared himself of the responsibility of the affray which had occurred. In conclusion he remarked, "I shall think myself most highly honored if I can be,
in the lowest degree, an instrument in procuring a perfect reconciliation between you and the parent state." [3] The dignity
of his excellency, however, was seriously shocked at the humiliating position in which he was placed, and the wound which
his pride had received rankled too deeply to be easily healed.
Hence no sooner had he delivered this message than he joined
with the officers in magnifying the " riot" into an "insurrection," and in soliciting an armed force to be sent to their relief.
The comptroller and the collector, as well as his excellency,
reported a "general spirit of insurrection, not only in the town,
but throughout the province;" and the commissioners, in a
body, applied to Commodore Hood, who was at Halifax, and
to Gage, who was at New York, for further protection. [4]
Their despatches to England were of the same tenor; and,
after remarking that the "long-concerted and extensive plan
of resistance to the authority of Great Britain" had broken
out in " actual violence sooner than was intended," they urged
that "nothing but the immediate exertion of military power

[1] Boston News Letter for June 23,
1768; Bradford, State Papers, and
Hist. i.; Prior Doc'ts, 263; Franklin's Works.

[2] " I received them," says his excellency, " with all possible civility,
and, having heard their petition, I
talked very freely with them upon the
subject, but postponed giving a formal
answer till the next day, as it should

be in writing. I then had wine hand-
ed round; and they left me, highly
pleased with their reception, especially
that part of them which had not been
used to an interview with me."

[3] Reply of Bernard, in Mass. Gazette, &c.

[4] Gage and Hood to the Commissioners, in Mems., July 11, 1768.

CHAP. could prevent an open revolt of the town of Boston, and prob-
XI.   ably of the provinces." [1]

1768.   The General Court was in session at this time, but did not
interpose, leaving the people to settle the affair in their own
way. But the inhabitants of Boston, though they deprecated
Jun. 17. violence, did not hesitate to speak their minds freely, and drew
up a series of instructions to their representatives, in which,
after affirming their "fixed resolution to maintain their loyalty
and duty to their most gracious sovereign, a reverent and due
subordination to the British Parliament as the supreme legislature in all cases of necessity for the preservation of the whole
empire, and to use their utmost endeavors for the preservation
of peace and order among themselves, — waiting with anxious
expectation for a favorable answer to the petitions and solicitations of the continent for relief, — they declared that it was
their "unalterable resolution to assert and vindicate their dear
and invaluable rights and liberties at the utmost hazard of
their lives and fortunes," and expressed the "full and rational
confidence that no design formed against them would ever
prosper." In conclusion, they instructed them to "forward, if
they thought expedient, in the House of Representatives, resolutions that every person soliciting or promoting the importation of troops should be pronounced an enemy to the town
and province, and a disturber of the peace and good order of
both." [2]

In the midst of this excitement, the instructions which had
been sent over by the secretary of state, that Massachusetts
should rescind her resolutions against importing goods from
England, came to hand ; and the governor, after consulting

---

[1] Mems. of the Commissioners, June 16, 1768. "Unless we have immediately two or three regiments, 'tis the opinion of all the friends to government that Boston will be in open rebellion." Letter of Paxton, June 20, 1768.

[2] Bernard to Hillsborough, June 16 and 18, 1768 ; Boston News Letter for June 23, 1768 ; Hutchinson, iii. App. K. "They broke up quietly," says the governor, "and there is an end of the meeting."

with Hutchinson and Oliver, sent to the House a message, CHAP.
accompanied with extracts from the letter of Hillsborough.[1] XI.
This message was read once, and was ordered to a second 1768.
reading in the afternoon, when floor and gallery were filled Jun. 21.
with auditors; and Otis, whose clarion voice rang through the
hall, in a masterly speech of two hours' length, filled with vol-
canic bursts of passion, set forth his objections to a compliance
with the requisition.[2]

It was well known that the governor had diligently corresponded with the secretary, and had misrepresented the views
and the conduct of the people; and, as he had communicated
to the House but part of the letter just received, and none of
his own letters, they desired him to lay before them, not only Jun. 23.
the whole of the letter of Hillsborough and the king's instructions, but that "he would be pleased to add copies of his own
letters relating to the subject of the aforesaid message." With
this request he was unwilling to comply. He was ready to Jun. 24.
submit the letter of Hillsborough; but his own letters, he assured them, he "would never make public but upon his own
motion and for his own reasons." But this refusal availed him
nothing. Copies of the letters had been obtained, and the
House knew their contents.[3] They were not, therefore, acting
in the dark. They were well informed of his excellency's
proceedings, and were determined to call him to an account.
Hence their course was decided. The ministry, they were sensible, was bent on humbling them; the eyes of all were fastened

[1] Bernard to Hillsborough, June 25, 1768; Boston Gazette for July 4 and 18, 1768; Mass. Gazette for June 23 and July 7, 1768; Bradford, State Papers, 145–150; Prior Doc'ts, 203; Jour. H. of R. for 1768, 68, 72, 75. A similar controversy occurred earlier in this year, when a portion of the let-ter of Shelburne was communicated to the House. Bradford, State Papers, 113–118.

[2] Bernard, to Hillsborough, June 25, characterizes this speech as "of the most violent and virulent nature." "He abused all persons in authority," he adds, "both here and at home. He indeed excepted the king's person, but traduced his government with all the bitterness of words."

[3] They were published in pamphlet form by "Edes and Gill, in Queen Street," in 1769. Resolve of H. of R. in Jour. for June, 1769, and Brad-ford, State Papers, 160. Comp. Hutch-inson, iii. 184, 195.

CHAP. upon them ; and in the hour of peril should they shrink from
XI.   the encounter ? From Virginia, from New Jersey, from Con-
1768. necticut, and from Georgia letters had been received approving
       their proceedings, and tendering sympathy.[1] Should they dis-
       appoint the expectations which had every where been formed ?
       Then would they deserve to be left to their fate.

           For a full week the affair was in suspense. To comply
       with the mandate of the king was to give up all. And should
Jun. 28. they retrace their steps when they had gone so far ? At length
       the governor demanded a definite answer, and informed them
       that longer delay would be construed as a refusal. The House
Jun. 29. asked a recess to consult their constituents ; but it was refused.
       Upon this the question was taken *viva voce ;* and out of one
       hundred and nine votes cast, but seventeen were in the affirm-
       ative.[2] A message was sent to the governor informing him of
Jun. 30. this decision, and a long letter was draughted to be sent to
       Hillsborough.[3] In accordance with his instructions, the gov-
July 1. ernor prorogued the House, and the next day, by proclamation,
       dissolved the court.[4] Thus Massachusetts was without a legis-
       lature, and the liberties of the people were at the mercy of
       their foes.

July.   In July, Hallowell, the commissioner of the customs, arrived
       in England as the accuser of the province. The letters he
       took with him were numerous, and great was the dismay caused
       by his appearance. At London, at Liverpool, at Bristol, and
       at other ports, the excitement was general. Stocks fell ; mer-
       chants grew anxious ; and those who had debtors in the colo-
       nies fancied themselves ruined.[5] The anger of the ministry

---

[1] Jour. H. of R. for 1768, App. 6
et seq. ; Boston Gazette for June 27,
1768 ; Prior Doc'ts, 213–220 ; Hutchinson, iii. 196 ; Bancroft, vi. 164.

[2] Bernard to Hillsborough, July 1,
1768 ; Hutchinson, iii. 197 ; Jour. H.
of R. for 1768, 85, 86, 88, 89–94.
" Among the majority," says Bernard,
" were many members who were scarce
ever known upon any other occasion

to vote against the government side
of a question — so greatly have infatuation and intimidation gained ground."

[3] This letter is given in full in Bradford, State Papers, 151–158 ; Jour.
H. of R. for 1768, App. ; Prior Doc'ts,
206–210.

[4] Bernard to Hillsborough, June
17 and July 1, 1768.

[5] Hutchinson's Letter of Oct. 4,

knew no bounds. To be thus bearded and set at defiance by
a "parcel of renegades," a "factious mob," a "rascally rabble,"
was "a thing not to be endured;" and the violent denounced
"vengeance against the insolent town of Boston."[1] "If the
government," they urged, "now gives way, as it did about the
stamp act, it will be all over with its authority in America."[2]
They had forgotten the memorable predictions of Pownall:
"Believe me, there is not a province, a colony, or a plantation
that will submit to a tax thus imposed. Don't fancy that you
can divide the people upon this point. You will by this conduct only unite them the more inseparably. The people of
America, universally, unitedly, and unalterably, are resolved not
to submit to any internal tax imposed upon them by any legislature in which they have not a share by representatives of their
own election. This claim must not be understood as though
it were only the pretences of party leaders and demagogues;
as though it were only the visions of speculative enthusiasts;
as though it were the ebullition of a faction which must subside; as though it were only temporary or partial. It is the
cool, deliberate, principled maxim of every man of business in
the country."[3] Such words, spoken by one who knew the
people, should have received more attention. But the statesmen of England were too obstinately bent on humbling America to listen to warnings; and they preferred the risk of losing
the colonies to yielding the claim of authority over them.

The examination of the collector took place at the treasury
chambers, in the presence of Lord North, Jenkinson, and
Campbell; and, though he subsequently saw fit to file certain
"corrections" to his testimony,[4] there was enough in it as ori-

---

1768. "It is not strange that measures should be immediately taken to
reduce the colonies to their former
state of government and order; but
that the national funds should be affected by it, is to me a little mysterious and surprising."

[1] Johnson to Pitkin, July 23, 1768;
Bancroft, vi. 174.
[2] Bancroft, vi. 174.
[3] Speech of May 15, 1767, in Pri-
or Doc'ts, 162, 163.
[4] MS. Letters and Papers, 1761–
1776, fol. 80, in Lib. Mass. Hist. Soc.

ginally given to prompt to action. True, he did not affirm that the determination to break the revenue laws was unanimous; for Salem and Marblehead had not resisted them, and "the better sort of people would be for government if they could be protected;" but the "Bostoneers" had defied the laws, and the infection might spread. Nor did he assert that the officers who remained were insulted after the first outbreak; but they were daily expecting to be driven away, for the "vermin" were to be expelled. He insisted, however, — and in this he echoed the representations of Bernard, — that "there had been a long-concerted and extensive plan of resistance to the authority of Great Britain;"[1] and, a copy of the memorial being sent to Hillsborough,[2] the lords of the treasury united in declaring that "nothing short of the immediate exertion of military power could prevent an open revolt of the town, which would probably spread throughout the provinces."[3] The coun-

July 24. ter memorial of the province, presented by De Berdt, charged the blame of the riot to the imprudence of the officers, and the commander of the Romney; and this memorial was strengthened by affidavits taken on the spot. But of what avail was such a defence, or any defence, to those who had beforehand resolved what to do? Bedford and his followers clamored for troops to be sent over to subdue the inhabitants of Boston, and for a striking example to be made of the most forward, to inspire the other colonies with terror. Weymouth fell in with this proposal. But Shelburne, more friendly to America, declared that it would be absurd to send a single additional soldier, or a vessel of war, to reduce the colonies, as they would return to their allegiance from affection and from interest, if

and fol. 83, where the corrections are given; Bradshaw to Pownall, Nov. 22, 1768.

[1] Copy of the Examination of Hallowell, in the pamphlet printed in Boston.

[2] Letter of Bradshaw, in MS. Letters and Papers, 1761–1776, fol. 82; Bradshaw to Pownall, July 22 and Aug. 31, in the pamphlet published in Boston.

[3] Narr. of Facts; Bradshaw to Pownall, July 22, 1768; Bancroft, vi. 174.

once the laws of which they complained were modified. But CHAP.
moderate counsels were despised ; and the king, who was per- XI.
sonally concerned to enforce his authority, became importunate 1768.
that Shelburne should be dismissed.[1]

A few days later a meeting of the cabinet was held, and a July 27.
union of parties was sought to be effected on the basis of the
declaratory act. With Massachusetts, it was thought, it would
not be difficult to deal, if that was the only refractory province ;
and Boston was to be proceeded against " with the utmost
severity." Scarcely a voice opposed these measures ; and when
the proposition was advanced that two additional regiments,
of five hundred men each, should be sent over, and that a
change should be made in the provincial charter, it was assented to without division, and almost without debate.[2] Bernard,
in the mean time, received from Gage an offer of troops when July 2.
he should desire them ; but the Council, to whom he communicated this offer under an injunction of secrecy, did not consider July 23
the troops necessary.[3] The governor dared not dissent from and 27.
their opinion, and wrote to Hillsborough for positive orders
not to call " a new assembly until the people should get truer
notions of their rights and interests."[4] The merchants of Boston, whose attempts to prevent importations had been hitherto
attended with but partial success, rallied once more ; and a Aug. 9
large number — all but sixteen, it is said — signed an agree- to 15.
ment, absolute in its terms, that they would send for no merchandise from Great Britain, articles of necessity only excepted,
for a year from the following January ; and tea, paper, glass,
painters' colors, &c., upon which duties had been imposed, were

[1] Mem. of De Berdt, of July 24,
1768; Francès to Choiseul, July 29,
1768; Grafton's Autobiog. in Bancroft, vi. 175.

[2] Camden to Grafton, Sept. 4, 1768,
in Grafton's Autobiog.; Mauduit to
Hutchinson, in Boston Chronicle;
Hillsborough to Bernard, July 30,
1768.

[3] Gage to the Commissioners of the
Customs, June 21, 1768, in Mems. of
Commissioners for July 11, 1768;
Bernard to Hillsborough, July 30,
1768; Postscript to Boston News
Letter for Oct. 13, 1768; Boston Ga-
zette for Oct. 10, 1768.

[4] Bernard to Hillsborough, Aug. 6,
1768.

CHAP. particularly prohibited.[1] Nor was the anniversary of the
XI.   outbreak against the stamp act forgotten. A vast concourse
1768. of people assembled at Liberty Tree, and, after rejoicing there,
Aug.14.
     a procession of chariots and fifty or sixty chaises proceeded to
Roxbury, to an entertainment provided for the occasion. The
selectmen of Boston and the representatives of the town formed
part of the company ; and the day passed pleasantly and without disturbance.[2]

Aug.19.   Five days later the vote of the legislature, refusing to rescind the resolutions against importation, reached England ;
and Lord Mansfield signalized the warmth of his zeal by proposing that the refractory members of the House should be
sent for to answer for their disloyal conduct. "Where rebellion begins," said he, "the laws cease ; and they can invoke
none in their favor." "The Americans," he insisted, "must
first be compelled to submit to the authority of Parliament ;
and it is only after having reduced them to the most entire
obedience that an inquiry can be made into their real or pretended grievances."[3] In every European court the progress
of the struggle was viewed with interest. It was the theme
of discussion and gossip in Paris ; at Madrid, the Spanish ministry were concerned lest their own colonies should "catch the
flame."[4] The discussion in England agitated all classes. Cam-
Sept. 4. den was alarmed "because the colonies were more sober, and,
consequently, more determined, in the present opposition than
they were upon the stamp act." "What, then, is to be done?"
was the inquiry of Grafton. "Indeed, my lord, I do not
know," was the reply. "Parliament cannot repeal the reve-

---

[1] Bernard to Hillsborough, Aug. 9, 1768 ; Hutchinson to ——, Aug. 10, 1768 ; Boston News Letter for Aug. 18, 1768.

[2] Bernard to Hillsborough, Aug. 29, 1768 ; Boston Gazette for Aug. 22, 1768 ; Hutchinson, iii. 201, 202 ; Bancroft, vi. 179. The observance this year was on Monday, Aug. 15, and

the toasts drunk were 45 in number. "The joy of the day was manly, and an uninterrupted regularity presided through the whole."

[3] Francès to Choiseul, Sept. 16 and 29, 1768, in Bancroft, vi. 182.

[4] Walpole's George III. iii. 253 ; Bancroft, vi. 182.

nue act, for that would admit the American principle to be right, and their own doctrine erroneous. The law must be executed ; but how it shall be executed I cannot say. Boston is the ringleading province ; and if any country is to be chastised, the punishment should be levelled there." [1]

The patriots of Boston had long been admonished of the necessity of vigilance, if they would defeat the schemes which threatened their ruin ; and Samuel Adams, in whom independence was an "original sin," [2] pleaded for it earnestly at all times and in all places. " We will never become slaves," said he. " We will submit to no tax. We will take up arms, and shed our last drop of blood, before the king and the Parliament shall impose on us, or settle crown officers, independent of the colonial legislature, to dragoon us." [3] Nor was Adams the only one in whose breast the fires of liberty were kindling. All of the resolute burned to vindicate their rights which had been trampled upon ; and early in the ensuing month a paper appeared in the Boston Gazette, in the form of " queries," designed to concentrate the action of the people. " If any should be sent to reduce us to slavery," — such was the language it held, — " we will put our lives in our hands, and cry to the Judge of all the earth, who will do right, saying, ' Behold, how they come to cast us out of this province, which thou hast given us. Help us, O Lord our God ; for we rest on thee, and in thy name we go against this multitude." [4]

Two days later the Senegal, one of the vessels stationed in the harbor, weighed her anchor, and left the port ; and on the following day the Duke of Cumberland sailed for Nova Scotia. Bernard himself gave out that both these vessels had gone for

[1] Campbell, v. 279; Camden to Grafton, Sept. 4, 1768, in Grafton's Autobiog.; Bancroft, vi. 183.
[2] T. Hollis to A. Eliot, July 1, 1768, relative to the American people generally. " You are an ungracious people. There is original sin in you. You are assertors of liberty and the principles of the revolution."
[3] Affidavits in the State Paper Office, London, quoted in Bancroft, vi. 193, 194.
[4] Clericus Americanus, in Boston Gazette for Sept. 5, 1768.

CHAP.
XI. troops; and the intelligence startled the people.[1] Immediately
a petition was signed for a town meeting, to be held on the

1768.
Sept. 9. following Monday, "to consider of the most wise, constitutional, loyal, and salutary measures" to be taken in this emergency.   Already had an officer arrived in Boston to provide

Sep. 10. quarters for the troops; and on Beacon Hill, the highest
ground in the town, where, from colonial days, it had been
customary, when the country was to be alarmed, to kindle a
signal fire, the old iron "skillet," of enormous dimensions,
which held the barrel of tar, was privately filled, and word
was given that it should be lighted when the fleet appeared in
sight.[2] The governor, in a panic, ordered the barrel to be
removed; and the selectmen communicated his request to the

Sep. 12. town meeting, but no action was taken upon it.   The Council,
therefore, advised the governor to direct the sheriff to remove
the barrel; and, taking with him a posse of six or seven men,
he executed his order stealthily, while the people were at
dinner.[3]

But more serious questions were to be discussed and
decided than those which related to mere matters of form.
Preparations for the meeting had been previously made by
Otis, and Adams, and Warren, who, at the house of the lat-

Sep. 10. ter, drew up the resolves which were to be presented, and
settled the order of debate.[4] When, therefore, the crowd gath-

Sep. 12. ered in Faneuil Hall, every thing was ready; and the people,
as they looked with a grim smile upon the burnished muskets,
four hundred in number, which lay in boxes along the floor,[5]

[1] Bernard to Hillsborough, Sept. 16, 1768. "The faction," he says, "immediately took the alarm."

[2] Bernard to Hillsborough, Sept. 16, 1768; Hutchinson to ——, Oct. 4, 1768, and Hist. iii. 202, 203.

[3] Bernard to Hillsborough, Sept. 16, 1768.

[4] Bernard to Hillsborough, Sept. 16, 1768. The governor falsely asserts that at this meeting "it was re-solved to surprise and take the Castle on the Monday night following."

[5] "In the Massachusetts government," wrote Hamilton to Calcraft, in 1767, "there is an express law by which every man is obliged to have a musket, a pound of powder, and a pound of bullets always by him; so there is nothing wanting but knapsacks (or old stockings, which will do as well) to equip an army for marching, and

entered upon the business for which they had convened. CHAP
Prayer was offered by the eloquent Cooper, pastor of the XI.
Brattle Street Church; Otis was chosen moderator; and a 1768.
committee was appointed to wait upon the governor, to inquire
his reasons for supposing that troops were expected, and to
request him "immediately to issue precepts for a General Assembly." The meeting then adjourned to the following morn- Sep. 13.
ing, when the committee reported that the governor had no
official announcement to make relative to the troops, and had
refused to call an assembly.[1] A "Declaration" was then read,
equalling in spirit the declaration from the same spot eighty
years before. "The inhabitants of Boston," it was resolved,
"will, at the utmost peril of their lives and fortunes, maintain
and defend their rights, liberties, privileges, and immunities."
Some counselled instant resistance, and insisted that no time
was better than the present. But rashness at such a juncture
might have defeated all. The prudent, therefore, gave different advice, and the people submitted. "There are the arms,"
said Otis, as he pointed to the boxes on the floor. "When an
attempt is made upon your liberties, they will be delivered."[2]
As the result of the meeting, a convention of all the towns was
proposed, to be held in Faneuil Hall within two weeks; and
Boston chose as its representatives Thomas Cushing, James

nothing more than a Sartorius or a Spartacus at their head requisite to beat your troops and your custom house officers out of the country, and set your laws at defiance. There is no saying what their leaders may put them upon; but if they are active, clever people, and love mischief as well as I do peace and quiet, they will furnish matter of consideration to the wisest among you, and perhaps dictate their own terms at last, as the Roman people formerly in their famous secession upon the Sacred Mount. For my own part, I think you have no right to tax them, and that every measure built upon this supposed right stands upon a rotten foundation, and must consequently tumble down, perhaps upon the heads of the workmen." Chatham Corresp. iii. 203, note. "This very morning," wrote Bernard to Hillsborough, July 9, 1768, "the selectmen of the town ordered the magazine of arms belonging to the town to be brought out to be cleaned, when they were exposed for some hours at the town house." See also Bernard to Hillsborough, Sept. 16, 1768; and comp. the Vindication of the Town of Boston, p. 28.

[1] Hutchinson, iii. 205; Boston Weekly News Letter for Sept. 15, 1768; Boston Gazette for Sept. 19, 1768.

[2] Bernard to Hillsborough, Sept. 16, 1768.

Otis, Samuel Adams, and John Hancock.[1] The selectmen
were directed to write to the several towns, informing them of
this design ; and it was recommended that all the inhabitants
should be provided with firearms and suitable ammunition.[2]
Nor was the time-honored custom of the fathers of New England forgotten ; and a day of fasting and prayer was appointed, and observed by all the churches except the Episcopal.[3]

By royalists the proceedings of this meeting were loudly
condemned. "They have delivered their sentiments," wrote
Gage, "in the style of a ruling and sovereign nation, who acknowledge no dependence."[4] The "Sons of Liberty" were
stigmatized as "Catilines;"[5] and Bernard was sure that, but
for the Romney, a rebellion would have broken out. Nay, he
even asserted that a design had been concerted to seize the
Castle, and talked of divulging the names of five hundred
who had enrolled for the service.[6] "I wish I were away," he
sighed, as he felt the perplexities of his situation increasing
upon him ; and when the offer of a baronetcy and the vice
government of Virginia was made to him, he accepted it
"most thankfully," and "hoped to embark for England in a
fortnight." But his hopes were dashed by the appointment
of Botetourt, and he began to fear lest he should lose Massachusetts.[7]

[1] "Surely," wrote Bernard to Hillsborough, "so daring an assumption of
the royal authority was never practised by any city or town in the British dominions, even in the times of
greatest disorder — not even by the
city of London when the great rebellion was at the highest, and the confusion arising from thence most urgent
for some extraordinary measures."

[2] Hutchinson, iii. App. L., where
the letter is given in full ; also, Postscript to Boston News Letter for
Sept. 22, 1768.

[3] Hutchinson, iii. 203–205 ; Bancroft, vi. 199.

[4] Gage to Hillsborough, Sept. 26,
1768.

[5] Auchmuty to Hutchinson, Sept.
14, 1768.

[6] Bernard to Hillsborough, Sept.
16, 1768. Comp. Vindication of the
Town of Boston, 30. The printed
copy of the former document reads,
nine hundred, and of the latter, five
hundred, men. Hutchinson, Hist. iii.
167, note, says, "Mr. Molineaux" was
the one who "proposed, at the head
of 500 men, to surprise the garrison
at the Castle;" "a strange, mad proposal," he adds, "*if such a one were
ever made.*"

[7] Hillsborough to Gage, Sept. 16,
1768; Bernard to Hillsborough, Sept.
17 and 18, 1768; Captain Corner's
Diary for Sept. 15, 1768, in Bancroft,

Three days before the convention was to meet, Bernard CHAP. announced to the Council that two regiments were expected XI. from Ireland, and that two others had been ordered by General Gage from Halifax, for which quarters should be provided. 1768.
Sep. 19. As the mutiny act formerly stood, the civil officers had a general discretionary power of quartering troops in inns, livery stables, retailing houses, &c. ; but that act had been changed ; and the Council, in their reply, suggested that " the process in quartering should be regulated accordingly, by sending the troops to the barracks ; and only in case of a lack of room there were they required to find other quarters." There was sufficient room at the barracks, they added, for a thousand men, and, consequently, enough to accommodate the two regiments from Halifax. But as for the orders of General Gage, " it was no disrespect to him to say, that no order whatever, coming from a less authority than his majesty and Parliament, can supersede an act of Parliament ; " and " if any military officer should take upon himself to quarter soldiers in any of his majesty's dominions in America otherwise than was limited and allowed by the act, he should be *ipso facto* cashiered, and disabled to hold any military employment in his majesty's service." [1]

The convention called by the people of Boston met accord- Sep. 22. ing to appointment ; and, on the first day, about seventy persons appeared as the representatives of sixty-six towns. This number was increased by daily arrivals, until ninety-six towns and eight districts, nearly every settlement in the province, were represented.[2] Otis was at first absent ; and Thomas Cushing, the speaker of the House, was chosen moderator, and

vi. 200. Comp. Hutchinson, iii. 199. Junius describes Botetourt as a " cringing, bowing, fawning, sword-bearing courtier, who had ruined himself by an enterprise which would have ruined thousands had it succeeded."

[1] Bernard to Hillsborough, Sept. 23 and 26, 1768 ; Hutchinson, iii. 207, 208 ; Mass. Gazette for Sept. 22, 1768.

[2] Boston News Letter for Oct. 6, 1768 ; Holmes's Ann. ii. ; Hutchinson, iii. 208, 209 ; Grahame, ii. 437 ; Bancroft, vi. 203.

CHAP.
XI.

1768.

the clerk of the House was chosen clerk of the convention. "They have committed treason," shouted the officers of the crown. "At least, the selectmen of Boston have done so." "Boston," wrote Gage, "is mutinous; its resolves treasonable and desperate." "Mad people procured them; mad people govern the town and the province."[1]

The first step of the convention was to petition the governor to "cause an assembly to be immediately convened;" but this petition he refused to receive, on the ground that it would be an admission of the legality of the convention, which he would by no means acknowledge; and he advised the "gentlemen assembled at Faneuil Hall under the name of a committee of convention" to separate at once, or he would publicly assert the prerogative of the crown, and they who persisted in usurping its rights should be made to "repent their rashness;" but the message was received with derision.[2]

The Council, as a branch of the legislature, had held meetings from time to time, with the consent of the governor, and had been consulted by him in their official capacity in several instances; but when the question of quartering the troops was referred to them a second time, in order to shake their former resolution, they replied, "We do not desire to be knocked on the head,"[3] and reduced to writing their reasons for adhering to the billeting act. This decision was communicated to the governor, was published in the Gazette, and a copy of the same was sent to Lord Hillsborough.[4] It was the "greatest blow," in the estimation of Bernard, "that had been given to

Sep. 26.

[1] Paper enclosed in Gage's letter of Sept. 26, 1768, in Letters, &c. 41; Bancroft, vi. 203. For a defence of the province against the charge of treason, see Pownall's Speech of Feb. 1769, p. 5.

[2] Bernard to Hillsborough, Sept. 27 and Oct. 3, 1768; Hutchinson, iii. 210. "It is now made a great question," writes Bernard, "in what man-

ner Great Britain will resent this proceeding. It is concluded that the most probable consequence will be the forfeiture of the charter. If this is the worst, it is an event most devoutly to be desired by every well wisher to the province."

[3] Comp. Bernard to Hillsborough, June 13, 1768.

[4] Bancroft, vi. 204.

the king's government." "Nine tenths of the people considered the declaration of the Council just ; " "throughout the
province they were ripe for almost any thing ; " and the ministry, astonished at the storm they had raised, dared not insist
further.[1]

The convention continued in session six days, and repeated
the protest of the people against the taxation of the colonies
by Parliament, against a standing army, and against the danger
to the "liberties of America from a united body of pensioners
and soldiers ; " and, after renewing their petition to the king,
which their agent was enjoined to deliver in person as soon
as possible, they dissolved.[2] "Some feared, others hoped, for
much more serious consequences from this extraordinary assembly ; " but its members, aware of the necessity of prudence,
displayed in all their proceedings remarkable caution ; and
when the result of their labors was transmitted to England,
though many would gladly have seized upon the slightest flaw
to justify their exemplary punishment, "no traces of high treason could be found in what had been done." [3]

On the very day that this convention was dissolved the Sep. 28
squadron from Halifax, consisting of seven armed vessels, entered the bay, and at noon was anchored off Nantasket. But
few of the members had left for their homes ; and curiosity
was awakened to see with what reception the troops, which
had been embarked in the squadron, would meet. Their commander, Colonel Dalrymple, on reaching the town, expressed
great surprise "that no quarters had been prepared ; " but the
Council, which was convened, declared their intention to ad- Sep. 29.
here to the law. Nothing remained, therefore, but for the
colonel to act in obedience to his instructions ; and he did so.

[1] Bernard to Hillsborough, Sept.
27, 1768 ; Hutchinson to Whateley,
Oct. 4, 1768 ; A. Eliot to T. Hollis,
Sept. 27, 1768 ; Bancroft, vi. 204,
205.
[2] Letter to De Berdt, Sept. 27,

1768, in Boston Gazette for Sept. 26
and Oct. 10, 1768, and Postscript to
Boston News Letter for Oct. 13,
1768.
[3] Cavendish Debates, i. 196 ; Hutchinson, iii. 212 ; Bancroft, vi. 206.

The governor, anticipating resistance, had slipped into the country; and the colonel was left to "take the whole upon himself."[1] The preparations for the landing were made with a view to prevent resistance; and the eight ships of war, which were in the harbor, including the Romney, with their tenders, were placed off the wharves, with cannon loaded and springs on their cables. Never before had the citizens of Massachusetts witnessed such a spectacle; and the indignation of all classes may be easily imagined. Yet no outcry was made; no resistance was shown. In perfect silence the crowd looked on as the fourteenth, and twenty-ninth, and part of the fifty-ninth regiments stepped on Long Wharf. The troops were all armed, and their bayonets were fixed; and in this warlike attitude they marched through the streets, with drums beating and colors flying, until they reached the Common, where they halted.[2]

As the twenty-ninth regiment was provided with field equipage, they proceeded to encamp. For the rest there was no shelter. Application was accordingly made to the selectmen for quarters; but, in imitation of the Council, they chose to abide by the law. As the night was cold, however, compassion prevailed, and, at a meeting hastily called, the benumbed troops were allowed to shelter themselves in Faneuil Hall. "I have got possession of the School of Liberty, and thereby secured all their arms," was the triumphant exclamation of Dalrymple. "I will keep possession of this town, where faction seems to prevail beyond conception." Nor was it difficult to carry out this threat; for who was there to oppose? The people stood on the defensive, and were determined not to be the aggressors. Secure in their integrity, and with the law on their side, they left the blustering officer to follow his own bent.[3]

---

[1] Dalrymple to Hood, Oct. 4, 5, 1768.
[2] Hutchinson to ——, Oct. 4, 1768, and Hist. iii. 212; Holmes's Ann. ii.; Gordon's Am. Rev. i. 247; Grahame, ii. 437; J. Adams's Diary, in Works, ii. 213; Bancroft, vi. 207; Drake's Boston.
[3] Hutchinson, iii. 212; Bancroft, vi. 209.

The requisition for allowances to the troops was laid before CHAP. the Council. "We are ready," was the reply, "to comply on XI. our part with the act of Parliament, if the colonel will on his." 1768. But the colonel would make no concessions, and "took the Oct. 3. liberty" to inform them that "he would represent the affair to the general, and would also send an express to England, to give advice of their refusal." After further deliberation, the Oct. 5. Council consented to appoint a commissary, if that person would "take the risk of being paid by the province." In this they acted warily; for they well knew that the power of appropriating moneys belonged to the House; and the legislature had been dissolved.[1]

At length General Gage came personally to Boston, before the arrival of the Irish regiments, and demanded quarters for the regiments in the town. "The barracks are not yet filled," was the reply; "and we are under no obligations to make further provisions until the law has been complied with."[2] Attempts were then made by the governor and sheriff to take possession of the old manufactory house, which was in a ruinous condition; but the occupants had counselled with the best lawyer in the province, and, "encouraged by several of the first-rate sons of liberty," they refused to quit. A day or two after, the sheriff "entered the house by surprise;" but the clamor against him was so great that he was compelled to leave.[3] "I am at the end of my tether," said Bernard. "I can do no more." And the general was left to shift for himself.

The weather was daily increasing in severity; and the condition of the troops, even of those who had tents, was far from agreeable. The commanding officer, therefore, was "obliged to hire houses at very dear rates," and to procure supplies at the charge of the crown. All that he could do, under the

---

[1] Postscript to Boston News Letter for Oct. 6 and 13, 1768; Boston Gazette for Oct. 10, 1768; Hutchinson, iii. 213; Bancroft, vi. 210.

[2] Gage to Hood, Oct. 18, 1768.
[3] Narr. of Boston Massacre, 17; Hutchinson, iii. 215; Bancroft, vi. 210.

CHAP.
XI.
1768.

Oct. 27.

Oct. 28.

circumstances, was to threaten; and, as a measure of intimidation, the main guard was stationed directly opposite the State
House, which was occupied by the troops, and cannon were
pointed towards the rooms in which the legislature was accustomed to sit.[1] Still, every thing was quiet; and the Council,
as an act of justice to the province, prepared a memorial,
signed by fifteen out of nineteen, appealing to the general to
testify, from his own observation, that the town was in a peaceful state, and accusing the commissioners of giving rise to the
principal riot, and of unnecessarily withdrawing to the Castle,
to induce a belief that they needed protection. If, upon inquiry, he should find their statements to be true, and should be
satisfied that his majesty's service did not require the regiments
from Halifax to remain in the town, they suggested that it
would be a "great ease and satisfaction to the inhabitants" if
he would be pleased to "order them to Castle William or Point
Shirley, and to order to the place where they were first intended the two regiments from Ireland."[2] The reply of the general contained a partial acknowledgment of the justness of
these representations; yet, in compliance with the wishes of
Bernard, he was unwilling to remove the troops, and advised
barracks, &c., on Fort Hill, to command the town. Thus a
military despotism was established in the province. "These
red coats make a formidable appearance," said Hutchinson,
exultingly. But Bernard, more timid and irresolute in his
character, feared that "troops would not restore the authority
of government," and urged anew a forfeiture of the charter.

[1] Supp't to Mass. Gazette for Nov.
3, 1768; Narr. of Boston Massacre,
16, 17; Hutchinson, iii. 215; Bancroft, vi. 211.
[2] Address of Council, Dec. 27,
1768, in Letters, &c. 129, 134; Mass.
Gazette for Nov. 3, 1768; Boston Gazette for Oct. 31, 1768; Hutchinson,
iii. 215, 216.

CHAPTER XII.

MILITARY RULE. THE BOSTON MASSACRE.

BOSTON was a garrisoned town. The people were subjected
to the evil they dreaded. Their liberties were at the mercy
of a hireling soldiery. It was evident to all that it had been
resolved in England to enforce the power of Parliament at
the point of the sword, and that the menaces which had been
thrown out were not idle.[1] How soon these threats would
be executed depended upon the course of the officers of the
crown. Should they assume arrogant airs, or instigate the
soldiery to deeds of violence, the struggle would be precipitated. Should they adopt a more prudent course, it might be
delayed. That it must come before long few could doubt, for
the signs of the times were threatening and ominous. Every
one felt that the die was thrown, and that, if England did not
recede from the position she had assumed, a popular outbreak
would be the result. It is not in the nature of man to submit
with tameness to continued encroachments upon his real or conceived rights. He may forbear for a time; but when the yoke
presses too heavily, an effort will be made to throw it off; and
the success of that effort rests with God. The reverent spirit
with which the people of New England had been accustomed,
from the infancy of their settlements, to speak of the "mother

---

[1] "My daily reflections for two
years," writes John Adams, (Diary, in
Works, ii. 214,) "at the sight of those
soldiers before my door, were serious
enough. Their very appearance in
Boston was a strong proof to me that
the determination of Great Britain to
subjugate us was too deep and invet-
erate ever to be altered by us; for
every thing we could do was misrepresented, and nothing we could say
was credited."

country ; " the sincere attachment which they had always felt to the homes of their ancestors ; the conviction which was cherished that the land of their fathers was blessed above all others in the possession of a wise and beneficent constitution, — these might lead them to weigh well the consequences of a rupture with that country, and to deprecate every step tending to disunion. But if forced to resist by a course of legislation from which relief was sought in vain, they argued, and justly, that the responsibility must rest, not with them, but with those who sanctioned that course and persisted in adhering to it. The state papers of Massachusetts commemorate the wisdom of the men who framed them. Their tone is firm, yet prudent and respectful. They were not the productions of visionary enthusiasts, ignorant of the principles of natural law. They were the effusions of an ardent and enlightened patriotism. And the men who guided the destinies of the province — those, at least, upon whom the greatest reliance was placed — were clear-headed, far-seeing, deep-thinking men. They pondered well every word they sent forth to the world. Not a hasty sentence escaped from their pens. They knew what they were doing ; had counted the cost ; had looked into the future as far as was possible ; and had formed their conclusions after mature deliberation. Hence a resolute spirit breathes throughout their acts. They wrought for themselves, and they wrought for posterity.[1]

The soldiers who had been quartered in Boston soon fell in love with the country, and numbers deserted.[2] But there were still enough left to parade the streets, to the scandal of the town ;[3] and the officers of the customs, inspired by their pres-

---

[1] I speak here of state papers. In newspaper effusions greater license is taken ; and many of the pieces in the journals of the day were written under the impulse of glowing passions. Yet the prudent wrote more calmly, though even their productions were often spicy.

[2] Eliot to Hollis, Oct. 17, 1768.
[3] "Through the whole fall and winter," writes John Adams, (Diary, in Works, ii. 213,) "a regiment was exercised by Major Small, in Brattle Square, directly in front of my house. The spirit-stirring drum and the ear-piercing fife aroused me and my fam-

ence, ventured once more to gratify their spite by arresting, on
charges which were never established, a few who had formerly
resisted their authority.[1] To this exceptions were taken ; but
the people waited patiently for intelligence from abroad, and
were especially anxious to know the decision of the king and
of Parliament. By early advices they were informed that
Shelburne had been dismissed, that Pitt had resigned, that the
privy seal had been conferred upon the Earl of Bristol, and
that the Earl of Rochford, lately ambassador at Paris, had
become secretary of state.[2] But these changes, eventful as
they were, produced less sensation than the speech of the king
at the opening of Parliament, who railed at " the spirit of faction " which he had hoped was " well nigh extinguished," but
which had broken out " afresh in some of the colonies." Boston, in particular, appeared to be " in a state of disobedience
to all law and government," and had " proceeded to measures
subversive of the constitution, and attended with circumstances
that might manifest a disposition to throw off its dependence
on Great Britain." " With your concurrence and support," he
added, " I shall be able to defeat the mischievous designs of
those turbulent and seditious persons who, under false pretences,
have but too successfully deluded numbers of my subjects in
America, and whose practices, if suffered to prevail, cannot fail
to produce the most fatal consequences to my colonies immediately, and, in the end, to all the dominions of my crown."[3]

The debate which followed was warm and animated. Lord
Henly, the son of Lord Northington, in moving the address in
the House of Commons, charged the Bostonians with " defying

Nov. 8

---

ily early enough every morning, and
the indignation they excited, though
somewhat soothed, was not allayed
by the sweet songs, violins, and flutes
of the serenading Sons of Liberty
under my windows in the evening."
[1] Gage to Hillsborough, March 5,
1769. Hancock and Malcom were
among those who were arrested.

[2] Chatham Corresp. iii. 336–348 ;
Mass. Gazette for Jan. 16, 1769 ; Belsham's George III. i. 218 ; Lord Mahon's Hist. Eng. v. 200–204 ; Bancroft, vi. 214, 215.
[3] Debates in Parl. v. 11, 12 ; Mass.
Gazette for Jan. 16, 1769 ; Boston
Gazette for Jan. 16, 1769.

CHAP.
XII.
———
1768.

all legal authority;" and Stanley, in seconding his motion,
declared that the "difficulties in governing Massachusetts"
were "insurmountable, unless its charter and laws should be
so changed as to give the king the appointment of the Council,
and to the sheriffs the sole power of returning juries." Burke
replied, defending the colonies,[1] and insisting that the order
requiring the General Court to rescind their resolutions, under
a penalty, was absolutely illegal and unconstitutional; and in
this, surprising as it may seem, Grenville agreed with him, as
did also Wedderburne. Barrington "wished the stamp act
had never been passed;" yet he accused the Americans as
"traitors," and "worse than traitors, against the crown."
"The troops have been sent thither," he added, "to bring riot-
ers to justice." Rigby spoke in the same strain; but Beckford,
who represented the city of London, suggested that "it were
best to repeal the late act, and conciliate the colonies by moderation and kindness." At length Lord North, the organ of
the ministry, gave his opinion. "I am against repealing the
last act of Parliament," said he; "I will never think of repealing it until I see America prostrate at my feet."[2] This speech
decided the question. The address was carried in the Commons without a division; and the House of Lords readily
acquiesced.[3] "We shall always," was the language of this
address, "consider it as one of our most important duties to
maintain entire and inviolate the supreme authority of the

---

[1] Some writers have insinuated that
Burke's defence of America was insincere, and that, "while vague rhapso-
dies about liberty decorated his harangues, his object was to introduce
his party to power, and, by equivocal
concessions to the American people,
and flattering patronage of the American chieftains, to purchase a pacific
reconciliation capable of being corrupted afresh into dependence." Ann.
Review, and Grahame, ii. 439, note.

[2] On this debate see Lee's Lee,
261, 262; Cavendish Debates, i. 32–

43, 90, 91; Johnson to Pitkin, Nov.
18, 1768; Boston Gazette for Jan. 23,
1769; and comp. Hutchinson, iii. 219.

[3] For the address, see Debates in
Parl. v. 13–15. In a pamphlet entitled "The State of the Nation," &c.,
published in Oct. 1768, Grenville appears as the advocate of American
representation. "The number of
electors," said he, "is become too
small in proportion to the whole people, and the colonies ought to be allowed to send members to Parliament."

legislature of Great Britain over every part of the British CHAP.
empire." "We will, by every means in our power, cheerfully XII.
and zealously support your majesty in all such future measures 1768.
as shall be found requisite to enforce a due obedience to the
laws, restore order and good government where they have
been disturbed, and to establish the constitutional dependence
of the colonies of Great Britain, so essential to the interest
and prosperity of both."

Thus war against the colonies was virtually declared. "Depend upon it," said Hillsborough, "Parliament will not suffer
their authority to be trampled upon. We wish to avoid severities towards you; but if you refuse obedience to our laws, the
whole fleet and army of England shall enforce it." [1] In the
spirit of this threat, he communicated to the agents of the dif- Dec. 6.
ferent provinces the result of a council held by the cabinet.
"Administration," said he, "will enforce the authority of the
legislature of Great Britain over the colonies in the most
effectual manner, but with moderation and lenity." [2] De
Choiseul, the French minister at St. James's, foresaw the consequences which must spring from such conduct; and to the
question of Du Chatelet, "Can the ministry reduce the colonies?" he replied, "To the menace of rigor they will never
give way, except in appearance and for a time. The fire will
be but imperfectly extinguished unless other means than those
of force conciliate the interests of the metropolis and its colonies. The Americans will not lose out of their view their
rights and their privileges; and next to fanaticism for religion
the fanaticism for liberty is the most daring in its measures
and the most dangerous in its consequences." [3]

The question of taxation was of vital importance; and this
was the question principally in dispute. "No force on earth,"

[1] Johnson to the governor of Connecticut, Nov. 18, 1768; Bancroft, vi.
216.
[2] Johnson to the governor of Connecticut, Jan. 3, 1769; Bancroft, vi.
238.
[3] Choiseul to Du Chatelet, Nov. 22, 1768, quoted in Bancroft, vi. 236.

CHAP. wrote the governor of New Jersey, "is sufficient to make the
XII. assemblies acknowledge, by any act of theirs, that the Parlia-
1768. ment has a right to impose taxes on America;" and this declaration was every where echoed.[1] The papers relating to the
colonies, including the letters of Bernard and Gage and those
of the commissioners of the customs, were laid before Parlia-
Nov.28. ment towards the close of the year, and referred to a commit-
Dec. 10. tee to consider and report what measures should be adopted.
This subject was for several weeks under consideration ; and
the debates which ensued covered a wide field.[2]

It is not unworthy of notice here that, at the very time Parliament was censuring the colonies for their "riotous" behavior, England itself was agitated by a worse spirit. "Look
at home," wrote Franklin. "I have seen, within a year, riots
in the country about corn ; riots about elections ; riots about
workhouses ; riots of colliers ; riots of weavers ; riots of coal-
heavers ; riots of sawyers ; riots of Wilkesites ; riots of government chairmen ; riots of smugglers, in which custom house
officers and excisemen have been murdered, and the king's
armed vessels and troops fired at." [3] These disturbances, however, were at home ; those in the colonies were abroad ; and
distance so magnified them that they became gigantic. Hence
the ministry were deluded, and relied too confidently upon the
exaggerated statements of Bernard and Hutchinson. True,
some members of the House of Commons were better informed,
and viewed things more calmly. "The Americans," said Beckford, "believe there is a settled design in this country to rule
them with a military force." "Want of knowledge, as well as
a want of temper," added Lord Beauchamp, "has gradually led
us to the brink of a precipice, on which we look down with
horror." "My heart will bleed," said Phips, "for every drop

[1] W. Franklin to Hillsborough,   in the Boston News Letter for April
Nov. 22, 1768.   7, 1769, and Boston Gazette for April
[2] Bradford, i. 174. A list of these   3, 1769.
papers, over 60 in number, is given   [3] Works, iv. 293, 294.

of American blood that shall be shed, whilst their grievances CHAP.
are unredressed. I wish to see the Americans in our arms as XII.
friends, not to meet them as enemies." [1] But these prudent 1768.
counsels were uttered in vain ; for, when the House divided,
out of two hundred who were present, one hundred and twenty-
seven voted to confine the inquiry.

Hillsborough exulted at the victory thus gained. "The
matter," said he, "is now brought to a point. Parliament
must give up its authority over the colonies, or bring them to
effectual submission. Legislation and taxation will stand or
fall together. The notion of the Americans is a polytheism in
politics, absurd, fatal to the constitution, and never to be admitted." In conclusion, he proposed a series of resolutions
expressive of the sense of the legislature. "If this is not sufficient," he added, "the hand of power must be lifted up, and
the whole force of this country exerted to bring the colonies
into subjection." [2] Bedford seconded these resolutions, and
moved, in addition, an address to the king, to bring "to condign punishment the chief authors and instigators of the late
disorders, pursuant to the provisions of the statute of the 35th
of Henry VIII. ;" and both the resolutions and the address
were adopted, with no opposition except from Richmond and
Shelburne. [3]

In the following month the resolutions and the address came 1769.
before the Commons for discussion; and "the grand debate on Jan. 26.
the North American affairs commenced." [4] The speakers were
numerous, and were listened to with attention. The ministry
showed what they had done, and what they intended to do ;
"that, on the representation of Governor Bernard and the

[1] Bancroft, vi. 239, 240.
[2] Parl. Hist. Eng. xvi. 476, 477 ;
Johnson to the governor of Connecticut, Jan. 3, 1769 ; Bancroft, vi. 245,
246.
[3] Parl. Hist. Eng. xvi. 479, 480 ;
Bancroft, vi. 246.
[4] Debates in Parl. v. 21 ; Parl.

Hist. xvi. 485, &c. Bollan presented
a petition at this time against the
pending resolutions, a debate ensued
on the question of its reception, and
it was rejected by a vote of over two
to one. Debates, &c. ; Bradford, i.
175 ; Cavendish Debates, i. 185 ; Boston Gazette for April 17, 1768.

commissioners of the customs, they had ordered troops and ships to Boston, by whose assistance every thing was now quiet; that they intended to keep them there; that by not repealing the tax bills they would show to North America their intentions to be steadily and firmly their masters; that, by bringing over the culpable, they hoped to strike a greater terror than any trials could do in that country, where it would be impossible to get a jury not involved in the same guilt; and several law arguments to show that the act of 35 Henry VIII. subsisted in full force against the North Americans."[1] The opponents of the resolves attacked them with vigor. "No lawyer," said Dowdeswell, "will justify them; none but the House of Lords, who think only of their dignity, could have originated them." "God and nature oppose you," said Burke. Even Grenville scoffed at the plan as "the wisdom which fools put on." Barré declared, "The question is not of one refractory colony. The whole country is ripe for revolt. If we do not change our conduct towards her, America will be torn from our side. I repeat it, unless you repeal this law, you run the risk of losing America." And Pownall, the former governor of Massachusetts, from his acquaintance with the character and feelings of the people and the state and resources of the country, expressed his conviction that they could not be coerced into submission to the laws; that, though faithful and loyal, they might be exasperated beyond endurance; and that conciliatory measures would be far more effectual in securing their allegiance. "The Americans," said he, "do universally, invariably, and unalterably declare that they ought not to submit to any internal taxes imposed upon them by any legislature wherein they have not representatives of their own election. The people of that country and the king's troops are, as it were, set in array against each other. The sword, indeed, is not drawn; but the hand is upon it. The word for action

---

[1] Debates in Parl. v. 22.

is not, indeed, yet given; but mischief is on tiptoe, and the CHAP.
slightest circumstance would in a moment throw every thing XII.
into confusion and bloodshed. And if some mode of policy 1769.
does not interpose to remove this exertion of military power,
the union between Great Britain and North America is broken
forever, unless — what is worse — both are united in one
common ruin."[1] Eloquence, however, was of no avail. At
four in the morning, "the whole House in confusion, laughing, Jan. 27.
&c," the resolutions were adopted by nearly three votes to one,
and the address was carried by a decided majority.[2]

The soldiers quartered in Boston found nothing to do but
to insult defenceless females, and parade the streets with clubs
in their hands as if provoking a brawl.[3] But the spirit of the
people was unawed. It was well known that a design was on
foot to seize several of the foremost of the "Sons of Liberty,"
to be sent to England on a charge of treason. In the previous
fall word was given out that, on the arrival of the regiments 1768.
from Ireland, Cushing and sixteen others, who had been mem- Nov. 4.
bers of the convention, would be arrested;[4] and all through
the winter similar rumors were circulated.[5] "I have entertained the opinion for a long time," wrote Oliver,[6] that, if
there be no way to take off the original incendiaries, they will
still continue to instil their poison into the minds of the people
through the vehicle of the Boston Gazette." But whatever
apprehensions may have been awakened by these rumors, the
ferment was increased by the conduct of the governor, who, in

[1] Pownall's Speech of Feb. 1769, p. 8; Debates in Parl. v. 21–24; Grahame, ii. 439; Bradford, i. 176; Bancroft, vi. 253, 254.

[2] Boston News Letter for March 23 and April 20, 1769; Grahame, ii. 440; Lord Mahon's Hist. Eng. v. 241; Bancroft, vi. 255. For the resolves and address see Debates in Parl. v. 64–67. The address is given in the Mass. Gazette for April 13, 1769.

[3] See the indictments of the officers and soldiers by the justices of the peace for Suffolk, at their quarter session, and the grand jury; and comp. Bradford, i. 178, and note.

[4] Francès to Choiseul, Nov. 4, 1768, in Bancroft, vi. 230.

[5] See Hood to Stephens, Dec. 12, 1768, in Letters, &c. 113, and comp. S. Adams, in Boston Gazette for Dec. 5, 12, and 19, 1768, under the signature of "Vindex."

[6] Letter of Feb. 13, 1769, in Representations, &c. 28.

CHAP.
XII.

1769.
Jan. 26.

conjunction with Hutchinson, as the season drew near for the choice of a new assembly, sought to prevent the election of councillors, and solicited their appointment by the ministry, furnishing for that purpose a list of persons favorable to government.[1] "There must be," said Hutchinson, "an abridgment of what are called English liberties." "If no measures are taken to secure the dependence of this people, or nothing more than some declaratory acts or resolves, it is all over with us. The friends of government will be utterly disheartened, and the friends of anarchy will be afraid of nothing, be it ever so extravagant."[2]

In accordance with these views, Bernard, and Hutchinson, and Oliver, in connection with the attorney general, busied themselves in seeking evidence against the leading patriots of the town, especially against Otis and Samuel Adams ; and affidavits were sworn to, and sent to England, attainting them of treason.[3] Proceedings were likewise instituted against Edes and Gill, the publishers of the Boston Gazette and the " trumpeters of sedition ; " and through them a blow was aimed at " all the chiefs of the faction " and " all the authors of numberless treasonable and seditious writings."[4] Already had Par-

Feb. 8.

liament requested the king to " make inquisition for treason in Boston, and to bring over the accused to England for trial ; "[5] and, thus strengthened, the enemies to colonial freedom were encouraged to persevere. De Grey and Dunning, the attor-

1768.
Nov. 25.

ney and solicitor general, had indeed given it as their opinion that the statute of the 35th of Henry VIII. was the only one by which criminals could be tried in England for offences committed in America ; but they declared at the same time that

[1] Bernard to Hillsborough, Jan. 26, and Feb. 4, 14, and 21, 1769 ; Hutchinson to Williams, Jan. 26, and to Jackson, Jan. 28, 1769 ; Oliver's Letter of Feb. 13, 1769, in Representations, &c. 29–32 ; Bancroft, vi. 249.

[2] Letter of Jan. 20, 1769, in Representations, &c. 16.

[3] Bernard to Hillsborough, Jan. 24, 1769 ; Bradford, i. 175 ; Bancroft, vi. 251.

[4] Bernard to Hillsborough, Jan. 25, 1769 ; Bancroft, vi. 251.

[5] Debates in Parl. v. 53, 67 ; Hutchinson, iii. 221 ; Grahame, ii. 440.

its provisions extended only to treason; and that there was CHAP.
no sufficient ground to fix the charge of high treason upon any XII.
persons named in the papers laid before them.[1] To such a 1769.
decision Hillsborough and his associates were unwilling to submit; and, determined to do all in their power to enforce the
measures which they had long advocated, they clamored for
judicial victims, and denounced the charter as encouraging
sedition.

The public despatches, which informed the province of the
action of Parliament and of the resolves which had been
adopted, were accompanied by private letters from friends
to America, assuring the people that "they need not be afraid
of the statute of Henry VIII., which was held up *in terro-
rem* only, and which even the crown lawyers did not intend
should be carried into execution;" and the opinion was generally expressed that "no vigorous measures were intended;"
"lenient and healing measures" were said to be the plan;
and "it was agreed that the last act for duties on paper,
&c., would be repealed, if not that session, certainly in the
next."[2] These assurances were as inspiring to the "Sons of
Liberty" as they were disheartening to the servants of the
crown. And the events which followed convinced the former
that the intelligence they had received was not mere rumor;
for the plan of altering the charter was for the present laid

---

[1] Grey and Dunning to Hillsborough, Nov. 25, 1768; Andrews's Hist.
of the War, i. 97; Bancroft, vi. 233,
234. "Thus," says Lord Mahon,
"was it designed to draw forth the
mouldering edict of a tyrant from the
dust where it had long lain, and where
it ever deserved to lie, and to fling it,
— instead of bread, a stone, — not
merely at the guilty, but also at the
innocent, whom it equally despoiled of
their rightful native juries. Such a
proposal, made at such a time, to me
at least appears utterly unjustifiable."

[2] Hutchinson, iii. 222. "The ma-

jority in the House of Commons is so
great," writes a correspondent from
Manchester, March 8, in Boston News
Letter for May 18, 1769, "and so ve-
nal, that they vote any thing they are
directed; and all our hopes of redress
seem now to rest in the expectation
that they will go such lengths the
people will bear no longer. We hope
for, nay, we doubt not, the firmness
of the Americans; that they will
calmly, without the last rioting or
disobedience to the laws, abide by the
constitutional principles they have so
universally adopted."

CHAP.
XII.
1769.

April.

aside;[1] discretionary orders were transmitted to Gage to "send back to Halifax the two regiments which were brought from that station, and to restore the regular rotation by sending the two other regiments to Ireland;"[2] and Bernard received the king's orders to leave his government and return to England.[3] The tendency of these steps was to allay the fever into which the people had been thrown. But the soldiers were not immediately removed; and disturbances between them and citizens of Boston frequently occurred. The Sabbath, too, was invaded, and its stillness was broken by the noise of drums and fifes. And the sentinels, who were posted at the barracks and at the gates of the principal officers, endangered the peace of the town by challenging passers.[4]

For nearly a year Massachusetts had been without a legislature. At length, in April, writs were issued by the governor, in the name of the king, for a General Court to be convened on the last Wednesday in May, according to the charter. A large number of soldiers were still stationed in Boston, where the assembly was to meet, and several ships of war were lying in the harbor; and these circumstances confirmed the belief, which was generally entertained, that the troops had been quartered in the metropolis, not only to assist in the execution of the laws of Parliament, but to influence the election, and even the votes and proceedings of the General Court. But neither the town nor the assembly was intimidated; and their decision and firmness were never more marked than on this

[1] Hutchinson to Williams, Jan. 29, 1769.
[2] Hillsborough to Gage, March 24, 1769; Mass. Gazette for Jan. 9, 1769. "It is reported that some of the troops here have received marching orders from General Gage; some say they are destined for Newport and New York." Boston Post Boy for Jan. 2, 1769.
[3] Hutchinson, iii. 225. Bernard had recently had the dignity of bar-

onet bestowed on him; "a most ill-timed favor," says Lord Mahon, "when he had so grievously failed in gaining the affections or the confidence of any order or rank of men within his province." Hist. Eng. v. 241. Comp. Hutchinson, iii. 226; London Gazette for March 23, 1769; Mass. Gazette for June 15, 1769.
[4] Narr. of Boston Massacre, 17. Comp. Hutchinson, iii. 224.

trying occasion. The selectmen of Boston requested General Mackay, the commander of the troops, to have them removed from the town on the day of the election. This request he declined, on the plea that it exceeded his authority; but he gave strict orders for the men to remain in their barracks. After the election was over, the citizens instructed their repre- May 8. sentatives to maintain freedom of debate, which was esteemed an essential and a sacred privilege; to require the troops to be removed from the town, as their presence was "inconsistent with the spirit and principles of the British constitution;" to oppose the raising of money to pay for the support of the troops; and to make diligent inquiry respecting the letters of Governor Bernard to ministers in England, in which both the town and the province had been misrepresented.[1] Nor did Boston stand alone; for Salem, Marblehead, Cambridge, Roxbury, Braintree, and other towns gave similar instructions to their representatives; and Roxbury, in particular, recommended a correspondence between the House of Representatives and the assemblies of the other colonies.[2]

Before the court met the American question was again a subject of discussion in England; and Thomas Pownall, the April 26 predecessor of Bernard in the government of Massachusetts, to introduced a motion in the House of Commons for the repeal May 8. of the revenue acts. "There is a general dissatisfaction and uneasiness," said he, "as well here as in America, at our falling back into that controversy and contest between the govern-

---

[1] Boston News Letter for May 11, 1769; Boston Gazette for May 15, 1769; Bradford, i. 179, 180; Bancroft, vi. 284. Of the 508 votes cast in Boston at this election, Otis, Cushing, Samuel Adams, and Hancock received each more than 500; and of the 92 members of the old legislature who voted not to rescind the resolutions of the House 81 were returned. Of the 17 rescinders but 5 were returned. Salem, especially, condemned the conduct of its former representa-

tives, and in their stead substituted two of the "Sons of Liberty." See Boston News Letter for May 11, 1769, and comp. Snow's Hist. Boston, 277.

[2] Boston News Letter for May 11 and 25, and June 1, 1769; Mass. Gazette for June 8, 1769; Hutchinson, iii. 231; Bradford, i. 181; Bancroft, vi. 285. Of the "other towns," alluded to in the text, I find named Brookline, Spencer, Paxton, and Great Barrington.

CHAP. ment and the colonies which we were once so happily delivered
XII. from. All now are convinced that there are no means of
1769. deciding this controversy ; that there are no hopes of putting
an end to the contest. Every event that arises raises fresh
difficulties ; nothing but power can operate, and that can operate only to mischief. Power, thus used, will inflame and unite
the colonies as in one common cause ; and every further exertion of that power will only press the people closer together,
and render more intense and ardent that heat with which they
are already inflamed. Times and occasions we cannot make ;
when they arise, all we have to do is to profit by them. If,
now, I can show that this is the proper occasion, the very
crisis, in which government should interpose to extricate itself
with honor and safety, — perhaps the only occasion in which it
can interpose, — I shall not only vindicate myself for having
made this motion, but, if I can explain this truth with that
conviction with which it lies in my own breast, I shall be able
also to persuade the House to act." "There have been strange
violences and outrages in America ; the winds have beaten
hard ; the storm has been high. The state, like a ship, has
been driven into extreme danger, amidst shoals and breakers.
But the people are now in a state of submission ; they are in
suspense ; all is peace ; there is a lull in the storm. Now,
therefore, is the moment to refit your rigging ; to work out
the vessel from amidst these breakers, and to get her under
way in her old course ; then you may bring her to the harbor
you wish."[1]

The motion thus made was seconded by Trecothick and
Beckford, the former of whom recounted the steps which had
been taken in America to prevent the consumption of British,
and to promote domestic, manufactures ; but Lord North replied, "We will not consent to go into the question on account
of the combinations in America ; " and, under the plea that

[1] For the speech of Pownall, see Debates in Parl. v. 93–103.

" the late time of the sessions would not allow a matter of so CHAP.
much consequence to be properly agitated," the motion was laid XII.
over, and the acts continued in force.[1]   1769.

Thus, when the legislature of Massachusetts met, the griev- May 31.
ances which were complained of remained unredressed. The
first act of the representatives, before proceeding to organize
the House, was to draw up a protest, and appoint a committee
to prepare and bring in an address to the governor, remonstrating against the breach of their privileges, and assuring him
of their "firm resolution to promote the welfare of the subject
and support his majesty's authority; to make a thorough inquiry into the grievances of the people, and have them redressed;
to amend, strengthen, and preserve the laws of the land; to
reform illegal proceedings in administration, and support the
public liberty." "We have a right to expect," were the closing
words of this address, "that your excellency will, as his majesty's representative, give the necessary and effectual orders for
the removal of the forces, by sea and land, out of this port and
the gates of this city, during the session of this assembly."[2]

The reply of the governor was dry and laconic. "I have no
authority," were his words, "over his majesty's ships in this
port or his troops in this town; nor can I give any orders for
the removal of the same."[3]   But the House was not satisfied,
and criticised this message with ability and spirit. "We Jun. 13.
clearly hold," say they, "that the king's most excellent majesty,
to whom we have borne and ever shall bear true and faithful

[1] Johnson to Trumbull, April 26,
1769; Debates in Parl. v. 103; Boston News Letter for July 6, 1769;
Bancroft, vi. 273–278.
[2] Narr. of Boston Massacre, 17;
Boston Gazette for June 5, 1769;
Bradford's State Papers, 166–168;
Jour. H. of R. for 1769, 5–7; Hutchinson, iii. 233, 497, 498. The pream-
ble to the order of the House was as
follows: "Whereas the Great and
General Court or Assembly of this
province is here convened by his ma-

jesty's writ, issued by the governor
under the great seal of the province;
and whereas a standing army is now
posted in this metropolis, and a military guard is kept with cannon pointed at the very door of the State House,
where this assembly is held; ordered,"
&c. Otis, Sheafe, Hawley, Adams, and
Cushing were the members of the
committee.
[3] Bradford's State Papers, 168, and
Hist. i. 183; Jour. H. of R. for 1769,
p. 8.

allegiance, is the supreme executive power through all the parts of the British empire; and we are humbly of opinion that, within the limits of this colony and jurisdiction, your excellency is the king's lieutenant and commander-in-chief, in as full and ample manner as is the lord lieutenant of Ireland, or any other of his majesty's lieutenants, in the dominions to the realm of Great Britain appertaining." [1]

Nor did the struggle cease here; for, when the councillors were chosen, and the list was sent to the governor for approval, no less than eleven were peremptorily rejected. Two of this number — William Brattle and James Bowdoin, who had received a unanimous vote — were of the council of the last year; four — Otis, Bowers, Gerrish, and Saunders — had been "repeatedly disapproved;" and the remaining five — Hancock, Ward, Greenleaf, Henshaw, and Spooner — "had not been before elected." Such an exercise of the veto power, if sanctioned by the charter, was certainly impolitic, and, in the excited state of the public mind, could not but increase the odium which attached to the conduct of the governor. [2] Gage, in the mean time, who had been intrusted with discretionary authority to withdraw the forces posted in Boston, ordered two of the regiments to Halifax, and requested Governor Bernard's written opinion respecting the disposition which should be made of the rest. [3] This was throwing upon the shoulders of his excellency a responsibility he was unwilling to assume; and, after conferring with his special advisers, Hutchinson and Oliver, he reported it to be their decided opinion that "the

May 31.
June 1.

[1] Jour. H. of R. for 1769, 18, 19; Boston Gazette for June 19, 1769; Bradford's State Papers, 169–171; Mass. Gazette for June 15, 1769.

[2] Jour. H. of R. for 1769, 10; Boston Gazette for June 5, 1769; Hutchinson, iii. 234; Bradford, i. 185; Bancroft, vi. 286.

[3] Gage to Mackay, June 4, 1769; Mackay to Gage, June 12, 1769; Bancroft, vi. 286. According to Hutchinson, iii. 241, 242, one of these regiments had sailed, and the other was embarking, when the resolves of the House appeared in print, on the 3d of July; and General Mackay, alarmed at their tone, determined, upon consultation with Governor Bernard and Commodore Hood, to put a stop to the embarkation; and an express was sent to General Gage, at New York, for his directions.

removal of the troops at that time would have very dangerous CHAP.
consequences, and that it would be quite ruinous to the cause XII.
of the crown to draw them all out of the town." "Two regi- 1769.
ments, one in the town and the other at the Castle, might be
sufficient," he added ; and these at least should be left, if the
others were removed.[1]

As the House had been in session for more than two weeks Jun. 15
without attending to the ordinary business of voting salaries
and replenishing the treasury, the governor charged them with
wasting the public money by needless debate, and threatened,
unless they altered their course, to adjourn them to some other
place. " It is an indifferent thing to me," said he, " where the
General Court is held. I know that it is not necessarily confined to any town. That town seems to me to be the most
proper for it where the business can be most conveniently, easily,
and readily done. And as it is apparent from your resolutions
that you do not think this is a proper town for the court to sit
in, I shall remove it to Cambridge, against which place no
objection that I know of can be formed." [2]

To this message the House replied, and reaffirmed their Jun. 19.
former resolutions. " No time," said they, " can be better
employed than in the preservation of the rights derived from
the British constitution, and insisting upon points which, though
your excellency may consider them as non-essential, we esteem
its best bulwarks. No treasure can be better expended than
in securing that true old English liberty which gives a relish
to every other enjoyment." [3] Dissatisfied with this reply, the
governor renewed his demand ;[4] but the House was intracta- Jun. 21.

[1] Bernard to Gage, June 12, 19,
and 26, 1769 ; Gage to Hillsborough ;
Bancroft, vi. 286.

[2] Message of Bernard, in Jour. H.
of R. for 1769, 20, and Bradford's
State Papers, 171, 172 ; Narr. of Boston Massacre, 17. The court was
adjourned to Cambridge June 16.
Jour. H. of R. for 1769, 21.

[3] Jour. H. of R. for 1769, 23, 24 ;
Boston Gazette for June 26, 1769 ;
Bradford's State Papers, 172, 173.

[4] Message of Governor Bernard of
June 21, 1769, and Reply of House,
in Mass. Gazette for June 29, 1769 ;
Bradford's State Papers, 174, 175 ;
Jour. H. of R. for 1769, 27.

CHAP.
XII.

1769.
June 27
to 29.

ble ; and as his excellency had informed them that " his majesty had been pleased, by his sign manual, to signify his will and pleasure that he should repair to England to lay before him the state of the province," [1] by a unanimous vote, when one hundred and nine members were present, a petition to the king was draughted " to remove Sir Francis Bernard *forever* from this government," [2] and a series of pungent resolves was passed, expressive of the discontent of the people on account of the revenue acts, and censuring severely the misrepresentations of his excellency, in which he " discovered his enmity to the true spirit of the British constitution and to the liberties of the colonies," and " struck at the root of some of the most invaluable constitutional and charter rights of the province ; " " the perfidy of which," they added, " at the very time he professed himself a warm friend to the charter, is altogether unparalleled by any in his station, and ought never to be forgotten." [3]

No one can read the papers which proceeded from the House at this period without being struck with the contrast between them and the papers of former years. Their tone was gradually becoming more firm. Both branches of the court acted in harmony. The conservative party was in a decided minority. The influence of Hutchinson was no longer potent. And the encouragement which the patriots of Boston had received from

[1] Message of Bernard of June 28, 1769, in Jour. H. of R. for 1769, 38, 85–87; Mass. Gazette for June 29, 1769 ; Boston Gazette for Sept. 4, 1769 ; Bradford, State Papers, 175, 176 ; Hutchinson, iii. 238. The fact of the recall of Bernard was known a fortnight earlier. See Mass. Gazette for June 15, 1769.

[2] Petition of the House of June 27, 1769, in Jour. H. of R. for 1769, 36 ; Mass. Gazette for Sept. 7, 1769 ; Bradford's State Papers, 188–191 ; Hutchinson, iii. 238. This petition, or " remonstrance," was " a disagreeable thing to the ministry, and was received with coldness, like the petition

of the livery of London." Extract of letter from London, in Boston News Letter for Nov. 30, 1769. The year previous, i. e. June 30, 1768, a motion was made that a petition be prepared and sent to the king for the removal of Governor Bernard ; and a committee was appointed to draught such a petition, which was done. Jour. H. of R. for 1768, 94, 95.

[3] Resolves of the House of June 29, 1769, in Jour. H. of R. for 1769, 56–60 ; Boston News Letter for July 13, 1769 ; Boston Gazette for July 3 and 10, 1769 ; Bradford's State Papers, 176–180, and Hist. i. 188 et seq. ; Hutchinson, iii. App. O.

abroad, especially the concurrence in their views upon taxa- CHAP.
tion expressed by several of the leading statesmen of England, XII.
confirmed them in their opinion of the justness of their cause, 1769.
and inspired them with renewed zeal to resist the encroachments of arbitrary power. Yet, boldly and manfully as they
contended for principles, in no case were they transported
beyond the bounds of equitable moderation ; nor did they fail
to acknowledge, while fearlessly asserting and vindicating their
rights, their " firmest allegiance " to their " rightful sovereign,"
and their readiness " with their lives and fortunes to defend his
majesty's person, family, crown, and dignity." A people thus
loyal could neither be terrified by menaces nor seduced by flattery. To bend their opinions was found to be impossible.
They would listen to reason, but not submit to dictation.
They had planted themselves firmly on the impregnable position that taxation and representation are inseparably connected, and that, as the colonies were not represented in the Parliament of Great Britain, Parliament had no right to impose
taxes upon them. By this position they were determined to
abide. For it they were ready to hazard their all. Shall we
be slaves or freemen ? was the question to be decided. A
nation is forever enslaved when it has neither an assembly nor
any other political body to defend its rights against the encroachments of the governing power ; nor can any society
preserve for a long time the shadow of liberty when it has lost
the privilege of voting in the sanction and promulgation of its
fiscal laws.[1]

One more attempt was made by the governor to coerce the
House, which, like all others, proved ineffectual. Towards the
close of the session he laid before that body an account of the July 6
expenditures incurred by quartering his majesty's troops in and 12.

---

[1] Raynal, Hist. Philos. et Polit. la promulgation des loix fiscales. Une
des deux Indes, vii. 174. " Aucun nation est à jamais esclave, quand elle
société n'a conservé une ombre de li- n'a plus d'assemblée ni de corps qui
berté dès qu'une fois elle a perdu le puisse défendre ses droits contre les
privilege de voter dans la sanction et progrès de l'autorité qui la gouverne."

CHAP.
XII.

1769.
July 15.

July 15.

July 31.

Boston, that funds might be provided for discharging the same;[1] but the House, in their reply, iterated their views "of the sudden introduction of a fleet and army here; of the unparalleled methods used to procure this armament; and of the indefatigable pains of his excellency, and a few interested persons, to keep up a standing force in a time of profound peace, under the mere pretence of the necessity of such a force to aid the civil authority." "Your excellency must therefore excuse us," they added, "in this express declaration, that as we cannot, consistently with our honor or interest, and much less with the duty we owe our constituents, so we NEVER shall, make provision for the purposes you have mentioned."[2] To this message the governor could return but a menacing reply, threatening to report their conduct to the king; and the court was prorogued "to the usual time of its meeting for the winter session."[3]

Thus closed the administration of Francis Bernard. He had been governor of the province for nine years, and in that time had done more than all other governors combined to inflame the jealousy of the ministry, to irritate the people over whom he ruled, and to strengthen the spirit of discord and disunion. He embarked for England on the last day of July,[4] regretted "by none who were sincerely desirous of the freedom and welfare of the province, but followed by the honest indignation of every intelligent and upright patriot for the misrepresentations he had often made of the views and conduct of the oppressed citizens, and the arbitrary and unfeeling manner in which he had executed the obnoxious laws of the British ministry." His cen-

---

[1] Messages of Bernard of July 6 and 12, 1769, in Jour. H. of R. for 1769, 52, 68; Mass. Gazette for July 13, 1769; Bradford's State Papers, 183, 184, and Boston Gazette for July 17, 1769.

[2] Reply of the House of July 15, 1769, in Jour. H. of R. for 1769, 80–83; Mass. Gazette for July 20, 1769;

Bradford's State Papers, 184–187; Hutchinson, iii. 244–248.

[3] Speech of Governor Bernard of July 15, 1769, in Jour. H. of R. for 1769, 84; Mass. Gazette for July 20, 1769; Bradford's State Papers, 187, 188; Bradford's Hist. i. 194–197.

[4] Mass. Gazette for Aug. 3, 1769.

sures and reproaches, however, were no longer heeded ; on his CHAP.
arrival in England he was treated with but little respect ; and XII.
it was soon evident, even to the most violent advocates of the 1769.
taxation of the colonies, that to his rash and imprudent conduct most of the difficulties which had occurred should be
imputed.[1] The day of his departure was a day of public rejoicing in Boston. " The bells were rung, guns were fired
from Mr. Hancock's wharf, Liberty Tree was covered with
flags, and in the evening a great bonfire was made upon Fort
Hill." [2]

It has been justly remarked that, " had the successor of Governor Bernard been a sincere and firm friend to the rights of
the province, though, at the same time, duly disposed to maintain the prerogative of the king and the just authority of Parliament, — one who had been disposed to conciliate, rather
than to criminate, and to represent favorably, rather than to
exaggerate, the temper and conduct of the people, — harmony
would probably have been in a good degree restored to the
province, and the separation of the colonies from the parent
state delayed for many years." [3] But, unfortunately for England, Thomas Hutchinson, who succeeded to the chair as chief
magistrate, was not the man to meet such expectations. Some,
indeed, were disposed to predict favorably of his administration because he was a native of the province, acquainted with
the feelings of the people, and possessed of abilities which
might have been exercised effectually in their behalf. Besides,
he had been long in public business. For ten years he had

[1] Bradford, i. 199. Hutchinson, of course, takes the part of the governor, and attempts to palliate his miscon-duct, and screen him from the charge of wilfully infringing upon the liber-ties of the people. See Hist. iii. 249, 254. Lord Mahon, however, Hist. Eng. v. 235, while he admits him to have been a " man of ability and firm-ness," does not hesitate to charge him with being " wilful and quarrelsome," and admits that the conviction which prevailed among the people of his having written home " the most unfa-vorable statements of their motives and designs " was " certainly well founded." Comp. Bancroft, vi. 291.
[2] Hutchinson, iii. 254.
[3] Bradford, i. 200.

CHAP.
XII.

1749
to
1766.
1758.
June.
1760.
Sept.

represented the town of Boston, during three of which he was speaker of the House. For seventeen years he had been a member of the Council, and for a large portion of that time was judge of probate. Since 1758 he had been lieutenant governor; and since 1760 he had been chief justice. He had likewise been twice chosen colonial agent, though he never visited England in that capacity. He had therefore had " sufficient opportunity to acquaint himself with the constitution and public affairs of the province ; " [1] and, taking the chair with such antecedents, he might have filled it with honor to himself and with credit to his country, had it not been for his avarice and his confirmed duplicity. That he had some good qualities no one can question. In cases where his own interests were not immediately involved, he had acted under the impulse of a genuine patriotism. As a commissioner in adjusting disputed boundaries, he had distinguished himself by his zeal, his prudence, and his integrity. And in the capacity of judge, " though he decided political questions with the subserviency of a courtier, yet, in approving wills, he was considerate towards the orphan and the widow ; and he heard private suits with unblemished integrity." [2] But he lived in a peculiar age and country. He could not at once be an Englishman and an American ; for between the two nations the differences of opinion, which had sprung up and increased, were such that no one could expect to please both parties. If he sided with

[1] Hutchinson's Hist. iii. 75, note, and 256 ; Bancroft, vi. 303, 304.

[2] Bancroft, vi. 304. "That Hutchinson was amiable and exemplary in some respects, and very unamiable and unexemplary in others, is a certain truth ; otherwise he never would have retained so much popularity on the one hand, nor made so pernicious a use of it on the other. His behavior in several important departments was with ability and integrity, in cases which did not affect his political system ; but he bent all his offices to that. Had

he continued steadfast to those principles which in his former life he professed, and which alone had procured him the confidence of the people, he would have lived and died respected and beloved, and have done honor to his native country. But by renouncing those principles and that conduct which had made him and all his ancestors respectable, his character is now censured by all America," &c. Almon's Remembrancer for 1775, 25, 26.

England, he must expect to incur the enmity of America. If he sided with America, he must expect to incur the enmity of England. He could not serve both God and Mammon; and he chose the latter, as more conducive, in his estimation, to his worldly advancement, and as more in accordance with his natural temperament.

Yet his professions of regard for the liberties of America were often obtrusive; and while, at one moment, he penned despatches rivalling in fervor the speeches of Otis, at the next he was careful to take back all by secretly informing particular friends that nothing was meant by these effusions — that they were chiefly designed for political effect. From his manuscript correspondence, which gives the best clew to his character, it would not be difficult to quote many passages in proof of his duplicity.[1] Favorable letters, addressed to persons of influence in England, were written, and sent round to be read in the province; but none of them reached the other side of the water. He repudiated in Boston the idea that he sanctioned the conduct of Bernard; yet in his first message to the colonial office he was careful to say, "I have lived in perfect harmony" with his excellency.[2] To the friends of America he artfully insinuated that they were deceived in their opinion of the colonists — that they were unworthy of the favor with which they were treated. The abettors of despotism he was ready to encourage, by assuring them that their measures were necessary and just.[3] Yet all this time he was exceedingly anxious to conceal the fact that he was laboring to subvert the liberties of his country. "Keep secret every thing I write," was his language to one; and to another his words were, "Suffer no parts of my letters to transpire."[4] To such a man

[1] This correspondence, in three folio volumes, is preserved at the State House, among the archives in the office of the secretary of state.

[2] Cooper to Thomas Pownall, Sept. 8, 1769; Hutchinson to John Pownall, July 25, 1769; Bancroft, vi. 305.

[3] See his MS. Corresp., especially his letters to Bollan, to Jackson, to Pownall, and others, and his letter to Franklin of July 29, 1769.

[4] Hutchinson to Whateley, Oct. 20,

CHAP. was the government of Massachusetts intrusted.   Is it surpris-
XII. ing that his conduct should have met its reward?   He sowed
1769. the wind, and reaped the whirlwind.   Making every allowance for the virtues he possessed, his faults were so glaring as
to more than balance them.   He was the Harpagon of America ; and, like Judas of old, who betrayed his master, he betrayed his country for paltry gain.[1]

Before the recall of Governor Bernard the circular letter
of the Earl of Hillsborough arrived, acquainting the colonies
that " it was the intention of his majesty's ministers to propose,
in the next session of Parliament, taking off the duties upon
glass, paper, and colors, on consideration of such duties having
been laid contrary to the true principles of commerce, and assuring them that at no time had they entertained any design
to propose to Parliament to lay any further taxes on America
for the purpose of raising a revenue."[2]   This letter, however,
July 26. did not satisfy the merchants of Boston ; for they argued, and
justly, that if the tax on glass and paper was " contrary to the
true principles of commerce," the tax on tea must be equally
so.   Hence they voted unanimously that this repeal was a
mere pretence, and that the duty on tea was retained to save
the " right " of taxing.   At once, therefore, they renewed the
obligation, formerly made, to import no more goods from Eng-

1769, to I. Mauduit, Oct. 27, 1769,
and to J. Pownall, July 27, 1770, and
Nov. 26, 1773.

[1] For a defence of the character
of Hutchinson, from the pen of Rev.
George E. Ellis, see the Christian Ex-
aminer for Nov. 1854, 403 et seq.

[2] Hillsborough to the Governor of
Connecticut, May 13, 1769, in Trumbull MSS. ii. 207 ; Grahame, ii. 451 ;
Belsham's George III. i. 246, 247 ;
Hutchinson, iii. 252.   " The whole legislature," wrote Hillsborough, " concur in the opinion adopted by his
majesty's servants, that no measures
ought to be taken which can in any
way derogate from the legislative au-

thority of Great Britain over the colonies.   But I can take upon me to
assure you, notwithstanding insinuations to the contrary from men of
factious and seditious views, that his
majesty's present administration have
at no time entertained a design to
propose to Parliament to lay any further taxes upon America for the purpose of raising a revenue; and it is at
present their intention, in the next
session of Parliament, to take off the
duties upon glass and colors, upon consideration of such duties being laid
contrary to the true principles of commerce."   See the reply of Pitkin, in
Trumbull MSS. ii. 233.

land, a few specified articles only excepted, unless the revenue CHAP.
laws should be fully repealed ; the inhabitants of the town XII.
were invited to an agreement to purchase nothing from those 1769.
who violated this engagement; the names of recusant importers were to be published ; and a committee was appointed
to consider the acts of trade, and to prepare a statement
of the embarrassments to which commerce was subjected
thereby.[1]

In accordance with these proceedings, the first step taken
was to publish in the newspapers the names of those who per- Aug.11.
sisted in importing goods contrary to agreement, " that there
might be the concurrence of every person upon the continent in
rendering their base and dangerous designs abortive ; "[2] and,
shortly after, two of the principal merchants, whose ship had Aug.23.
recently arrived, were waited upon by the committee, and compelled to subscribe an engagement to sell none of their goods
until the time fixed upon for non-importation had expired.[3]
Factors, to whom goods had been consigned, were likewise
compelled to reship them to their principals in England. And
there was a general determination that the agreement should
be complied with, and that those who were refractory should
be dealt with summarily to reduce them to obedience.[4]

The son of Bernard and two sons of Hutchinson were
among the few who refused to submit to these measures ; and,
at a public meeting in Faneuil Hall, Hancock proposed to send Aug.
for the latter, to reprove them for their stubbornness — hint-
ing, what was true, that their father was himself " a partner
with them in their late extraordinary importations of tea."
But a more prudent course was adopted ; and, as the best
means of coercion, a paper was circulated from house to house,

[1] Mass. Gazette for July 27, 1769;
Boston Gazette for July 31, 1769;
Observ. on several Acts of Parl., pub.
by the Merchants of Boston, 1769;
Hutchinson, iii. 252, 253; Grahame,
ii. 452.

[2] Hutchinson, iii. 258.
[3] Boston News Letter for Aug. 31,
1769; Hutchinson, iii. 258.
[4] Hutchinson to Bernard, Oct. 19,
1769; Hutchinson's Hist. iii. 258.

CHAP. which nearly every one signed, agreeing not to purchase of
XII. them until they yielded.[1]

1769. The anniversary of the outbreak against the stamp act was
Aug.14. celebrated this year with great parade. At Dorchester, John
Adams "dined with three hundred and fifty Sons of Liberty at
Robinson's, the sign of the Liberty Tree." Two tables were
"laid in the open field, by the barn, with between three and
four hundred plates, and an awning of sailcloth over head;"
and, though the rain poured without, which made "some abatement of their pleasures," the day was for the most part agreeably spent. "Mr. Dickinson, the Farmer's brother, and Mr.
Reed, the secretary of New Jersey," were there, as was also
Balch, the wit of the province, who diverted the audience with
his wonderful mimicry. The "Liberty Song" was sung as a
duet; and the whole company joined in the chorus. The
toasts which were drunk were appropriate and spirited; and
"strong halters, firm blocks, and sharp axes, to such as deserve
either," were the words of the forty-fifth. In the afternoon,
between four and five, the company broke up; the "carriages
were got ready," and a procession of a mile and a half in
length was formed, which entered the town before dark,
marched round the State House, and then dispersed. "Otis
and Samuel Adams," wrote the kinsman of the latter, "are
politic in promoting these festivals; for they tinge the minds
of the people, they impregnate them with the sentiments of
liberty; they render the people fond of their leaders in the
cause, and averse and bitter against all opposers." "To the
honor of the Sons," he adds, "I did not see one person intox-
icated, or near it." [2]

Copies of letters from public officers to the ministry, taken
by Beckford, had been published in Boston.[3] Otis was cen-

---

[1] Boston Gazette for Aug. 14 and
Sept. 4, 1769; Hutchinson to Bernard, Aug. 8, 1769.
[2] John Adams's Diary, in Works,

ii. 218; Boston Gazette for Aug. 21,
1769; Bancroft, vi. 309.
[3] Hutchinson to Mauduit, April 16,
1769. Authentic copies of letters,

sured in these letters as a "demagogue;" and, as the warmth CHAP. of his zeal in the cause of liberty had sensibly wrought upon XII. his susceptible nerves, he was nearly beside himself with anger. 1769. In this sad condition he provoked an affray with Robinson, Sept. 5. one of the revenue officers, at the British Coffee House, on King, now State, Street, and was severely wounded by a blow on the head. The sympathy that was felt for him, and the odium with which the conduct of the officers was viewed, tinged this transaction with a tragical hue, and quarrels between the people and the officers increased.[1] The merchants of Boston were likewise again aroused to action by letters from New York, inviting them to extend indefinitely the non-importation agreement; and, by the influence of Molineux, Samuel Oct. 17. Adams, and William Cooper, they were readily induced to comply with this request.[2] The next day the town published Oct. 18 its "Appeal to the World," or "vindication from the aspersions" of Bernard and others.[3] The tone of this appeal was fearless, yet candid; but Hutchinson, who felt that his own

memorials, &c., written by Bernard, Hood, and the commissioners to the ministry, were transmitted to the selectmen of Boston by Bollan, and read at a town meeting, Oct. 4. Boston News Letter for Oct. 5, 1769.

[1] Mass. Gazette for Sept. 7, 11, and 14, 1769; Boston Gazette for Sept. 11 and 18, 1769; Boston News Letter for Sept. 21, 1769; Tudor's Life of Otis, 362; Snow's Hist. of Boston, 277; Bancroft, vi. 310. Otis sued Robinson for the injuries he had received, and obtained a verdict for £2000 damages; but on receiving a suitable apology from the defendant, he remitted the fine. That nervous irritability, which ended in insanity, was at this time fast increasing upon the once noble patriot. "Otis," writes John Adams, Diary, in Works, ii. 226, 227, "is in confusion yet; he loses himself; he rambles and wanders like a ship without a helm. . . . I fear, I tremble, I mourn for the man

and for his country; many others mourn over him with tears in their eyes."

[2] Hutchinson to ——, Oct. 17, 1769; Dalrymple to Gage, Oct. 22, 1769; Bancroft, vi. 311.

[3] The title of this document was, "An Appeal to the World, or a Vindication of the Town of Boston from many False and Malicious Aspersions contained in certain Letters and Memorials written by Governor Bernard, General Gage, Commodore Hood, the Commissioners of the American Board of Customs, and others, and by them respectively transmitted to the British Ministry. Published by Order of the Town. Printed and sold by Edes and Gill, in Queen Street, Boston, 1769," pp. 34. This appeal was most probably written by Samuel Adams, as large fragments of the draught in his handwriting are still in existence. Comp. Boston News Letter for Oct. 26, 1769, and Boston Gazette for Oct. 30, 1769.

conduct was rebuked in it, endeavored to wipe off the unfavorable impressions it might produce in England by renewing his charges against the people ; and, by secret despatches, he sent word to Grenville, to Jenkinson, and to Hillsborough that " all would be set right if Parliament, within the first week of its session, would change the municipal government of Boston, incapacitate its patriots to hold any public office, and restore the vigor of authority by decisive action." [1] At the same time, to prepare for the inaction of Parliament, he sent orders for a large supply of teas for the shop of his sons, and instructed his correspondents how to forward them so as to elude the vigilance of the committees of Boston. [2]

Hitherto the conduct of the people had been decorous. But, considering the provocations they were constantly receiving, not only from the soldiers, but from refractory merchants and headstrong loyalists, they should not be too sharply censured if, in a few cases, they departed from their usual course, and expressed their feelings by peculiar and decisive marks of displeasure. One such instance occurred at this time, when a " great number of people," a " little after sunset," seized " an informer against the breaches of the acts of trade," and, having stripped him of a " great part of his clothing," and " tarred and feathered him upon his naked body," " carted him about the town, requiring the inhabitants to place lights in their windows, and terrifying them with confused noise, tumult, and uproar." [3] Mein, a printer, whose publications had given offence, was likewise assaulted on King Street, and in the scuffle which ensued pistols were fired. For protection he fled to the main guard ; but the people followed, and insisted upon

Oct. 28.

---

[1] Hutchinson to Bernard, Oct. 19, to Whateley, Oct. 20, and to Pownall, Oct. 23, 1769; Grenville Corresp. iv. 486; Bancroft, vi. 313.

[2] Hutchinson to W. Palmer, Oct. 5 and 24, 1769.

[3] Proclamation of Hutchinson, of Oct. 30, in Mass. Gazette for Nov. 2, 1769; Dalrymple to Gage, Oct. 29, 1769; Hutchinson to Bernard, Oct. 30, and to Hillsborough, Oct. 31, 1769; Boston Gazette for Nov. 6, 1769.

his being delivered up to them. He finally escaped in disguise, CHAP.
and absconded from the town.[1] The soldiers, in the mean XII.
time, were "rendered desperate;" and a captain of the twenty- 1769.
ninth regiment said to his men, "If they touch you, run them
through the bodies."[2] For this speech he was indicted; and,
shortly after, the grand jury for the county of Suffolk found a Nov.
true bill against Gage and others for "slandering the town of
Boston."[3] The troops were rapidly becoming "the objects of
the contempt even of women and children;" and the position
in which they were placed, to persons of their temper, was
exceedingly humiliating.[4]

Hutchinson was appalled by the spirit of the people. To
his mind it was evident that, "without a further exertion of
power and authority from the kingdom, acts of Parliament for
raising money by taxes from the inhabitants of the colonies
could never be carried into execution." "The people," says
he, "were determined to resist them. There was no power,
legislative or executive, within the colonies, which would exert
itself in checking this resistance. A military force was of no
sort of use. Without the direction of a civil magistrate, it
remained perfectly inactive in all times of tumult and riot."[5]

Early in January Parliament met, and the American ques- 1770.
tion was a topic of debate. Chatham, who for more than two Jan. 9.
years had been unable to take part in the transaction of business,[6] had so far recovered as to venture to appear in the
House of Lords; and curiosity was excited to hear what he
would say. The king, in his speech, with the "misery of a

---

[1] Hutchinson, iii. 258–260. Comp.
Boston News Letter for Aug. 31,
1769, and Mass. Gazette for Sept. 7,
1769.
[2] Bancroft, vi. 314.
[3] Hutchinson, iii. 262, 263; Bancroft, vi. 314.
[4] S. Adams to De Berdt, Nov. 6,
1769; Hutchinson, iii. 263.
[5] Hist. iii. 263.
[6] He had recently effected a recon-

ciliation, which he had long anxiously
sought, with his brother-in-law, Lord
Temple, whom he had ever loved and
esteemed, but whose friendship, in a
moment of political elation, he had
unhappily lost. This event, in conjunction with others, is supposed to
have had a favorable influence upon
his health. Political Register for Nov.
25, 1768; Belsham's George III. i.
255; Lord Mahon's Hist. Eng. v. 244.

CHAP.
XII.

1770.

ruined grazier rather than with the dignity of an English sovereign," found himself obliged, before proceeding to other matters, to announce to the guardians of the public welfare that "the distemper among the HORNED CATTLE had lately broken out in the kingdom, notwithstanding every precaution that had been used for preventing the infection from foreign parts." This reference in itself appeared so ridiculous that it excited the merriment of the witlings of the court; and the whole session, in consequence, was named "THE HORNED CATTLE SESSION."[1] But it was perhaps well that there was something to excite good humor; for, when graver questions came to be discussed, there was need of such humor to temper the heated passions of the disputants.

The speech of Pitt, on the motion for an address to the king, was marked with his wonted intellectual vigor. To his enemies he seemed as one risen from the dead, armed with supernatural power to scatter confusion and dismay in their camp. His friends were reminded of the fable of the swan, whose latest notes are said to be the sweetest.[2] Every one hung on his lips with attention; and the House of Lords was hushed to silence. Commencing with a compliment to the Duke of Ancaster, the mover of the address, and acknowledging his personal obligations to the king, he proceeded to bewail the unsatisfactory state of foreign affairs, which he principally ascribed to the manner in which the treaty of Paris was concluded. But, important as were these matters, there were others of greater consequence which demanded attention — the measures which had led to the estrangement of the colo-

[1] Debates in Parl. v. 202; Lord Mahon's Hist. Eng. v. 246; Boston News Letter for March 22, 1770. The address of the Lords and Commons in reply may be seen in the News Letter for April 6, 1770.

[2] "With his health," says Belsham, George III. i. 255, "his intellectual faculties, so long clouded and op-

pressed, resumed their pristine force and vigor; and it is remarkable that, from this time to the termination of his life, they shone out with a brightness and lustre in no respect inferior to that which they displayed in the full meridian of his long and glorious career." See also Lord Mahon's Hist. Eng. v. 244.

onies. "I own," said he, "my natural partiality to America, and am inclined to make allowance for all excesses. The people of the colonies should be treated with tenderness. Their ebullitions of liberty, which have broken out upon the skin, are a sign, if not of perfect health, at least of a vigorous constitution, and must not be driven in too suddenly, lest they strike to the heart. With these views, I object to the word 'unwarrantable' in the address. It is passing sentence without hearing the cause or knowing the facts. What I have heard of the combinations in America, and of their success in supplying themselves with goods of their own manufacture, has indeed alarmed me for the commercial interests of the mother country; but I cannot conceive in what sense they can be called illegal, much less how a declaration of this house can remove the evil. They may be dangerous; and I could wish to have this word substituted for unwarrantable.

"The discontent of two millions of people deserves consideration, and its foundation should be removed. But I shall give my opinion more fully on this subject when authentic information shall be laid before the house. For the present I will only say that we should be cautious how we invade the liberties of any part of our fellow-subjects, however remote in situation or unable to make resistance. Liberty is a plant that deserves to be cherished. I love the tree, and wish well to its branches, wherever they are. Like the vine in the Scriptures, it has spread from east to west, has embraced whole nations with its branches, and sheltered them under its leaves. The Americans have purchased their liberty at a dear rate; since they quitted their native country, and went in search of freedom to a desert." [1]

---

[1] Debates in Parl. v. 127–131; Johnson to Trumbull, Jan. 10, 1770, in Bancroft, vi. 323; Lord Mahon's Hist. Eng. v. 246–248; Belsham's George III. i. 256. Bancroft gives the preference to the sketch of Johnson, and says, "The report of the American on America is the safest guide. The American understood the figure of the vine to refer to liberty in America. Chatham never meant to say it had embraced whole nations." I see

CHAP. Camden, who had once resisted oppressing the colonies, but
XII. who afterwards retracted, was aroused by this speech, and,
1770. rising from the woolsack, pledged himself thenceforth to take
a nobler course. " I have suffered myself too long," said he,
" to be trammelled by the ministers of his majesty. For some
time I have beheld with silent indignation their arbitrary
measures. I have often drooped and hung down my head in
council, and disapproved by my looks those steps which I
knew my avowed opposition could not prevent. I will do so
no longer, but openly and boldly speak my sentiments. I now
proclaim to the world that I entirely coincide in the opinion
expressed by my noble friend, whose presence reanimates us,
touching this illegal and unconstitutional vote." [1]

The debate in the House of Commons was equally spirited ;
and, on the article of the American affairs, the ministry were
sharply treated, and condemned for having done every thing
without success. In reality, it was said, they had done very
little — and that little injudiciously, weakly, and inconsistently.
Last year the king had declared America in actual rebellion.
The House had desired him to send for the rebels, to be tried
in England. The Americans had resolved this vote to be illegal and unconstitutional ; yet no notice had been taken of
their behavior. This had rendered the resolutions of Parliament ridiculous and contemptible. Barré, as usual, appeared
as the defender of the colonies. " The people of England,"
said he, "know, the people of Ireland know, and the American
people *feel*, that the iron hand of ministerial despotism is lifted
up against them ; but it is not less formidable against the
prince than against the people." " The trumpeters of sedition," was the reply of Lord North, " have produced the disaf-

no reason, however, to doubt the substantial correctness of the general reports. The American is as likely to
have Americanized the speech as the
Englishman to have Anglicized it.
[1] Debates in Parl. v. 141, 142;

Lord Mahon's Hist. Eng. v. 248.
This speech of Camden had immediate
reference to the vote incapacitating
Wilkes from holding a seat in the
House of Commons; but the pledge
was general.

fection. The drunken ragamuffins of a vociferous mob are CHAP.
exalted into equal importance with men of judgment, of mor- XII.
als, and of property. I can never acquiesce in the absurd 1770.
opinion that all men are equal. The contest in America,
which at first might have been easily ended, is now for no less
than sovereignty on one side and independence on the other." [1]

From the temper of both Houses it was evident that nothing
would be immediately done tending to the relief of the colonies. Changes in the ministry followed; the new tory party Jan. 22
took possession of the cabinet; difficulties increased; and ‑31.
political grievances remained unredressed. "The ship of
state," said Barré, "tossed on a stormy sea, is scudding under
a jury mast, and hangs out signals for pilots from the other
side." "The pilots on board," was the reply of Lord North,
"are capable of conducting her into port." How capable they
were time soon proved.

The legislature of Massachusetts was to meet in January; Jan. 10.
but just as the members were preparing for their journey to
the metropolis, Hutchinson prorogued the court to the middle
of March.[3] The reason assigned for this step was an arbitrary
instruction from the Earl of Hillsborough, the validity of which
Samuel Adams denied.[4] The non-importation agreement had
expired by limitation; and the sons of Hutchinson, "supposing Jan. 1.
they had a right to be repossessed of their goods and to dispose of them as they thought fit," broke the padlock which the
committee had placed on their warehouse, and secretly made
sales of the teas deposited there, which had advanced in value
one hundred per cent.[5] A meeting of merchants was imme- Jan. 16

---

[1] Debates in Parl. v. 203, 204;
Bancroft, vi. 322.

[2] Lord Mahon's Hist. Eng. v. 250
‑253; Bancroft, vi. 325–327.

[3] Hutchinson to Bernard, Jan. 10,
1770; Jour. H. of R. for 1770, 90.

[4] Hillsborough to Hutchinson, Nov.
4, 1769; Vindex, in Boston Gazette
for Jan. 8, 1770; Bancroft, vi. 329.

[5] Hutchinson's Hist. iii. 266, 267;

Lord North, in Cavendish Debates, i.
488. The sons of Hutchinson, with
Theophilus Lillie and others, entered
into an agreement in October, 1769,
to abide by the resolutions of the merchants, and to deliver up the tea they
had imported. Boston News Letter
for Oct. 5, 1769. See also ibid. for
Dec. 14, 1769, and Jan. 4, 1770, for
other names.

diately called, and the committee demanded the restoration of the goods; but compliance was refused. The whole body then went to Hutchinson's house, and repeated the demand; but, instead of opening his doors to them, a window was thrown up, at which his honor appeared, "warned them of the consequences of their illegal, riotous proceedings, and required them to disperse." [1] "We come," was the reply, "to treat with your sons, who have violated their contract, to which their honor was pledged." "A contract without a valuable consideration is not valid in law," was the rejoinder. Yet the chief magistrate was perplexed; and early the next day, after consulting with Phillips, the moderator of the meeting, he consented to return the goods which were unsold, and to make compensation for the rest. But no sooner had he entered into this agreement than he began to "repent," and, according to his own statement, "felt more trouble and distress from this error in his public trust than he had done from the loss and damage to his private fortune, when his house and great part of his property were destroyed." [2] The friends of Bernard censured him for his cowardice, said it "was as good a time as any to have called out the troops," and that it was best to "bring matters to extremities." Dalrymple was ready, and his men were armed; but no orders were given.

Yet the peace of the town was not restored; and meetings were held from day to day. Hutchinson felt the embarrassment of his position, and the Council was convened, and the members were urged to join in quieting the people; but they declined interfering. The justices were then called upon; but they, too, declined, saying that, "though these assemblies might be deemed unwarrantable, there were times when irregularities could not be restrained; and this was a time when the minds of the people were greatly agitated and disturbed from a sense

---

[1] Hutchinson to Hillsborough, Jan. 24, 1770, and Hist. iii. 267; Cooper to Pownall, Jan. 30, 1770; Boston   News Letter for Jan. 25, 1770.
[2] Hist. iii. 267.

of danger to their just rights and liberties." The sheriff was then sent to the adjourned meeting, which was in session, with a paper requiring them, in his majesty's name, to disperse; but, though the paper was read, the meeting unanimously voted that their assembly was warranted by law, and that they were determined "to keep consciences void of offence towards God and towards man." Hutchinson saw that the answer which was sent to him was in the handwriting of Hancock; and he preserved the autograph as evidence against him, should he ever be tried for treason.[1]

CHAP.
XII.
1770.
Jan. 23.

The next step of the meeting was to proscribe by name four persons who had begun to sell contrary to agreement; and they were declared enemies to their country, who should be treated as such, "by withholding, not only all commercial dealing, but every act and office of common civility."[2] To give greater effect to this proscription, posts were planted before the doors of the recusants, with a hand affixed pointing towards them in derision. One of these posts was placed before the door of Theophilus Lillie; and Richardson, a neighbor and an informer, endeavored to persuade some teamsters from the country, who were passing by, to break it down by driving against it the wheels of their carts. A crowd soon gathered; Richardson was chased home; his house was surrounded; and bricks and stones were thrown at the windows. To repel the assailants, a random shot was fired among them; and a lad of eleven or twelve years of age — the son of a poor German —

Feb. 22.

[1] Boston News Letter for Feb. 1, 1770; Hutchinson to Hillsborough, Feb. 28, 1770, and Hist. iii. 267, 268; Bancroft, vi. 331. "While these combinations are tolerated," wrote Hutchinson to Bernard, Feb. 28, 1770, "government can never be restored. They never will be suppressed by any power within themselves; for both the legislative and executive power join with the body of the people in the combination." Almon's Remembr. for 1775, 45.

[2] Hutchinson, iii. 268. On the 4th of October, 1769, at a town meeting, the names of several violators of the agreement were ordered to be entered on the records, "that posterity may know who those persons were that preferred their little private advantage to the common interests of all the colonies in a point of the greatest importance." Boston News Letter for Oct. 5, 1769.

CHAP. was mortally wounded. The excitement became intense ; and
XII. the murderer was seized and cast into prison.[1]

1770. The funeral of the lad was attended by "all the friends of
Feb. 26. liberty," and the coffin was covered with appropriate inscrip-
tions.[2] Five hundred children walked in couples in front of
the bier ; six of his playmates held the pall ; his relatives followed ; after them came thirteen hundred inhabitants on foot ;
and chaises and chariots closed the procession. A more imposing spectacle had seldom been witnessed ; and, as the long
cortege moved on from Liberty Tree to the "burying place,"
the impression which it made upon the minds of all was deep
and lasting. The first blood had been shed ; the first victim
had fallen. And the thoughtful asked, "Where will this
end?"

The murder of Snider — for such was the lad's name — was
Mar. 2. the prelude to scenes of greater violence ; and, early in March,
an affray occurred in which the soldiery were engaged. One
of their number, a private in the twenty-ninth regiment, went
to Gray's ropewalk, and demanded satisfaction for an insult
he had received, but was repulsed. He then challenged any
one to turn out and fight him ; his challenge was accepted, and
he was beaten. Several of his companions joined him, but were
driven off. A still larger number next entered the field, with
clubs and cutlasses ; but they, too, were defeated. The pro-
prietor of the works then interposed, and for that day further
disturbance was prevented.[3]

The defeated soldiers, feeling that the honor of their regiment was involved, nourished their anger through Saturday

[1] Hutchinson to Bernard, Feb. 28,
1770, to Hillsborough, Feb. 28, 1770,
and Hist. iii. 269 ; Snow's Hist. Boston, 278.

[2] On the foot of the coffin were the
words, " Latet anguis in herba ; " on
the sides, " Hæret lateri lethalis arun-
do ; " and on the head, " Innocentia
nusquam tuta." Snow's Boston, 279.

[3] Postscript to Boston News Letter
for March 8, 1770 ; Testimony of
Nicholas Ferriter, in Trial, &c. 23,
and of Ferriter, Richardson, Fisher,
and Hill, in Narr. of Boston Massacre, 39, 40. Gray's ropewalk was
near Green's barracks, in Atkinson
Street. Narr. Boston Massacre, 21,
note, ed. 1849.

and Sunday, and on Monday were ready to revenge the affront
they had received. One of their number was heard to say, some days before, "I will never miss an opportunity of firing
upon the inhabitants. I have wanted such an opportunity ever since I landed." [1] And there can be little doubt that his companions cherished the same feelings. For had they not all been subjected for a long time to derision and contempt? Had not their temper been soured by insults? And had not their passions been imbittered by strife? [2] True, such provocations, however great, could not justify them in assuming the offensive; nor did they warrant a resort to violence for redress. Yet the conduct of those who fanned the embers of strife, and who sought to provoke a quarrel with the troops, was certainly culpable. "The cause of liberty," says Dickinson, in one of his letters, "is a cause of too much dignity to be sullied by turbulence and tumult. It ought to be maintained in a manner suitable to her nature. Those who engage in it should breathe a sedate, yet fervent spirit, animating them to actions of prudence, justice, modesty, bravery, humanity, and magnanimity." [3] There are always some, however, over whom such counsels, though well meant, have very little influence; and a distinction should be made between the conduct of the prudent, who deprecate violence, and of the headstrong, who can brook no restraint. It is generally the latter who, in all revolutions, have precipitated the struggle; and to their rashness the effusion of blood must be attributed.

The narrative of the massacre of the fifth of March is a

[1] Testimony of Hemmingway, in Trial, &c. 22, ed. 1807.

[2] See Quincy's speech at their trial. "No room was left for cordiality and friendship. Discontent was seated on almost every brow. Instead of that hospitality that he thought himself entitled to, scorn, contempt, and silent murmurs were his reception. Almost every countenance lowered with a discontented gloom, and scarce an eye but flashed indignant fire." See also J. Adams's Diary, in Works, ii. 229. "Endeavors had been systematically pursued for many months, by certain busy characters, to excite quarrels, rencounters, and combats, single or compound, in the night, between the inhabitants of the lower class and the soldiers, and at all risks to enkindle an immortal hatred between them."

[3] Farmer's Letters.

melancholy proof of the evils which spring from the wild
turbulence of human passions. The soldiers had prepared
for an assault before the evening, by arming themselves
with bludgeons,[1] and warning their friends to tarry at home.[2]
How far the officers were aware of these proceedings it is
difficult to say. That they must have had some cognizance of
what was passing can hardly be doubted, unless they were
uncommonly devoid of intelligence. Nor do they seem to have
taken the necessary precautions to prevent bloodshed by con-
fining their men in the barracks at the earliest hour prescribed
by military rule. A laxness of discipline prevailed ; and the
troops were left to do much as they pleased.

During the day there had been a fall of snow ; but as night
drew on the weather cleared, and the moon, which was in its
first quarter, shone brightly upon the earth.[3] At an early
hour "clusters of the inhabitants were observed in different
quarters of the town," and "parties of soldiers were driving
about the streets, as if the one and the other had something
more than ordinary upon their minds."[4] A crowd of boys
gathered ; and the soldiers, as they hurried along, struck at
the inhabitants indiscriminately with sticks and cutlasses.[5] A
few minutes after nine o'clock, four young men came down
Cornhill towards Dock Square ;[6] and, in passing the narrow
alley leading to Murray's barracks,[7] they were attacked by a
soldier, who stood in the alley with a huge broadsword in his

[1] Deposition of John Fisher, in
Boston Narr. 40 ; S. Adams, in Boston Gazette for Dec. 31, 1770 ; Postscript to Boston News Letter for
March 8, 1770. " 'Tis said many of
the 29th regiment have armed themselves with bludgeons of about two
feet long, a round handle, and the body
of the club three square."
[2] S. Adams, in Boston Gazette for
Dec. 24, 1770 ; Testimony of Mary
Brailsford, Mary Thayer, Asa Cope-
land, and Matthew Adams, in Narr.
&c. 23, 42, 43, 46.

[3] R. T. Paine, at the trial of the
soldiers.
[4] Hutchinson, iii. 271.
[5] Narr. of Boston Massacre, and
Trial, &c., Testimony of Bass.
[6] Boston Evening Post for March
12, 1770. The names of these young
men were Edward Archbald, Francis
Archbald, William Merchant, and
John Leech.
[7] Known as Boylston's Alley.
Snow's Boston, 279.

hand, which he was brandishing and striking against the walls CHAP.
of the buildings. The youths returned the blow; and an XII.
Irishman, who was in company with the soldier, ran to the 1770.
barracks for assistance. Two men came, armed with shovel
and tongs; but they were driven back. A moment after, ten
or twelve soldiers, armed with clubs, cutlasses, and bayonets,
tumultuously rushed out, and a fray ensued, in which blows
were exchanged.[1] Presently a voice cried, "Town born, turn
out!" and the cry was repeated, until a large concourse filled
the streets.[2] The cry of "Fire!" was likewise raised, and the
bells were rung. More of "the town's people" came from
towards the market, and "there was a squabble and a noise
between them and the officers."[3] The tumult increased; and
from every quarter citizens hurried to the scene of strife.
The rage of the soldiers was fast becoming ungovernable;
and, as a lad came running along, with his hand to his head,
crying that "he was killed," one of the officers "damned him
for a little rascal," and a soldier hastened from the barrack
gate with his musket, and kneeling on one knee, with his face
towards the alley, shouted, "Damn your blood, I will make a
lane through you all." A lieutenant interposed in season to
prevent his firing, and pushed him towards the barrack; and
when he, or an associate, came forth and renewed his threats,
he was a second time driven back, and his musket was taken
from him.[4]

A few prominent citizens had by this time ventured into the
streets; and one of these requested the officers to confine the

[1] Testimony of Coburn, Polley, Atwood, and Archbald, in Narr. &c. 53–
55, 67.
[2] Testimony of Dr. Hirons, in Trial, &c. 53.
[3] Testimony of Dr. Hirons, in Trial, &c. 54.
[4] Testimony of Dr. Hirons, Trial,
&c. 54, and of Kirkwood, in Narr. &c.
56. Ensign Maul, according to the
testimony of Kirkwood, is said to

have encouraged the soldiers to attack
the people by shouting, "Turn out! and
I will stand by you. Kill them! stick
them! knock them down! Run your
bayonets through them!" There is,
however, some discrepancy in the testimony relative to his conduct, and I
have preferred not to bring the charge
directly against him. Comp. Narr.
&c. 56.

soldiers to the barracks. This they promised to do ; upon which the person who had made the request advised the people to disperse, and the cry was circulated, "Home! home!" But some shouted, "Hurrah for the main guard! there is the nest!" and thither they hastened.[1] The station of the main guard was at the head of King, now State, Street, opposite the door on the south side of the town house ; and, as the crowd dispersed, some ran up Cornhill, others up Crooked, now Wilson's, Lane, and others up Royal Exchange Lane, now Exchange Street.[2] A sentinel was stationed at the door of the Custom House, which was at the corner of Exchange Lane ; and, as the crowd drew near, the boys in the street pelted the sentinel with snowballs.[3] Immediately he loaded his musket, and, with bayonet fixed, pushed at the boys, and commanded them to stand off.[4] Captain Goldfinch passed by ; and a barber's lad shouted, "There goes a mean fellow, who has not paid my master for dressing his hair ; " upon which the sentinel left his post and struck the lad, who staggered, and cried from the pain of the blow.[5] Soon ten or twelve soldiers, armed with cutlasses, &c., came rushing through Silsby's Alley, or Crooked Lane, crying, "Where are your Sons of Liberty ? Where are the cowards ? Knock them down."[6] "Do you intend to murder the people ?" was asked by Atwood. "Yes, by God ! — root and branch," was the reply ; and they struck at him, and at other citizens, in their doorways, as they passed, compelling them to retire.[7] Nearly at the same time another party of soldiers, twelve or fifteen in number, came from the southward,

[1] Testimony of Palmes, in Narr. &c. 70, and of Mitchelson and Hirons, in Trial, &c. 48, 53, 54.
[2] Snow's Boston, 280.
[3] Testimony of Usher, in Narr. &c. 86.
[4] Testimony of Usher, in Narr. &c. 86.
[5] Testimony of Tyler and Le Bar-

on, in Narr. &c. 48, 50, and of Captain Goldfinch and Davis, in Trial, &c. 56.
[6] Testimony of Tyler, Le Baron, Broaders, and Drowne, in Narr. &c. 48, 50, 58, 83.
[7] Testimony of Atwood, in Narr. &c. 55.

into King Street, and passed through Cornhill towards Murray's barracks.[1]

Thirty or forty boys had by this time assembled in King Street; and, more from bravado than from malice, it would seem, they commenced annoying the sentinel, and dared him to fire. Provoked by their conduct, he knocked at the door of the custom house, and asked for assistance. The boys pressed round him, shouting, "Fire, and be damned! The lobster dares not fire."[2] "Stand off!" he cried; and a servant ran to the guard house, which was near by, saying, "They are killing the sentinel; turn out the guard."[3] At the command of Preston, seven or eight soldiers were detached, and, headed by a corporal, and followed by Preston, sword in hand, they were hastily marched and posted in a semicircle between the custom house door and the west corner of the building, where the sentry box stood.[4] No sooner were they thus placed than snowballs and even sticks were thrown from the crowd; and, as they pressed upon the soldiers, the latter pushed at them with their bayonets, and bade them "Stand off."[5] Finding the people still fractious, Captain Preston ordered his men to load and prime. They did so, and stood with their guns breast high and bayonets fixed. "You are not going to fire?" queried several bystanders. "By no means," was the reply, "unless I am compelled to." "For God's sake," said Knox, grasping at Preston's coat, "take your men back again; if they fire, your life must answer for the consequences." "I know what I am about," was the reply, while the agitation of his countenance belied his words.[6]

---

[1] Testimony of Appleton, in Narr. &c. 52.
[2] Testimony of Tant, Cain, Knox, Payne, and Morton, in Narr. &c. 63, 64, 73, 74, 78.
[3] Testimony of Cunningham, in Trial, &c. 65.
[4] Testimony of Polley, Hill, Cain, Cunningham, Condon, Wyat, Read, Goddard, and Whiston, in Narr. &c. 54, 62, 65, 66, 72, 77, 87, 89, and Wilkinson, in Trial, &c. 19.
[5] Testimony of Cain, Usher, Goddard, and Hickling, in Narr. &c. 65, 86–88, and of Dodge, in Trial, &c. 9.
[6] Testimony of Palmes, Wyat,

When the soldiers had loaded, a party of ten or twelve,
with sticks in their hands, gave three cheers, passed before
them, and struck at their muskets, saying, "You are cowardly
rascals for bringing arms against naked men. Lay aside your
guns, and we are ready for you." Others shouted, "Come on,
you rascals! you bloody backs! you lobster scoundrels! Fire,
if you dare! You dare not fire!"[1] The boys, who had sticks
in their hands, joined in the cry, and huzzaed, and whistled, and
pelted the soldiers with snowballs. At length a stick was
thrown, and at the same time one Burdick struck at the musket
of Montgomery. A voice cried, "Fire!" and, stepping a little
aside, he discharged his gun. The shot took effect; and Crispus Attucks, a negro, who had been active in the fray, fell.[2]
The order to "fire" was repeated; and a voice — said to have
been Preston's[3] — shouted, "Damn you, fire! be the consequence what it will."[4] "Don't fire," said Langford to Kilroi.
one of the soldiers who had been worsted in the affray at the
ropewalk; but he fired, and Samuel Gray fell.[5] Other guns

Knox, Simpson, and Hickling, in
Narr. &c. 71, 73, 81, 88, and of
Brewer and Simpson, in Trial, &c.
12, 20.

[1] Testimony of Tant and Greenwood, in Narr. &c. 64, 102, and of
Bridgham, in Trial, &c. 7. There is
a conflict of testimony on this point —
some swearing positively that there
was not the least provocation given to
Preston or his soldiers, the backs of
the people being towards them when
they were attacked. See Testimony
of Palmes, Frizel, &c.

[2] Testimony of Hinckley, in Narr.
&c. 67, and of Bailey, Palmes, Dan-
brooke, Bass, and Simpson, in Trial,
&c. 14, 16, 17, 20. Burdick, in Trial, &c. 24, swears that he personally
struck Montgomery, who was pushing
at him with his gun. Crispus Attucks
was the slave of William Brown, of
that part of Sutton which is now Mill-
bury. He was freed previous to 1770,

and came to Boston, and let himself
as a servant. Communication of
Charles H. Morse, Cambridgeport,
Mass., May 27, 1856.

[3] Testimony of Hobby, Hooton, and
Drowne, in Narr. &c. 63, 70, 84. Preston himself was often heard to assert,
at a later period, that he never ordered
the soldiers to fire, but, on the contrary, did all he could to prevent their
firing — even hazarding his own life in
so doing. There was a great uproar at
the time, so that it was difficult to tell
from whom the order came. Communication of Caleb Bates, of Hingham.

[4] Testimony of Wyat, Simpson,
Wilson, and Goddard, in Trial, &c.
72, 81, 82, 87, and of Wilkinson, in
Narr. &c. 19. Hinckley says this
voice came from an officer at a chamber window. Testimony, in Narr.
&c. 16.

[5] Boston Narr.

were discharged ; and one of the soldiers deliberately aimed CHAP
at a boy, who was running to get clear of the crowd.[1] In all, XII.
three persons were killed, and eight were wounded.[2] Some 1770.
say guns were fired from the custom house.[3]

King Street was speedily thronged with people, and more
than a thousand were gathered together.[4] The soldiers were
infuriated ; and, as some stooped to remove the dead, they prepared to fire again, but were checked by Preston.[5] The
twenty-ninth regiment turned out in a body, as if bent on a
further massacre ; and soldiers of the fourteenth, like dogs
eager for their prey, cried, "This is our time!"[6] Hutchinson,
in the mean time, was informed of what was passing ; and,
while the bells of all the churches were rung, and the town
drums were beaten, the cry was raised, "To arms — to arms!"
"Our hearts," says Warren, "beat to arms — almost resolved
by one stroke to avenge the death of our slaughtered brethren."[7] But calm and collected the patriots stood ; and the
advice which they gave was worthy the men. His honor was
requested to order the soldiers to withdraw to their barracks.
"It is not in my power," was his reply. "It lies with Colonel
Dalrymple, and not with me. I will send for him, however ;"
and he did so. But this did not satisfy ; and his attention
was called to the position of the soldiers, drawn up in platoons
ready to fire. After "much persuasion," he called for Colonel
Carr ; and the troops were ordered to shoulder their guns, and
were marched to the barracks.[8] The body of the people then

[1] Testimony of Bridgham, in Trial,
&c. 8.
[2] Testimony of Langford, in Trial,
&c. 10. Most of the witnesses who
testified at the trial say there were but
six or seven shots fired.
[3] Several affirmed that two or three
shots were fired from the windows of
the custom house. Testimony of Char-
lotte Bourgate, Gillam Bass, Benjamin
Frizel, Jeremiah Allen, George Costar,
and Samuel Drowne, in Narr. &c. 75,
76, 79, 80, 83, 84.

[4] Testimony of Palmes, in Narr
&c. 71.
[5] Preston's Narr.
[6] Testimony of Mary Gardner and
William Fallass, in Narr. &c. 96.
Comp. Boston Gazette for Dec. 31,
1770.
[7] Oration of March 5, 1772, in Lib.
Mass. Hist. Soc. ; Bancroft, vi. 340.
[8] Testimony of Palmes, Pierce, and
Dorr, in Narr. &c. 71, 93, 94 ; Hutchinson, iii. 273.

retired, leaving about a hundred to keep watch on the examination, which was immediately commenced, and continued until
after midnight.[1] As the result, a warrant was issued for the
arrest of Preston, and the soldiers whom he had called out
were committed to prison.[2]

Early the next morning the selectmen of the town and the
justices of the county waited upon Hutchinson at the council
chamber, and assured him that a meeting of the inhabitants
would shortly be held, and that nothing would satisfy them but
positive orders for the removal of the troops. Quincy, of
Braintree, especially warned him of the " terrible consequences " which a refusal might provoke ; but his honor replied, " I have no power to remove the troops, nor to direct
where they shall be placed." He consented, however, to send
for Dalrymple and Carr, the commanding officers, for their
advice ; and they attended the Council, where the question was
" largely discussed." [3]

An hour before noon the town meeting convened, and was
opened by prayer from the eloquent Cooper. A committee of
fifteen, with Samuel Adams at their head, was appointed to
proceed to the council chamber, and, in the name of the town,
demand the removal of the troops. "It is our unanimous
opinion " — such was their message — " that the inhabitants
and soldiery can no longer live together in safety ; that nothing can rationally be expected to restore peace, and prevent
blood and carnage, but the immediate removal of the troops;
and we most fervently pray that your power and influence may
be exerted for their instant removal." [4] The reply of Hutchinson, after some parley, was much as before. He expressed
regret at the " unhappy differences " which had arisen between

---

[1] Hutchinson to Gage, March 6,
and to Bernard, March 12, 1770;
Preston's Narr. ; Bancroft, vi. 341.
[2] Dalrymple's Narr. of the late
Transactions in Boston; Hutchinson,
iii. 273.

[3] Postscript to Mass. Gazette for
March 8, 1770; Hutchinson, iii. 273,
274.
[4] Boston News Letter for March
15, 1770.

"the inhabitants and the troops," but added, "I have consulted CHAP. with the commanding officers. They have their orders from XII. the general, at New York. It is not in my power to counter- 1770. mand those orders. The Council have desired the regiments to be removed; and Colonel Dalrymple has signified to me that the regiment of which he has the command shall, without delay, be placed in the barracks at the Castle, until he can send to the general and receive his orders for both regiments. The main guard, he also assures me, shall be removed; and the fourteenth regiment shall be laid under such restraint that all occasion of future disturbances may be prevented." [1]

The reply of his honor was brought before the adjourned meeting in the afternoon, which, from the greatness of the crowd, was held in the Old South Meeting House, instead of in Faneuil Hall. "Make way for the committee," was the shout of the multitude, that thronged the street from the State House to the church, as Samuel Adams and his associates made their appearance. They were ushered into the house, which was crowded in every part; their report was read; and dissatisfaction was painted on every face. A new committee was forthwith chosen, consisting of seven persons, who bore to the chief magistrate their final message. They found him in the council chamber, surrounded by the Council and by the highest officers of the army and of the navy. Samuel Adams acted as prolocutor, and, in the name of the town, renewed the demand for the removal of the troops — declaring that it was the irrevocable determination of the meeting, which consisted of nearly three thousand persons, to insist upon the withdrawal of all the forces, and that they would be satisfied with nothing short of an immediate compliance. "The troops are not subject to my authority; I have no power to remove them," was the reply. Adams, upon this, drew up to his full height; and, while his "frame trembled at the energy of his

[1] Boston News Letter for March 15, 1770.

CHAP. soul," [1] he stretched forth his hand, "as if upheld by the
XII.   strength of thousands," and in a dignified and resolute tone
1770. rejoined, "If you have power to remove one regiment, you
have power to remove both. It is at your peril, if you refuse.
The meeting is impatient. The country is in motion. Night
is approaching ; and your answer is expected." [2] The officers
were abashed in the presence of the patriot, and " the air was
filled with the breathings of compressed indignation." Yet
his gaze was steadfastly riveted upon the chief magistrate.
Hutchinson trembled, and his face grew pale. [3] His mind
reverted to events which had occurred on the same spot in
former days, when Andros, the arbitrary minion of James, was
seized and imprisoned, and the people, in their majesty, asserted their rights. [4] " It is not such a people as formerly pulled
down your house who conduct the present measures," was remarked by Tyler, one of the Council. " They are people of
the best characters among us — men of estates, men of religion.
Their plans are matured, and it is useless to resist them. The
people will come in from the neighboring towns ; and there
will be ten thousand men to effect the removal of the troops,
be the consequence what it may." [5]

Dalrymple, who stood by, repeated the assurance that it was
" impossible to go any further lengths in this matter," and that
the information which had been given of the intended rebellion
was a sufficient reason against the removal of his majesty's
forces. [6] But Gray remarked to the lieutenant governor, " You
have asked the advice of the Council ; they have given it
unanimously, and you are bound to conform to it." " Besides,"
added Irving, " if mischief should come by means of your not

[1] John Adams to Jedediah Morse, and to Judge Tudor. Gordon, Am. Rev. i. 192, 2d ed., says Adams was " trembling under a nervous complaint."

[2] Hutchinson to Bernard, March 18, 1770.

[3] S. Adams to James Warren, March 25, 1771.

[4] Hutchinson to Hillsborough, March 12, 1770.

[5] Gordon's Am. Rev. i. 192.

[6] Dalrymple's Narr. in Bancroft, vi. 346.

joining with us, the whole blame must fall upon you ; but if CHAP.
you join with us, and the commanding officer, after that, should XII.
refuse to remove the troops, the blame will then be at his 1770.
door." [1] For some time Hutchinson stood irresolute. Oliver,
at length, whispered in his ear, "You must either comply, or
determine to leave the province ; " prudence constrained him
to yield ; he signified his readiness to adopt the advice of the
Council, and Dalrymple assured him that his commands should
be obeyed. The committee, having received his decision, hastened to communicate it to the waiting assembly ; the people
listened with the highest satisfaction ; and the meeting broke
up, after taking the precaution to provide for the appointment
of a strong military watch until the regiments should leave
the town. [2]

The funeral of the slain was attended with great ceremony. Mar. 8.
Many of the shops in Boston were shut ; and the bells of that
town, and of Charlestown, Cambridge, and Roxbury were solemnly tolled. Attucks, the mulatto, and Caldwell, who was a
stranger, were borne from Faneuil Hall ; Maverick from the
house of his mother, in Union Street ; and Gray from his
brother's, in Royal Exchange Lane. The procession was of
great length ; and, after the four hearses had joined in King
Street, near the scene of the tragedy, it marched in columns
of six deep through the main street to the middle burial
ground, where the four victims were deposited in one grave.
The aggravated circumstances attending their death, the presence of the soldiers, who had not yet removed, and the distress
and sorrow of relatives and friends, — all conspired to invest
the scene with a peculiar solemnity. [3] It was a mournful day
to the people of Boston. They well knew that exaggerated
narratives of the affair would be published, and that no pains
would be spared to insist upon harsher measures, and to justify

[1] Oliver's Narr. in Bancroft, vi. 346.
[2] Boston Narr. ; Gordon's Am.
Rev. i. 192.

[3] Boston Post Boy for March 12,
1770 ; Boston Gazette for March 15,
1770.

CHAP. high-handed attempts to enslave them.   Yet, withal, there was
XII. a feeling in the breast of every one that, come what would, the
1770. province must on no account recede from its position.

Oct.   The trial of Preston was held in October ; every indulgence
was shown him by the citizens, and he was soon acquitted.[1]
Nov.27. The trial of the soldiers took place in November, and they
were ably defended by Josiah Quincy and John Adams. Six
of the accused were brought in " not guilty ; " two, Kilroi and
Montgomery, were declared " guilty of manslaughter," but,
praying the " benefit of clergy," they were " each of them burnt
in the hand, in open court, and discharged." [2] Four others,
who were charged by the grand jury with being present and
Dec. 12. abetting, were tried in December ; but the jury acquitted them
without leaving their seats.[3] For several years, on the anniversary of the massacre, orations were delivered by prominent
citizens ; but, after the war of the revolution had ended, the
observance ceased to engross attention, and the natal day of
the freedom of the country was preferred as the time for a
public address.[4]

In reviewing the circumstances attending this " massacre,"
it will, perhaps, be acknowledged by the candid and thoughtful
that there was blame on the part of the citizens of Boston as
well as on the part of the soldiers of the king. Both the
troops and the populace were highly excited. For a long time
there had been grudges and collisions between them. In more

[1] Bancroft, vi. 373 ; Snow's Boston,
284, 285.
[2] Trial, &c. 120 ; Hutchinson to
Bernard, Dec. 6 and 10, 1770. The
names of the prisoners were William
Weems, James Hartegan, William
M'Cauley, Hugh White, William
Warren, John Carroll, Matthew Kilroi, and Hugh Montgomery.
[3] Trial, &c. 120.   The names of
these four were Edward Manwaring,
John Munro, Hammond Green, and
Thomas Greenwood.

[4] For particulars relative to the ora-
tions on the 5th of March, see Loring's
Hundred Boston Orators. A number
of these orations are preserved in the
archives of the Mass. Hist. Soc., in the
Boston Athenæum, the Library of
Harvard College, and other public in-
stitutions.   The earliest orators were
Thomas Young, James Lovell, Joseph
Warren, Benjamin Church, and John
Hancock.

than one instance they had resorted to blows.   And the trage- CHAP.
dy of the fifth was the natural result.   On which side there XII.
was most blame it may be difficult to decide.   Among the 1770.
citizens the opinion prevailed that the soldiers could not fire
without the order of the civil magistrate ; and this, doubtless,
emboldened them to persist in their insults.   The soldiers,
governed by a different rule, looked to their own officers for
the word of command.   In the uproar which prevailed, it may
have been difficult to distinguish from what quarter the order
to fire came ; and, smarting under provocations and eager for
revenge, the soldiers may not have been over-scrupulous in
assuring themselves that they acted under proper authority,
and may have availed themselves of the confusion and uncertainty of the occasion to redress their own wrongs, trusting to
the influence of their superiors to clear them, should their conduct be blamed.   We should not too harshly judge Captain
Preston.   It is not certain that the order to fire proceeded
from him.   The evidence against him was not conclusive, and
he personally denied having given such orders.   The outbreak
was one which will ever be lamented.   Yet back of the incidents attending the tragedy there still lies the fact that the
presence of the soldiery was the cause of the strife ; and if
responsibility rests any where, it must rest upon those who sent
them here, and, more than all, upon those who clamored for
having them sent.   Hillsborough and Bernard were the culpable parties — the latter the more so, as it was at his instigation
that the troops were quartered in Boston ; and the former, as
the executive minister of the king, should be blamed for listening to his insidious proposals.

CHAPTER XIII.

PROGRESS OF THE STRUGGLE. COMMITTEES OF CORRESPONDENCE.

THE fifth of March, 1770, was doubly memorable in the annals of New England — memorable as the day of the "massacre" in Boston, and memorable as the day on which, in the Parliament of Great Britain, the "American question" was again under debate. A "petition from the merchants and traders of London trading to North America" was presented in the House of Commons, setting forth the "alarming state of suspense" into which commerce had fallen, and that this "interruption of trade," in the apprehension of the petitioners, was "principally owing to certain duties imposed on tea, paper, glass, and painters' colors imported into the colonies." They "therefore presumed to lay the distressed situation of this trade before the House, and, for the recovery of so important a branch of commerce, to pray for such relief as to the House shall seem meet." [1] Lord North, who had been recently appointed first lord of the treasury,[2] moved the reading of the act to which the petitioners referred ; and, after it had been read, he observed that the act thus petitioned against had been "the occasion of most dangerous, violent, and illegal combinations in America ;" yet as "many of the articles contained in the tax" it was "absurd to have imposed a duty upon," for "these commercial reasons" it was "necessary to move the repeal of such duty."

---

[1] Debates in Parl. v. 253.
[2] The resignation of the Duke of Grafton occurred January 28, 1770, and Lord North took his place. Belsham, i. 266.

"He had favored," he added, "with the rest of the ministry, at the end of the last sessions, the circular letter to the governors of the colonies, promising to repeal, on certain commercial principles, that part of the law which was repugnant to them; that he did this as a persuasive to bring them back to their duty, by a measure which would not at the same time relax the reins of government over them; and he could have wished to have repealed the whole, if it could have been done without giving up such absolute right. But he was sorry to say that the behavior of the Americans had by no means been such as to merit this favor, their resolutions being more violent this summer than ever; neither did he think a total repeal would by any means quell the troubles there; as experience had shown that to lay taxes when America was quiet, and repeal them when America was in flames, only added fresh claims to those people on every occasion; and now, as they totally denied the power of Great Britain to tax them, it became more absolutely necessary to compel the observance of the laws, to vindicate the rights of Parliament." On these grounds he would not move an absolute repeal of the act, but only that "leave be given to bring in a bill to repeal the tax act as far as related to the tax on paper, glass, and painters' colors."[1]

The speech of Pownall was an elaborate defence of the petition; and at its close he moved, as an amendment, a clause including tea with the articles enumerated.[2] "I do not," said he, "argue this repeal as asking a favor for the Americans; they do not now ask the repeal as a favor. Nor do I move in this matter as seeking redress of a grievance complained of by them; they have not complained to Parliament, nor do they come for redress. Although they feel deeply, they suffer and endure with a determined and alarming silence. They are

[1] Debates in Parl. v. 253–255; Lord Mahon's Hist. Eng. v. 265; Boston News Letter for April 26, 1770. The report of Johnson, the agent of Connecticut, is somewhat different from the above, and an abstract of the same is given in Bancroft, vi. 351, 352.

[2] Debates in Parl. v. 255–268; Boston News Letter for April 26, 1770.

CHAP. under no apprehension for their liberty. They remember that
XIII. it was planted under the auspicious genius of this constitution ;
1770. it hath taken root, and they have seen it grow up, under the
divine blessing, to a fair and blooming tree. And should any
severe strokes of fate again and again prune it down to the
bare stock, it would only strike the deeper and the stronger.
It would not, perhaps, rise in so straight and fair a form ; but
it would prove the more hardy and durable. They trust, therefore, to Providence ; nor will they complain."

Grenville followed ; and, after lauding the stamp act, his
own favorite measure, and censuring the subsequent policy of
the ministry, declared his intention to remain neutral in the
present controversy, and "not vote in the question."[1] Conway
expressed his "concurrence in repealing the whole of the present act ; "[2] and Sir William Meredith declared the tax "ought
to be repealed totally."[3] Barrington and Ellis opposed both
the amendment and the original motion ; but the uncompromising Barré "was for the whole repeal." The act was unjust in
every sense of the word, and as impolitic as unjust ; and too
soon the ministry could not retrace their steps, if they wished
to restore peace to the kingdom.[4] When the question was
taken, however, upon the amendment of Pownall, it was rejected by a vote of two hundred and four against one hundred and
forty-two ; and the repeal was lost, so far as the article of tea
was concerned, though carried on the other points.[5]

The General Court of Massachusetts had been prorogued
by Bernard to the tenth of January ; but before that day
arrived, a "further signification of the king's pleasure" was
received by Hutchinson, that the court "should be held at
Cambridge, unless the lieutenant governor had more weighty

[1] Debates in Parl. v. 268, 269 ;
Boston News Letter for April 26,
1770. Comp. Du Chatelet to Choiseul, Feb. 27, 1770, in Bancroft, vi.
353 ; Franklin's Works, vii. 466.
[2] Debates in Parl. v. 269.

[3] Debates in Parl. v. 269.
[4] Debates in Parl. v. 269. Comp.
Lord Mahon's Hist. Eng. v. 266, 267.
[5] Debates in Parl. v. 270 ; Boston
News Letter for April 26, 1770.

reasons for holding it at Boston ; " and, considering the " in- CHAP.
struction tantamount to a peremptory order," contrary to his XIII.
own judgment, as he afterwards affirmed,[1] he convened the 1770.
legislature at Cambridge.[2] This step was displeasing to the Mar. 15.
House ; and a remonstrance was prepared against the proroga- Mar. 16.
tion of the assembly by the " mandate " of the minister as " an
infraction of their essential rights as men and citizens, as well
as those derived from the British constitution and the charter
of the colony," and praying that the assembly should be adjourned " to its ancient place, the court house in Boston." [3]
But his honor, in reply, stood upon his reserved rights as commander-in-chief, and declared his determination not to depart
from his duty to the king.[4] For some days the controversy Mar. 16
was continued ; the Council joined with the House in petition- to 24.
ing for the removal of the court ; and the House, by a verbal
message, desired of his honor a copy of his instructions from
the king, and drew up a memorial, based upon the act of 10
William III., authorizing the General Court or Assembly to
be held " *at the town house in Boston,*" as a warrant for their
petition ; but all was to no purpose. Hutchinson was inflexible, and the session of the court was continued at Cambridge.
" We proceed to business under this grievance," the House
then resolved, " only from *absolute necessity* — hereby protesting against the illegality of holding the assembly as aforesaid,
and ordering this our protest to be entered on our journals, to
the end that the same may not be drawn into precedent at any
time hereafter." [5]

---

[1] Hutchinson to Gage, Feb. 25, 1770. Comp. the first draught of his letter to Hillsborough, of Feb. 28, 1770, in Almon's Remembrancer for 1775, 44.

[2] Hutchinson to Hillsborough, Feb. 28, 1770, and Hist. iii. 280, 281; Almon's Remembrancer for 1775, 44, 45.

[3] Jour. H. of R. for 1769–70, 91; Hutchinson, iii. 281.

[4] Jour. H. of R. for 1769–70, 92; Hutchinson, iii. 282.

[5] Jour. H. of R. for 1769–70, 92–103; Hutchinson, iii. 282, 283; Bradford, i. 212 ; Boston News Letter Extra for March 23, 1770, and News Letter for March 29, 1770. " The court," wrote Hutchinson, March 25, 1770, " has been sitting at Cambridge ever since the 15th, refusing to do any business, and urging me to re-

CHAP.   Under such duress, the temper of the House was by no
XIII.   means softened to a conciliatory tone. Yet one more attempt
1770.   was made in England in behalf of the colonies; and several
April 9. members of the House of Commons — Trecothick, Beckford,
Beauchamp, and Dowdeswell [1] — proposed the repeal of the
duty on tea. But the king, who was exceedingly jealous of
his prerogative, was indignant at this "debate in the teeth of
a standing order," and through his mouthpiece, Lord North,
declared that, though he wished to "conciliate the Americans,
and to restore harmony between the two countries," he would
"never be intimidated by the threats nor compelled by the
combinations of the colonies to make unreasonable or impolitic concessions." This decided the question; the matter was
passed over; and the next order of the day was called for by
a vote of eighty to fifty-two. [2]

It is not a little singular that, in the messages of Hutchinson
to the General Court, no notice was taken of the event which
had convulsed the province from one end to the other. To the
tragedy of the fifth of March he made no allusion. Yet minor
disturbances attracted his attention; and, as a "riotous trans-
April 7. action" had occurred in Gloucester, he "thought it proper to
communicate it to the House and to the Council, that, if any
act or order of the whole legislature should be judged necessary for strengthening or encouraging the executive powers of
government, there might be an opportunity for it." [3] For
more than a fortnight this communication remained unan-
Apr. 23. swered; then, in an address to his honor, the House assured

move them to Boston; but I shall not
do it. I hope no copy of my Lord
Hillsborough's letter to me on the
9th of December will be suffered to
be made public, nor of mine to his
lordship in answer; for I have followed your advice, and they *do not
know that I had any sort of* discretion left in the matter." Almon's Remembrancer for 1775, 41.
   [1] Conway, Dunning, and Sir George

Saville likewise took part in this debate in favor of America.
   [2] Debates in Parl. v. 305, 306;
Bancroft, vi. 360.
   [3] Jour. H. of R. for 1769–70, 139;
Boston News Letter for May 3, 1770;
Hutchinson, iii. 283. The "riotous
transaction" consisted in tarring and
feathering a custom house officer who
had given offence by his proceedings.

him of their "abhorrence of all disorderly and riotous pro- CHAP.
ceedings," and of their "disposition and duty to take the most XIII.
effectual measures to discountenance the same." But, while 1770.
complaints were made of "riots and tumults," it became them
to inquire into the "real causes" of such disturbances. "It
may justly," they added, "be said of the people of this province
that they seldom, if ever, have assembled in a tumultuous manner, unless they have been oppressed. It cannot be expected
that a people accustomed to the freedom of the English constitution will be patient under the hand of tyranny and arbitrary
power. They will discover their resentment in a manner
which will naturally displease their oppressors. And, in such
case, the severest laws and the most rigorous execution will be
to little or no purpose. The most effectual method to restore
tranquillity would be to remove their burdens, and to punish
all those who have been the procurers of their oppression."

They then reviewed more fully the subject of the message,
complained of the "enormities committed by the soldiery," and
closed with a protest against a military force posted among
the people without their consent, which, in their estimation,
was in itself "one of the greatest grievances, threatening the
total subversion of a free constitution — much more, if designed
to execute a system of corrupt and arbitrary power, and even
to exterminate the liberties of the country." "Surely, then,"
say they, "your honor cannot think this House can descend to
the consideration of matters comparatively trifling, while the
capital of the province has so lately been in a state of actual
imprisonment, and the government itself under duress."[1]

Three days after the General Court had sanctioned this Apr. 26
message, the news of the massacre in Boston having reached
England, Alderman Trecothick, in the House of Commons,
moved that an address be presented to the king for "copies of

---

[1] Jour. H. of R. for 1769–70, 178   App. P.; Boston News Letter for
–181; Hutchinson, iii. 283, 284, and   April 26, 1770.

CHAP.   all narratives of disputes or disturbances between his majesty's
XIII.   troops and the inhabitants of any of the colonies, since the
1770.   twenty-fourth of June last, which had been received by the
commissioners of the treasury or either of the secretaries of
state, with copies of all orders and instructions to the governors or other officers relative to such disputes." [1] The debate
which ensued was highly interesting. Even Grenville, who
spoke "exceedingly well," exclaimed, " God forbid we should
send soldiers to act without civil authority."   " The officers,"
said Barré, "agreed in sending the soldiers to the Castle ; and
what minister will dare send them back to Boston ? "   " Let us
have no more angry votes against the people of America," cried
Beauchamp.   And William Burke, in the same spirit, declared
that " the very idea of a military establishment in America "
was " wrong." [2]

May 8.   Early in the ensuing month the discussion was renewed ;
and Pownall introduced a motion, which he defended at length,
and which was seconded by Beckford, praying his majesty to
examine the commissions issued to officers in America, that
they might be amended in all cases in which they clashed or
interfered with each other, or contained any powers not warranted by the constitution.[3] This motion was debated by
Johnstone, Barrington, Beckford, Barré, Conway, and Sa-
May 9.   ville ; [4] and on the following day, on the motion of Burke,
who acted in thorough conjunction with Grenville, a series of
resolves, seventeen in number, was reported in the House, condemning the measures of the ministry, but carefully abstaining
from indicating the policy they should adopt ; [5] but these resolves, after considerable debate, were all negatived except the
first, declaring that, " in several of his majesty's colonies in

---

[1] Debates in Parl. v. 308.
[2] Boston Gazette for June 25,
1770 ; Bancroft, vi. 360, 361.
[3] Debates in Parl. v. 312–325 ;
Boston News Letter for July 12,
1770. Beckford died a few weeks

after this debate ; and thus the colonies lost one of their friends. Comp.
Lord Mahon's Hist. Eng. v. 273.
[4] Debates in Parl. v. 325–329.
[5] Johnson to Trumbull, May 21,
1770 ; Debates in Parl. v. 329–333.

North America, disorders had of late prevailed prejudicial to CHAP.
the trade and commerce of this kingdom, and destructive to XIII.
the peace and prosperity of the said colonies," which was "car- 1770.
ried by a majority of one hundred and ninety-seven to seventy-
nine." [1]

In the House of Lords, the "affairs of America" were called May 18.
up by the Duke of Richmond; and the resolves which had
been reported by Burke in the House of Commons were read.[2]
His grace then proceeded to charge on Lord Hillsborough the
disorders which had latterly occurred in America, and was
particularly severe upon his letter of September 8, 1768, directing some of the American governments to dissolve their
assemblies, which he characterized as an "ill-written, unconstitutional, official letter, wanting the weight and advice of Parliament, as well as the leniency of authority." [3]

This charge brought Hillsborough to his feet, who expressed
his surprise that his conduct should be thus questioned; yet,
as it ever had been, so it should be, his principle to attach himself to no particular party, but to pursue steadily those objects
which he thought were most conducive to the good of the constitution and the honor of the crown. The ground on which
he stood he knew was slippery; and hence he had always
sought to be circumspect. Yet, in relation to quartering the
troops in Boston, he acknowledged that he was the "culprit,"
nor did he attempt to defend the measure; and, to avoid the
effect of further debate, he moved an adjournment. "Adjourn!
adjourn!" was cried by his friends. But the Marquis of
Rockingham prevented it by rising; and Lord Temple, in
seconding his motion, took occasion to animadvert upon the
unwillingness of the administration to trust to the goodness
of their cause, and asked how the promises which had been
made relative to America had been complied with. "I must

[1] Debates in Parl. v. 336.   [3] Debates in Parl. v. 198; Supp't
[2] Debates in Parl. v. 196–198.   Boston News Letter for July 31, 1770.

CHAP.
XIII.

1770.

confess," said he, " that these promises have been performed in a most singular manner, and that the business of the government has been done in a style still more singular — a style which reminds me of the French gasconade, —

> 'The King of France, with forty thousand men,
> Marched up the hill, and so marched down again.' "

But the ministry was immovable. The weight of authority was on their side ; and the resolves were rejected by a large majority.[1]

By the terms of the charter, the General Court was to commence its session on the last Wednesday in May. The election of members, accordingly, soon followed the dissolution of the old court ; and in most of the towns the people were careful to return men favorable to the cause of liberty.[2] The town of
May 15. Boston, at the instance of Quincy, instructed its representatives to resist the " unwarrantable and arbitrary exactions made upon the people, from which, under God, nothing but stern virtue and inflexible fortitude could save them." " A series of occurrences," say they, " many recent events, and especially the late journals of the House of Lords, afford good reason to believe that a desperate plan of imperial despotism has been laid, and partly executed, for the extinction of all civil liberty. For years we have with sorrow beheld the approaching conflict. Every thing now conspires to prompt us to vigilance. And, as the exigencies of the times require, not only the refined abilities of true policy, but the more martial virtues, — conduct, valor, and intrepidity, — so, gentlemen, in giving you our suffrages at this election, we have devolved upon you a most

---

[1] Debates in Parl. v. 199–201 ; Supp't to Boston News Letter for July 26, 1770. Comp. Boston Gazette for Nov. 9, 1772.

[2] Not in all ; for, according to John Adams, Diary, in Works, ii. 263, the House, in the sessions of 1770, was " very near equally divided." Yet the opponents of Hutchinson were in the majority, — decidedly so, — and able to carry their measures on almost every occasion.

important trust, to discharge which, we doubt not, you will CHAP.
summon up the whole united faculties of both mind and XIII.
body." [1]

1770.

The message of the House, at the opening of the sessions at May 31.
Cambridge, was conceived in the same spirit. "The town
house in Boston," said they, "is the *only place* where the General Court is to be convened and held. We do not conceive
that it is in your honor's discretion to remove it to this or to
any other place ; nor does the prerogative of the crown extend
so far as to suffer you to exercise power to the injury of the
people. We therefore esteem it our indispensable duty, before
proceeding to the business of this assembly, to remonstrate
against its being held in any other place than the town house
in Boston." [2]

From the former course of the court in remaining at Cambridge, his honor "flattered himself" that he might be "soon
able to hold the assembly at Boston again ; " but this message
"blasted all his hopes ; " and, as ninety-six out of one hundred
and two members had protested against proceeding to business,
in less than four weeks he prorogued the assembly for a Jun. 25.
month. [3] But this did not mend the matter ; for, when the
court reassembled, they declared their adherence to their for- July 25.

---

[1] Hutchinson, iii. App. R.; Boston News Letter for May 17, 1770.
Hutchinson, about this time, received
notice that "it was intended he should
succeed Sir Francis Bernard as gov-
ernor-in-chief ; " but he was not confirmed until some months after. Hist.
iii. 288.

[2] Jour. H. of R. for 1770 ; Bradford's State Papers, 206–208 ; Boston
News Letter for May 31, 1770. "It
was, no doubt," says Hutchinson, Hist.
iii. 291, "unpleasant to the inhabitants
of Boston to see the concourse of all
ranks of people, which had always
been assembled upon the day of election, carried to another town ; and the
selectmen, and many of the principal
inhabitants, resolved to retain as much

of the ceremony, and to draw as much
of the concourse from Cambridge, as
was in their power. They therefore
desired Dr. Chauncy, as senior minister of the town, and zealously affected
to the popular side, to preach a sermon in the usual place, invited many
of the ministers of the country to
their houses, and caused an ox to be
roasted for the populace." "The appearance, however," he adds, "was
decent at Cambridge, though the number of people was less than common."
Comp. with this the Boston News Letter for May 31, 1770.

[3] Hutchinson, iii. 305, 306 ; Jour.
H. of R. for 1770 ; Bradford's State
Papers, 236.

CHAP.   mer resolution, and were again prorogued to the following
XIII.   September.[1]

1770.   In this interval intelligence was received of an order in
July 6. council, of the previous July, making a beginning of martial
law in Massachusetts, and preparing the way for closing the
port of Boston. By the terms of this order, the harbor of
Boston was made " the rendezvous of all ships stationed in
North America," and the fortress which commanded it was to
be delivered up to such officer as General Gage should appoint,
to be garrisoned by regular troops, and put into a respectable
state of defence.[2] The instructions of Gage to Hutchinson
were to deliver up the Castle to Colonel Dalrymple. But the
charter of the province expressly reserved to the governor the
command of the militia and the forts ; and, as the Castle was
plainly included in this reservation, to divert the command
from the chief magistrate to another person was obviously a
violation of the charter as well as of usage. Fearing the displeasure of the people, for a day Hutchinson hesitated — first
inclining to write to the general, and to delay the execution
of the order. But, conceiving that hesitation might be construed as a refusal, he " altered his mind," and " resolved to
carry the order into execution while it was in his power to do
so." Hence a message was sent to the commanding officer to
remove the sentinels and guards from their posts, and to admit
in their place such of the king's troops as Dalrymple should
appoint. His honor then repaired to the council chamber, and,
under an injunction of secrecy, disclosed his instructions ; but
finding that body was " struck with amazement," he stole into
a barge, was rowed to the Castle, invested Dalrymple with the
" custody of the fort," and then withdrew to his country house
at Milton.[3]

[1] Jour. H. of R. for 1770; Bradford's State Papers, 254.
[2] Hillsborough to Hutchinson, July,
1770 ; Bancroft, vi. 367, 369.
[3] Hutchinson to Gage, Sept. 9,

1770, and to Bernard, Sept. 15, 1770,
and Hist. iii. 307–310 ; Boston News
Letter for Sept. 13, 1770 ; Bancroft,
vi. 369, 370.

Upon the reassembling of the court, a day of solemn prayer CHAP.
and humiliation was appointed and observed ; and the House ___XIII.___
sent a committee to the lieutenant governor, informing him 1770.
that a quorum was present, and requesting that the assembly
might be removed to Boston.[1] But his honor declined, assign-
ing as his reason that the king had expressed his " entire approbation " of his summoning the court at Cambridge. " I am
restrained," said he, " from removing it to Boston, but am not
confined to the town of Cambridge ; and I am willing to meet
the court at any town in the province which shall appear to
me most for the convenience of the members, and which shall
not militate with the spirit of my instructions." [2] But the
House was not satisfied ; and, alarmed at the new and insup-
portable grievances to which they had been subjected, — which,
in their opinion, should be " radically redressed," — by a vote
of fifty-nine to twenty-nine another message was prepared and Oct. 13.
sent to his honor, requesting to know " whether he still held
command of the Castle." [3] To this message he returned an Oct. 16.
equivocal reply ; [4] upon which the House renewed their inqui- Oct. 23.
ry, and, being again repulsed, the Council draughted a mes- Oct. 25.
sage desiring his honor to " lay before the board an authentic
copy of the report and order, and so much of the letter from
the Earl of Hillsborough as concerned the Council or province," that they might " take such measures as should be judged
most advisable to vindicate their character, and prevent any
infringements on the charter rights of the province." [5]

Meanwhile, in England, Hillsborough himself, possessed with

[1] Jour. H. of R. for 1770 ; Bradford's State Papers, 257.
[2] Jour. H. of R. for 1770 ; Bradford's State Papers, 258.
[3] Jour. H. of R. for 1770 ; Bradford's State Papers, 258. Hutchinson,
Hist. iii. 307, says, the " principal, if
not the only additional grievance," of
which the people complained, " was
the exchange of a garrison, at Castle

William, of inhabitants in the pay of
the province, for a garrison of regular
troops in the pay of the crown." Perhaps so ; but was there nothing peculiar in this exchange, which constituted the grievance ?
[4] Jour. H. of R. for 1770 ; Bradford, 259.
[5] Jour. H. of R. for 1770 ; Bradford, 262.

CHAP.   the fear that the American colonies were on the eve of a revolt,
XIII.   exerted all his power to maintain the tottering supremacy of
1770.   Parliament. "No more time should be lost in deliberation,"
        said he ; and he prepared to act.[1] Hutchinson was ready to
Oct. 26. aid in•this work, and wrote that "no measure could have been
        pitched upon more proper " for the purpose "than the posses-
        sion of the harbor of Boston by the king's troops and ships."[2]
        Already had he boasted to Gage that he had "managed this
        affair with much prudence ; "[3] and, elated at the prospect of
        rising to still higher dignity, he advised "a bill for vacating or
        disannulling the charter in all its parts, and leaving it to the
        king to settle the government by a royal commission." "If
        the kingdom," said he, "is united and resolved, I have but very
        little doubt we shall be as tame as lambs."[4] But his honor
        misjudged the temper of the people. Tameness in submitting
        to an infraction of their charter was no article in the creed of
        the politicians of Massachusetts.[5]

        The death of De Berdt, which occurred about this time, ren-
        dered it necessary to choose a new agent; and Samuel Adams,
        with a number of others, following the advice of Reed, of
        Philadelphia, gave their suffrages for Arthur Lee ; but, by the
        influence of Bowdoin and Dr. Cooper, Franklin was chosen,
Oct. 24. with Lee as his substitute in case of his death or absence.[6] By
        this step the province was served by one of its ablest native

---

[1] Hillsborough to Hutchinson, Oct. 3, 1770 ; Bancroft, vi. 371.

[2] Hutchinson to Hillsborough, Oct. 26, 1770.

[3] Bradford's Hist. Mass. i. 233, note.

[4] Hillsborough to Hutchinson, Oct. 3, 1770 ; Hutchinson to Hillsborough, Oct. 8 and 26, 1770, and to Bernard, Oct. 20, 1770, in MS. Corresp. ii. 181, and iii. 22, 23.

[5] "With all his advantages," says Almon's Remembrancer for 1775, 26, "he never was master of the true character of his native country, not even of New England and the Massa-

chusetts Bay. Through the whole troublesome period since the last war, he manifestly mistook the temper, principles, and opinions of the people. He had resolved upon a system, and never could or would see the imprac-ticability of it."

[6] S. Adams to S. Sayre, Nov. 16, 1770 ; Hutchinson to Pownall, Nov. 11, 1770 ; Cooper to Franklin, Nov. 6, 1770 ; T. Cushing to Sayre, Nov. 6, 1770, in MS. Letters and Papers, 1761–1776. There is a portrait of De Berdt in the office of the secretary of the Board of Education, at the State House.

born sons, whose devotion to liberty was known to be sin- CHAP.
cere, and whose inflexible integrity and large experience were XIII.
a pledge that his best efforts would be used in their behalf. 1770.
The service demanded of him was, indeed, of the most delicate
and difficult nature ; and he entered upon his duties at a critical period. But, possessing the confidence of statesmen in
England, genial in his manners, and with a ripened wisdom
which knew how to meet difficulties and successfully surmount
them, no one was better qualified to discharge the onerous yet
honorable trust to greater advantage.[1]

In the mean time the ministry were perfecting their scheme
for the reduction of the colonies ; and the project was started
of producing divisions by arraying them against each other.
The merchants of New York had, some time before, agreed
to a general importation of all articles except tea. Most of
the other colonies censured this agreement as a desertion of
the cause which all were equally pledged to uphold ; but in
England the tidings were received with joy.[2] The tax on
tea remained unrepealed ; and as assurances had been given
to Hutchinson and his associates that a portion of the income
derived from this tax should be appropriated to their benefit,
the zeal of his honor was wonderfully increased, and he exultingly cried, "I can find bones to throw among them, to
continue contention, and prevent a renewal of their union."[3]

---

[1] A committee was at the same
time appointed by the House to communicate intelligence to the agent and
others in Great Britain, and to the
speakers of the several assemblies
throughout the continent, and to confer with a committee of the Council
appointed to correspond with their
agent, as far as they should judge necessary. Hutchinson, iii. 318.

[2] Votes of the meeting at Faneuil
Hall, July 24, 1770 ; J. Adams's Diary, in Works, ii. 364 ; Hutchinson,
iii. 330 ; Bancroft, vi. 365. On Tuesday, September 4, a notification for a

meeting was posted in Boston, to be
held on the 5th, to concert measures
to strengthen the union of the colonies and support the non-importation
agreement, which should be executed
"with that undaunted fortitude which
becomes those only who are resolved
to be free." Boston News Letter for
Sept. 6, 1770.

[3] Hutchinson to Mauduit, Dec.
1770, in MS. Corresp. iii. 68–70;
Bancroft, vi. 385. Hutchinson, by his
own acknowledgment, interested himself in encouraging the breach of the
combination made by the merchants,

CHAP. But the Bay Province was little disposed to second him in
XIII. these views; and at the November session of the General
1770. Court resolutions were passed discouraging extravagance and
Nov. the use of superfluities, and encouraging industry and frugality; manufactures in the towns were likewise fostered; and
the wives and daughters of the yeomen of Massachusetts,
catching the spirit which every where prevailed, held — as,
indeed, for a long time they had done — social gatherings at
different houses; and it was a point of pleasing and generous
rivalry among them who should spin the most yarn or weave
the most cloth.[1] Nor did they stop here, but cheerfully ab-
stained from the use of tea, the favorite beverage of their
sex, and substituted in its place an infusion of herbs indigenous to the soil.[2] Thus were the people ripening for independence; and the devotion to principle, the vigorous intellect, the clear perception, the breadth of purpose, and the
executive energy, which were distinguishing traits of the
sons of New England, tempered with the virtues and graces
of the daughters, were excellent preparatives for the enjoyment of the priceless blessings of freedom.

For a few months quiet reigned in the province. The ministry, indeed, were still pursuing their system of strengthening
the power of Parliament; but with whatever steadfastness
they adhered to this purpose, there were many, in both Houses,
who were more than ever disposed to lenient and indulgent
measures; the raising of a revenue from the colonies ceased

---

and declared that, "however it might
be called Machiavelian policy, it was
certainly, in such a case, to be justified." Hist. iii. 331, note.

[1] See the Boston newspapers for
1769 and 1770, and comp. Bradford,
i. 236. The following is given as a
sample of numerous similar advertisements: "Boston, May 21, 1770.
Last Wednesday 45 Daughters of Liberty met in the morning at the house
of the Rev. Mr. Morehead, in this

town; in the afternoon they exceeded
50. By the evening of said day they
had spun 232 skeins of yarn, some
very fine. Their labor and materials
were all generously given the worthy
pastor." Boston News Letter for May
24, 1770.

[2] See the papers of the day. Tea
had for some time been a prohibited
article — at least, that imported from
England.

with them to be an object of paramount interest and importance ; and if some inclined to assert the abstract right of Parliament, as an offset to the claim of exemption from its authority, they were indisposed to make such an application of the
doctrine as to provoke resistance, and carefully avoided a sudden collision with the prejudices of the people, which, it was
evident, were too strong to be easily removed.[1]

At length Hutchinson, who had for some time been dallying
for a commission as governor, with the doting of a lover upon
the charms of his mistress, and who had affected coyness, diffidence, and distrust, only the more surely to accomplish his
object, was unspeakably delighted at the reception of the
parchment upon which his name was fairly engrossed, and
viewed it with a complaisance which he could not conceal.[2]
The goal of his ambition was finally reached. He could rise
no higher on this side of the waters ; and as he professed
attachment to the land of his birth,[3] it was to him an exceedingly gratifying idea that he had become its chief magistrate ;

---

[1] George Grenville, the author of
the stamp act, died in the autumn of
1770. Lord Mahon's Hist. Eng. v.
275. His last recorded expressions
on American taxation are said to have
been, "Nothing could ever induce me
to tax America again but the united
consent of the King, Lords, and Commons, supported by the united voice
of the people of England. I will never
lend my hand towards forging chains
for America, lest in so doing I should
forge them for myself." Cavendish
Debates, i. 496.

[2] "Before the arrival," says he,
Hist. iii. 332, 333, "of the lieutenant
governor's letters in England, desiring
to be excused from any further share
in the administration, the king had
been pleased to direct a commission
to be prepared, constituting him governor of the province in the room of
Sir Francis Bernard, and to promote
Mr. Oliver to the place of lieutenant
governor; but Lieutenant Governor

Hutchinson's letters arriving in a short
time after, a stop was put to any further progress. The secretary of state
however, condescended to inform him
that an opportunity was given him for
further consideration, and that there
would be no appointment of any other
person in the mean time. The advice of so *unexpected* a mark of favor,
with the assurances given him by his
friends of support as far as should be
in their power, together with the
abatement of the tumultuous, violent
spirit which had prevailed, caused a
change of his former determination,
and a grateful acknowledgment of the
honor done him." For John Adams's
views on the character of Hutchinson,
see his Diary, in Works, ii. 278.

[3] "I cannot," said he, (letter to
Hillsborough, March 25, 1770,) "help
an attachment to the place of my
birth ; and I have some *personal interest*, 140 or 150 *pounds sterling annual rents, besides the house I live in.*"

CHAP. and pleasing visions of a successful administration floated before
XIII. his eyes.[1]

1771. To realize these visions, he first applied himself to weaken the influence of his political opponents.[2] Otis, once the foremost in defending the liberties of his country, was shattered in intellect, and possessed with a morbid sensitiveness and jealousy which were fast obscuring the brightness of his talents.[3] John Adams had withdrawn from public life, and was devoting himself principally to his farm and his office.[4] But Samuel Adams remained at his post; and his vigilance increased, and his spirit became more daring, as the crisis approached.[5] Bowdoin, too, and Cushing, and Hawley, and Warren, and Phillips, were men of such temper that the hopes of his excellency of seducing them were dashed. Upon Hancock alone did he flatter himself that he might operate with success; for with him vanity was so mingled with patriotism that adulation served to intoxicate and betray him. But, fortunately, his sympathies were so deeply enlisted, and the generous qualities of his heart so prevailed, that he spurned the caresses which were treacherously lavished upon him; and such was the confidence of his countrymen in his integrity, that, when the struggle came, he was the first to enroll his name on that

[1] "It is very probable," says he, Hist. iii. 333, "that, notwithstanding the disputes in which Mr. Hutchinson had been engaged with the Council and the House, the major part of the people of the province was not displeased with this appointment, though his principles in government were known in times past, when a member of the House, and afterwards of the Council, to be favorable to the prerogative." He also refers to the addresses which he received from the Episcopal, Presbyterian, and Baptist ministers as further evidence of the regard felt for his person.

[2] The emissaries of Hutchinson were abroad in all parts of the province, busy instilling, insinuating their notions and principles," and laboring to reconcile the people to his sway. J. Adams, Diary, in Works, ii. 285.

[3] Hutchinson, iii. 347.

[4] J. Adams, Diary, in Works, ii. 260. "I have stood by the people much longer than they would stand by themselves. But I have learned wisdom by experience. I shall certainly become more retired and cautious. I shall certainly mind my own farm and my own office."

[5] "Samuel Adams," wrote Hutchinson to J. Pownall, Oct. 17, 1771, "abates not his virulence. He would push the continent into a rebellion tomorrow, if it was in his power."

instrument which declared to the world that America would be free.[1]

The fifth of March, the first anniversary of "the Boston Massacre," was observed in the metropolis with great solemnity. The bells of the churches were tolled at noon and tolled in the evening; an "oration" was delivered in Faneuil Hall; and figures representing "the murder of the inhabitants" were exhibited from a window at the north part of the town.[2] In Salem there were similar observances; and the talented Whitaker, who officiated on the occasion, in his prayer implored that the guilt of blood might be taken from the land; and in his sermon represented the fatal effects from the terror of an armed force over the civil magistrate, and hinted very plainly at the pusillanimity of Hutchinson at that time.[3]

The General Court had been prorogued in November to the following April; and soon after Hutchinson's commission was published, he met both houses at Cambridge. In his opening address, after expressing his "sense of the honor" which had been conferred upon him, he declared that it was "his sincere desire and resolution to employ the powers with which he had been intrusted for his majesty's service, and for the best interests of the people;" and that, to this end, he should "cheerfully join, at all times, with the other branches of the legislature, in such measures as might tend completely to restore and constantly to maintain that state of order and tranquillity upon which the prosperity of the province depended."[4] The House, however, was little inclined to notice this message without first protesting against the continuance of the court at Cambridge; and a verbal message was sent to

---

[1] Hutchinson to ———, June 5, 1771, and Hist. iii. 346. The king sent word to tempt Hancock by marks of favor; and the difference which had taken place between him and Samuel Adams seemed to favor the idea that he might be gained over; but the hopes of the governor proved delusive. Comp. J. Adams, Diary, in Works, ii. 279, note, and Bancroft, vi. 407.

[2] Hutchinson, iii. 335.

[3] Hutchinson, iii. 335; Felt's Hist. Salem, ii. 550.

[4] Jour. H. of R. for 1770–71; Bradford's State Papers, 294.

CHAP. the governor, desiring the removal of the court to Boston.[1]
XIII. But his excellency, in reply, refused to accede to this request,
1771. as it would be yielding to the House "a right which would
April 5. have remained in the crown if no notice had been taken of it
Apr. 24. in the charter."[2]   Nearly three weeks elapsed before the
House rejoined ; then they declared that it would have "given
them no uneasiness if an end had been put to the present
assembly, rather than to have been again called to this
place ;" and they were "unwilling to admit the belief that,
when the season for calling a new assembly should arrive, his
excellency would continue an indignity so flagrant, and so
repeatedly remonstrated by both Houses, as the deforcement
of the General Assembly of its ancient and rightful seat."[3]

May 29.   Yet the new court was convened at Cambridge ; and no
sooner had the House chosen their speaker than they proceeded to remonstrate upon "the old subject."[4]   At the
instance of Samuel Adams it was likewise moved that "the
House should come into a resolve to do no business except in
the town of Boston ;"[5] but Otis, who had been chosen to
represent Boston in the place of John Adams, who had
changed his residence,[6] opposed this motion ;[7] and as a portion of the members were friends to the governor and friends
to the prerogative, and few were inclined to come to an open
rupture while matters of great importance might claim their
attention, the motion was negatived.[8]

[1] Bradford, i. ; Bancroft, vi.
[2] Jour. H. of R. for 1770–71 ;
Bradford's State Papers, 295, 296.
[3] Jour. H. of R. for 1770–71 ;
Bradford's State Papers, 296, 297 ;
Hutchinson, iii. 336, 337.
[4] Bradford's State Papers, 299,
note ; Hutchinson, iii. 339.
[5] Hutchinson, iii. 339.
[6] He moved to Braintree in April,
1771. Diary, in Works, ii. 255, note.
[7] Hutchinson, iii. 339. Comp. J.
Adams, Diary, in Works, ii. 266.

[8] J. Adams, Diary, in Works, ii.
263, says, "The House was very near
equally divided the whole of the last
session ; and these two members
(Colonel Edson, of Bridgewater, and
Colonel Gilbert, of Freetown) will be
able to make a balance in favor of timidity, artifice, and trimming." Hutchinson, on the other hand, Hist. iii. 338,
represents the majority against government as greater this year than ever
before, and says, "Except in two or
three instances, the new members

One such matter came before the House. It had long been CHAP.
suspected, and was now publicly known, that a salary of XIII.
fifteen hundred pounds per annum had been established for 1771.
the governor by grant of the crown ; and this, joined to other Jun. 19.
grievances, called forth a protest against the removal of the
assembly from Boston by force of an instruction from the
king, and against the establishment of a salary for the chief
magistrate.[1] "If a British king," say they, "should call a
Parliament, and keep it seven years in Cornwall, however
his ministry, as usual, might shift for themselves, their master
and his affairs would be irretrievably embarrassed and ruined.
And a governor of this province, who, in order to harass the
General Assembly into unconstitutional and unconscionable
measures, should convene and hold them in the county of Berkshire or Lincoln, would render himself and his administration
justly ridiculous and odious."[2] On the latter point, it will be
remembered, a controversy had arisen during the administrations of Shute and Burnet ; and its renewal at this time shows
that the same spirit animated the House, and that they were
determined to resist all invasions of their chartered rights.
The consolidation of power in the hands of the executive,
which would naturally flow from his independence of the provincial legislature, and the paramount authority given to the
instructions of the king, could not but awaken jealousy and
alarm ; and the disposition evinced on the part of the governor
to abide by those instructions and use that power satisfied the
people that his professions, as usual, were but a courtly pretence.

An incident, slight in itself, and only important for the principle involved, may be adduced in evidence of the arbitrary

were in the opposition." The list of
friends to government, in his note,
gives only eight names.
[1] "The subject of the governor's
independency is a serious, a dangerous, a momentous thing." J. Adams,
Diary, in Works, ii. 290.

[2] Jour. H. of R. for 1771 ; Bradford's State Papers, 302–304, and
Hist. i. 408–410 ; Hutchinson, iii.
App. T. Otis was chairman of the
committee which draughted this protest.

CHAP. manner in which the governor was disposed to use his author-
XIII. ity. The tax bill reported in the House this year did not
1771. exempt the estates of the officers of the crown in the province ;
July 4. and when it was presented to his excellency for approval, he
rejected it, on the ground that he was " expressly forbidden by
his majesty's twenty-seventh instruction from giving his consent to such an act upon any pretence whatsoever."[1] Indig-
July 5. nant at this assumption, the House, in their reply, declared
that " they knew of no commissioners of his majesty's customs,
nor of any revenue his majesty had a right to establish in
North America ; " and that to withhold his assent by " force
of instruction" alone was " effectually vacating the charter, rendering the representatives mere machines, and reducing them
to this fatal alternative — either to have no taxes levied at all,
or to have them raised in such a way and manner, and upon
those only whom his majesty pleased."[2]

The rejection of the grants made by the court for the support of their agents was another step which called forth the
displeasure of the House ; and they commented upon it with
becoming severity.[3] Nor was this the greatest grievance ; for
Aug.12. during the summer, twelve vessels of war, carrying two hundred and sixty-two guns, and commanded by Montagu, rear
admiral of the blue, and the brother of Sandwich, anchored
in the harbor, and displayed their frowning batteries to the
town.[4] Few, after this, could doubt the intentions of the min-

---

[1] Jour. H. of R. for 1771; Bradford's State Papers, 306 ; Hutchinson,
iii. 344.

[2] Jour. H. of R. for 1771; Bradford's State Papers, 307.

[3] Jour. H. of R. for 1771; Bradford's State Papers, 308.   Comp.
Hutchinson, iii. 345. The cause of
this rejection was the fact that the
Council and House had appointed
committees to correspond with their
agents. Comp. Hutchinson, iii. 318.

[4] Boston Gazette for Aug. 19,
1771 ; Boston Post Boy for Aug. 19,

1771. " Monday, being the anniversary of the birthday of his royal high-
ness the Prince of Wales, at one
o'clock the guns at Castle William
were fired on the occasion. The same
afternoon arrived in King Road the
Hon. John Montagu, Esq., rear admiral of his majesty's blue squadron,
in his majesty's ship, the Captain. The
Lively, Tamar, and Swan, which sailed
from England with the admiral, are
also arrived." On the character of
Montagu, see J. Adams, Diary, in
Works, ii. 306.

istry;[1] and it was no easy task to persuade the people that such an armament was necessary to insure obedience or loyalty. The apprehension of a war with Spain, which had dispossessed his majesty's subjects of their settlement at Port Egmont, in the Falkland Islands, and the necessity of obtaining satisfaction for this insult, was indeed alleged as the reason for sending such a fleet to America; but it was easy to see through the pretext; for why was not the fleet sent to New York?[2]

The patriots of the province beheld these proceedings with dismay; and Samuel Adams, more than ever convinced that the time for action had arrived, revolved in his mind the project, which was afterwards matured, of effecting a general union of the colonies. "It would be an arduous task," said he, "to awaken a sufficient number to so grand an undertaking. Nothing, however, should be despaired of. The tragedy of American freedom is nearly completed. A tyranny seems to be at the very door. Yet the liberties of our country are worth defending at all hazards. If we should suffer them to be wrested from us, millions yet unborn may be the miserable sharers in the event. Every step has been taken but one; and the LAST APPEAL would require prudence, unanimity, and fortitude. America must herself, under God, finally work out her own salvation."[3]

By such stirring words did this eloquent man seek to infuse into others' breasts his own courageous, resolute spirit. Nor did he labor in vain; for when, in the fall, the governor issued his proclamation for the customary day of thanksgiv-

---

[1] "These," says Hutchinson, Hist. iii. 332, "were evident marks of the jealousy of the government."

[2] "I have learned," wrote Arthur Lee from London, Sept. 22, 1771, "with very great satisfaction, that you have determined to resist any new invasions of your rights, as well as to remonstrate against those that are already passed. It was such vigilance and perseverance in our illustrious ancestors that redeemed our constitution when equally invaded; and I trust in God that these virtues in you will be crowned with the same success." Bradford's State Papers, 313.

[3] S. Adams, in the Boston Gazette for Oct. 14, 1771; Adams to Lee, Oct. 31, 1771.

CHAP. ing, and called upon the people to express their gratitude that
XIII. "civil and religious liberties" were continued, the ministers
1771. of Boston, with but one exception, refused to read the paper;
and on the day appointed, instead of the prayer which they
were expected to offer, they "implored of Almighty God the
restoration of *lost* liberties."[1]

Nothing of importance occurred during the winter. The
reunion of the colonies against importation was urged by the
prudent; and in different parts of the country it was under
discussion. "I heartily wish with you," wrote Cushing to
1772. Sherman, of Connecticut, "that some measures might be come
Jan. 21. into to revive the union of the colonies. To place any great
dependence on the virtue of the people in general, as to their
refraining from the use of the destined articles, will be in vain.
The only thing we can at present depend upon is the conduct
of the several assemblies through the continent; and however
the people in general may be induced, for peace' sake, or from
a sense of inability, to submit at present to what they apprehend the usurped authority of Parliament, the assemblies
ought to keep a watchful eye upon their liberties, and, from
time to time, assert their rights in solemn resolves, and con-
tinually keep their agents instructed upon this important subject, and renew their memorials to the king for the redress of
their grievances and the restoring their privileges."[2]

April. At the spring session of the legislature, Mr. Cushing, the
speaker of the House, being confined by indisposition, John
Hancock was chosen to his place. As a councillor, Mr. Hancock had been often rejected by Bernard and Hutchinson;
but, in pursuance of the policy which had been commended to
his notice, the latter now ventured to confirm him as speaker.

[1] Life of Lee, ii. 186; S. Adams's
Papers, in Bancroft, vi. 408; Hutchinson, iii. 347. Pemberton, of Boston, of whose church Hutchinson was
a member, was the one who read the
proclamation; and, as he began to
read, the patriots of his congregation,
turning their backs upon him, walked
out of the meeting in great indignation. Bancroft, vi. 408.
[2] T. Cushing to R. Sherman, Jan.
21, 1772, in MS. Letters and Papers,
1761–1776, 108, in Lib. Mass. Hist.
Soc.

A motion had been previously made by Hancock, in the House, that a message be sent to the governor, to desire, "in consideration of the inconveniences attending their sitting at Cambridge," that the court should be removed to Boston ; and as such a message, which waived the point of right, was all his excellency wanted, he was prepared to comply ; but, unfortunately for his purpose, Samuel Adams rose in opposition ; a similar motion in the Council was opposed by Bowdoin, and the matter dropped.[1]

The new session of the court, therefore, was held at Cambridge ; and the claim of right was once more insisted upon.[2] Say the House, in their message, "The town house in Boston is the accustomed, ancient place for holding the General Assembly, and where alone provision is made for it. It does not appear to us that there was any necessity for convening the assembly in this place, nor can we conceive of any for continuing it here. It is, therefore, our earnest request that you would remove the assembly to the town house in Boston, where we may, with the greatest advantage and despatch, transact all such public matters as are now before us, together with such others as your excellency shall propose for our consideration."[3] To this message the governor "imprudently" returned a negative answer ; but, upon maturer deliberation, and after consulting with the Council, who favored the removal, he consented to yield the disputed point, and the assembly was adjourned to Boston.[4]

In less than a month new difficulties arose. The governor had accepted a salary from the king. This was known, and

CHAP XIII.

1772.

May 28.

May 29.

Jun. 13.

July 10.

---

[1] Jour. H. of R. for 1771–72 ; Hutchinson, iii. 348.

[2] In consequence of the difficulty between Hancock and S. Adams, an attempt was made at the election in Boston this year to defeat the latter ; but he was triumphantly elected by a vote of 723 against 218. Happily, a reconciliation between the parties was soon after effected, and harmony was restored. See Hutchinson, iii. 356, and Bancroft, vi.

[3] Jour. H. of R. for 1772 ; Bradford's State Papers, 321.

[4] Jour. H. of R. for 1772 ; Bradford's State Papers, 322–325 ; Hutchinson, iii. 356, 357.

CHAP.
XIII.
    had already been censured. But the House now took more definite grounds; and a series of resolves draughted by Haw-

1772.
    ley was passed by a vote of eighty-five to nineteen, to the effect that "the making provision for the support of the governor of the province, independent of the acts and grants of the General Assembly, is an infraction upon the rights granted to the inhabitants by the royal charter, and in derogation of the constitution." [1]

    His excellency was displeased with these proceedings; and, in revenge for the affront which had been put upon his dignity, not only in this particular, but in the refusal of the Court to repair the Province House, which he occupied as his residence,[2]

July 21.
    he wrote to Hillsborough that "if the nation would arouse, and unite in measures to retain the colonies in subordination, all this new doctrine of independence would be disavowed, and its first inventors be sacrificed to the rage of the people whom they had deluded." [3] But the secretary had not been idle,

Aug. 7.
    and, on his part, announced that the king, "with the entire concurrence of Lord North, had made provision for the support of his law servants in the Massachusetts Bay." [4] This was his last act as a minister of the king; a patent for an

Aug. 14.
    earldom soothed his fall; and William Legge, Earl of Dartmouth, commemorated by Cowper as one

---

[1] Jour. H. of R. for 1772; Bradford's State Papers, 325–329; Hutchinson, iii. 357, and App. V. The governor, in his message of June 13, informed the House that he had received and accepted a salary from the king; and this was the cause of the present rejoinder. Bradford's State Papers, 324, 325.

[2] Jour. H. of R. for 1772; Bradford's State Papers, 330, 331.

[3] Hutchinson to J. Pownall, July 21, 1772, in Almon's Remembrancer for 1776, 57. Hutchinson's views upon the subject of independence may be seen in his Hist. iii. 355. "After all," says he, "a new independent state

may be added to the empires of the world, with perhaps the name of a free state; a few individuals may attain to greater degrees of dignity and power; but the inhabitants in general will never enjoy so great a share of natural liberty as they would have done if they had remained a dependent colony. Thus, for an imaginary good, and even that improbable to be obtained, we are parting with real, substantial happiness."

[4] Hillsborough to Hutchinson, Aug. 7, 1772. Comp. Hillsborough to Hutchinson, June 6, 1772, and to the Board of Trade, July 27, 1772; and Bancroft, vi. 419.

"Who wears a coronet, and prays,"

took his place as secretary for the colonies.[1]

As the court was not sitting when Hillsborough's letter
arrived, an informal meeting of the inhabitants of Boston was
called. A petition for a town meeting was then draughted ;   Oct.
and, though some opposed, the people insisted that "the crisis
had come," and that "from this time forward posterity must
date their freedom or their slavery."[2] On the appointed day Oct. 28.
the inhabitants assembled, and John Hancock was chosen moderator.[3] "We must now strike a home blow," was the language of the boldest, "or the chains of tyranny are riveted
upon us." An address to his excellency was prepared and
sent, requesting information of the truth of the report that
"stipends had been affixed to the offices of the judges ;" but Oct. 30
the request was declined on the ground of its impropriety.[4]
A new petition was then draughted, declaring "such an establishment contrary, not only to the plain and obvious sense of
the charter of the province, but also to some of the fundamental principles of common law, — to the benefit of which all
British subjects, wherever dispersed, are indubitably entitled,"
— and requesting that the subject might be referred to the
General Court.[5] But this petition was likewise rejected ; nor Nov. 2.
would the governor consent that the court should meet in December, the time to which it had been prorogued.[6] "If," said

---

[1] Dartmouth to the Governor of
Connecticut, Aug. 14, 1772, in MS.
Letters and Papers, 1761–76, 106 ;
Belsham's George III. i. 326 ; Lord
Mahon's Hist. Eng. v. 320 ; Hutch-
inson, iii. 361, note ; Bancroft, vi. 420.

[2] Hutchinson, iii. 361 ; Bancroft, vi.
426.

[3] Boston Post Boy for Nov. 2,
1772. Bancroft, vi. 426, says, Hancock, who disapproved of what seemed
to him rash measures, joined with
three or four others of the selectmen
of Boston, and rejected the prayer of
the first petition for a town meeting,

and gives as his authority the statement of Hutchinson, Hist. iii. 361.
But if Hancock was one of those who
opposed the meeting, it seems hardly
credible that he should afterwards
have been chosen moderator.

[4] Boston Post Boy for Nov. 2,
1772 ; Boston News Letter for Oct.
29 and Nov. 5, 1772. Comp. J. Adams's Diary, in Works, ii. 300, 301.

[5] Boston Post Boy for Nov. 2,
1772.

[6] Boston Post Boy for Nov. 9,
1772 ; Hutchinson, iii. 363. The attendance at the meetings, both of the

CHAP.
XIII.

1772.

he, " in compliance with your petition, I should alter my determination, and meet the assembly, contrary to my own judgment,
at such time as you judge necessary, I should in effect yield to
you the exercise of that part of the prerogative, and should be
unable to justify my conduct to the king.   There would, moreover, be danger of encouraging the inhabitants of the other
towns in the province to assemble, from time to time, in order
to consider the necessity or expediency of a session of the General Assembly, or to debate and transact other matters which
the law that authorizes towns to assemble does not make the
business of a town meeting." [1]

This reply, which invaded the rights of the little republics
of New England, was communicated to the meeting, and read
several times ; after which it was unanimously voted that the
inhabitants of Boston "have ever had, and ought to have, a
right to petition the king for the redress of such grievances as
they feel, or for preventing of such as they have reason to apprehend, and to communicate their sentiments to other towns." [2]
Then followed the step "which included the whole revolution ; " and Samuel Adams, the master spirit of the times, who
had matured his plans by consulting the ablest men in the
province, moved " that a committee of correspondence be appointed, to consist of twenty-one persons, to state the rights
of the colonists, and of this province in particular, as men and
Christians, and as subjects ; and to communicate and publish
the same to the several towns and to the world, as the sense
of this town, with the infringements and violations thereof
that have been, or from time to time may be, made." [3]   This
motion was carried without a division, the vote in its favor

28th October and the 2d November,
is said not to have been large — not
much larger than on ordinary occasions. S. Adams to Arthur Lee, Nov.
3, 1772 ; Bancroft, vi. 427, 428.
    [1] Boston Post Boy for Nov. 9,
1772 ; Boston Gazette for Nov. 9,
1772.

[2] Boston Post Boy for Nov. 9,
1772 ; Boston Gazette for Nov. 9,
1772.
    [3] Boston Post Boy for Nov. 9,
1772 ; Bancroft, vi. 428, note, and
429.

being nearly unanimous ; but, when an attempt was made to CHAP.
raise the committee, difficulties arose. Three of the four XIII.
representatives, and two of the selectmen, of Boston pleaded 1772.
private business, and declined to serve ;[1] and their example
was followed by others.[2] The committee was filled, however,
and, with Otis as its chairman, held its first session at the representatives' chamber on the following day, and organized by Nov. 3.
electing William Cooper as its clerk.[3] Thus the foundation
was laid for AMERICAN UNION. "The people in every town,"
an "American" had written, "must instruct their representatives to send a remonstrance to the King of Great Britain,
and assure him, unless their liberties are restored whole and
entire, they will form an independent commonwealth, after the
example of the Dutch provinces, and offer a free trade to all
nations. Should any one province begin the example, the
other provinces will follow ; and Great Britain must comply
with our demands, or sink under the united force of the French
and Spaniards. This is the plan that wisdom and Providence
point out to preserve our rights, and this alone."[4]

The first step of the committee, after its organization, was
to pass a vote pledging their "honor not to divulge any part
of the conversation at their meetings to any person whatsoever,
excepting what the committee itself should make known ;" and

---

[1] Cushing, Hancock, and Phillips
were the representatives who declined ; and Scollay and Austin were
the selectmen. See Cooper to Franklin, March 15, 1773, in Franklin's
Works, viii. 37 ; Hutchinson to Pownall, April 19, 1773 ; L. in the Boston
Gazette for Nov. 9, 1772 ; Bancroft,
vi. 429, 430. The latter, Hist. U. S.
vi. 426, says, when Adams "proposed
his great invention," "every one of
his colleagues in the delegation from
Boston opposed him." "Especially
Cushing," he adds, "dissuaded from
the movement, and had no confidence
in its success." But the authority
upon which the last statement is

based — being the assertion of Hutchinson alone — does not seem to me
sufficient to warrant the charge, especially in view of the letters of Cushing
advocating a union against importation.

[2] Comp. Boston Gazette for Nov.
9, 1772. Hutchinson described this
committee as in part composed of
"deacons," and "atheists," and
"black-hearted fellows whom one
would not choose to meet in the
dark." Hutchinson to J. Pownall,
Nov. 13, 1772.

[3] Bancroft, vi. 430.

[4] Boston Gazette for Nov. 2, 1772.

CHAP. this pledge was fully redeemed.[1] Next, Samuel Adams was
XIII. appointed to prepare a statement of the rights of the colonies ;
1772. Joseph Warren was to report upon the grievous violations of
those rights ; and Benjamin Church was to draught a letter to
the several towns in the province.[2] The coöperation of the
Old Colony was likewise sought, by advising with James Warren, of Plymouth, who favored the scheme of union, and lent to
it the weight of his influence at home.[3]

In about two weeks the report of the Boston committee was
Nov.20. prepared ; and James Otis, the chairman, was appointed to
present it. The natural rights of the colonists were claimed
to be " a right to life, to liberty, and to property, together with
the right to support and defend them in the best manner they
can." " All men," say they, " have a right to remain in a state
of nature as long as they please ; and, in case of intolerable
oppression, civil or religious, to leave the society they belong
to, and enter into another. When men enter into society, it is
by voluntary consent ; and they have a right to insist upon the
performance of such conditions and previous limitations as
form an equitable original compact. Every natural right, not
expressly given up, or from the nature of a social compact
necessarily ceded, remains. All positive and civil laws should
conform, as far as possible, to the law of natural reason and
equity. Every man has a right peaceably and quietly to
worship God after the dictates of his conscience ; and, in regard to religion, mutual toleration in the different professions

[1] Bancroft, vi. 430, from the MS.
journals of the committee, in his possession — an invaluable source of information on this period.
[2] Journals, in Bancroft, vi. 431.
[3] According to Gordon, Am. Rev.
i. 207, Warren was the first to propose
" to originate and establish committees of correspondence in the several
towns of the colony, in order to learn
the strength of the friends to the
rights of the continent, and to unite

and increase their force." But Bancroft, Hist. U. S. vi. 429, note, attrib-
utes the invention of this system to
Samuel Adams, and quotes the statements of John Adams and of Hutchinson. It is not, however, improbable
that several persons may have contemporaneously favored such a scheme,
though it was the good fortune of
Adams to bring it to maturity and secure its benefits.

thereof is what all good and candid minds in all ages have
ever practised, and, both by precept and example, inculcated
on mankind. The natural liberty of man, by entering into
society, is abridged or restrained so far only as is necessary for
the great end of society — the best good of the whole."

The rights of the colonists as subjects were set forth in language equally strong. "All persons," say they, "born in the
British American colonies are, by the laws of God and nature,
and by the common law of England, exclusive of all charters
from the crown, entitled to all the natural, essential, inherent,
and inseparable rights, liberties, and privileges of subjects born
in Great Britain, or within the realm. The legislative power
is for the preservation of society; and it has no right to absolute, arbitrary power over the lives and fortunes of the people;
nor can mortals assume a prerogative, not only too high for
men, but for angels, and therefore reserved to Deity alone.
An independent judiciary is likewise essential. There should
be one rule of justice for rich and poor — for the favorite at
court and the countryman at the plough. And the supreme
power cannot justly take from any man any part of his property, without his consent in person or by his representative." [1]

The "list of infringements and violations of these rights"
presents a formidable array of complaints: the assumption of
absolute legislative powers; the imposition of taxes without the
consent of the people; the appointment of officers unknown to
the charter, supported by the income derived from such taxes;
the investing these officers with unconstitutional powers, especially the "commissioners of his majesty's customs;" the
annulment of laws enacted by the court, after the time limited
for their rejection had expired; the introduction of fleets and
armies into the colonies; the support of the executive and the
judiciary independently of the people; the oppressive instruc-

[1] Votes and Proceedings of the
Freeholders of Boston, 2–12. For
an account of the meeting of Nov. 20
see Boston News Letter for Nov. 26,
1772.

CHAP. tions sent to the governor; the extension of the powers of the
 XIII. Courts of Vice Admiralty; the restriction of manufactures;
 1772. the act relating to dock yards and stores, which deprived the
people of the right of trial by peers of the vicinage; the attempt to "establish an American episcopate;" and the alteration of the bounds of colonies by decisions before the King and
Council.[1]

The letter to the towns was equally spirited; and it was
desired that the sense of the people should be explicitly declared. "A free communication of your sentiments to this
town"—such was its language—"of our common danger is
earnestly solicited, and will be gratefully received. If you
concur with us in opinion that our rights are properly stated,
and that the several acts of Parliament and measures of administration pointed out by us are subversive of these rights,
you will doubtless think it of the utmost importance that we
stand firm, as one man, to recover and support them, and to
take such measures, by directing our representatives or otherwise, as your wisdom and fortitude shall dictate, to rescue from
impending ruin our happy and glorious constitution. But if it
should be the general voice of this province that the rights, as
we have stated them, do not belong to us, or that the several
measures of administration in the British court are no violations
of these rights, or that, if they are thus violated or infringed,
they are not worth contending for or resolutely maintaining,—
should this be the general voice of the province, we must be
resigned to our wretched fate, but shall forever lament the
extinction of that generous ardor for civil and religious liberty
which, in the face of every danger and even death itself, induced our fathers to forsake the bosom of their native country, and begin a settlement on bare creation. But we trust

[1] Votes and Proceedings of the   the Boston News Letter for Oct. 29,
Freeholders of Boston, 13-29; Hutch-   and the Boston Gazette for Nov. 2,
inson, iii. 365-367. The act relative   1772.
to dock yards, &c., was published in

this cannot be the case. We are sure your wisdom, your regard to yourselves and the rising generation, cannot suffer you
to doze, or sit supinely indifferent on the brink of destruction,
while the iron hand of oppression is daily tearing the choicest
fruit from the fair tree of liberty, planted by our worthy predecessors at the expense of their treasure, and abundantly
watered with their blood. . . . Let us consider, brethren,
we are struggling for our best birthrights and inheritance,
which being infringed, renders all our blessings precarious in
their enjoyments, and, consequently, trifling in their value.
Let us disappoint the men who are raising themselves on the
ruin of this country. Let us convince every invader of our
freedom that we will be as free as the constitution our fathers
recognized will justify." [1]

The towns in the province responded to this call; and,
before the spring opened, committees of correspondence were
every where established.[2] Hutchinson pronounced the scheme
"such a foolish one that it must necessarily make them ridiculous;[3] but patriots thought otherwise; and Samuel Adams
exclaimed, " God grant that the love of liberty and a zeal to
support it may enkindle in every town." [4] The Earl of Chatham
read the accounts from America with pride, and said, " These
worthy New Englanders ever feel as Old Englanders ought to
do." [5] And many of his colleagues echoed his words. Even
Lord North wavered between duty and a wish to conciliate;[6]
and the Earl of Dartmouth, the new secretary of state, desired
the king to "reign in the affections of his people," and would
have regarded conciliation as " the happiest event of his life."[7]

The expressions of opinion from the different towns show

---

[1] Letter to Towns, in Proceedings,
&c., 30–35; Boston News Letter for
Nov. 26, 1772; Hutchinson, iii. 368.

[2] "There was such concern to obtain a universal consent," says Hutchinson, Hist. iii. 368, note, "that even
a district of two hundred Indians,
called Mashpee, was not omitted."

[3] Hutchinson to the Secretary of
the Board of Trade, Nov. 13, 1772.

[4] Bancroft, vi. 431.

[5] Chatham to T. Hollis, Feb. 3,
1773; Bancroft, vi. 434.

[6] Bancroft, vi. 434.

[7] Dartmouth to Hutchinson, Dec.
1772; Bancroft, vi. 435.

how wide-spread was the sense of the wrongs which the people had suffered. In the vicinity of Boston earnest resolves were passed; and the inhabitants of Cambridge " discovered a glorious spirit, like men determined to be free," and were " much concerned to maintain and secure their own invaluable rights, which were not the gift of kings, but purchased with the precious blood and treasure of their ancestors."[1] Roxbury found " the rights of the colonists fully supported and warranted by the laws of God and nature, the teachings of the New Testament, and the charter of the province." " Our pious forefathers," said they, " died with the pleasing hope that we, their children, should live free. Let none, as they will answer it another day, disturb the ashes of those heroes by selling their birthright."[2] " Every thing dear to us, as men and as British subjects," said the people of Charlestown, " is held in trembling suspense. The fate of unborn millions is depending. Our rights are, in many instances, broken in upon and invaded."[3]

The towns in Essex county spoke in the same tone; and the people of Gloucester declared their readiness to stand for their rights and liberties, which were dearer to them than their lives, and to join with all others in appeal to the Great Lawgiver to crown their efforts with success.[4] Newbury and Newburyport declared their intention to do all in their power, " in order that the present and succeeding generations may have the full enjoyment of all those privileges and advantages which naturally and necessarily result from our glorious constitution."[5] Ipswich thanked the people of Boston " for informing the public of alarming encroachments on the rights of the province, and for seasonably endeavoring to obtain the sense

[1] Bancroft, vi. 438. William Brattle, who was wavering in his patriotism, opposed the action of the town. Letter of Dec. 28, in Boston Post Boy for Jan. 4, 1773.

[2] Boston Gazette for Nov. 30, 1772; Bradford, i. 262, note; Bancroft, vi. 438.

[3] Frothingham's Hist. Charlestown, 287, 288.

[4] Original Papers, 361; Jour. Com. of Corresp. i. 67, in Bancroft, vi. 440.

[5] Coffin's Hist. Newbury, 240, 241.

of the country," and advised that "the colonies in general, and the inhabitants of this province in particular, should stand firm as one man, to support and maintain all their just rights and privileges."[1] Even little Salisbury counselled an American Union;[2] Beverly, Lynn, Danvers, and Rowley advocated a like course;[3] and the fishermen of Marblehead expressed their readiness to "unite for the recovery of their violated rights," and declared that they "detested the name of a Hillsborough," and were justly "incensed at his unconstitutional, unrighteous proceedings."[4]

In Middlesex the freemen were equally fervent. "No power on earth," said the people of Concord, "can, agreeably to our constitution, take from us our rights, or any part of them, without our consent."[5] "It is our absolute duty," said the people of Framingham, "to defend, by every constitutional measure, our dear privileges, purchased with so much blood and treasure."[6] Medford, Acton, Stoneham, Medfield, Groton, Pepperell, and Shirley, spoke out firmly.[7] "We greatly applaud you," wrote the people of Newton, "and think ourselves and the whole province much obliged to you for your generous exertions. As far as in us lies, we would encourage your hearts to persevere in all legal, loyal, regular, and constitutional methods for the redress of the grievances we feel, and for preventing those we have reason to fear."[8] "Death," said the citizens of Marlborough, "is more eligible than slavery.

---

[1] Felt's Hist. Ipswich, 131; Original Papers, 441; Jour. Com. of Corresp. 50, in Bancroft, vi. 440.

[2] Original Papers, 815, in Bancroft, vi. 440.

[3] Stone's Hist. Beverly, 57; Gage's Hist. Rowley, 237–240; Hanson's Hist. Danvers, 78; Bancroft, vi. 447.

[4] Boston Gazette for Dec. 7 and 14, 1772; Bradford, i. 262, note; Bancroft, vi. 437. Hutchinson, iii. 369, says the report was opposed in Marblehead, and, after it was carried, "about 30 of the inhabitants, most of them

persons of the first character in the town, had firmness enough to declare and make public their dissent, with their reasons, in an instrument signed by them."

[5] Shattuck's Hist. Concord, 77.

[6] W. Barry's Hist. Framingham, 90.

[7] Brooks's Hist. Medford, 146–148; Butler's Hist. of Groton, Pepperell, and Shirley, 118–121, 330, 374.

[8] Jackson's Hist. Newton, 180.

CHAP. A freeborn people are not required by the religion of Jesus
XIII. to submit to tyranny, but may make use of such power as
1772. God has given them to recover and support their laws and
liberties." [1]

The towns at the west spoke; and the farmers of Lenox
were sure that "neither nature nor the God of nature required
them to crouch, Issachar like, between the two burdens of
poverty and slavery." [2] "We think it our duty" — such
was the voice of the people of Leicester, in conjunction with
the districts of Spencer and Paxton — "to risk our lives and
fortunes in defence of the liberties we prize so highly." [3] "The
time may come," wrote the small town of Petersham, "when
you may be driven from your goodly heritage; if that should
be the case, we invite you to share with us in our supplies of
the necessaries of life." [4] "Prohibiting slitting mills," said the
citizens of South Hadley, "is similar to the Philistines prohibiting smiths in Israel, and shows we are esteemed by our brethren as vassals." [5] "We will resolutely endeavor," said the
people of Brimfield, "by every just and constitutional way, to
maintain our rights and liberties yet continued, which were
purchased for us by the blood of our ancestors, and to recover
those which have been cruelly, not to say unrighteously, taken
from us." [6] "Posterity may rise up and curse us," said Lunenburg, "if we do not speak our minds with freedom." [7] And
Worcester, "the heart of the province," was loyal to freedom. [8]

In the old colony the flame caught; and even in Plymouth,
notwithstanding James Warren thought the people were
"dead," there were "ninety to one to fight Great Britain." [9]
"We inherit," was the glowing language of Duxbury, "the

[1] Hutchinson, iii. 369, note; Bancroft, vi. 442.
[2] Bancroft, vi. 442.
[3] Bancroft, vi. 442.
[4] Gordon's Am. Rev. i. 209–212;
Hutchinson, iii. 369, note; Bancroft,
vi. 442.

[5] Bancroft, vi. 447.
[6] Holland's Hist. Western Mass.
ii. 21.
[7] Bancroft, vi. 447.
[8] Lincoln's Hist. Worcester, 75.
[9] Judge Oliver, of Middleborough,
to Hutchinson, Dec. 16, 1772; Thach-

very spot of soil cultivated by some of the first comers to New
England, who emigrated from their native land to this then
howling wilderness, to escape the iron yoke of oppression, and
to transmit to posterity that fair, that amiable inheritance —
liberty, civil and sacred. We esteem it a virtue to oppose
tyranny in all its forms, and will use our utmost endeavors to
extricate ourselves from every dangerous and oppressive innovation."[1] "We view ourselves," said the people of Abington,
"under indispensable obligations to give our testimony against
all those arbitrary and despotic innovations which have lately
taken place in the province."[2] The people of Eastham declared their "right to communicate their sentiments, and ask
advice of any or all the towns in the province, or elsewhere,
if need be."[3] The citizens of Rehoboth deprecated the "unparalleled encroachments made on them by a ministry fond of
arbitrary sway."[4] The people of Pembroke predicted that
"if the measures so justly complained of were persisted in,
and enforced by fleets and armies," they would, "in a little
time, issue in the total dissolution of the union between the
mother country and the colonies."[5] And the little town of
Chatham, at the extremity of Cape Cod, declared "their civil
and religious principles to be the sweetest and essential part
of their lives, without which the remainder was scarcely worth
preserving."[6] "It will not be long," said the people of Rochester, prophetically, "before our assembling for the cause of liberty will be determined to be riotous, and every attempt to
prevent the flood of despotism from overflowing our land will
be deemed open rebellion."[7]

CHAP.
XIII.

1772.

---

er's Hist. Plymouth, 197; Bancroft, vi.
438. For an account of the meeting
at Plymouth see Boston Gazette for
Nov. 23 and Dec. 7, 1772, and Boston
News Letter for Nov. 26, 1772.

[1] Winsor's Duxbury, 121–123.
[2] Hobart's Abington, 118.
[3] Pratt's Hist. Eastham, 74; Original Papers, 322.
[4] Bliss's Rehoboth, 143–145.

[5] Town Records of Pembroke, Dec.
28, 1772; Jour. Com. of Corresp. i.
54, in Bancroft, vi. 440.
[6] Proceedings of Chatham, in Original Papers, 269; Jour. Com. of
Corresp. ii. 118, in Bancroft, vi. 440,
441.
[7] Original Papers, 772; Jour. Com.
of Corresp. in Bancroft, vi. 439.

CHAP.
XIII.

1772.

Thus did the people arise in their majesty, and assert their rights. "They succeed," wrote Hutchinson; and he earnestly invoked aid from Parliament.[1] "It is only some people in the Massachusetts Bay," was the language of others, "making a great clamor in order to keep their party alive."[2] But Samuel Adams was better informed, and predicted "a most violent political earthquake throughout the British empire." "This unhappy contest," he added, "will end in rivers of blood; but America may wash her hands in innocence."[3] And as he looked abroad into the other colonies, and watched the movements of the public mind, and as the news came from England that the burning of the Gaspee by the people of Rhode Island was denounced as a crime of a deeper dye than piracy, and that its authors and abettors were to be transported to England for trial,[4] his spirit was stirred to its utmost depths, and he was more earnest than ever to consecrate his all upon the altar of liberty.

1773.
Jan. 6.

The legislature of the province was convened early in the new year; and the governor, in his message, saw fit to comment with considerable severity upon the recent attempt to "call in question the authority of Great Britain to make and establish laws" for the colonies. "What was at first whispered with caution," says he, "was soon after openly asserted in print; and, of late, a number of inhabitants, in several of the principal towns of the province, having assembled together in their respective towns, and assumed the name of legal town

---

[1] Hutchinson to Jackson, Dec. 8, 1772, and to Pownall, in Bancroft, vi. 441. In his Hist. iii. 370, note, Hutchinson says, "Thus, all on a sudden, from a state of peace, order, and general contentment, as some expressed themselves, the province, more or less from one end to the other, was brought into a state of contention, disorder, and general dissatisfaction; or, as others would have it, were roused from stupor and inaction to sensibility and activity."

[2] W. Franklin to Dartmouth, Jan. 1773; Bancroft, vi. 443.

[3] S. Adams to D. Sessions, Jan. 2, 1773; Bancroft, vi. 443.

[4] On the burning of the Gaspee see Bancroft, vi. 416–418; and on the advices from England see Dartmouth to Hutchinson, and to Governor Wanton, of Rhode Island, Sept. 4, 1772; Grahame, ii. 467; Bancroft, vi. 441.

meetings, have passed resolves, which they have ordered to be CHAP.
placed upon their town records, and to be printed and pub- XIII.
lished in pamphlets and newspapers. In consequence of these 1773.
resolves, committees of correspondence are formed in several
of these towns, to maintain the principles upon which they are
founded." That this course was illegal he was fully persuaded;
and he added, " I know of no line that can be drawn between
the supreme authority of Parliament and the total independence of the colonies. It is impossible there should be two independent legislatures in one and the same state; for although
there may be but one head, the king, yet the two legislative
bodies will make two distinct governments, as distinct as the
kingdoms of England and Scotland before the union."[1] Having thus openly defined his position, he prepared a letter to be
forwarded to the ministry, informing them of his proceedings;
and so confident was he of victory that he closed by saying,
" I shall be enabled to make apparent the reasonableness and
necessity of coercion, and justify it to all the world."[2]

The issue thus raised was promptly met; and Samuel Adams,
in conjunction with Hawley and John Adams, prepared to
" take the fowler in his own snare."[3] The answer of the Coun- Jan. 25.
cil to the message of his excellency was draughted by Bowdoin; and from the laws of England, its constitution, and the
charter of William and Mary, it was argued that the power
of Parliament was limited, and did not extend to the levying
of taxes within the province.[4] The reply of the House was Jan. 26.
still more decided, and the reasoning of the governor was
thoroughly sifted. " If there be no such line " — was the lan-

---

[1] Message of Jan. 6, 1773, in Jour.
H. of R. for 1773; Bradford's State
Papers, 336–342; Hutchinson, iii.
371, 372. Comp. J. Adams, Diary, in
Works, ii. 311.

[2] Letter to J. Pownall, Jan. 1773,
in MS. Corresp.; Bancroft, vi. 446.

[3] That the message of the House
was in the handwriting of Samuel
Adams is admitted; nor is it denied

that Hawley was consulted in its preparation; and that John Adams was
advised with is asserted in his Diary,
Works, ii. 310–313, and by Hutchinson, Hist. iii. 374. Dr. Joseph Warren is said to have prepared the first
draught. J. Adams's Diary.

[4] Bradford's State Papers, 342–
351; Hutchinson, iii. 372, 373.

guage of this document — "between the supreme authority of Parliament and the total independence of the colonies, then either the colonies are vassals of the Parliament, or they are totally independent. And as it cannot be supposed to have been the intention of the parties in the compact that one of them should be reduced to a state of vassalage, the conclusion is, that we were thus independent." [1]

The controversy thus opened was continued for about two months; and several messages passed between the governor and both branches of the General Court, in which the question of the relation of the colonies to the Parliament of Great Britain was fully discussed.[2] "I stand amazed at the governor," wrote John Adams, "for forcing on this controversy. He will not be thanked for this. His ruin and destruction must spring out of it, either from the ministry and Parliament on the one hand, or from his countrymen. He has reduced himself to a most ridiculous state of distress. He is closeting and soliciting Mr. Bowdoin, Mr. Denny, Dr. Church, &c., and seems in the utmost agony." [3] But his excellency was not so thoroughly discomfited as not to have some crumbs of comfort in his troubles; and he sought to intimidate the court by telling them that "the English nation would be roused, and could not be withstood," and that "Parliament would, by some means or other, maintain its supremacy." [4]

The institution of committees of correspondence in Massachusetts prepared the way for the establishment of like committees in all the colonies; and Benjamin Church, in his oration upon the anniversary of the "Boston Massacre," as if gifted with the spirit of prophecy, predicted that "some future CONGRESS would be the glorious source of the salvation of

Mar. 5.

[1] Jour. H. of R. for 1772; Bradford's State Papers, 351–366; Hutchinson, iii. 374, 375.
[2] See Jour. H. of R. for 1772–3; Bradford's State Papers, 366–396; Hutchinson, iii. 376 et seq.

[3] J. Adams's Diary, in Works, ii. 315.
[4] Hutchinson to J. Pownall, Feb. 24, and to T. Pownall, Feb. 23, 1773; Bancroft, vi. 453.

America." "The Amphictyons of Greece," he added, "who CHAP
formed the diet or great council of the states, exhibit an excel- XIII.
lent model for the rising Americans."[1] The action of Vir- 1773.
ginia forwarded this object. In the legislature of that province a union of councils throughout the continent was advised ;
and the resolutions recommending this course were unani- Mar.12.
mously adopted.[2] The friends of independence in New England received these tidings with joy ;[3] and South Carolina, by
her "steady perseverance" in resisting the encroachments of
absolute power, inspired the hope that "the fire of liberty
would spread throughout the continent."[4] "An American
Congress," wrote Samuel Adams, "is no longer the fiction of
a political enthusiast."[5] "We trust," wrote Cambridge to
the Boston committee, "the day is not far distant when our
rights and liberties shall be restored to us, or the colonies,
united as one man, will make their most solemn appeal to
Heaven, and drive tyranny from these northern climes."[6]
Even Hutchinson was satisfied, from the tenor of his despatches
from England, that there was "no room to hope that argument
and persuasion would induce the colonies to yield due obedience to the laws of Parliament ;" and it was recommended to
him to "avoid any further discussion whatever upon those
questions, the agitating of which had already produced such
disagreeable consequences."[7]

It would have been well for his excellency had he heeded

[1] Church's Oration of March 5, 1773, in Lib. Mass. Hist. Soc.

[2] Circular of Peyton Randolph, dated March 19, 1773; Hutchinson, iii. 392, 393 ; Wirt's Patrick Henry, 105 –108; Warren's Hist. Am. Rev. i. 110, note ; Bradford, i. 276. "These measures," says Wirt, "were so nearly coeval in the two states as to render it impossible that either could have borrowed it from the other. The messengers who bore the propositions from the two states are said to have crossed each other on the way."

Hutchinson asserts that the congress was suggested by Dr. Franklin, "in a letter to the speaker of the Massachusetts assembly, if it should be necessary."

[3] Original Papers, 351.

[4] Bancroft, vi. 447, 448.

[5] S. Adams to Arthur Lee and to R. H. Lee, April 9, 1773; T. Cushing to A. Lee, April 22, 1773; Bancroft, vi. 456.

[6] Bancroft, vi. 456.

[7] Hist. Mass. iii. 385. Comp. Dartmouth to Hutchinson, April 10, 1773.

this advice ; but, instead of adopting conciliatory measures, he seems to have prided himself in displaying his entire subserviency to the crown. Hence, when the usual grants were made by the House to the justices of the Superior Court, the governor refused his assent, because he expected warrants for their salaries from the king.[1] To this the House replied that "no judge who had a due regard to justice, or even to his own character, would choose to be placed under such an undue bias as they must be under by accepting their salaries of the crown." And, not satisfied with this, they added, "We are more and more convinced that it has been the design of administration to subvert the constitution, and introduce an arbitrary government into this province ; and we cannot wonder that the apprehensions of this people are thoroughly awakened."[2] The reception of certain letters which had been written by the governor, some years before, to his friend Mr. Whateley, in England, stripped off the mask under which he had long concealed his hostility to the liberties of his country ; and his conduct was indelibly branded with infamy. How these letters were obtained no one has been able fully to determine.[3] They were forwarded by Dr. Franklin, the agent of the province, who kept his secret so well that it has never been penetrated.[4] At first they were communicated to the committee of correspondence and to the assembly, with the understanding that they were not to be published ; and in this form they were debated for a considerable time. But when the House, by a vote of

[1] Jour. H. of R. for 1773 ; Bradford's State Papers, 365.

[2] Jour. H. of R. for 1773 ; Bradford's State Papers, 366.

[3] For a full discussion of this point see Sparks's Franklin, iv. ; J. Adams's Diary, in Works, ii. 318 ; Bradford, i. 284–290 ; Bancroft, vi. 435–437, 461 –464 ; and comp. on the other side Lord Mahon's Hist. Eng. v. 322– 326, and Hutchinson, iii. 394 et seq. "The secrecy of these epistolary genii," says J. Adams, "is very remarkable, profoundly secret, dark, and deep."

[4] Bancroft, vi. 435, is of opinion that John Temple, formerly one of the Board of Commissioners, was privy to the plan of getting these letters, and adds, "English writers have not noticed that the English ministry and Hutchinson seem to have had the means of discovering the secret, that the ministry discouraged inquiry, and that Temple was subsequently forgiven, and appointed to a good place." Comp. J. Adams's Diary, in Works, ii. 319, and note.

one hundred and one to five, declared that "the tendency and
design of the letters was to subvert the constitution and government, and to introduce arbitrary power into the province,"
public curiosity was so excited to know their contents that,
after some hesitation, and after consulting with Dr. Franklin,
the prohibition was removed, the letters were circulated in
pamphlet form,[1] and a memorial was sent to the king for the
removal of the governor.

Hutchinson was at first inclined to deny the authenticity of
these letters ; but, when he found that this was of no avail, he
was obliged to acknowledge that they appeared to be in his
handwriting, though he denied that they were designed "to subvert the constitution of the government, but rather to preserve
it entire." Yet, conscious of his guilt, and fearful lest other and
more recent communications might be discovered, he wrote to his
friends in England to burn such of his letters as could be used
against him ; "for," said he, "I have written much that ought
not to be made public."[2] Franklin was bitterly denounced
for the part he took in this affair ; and, in his examination
before the privy council, Wedderburne took occasion to pour
out upon him a torrent of invective and biting sarcasm, which
excited the mirth of his associates, but which were received by
their subject with perfect composure.[3] His dismission from
the office of deputy postmaster general followed, and Hutchinson solicited to take his place.[4] But nothing was gained by
the adoption of such measures. If the English ministry were
disposed to assert the supremacy of Parliament, and to insist
upon the entire subordination of the colonies, the people of
America, aroused to the necessity of resisting such claims,
moved steadily on in the course which the prudent had marked
out for the continent, and, by cementing union, were strengthened for the contest which was rapidly approaching.

---

[1] This pamphlet was published in
1773.
[2] Hutchinson to ——, June 29,
1773.
[3] On this affair see Sparks's Franklin ; Lord Mahon's Hist. Eng. v. 326
–329 ; Bancroft, vi. 490–502.
[4] Hutchinson to Bernard, June 20,
1773.

CHAPTER XIV.

THE BOSTON TEA PARTY. THE BATTLE OF LEXINGTON.

CHAP.
XIV.
1773.

THE ministry in England were not entirely unfriendly to America, for Dartmouth, the secretary of state for the colonies, openly favored conciliatory measures.[1] Distinguished for his piety, his uprightness, and his candor, and demeaning at all times with "decency and propriety," his associates felt the power of his example; and had his influence at court been commensurate with his worth, his prudence might have averted the evils which threatened. The embarrassments of the East India Company hastened the struggle. The affairs of this company, through long mismanagement, had fallen into confusion; and the continued refusal of the merchants of America to import their teas had thrown upon their hands such quantities of this article that they were unable to pay either dividends or debts; and, reduced to a state of extreme distress, they were forced to apply to Parliament for a loan, to save themselves from bankruptcy and ruin. This loan was granted, accompanied by a bill for the better regulation of their affairs

May 10.

in the future, which empowered them to export teas direct from their own warehouses, and on their own account, and granted a drawback of the whole duty payable in England on such teas as were exported to the British plantations in America.[2] The colonial tax of threepence on the pound was still

[1] Grafton's Autobiog.; Lord Mahon's Hist. Eng. v. 320; S. Adams to J. Hawley, Oct. 4 and 13, 1773.
[2] Acts 13 Geo. III. c. xliv.; Boston Gazette for Oct. 18, 1773; Lord Mahon's Hist. Eng. v. 319; Bradford, i. 298; Bancroft, vi. 459, 465. Stedman, Hist. War, i. 85, and Grahame,

(464)

to be paid; nor would Lord North listen to the proposal of CHAP.
XIV. Trecothick that this should be abandoned. America was not to be relieved from taxation. Yet, as teas could be sold in 1773. the colonies under the new regulations at lower rates than formerly, and as the article itself was one which the people were willing to use, provided it was not made a badge of their servitude, it was supposed that they might be tempted, in view of the apparent reduction in their favor, to forego their scruples, and submit without further opposition to the wishes of the king.

But if the ministry calculated upon seducing the colonists by appealing to their cupidity, they were destined to find themselves sadly mistaken; for no sooner did the company apply Aug. 20. to the treasury for the customary license than they were warned that it would be useless to send teas to America; the merchants would not receive them, and the people were determined to resist at all hazards the claim of authority by the Parliament of Great Britain. In vain did Lord North say, "It is to no purpose making objections, for the king will have it so. He means to try the question with America."[1] The king might *try* the question, but he could not *decide* it. The measure was at once denounced as "insidious;"[2] a plan of resistance was matured; and it was publicly declared, in the papers of the day, that "whoever should purchase and use this article would drink political damnation to themselves."[3] Indeed, the excitement in the province was general. No meas-

---

ii., mistake in saying the company had leave to export their teas duty free wherever they could find a market for them. They were only entitled to a drawback of the whole duty payable in England on such teas as were exported to the British plantations in America.

[1] Almon's Anecdotes, c. xli.; B. Franklin to W. Franklin, July 14, 1773, in Works, viii. 75; Bancroft, vi. 465.

[2] W. Phillips, in Bradford, i. 298, note. "Nothing can more evidently prove the ill conduct or mismanagement of the affairs of the East India Company than their becoming exporters of tea to America—a paltry transaction, unworthy of one of the greatest associated bodies in Europe. How are the mighty fallen!" Boston Post Boy for Nov. 1, 1773.

[3] Bradford, i. 298, note.

CHAP. ure of administration, not even the stamp act, had created
XIV. more alarm.[1] It was now to be determined whether the Amer-
1773. icans should be freemen or slaves.

Concert of action throughout the continent could alone
insure success in this crisis; and Samuel Adams, impatient at
even the appearance of delay, urged, with his usual power and
eloquence, a Congress on the "plan of union proposed by Virginia." "When our liberty is gone," said he, "history and
experience will teach us that an increase of inhabitants is but
an increase of slaves."[2] The committee of correspondence
Sept. seconded his views; and, though Thomas Cushing, the speaker
of the House, advised forbearance,[3] assured of the concurrence
of the more ardent patriots, they fearlessly aimed at the "union
of the province," and advised "the confederacy of the whole
continent of America." "Watchfulness, unity, and harmony,"
they urged, "are necessary to the salvation of ourselves and
posterity from bondage. What oppressions may we not expect in another seven years, if, through a weak credulity, we
should be prevailed upon to submit our rights to the tender
mercies of the ministry? We have an animating confidence
in the Supreme Disposer of events, that he will never suffer a
sensible, brave, and virtuous people to be enslaved."[4] A "Congress of American states, to frame a bill of rights," or to
"form an independent state, an American commonwealth,"
was no longer the "sickly dream of an enthusiast."[5] It was
the opinion of Franklin[6] that such a step was necessary; and

[1] Hutchinson, iii. 422, asserts that
the intelligence "caused no alarm;"
that "the body of the people were
pleased with the prospect of drinking
tea at less expense than ever;" and
that "the only apparent discontent
was among the importers of tea."

[2] A., in the Boston Gazette for
Sept. 13, 1773. A writer under the
signature of "Time and Judgment,"
in the Gazette for Aug. 2, 1773, urges
a union of the colonies, or congress of

the states, for the "interest of Great
Britain as well as their own." See
also W. in the Gazette for Sept. 27,
1773.

[3] T. Cushing to A. Lee, Sept. 20,
1773; Bancroft, vi. 466.

[4] Circular of the Com. of Corresp.
Sept. 21, 1773; Bancroft, vi. 467.

[5] "Observation," in Boston Gazette for Sept. 27, 1773.

[6] Franklin to T. Cushing, July 7
1773; Bancroft, vi. 469.

Samuel Adams, whose vigorous intellect overpowered opposi- CHAP.
tion, persuaded even Cushing to act as one of a select commit- XIV.
tee to prepare a circular to be sent to the other colonies to 1773.
join with Massachusetts in resisting the designs of the English
ministry, and in preventing the landing of teas in their ports.[1]

The province of Pennsylvania was the first to act; and
Philadelphia, the largest town in the colonies, denied the Oct. 8
and 18.
authority of Parliament to tax America, condemned especially
the duty on tea, declared every one who should countenance
its importation an "enemy to his country," and requested the
resignation of the agents of the East India Company.[2] The
citizens of Boston followed this example; and as Hutchinson
himself, under the name of his sons, had been selected as one
of the consignees, the committee prepared to require of all a
resignation of their office. Accordingly, in the night between
the first and second of November, letters were left at their Nov. 1.
doors for their appearance at Liberty Tree on Wednesday, at
noon, then and there to resign their commissions; and printed
notices were posted in the town, requesting the freemen of
Boston and its vicinity to meet at the same time and place, to
witness the ceremony.[3]

On the appointed day, at an early hour, a flag was hung out Nov. 3.
on Liberty Tree; and at eleven o'clock the bells were rung. At
twelve, five hundred persons assembled. Samuel Adams, John
Hancock, and William Phillips, three of the four representatives of Boston, were present, with William Cooper, the resolute town clerk, and the board of selectmen; and as the consignees failed to appear, a committee was appointed to wait
upon them at their stores. The people in a body then proceeded to King Street, to the warehouse of Richard Clarke,
and Molineux, one of the committee, acted as spokesman.

[1] Bancroft, vi. 469.
[2] Hutchinson, iii. 423; Gordon's
Hist. Pa. 481, 482; Hazard's Pa. Register, ii. 368; Boston Post Boy for
Nov. 1, 1773; Ramsay's Am. Rev. i.
98; Bancroft, vi. 470, 471.

[3] Order on Thos. and Elisha Hutchinson, Nov. 2, 1773, and Handbills,
posted Nov. 2 and 3, 1773; Boston
Post Boy for Nov. 8, 1773; Boston
News Letter for Nov. 4, 1773; Hutchinson, iii. 423; Bancroft, vi. 473.

"From whom are you a committee?" was the inquiry of Clarke. "From the whole people," was the brief reply. "And who are the committee?" was the next inquiry. "I am one," was the answer of Molineux; and he named the rest. "What is your request?" "That you give us your word to sell none of the teas in your charge, but return them to London in the same bottoms in which they were shipped. Are you ready to comply?" "I shall have nothing to do with you," was the haughty response. The same answer was returned by the other consignees; upon which Molineux, in a clear voice, read a resolve passed at Liberty Tree, declaring that those who should refuse to comply with the request of the people were "enemies to their country," and should be dealt with accordingly; and, after a short tarry, "every one returned to his own home."[1]

Nov. 5.   On Friday a legal meeting of the citizens was held in Faneuil Hall; John Hancock was chosen moderator; and a series of resolves, eight in number, a transcript of the Philadelphia resolves, was passed, with an additional resolve to prevent the sale of the company's teas. The meeting then adjourned "till three o'clock in the afternoon," when the committee which had been appointed to wait on the consignees reported that the Clarkes and Benjamin Faneuil persisted in refusing to resign their commissions, on the ground that they wished to consult the Hutchinsons, who were absent at Milton. A committee was next appointed to wait on the Hutchinsons; an adjourn-

Nov. 6. ment was proposed; and, upon reassembling, a letter was read from Thomas Hutchinson, which, with the reply of the Clarkes and of Faneuil, was declared to be "daringly effrontive to the town," and the meeting was dissolved.[2]

---

[1] Boston Post Boy for Nov. 8, 1773; Bancroft, vi. 473, 474. Some were for immediately ejecting the consignees, and cried, "Out with them! out with them!" But Molineux dissuaded from violence, and succeeded in pacifying the crowd. Comp. Hutchinson, iii. 424.

[2] Hutchinson, iii. 424; Boston Post Boy for Nov. 8, 1773; Boston News Letter for Nov. 11, 1773.

Twelve days later, intelligence was received through Captain Scott, who arrived with Jonathan Clarke, "one of the East India factors," that the "Boston tea ships" had actually sailed, and might be shortly expected; whereupon a new meeting was called for the following day, at which fresh resolutions were passed, and the consignees were again desired to resign. "We have received no orders from the East India Company respecting the teas," was their reply. "Our friends in England have entered into general engagements in our behalf, merely of a commercial nature, which puts it out of our power to comply with the request of the town." This answer was "voted unsatisfactory, and the meeting was dissolved." [1] The consignees were alarmed, and applied to the governor for aid; upon which the Council was convened, and a petition was presented from the "tea commissioners," praying to "resign themselves and the property committed to their care to his excellency and their honors, as guardians and protectors of the people," and that measures might be taken "for the landing and securing the teas, until the petitioners can be at liberty openly and safely to dispose of the same, or until they can receive directions from their constituents." [2] But the Council declined acting on the petition, on the ground that they "might as well become the trustees of all the individuals, and, *ex officio*, be the storekeepers of every store, in the province;" and the gentlemen were left to shift for themselves. [3]

On Monday, the committees of Dorchester, Roxbury, Brookline, and Cambridge met the Boston committee at the selectmen's chamber, in Faneuil Hall; and the question being put, "Whether it be the mind of this committee to use their joint influence to prevent the landing and sale of the teas exported

CHAP.
XIV.

1773.
Nov.17.

Nov.18.

Nov.19.

Nov.22.

---

[1] Hutchinson, iii. 426; Boston Post Boy for Nov. 22, 1773; Boston News Letter for Nov. 26, 1773; Boston Gazette for Nov. 8, 1773. "This sudden dissolution," says Hutchinson, "struck more terror into the consign- ees than the most minatory resolves."
[2] Hutchinson, iii. 426, 427; Boston Post Boy for Nov. 22, 1773.
[3] Boston Post Boy for Nov. 22, 1773; Boston Gazette for Dec. 27, 1773.

CHAP. from the East India Company," it passed in the affirmative
XIV. unanimously; and a letter was prepared to be sent to the other
1773. towns, soliciting their concurrence.[1] The governor, alarmed
at this demonstration, prepared to "flee to the Castle, where he
might, with safety to his person, more freely give his sense of
the criminality of the proceedings;"[2] but he was dissuaded
from a step which would manifest his cowardice, and remained
in the town. Yet with trembling and fear he listened to the
declarations of the people that "the teas should never be
landed;" and the consignees were warned of the "dreadful
consequences that must in all probability ensue" if they persisted in their refusal to send them back.[3]

Nov. 26.   Before the week was out, the citizens of Cambridge adopted
the Philadelphia resolves, and declared that whoever should
harbor the East India factors in their houses were "unfriendly
to their country;" and that any inhabitants of the province
who should import any teas subject to the payment of a duty
in America were "in an eminent degree enemies to their country, and ought to be treated with equal contempt and detesta-
tion with the present supposed factors." "And as it is very
apparent," they added, "that the town of Boston are now
struggling for the LIBERTIES of their country, it is therefore
Resolved, that this town can no longer stand idle spectators,
but are ready, on the shortest notice, to join with the town of
Boston and other towns in any measure that may be thought
proper to deliver ourselves and posterity from slavery." The
Nov. 27. citizens of Charlestown imitated this example, and adjourned
their meeting until the following Wednesday.[4]

Nov. 28.   On Sunday one of the ships arrived, bringing one hundred
and fourteen chests of tea.[5] Immediately the selectmen held

[1] Boston Gazette for Dec. 6, 1773; Bancroft, vi. 476.
[2] Letter of Hutchinson, of Nov. 24, 1773.
[3] Boston Gazette for Nov. 22, 1773.
[4] Boston Post Boy for Nov. 29, 1773; Boston News Letter for Dec. 2, 1773; Boston Gazette for Nov. 29, 1773.
[5] This was the Dartmouth. Boston News Letter for Dec. 2, 1773.

a meeting; and the committee of correspondence obtained CHAP.
from Rotch, the owner of the vessel, a promise not to enter it XIV.
until Tuesday. The towns around Boston were then sum- 1773.
moned to meet on Monday; "and every friend to his country,
to himself, and to posterity" was desired to attend, "to make
a united and successful resistance to this last, worst, and most
destructive measure of administration."[1]

At an early hour the people gathered; and by nine o'clock Nov.29.
the concourse was so great that Faneuil Hall was filled to
overflowing. A motion to adjourn to the Old South Meeting
House, the "Sanctuary of Freedom," was made and carried;
and, on reaching that place, Jonathan Williams was chosen
moderator, and Hancock, Adams, Young, Molineux, and Warren fearlessly conducted the business of the meeting. At least
five thousand persons were in and around the building; and
but one spirit animated all. Samuel Adams offered a resolution, which was unanimously adopted, that "the tea should be
sent back to the place from whence it came, at all events, and
that no duty should be paid on it." The consignees asked
time for consultation; and, "out of great tenderness," their
request was granted. To prevent any surprise, however, a
watch of twenty-five persons, under Edward Proctor, was appointed to guard the ship during the night.

The answer of the consignees was given in the morning; Nov.30.
and, after declaring that it was out of their power to send
back the teas, they expressed their readiness to store them
until otherwise advised. In the midst of the meeting the
sheriff of Suffolk entered, with a proclamation from the governor warning the people to disperse; but the message was
received with derision and hisses, and a unanimous vote not to
disperse. The master and owner of the ship which had lately
arrived were then required to attend; and a promise was extorted from them that the teas should be returned, without

[1] Boston Post Boy for Nov. 29, 1773; Boston News Letter for Dec. 2,
1773; Bradford, i. 301.

CHAP.
XIV.

1773.

touching land or paying a duty. The factors of two other vessels, which were daily expected, were next summoned, and similar promises were given by them ; upon which the meeting, after voting to carry into effect, "at the risk of their lives and properties," their former resolves, quietly dissolved.[1]

After this dissolution the committees of correspondence of Boston and its vicinity held meetings daily, and gave such directions as circumstances required. The other ships, on their arrival, were anchored beside the Dartmouth, that one guard might serve for all ; and the inhabitants of a number of towns, at meetings convened for the purpose, promised to aid Boston whenever their services should be needed.[2] At the end of twenty days the question must be decided ; and if the teas were landed, all was lost. As the crisis drew near the excitement increased. Hutchinson was confident that no violent measures would be taken. The wealth of Hancock and others seemed a sufficient security against such measures. But the people had counted the cost, and had determined to risk all rather than be slaves.

Dec. 16.

The eventful day at last dawned ; and two thousand from the country, besides the citizens of Boston, assembled in the Old South, at ten o'clock, to decide what should be done. It was reported that Rotch, the owner of the Dartmouth, had been refused a clearance ; and he was immediately instructed to "protest against the custom house, and apply to the governor for his pass." But the governor had stolen to his residence at Milton ; and at three o'clock in the afternoon Rotch had not returned. What should be done ? "Shall we abide by our resolutions?" it was asked. Adams and Young were in favor of that course ; Quincy, distinguished as a statesman

[1] Hutchinson, iii. 429–433 ; Boston Gazette for Dec. 6, 1773 ; Bancroft, vi. 478, 479.

[2] Votes of the inhabitants of Marblehead, Plymouth, and Medford, in Boston Post Boy for Dec. 13 and 20, 1773. Roxbury, Brookline, Dorchester, Charlestown, Newburyport, Malden, Lexington, Leicester, Fitchburg, Gloucester, and other towns, passed similar votes. Original Papers, 495, 670 ; Jour. of Com. of Corresp. in Bancroft, vi. 482 et seq.; Boston News Letter for Dec. 9 and 16, 1773.

and a patriot, advised discretion ; but the people cried, " Our CHAP.
hands have been put to the plough ; we must not look back ; " XIV.
and the whole assemblage, of seven thousand persons, voted 1773.
unanimously that the tea should not be landed.[1]

Darkness, in the mean time, had settled upon the town, and
in the dimly-lighted church the audience awaited the return of
Rotch. At a quarter before six he made his appearance, and
reported that the governor had refused him a pass. " We can
do no more to save the country," said Samuel Adams ; and a
momentary silence ensued. The next instant a shout was
heard at the door ; the war whoop sounded ; and forty or fifty
men, disguised as Indians, hurried along to Griffin's Wharf,
posted guards to prevent intrusion, boarded the ships, and in
three hours' time had broken and emptied into the sea three
hundred and forty-two chests of tea.[2] So great was the stillness that the blows of the hatchets, as the chests were split
open, were distinctly heard. When the deed was done, every
one retired, and the town was as quiet as if nothing had occurred. The next day travellers upon Dorchester beach found
the tea heaped up in windrows along the shore.[3] " This,"
says Hutchinson, " was the boldest stroke which had yet been
struck in America." [4]

The die was now cast. It was impossible to recede. " They
had passed the river, and cut away the bridge." Nothing remained but to bide the issue.[5] The governor was " in a forlorn
state," and was unable to keep up even " a show of authority."

[1] Boston Post Boy for Dec. 20,
1773 ; Boston News Letter for Dec.
23, 1773 ; Hutchinson, iii. 435, 436.
[2] Boston Post Boy for Dec. 20,
1773 ; Boston News Letter for Dec.
23, 1773 ; Boston Gazette for Dec.
20, 1773, and Supp't for Dec. 27,
1773 ; Hutchinson, iii. 436.
[3] MS. Journals, in the possession
of the author.
[4] Hist. Mass. iii. 439. "This," says
John Adams, Diary, in Works, ii. 323,
" is the most magnificent movement

of all. There is a dignity, a majesty,
a sublimity in this last effort of the
patriots that I greatly admire. The
people should never rise without doing something to be remembered. The
destruction of the tea is so bold, so
daring, so firm, intrepid, and inflexible, and it must have so important
consequences, and so lasting, that I
cannot but consider it an epocha in
history."
[5] J. Adams's Works, ix. 333.

CHAP.
XIV.

1773.

Every one was against him. The House were against him ;
the Council were against him ; " the superior judges were
intimidated from acting ; " and " there was not a justice of the
peace, sheriff, constable, or peace officer in the province who
would venture to take cognizance of any breach of law against
the general bent of the people." [1] The committees of correspondence were never more animated ; and a "declaration"
was drawn up to be sent abroad ; letters were written to all
the colonies ; " old jealousies were removed, and perfect harmony subsisted between all." [2] " A common cause," it was
said in the papers, " is best supported by a common association. The defence and maintenance of our rights and liberties
is the common cause of every American ; and all should unite,
hand in hand, in one common association, in order to support
it." [3] " Union," was the cry ; " union from Florida to the
plains of Canada." " A Congress of the states is indispensable ; we can redress ourselves if we will ; and what the people
wills shall be effected." [4]

The General Court stood prorogued to the twelfth of January ; but the governor, fearing to meet it at that time, issued

Dec. 31. a proclamation further proroguing it to the twenty-sixth of

1774.
Jan. 26.
the month.[5] In his opening address no notice was taken of
the recent transactions in Boston, and such things only were
mentioned as, in his estimation, " were least likely to give
room for any harsh or unkind return." [6] One thing was alluded to, however, which could not be passed over. This was his
signification of " his majesty's disapprobation of the appointment of committees of correspondence," to sit and act during

Feb. 5. the recess of the court. To this signification the House re-

[1] Hutchinson, iii. 437.
[2] S. Adams to J. Warren, Dec. 28, 1773.
[3] Boston Post Boy for Dec. 20, 1773.
[4] Boston Gazette for Dec. 27, 1773.
"From Florida, where heat intensely reigns,
To where we sought the Gaul on icy plains,
One mortal flame through every breast may spread,
By insult prompted and by FREEDOM led."
[5] Boston Post Boy for Dec. 27, 1773 ; Boston News Letter for Dec. 23, 1773.
[6] Hutchinson, iii. 442 ; Bradford's State Papers, 410.

plied that, " while the common rights of the American subjects CHAP.
continued to be attacked, at times when the several assemblies XIV.
were not sitting, it was highly necessary that they should cor- 1774.
Feb. 5.
respond with each other, in order to unite in the most effectual
means for the obtaining a redress of their grievances." " We
would, moreover, observe," they added, " that, as it has been
the practice for years past for the governor and lieutenant
governor of this province, and other officers of the crown, at
all times, to correspond with the ministers of state and persons
of distinction and influence in the nation, in order to concert
and carry on such measures of the British administration as have
been deemed by the colonists to be grievous to them, it cannot
be thought unreasonable or improper for the colonists to correspond with their agents, as well as with each other, to the
end that their grievances may be so explained to his majesty
as that, in his justice, he may afford them necessary relief." [1]

The principal topic of discussion in this session was the salaries which had been settled upon the judges by the king ; and
the officers were called upon to refuse to accept the same.
Four of them yielded ; but Oliver, the chief justice, declined,
and the House impeached him before the Council.[2] Hutchinson, to evade a decision of the question, proposed to prorogue
the court, and, as a preliminary step, acquainted them by message, that he had " received discretionary leave from the king Feb. 24.
to go to England," and, as he intended to avail himself of it,
should put an end to the session, that he might prepare for his
voyage.[3] But both Council and House persisted in their
course, and continued to labor for the removal of the chief
justice, as " the most necessary business before them." " If,
when we complain," said they, " we cannot even be heard, our

[1] Bradford's State Papers, 411, 412, and Hist. i. 308.
[2] Hutchinson, iii. 442–449 ; Brad-ford, i. 309–314 ; Boston Post Boy for Feb. 21 and 28, and March 7 and 14, 1774 ; Boston News Letter for March 3, 1774 ; Boston Gazette for Feb. 14, 1774 ; Andrews's Am. Rev. i. 133.
[3] Jour. H. of R. for 1774 ; Brad-ford's State Papers, 413 ; Hutchinson, iii. 449 ; Boston News Letter for March 3, 1774.

CHAP.
XIV.
1774.

Mar. 7.

Mar. 14.

Mar. 18.

Mar. 22.

Mar. 23.

case is indeed deplorable. Yet we have the pleasure of contemplating that posterity, for whom we are struggling, will do us justice by abhorring the memory of those men who owe their greatness to their country's ruin."[1] The governor, upon this, prepared to execute his purpose, and sent a messenger to the Council to close the session; but the House refused to admit the messenger until they had completed their business, and authorized the committee of correspondence to act in the recess of the court.[2]

In the mean time, in England the affairs of America were under discussion; and early in March, the news of the destruction of the tea having arrived,— "the last drop which made the waters of bitterness overflow,"— a message from the king and the American papers were laid before the House, and ordered to be read on the eleventh instant. On Monday of the following week a debate ensued; and, amidst confusion, leave was given to bring in a bill for the punishment of Boston, "the principal object of attention."[3] Four days later, the bill was reported, and was read the first time without debate. On its second reading, there was a slight discussion; but the bill was committed without a division.[4] Before its third reading, a petition against it from "several natives of North America" was presented by the Lord Mayor of London.[5] The House then went into a committee of the whole; and the discussion which followed was exceedingly spirited. "You cannot," said Rose Fuller, "carry this bill into execution without a military force. But if you send over a small

[1] Hutchinson, iii. 450.
[2] Hutchinson, iii. 453, 454; J. Adams, Diary, in Works, ii. 328–332. The Superior Court, after the impeachment of Oliver, did not sit again "until a new one was appointed by the Council exercising the powers of a governor under the charter, after the battle of Lexington, on the 19th of April, 1775." J. Adams.
[3] Debates in Parl. vii. 69–75; Parl. Hist. xvii. 1164, 1279; Gordon's Am.

Rev. i. 230, 231; Lord Mahon's Hist. Eng. vi. 3; Ramsay's Am. Rev. i. 100. Bollan petitioned to be heard for the Massachusetts Council; but the Commons refused to hear him. The Lords, however, gave him an audience; but his protest was of no avail.
[4] Debates in Parl. vii. 75, 76; Gordon's Am. Rev. i. 231.
[5] Debates in Parl. vii. 83–86; Ramsay's Am. Rev. i. 105.

number of men, the Boston militia will immediately cut them
to pieces; if you send over a larger number, six or seven
thousand, the Americans will debauch them; and by these
means we shall only hurt ourselves. I would begin by an
amercement."[1] Lord North, in reply, declared that he was
not an enemy to lenient measures, but that he had found resolutions of censure and warning to avail nothing. "We must,
therefore," he added, "proceed to some immediate remedy.
Now is our time to stand out, to defy them, to proceed with
firmness, and without fear. They will never reform until we
take a measure of this kind. I hope this act will not, in any
shape, require a military force to put it into execution. Four
or five frigates will do the business without any military force.
But if the consequences of disobedience are likely to produce
rebellion, that consequence belongs to them, and not to us. It
is not what we have brought on, but what they alone have
occasioned. We are only answerable that our measures are
iust and equitable. Let us, then, proceed with firmness, justice, and resolution."[2] Montagu, the second son of Lord
Sandwich, as "a virgin orator," defended the bill.[3] Byng, in
reply, exclaimed, "You are not punishing the Bostonians; you
are punishing the English merchants."[4] Charles Jenkinson
sided with the ministry, and eulogized Grenville; Charles
Fox spoke on the opposite side. Van declared that "the
town of Boston ought to be knocked about their ears, and
destroyed;" Barré indignantly exclaimed, "Keep your hands
out of the pockets of the Americans, and they will be obedi-
ent subjects. Parliament may fancy they have rights in the-
ory, which I'll answer for they can never reduce to practice."[5]

Two days later, the discussion was resumed; and Dowdeswell, Pownall, and Edmund Burke defended the Americans;

---

[1] Debates in Parl. vii. 86.
[2] Debates in Parl. vii. 87, 88.
[3] Debates in Parl. vii. 89, 90.
[4] Debates in Parl. vii. 91.

[5] Debates in Parl. vii. 92–94. For
a further sketch of this debate see
Boston News Letter for May 19, 1774.

CHAP. but so strongly did the current set in favor of the bill, that
XIV. remonstrances against it were viewed with disfavor, or listened
1774. to with impatience; it was passed without division, and was
sent to the Lords as if it had been unanimously assented to by
the Commons.[1] In this body the bill was more fairly dis-
Mar. 29. cussed; and the amiable Dartmouth favored conciliation. But
Mansfield exclaimed, "The sword is drawn, and you must
throw away the scabbard. If you pass this act with tolerable
unanimity, Boston will submit, and all will end in a victory
without carnage."[2] This decided the question; no division
was made; and the journal of the Lords declares that the
bill "passed unanimously."[3] Thus was the port of Boston
closed.

Apr. 19. At a subsequent date, to "prove that conciliation, not
revenge, was predominant in Britain," an immediate repeal of
the tax on tea was proposed; and in the debate which ensued,
Edmund Burke, in a masterly speech, surveyed the whole
course of the ministry for the past ten years, and declared in
favor of the measure now proposed. "Let us," said he, "act
like men; let us act like statesmen. Let us hold some sort
of consistent conduct. Leave the Americans as they anciently
stood. Do not burden them by taxes. When you drive him
hard, the boar will surely turn upon the hunters. If our sovereignty and their freedom cannot be reconciled, which will they
take? They will cast your sovereignty in your face. Nobody
will be argued into slavery."[4] But splendid eloquence was of
no avail. The opponents of America were more numerous

---

[1] Debates in Parl. vii. 94–104.
[2] Speech of Barré, May 2, 1774;
Shelburne to Chatham; Life of Lord
Mansfield; Bancroft, vi. 518, 519.
[3] Jour. H. of Lords for 1774. This
bill was signed March 31, 1774, being
"smuggled through the House in seventeen days only from its introduction.
The evidence before the privy council
was suppressed, the agents refused a
hearing at the bar, and no member

for Boston or America in either
house." Boston Post Boy for May
23, 1774. The bill was published in
the colonies with a black border around
it, as though it contained funeral news;
and it was cried in the streets of many
towns under the title of "A Barbarous, Cruel, Bloody, and Inhuman
Murder." Andrews's Am. Rev. i.
134; Lord Mahon's Hist. Eng. vi. 10.
[4] Debates in Parl. vii. 123–174.

than its friends. Only forty-nine voted to repeal the tax, and CHAP.
nearly four times that number voted against the repeal.[1] XIV.

Three other measures summed up the action of Parliament, 1774.
so far as the old colonies were concerned. These were, a bill April and
for "the better regulating the government of the Province of May.
the Massachusetts Bay," which abrogated so much of the charter as gave to the legislature the election of the Council; abol-
ished town meetings, except for the choice of town officers, or
on the special permission of the governor; conferred on the
executive the appointment and removal of sheriffs at pleasure;
and intrusted to the sheriffs the returning of juries; — a bill
"for the impartial administration of justice," &c., which transferred the place of trial of magistrates, revenue officers, or
soldiers indicted for murder, or other capital offence, to Nova
Scotia or Great Britain; — and a bill for legalizing the quartering of troops in Boston.[2] All these bills were petitioned
against and opposed by the friends of America; but they were
triumphantly carried, and were approved by the king. In the
mean time, Hutchinson was recalled, Thomas Gage was appointed in his stead, and four regiments were ordered to enforce submission.[3] By his instructions the governor was to Mar 31
close the port of Boston, and to take measures for bringing to
condign punishment those patriots who had led the people in
the recent movements. Samuel Adams, in particular, was

[1] Ayes, 49. Noes, 182. Debates
in Parl. vii. 178; Andrews's Am.
Rev. i. 119.

[2] Boston News Letter for June 9,
1774, and Boston Post Boy for June
6 and 13, 1774, where two of the bills
are given, with the debates thereupon.
Gordon's Am. Rev. i. 232–235; Bradford, i. 331; Andrews's Am. Rev. i.
120, 124; Lord Mahon's Hist. Eng.
vi. 5, 6; Bancroft, vi. 517, 525, 526;
Frothingham's Siege of Boston, 8.
Copies of these acts were received
June 2, and were immediately circulated throughout the colonies.

[3] Hutchinson, iii. 458; Bancroft,

vi. 523. It is said that Dartmouth
proposed to confer the government of
Massachusetts upon Thomas Pownall,
with a view to conciliate and quiet the
people; but a majority of the ministry opposed his appointment. Boston
News Letter for Sept. 16, 1773; Boston Gazette for Oct. 4, 1773; Bradford, i. 316. Gordon, Am. Rev. i.
237, says the appointment of Gage
was "not thought of by Mr. Hutchinson;" that he expected to have
been personally "intrusted with the
execution of the ministerial plan," and
"was rather disconcerted when he
found it to be otherwise."

CHAP. marked out for sacrifice, as "the chief of the revolution;"
XIV.   and against him and his associates proceedings were to be im-
1774. mediately and formally instituted.[1]

Pending the passage of the bills just alluded to, the citizens
of Massachusetts were not idle; and as it was evident that the
struggle must soon commence, throughout the province companies were organized, under officers of their own choosing; and
arms were provided for them, in the use of which they were
diligently trained.[2] Nor was the proposal for a Congress
overlooked; and John Hancock, in his oration on the anni-
Mar. 5. versary of the "Boston Massacre," suggested a "Congress of
deputies from the several houses of assembly on the continent,
as the most effectual method of establishing a union for the
security of the rights and liberties" of the country.[3] As a
preparatory step to the calling of such a Congress, a plan was
May.   formed for frequent and stated communications between the
colonies; and as Franklin had been removed from his office of
deputy postmaster general for America, private posts were
established, which were found to be of great service in conveying intelligence from place to place.[4]

May 17. General Gage reached Boston in May, and, on landing at
Long Wharf, was received with great parade. The principal
officers of the government, the selectmen of Boston, and "a
number of other gentlemen," were in attendance, with the company of Cadets; and, amidst the discharge of cannon from the
admiral's ship and from the north and south batteries, he was
escorted through King Street, where the troop of horse, the
artillery company, the grenadiers, and other military compa-

---

[1] Frothingham's Siege of Boston, 5, note; Boston Post Boy for July 11, 1774; Bancroft, vi. 523. The letter of Dartmouth to Gage, with instruc- tions, was dated April 9, 1774.

[2] Hutchinson, iii. 455. The local histories of different towns prove that some such preparations were made in the latter part of 1773.

[3] Oration of March 5, 1774, in Lib.

Mass. Hist. Soc. J. Adams, Diary, in Works, ii. 332, characterizes this as "an elegant, a pathetic, a spirited perform- ance." "The composition, the pro- nunciation, the action," he adds, "all exceeded the expectations of every body. They exceeded even mine, which were very considerable."

[4] Bradford, i. 320.

nies, were drawn up to salute him as he passed. On his arri- CHAP.
val at the council chamber his commission was read, and the XIV.
oath of office was administered by the president of the Council. 1774.
A proclamation was then issued, continuing all officers in their
places; three volleys were fired; three cheers were given;
and the governor was escorted to Faneuil Hall, where "an
elegant dinner was provided for his welcome." [1]

Already had the people been warned that the "ministry
were determined to try their metal to the utmost." "The
spoils of England," it was said, "are insufficient to support the
luxury of the minions of power; they have fixed their vora-
cious appetites upon the possessions of the Americans, and
intend to make a prey of them." "Depend upon it," it was
added, "every colony is to be subdued into a slavish obedience
to the tyrannical impositions of Great Britain. Nothing less
will suffice; nothing less is intended. After the subjection of
Boston, and perhaps all the New England governments, New
Jersey and New York are to be the next in course; and they
talk of taking away Penn's charter." [2] True, the commanders-
in-chief were not authorized to fight, unless they could provoke
the colonists to be the aggressors; nor were they to commence
hostilities without further orders. But how soon such orders
might come no one could tell; and the appeal for vigilance
was not ill-timed.

"Shall the Boston port bill be enforced?" was the question
which first solicited the attention of Gage; and a consultation
was held with Hutchinson, the admiral, and the commissioners
of the customs as to what should be done. All agreed that
the act should be enforced; and on the appointed day, as the
clock struck twelve, it went into effect; the custom house was June 1.
closed, and the courts were suspended. No opposition was
made by the people; but the bells of the churches were sol-

[1] Boston Post Boy for May 23,
1774; Boston News Letter for May
19, 1774; Frothingham's Siege of
Boston, 6.

[2] Letters from England, of April 7
and 8, 1774, in Boston Post Boy for
May 23, 1774.

CHAP.
XIV.

1774.

May 31.

Jun. 14
and 15.
July 4
and 5.

Aug.

May.

emnly tolled, mourning emblems were exhibited, and the day was improved, not only in Massachusetts, but even in Virginia, and indeed in other colonies, in fasting and prayer.[1] Hutchinson, with his family, left on the same day, in the Minerva, for England. From some parts of the province public testimonials of respect were tendered him;[2] but in general his departure was little lamented. He had forfeited the esteem of the lovers of liberty ; and, leaving the country which gave him birth, the remainder of his days was passed in England, where his descendants still reside.[3]

The troops which had been sent to enforce the port bill had not arrived ; and the loyalists anxiously awaited their appearance. "Many are impatient," wrote Gage, "for the arrival of the troops ; and I am told that people will then speak and act openly, which they now dare not do."[4] But they had not long to wait ; for in a little over a month a large force was concentrated in Boston. The king's regiment and the forty-ninth landed about the middle of June, and encamped on the Common ;[5] and early in July the fifth and thirty-eighth regiments landed at Long Wharf.[6] At Salem, likewise, the fifty-ninth regiment from Halifax was posted ;[7] and additional troops, to be quartered in Boston, were ordered from New York, the Jerseys, and Quebec.[8]

The annual election was a season of unusual depression and gloom ; and "many felt sad with the apprehension that it would be the last of the kind."[9] Nor was the conduct of

---

[1] Boston Post Boy for May 23, 1774; Gordon's Am. Rev. i. 239; Andrews's Am. Rev. i. 135 ; Ramsay's Am. Rev. i. 118; Grahame, ii. 488; Lord Mahon's Hist. Eng. vi. 10; Wirt's Patrick Henry, 113.

[2] Addresses were sent to him from 120 merchants and gentlemen of Boston, from members of the bar, the episcopal clergy, the magistrates of Middlesex, and from a number of citizens of Salem and Marblehead. Hutchinson's Hist. iii. 459; Boston

Post Boy for May 30 and June 6, 1774 ; Boston News Letter for June 2, 1774.

[3] Hist. iii. 459; Allen's Biog. Dict.

[4] Frothingham's Siege of Boston, 7.

[5] Boston Post Boy for June 20, 1774.

[6] Frothingham's Siege of Boston, 7.

[7] Newell's Diary, in Frothingham's Siege of Boston, 7.

[8] Gordon's Am. Rev. i. 252 ; Frothingham's Siege of Boston, 7.

[9] Gordon's Am. Rev. i. 238.

Gage such as to encourage the belief that he was disposed to CHAP conciliate; for when the board of councillors was presented to XIV. him for approval, thirteen were rejected;[1] and in his opening 1774. address he declared his intention, in obedience to the instruc- May 26. tions of the king, to remove the General Court to Salem.[2] The reply of the Council was not sent in until after these measures had taken effect; and while they declared their readi- June 9. ness, "on all occasions, cheerfully to coöperate with his excellency" in every step tending to "restore harmony" and "extricate the province from their present embarrassments," which were attributable, in their estimation, to the conduct of his "two immediate predecessors," they at the same time affirmed that "the inhabitants of the colony claimed no more than the rights of Englishmen, without diminution or abridgment;" and that these, "as it was their indispensable duty, so would it be their constant endeavor, to maintain, to the utmost of their power, in perfect consistence with the truest loyalty to the crown, the just prerogatives of which they should ever be zealous to support."[3] To this message, which was certainly respectful, the answer of the governor was short and bitter. Jun. 14. "I cannot," said he, "receive an address which contains indecent reflections on my predecessors, who have been tried and honorably acquitted by the Lords of the Privy Council, and their conduct approved by the king. I consider this address as an insult upon his majesty and the Lords of the Privy Council, and an affront to myself."[4]

The course of the House was equally decided; and while they congratulated his excellency upon his safe arrival, and declared that "they honored him in the most exalted station in the province, and confided in him to make the known constitution and charter the rule of his administration," they

---

[1] Gordon's Am. Rev. i. 239.
[2] Bradford's State Papers, 413.
[3] Boston Post Boy for June 20, 1774; Boston News Letter for June

16, 1774; Bradford's State Papers, 414, and Hist. i. 327.
[4] Boston Post Boy for June 20, 1774; Bradford's State Papers, 415.

CHAP.   deprecated the removal of the court to Salem, but expressed
XIV.   the hope that " the true state of the province, and the charac-
1774.   ter of his majesty's subjects in it, — their loyalty to their sovereign and their affection for the parent country, as well as
their invincible attachment to their just rights and liberties, —
would be laid before his majesty ; and that he would be the
happy instrument of removing his majesty's displeasure, and
restoring harmony, which had been long interrupted by the
artifices of interested and designing men."[1] Nor did they
pause here ; for Samuel Adams, satisfied that the time for
action had come, conferred with Warren, of Plymouth, and
convened " caucuses,"[2] in which the plan of a union of the
colonies was matured. This was to be brought before the
House for adoption ; and as the measure was of the utmost
importance, it was kept secret from the governor, lest it should
be frustrated.

Jun. 17.   On the appointed day the doors were closed and the subject
was broached ; but before any action could be taken in the
premises, a loyalist member obtained leave of absence, and immediately despatched a messenger to Gage, to inform him of
what was passing. The governor, in great haste, sent the
secretary to dissolve the court. Finding the door locked, he
knocked for admission, but was answered that " the House was
upon very important business, which when they had finished
they would let him in." Failing to obtain entrance, he stood
upon the steps, and read the proclamation in the hearing of
several of the members and others, and after reading it in the
council chamber, returned.[3] The House took no notice of

---

[1] Boston Post Boy for June 13, 1774 ; Bradford's Hist. i. 328, 329. The House, before proceeding to business at Salem, protested against the removal of the court.

[2] The word " caucus," which is of American invention, and which seems to have been first used in Boston, is employed to denote a meeting of cit-

izens to agree upon candidates to be proposed for election to office, or to concert measures for supporting a party. Its precise origin is not known. See Gordon's Am. Rev. i. 240 ; Webster's Dictionary.

[3] For the proclamation see Boston Post Boy for May 20, 1774.

this message, but proceeded with their business; and, by a CHAP.
vote of one hundred and seventeen to twelve, having deter- XIV.
mined that "a committee should be appointed to meet, as soon 1774.
as may be, the committees that are or shall be appointed by
the several colonies on this continent, to consult together upon
the present state of the colonies," James Bowdoin, Thomas
Cushing, Samuel Adams, John Adams, and Robert Treat Paine
were selected for that purpose, and funds were provided for
defraying their expenses.[1]   Yet even now, whatever the ardent
may have wished, all did not "meditate an independency of
Great Britain; much less did they suppose that a resort to
arms would be necessary to support their liberties."[2]   But
they were resolved to show the ministry that a determination
prevailed throughout the colonies to oppose their arbitrary and
oppressive laws; and that, whatever the cost to themselves,
they were ready to take a decided stand in defence of their
rights.

Already had meetings been held in Boston,[3] to adopt measures for relief from the burdens of the detested port bill; and
on the day that the court was prorogued, the citizens, by ad- Jun. 17
journment, gathered in Faneuil Hall, and, with John Adams
in the chair, with but one dissentient, voted that the committee
of correspondence be "enjoined forthwith to write to all the
other colonies, acquainting them that we are not idle; that we
are deliberating upon the steps to be taken in the present exigencies of our public affairs; that our brethren, the landed
interest of this province, with an unexampled spirit and unanimity, are entering into a non-consumption agreement;[4] and

[1] Boston Post Boy for June 20,
1774; Boston News Letter for June
23, 1774; J. Adams's Diary, in Works,
ii. 339; Gordon's Am. Rev. i. 240,
241; Andrews's Am. Rev. i. 137,
138; Bradford, i. 329–331.
[2] Bradford, i. 330.
[3] A meeting was held, May 13, to
consider the act of Parliament for
shutting up the port and harbor; and

it was voted to make application to
the other colonies to refuse all importations from Great Britain, and to
withhold all commercial intercourse
with her, as the most probable means
to procure the repeal of the act complained of. Bradford, i. 320; Andrews's Am. Rev. i. 134.
[4] This non-importation agreement,
which was called "the solemn league

that we are waiting with anxious expectation for the result of a CONTINENTAL CONGRESS, whose meeting we impatiently desire, in whose wisdom and firmness we confide, and in whose determinations we shall cheerfully acquiesce." [1] And well might Boston, and Charlestown, which was also suffering, pause and deliberate; for in both towns laborers were thrown out of employment, the poor lacked bread to eat, business was suspended, and a general gloom pervaded the streets. But sympathy for their distress was every where manifested; throughout the province, and even from other colonies, large contributions were sent for their relief; and the different towns seemed to vie with each other in hearty expressions of interest and friendship.[2]

Meanwhile, attention continued to be paid to military discipline; and old guns were repaired, knapsacks were brought out, and every one was anxious to be properly accoutred. County conventions were likewise called, in which the affairs of the province were debated; and the people of the interior assured their friends in the metropolis and its vicinity that "they were never more firm and zealous, and that they looked to the *last extremity* with spirit and resolution."[3] Some, in-

---

and covenant," was vehemently opposed by Gage as an "unlawful, hostile, and traitorous combination;" and he charged all magistrates to apprehend and secure for trial such as should have any share in aiding or abetting the same. Boston Post Boy for June 27, 1774; Gordon's Am. Rev. i. 248; Andrews's Am. Rev. i. 141; Ramsay's Am. Rev. i. 126; Bradford, i. 323.

[1] Boston Post Boy for June 20, 1774; Boston News Letter for June 23, 1774.

[2] Gordon's Am. Rev. i. 247, 249; Frothingham's Siege of Boston, 7. Salem, in particular, sent to Gage a memorial against the port bill breathing the noblest and purest spirit, and declaring that they should be dead to every idea of justice, and lost to all

feelings of humanity, could they indulge one thought to seize on wealth, and raise their fortunes on the ruins of their suffering neighbors. Boston Post Boy for May 20, 1774; Andrews's Am. Rev. i. 138; Ramsay's Am. Rev. i. 124.

[3] Gordon's Am. Rev. i. 249; Bradford, i. 333. "Husbands and wives," writes Gordon, "parents and children, brothers and sisters, lovers, the young and the old, seem possessed of, or rather to be possessed by, a martial spirit, and are fired with an enthusiastic zeal for liberty. In most places, but particularly in Berkshire and Worcester counties, where the influence of government was supposed to prevail most, nothing is to be seen or heard of except the purchasing of arms and ammunition, the casting of balls,

deed, took still stronger ground, and declared that "if the CHAP.
king violates his faith to, or compact with, any one part of his XIV.
empire, he discharges the subjects of that part of their alle- 1774.
giance to him, dismembers them from his kingdom, and reduces
them to the state of nature ; so that, in such case, he ceases to
be their king, and his governor, set over such part as his representative, ceases to have any lawful authority to govern that
people ; and they are at liberty to form themselves into an
independent state."[1] With such a spirit abroad, which was
daily strengthening, there was reason to hope that when the
crisis came, it would be properly met. But the loyalists were
not inactive ; and Gage wrote to Dartmouth, "There is now
an open opposition to the faction, carried on with a warmth
and spirit unknown before, which it is highly proper and necessary to cherish and support by every means ; and I hope it will
not be long before it produces salutary effects."[2]

That the new governor was unfit for the position he filled
soon became evident to all except his particular friends. Arrogant in the discharge of his office, and adding to incapacity
gross insincerity in his intercourse with the people, his course
was, if any thing, more obnoxious than that of Bernard. Official copies of the recent acts of Parliament, which "cut away
the scaffolding of English freedom," were received by his excellency early in August ; and he was instructed at all hazards to Aug. 6.
put them in force.[3] With these orders there came a nomination of thirty-six councillors, twenty-four of whom immediately
accepted. Their first meeting was held two days after ; and a Aug. 8.
meeting of the whole was called on the sixteenth, soon after Aug. 16.
which the judges proceeded to hold courts, and the sheriffs to
summon juries. The question of obedience now came up ; and
the people were ready and prepared to meet it. The council-

and the making of all those preparations which testify the most immediate
danger and determined resistance."
[1] Bradford, i. 333, 334.
[2] Letter of Gage, in Parl. Reg. for

1775 ; Frothingham's Siege of Boston, 7.
[3] Andrews's Am. Rev. i. 145 ;
Frothingham's Siege of Boston, 9.

CHAP. lors who had accepted their appointments were compelled to
XIV. resign or to flee to Boston; and in one of the western towns,[1]
1774. the judges, on attempting to hold courts, were driven from the
bench.[2] At length the committee of Worcester suggested a
meeting of the different committees, to conclude upon a plan
of operation for the province ; and the Boston committee, at
Aug. 26 their request, called such a meeting at Faneuil Hall, in which
and 27.
it was resolved that a Provincial Congress was necessary to
counteract the systems of despotism ; that, previous to the
meeting of such Congress, the courts ought to be opposed, and
the officers holding them be branded as traitors ; that " every
defender of the rights of the province or of the continent
ought to be supported by the whole country, and, if need be,
by the province ; " and that, " as a necessary means to secure
the rights of the people, the military art, according to the
Norfolk plan, ought to be attentively practised." [3]

The inhabitants of Middlesex were the first to act on these
resolves ; and at a convention at Concord of one hundred and
Aug.30. fifty delegates, from every town and district in the county, it
was declared that to obey the recent acts of Parliament " would
be to annihilate the last vestiges of liberty in this province ;
and therefore we must be justified by God and the world in
never submitting to them." " No danger," they added, " shall
affright, no difficulties intimidate us ; and if, in support of our
rights, we are called to encounter even death, we are yet undaunted, sensible that he can never die too soon who lays down
his life in support of the laws and liberties of his country." [4]

The governor, in view of these proceedings, determined to
call in the aid of his troops to disperse public meetings and
protect the courts ; and his first attempt was made at Salem,

---

[1] Great Barrington. Gordon's Am.
Rev. i. 253.
[2] Ramsay's Am. Rev. i. 126, 127 ;
Gordon's Am. Rev. i. 253 ; Andrews's
Am. Rev. i. 145 ; Frothingham's Siege
of Boston, 10.

[3] Frothingham's Siege of Boston,
11, 361–363, from MSS. in the Mass.
Hist. Soc.
[4] Boston News Letter for Sept. 15,
1774 ; Frothingham's Siege of Boston, 12.

where a meeting was convened to elect delegates to a county CHAP.
convention to be held at Ipswich. But his proclamation did <u>XIV.</u>
not prevent the meeting of the convention; nor did the de- 1774.
tachment which he sent to enforce his orders awe the people, Aug.24.
who transacted their business and adjourned, much to the discomfiture of his excellency, who gratified his resentment by
arresting three of the originators of the assembly.[1]

His next step was to secure the cannon and powder of the
province; and at the instance of Brattle, a detachment of two
hundred and sixty men, under Lieutenant Colonel Maddison,
was sent at an early hour, in thirteen boats, to the powder Sept. 1.
house on Quarry Hill, in that part of Charlestown now called
Somerville; and two hundred and fifty barrels of powder —
about thirteen tons in all — were seized and carried off. Another detachment was likewise sent to Cambridge, and two
field pieces, lately procured for the regiment of that place, were
taken, with which the party proceeded to Castle William.[2]
The people, indignant at these movements, collected in great
numbers, and many were in favor of attempting to recapture
the powder and cannon; but more prudent counsels prevailed;
and on the following day they repaired in a body to the resi- Sept. 2.
dence of Lieutenant Governor Oliver, and obliged him to resign
his office, and procured the resignation of other important
officers.[3] The seizure of the stores of the province, in the
mean time, was magnified into a report that Boston had been
cannonaded; and bells were rung, and beacon fires were lighted, which called in crowds from the country towns, and even
from other provinces, who, with arms in their hands, hastened
to the supposed scene of danger.[4]

---

[1] Gordon's Am. Rev. i. 253; Frothingham's Siege of Boston, 13.

[2] J. Adams, Diary, in Works, ii. 370; Gordon's Am. Rev. i. 254; Frothingham's Siege of Boston, 13, and Hist. Charlestown, 301, 302.

[3] Boston Gazette for Sept. 5, 1774; Gordon's Am. Rev. i. 254; Ramsay's Am. Rev. i. 127; Frothingham's Siege of Boston, 14, and Hist. Charlestown, 302-305.

[4] J. Adams's Diary, in Works, ii. 368; Gage to Dartmouth, Sept. 25, 1774; Frothingham's Siege of Boston, 14, and Hist. Charlestown, 302-305; Lincoln's Hist. Worcester, 96.

CHAP.   Satisfied by this time that he had kindled a fire which could
XIV.   not be easily quenched, the governor, in his despatches to Eng-
1774.   land, declared that "the flames of sedition had spread universally throughout the country beyond conception;" and that
nothing could be done but by forcible means.[1] But the people
scorned his most violent menaces; and no pains were spared
to secure and secrete their remaining stores. Hence cannon
and muskets were stealthily removed from Boston to the coun-
Sep. 15. try; and the guns were taken from an old battery in Charlestown, where the navy yard now is.[2]

Previous to this date, Gage had resolved to erect fortifications on the neck, which commanded the entrance to the town;
Sept. 5. and the people, alarmed at these demonstrations, protested,
through the selectmen, against his proceedings. His excellency replied that it was necessary to provide for the safety
of the troops, and that he had no design to stop up the avenue,
or to check the ingress or egress of the peaceably disposed.
Accordingly he went on with the works, and soon mounted
two twenty-four pounders and eight nine pounders. The select-
Sept. 9. men again protested, and declared that such conduct, in their
estimation, evinced a determination to reduce the metropolis
to the state of a garrison; but his excellency repeated his former assurances, and suggested that, as he was peaceably disposed, if the people would be likewise peaceable no difficulties
would arise. Thus the controversy continued. The governor
persisted in adhering to his plans, and the people commented
upon his course with asperity.[3]

Sept. 5. In the mean time the CONTINENTAL CONGRESS assembled at
Carpenter's Hall, in Philadelphia. Peyton Randolph was
chosen president, and Charles Thomson secretary. The meetings were opened with prayer, and the convention was organ-

[1] Frothingham's Siege of Boston,
14.
[2] Frothingham's Siege of Boston,
15, and Hist. Charlestown, 306.

[3] Gordon's Am. Rev. i. 254, 255;
Jour. Cont. Cong. i. 14–19; Frothingham's Siege of Boston, 16, 17.

ized with all the solemnities of a regular legislature.[1] The CHAP.
most eminent men of America were there; and all were im- XIV.
pressed with the importance of the business they had met to 1774.
transact.[2] The liberties of three millions of people were at
stake; the waves of tyranny were sweeping over the land;
and whether they would be able to breast those waves depended upon their prudence, their calmness, and unity. Is it surprising that, at first, a deathlike silence pervaded the meeting?
This silence was broken by Patrick Henry, the Demosthenes
of his day, who, with the glowing eloquence for which he was
distinguished, recited the wrongs which the people had endured,
for which redress was imperiously demanded. His speech was
at once both noble and manly; and on taking his seat, murmurs of applause and astonishment were heard. The gifted
Lee, who has been compared to Cicero, participated in the
debate, in an address of classic elegance, which filled the ear
with bewitching harmony, and charmed the senses with exquisite imagery. But eloquence alone did not carry the day.
Ripened wisdom, calm reflection, delicacy, caution, and all the
elements which are essential to the conduct of a deliberative
assembly, were possessed by that body in a remarkable degree;
and these qualities, which can alone direct with entire success
measures affecting the destinies of a continent, enabled them to
move on with dignity and power.[3]

Three weeks were spent in reading addresses, appointing

---

[1] For a list of the members, nearly half of whom were lawyers, see the Journals of the Congress, i. 3, 4. The committee for Massachusetts took their departure from Boston on the 10th of August. J. Adams's Diary, in Works, ii. 340; also, ibid. 365, 368.

[2] "Mr. Deane says the sense of Connecticut is, that the resolutions of the Congress shall be the laws of the Medes and Persians; that the Congress is the grandest and most important body ever held in America; and that the *all* of America is intrusted to

it and depends upon it." J. Adams's Diary, in Works, ii. 341. Comp. Reed's Reed, i. 75; Ramsay's Am. Rev. i. 133; Grahame, ii. 493; and Lord Mahon's Hist. Eng. vi. 14.

[3] J. Adams's Diary, in Works, ii. 365–368; Lord Mahon's Hist. Eng. vi. 15; Wirt's Patrick Henry, 124–126. It is said that the ministry in England sent large sums to New York to bribe the delegates from that colony to oppose the proceedings of the Congress. Gordon's Am. Rev. i. 284, 285.

CHAP.
XIV.

1774.
Sep. 27.

Sep. 30.

Oct. 1.

Oct. 14.
Oct. 18.
Oct. 19.

Oct. 20.

Oct. 26.

committees, and preparing for business; when, having approved the Boston resolutions, towards the last of the month it was resolved unanimously "that from and after the first day of December next there be no importation into British America, from Great Britain or Ireland, of any goods, wares, or merchandise whatever, or from any other place of any such goods, wares, or merchandises as shall have been exported from Great Britain or Ireland; and that no such goods, &c., imported after the said first day of December next be used or purchased."[1] Three days later another resolve was passed, that "from and after the tenth day of September, 1775, the exportation of all merchandise, and every commodity whatsoever, to Great Britain, Ireland, and the West Indies, ought to cease, unless the grievances of America are redressed before that time."[2]

With these preliminaries settled, the convention was prepared for the adoption of further measures; and a committee was appointed to bring in a loyal address to the king, dutifully requesting his attention to the grievances which alarmed and distressed his subjects in North America; an able declaration of rights, embodied in eleven articles, was reported, debated, and passed; an address to the people of England was draughted, another to the people of Canada, and a memorial to the inhabitants of the British American colonies; a non-importation agreement was drawn up and subscribed; and a letter to the agents of the colonies in England was prepared.[3] In all things the business of the convention was conducted with propriety; and after its session had continued for seven weeks, the meeting was dissolved.

Every eye was now fixed upon Boston, once the seat of

---

[1] Jour. Cont. Cong. i. 21.
[2] Jour. Cont. Cong. i. 21.
[3] Jour. Cont. Cong. i. 22, 26–68; Andrews's Am. Rev. i. 157–170; Gordon's Am. Rev. i. 258–268; J. Adams's Diary, in Works, ii. 370 et seq.; Lord Mahon's Hist. Eng. vi. 15, 16. The declaration of rights was substantially the same as that adopted by the people of Boston, an abstract of which has already been given.

commerce and plenty, and inhabited by an enterprising and CHAP.
hospitable people. The cause in which it suffered was regarded XIV.
as the common cause of the country. A hostile fleet lay in its 1774.
harbor; hostile troops paraded its streets. The tents of an
army dotted its Common; cannon were planted in commanding
positions. Its port was closed; its wharves were deserted;
its commerce was paralyzed; its shops were shut; and many
were reduced from affluence to poverty. Yet a resolute spirit
inspired them still. Loyalists, indeed, were numerous and
ardent, exulting over the sorrows and distresses of their neighbors. But with whatever confidence they relied upon the military talents of the governor, and his fixed resolution to enforce
his instructions, the "Sons of Liberty" knew no despair; and
the "Liberty Song," set to the tune of "Smile Britannia," bade
the citizens of the beleaguered town

> "Be not dismayed!
> Though tyrants now oppress,
> Though fleets and troops invade,
> You soon will have redress.
> The resolution of the brave
> Will injured Massachusetts save." [1]

For a time unusual quietness reigned; so much so that Gage
and the officers of the army began to flatter themselves that
the people were subdued.[2] But this stillness was ominous, and
would have been so construed by his excellency, had he been
thoroughly acquainted with the temper of the people. Submission was the last thought of the patriots of Boston. They
were preparing for resistance, preparing in secret, preparing

---

[1] Essex Gazette for Oct. 25, 1774;
Frothingham's Siege of Boston, 39,
where the whole song, in six verses,
is given.

[2] "The faction in Boston is now
very low. Believe me, all ranks of
people are heartily tired of disorder
and confusion; and, as soon as the determination of Great Britain to despise
their resolves and petitions is known,
all will be very quiet." Letter of Nov.
3, 1774, in Frothingham's Siege of
Boston, 40, note.

CHAP. with a fixed, determinate purpose. The town was full of clubs
XIV. and caucuses, which were used with effect to secure unity of
1774. action ; and the hardy mechanics, who had done so much to
promote the industrial prosperity of the metropolis, and who
now acted as patrols, were the steady supporters of the patriot
cause. In vain were the artifices of loyalists employed to
seduce them to compliance with the wishes of his excellency ;
and when their services were required at the barracks, "all
Sep. 26. the carpenters of the town and country" left off work ; and
British gold was powerless to tempt them, though "hundreds
were ruined, and thousands were half starved." [1] Nay, they
went farther, and obstructed the works of the governor. His
supplies of straw were set on fire ; his boats conveying bricks
were sunk ; and his wagons laden with timber were over-
turned. [2]

Nor should the noble example of woman be forgotten.
Mothers and daughters infused their own earnest, principled
spirit of resistance to tyranny into the bosoms of fathers and
sons, and addressed to them words of persuasion and encouragement ; and none more cheerfully than they submitted to priva-
tions, or encountered the trials which fall with peculiar hardship
on their sex. Exposed to the brutal passions of the soldiery,
and conscious that they were bringing upon themselves manifold
sorrows, they yet counselled not with fear ; but, devoting themselves to the cause of their country, they were ready to sacrifice
home and its charms, life and its endearments, and all the
countless blessings of peace, rather than give up — what was
dearer than all — liberty, without which life is a curse. Those
gentler emotions which are their ornament and pride, and even
their natural aversion to blood, were, for the time, to give way
to a sterner and more resolute temper. Yet, withal, they
moved in the new sphere opened to them with the same quiet
dignity and the same deep tenderness which render their pres-

[1] Gordon's Am. Rev. i. 270; Froth-   [2] Gordon's Am. Rev. i. 252; Lord
ingham's Siege of Boston, 25, 26.   Mahon's Hist. Eng. vi. 12.

ence a blessing at all times; and the delicate offices which CHAP
none but their hands could so well perform, in the hour of trial XIV.
assuaged the pain of many a wound, and relieved the ghastli- 1774.
ness and horrors of death.

Writs were issued early in September convening the General Sept. 1.
Court at Salem on the fifth of October; but before that time
arrived, a proclamation from the governor dissolved the assem- Sep. 28.
bly. For this step the patriots of the province were prepared;
and, pursuant to the course which had been already agreed
upon, after meeting on the appointed day, they resolved them- Oct. 5.
selves into a PROVINCIAL CONGRESS.[1] The first session of this
body, so memorable in our annals, was held at Salem on Friday, the seventh of October; the meeting was temporarily Oct. 7.
organized by choosing John Hancock chairman and Benjamin
Lincoln clerk, and was adjourned to the following Tuesday,
then to meet at the court house in Concord.[2] Finding the
court house too small for their purpose, however, the meeting Oct. 11.
house was procured; the Congress was permanently organized
by choosing John Hancock president and Benjamin Lincoln
clerk; and provisions were made for opening the session each
day with prayer.[3] A committee on the state of the province
was next appointed; and an address to his excellency the governor was reported, which was ordered to be printed in the Oct. 13
Boston newspapers;[4] the several constables and collectors
throughout the province, having moneys in their hands payable to the order of Harrison Gray, Esq., were advised to retain
the same, subject to the advice of a constitutional assembly;[5]
and the convention was adjourned to the town of Cambridge.

On assembling at this place, a message from the governor Oct. 17
was read to the meeting, in which, after speaking of his inten-

[1] Jour. Prov. Cong. 3, 4; Gordon's Am. Rev. i. 268; Ramsay's Am. Rev. i. 129; Andrews's Am. Rev. i. 150; Lord Mahon's Hist. Eng. vi. 17; Frothingham's Siege of Boston, 41.

[2] Jour. Prov. Cong. 7–15, where the list of the members is given; Gordon's Am. Rev. i. 269.

[3] Jour. Prov. Cong. 15, 16; Gordon's Am. Rev. i. 269.

[4] Jour. Prov. Cong. 17, 18; Gordon's Am. Rev. i. 269.

[5] Jour. Prov. Cong. 19.

CHAP.
XIV.

1774.

tion to pursue his measures for constructing a fortress in Boston, he declared that Britain could "never harbor the black design of wantonly destroying or enslaving any people on earth," and warned them of the "rock they were upon," and required them to "desist from such illegal and unconstitutional proceedings." [1] For some days the business of the Congress was conducted with closed doors; committees of safety, of inquiry, and on the state of the province were appointed; and every thing was done that could be to prepare for the crisis which was rapidly hastening. A protest against slavery was likewise introduced, "purporting the propriety, that, while we are attempting to free ourselves from our present embarrassments, and preserve ourselves from slavery, we also take into consideration the state and circumstances of the negro slaves in this province." And it should be said, to the honor of the people of Massachusetts, — who had ever at heart been opposed to this institution, who had legislated for its suppression, and who felt the inconsistency of holding in bondage one class of their fellow-beings while they were struggling to secure their own freedom, — that this subject, once introduced, was never lost sight of until measures were taken which ended in the extinction of so great an evil. [2]

Oct. 26.

As the improvement of the militia was an object of importance, arrangements were made for increasing the quantity of warlike stores, and organizing an army; and the several towns and districts in the province were advised to "see that each

Dec. 10.

of the *minute men* not already provided therewith should be immediately equipped with an effective firearm, bayonet, pouch, knapsack, and thirty rounds of cartridge and balls, and be disciplined three times a week, and oftener as opportunity may offer;" [3] and in the second Congress, where any deficiency in

[1] Jour. Prov. Cong. 20, 21; Gordon's Am. Rev. i. 269.

[2] Jour. Prov. Cong. 29.

[3] Jour. Prov. Cong. 33, 34, 47, 71. Jedediah Preble, Artemas Ward, and Seth Pomeroy were elected general officers, to have the command of the militia if called into action; but Preble did not accept, and John Thomas and William Heath were subsequently appointed. Gordon, i. 270; Ramsay's Am. Rev. i. 130; Frothingham's Siege of Boston, 41, 42.

arms or accoutrements was found, the selectmen of the towns CHAP.
were instructed to supply the same "out of the town stock; XIV.
and in case of a deficiency there, to apply to such inhabitants 1774.
as can best spare their arms or accoutrements, and to borrow
or purchase the same for the use of the inhabitants so enlisting."[1] A receiver general was likewise chosen, to act as the Oct. 28.
treasurer of the province, and Henry Gardner was selected for
that purpose;[2] sympathy was expressed for the town of Boston and its neighbor, Charlestown;[3] the proceedings of the
Continental Congress were approved, and delegates to a new
Congress were chosen;[4] an address to the clergy was prepared;[5] a committee was appointed to report on the population of the province, and the state of manufactures;[6] an address was sent out "to the freeholders and other inhabitants
of the towns and districts of Massachusetts Bay;"[7] and after
providing for calling a future Congress, the meeting was dis- Dec. 10.
solved.[8]

Loyalists, in the mean time, had also been active; and
throughout the province they had been concocting measures
for the furtherance of the work in which the governor was
engaged. Timothy Ruggles, of Hardwick, was one of their
leaders; and, at his instance, papers were drawn up, to be circulated in every town, calling upon the "friends to government" to form an association to counteract the designs of the
Provincial Congress.[9] Nor was this all. The number of
troops quartered in Boston had been greatly augmented; so
that in November the force consisted of eleven regiments and Nov.
the artillery; and in December five hundred marines landed Dec.
from the Asia.[10] This army was in "high spirits;" provisions

---

[1] Jour. Prov. Cong. 209, 210.
[2] Jour. Prov. Cong. 38, 39, 45.
[3] Jour. Prov. Cong. 54, 59.
[4] Jour. Prov. Cong. 56, 57. John
Hancock, Thomas Cushing, Samuel
Adams, John Adams, and Robert
Treat Paine were the persons selected.
[5] Jour. Prov. Cong. 60.
[6] Jour. Prov. Cong. 61–65.

[7] Jour. Prov. Cong. 69–72.
[8] Jour. Prov. Cong. 73, 74.
[9] Jour. Prov. Cong. 68, and Boston
News Letter for Dec. 29, 1774, where
the form of association is given.
[10] Boston News Letter for Oct. 20,
1774; Frothingham's Siege of Boston, 43.

CHAP.
XIV.

1774.

were plenty, and they had little to do but to mount guard, parade, and boast of their prowess. The calmness of the people was viewed as an evidence of timidity or cowardice; and officers wrote to their friends, "As to what you hear of their taking arms to resist the force of England, it is mere bullying, and will go no further than words. Whenever it comes to blows, he that can run the fastest will think himself best off. Believe me, any two regiments here ought to be decimated if they do not beat, in the field, the whole force of the Massachusetts province; for though they are numerous, they are but a mob, without order or discipline, and very awkward at handling their arms." [1]

1775.
Jan.

Jan. 17.

At the opening of the new year, Boston was garrisoned by thirty-five hundred soldiers of the king; and Gage, who was already confident of success, wrote to Dartmouth that, "if a respectable force is seen in the field, the most obnoxious of the leaders seized, and a pardon proclaimed for all others, government will come off victorious, and with less opposition than was expected a few months ago." [2] But his excellency misestimated the forbearance of the people. Hitherto, violent counsels had been deprecated, not from the want of a will to resist, but because such resistance, without sufficient provocation, might have been used to their disadvantage, and would have been regretted by the prudent in other colonies. The patriots of Boston, therefore, were determined not to be the aggressors, but to submit to indignities and insults, if possible, without retaliating. Besides, delay was necessary to perfect their measures and increase their resources; and as a resort to arms at this stage of affairs would have found the province poorly supplied with the munitions of war, there was nothing to be lost, but every thing to be gained, by patiently awaiting

[1] Gordon's Am. Rev. i.; Frothingham's Siege of Boston, 44.
[2] Gage to Dartmouth, Jan. 17, 1775; Boston News Letter for Jan. 5, 1775; Frothingham's Siege of Boston, 46.

the action of the governor, and leaving events to shape them- CHAP.
selves.[1] XIV.

The first symptoms of the approaching struggle came from 1775.
a quarter least expected. The Ruggles covenant, which has
already been alluded to, had been diligently circulated ; and
in the old colony it found a number of signers. In Marshfield,
in particular, the " loyal association " became quite large ;[2]
and as the patriots of the neighborhood evinced a determination to make them recant, they hastily applied to Gage for
relief, who sent a detachment of one hundred men, under Cap- Jan. 23.
tain Balfour and three subalterns, with two field pieces and
three hundred stands of arms, for their protection. But the
presence of such a force, however exact the discipline preserved, could not fail to excite alarm ; and though they boasted that " every faithful subject to his king " was enabled
" freely to utter his thoughts, drink his tea, and kill his sheep
as profusely as he pleases," an address was sent to the governor from the selectmen of Plymouth, Kingston, Duxbury, Feb.
Pembroke, Hanover, and Scituate, protesting against the course
he had pursued, and requesting their recall.[3] The second Provincial Congress was in session at this time ;[4] and upon the
reception of a copy of this address, passed a vote approving Feb. 14
the vigilance of the patriots, and recommending them " steadily to persevere in the same line of conduct which has, in this
instance, so justly entitled them to the esteem of their fellow-

---

[1] " The fortitude," says Gordon,
Am. Rev. i. 279, " with which the
town of Boston supports its present
distresses, and the determination it
discovers to endure as much as human
nature can, rather than betray the
American cause and endanger the liberties of posterity, will secure it the
encomiums of future generations. Not
a town or city in all the colonies would
have been likely to have exhibited so
glorious a spectacle, had it been called
out to a similar trial ; and all the
friends of American liberty throughout the continent may congratulate

themselves that the storm of ministerial vengeance has fallen first on the
capital of Massachusetts, as in consequence of it they have enjoyed the
opportunity of providing against the
worst that may be attempted in order
to reduce them to subjection."
[2] An article in Rivington's Gazette
of Feb. 9, 1775, represents the number as two hundred.
[3] Boston Post Boy for Feb. 27,
1775 ; Winsor's Duxbury, 127, 128.
[4] It met at Cambridge, Feb. 1,
1775. Jour. 77.

CHAP. countrymen, and to keep a watchful eye upon the behavior of
XIV. those who are aiming at the destruction of our liberties."[1]

1775.   The expedition to Marshfield was followed by one to Salem,
Feb. 26. where a few brass cannon and gun carriages were deposited.
The troops detached for this purpose were placed under Colonel Leslie, and embarked on Sunday, landed at Marblehead in
the afternoon, while the people were at meeting, and marched
to the town by the way of the North Bridge. On arriving at
this spot, however, they found their progress arrested, the
draw of the bridge being hoisted to prevent their passage.
The colonel ordered it to be lowered, but was answered, " It is
a private way, and you have no authority to pass over it."
He then prepared to seize two gondolas which were moored
near by ; but their owners jumped in, and began to scuttle
them. A scuffle ensued, and the soldiers thrust at the people
with their bayonets ; but, by the intervention of Mr. Barnard,
a clergyman of Salem, a compromise was effected, and the
bridge was lowered, after Leslie had given a pledge that he
would not march more than thirty rods beyond it. Thus
bloodshed was prevented, and the brave colonel,

> " Without loss of time or men,
>   Veered round for Boston back again,
>   And found so well their projects thrive,
>   That every soul got home alive."[2]

Meanwhile, in England, the affairs of America were again
discussed, and the debates in both Houses were full and animated. Josiah Quincy, one of the truest of the Boston patriots, had recently arrived in London, and was present in Parliament ; and the minutes from his pen are the more valuable

---

[1] Jour. Prov. Cong. 103, 104.
[2] Gentleman's Magazine for 1775 ;
Boston News Letter for March 2,
1775 ; Almon's Remembrancer for
1775, 60 ; Essex Gazette for Feb.
1775 ; Gordon's Am. Rev. i. 305, 306 ;
Andrews's Am. Rev. i. 287 ; Bradford, i. 365, 366 ; Felt's Hist. Salem ;
Frothingham's Siege of Boston, 47,
48. The lines in the text are from
Trumbull's M'Fingal.

from the fact that this was the last service he was able to ren- CHAP.
der his country, his death following soon after.[1] Bernard and XIV.
Hutchinson were "incessant in their applications to adminis- 1775.
tration;" all the "measures against America were planned
and pushed on" by them; and they "gave the most positive
assurance of success."[2]   Lord North had repeatedly said,
"We must try what we can do to support the authority we
have claimed over America; if we are defective in power, we
must sit down contented, and make the best terms we can;
and nobody then can blame us after we have done our utmost;
but till we have tried what we can do, we can never be justified in receding; and we ought to and shall be very careful
not to judge a thing impossible because it may be difficult;
nay, we ought to try what we can effect, before we can determine upon its impracticability."[3] Such being the state of
feeling in England, is it surprising that arbitrary measures
should have been vehemently counselled? Indeed, it is acknowledged by a recent historian of that country that "there
was then a general tendency at home to undervalue the colonies; and they, and more especially the natives of New England, were often called by the name of YANKEES, which had
grown to be, in some measure, a term of reproach." "To
such an extent," he adds, "did these disparaging reflections
proceed, that a doubt was even uttered whether the Americans
possessed the same natural courage as the English."[4]

It was at the commencement of the new year, after the usual Jan. 20
holiday recess, that the American question was brought forward in the House of Lords by the Earl of Chatham, when

---

[1] Gordon, Am. Rev. i. 282 et seq.,
quotes from Quincy's Journal. Comp.
Grahame, ii. 501; Quincy's Life of
Quincy.

[2] Quincy, in Gordon, i. 283. "Governor P[ownall] assured me that all
the measures," &c. Comp. Lord Mahon's Hist. Eng. vi. 7. "Hutchinson,
on his arrival in England, was admit-

ted to an audience of his majesty, and
tended much by his misrepresentations
to confirm the government in the
hopes which they had formed."

[3] Quincy, in Gordon, i. 283. "Lord
N. repeatedly said to me," &c.

[4] Lord Mahon's Hist. Eng. vi. 7.
Comp. Andrews's Am. Rev. i. 130.

the bar was crowded with Americans, among whom stood conspicuous the venerable Franklin. An address to the king was moved, to open a way towards allaying the ferments and softening the animosities in America, requesting him to order the removal from Boston of the troops under Gage as soon as possible. "The hour of danger," said the eloquent speaker, "must arrive unless these fatal acts of the last session are done away; it must arrive in all its horrors. There ought, therefore, to be no delay in this matter; we should proceed to it immediately. But it is not merely repealing these acts that can win back America to your bosom. You must repeal her fears and her resentments; and you may then hope for her love and gratitude. Now, insulted with an armed force, irritated with a hostile array before her eyes, which is a bar to all confidence and cordial reconcilement, her concessions, even if you could force them, would be suspicious and insincere. We shall be forced ultimately to retract; let us retract while we can, not when we must. Whoever advises the enforcement of these acts must do so at his peril. They must be repealed; you will repeal them; I pledge myself for it that you will in the end repeal them. I stake my reputation on it. I will consent to be taken for an idiot if they are not finally repealed. There is no time to be lost; every moment is big with danger. Nay, while I am now speaking, the decisive blow may be struck, and millions involved in the consequence. The very first drop of blood will make a wound that will not easily be skinned over. Years, perhaps ages, may not heal it. It will be *irritabile vulnus* — a wound of that rancorous, malignant, corroding, festering nature, that in all probability it will mortify the whole body. Repeal, therefore, my lords; REPEAL, I say! Thus will you convince America that you mean to try her cause in the spirit and by the laws of freedom and fair inquiry, and not by codes of blood. How can she trust you, with the bayonet at her breast? She has all the reason in the world to believe you mean her death or bondage. Avoid, then, this

humiliating, disgraceful necessity. To conclude, if the minis- CHAP.
ters thus persevere in misadvising and misleading the king, I XIV.
will not say that they can alienate the affections of his sub- 1775.
jects from the crown, but I will affirm that, the American jewel
out of it, they will make the crown not worth his wearing. I
will not say that the king is betrayed ; but I will say that the
nation is ruined."[1]

This motion of Chatham was ably supported by Shelburne
and Camden, and Rockingham also said a few words in its
favor ; but the ministers opposed it, and declared that, instead
of recalling the troops, they would send more if necessary.
Hence, when the question was taken, but sixteen favored the
motion, and sixty-eight opposed it.[2] Petitions from the trading
and manufacturing towns of the kingdom — Bristol, Glasgow,
Norwich, Liverpool, Manchester, and Birmingham, and even
from London, the great metropolis — were presented in vain ;
and the petition of the Congress of America, offered by Bollan, Franklin, and Lee, was scornfully rejected by a vote of
more than three to one. It was evident that both Houses
were bent upon violent measures. Already had Dartmouth, Jan. 4.
by order of the king, written to the governors of the colonies
to allow no more Congresses to be held ; and though it may
possibly be doubted whether it was suspected that the contest
would actually end in blood, no steps were taken to prevent
such a catastrophe, and the measures which were adopted were
eminently calculated to exasperate and inflame.[3]

Far from being daunted by his recent repulse, one more
effort was made by Chatham, who had consulted with Frank- Feb. 1.
lin,[4] to arouse the nation to a sense of its danger, by intro-

---

[1] For a fuller report of this speech
see Gordon's Am. Rev. i. 286–290,
where the date, by mistake, is Dec.
20; Belsham's George III. ii. 75 et
seq. ; Lord Mahon's Hist. Eng. vi. 21
–23.

[2] Gordon's Am. Rev. i. 290–292 ;
Lord Mahon's Hist. Eng. vi. 23. Quin-

cy, in Gordon, says there were " 18
contents, and 77 non-contents, including proxies."

[3] Gordon's Am. Rev. i. 292–294 ;
Ramsay's Am. Rev. i. 150.

[4] On these interviews see Writings
of Franklin, and Lord Mahon's Hist.
Eng. vi. 23–26.

CHAP. ducing a provisional bill "for settling the troubles in America,
 XIV. and for asserting the supreme legislative authority and super-
1775. intending power of Great Britain over the colonies." But
this bill was as objectionable to the ministry as his former proposal. It caused, indeed, "a variety of discussion, within and
without doors." Several peers, as Shelburne and Camden,
argued in its favor, while others, as Lyttleton and Temple,
objected to some points in it; but when a division took place,
it was rejected by a vote of sixty-one to thirty-two, and was
immediately printed by Chatham, as an appeal to the public
judgment.[1] The "conciliatory scheme" of North, proposed
Feb. 20. shortly after, which contained a conditional renunciation of
the right of taxation, met with a different fate; but it was too
defective in its character, and was adopted at too late a period,
to remedy the evils which existed.[2] Nay, even had this scheme
been good in itself, it could have accomplished but little; for
Feb. 10. a bill had been reported, and was passing, for restraining the
commerce of New England with Great Britain, as a retaliation
for the non-importation agreement of the colonies; and this
bill, which was, in effect, an extension of the obnoxious Boston
Port Bill, was "calculated in no slight degree to heap fresh
fuel on the flames already burning in America."[3] Hence conciliation was out of the question; and the address to the king,

---

[1] Gordon's Am. Rev. i. 295; Ramsay's Am. Rev. i. 151–153; Belsham's
George III. ii. 90; Lord Mahon's
Hist. Eng. vi. 26–28. Lord Mahon,
in a passage covering two pages of his
excellent work, queries what consequences might have resulted from an
opposite decision. "Would the Americans have accepted the measure cheerfully and readily? Would it for a
long time to come have closed the
breach and cemented the union with
the mother country? From all the
facts and testimonies then or since
made public, I answer, without hesitation, that it would. On both sides
there were injuries to redress, but not
as yet bloodshed to avenge. It was

only a quarrel; it was not as yet a
war."
  [2] Gordon's Am. Rev. i. 301, 302;
Ramsay's Am. Rev. i. 161–168; Belsham's George III. ii. 95. The ministry, it seems, condescended at length
to consult with Franklin relative to
this scheme; and the latter drew up
a paper of "Hints," tending to an adjustment of the differences between
the countries; but his "Hints" contained some inadmissible conditions,
and were not approved. Sparks's
Franklin; Lord Mahon's Hist. Eng.
vi. 30, 31.
  [3] Gordon's Am. Rev. i. 300, 301;
Ramsay's Am. Rev. i. 159; Lord
Mahon's Hist. Eng. vi. 32.

previously adopted, which declared that "a rebellion actually CHAP
existed within the province of the Massachusetts Bay," and in XIV.
which the Houses pledged themselves, "at the hazard of their 1775.
lives and properties, to stand by his majesty, against such
attempts, in the maintenance of his just rights and the rights
of Parliament," was too palpable a proof of the intentions of
the ministry, to admit the supposition that lenient or healing
measures would ever be favored by them.[1]

While ministers in England were thus preparing to enforce
their decrees at the cannon's mouth, statesmen in America
were coolly and deliberately preparing for resistance. In
Boston, the governor and his adherents maintained their position, surrounded by troops, ready at a moment's warning to
obey their commands. At Cambridge, and afterwards at Con- Feb. 1.
cord, the new Congress, convened in February,[2] chose delegates to the next American Congress, and passed resolutions
for strengthening the militia of the province, improving the
discipline of the troops, and furnishing them with arms. No
disposition, however, was evinced on either side to commence
hostilities, though collisions occasionally occurred, which seriously threatened a civil disturbance. Letters had indeed been
received from abroad, counselling bolder steps, and saying
"Your countrymen must SEAL THEIR CAUSE WITH THEIR BLOOD.
THEY MUST NOT DELAY. They must resist, or be trodden down
into the vilest vassalage — the scorn, the spurn of their enemies, a by-word of infamy among all men."[3] But such counsels were censured by the prudent as rash; and the patriots
of the Bay Province, conscious that one misstep might ruin all,
bore with inflexible fortitude the bitterest taunts, and soothed
the excited passions of the turbulent.

[1] Gordon's Am. Rev. i. 296–300 ; Ramsay's Am. Rev. i. 157; Belsham's George III. ii. 90–93. A number of lords protested against this address, as holding out no substantial offer for the redress of grievances.

[2] This Congress met at Cambridge Feb. 1, 1775, and adjourned Feb. 16. It then met at Concord, March 22, and adjourned April 15, shortly before the battle of Lexington. Its subsequent history will be hereafter given. Jour. Prov. Cong. 75.

[3] Gordon's Am. Rev. i. 284.

CHAP.   What if the gallant Warren was hissed at as he delivered
XIV.   his "oration" in the Old South, on the anniversary of the
1775.   Boston Massacre? What if Ditson, a citizen of Billerica, was
Mar. 5.
Mar. 9.   tarred and feathered, fastened to a chair on trucks, and drawn
through the streets, surrounded by a party of soldiers of the
forty-seventh, playing in derision "Yankee Doodle"? What
Mar.16.   if the day of fasting and prayer was made an occasion of un-
manly annoyance, while marquee tents were pitched before the
west meeting house, and drums and fifes were played to dis-
Mar.17.   turb the devotional services? What if the house of Hancock
was assaulted, and his fences hacked by a party flushed with
bravado and liquor? All such outrages, however annoying,
were borne with a calmness which discerning loyalists, had
they been wise, would have construed as ominous of a fearful
retribution, should the day of reckoning be hastened by their
folly.[1]

Yet the people moved steadily on in their course, adopting
the means which prudence prescribed to prepare for the struggle, whenever it should come. Some of their devices were
exceedingly ingenious. Cannon were conveyed from the town
to the country in carts, under the appearance of loads of
manure; half barrels of gunpowder were put into butcher's
pads, or the hampers of marketmen, as they returned home in
the evening ; and cartridges were packed in candle boxes, and
Mar.18.   sent off. Sometimes prizes were made; and in one instance
over thirteen thousand cartridges and three thousand pounds
of balls were seized. But this mishap, so far from disheartening, only stimulated to increased vigilance ; and provisions
were made for concentrating in places the most secure the supplies which had been provided by the Congress for the army.[2]
Indeed, every where, lynx-eyed men were abroad, secretly

---

[1] Mass. Spy for March 10, 1775 ;   Letter for March 17, 1775 ; Froth-
Almon's Remembrancer for 1775, 62 ;   ingham's Siege of Boston, 50.
Gordon's Am. Rev. i. 307, 308; Jour.   [2] Gordon's Am. Rev. i. 309; Froth-
Prov. Cong. i. 131–133 ; Boston News   ingham's Siege of Boston, 51.

watching the motions of the enemy, and reporting their doings CHAP.
to the committees of safety. The country was aroused. De- XIV.
termination was stamped upon every brow. Companies of 1775.
minute men flitted about, and were here at one moment and
there at another. Not a red coat could be seen in the neighboring villages but the wearer was followed, and his errand
discovered.

A large quantity of stores had been deposited at Concord,
and it was rumored that Gage was determined to destroy
them. A guard was accordingly stationed for their security, Mar.14.
and couriers were engaged in Charlestown, and Cambridge,
and Roxbury, the three avenues from Boston, to alarm the
country, should the attempt be made. The disguised officers
sent out by the commander-in-chief to sketch the roads were
narrowly watched by vigilant patriots. The bodies of troops
which were occasionally sent out were likewise watched; and
"great numbers" were prepared to attack them if necessary.[1]
It was known that Howe, and Clinton, and Burgoyne, officers April 4.
of established reputation for courage, had been ordered to
Boston to join General Gage, and that troops were to accompany them, to strengthen his forces; and it was also known
that Parliament had prohibited the exportation of military
stores to the colonies, to deprive the people of the means of
defence.[2] Gage had now four thousand men under his command — veteran troops, trained to war, under leaders of approved ability and courage.[3] Sanguine of success, he did not
for a moment harbor the thought that his designs would be
defeated. He had no confidence whatever in the gallantry of
the provincials, but regarded them as poltroons, easily intimidated. But the people were not dismayed. "Should administration," wrote Cushing, "determine to carry into execution

---

[1] 2 M. H. Coll. iv. 204–215. Captain Brown and Ensign De Bernicre
were the officers sent to sketch the
country.
[2] Boston Gazette for April 4, 1775;

Almon's Remembrancer for 1775, 56;
Frothingham's Siege of Boston, 52,
54.
[3] Frothingham's Siege of Boston,
53.

CHAP.
XIV.

1775.

Apr. 15.

Apr. 17.

Apr. 18.

the late acts of Parliament by military force, they will make the last appeal. They are determined life and liberty shall go together."[1]

Towards the middle of April it was discovered that there were movements on foot which looked to the accomplishment of the attack upon Concord; for the grenadiers and light infantry were relieved from duty, "upon the plea of learning a new exercise;" and at night the boats of the transport ships, which had been hauled up to be repaired, were launched and moored under the sterns of the men of war.[2] Immediately the committee of safety took additional measures for the security of the stores, and ordered the cannon to be secreted, and a part of the munitions to be removed to Sudbury and Groton.[3]

On the following day, ten or twelve British officers, who had dined at Cambridge, were directed at nightfall to station themselves along the roads leading to Concord, to intercept expresses sent out to alarm the country. The committees of safety were at the same time in session at Wetherby's tavern,[4] in what is now West Cambridge; and Gerry, and Orne, and Lee, three of the members, remained to pass the night. Two others, Devens and Watson, rode towards Charlestown, and, meeting on the way several officers on horseback, they returned to inform their friends of the fact, and proceeded on their journey. Gerry at once sent a messenger to Hancock and Adams, who were stopping at Mr. Clark's, the minister of Lexington, to acquaint them with what was passing; and precautionary measures were adopted at Lexington.[5] Upon his arrival in Charlestown Devens learned that the British troops were on the eve of

---

[1] Frothingham's Siege of Boston, 53.

[2] Gordon's Am. Rev. i. 309; Everett's Lexington and Concord Addresses; Frothingham's Siege of Boston, 56.

[3] Shattuck's Concord, 95; Everett's Lexington Address; Frothingham's Siege of Boston, 56.

[4] Some authorities say, at Newell's tavern.

[5] Austin's Life of Gerry, i. 68; Frothingham's Siege of Boston, 57; Shattuck's Concord, 101. Information of the movements of the officers had already been received at Lexington through Solomon Brown. Everett's Lexington Address.

embarking ; and a lantern was displayed by Paul Revere in the CHAP.
upper window of the tower of the North Church, in Boston — XIV.
the signal which had been agreed upon. Gage, who supposed 1775.
that nothing was known of his movements, communicated them
in confidence to Lord Percy, at nine in the evening ; but the
latter, shortly after, in returning to his quarters, overheard a
conversation which satisfied him that the affair was no longer
secret ; [1] and, hastening to Gage, orders were issued that no
one should be suffered to leave the town. Dr. Warren, however, but a few moments before, had sent into the country two
trusty messengers, — Paul Revere and William Dawes, — who
eluded the vigilance of the guards, and spread the alarm. At
midnight one of the messengers, Paul Revere, reached the
house of the Rev. Mr. Clark ; and, though the family were at
rest, they were promptly aroused.[2]

At one in the morning the minute men of Lexington and Apr.19
the militia of the town were summoned to meet at their place
of parade, on the green near the meeting house ; and messengers were sent towards Cambridge for additional information.
At two the soldiers, one hundred and thirty in number, assembled ; the roll was called, and every gun was loaded ; [3] but, by
the return of the messengers, they were informed that all was
quiet ; and, as the night was chilly, they dispersed into the
neighboring houses — most of them going to Bucknam's tavern.[4]

In Concord the alarm was likewise spread ; [5] and Dr. Pres-
cott agreed to assist in rousing the people. While thus engaged, with Revere and Dawes, he was met by a party of

[1] Everett's Concord Address;
Frothingham's Siege of Boston, 58.
[2] Phinney's Hist. of the Battle, 33;
Everett's Lexington and Concord Addresses; Frothingham's Siege of Boston, 59; Shattuck's Concord, 101. A
guard of eight men had been stationed
at Mr. Clark's house for the protection
of Adams and Hancock. Everett's
Address.

[3] Gordon's Am. Rev. i. 310; Everett's Lexington Address; Frothingham's Siege of Boston, 60.
[4] Gordon's Am. Rev. i. 310.
[5] Three persons — Sanderson, Loring, and Brown — had been sent up
from Lexington towards Concord, to
watch the movements of the officers.
Everett's Address.

CHAP. officers, armed and mounted ; and, in the scuffle which ensued,
XIV. Revere was captured, but was subsequently liberated.[1] There
1775. could now be no doubt that the regulars were on their march ;
and it was afterwards ascertained that Lieutenant Colonel
Smith, at the head of about eight hundred men, had embarked
at ten o'clock, on the evening of the eighteenth, at the foot of
the Common, in Boston, in the boats of the ships of war. Just
as the moon rose he landed, with his men, in perfect stillness,
at Lechmere's Point, crossed the marshes, and entered the old
Charlestown and West Cambridge road, near the foot of Prospect Hill. As they passed the tavern where the " rebels"
were lodging, the latter arose from their beds to gaze on the un-
wonted spectacle ; and, when a party was detached to surround
the tavern, they hastily escaped to an adjoining field.[2] Colonel
Smith had marched but a few miles before he was satisfied, by
the ringing of bells and the noise of guns, that the country
was alarmed. He therefore detached six companies of infantry and marines, under Major Pitcairn, with orders to press
on and secure the bridges at Concord, while a messenger was
sent to Boston for a reënforcement.[3]

Pitcairn, in obedience to his orders, hurried his men forward ; but, within a mile and a half of the Lexington meeting
house, Thaddeus Bowman escaped his advanced guard, galloped
to the Common, and sounded the alarm.[4] It was now half
past four ; and, by the orders of Captain Parker, the drums
were beaten, guns were fired, and Sergeant Monroe was instructed to form his company in two ranks a little north of the
meeting house. A short time after Pitcairn arrived, halted for
a moment, ordered his men to " prime and load," and then to
march forward in double quick time. Sixty or seventy of the
militia had collected, and about forty spectators, a few of whom

[1] Everett's Concord Address ;
Frothingham's Siege of Boston, 60 ;
Shattuck's Concord, 101.
[2] Almon's Remembrancer for 1775,
69 ; Everett's Addresses ; Frothingham's Siege of Boston, 61.
[3] Everett's Addresses ; Frothingham's Siege of Boston.
[4] Everett's Concord Address.

were armed; and, as Pitcairn rode up, he shouted, "Disperse, CHAP.
you rebels! Throw down your arms! Villains, disperse!" XIV.
Finding they did not obey, he ordered his men to fire. A few 1775.
guns were discharged, but no one was killed. A general discharge followed, with fatal results.[1] The militia immediately
returned the fire; and, both from the ranks of the company,
and from behind a stone wall, and from the back door of
Bucknam's house, shots were aimed at the regular troops.[2]
The skirmish became general; and the troops under Pitcairn
continued their fire as long as the militia continued in sight —
killing eight and wounding ten. Parker,[3] Muzzy, the Har-
ringtons,[4] Monroe,[5] Hadley, Brown, and Porter, of Woburn,
were the persons killed.[6] The British suffered but little. "A
private of the tenth regiment, and probably one other, were
wounded, and Major Pitcairn's horse was struck."[7]

The citizens of Concord had been aroused at an early hour;
and the committee of safety, the military officers, and prominent citizens met for consultation. The soldiers were likewise
mustered, and formed on the parade ground, near the meeting
house; messengers were sent towards Lexington for information; and a portion of the militia, under Colonel Barrett,
labored in removing the stores to the woods. Soon word came

[1] Rev. J. Clark, in Shattuck's Concord, 102, 103; Gordon's Am. Rev.
i. 310; Everett's Addresses; Frothingham's Siege of Boston, 62.
[2] Phinney's Hist. of the Battle;
Everett's Concord Address; Frothingham's Siege of Boston, 63, and note.
[3] "Roman history does not furnish
an example of bravery that outshines
that of Jonas Parker. A truer heart
did not bleed at Thermopylæ." Everett's Address.
[4] Jonathan and Caleb Harrington.
Of the former Everett says, "Harrington's was a cruel fate. He fell in
front of his own house, on the north
of the Common. His wife, at the
window, saw him fall, and then start
up, the blood gushing from his breast.

He stretched out his hands towards
her, as if for assistance, and fell
again. Rising once more on his hands
and knees, he crawled across the road
towards his dwelling. She ran to
meet him at the door, but it was to
see him expire at her feet."
[5] Robert Monroe had served in the
French wars, and was the standard
bearer of his company at the capture
of Louisburg, in 1758. Everett's Address; Frothingham's Siege of Boston.
[6] For the list of the killed see Jour.
Prov. Cong. and Frothingham's Siege
of Boston.
[7] Gage's Account, in Frothingham's
Siege of Boston, 64.

that the British had fired upon the provincials at Lexington. The excitement was intense; and a portion of the militia of Concord, and of Lincoln, the adjoining town, resolved to push on to the assistance of their neighbors, while Captain Minot, with the alarm company, remained in town, and took possession of the hill near the liberty pole.[1] No sooner had he gained this position than the companies which had left returned, with the intelligence that the number of the British was treble that of the Americans; and the whole force fell back to an eminence back of the town, and formed in two battalions.[2] Scarcely were they thus posted when the British appeared in sight, rapidly advancing on the Lincoln road, with their guns glittering in the early sunshine. Deeming resistance useless, Colonel Barrett, who had joined his townsmen, ordered a retreat, over the North Bridge, to an eminence about a mile from the centre of the town.[3]

Shortly after the withdrawal of the Americans the British troops marched into Concord, in two divisions — the one by the main road, and the other by the hill which the Americans had just left. The grenadiers and light infantry, under Colonel Smith, were posted in the centre of the town; and Captain Parsons, with six light companies, was detached to secure the North Bridge, while Captain Pole was sent to secure the South Bridge.[4] On reaching the North Bridge, three companies, under Captain Lawrie, were left to guard it; and the other three, under Captain Parsons, proceeded to Colonel Barrett's house, in search of stores. In the mean time, the militia of Concord and Lincoln, joined by their brethren from Carlisle, Chelmsford, Weston, Littleton, and Acton, formed under Hosmer. Captain Smith, with his company, volunteered to dis-

---

[1] The minute men from Lincoln were under Captain William Smith, and the militia under Captain Samuel Farrar. Frothingham's Siege of Boston, 66.

[2] Shattuck's Concord, 105; Frothingham's Siege of Boston, 66.
[3] Shattuck's Concord, 106; Frothingham's Siege of Boston, 66.
[4] Shattuck's Concord, 107; Frothingham's Siege of Boston, 66.

lodge the guard at the North Bridge ; Captain Isaac Davis, CHAP. with his company from Acton, was equally patriotic ; and, by XIV. the orders of Colonel Barrett, they were detached, under Major 1775. John Buttrick, with Lieutenant Colonel Robinson as an assist- ant, for the discharge of this difficult service. As they drew near the bridge, the British fired ; and at the second volley Captain Davis was killed, and Hosmer, a private in his com- pany, fell at his side. "Fire, fellow-soldiers! for God's sake, fire!" exclaimed Major Buttrick ; and a general action ensued, when the British, in confusion, retreated. A detachment was sent to their relief ; and the provincials pursued them over the bridge, until they joined the main body in the centre of the town.[1]

By this time the old New England drums, that had beat at Louisburg, at Quebec, at Martinique, and at the Havana, were sounding on all the roads leading to Concord ;[2] and Colonel Smith, after resting for two hours, prepared about twelve o'clock to march for Boston. The militia of Reading and Bil- lerica came hurrying in to lend their aid to their countrymen ; the Sudbury company was there ; and the roads all along the route were occupied by the Americans, posted behind trees, and walls, and rocks. Smith pushed on, but was met by a fire so hot that his ranks were speedily thinned, and his situation became perilous. At this critical moment a reënforcement arrived, consisting of three regiments of infantry and two divisions of marines, with two field pieces, under Lord Percy, who had marched through Roxbury to the tune of Yankee Doodle.[3] By the aid of the field pieces the Americans were kept at bay for a time, and the retreat was resumed. Yet every height was filled, and at every defile the contest was bloody. Below West Cambridge the militia from Dorchester, Roxbury, and Brookline came up ; the Danvers company had

---

[1] Shattuck's Concord, 112 ; Ever- ett's Concord Address ; Frothing- ham's Siege of Boston, 70.

[2] Everett's Concord Address.

[3] Frothingham's Siege of Boston, 72–75.

CHAP. previously arrived ; and, thus recruited, the gallant provincials
XIV. fell with overwhelming force upon their assailants.   The Brit-
1775. ish were nearly exhausted ; and as they reached Prospect Hill,
their situation was critical.   Their progress was obstructed by
the number of wounded ; they had but a few rounds of cartridges left ; the roads were alive with pursuers, as if they had
" dropped from the clouds ; " and volley on volley was poured
in upon them.   At length, about sunset, almost on the run,
they reached Charlestown Common, where they were sheltered
by the guns from the ships, and the pursuit was stopped.   Of
the Americans, forty-nine were killed, thirty-nine were wounded,
and five were missing.   Of the British, seventy-three were
killed, one hundred and seventy-four were wounded, and
twenty-six were missing.[1]   This was THE COMMENCEMENT OF
THE WAR OF THE REVOLUTION.   The blood of the English
and of the Americans had flowed ; the union of the colonies
with Great Britain was severed ; and from this hour the era
of INDEPENDENCE properly dates.   " What a glorious morning
is this ! " exclaimed Samuel Adams, as he heard the sound of
the guns at Lexington.   It was the morning of FREEDOM.
The day star of liberty had risen upon America.

[1] Almon's Remembrancer for 1775, 70 ; Everett's Concord Address ; Frothingham's Siege of Boston, 79. For minute details of this whole ex-pedition see Almon's Remembrancer for 1775, 72–82 ; Phinney's Account ; the different orations at Lexington and Concord ; Frothingham's Siege of Boston ; the local histories of Con-cord, &c. ; Jour. Prov. Cong. 660-694, &c.